SPANISH-
AMERICAN
LITERATURE

SPANISH-AMERICAN LITERATURE

A History

by Enrique Anderson Imbert
THE UNIVERSITY OF MICHIGAN

translated from the Spanish
by John V. Falconieri

Detroit / 1963
Wayne State University Press

Published simultaneously in Canada by Ambassador Books, Limited /
Toronto, Ontario, Canada

Library of Congress Catalog Card Number 63-8294

Grateful acknowledgement is made to the Rockefeller Foundation
for financial assistance in publishing this translation.

CONTENTS

South / B. MAINLY PROSE: 1. NOVEL AND SHORT STORY: (*1*) *Mexico;* (*2*) *Central America: Magón;* (*3*) *Antilles;* (*4*) *Venezuela: Picón-Febres;* (*5*) *Colombia: Carrasquilla;* (*6*) *Ecuador;* (*7*) *Peru;* (*8*) *Bolivia;* (*9*) *Chile: Lillo, Orrego Luco, Gana;* (*10*) *Paraguay;* (*11*) *Uruguay: Viana, Reyles;* (*12*) *Argentina: Payró* / 2. ESSAY: *Korn, Sanín Cano* / C. THE THEATER

XI. 1895-1910

Authors born between 1870 and 1885 / *p. 264*

Historical framework: Industrialization. Growth of international capitalism.
Cultural tendencies: Height of Modernism.

THE CHARACTERISTICS OF MODERNISM / A. MAINLY VERSE: 1. MODERNIST POETS: *Rubén Darío; Central America; Argentina: Lugones, Carriego; Bolivia: Jaimes Freyre; Uruguay: Herrera y Reissig; Peru: Chocano, Eguren; Colombia: Valencia; Mexico: Nervo, Urbina, Tablada, González Martínez; Other Countries, from North to South* / 2. NON-MODERNIST POETS / B. MAINLY PROSE: 1. NOVEL AND SHORT STORY: (*a*) *Estheticizing Narrators:* (*1*) *Mexico;* (*2*) *Central America: Gómez Carrillo;* (*3*) *Antilles;* (*4*) *Venezuela: Díaz Rodríguez;* (*5*) *Colombia;* (*6*) *Ecuador;* (*7*) *Peru;* (*8*) *Bolivia;* (*9*) *Chile: D'Halmar;* (*10*) *Paraguay;* (*11*) *Uruguay: Horacio Quiroga;* (*12*) *Argentina: Larreta* / (*b*) *Realist Narrators:* (*1*) *Mexico: Azuela;* (*2*) *Central America: Blanco-Fombona;* (*3*) *Antilles: Cestero;* (*4*) *Venezuela: Blanco-Fombona;* (*5*) *Colombia;* (*6*) *Ecuador;* (*7*) *Peru;* (*8*) *Bolivia: Arguedas;* (*9*) *Chile;* (*10*) *Paraguay;* (*11*) *Uruguay;* (*12*) *Argentina: Gálvez* / 2. ESSAY: *Ingenieros; José Enrique Rodó / Other Essayists* / C. THE THEATER: *Florencio Sánchez*

PART THREE: CONTEMPORARY PERIOD

XII. 1910-1925

Authors born between 1885 and 1900 / *p. 327*

Historical framework: Social Revolution in Mexico and the effects of World War I.
Cultural tendencies: Modernist artifice set aside in favor of a simpler expression of American reality. Experimentation in new "isms."

A. MAINLY VERSE: 1. NORMALITY: (*1*) *Mexico: López Velarde;* (*2*) *Central America: Cardona, Miró and Others;* (*3*) *Antilles: Poveda, Acosta and Others;* (*4*) *Venezuela: Andrés Eloy Blanco;* (*5*) *Colombia: Porfirio Barba Jacob;* (*6*) *Ecuador: Medardo Ángel Silva and Others;* (*7*) *Peru: Valdelomar and Others;* (*8*) *Bolivia: Peñaranda;* (*9*) *Chile: Gabriela Mistral;* (*10*) *Paraguay: Fariña Núñez;* (*11*) *Uruguay: Agustini, Ibarbourou and Others;* (*12*) *Argentina: Banchs, Fer-*

PROLOG

OF THE MANY dangers an historian of literature risks, two are quite serious: that of specializing in the study of isolated great books, and that of specializing in the study of the circumstances under which those books were written. If the historian elects to go down the first path, he produces a collection of unconnected critical essays, that is, a history of literature containing very little history. If he chooses to follow the second, the result will be a series of external references to the process of civilization, that is, a history of literature containing very little literature. Is a History-history of Literature-literature possible? At least, it is possible to attempt one. It would be a history that gave meaning to the expressive moments of certain men who, through the passing of the centuries, set themselves to write. Each writer asserts those esthetic values that he has formed while contemplating the possibilities of his historical environment, and these are the values that should constitute the real subject matter of any History of Literature.

This is all well and good, as theory. But if we were mindful only of esthetic expression, to what thin line would this history which we are about to offer reduce itself? The effective contributions of Spanish-American literature to international literature are minimal. Yet we Spanish-Americans have done a great deal if one were to consider the many obstacles with which our literary creation has had to contend and is still contending. The Inca Garcilaso, Sor Juana Inés de la Cruz, Andrés Bello, Domingo Sarmiento, Juan Montalvo, Ricardo Palma, José Martí, Rubén Darío, José Enrique Rodó, Alfonso Reyes, Pablo Neruda, Jorge Luis Borges, and a dozen more, are figures who would do honor to any literature. But, in general, we are afflicted by improvisation, disorder, fragmentation, and impurity. Necessarily, many unaccomplished writers will have to be included here.

We cannot prevent a certain amount of farrago from slipping into this history. But to be sure, what does interest us here is the reality which has been transmuted into literature. Although we witness, respectfully and patiently, a long procession of writers and try to understand their contribution, the fact is that we anxiously look for the few who have expressed esthetic values. Our subject is Literature, that is to say, those writings that can be assigned to the category of beauty.

Of course, in the first chapters we had to admit many men of action or thought who wrote chronicles and treatises without any artistic intentions; yet, even in these cases, it was the literary portion of their writings that we valued. But as we approach our own times we must be more demanding in drawing limits to what is and what is not literature. Once we reach our own age, we are only interested in those writers who cultivate poetry, prose poems, the short story, the novel, and the theater. We only consider essayists insofar as they are men of letters. Had this been an extended history of culture instead of a compressed history of literature, we would also have included critics, philosophers, historians and patrons of art; or even had sociology been our aim, we would have included information about journals, literary gatherings, prizes, and the like. But this book does not aspire to include all. We are fully aware that in Spanish-America there are often extraordinary personalities in literary life who study and promote literature, but who do not produce it. Furthermore, at times the men who most influence literary groups are precisely the ones who write neither poetry, nor novels, nor dramas. It may be lamentable, but it is obvious that they do not belong to a history of poetry, novels, and dramas.

The literature of the Americas we are going to study is the one which was written in Spanish. We do not ignore the importance of the masses of Indians; however, in a history of the expressive uses of the Spanish language in America, it behooves us to listen only to those who expressed themselves in Spanish. For this same reason we will not refer to the writers who were born in Spanish-America, but who wrote in Latin (like Rafael Landívar), in French (like Jules Supervielle), or in English (like W. H. Hudson). Nor will we consider those authors who, although they wrote in Spanish, did not write of American experiences (like Ventura de la Vega). On the other hand, we will include in our history those foreigners who lived among us and used our language (like Paul Groussac).

It is well known that history is a continuous process. We will, therefore, introduce writers in the order in which they came into the world and entered into literary life. But, although history is an indivisible succession of events, we could not represent it without certain conventions which we call periods. In order to be useful, this breaking up of history into periods should adjust itself to historical facts and respect the complexity of each epoch. Thus, a system of periods must be consistent with the principle which it adopts, but it does not need to be regular. On the contrary, excessive regularity would indicate that the historian, through his great desire to embellish his vision, is allowing himself to be carried along by symmetries and metaphors. There are periods of long stability. There are short, rapid periods. In the fear of falsifying literary development through the use of subjective figures, we have chosen an inoffensive criterion: an historical-political classification in three parts, "The Colony," "One Hundred Years of the Republic," and the "Contemporary Period." But within these broad divisions we have shaded in certain generations, attempting to make the external framework of political history coincide with esthetic tendencies. The dates heading each chapter indicate the years during which these generations came into being and produced: *"Gestación"* and *"Gestión,"* as Ortega y Gasset put it. In order that the outline might be more useful, we have also indicated the approximate birthdates of the authors. But, when historical sense demands, we shall alter the outline and situate a borderline author on whatever side best suits our purposes.

That we should be arranging the materials of this history into periods does not mean that we are neglecting other regulative criteria: those of nationality, genre, schools, and themes. What we have done is to subordinate these criteria to chronology. In other words, our method is systematic when it groups fundamental literary phenomena chronologically, and asystematic with regard to everything else. It is more difficult this way, but there is less falsification of history.

To have grouped the authors by country would have been to break the cultural unity of Spanish America into nineteen illusory national literatures. To have had recourse to the rhetorical categories of genres would have obliged us to have dismantled the work of any writer who cultivated various types of literature and to have distributed the pieces throughout several chapters under the headings of "poetry," "narrative," "essay," and "theater," not to mention the difficulty involved in classifying the subgenres. To have insisted on schools and "isms" would have caused us to fall into the vice of giving substance to mere ideal concepts, thus, lending more attention to collective styles than to individual ones. To have made our history revolve around certain themes would have been superficial: what counts, after all, is the treatment of the theme, not the theme itself. In spite of what has been said, the reader will find, especially in the last chapters, an arrangement according to nationality (from north to south), in genres (from verse to prose and, within prose, fiction, essay, and theater) and in schools (from the more imaginative to the more realist).

We must remind the reader who opens the book here and there, with the intention not of reading it, but of consulting it, that what he has before him is a history and not an inventory of names. In other words, its value lies in the total interpretation of a continuous process; a series of names, even a series of sentences, only makes sense if it is reached after first reading many pages back. Trusting in the fluidity with which the themes are formed and developed we have boldly incorporated into the text those lists that other historians prudently hide in separate notes. To read just the lists would be tantamount to ignoring the esthetic category to which the names belong. One might ask, why not delete those ugly pieces of census? But they are not pieces of census, they are clouds, constellations, woods, highlands, and dales in an historical landscape. The great quantity of names brings out the fact that, because there is so little communication among the Spanish-American countries, literary values are fixed in local markets: to omit these names would hurt national pride. Now that we have touched on the matter of national honor, the reader must remember that in a history, constructed in one unit as this one is, the number of pages devoted to any particular writer is no measure of his importance. There are writers of really great stature who can be dealt with in brief critiques. On the other hand, other writers of less value require a more extensive treatment if they illustrate a movement, a genre, a theme, or a cultural reality. So that the reader will not lose the thread of what is really noteworthy, those sections of minor importance will be set in reduced type.

An historian of literature cannot read every book (an entire life would not be enough) but neither can he limit himself to commenting only on those books that he has read (if he did this, he would not set down an objective historical process but his autobiography as a reader). In order to offer a complete panorama of what has been written during the past four hundred years in a continent that is now divided into nineteen republics, the historian is obliged to utilize the data and judgments of others. There are several ways of promoting this huge informative enterprise. One way, the most serious from a scholarly point of view, but the least practical from the point of view of a manual, is to interrupt the exposition at every step with bibliographical references, footnotes, citations within the text, appendices, and careful acknowledgement of the works of hundreds of colleagues which are used and reworked. Another way, the one we have risked, is to appoint oneself the Editing Secretary of an imaginary Stock Company of Spanish-Americanists and to invert into a fluid history all that is known among all of us. In this case the historian constructs an optical apparatus, with lenses and mirrors, through which he looks out on the range of letters; and he consolidates his own observations and those of other observers in a book with "form"—a form with unity, continuity, smoothness, and roundness. Composite art. In this way, pages based on a direct knowledge of texts are intermingled and occasionally integrated with others that indirectly summarize scattered studies. The bibliography is only a guide for the reader; it is not a listing of the sources that we have used. These sources are innumerable. Each time we found something that was compatible with the plan of the book, we unhesitatingly incorporated it: there is, then, the manipulation of over-all histories, partial monographs, journal articles, and book reviews. We even went further by writing to critics in different places and using their replies in the systematic construction of this vast synthesis. As we traveled through the countries of Spanish-America, we approached literary groups and, pen in hand, took notes which later were utilized. For this reason, in some cases, this *History* may give first-hand the fruits of research. That is to say that we conceived this *History* as a living and voracious body: the peril lies in our having created a Frankenstein! Our desire has been to render a public service: to bring together dispersed material, to classify the medley of data, to illuminate with a single light the dark corners of a Spanish America inwardly shattered and badly misunderstood, and to put into the hands of the reader a *Summa*. Although the *History* has been raised with the contributions of many, it advances in a single, uninterrupted line. It is a collective yet uniform work. Although in our desire for verbal economy we have not had room even to cite the most authoritative specialists, we hereby declare our debt to their investigations. We have worked, therefore, in part as architect and in part as bricklayer. In the entire *History* there is not a single citation, not even when the criticism follows other historians closely. Nor do we cite our own scholarly contributions published elsewhere. In those contributions we rigorously analyzed textual styles; but in this *History* we occasionally recast what we have not before analyzed directly. Yet, let us not exaggerate. This *History* is personal in conception, in arrangement, and in a good deal of its commentary.

TRANSLATOR'S FOREWORD

THIS *History* is the most comprehensive compilation of studies of the literature of Hispanic America ever written. It is vast not for the number of pages but for the breadth of its topics, for the depth of its chronology, for the scope of its geography, and for the magnitude of its philosophic, historical, and cultural framework in which it is neatly ensconced; it is intense for the compactness of its organization and of its prose: all the chaff has been threshed out. This compact prose reflects perfectly the manner in which the author has compressed almost six centuries of literature into such few pages. What is more stunning is that withal it remains a history of *literature*, achieved without sacrificing non-literary data. The key to this accomplishment lies in the richness of the author's language as he dissects literary forms, literarily; that is, with the very instruments of the creative artist. The *History* is replete with unexpected vocabulary, turns of syntax, plays on words and ideas, tropes, metaphors which, instead of obfuscating, illuminate the creative process of so many of the writers.

It has been our intention to mirror this prose style in every respect, but all translation-mirrors have their imperfections, and images sometimes yield untrue refractions. (May there not be any distortions!) We tried to trade expression for expression, figure of speech for figure of speech, and if the trading were not possible in one place, we tried to make up the deficiency elsewhere; yet, we may not have been able to liquidate all our indebtedness to the original. If the rhythm of the English prose is not the accustomed or traditional one it is because the original is likewise an unusual and non-traditional Spanish. We hope the readers will become attuned to the new beats.

This is the translation of the greatly augmented third edition of Professor Enrique Anderson Imbert's *Historia de la literatura hispanoamericana* published by the Fondo de Cultura Económica of Mexico City. Since this edition Professor Anderson has added some authors and data pertaining to them, as well as slight modifications of the text. In this respect, the translation has taken one step beyond the original.

Enrique Anderson Imbert, a native of Argentina, has been for close to a score of years Professor of Hispanic American Literature at the University of Michigan, the most outstanding authority in this field, and a teacher revered and admired by many students. Professor Anderson's literary tools, alluded to above, come to him naturally: he is a very respected author in Spanish American letters forming part of the very history he writes.

The introduction of this *History* to Anglo-America is propitious at this time because interest in Hispanic-American art and literature in increasing. With the passage of time the artistic and literary production of Hispanic America multiplies at an incredible rate. We need only cast a glance at the table of contents of this *History* to note that the first half encompasses the years 1492 to 1910, while the second half covers the last 50 years or so. The acceleration is patent; the character of the literature, from what once may have been imitative and lagging, now takes on greater variety, newness and autonomy.

As a great number of the works have not been put into English, it was deemed proper to include the original titles with the translated titles. If a title reoccurs after it has been translated, the English title is repeated and not the original. Only Hispanic-American titles are translated; others, including Spanish, are left in their original tongue. Titles of short stories or of poems are translated, but the original is omitted, especially when the full title of the collection is given. Orthodox American English spelling was used throughout the work. In those cases where "ink-saving" orthography appears (e.g. *prolog* rather than *prologue*) it is solely due to the dictates and policies of the Wayne State University Press.

I wish to record here my appreciation and indebtedness to Professor Claude C. Hulet, of the University of Southern California, for having read the greater portion of the translation and to Professor James R. Stamm, of Michigan State University, for having read sections of the work. Their observations, suggestions, and criticisms were well received and of great value. To Professor Harold Murphy of Marshall University go my thanks for his courteous and patient aid in reading the manuscript. Grateful acknowledgment is made to Mrs. Patricia Davis of the Wayne State University Press for her efforts in preparing the text and index for printing. To Professor Anderson Imbert I extend my eternal and humble gratitude for his faith in me, for his patience with me, and for the guiding hand which led me through so many reefs and pitfalls. And finally I wish to thank Mrs. Diana N. Falconieri for the material aid and spiritual comfort than can only be repaid in the heavens.

I. 1492-1556

Authors born between 1451 and 1530

Historical framework: Discovery, exploration, conquest, and colonization under the Catholic Monarchs and Charles V.

Cultural tendencies: First renaissance. From the obsolescent genres of medieval aspect (chronicles, missionary theater) to the importation of ideas (Erasmism) and forms (Italianate poetry).

' Spanish literature of this period is generally considered a first renaissance and is characterized by its importation of forms and ideas, especially from Italy. The conquistadors and the missionaries brought the literature of Spain to the New World. They brought it in their ships and in their heads. Even writers came. And as these Spaniards began to write in America, they naturally relied upon the literary trends dominant in Spain. Although there were a few isolated Erasmists, in general this early phase of the colonization reflects, at first glance, medieval features.

The books which were being circulated and printed were, in the main, ecclesiastical and didactic, to be sure. But, putting aside those written in Latin and in the indigenous tongues (only that literature produced in the Spanish language interests us here), there remain two genres, the chronicle and the theater, which, although medieval in appearance, acquire creative power upon contact with the new American reality. |

The Chronicles

To reiterate, the men who came to the New World were driven by the spiritual force of the Renaissance, but they were still guided by a medieval vision. They came from Spain, where the Renaissance never gave up its medieval legacy; they came from the people, normally slow in accepting change; and even those who came from the educated classes were neither contemplative nor creators of beauty, but men of action. The last sight of their homeland must have been the Gothic cathedrals. In fact, on reading their chronicles, we seem to be reading contemporaries of the Gothic era rather than contemporaries of the Renaissance. Their chronicles penetrate reality without defining it, without enclosing it, in the same manner that Gothic churches pierce the sky with aery structures in which sculpture and stained glass triumph. Chronicles without architecture—fluid, complex, free, disproportionate—wherein realistic anecdotes range on one side and Christian symbolism on the other, just as in a conversation. These chronicles lack the composition, the unity, the congruence, the artistic and intellectual loftiness of the Renaissance creations. In spite of their apparent medievalism, the chroniclers gave to their pages a new kind of vitality and unconventional emotion, perhaps because they wrote spontaneously and almost without training about actual experience, or because, no matter how sophisticated they were, they allowed the marvels of the New World to penetrate and exalt them.

The first chronicler was, naturally, CHRISTOPHER COLUMBUS (1451–1506). The letter which tells of his first voyage was printed in 1493. With a Spanish prose learned in Portugal, the Genovese Columbus set about to describe clumsily what he had seen. But he barely saw America—he believed himself to be sailing toward Asia; moreover, he was blinded by greed for gold. He must have been disappointed with his own discovery—wretched islands inhabited by naked beings. And although he made an effort to appear enthusiastic—thus complying with his own need for publicity—he was unable to appreciate either the American landscape or the American himself. Upon reading Columbus' narrative, the Europeans confirmed old Utopian dreams and were able to give substance to two of the great themes of the Renaissance: natural man, happy and virtuous; and Nature, luxuriant and paradisiacal. Nevertheless, at the heart of the most vivid passages in Columbus' chronicle there was not a direct insight into America, rather a reflection, like clouds on a quiet lake, of traditional literary figures. Columbus moved with the Renaissance man's impulse of discovery, but his mind was still tempered in the medieval forge. Although he was not a man of letters, he had read enough of real and imaginary voyages, of myths, ballads and folk tales that they had slipped into his spirit, coloring and transfiguring the reality of the New World: vegetation became a garden landscape; the birds of the Antilles, Provenzal nightingales; even the natives were poetized into ennobling engravings or into prodigious monsters. The promise of earthly paradise or of the land of the Amazons forever trembled on the horizon. The constant comparisons with Europe also clouded his perception of the singular aspects of the New World; his words began to classify the new objects into European categories. He did not describe for the sheer love of describing as some conquistadors did later. He was taking inventories—an inventory of riches (future rather than present). But Columbus observed details, and even today, on reading his words, we feel every now and then the esthetic pleasure that a witness of faraway and awesome places always communicates to us. Because we respond imaginatively to Columbus, his unadorned remarks on the naked beauty of the Indian, the gentleness of his laughter and gestures, the soft warm air of the green isles, the minuscule life of the cricket and the grass, appear to take on literary style.

His observations on the appearance and customs of the natives are more numerous, meticulous, and discerning than those on the natural setting of the islands. This interest in the human element rather than in the panoramic was typical of an entire tradition of travel chronicles, ranging from the real adventures of Marco Polo to the fantastic ones of Amadis de Gaula. Columbus, feeling himself more an adventurer than a man of science—after all, it had been the men of science who rejected his computations—wrote to satisfy his readers' curiosity about adventures among unknown peoples, not to supply information for cosmographers, mathematicians, navigators, and naturalists. Only on his third voyage did he note down the position of the stars, but even in this instance his inspiration was more poetic than scientific: "I was taken by a great admiration" for the North Star, he says. He adds that the differences in measurements in the newly discovered sky convinced him that the earth was not spherical as he had believed, but possessed the form of a woman's breast, with the nipple high up near the sky, and for this reason "ships could rise on a gentle incline, there to enjoy a more gentle climate." On this lovely nipple of land with the curves of a woman, Columbus situated Paradise, a fountain of "precious things" crowned with an even greater "diversity of stars."

Columbus' Men / Those who accompanied Columbus also left accounts. The Sevillian physician, DIEGO ÁLVAREZ CHANCA, was the first to describe the flora of the new world, although, like others, he preferred to speak of human marvels rather than the marvels of nature. FRIAR ROMÁN PANE (or PAN) was the first European, so far as is known, to speak an American tongue; he was the first teacher of Indians. He initiated American ethnography. His notes on the religious and artistic culture of the Indians on the island of Hispaniola are first-hand accounts. He heard the songs through which the Indians transmitted their cosmogony and their history ("by which they were ruled as the Moors are by their writings")—songs which were accompanied with musical instruments which Pane also described. HERNANDO COLÓN (1488–1539) who accompanied his father on his fourth voyage, was one of those bookish Renaissance men attached to everything European. Incited by the need to defend his family's prerogatives, he wrote *The Life of Admiral Christopher Columbus* (*Vida del Almirante Don Cristóbal Colón*), of which only an Italian version is extant.

As can be seen, the most notable feature in the writings of this entire first group of travelers is the attention given to the inhabitants rather than to the land itself. (An exception is the *Compendium of Geography* [*Suma de geografía*, 1519] written by the explorer Martín Fernández de Enciso, which was one of the first scientific systematizations that embraced the New World.) The same can be said of the letters of Amerigo Vespucci which are not included in this history, for they were not written in Spanish. However, it was because of them that some mapmakers from Lorraine baptized the New World as the world of Amerigo: America.

The Controversy over the Indians / As we have already said, it was by virtue of the first reports on the discovery of America that the Utopian dreams of a paradisiacal landscape and of a noble savage were reaffirmed. But also at an early date there were a few chroniclers who on occasion denigrated the American landscape and who declared its inhabitants to be inferior men without souls—in the eighteenth century de Pauw will use such testimonials upon which to base his theories of a degenerate America.

The Indian, then, had his detractors and panegyrists. The controversy went from words to deeds. If, as Columbus himself says, the Indians believed that the white men had come down from heaven, they were soon to be disenchanted. The Spaniards threw themselves forward with such violence and candor that the conquest quickly took on a human, all-too-human, quality. The transplanting of European culture, the servitude of the Indian, intermarriage, and the shaping of an original society had begun. The conquest was a military undertaking and yet at the same time there was an amazing effort to have Christian precepts prevail everywhere. Since the Church had given the Spanish Crown the power to direct ecclesiastical affairs as well as affairs of state in the New World, political thinking was inspired by theological thinking; and, as a consequence, abstract ideas affected the behavior of the most remote lives. Theologians and jurists not only had counseled the Catholic monarchs to proclaim the freedom of the natives, but they also had advised the assignment of Indians to different *repartimientos*, where they would be forced to work. (Under the system of *repartimientos* a group of Indians was assigned to a Spanish employer or landowner.)

The Dominican fathers, who had arrived on the island of Hispaniola (today the Dominican Republic and Haiti) in 1510, protested against the *repartimientos*. Thus a few short years after the founding of the first colony in America, there originated one of the most profound moral lessons in history: men of a conquering nation bring under discussion the righteousness of conquest itself. If it were not literature that changed the outlook of the Spaniard toward the life of the Indian, it was the artistic use of language in the sacred oratories of Friar Antonio Montesinos and others. The Dominicans denied absolution to any Spaniard who reaped benefits from the *repartimientos*. Complaints and threats finally resulted in King Fernando's convening a body of learned and conscientious men in 1512. As a result, the *repartimientos* were not abolished, but they were regulated in such a way as to allow free labor in theory and forced labor in practice.

These theological and juridical opinions were based on the medieval philosophy concerning the nature of monarchical power, the delimitations between spiritual and temporal matters, and the relation between Christianity and the infidels. This philosophy, insofar as it applied to America, meant the following: the Indians are free and rational individuals. When they defend themselves unaware of the evangelizing intentions of the Spaniards, they are within their rights and cannot be deprived of their property nor enslaved; but, of course, they are not in any way entitled to political power. If after teaching the Indians the truths of the Church-State of Spain (that is, the power of the world resides in the Pope and he gave the Indian lands to the Spanish king), they insist on resisting the preachings of the Catholic faith, then the wars are just and the Indians may be invaded, despoiled, and subjugated. They were free so long as they conformed to the Church. If they did not, the Spaniards would change from "peacemakers" to "conquerors."

This Christian imperialism had its repercussions in certain practices during the occupation of the New World. One was the custom, initiated in 1513, of "requirements." Each captain was obliged to explain briefly the Christian concept of the world to the Indians so that they might know what to abide by; then they were required to deliberate and recognize the overlordship of the Church, and (because of the papal donation of the lands to Spain) also of the king. If they did this, they were received with love; if not, they were warred upon. The captains complied with these formulas, serving them up in a platter of official language, but naturally, the Indians did not partake of what they did not understand. This was neither farce nor foolishness, but a curious example of the desire to weld abstract ideas to deeds. These ideas were stirred up by the controversies concerning the freedom of the Indians that had been enkindled by the Dominicans of Hispaniola: FRIAR PEDRO DE CÓRDOBA (1482–1521), who wrote a manual *Christian Doctrine for the Instruction of Indians* (*Doctrina cristiana para instrucción de los indios,* Mexico, 1544); FRIAR ANTONIO MONTESINOS; and others.

Father Las Casas / These friars defended the Indian from military rapacity and enlisted in their crusade the most intractable chronicler of America, BARTOLOMÉ DE LAS CASAS (1474–1566). In his long and turbulent life, this tumultuous Andalusian defended the principle that only the peaceful conversion of the Indians was legitimate. Those who had despoiled and subdued them had to return all properties if they wanted to save their own souls. Either the Spaniards returned to Spain, leaving things as they had found them, or they had to conquer by dint of holy water and scapularies, and with the Indians' permission. While he defended this principle, he penned a whole gallery of portraits and scenes which are among the most interesting of the age. He wasn't a writer, but a writing paladin. His prose flowed like a wide, slow, and unending river, rock-studded, difficult to navigate, and open to a thousand digressions; yet, the reader occasionally discerns an evocative phrase skimming on the surface. The fire of his indignation when he tells of the iniquities of the Spaniards, the intellectual keenness of his irony when he removes the hypocritical Christian mask from the face of avarice, the aggressive polemics against other chroniclers and doctrinaires, and the sagacity with which he associates the physical and psychological in his biographical sketches, reveal a writer in Las Casas. He was morally superior to his fellow countrymen in America, but he was not so lofty that he could not enjoy their gossiping. There he was, watching and hearing humanity agitated by ambitious passions, power, faith, rebellion, adventure, glory, and knowledge. And he understood these men well, even when their actions were impelled by non-spiritual motives. He poked and stirred up their consciences (hence, the psychological quality of many of his pages) and there is a malicious mockery in the way he exposed their selfishness. As he sketched them, he would reduce their heroic stature. For example, he showed Cortés as timid, "withdrawn and humble" before Velazquez's servants, and later Cortés is shown laughing cynically, recalling his depredations as "the pagan pirate." Or if he depicted his subjects as being heroic, he also projected their rabid quality, as he did in the admirable picture of the slight, quick, and fearless Alonso de Ojeda who was so short that in order to shield himself completely all he had to do was to kneel behind his buckler. Ojeda had never seen his own blood until, wounded by an arrow, he orders the torn muscle to be cauterized with white-hot searing irons. He threatens the hesitating doctor with the gallows; then he wraps himself in vinegar-saturated bedsheets and without a complaint awaits the return of his health in order to resume running Indians through with his sword.

To demonstrate the terrible impact that the Spaniards produced, even while mortally wounded, he describes the scene in which Pedro de Ledesma, his brains exposed, his body broken and bloody, was putting Indians to flight while lying on his back yelling: "If I get up!— with this threat alone they [the Indians] would bolt and flee in astonishment, for which we should not marvel, for he was a fierce man, large in body and with a deep voice." Las Casas was also sensitive to the physical beauty of these men when, for example, he evokes the scene in which the youth Grijalva is bedecked by one of the chieftains with leaves of gold, saying: "the handsomeness that Grijalva assumed was worthy of being seen." A great portraitist was Las Casas—depicting the voice, the figure, the countenance, how well this or that man played the guitar, the headaches that prevent studying, the way a horse was made to gambol, the way one laughed, or gazed, or held his head, and so on. His indignation prompted sermons which were not his best writings. But it also prompted episodical adventures in which the Spaniards had the role of villains and the Indians "that of people of the Golden Age lauded for so long by poets and historians"; here indeed we can enjoy the fruits of his literature. His *History of the Indies* (*Historia de las Indias*) was begun in 1527 and included the period up to shortly before his death. His *Brief Account of the Destruction of the Indies* (*Brevísima relación de la destrucción de las Indias*) was published in 1552. It has more historic exactness than his opponents have claimed. In this respect he was superior to Oviedo, to Pedro Mártir, to Gómara, and to Herrera. But Las Casas possesses merit not because he may have been the first to proclaim those ideas which aroused his passions, but because he defended them with valor, enkindling them with love, setting forth problems in a new and vast reality. In a history governed by Providence, he considered himself a man of destiny. The Indians, his protégés, were descendants of the lost tribes of Israel. These peoples were those who would embrace the Church if, as Las Casas prophesied, the destruction of the Indies were punished one day by the destruction of Spain.

Conquest and Learning: Oviedo / Although Las Casas moved from place to place, he centered his activities in Santo Domingo because this was the cultural center of the New World. It was there that the first convents and schools were established; it was there the first pedagogical books were written; and there the colonial expansion was initiated.

Certainly of an extraordinarily virile temper were these men who emerged from ordinary people to make their way through uncharted mountains, rivers, jungles, deserts and seas, to raise everywhere the pillars upon which the Spanish Empire was to be built. They explored the Antilles, they discovered the Pacific Ocean and the Río de la Plata, they took possession of Mexico and Peru, they trod from Florida to the Mississippi, they fought the Arauco Indians of Chile, they founded cities in Nueva Granada, they colonized Argentina and Paraguay, and they explored the Amazon River. Out of these expeditions came chroniclers—soldiers and missionaries—aware of the importance of their deeds, who wrote what they saw, and the pleasure with which they wrote compelled them to improve their unpolished prose. They have left not only documents for the understanding of sixteenth-century history, but also the secrets necessary for the understanding of their souls. It was America that awakened in the majority of them the desire to write, and they did so in a language that was fairly uniform though hasty, turbulent, and murky.

While others in Europe were rediscovering the value of ancient cultures, GONZALO FERNÁNDEZ DE OVIEDO (1478–1557) discovered in America the value of new experiences in an original environment. He preferred a historiography founded on direct observation as opposed to the humanist historiography of his times: "I am not writing on the authority of any historian or poet, but as my own eyewitness." To him the New World appeared as "one of those things worthy of being known." "Do not look," he wrote to Charles V, "but on the newness of what I wish to say." That "newness" was not just American geography, but also the philosophic meaning that Oviedo gave, for the first time, to the discovery. In his *Summary of the Natural History of the Indies* (*Sumario de la natural historia de las Indias*, 1526), he described the non-European elements, the uniqueness "of the secrets and things that nature produces" in the newly explored lands. A man of the Renaissance, but of the Spanish Renaissance, Catholic, and preserver of medieval traditions, Oviedo gave a tranquil vision of the universal order —God, Nature, Man are part of an intelligible system. We know God by studying nature; then nature invites us to a superior spiritual life for which God has endowed us appropriately. And because the nature of the New World was unknown, to contemplate it was to complete our knowledge of God.

The *Summary* was expanded into the *General and Natural History of the Indies* (*Historia general y natural de las Indias,* 1526–1549) with an interpretation which, departing from the new American reality, arrived at the justification of the imperial policies of Charles V. God had elected the Spaniards to implant a universal Catholic monarchy. Oviedo saw, of course, the rapacity of the conquistadors, but to him it seemed accidental. On the other hand, the defects that he saw in the Indians seemed to him inherent. It was the defects of their savageness which, depriving them of their understanding of the true religion, deformed their souls. Yes, Oviedo admitted that the Indians had souls; what they lacked was rational sufficiency. The ugliness of soul was converted into ugliness of body. Spiritual inferiority, of historic origin, was converted into material inferiority, of ethnographic origin. Christianity, with its moral perfections, would give light to the spirit and, in turn, the spirit would give light to the countenance. Meanwhile, the Indians must pay for their idolatry.

In his moments of greatest impatience, Oviedo believed that the Indians were shades of Satan that had to be exterminated. They were men, not beasts, but so vicious, vile, cowardly, degenerate, superstitious, ungrateful, deceitful, lazy, and stupid that they had to be treated like beasts. They were to blame for their own destruction because they were incapable of forming part of the Catholic empire of Charles V. When Las Casas accused Oviedo of speaking about things he had not seen, he was referring to the latter's deprecation of the Indian. The fact is that the real Indian could not be seen in the sixteenth century— he was either the abstraction of the good man or the evil man. And for Oviedo he was the evil man whom God had punished by the hand of the conquistador. He was not enthused, then, with what he saw; yet, upon describing an *areyto* (dance with recitative) that he saw in Hispaniola in 1515, he remembered that this indigenous custom of commenting on historical facts and of preserving traditions was similar to the old Spanish ballads which he remembered and occasionally felt called upon to recite. Down deep Oviedo failed to comprehend native customs. He saw things through European eyes and was determined, furthermore, to belittle the Indians. In the beautiful Anacaona, first American poetess of record—although her lyrics, intoned by the Indians in the *areytos*, are lost—Oviedo saw beauty, indeed, but also moral dissolution. He had a taste for literature as can be seen from the first book he put together (more as a translator than as an author), *Claribalte*

(1519), a book of chivalry and adventure. Later, perhaps because of Erasmistic influences, he became ashamed of this useless fiction and severely condemned all novelistic genres. By now his life was oriented by an imperious ethical sense which made him value the truth of history and not the beauties of fantasy. The heart of his great body of writings, then, was history. He was a self-taught man who tried to please whoever employed him (this is the reason for his thesis that the Indies belonged to the early Spanish kings—even before Columbus), but he did all he could to gather documentation, and in this sense, he was a conscientious historian. Nevertheless, his early fondness for the novels of chivalry and for the wonders of the imagination slips into his historical works without his realizing it. The marvelous monsters of literary history reappear on the American landscape; knights-errant reappear costumed as conquistadors. And is not there an after-taste of chivalric literature in his enjoyment of ancestral lineages and coats of arms described in his treatises on nobility, though he says that his models were the *Portraits and Generations* (*Generaciones y semblanzas*) of Fernán Pérez de Guzmán and *Illustrious Men* (*Claros varones*) of Fernando del Pulgar? We are referring to Oviedo's *Fifty Stanzas on Spanish Nobility* (*Quincuagenas de la nobleza de España*) and *Fifty Stanzas on Illustrious Men or Battles* (*Quincuagenas de varones ilustres o Batallas y quincuagenas*). The latter is in the form of a dialog between Sereno, who interrogates, and the Mayor (or rather Oviedo, mayor of Santo Domingo, in Hispaniola), who answers.

Conquistadors in Mexico / Not all the chroniclers had something all their own to say. From the viewpoint of literary history only a few of the testimonials concern us, for example, those of two really distinctive men, Hernán Cortés and Bernal Díaz del Castillo, who were associated in the same enterprise.

HERNÁN CORTÉS (1485–1547) dispatched five letters to Charles V between the years 1519 and 1526. The first one has been lost and is replaced by another also addressed to Charles V by the City Council of Veracruz. In his *Letters* Cortés speaks unemotionally, and one can only guess the sudden animation in his face when he relates, not so much what he does, but what he sees in his walks about the city and the marketplace. He was the first soldier to discover the greatness of an indigenous civilization. Soldier indeed he was, and his goal was conquest; but while he was overpowering everything through persuasion, intrigue, politics, falsehood, and brutality, he knew how to appreciate the value of the social organization of the Aztecs. It is not because of literary lassitude that Cortés confesses his inability to communicate to the king the wonders that he sees; it is really the feeling that Mexican reality was greater than the mental framework that he brought from Spain. He feels that the very language he speaks is a wide-meshed net that cannot pull up all the new things he sees. "Since I cannot name them I shall not express them." While describing a temple he says: "there is no human tongue than can interpret its grandeur and singularness."

Cortés perceived the ideal forms of an indigenous culture. However, after contemplating them, he destroyed them. He had, like all of his companions, a soul shaped by the hierarchical notions of Church and Empire. The obedience to Church and Empire gave his soul a swordlike hardness with which to cut the knots that his admiration had tied earlier. The first sign of disrespect on the part of the Indians would occasion a "we Spaniards" and "those Indians" attitude that reduced the moral radiance of his letters though not the value of his evocative prose. He is an audacious man who demands the vassalage of all the Indians and their immediate conversion to Catholicism. He decrees and threatens. If they acquiesce, there will be peace; if not, he will torture, he will assassinate, he will scorch, he will massacre. He advances dauntlessly, friendly to the submissive, terrible to the rebellious. As he relates, he does not obstruct the image of the Indians by interposing his own massive personality. Quite the contrary, if we sympathize with the Indians, as we make our way through the chronicle, it is partly due to Cortés' sympathetic treatment. He shows them frightened, confused. At times they take recourse to diplomacy or to conspiracy; at times they are scandalized or contemptuous, determined in every way to rid themselves of those Spaniards who, with their horse, their gunpowder, their armor, do not retreat before anything. And when the Indians finally rise up in arms, Cortés puts words in their mouths that justify their warring upon the Spaniards. Cortés was not sincere in the aims he proposed in his *Letters* to the Emperor, and if there is anything lacking in them, it is frankness. But if he did not reveal the Indians' true temper of mind, it was not because of insincerity, but because he was unable to conceive of it.

Having demolished the indigenous culture, Cortés begins to set up the Colony. In his fourth letter he points out the defects of the Spanish colonization—the unworthy friar and the rapacious *encomendero*. (*Encomendero* was the recipient of an *encomienda,* an assignment by Royal decree of lands to be exploited, not unlike a feudal estate.) The restrained tone of his *Letters* was not so much a reflection of his temperament as it was of his ability. He was an irascible leader whose temple veins used to swell, Bernal tells us, during his frequent disputes. But, like most leaders he knew how to control himself and domineer with coldly contained words. And in this manner he shows himself to us in his *Letters*—cool, with the coolness of one who puts up a front. He was a Caesar, more like Borgia than Julius. "He was somewhat of a poet, who knew Latin very well and conversed with good rhetoric," reports Bernal.

BERNAL DÍAZ DEL CASTILLO (1495 or 1496–1584) who was one of Cortés' soldiers, recognized the courage, the effectiveness, and the dignity of Cortés; but he added to the idea of Hero (so dear to the Renaissance biographers of Cortés) his own idea of the importance of Masses (the body of the Spanish army, the populace). He did not belittle Cortés; he humanizes him. He surrounds him with people, he has him move and speak with everyday gestures, and in this fashion another history of the conquest of New Spain emerges, not the true one but a more colorful one. *The True History of the Conquest of New Spain* (*Verdadera historia de la conquista de la Nueva España*) is one of the most impassioned chronicles ever written in Spanish, and perhaps the one most passionately discussed. Say what one will, reading Bernal is pleasurable. The reader is taken by the contrast between the extraordinary value of the narration and the simplicity of materials with which it is woven. Bernal was not trained to write, nor was he a soldier who had great deeds to recount. He was an obscure person who never distinguished himself in anything, but he was so ambitious that thanks to these defects—not being a writer and not being a hero—he succeeded in producing a genial work. Bernal, a man from the masses, democratizes historiography and during his prolonged old age he writes about what no one knows better than he. "And I say again that I, I and I, and many times I say, that I am the oldest [of the conquistadors], and I have served His Majesty as a good and dutiful soldier." The force with which the "I" pounds down throughout the *True History* produces a new sound to which we must attune our ears in order to be able to enjoy it; because it is not the heroic I, but rather the slightly discontented, resentful, covetous, vainglorious, vituperative I, of an intelligent plebeian who says everything in a cataract of minutely detailed recollections. Bernal does not adorn, does not pick and choose, does not organize, does not dissemble. And because he lacked a feeling for literary form he gave us the most informative and complete of the Mexican chronicles. The literary form that he does, indeed, handle well is the narrative—he relives the past minute by minute, confusing the essen-

tial with the accidental, as in a vivid conversation. With one jerk he
pulls us from our seats, placing us in the sixteenth century, and we see
what the Spanish people were like during their first days in the Americas. He even records the slightest phenomena of New World phonetics.
Although Bernal was a Castilian, there is evidence that he mixed the
consonants *c* and *s* as the Andalusians do. The first linguistic sediments
in America were from Andalusian pronunciation (sixty-seven per cent
of the Spanish population was from Andalusia by 1509; seventy per
cent by 1519), and Bernal learned to *sesear,* that is, to pronounce *c*
before *e* and *i* as *s,* in America. On the other hand, his vocabulary
comes from the language he heard in Spain: it has been estimated that,
out of the 4,300 words he uses, less than 100 are of American origin. He
speaks with the breath of an entire social group. A chronicler of the
masses, his "I" becomes "we." Bernal remembers the heroic romances
of literature, so that he knows it would be easier to simplify his account with individual actions adorned rhetorically in the manner of
the epics, but what he desires to relate is the efforts of the masses and
therefore he chooses that difficult road, suspecting that he cannot accomplish his end with vividness. He was aware of the strength of his
chronicle and would even call himself coquettishly "unlettered idiot."
In his final chapter Bernal refers to a conversation in which two licenti-
ates reproach him for speaking so much about himself. And of whom
else should he speak? says he. "Would you have the birds babble about
the battles as they flew over them, or the clouds that passed by, or
should it not be the very officers and soldiers who took part in them?"
"It is not my intent to praise myself in this, for it is the simple truth;
and these are not old accounts of many years gone by, of Roman history
nor of imaginative tales of poets . . ."

Las Casas is the chronicler who defends the Indian from the rapacity of the Spaniard, and Bernal is the chronicler of rapacity itself. And
precisely for this reason we can see how Las Casas exaggerated his
accusations, and how unjust are those who, misusing his *Brief Account
of the Destruction of the Indies,* consolidated the black legend against
Spain. Because in Bernal not everything is covetousness—there were also
the idealistic drives of glory, Christianity, loyalty to king, concept of
empire—something chivalric, in short. In fact, he is the only chronicler
who ventures to cite novels of chivalry, which, as is well known, constituted the favorite reading from the end of the fifteenth century to the
middle of the sixteenth. Those tales of knights-errant who sallied forth
into enchanted lands excited the imagination of the conquistadors at a
time when every printed book was taken to be the truth and moved

their spirits to heroic undertakings in which they hoped to find treasures, wonders, and glorious adventures. The influence of these novels reflects itself subtly, but the chroniclers did not cite them, partly because the moralists and humanists of the sixteenth century railed against them (the point was reached where they were prohibited), and it would not have been proper, in "service reports," to support one's own chronicle on the basis of such scorned material. Bernal Díaz, on the other hand, upon describing his first impressions of the Aztec capital cannot help but bring to the surface his *Amadís:* "We were all amazed and remarked that those towers, temples and lakes resembled the enchanted places described in the *Amadís.*" Indeed, these men had read the *Amadís.* From one of the *Amadís* sequels came the place name of California—the name of the island of black Amazons in the *Exploits of Esplandián* (*Sergas de Esplandián*). They also read *Palmerín,* and from the second offspring of the *Palmerín* series came the place name of Patagonia—in the *Primaleón,* Patagón was the name given to a monster with a human trunk and a canine face. Offshoots of these first Mexican chronicles would be those of Hernando Alvarado Tezozómoc (*ca.* 1520–*ca.* 1600) and Diego Muñoz Camargo (*ca.* 1526–*ca.* 1600).

Missionaries in Mexico / The conquest and colonization of Ibero-America are too complex to form any rash judgments—they were neither the black legend of monsters nor the white legend of saints. It was a violent collision of civilizations, and if the Spaniard could not respect the culture of the Indian, at least he made an effort to understand it. No other people did so. Spain, especially through the work of its friars, demonstrated a new kind of intellectual curiosity. The friars wanted to Christianize the Indians; that is, they wanted them to stop being Indians. But in order to attain this profound change in the personality of the peoples of the New World, the friars had to become part of that personality. Consequently, before they could Christianize they were Indianized themselves. They began by learning the indigenous languages in order to catechize better. They constructed grammars and dictionaries; they wrote in the native language. The Crown required the teaching of Castilian. By 1550 it had been repeated over and over again that it was necessary "that those peoples learn our Castilian tongue and that they accept our good-breeding and customs." However, there were times when the friars dedicated themselves more resolutely to the learning of indigenous languages than to the teaching of Castilian. What was the reason for this? Were they afraid that along with the Castilian the Indians would adopt the blasphemies, heresies, deviational tendencies, sorceries, and new ideas that were perturbing the religious conscience of sixteenth-century Spain? Did they believe that ignorance of the Castilian language would be a holding dike to allow time to catechize the uncorrupted minds with purity? Did they wish to become indispensable? If they, and only they, were able to communicate with the Indians, they would possess an advantage over all other Spaniards. Were they learning indigenous languages in order to better implant Spanish? What *is* certain is that the friars had slipped into the inner recesses of the indigenous soul; and there, before building Christian faith, they admired the spirit of non-European cultures. The indigenous past—customs, traditions—appeared before European eyes, not so much because friars had moved to the New World, but because they had moved into the souls of the inhabitants of the New World.

FRIAR ANDRÉS DE OLMOS (1500–1571), for example, put into Castilian "Preachments of the Elders" (*"Pláticas de los ancianos"*) recalled by the oldest of the Indians in Mexico. With these dissertations the Indians educated their youth. A disciple of his was FRIAR BERNARDINO DE SAHAGÚN (1500–1590) who defended the existence of rhetorical art among the Indians and who transcribed their discourses (comparing them to those of classical European culture) and their hymns to the gods. As a Christian of zealous faith, Sahagún believed that Satan hid himself in the religious chants of the Mexican Indians in order that he might better plot his evils; however, Sahagún made an effort to study in Nahuatl to understand the Indians better and to educate them so that they themselves could record their traditions in Castilian script. In his *General History of the Things of New Spain* (*Historia general de las cosas de Nueva España*)—written in the Mexican language and later rewritten by himself in Castilian—this Franciscan missionary collected ethnographic and folkloric information in an objective manner, that is, respectful of the objects studied. This affection for the Indians induces FRIAR TORIBIO DE BENAVENTE (d. 1569) to change his name to MOTOLINÍA, "the poor one." His attitude is symbolic: "This is the first word that I know in this language, and so that I may not forget it, from this point on it shall be my name." His *History of the Indians of New Spain* (*Historia de los indios de Nueva España*) opposed Las Casas, not because he excuses the conquistadors, but because he places their cruelty on a relative basis comparing it with that of the Spaniards in Spain. Other religious chroniclers were: Pedro Simón, Jerónimo de Mendieta, Alonso de Fuenmayor (d. 1554), Friar Domingo de Betanzos (d. 1538), and Friar Martín Ignacio de Loyola, whose *Itinerary of the New World* (*Itinerario del Nuevo Mundo*) was revised by Juan González de Mendoza (1545–1618).

The defenseless Spaniard: Cabeza de Vaca / Of the contact between Europeans and Indians, the only extant impressions are those of the Europeans; nevertheless, the Indians were discovering the white man at the same time that they were being discovered by him. How did they look upon the white man? We do not know. Generally he appeared

disfigured by the complicated apparatus of civilization. But in the case
of ALVAR NÚÑEZ CABEZA DE VACA (1490?–1559?) we see European man
and American man, for the first time face to face in their naked state.
And we can imagine how the Indians looked upon this fellow creature,
an exhausted and defenseless Spaniard. The "relation" of his wanderings has come to us in three versions. In modern editions it is known
under the title *Shipwrecks* (*Naufragios*). The *Shipwrecks* scarcely is
of interest to the historian (although it has much for the ethnolo-
gist in view of the strange information it yields on the customs of the
Indians), but that is where its merit lies. Its interest does not depend,
as in other chronicles, on heroic deeds, or on conquests, or on the background of opulent indigenous civilizations, but rests purely and exclusively in its narrative quality. Cabeza de Vaca left Spain in 1527. He
suffered so many shipwrecks that his vessels were finally scattered with
the cry, "every man for himself." He arrived on land with a handful of
Spaniards. Hunger, struggles with the Indians, hardships, disease. Little by little they began dying off. Finally four remain: he, Dorantes,
Castillo, and the Negro Estebanico. Captured by the Indians, he was
maltreated by some, idolized by others. Yet Cabeza de Vaca covered
a great distance on foot (from the Gulf of Mexico to the Gulf of California). Nine years of captivity converted him, in physical appearance
at least, into another Indian. He can only be proud of one thing—
being a man. He walks about as nude as the day he was born, eating
what the Indians eat, living and speaking like them, different only in
his Christian faith. When in 1536 he stumbled upon some Spaniards
on horseback, he relates "they were put in a state of contention upon
seeing me so strangely dressed and in the company of Indians. They
kept looking at me for some length of time, so astonished, that they
neither spoke to me nor managed to ask me anything."

Cabeza de Vaca knows how to tell a story. He centers his stories
around the "I," and without losing sight of his reader (he is one chronicler who writes for his reader) he evokes his adventures in a style
which is rapid, rich in detail, impressive, and conversational yet dignified. It is one chronicle that can be reread with pleasure. While
reading, one visualizes constantly—such is the strength of his description. There is not a single obscure page in this adventure story with a
happy ending.

Chronicles of the Conquest of Peru / The conquest of the Aztec empire and its adjacent territories was now complete and the conquistadors
looked for another Mexico. The Garden of Eden, El Dorado, the City

of the Caesars, the realm of the Amazons, in short, everything that they did not find in the campaigns of the North, now they feverishly sought in the South. Sea explorations had already touched the outer edges of South America (Vespucci, Magellan, Solís, Cabot), but it was after 1530 when land explorations opened the mysterious interior to the geographic eyes of the epoch. Francisco Pizarro discovered in Peru, as Cortés had done in Mexico, a stupendous civilization—the Inca. And new riches of the conquered lands appeared and new chronicles by the conquerors. It is possible that Spain might not have understood until then the value of its own imperial undertaking. But the great riches that the conquest of Peru produced and the chronicles that were revealing the growing expanse of territorial possessions must have opened the eyes of Charles V—perhaps he began suspecting that America was something more than an obstacle on the road to the Orient. Had not Francisco López de Gómara just told Charles V, upon dedicating to him his *General History of the Indies,* that "the greatest thing next to the creation of the world, omitting the incarnation and death of He who created it, is the discovery of the Indies; and for this reason, they call it The New-World"? We will mention several chroniclers, pointing out that those who contributed most in forming a picture of the history of the Incas were Cieza de León, Agustín de Zárate, and Sarmiento de Gamboa.

PEDRO CIEZA DE LEÓN (b. between 1520 and 1522 and d. in 1560) left one of the most extensive and objective chronicles on the conquest of Peru, the internecine struggles of the Spaniards, the Inca civilization, and its geographic setting. "Many times," says Cieza, "when the other soldiers rested, I busied myself writing." But this soldier who writes his own recollections is following a plan, that of a vast history. The *First Part of the Chronicle of Peru (Parte primera de la Crónica del Perú)* was published in 1553. The second part or *The Dominion of the Incas (Del señorío de los Incas)* was published only in 1880. The third part began to be published in 1946, and the fourth seems to have been lost. Cieza looks upon the Indians from above—savages capable of cruelty and of the "impious sin of sodomy."

From a literary point of view one of the best chroniclers was AGUSTÍN DE ZÁRATE (d. after 1560). He witnessed the rebellion of Gonzalo Pizarro. His *History of the Discovery and Conquest of Peru (Historia del descubrimiento y conquista del Perú)* is meritorious for its commentaries written in "awkward and badly assorted words," according to the author, but in reality very profuse in movement, method, and even style. In judging the overlords of Cuzco his tone is condemnatory.

He left us a historical monument, beautiful for its clarity and elegance, even though his work elaborates on the materials of other chroniclers.

PEDRO SARMIENTO DE GAMBOA (1530–1592), who considered the Incas tyrannical usurpers, was the favorite of Viceroy Toledo, the up-rooter of the Inca line. Gamboa's *History of the Incas (Historia de los Incas)* gives us vivid pictures of the terror and infamies perpetrated by the natives.

FRANCISCO LÓPEZ DE JEREZ (1504–1539), secretary to Francisco Pizarro under whose charge he wrote the *True Account of the Conquest of Peru and the Province of Cuzco (Verdadera relación de la conquista del Perú y provincia de Cuzco, 1534)*, with painstaking care ponders the deeds of the conquistadors up to the death of Atahualpa. Other chroniclers were: JUAN POLO DE ONDEGARDO (d. 1575); JUAN DE BETANZOS (1510–1576); the two clerics of the same name, CRISTÓBAL DE MOLINA ("the Chilean," 1494–1580? and "the Cuzqueño," d. 1585); PEDRO DE VALDIVIA (1500–1553) whose *Letters (Cartas)* describe beautifully the founding of Serena in Chile.

Among the first chroniclers of Peru, ALONSO HENRÍQUEZ DE GUZMÁN (1500 and d. after 1544) is noteworthy, if not for his literary value (although he did write verse and knew the poetry and theater of his times), for his originality. Traces of picaresque literature have been noticed in his autobiography. Nevertheless, his unscrupulous impulsion to adventure is not that of a rogue. Unlike the rogue, he does believe in a respectable social order; the trouble is that he does not occupy in that social order the position that he would like. Even so, he was somewhat roguish, especially in the first part of the *Life and Customs of Don Alonso Henríquez de Guzmán, Destitute Nobleman (Vida o Libro de la vida y costumbres de Don Alonso Henríquez de Guzmán, caballero noble desbaratado)*.

Chroniclers of New Granada

Together with the rogue-conquistadors were the knight-errant-conquistadors. We know that the novels of chivalry were slowly losing their fascination and that Cervantes, in that superb exercise of literary criticism—*Don Quijote*—reduces them to the ridiculous. Something of the Don Quijote, with his bewildering fluctuation between reality and fantasy, could be seen in a number of conquistadors who were capable of cruelty and self-denial.

And one of the conquistadors sounds to us like the real Don Quijote —GONZALO JIMÉNEZ DE QUESADA (1499–1579). He was a humanist who wore his Latin learning well, but almost everything he wrote has been lost. There are good reasons for attributing to him the *Compendium of the Conquest of New Granada (Epítome de la conquista del Nuevo de Granada)* which is extant. Rodríguez Freyle reproaches him for "not writing the events of his times, although he was a learned man." His contemporaries were wont to cite him and profit by his writ-

ings and his oratory. His sphere of action and observation was the
"new realm of Granada." As a tangent to his sphere was *The Antijovio,*
a refutation of the Italian historian Paolo Jovio. He had a taste for
poetry and even wrote some. He was a protagonist in the polemic (still
alive in America even though in Spain it had already passed away) between pure Spanish verse and Italianate verse. The short meters of
the old ballads and lays were arriving without interruption; and for
serious poetry, there were the strophes made famous by Juan de Mena.
The oldest anonymous poem on the conquest of Peru was written around
1548 in couplets of *arte mayor.* Gonzalo Jiménez de Quesada and
other poet-soldiers had their ears trained to the octosyllable. When
they heard for the first time the Italianate hendecasyllables they did
not know how to enjoy them. "The verses left such a bad sound in
their ears / that they judged them to be prose / with superfluous
rhymes," says Juan de Castellanos quoting Lorenzo Martín, the captain who heartened his starving soldiers with his pleasantries, torrents
of couplets and improvised quatrains. And referring to Jiménez de
Quesada, he would add, "And he contended with me many times /
that the old Castilian meters were / those fitting and proper for having been brought forth / from the bosom of that language / and that
the hendecasyllables were alien newcomers, adopted / from a different
and foreign mother."

The anxiety for discovery was such that three expeditions, Jiménez
de Quesada's, Belalcázar's, and Federmann's, suddenly ran across each
other in the valley where Bogotá rises today. The legend of El Dorado
had attributed fantastic riches to this region. It was said that a chieftain,
surrounded with treasures greater than those of Mexico and Peru, had
the habit of bathing in the nude with his body covered with gold dust.
There were other legends: the fountain of youth, the silver mountain
range, the land of cinnamon. This last legend attracted Orellana in
his exploration of the Amazon.

The Amazons / No sooner had the followers of Orellana become disillusioned with the cinnamon, when they were taken by the illusion of
the legend of the Amazons—certain women who lived separated from
men. The chronicler of Orellana's voyage was FRIAR GASPAR DE CARVA-
JAL (1504–1584). His *Account of the Recent Discovery of the Famous
Great River of the Amazons* (*Relación del nuevo descubrimiento del
famoso río Grande de las Amazonas*) relates without embellishments,
without emphasis of expression, his impressions of 1541–42. The merit
of these writings depends on the real, direct, and faithful experience

that he transmits, and not on his style. And, observed Gonzalo de Oviedo, Friar Carvajal "should be believed if only for those two arrow wounds, one of which tore out or crushed his eye." The stamp of validity for this literature rests on the fact that the author's eyes were looking upon the reality being described, pierced by the arrow of this same reality. Carvajal is an observer of reality. He would like to see everything. He left us observations on the character of the Indians in war and in peace, on their musical instruments and dances, on their weapons and dugout canoes. In spite of his lack of resources, in spite of his wounded eye, he does appreciate the gayness of the island that the brigantines were beginning to leave behind. He is a realist-observer; yet the myth of the Amazons so obsessed him that he believed that the women who fought alongside their husbands were Amazons, and he describes them as captains from the "good land and dominion of the Amazons." His fantasy poetizes his chronicle, as in the case of the rare bird who was perched on an oak by the shore, and "began to screech at great speed flee, flee, flee . . ." Not mentioning such Christian prodigies as God's intervening to save him, he adds brush strokes of light to the adventures of this spirited and pious one-eyed friar on the great river labyrinth until he emerges from "the mouths of the watery dragon" into the Atlantic.

In the Region of the Río de la Plata / In 1536 Don Pedro de Mendoza founded the city of Buenos Aires on the shores of the Río de la Plata. Friar LUIS DE MIRANDA (1500?), who accompanied him, was to describe later (between the years 1541 and 1545) the native siege, the hunger, and the destruction of the city in a *Folk-poem* (*Romance*) of 150 octosyllables in *pie quebrado* (combination of verses of eight and four syllables). Faced with this scene of horror, Luis de Miranda, without poetic inspiration but with ingenuity, allegorically converts the Argentinian lands into a treacherous woman who kills off her Spanish husbands, one by one. Only God, he says, could give such a widow a "wise, strong and daring" husband. This husband was to be in 1580 Juan de Garay. But until then the first permanent colony in the south of the continent was Asunción in Paraguay. Luis de Miranda went there; Cabeza de Vaca arrived there in 1540 with his secretary Pero Hernández; and there the three were victims of the same political disturbance.

PERO HERNÁNDEZ (*ca.* 1513?) wrote his *Commentaries* (1554) in which he narrates the unfortunate lot of Alvar Núñez Cabeza de Vaca in Asunción from 1540 to 1545. It is the first Spanish book on the conquest of the Río Plata region. He who approaches the struggles between Spaniards in sixteenth-century Asunción with historical sympathy can move through the pages of the *Commentaries* with ease, because its defects are not too disturbing. It stands in defense of Cabeza de Vaca and in opposition to Irala. His factious nature, on one hand, denounces the impetuous Spanish customs, and on the other, reveals a basic pity for the ill-treated mass of Indians. That is what makes the accusations dramatic. Since accusatory literature is made with gestures ("he did that," "I did this"), the prose, which otherwise would ramble on sluggishly, moves in impulsive strides. Cabeza de Vaca helped Hernández edit the first chapters. In one of these chapters, where reference is made to Cabeza de Vaca's second crossing from Spain to the New World, we have the pleasant episode about the cricket: a soldier, upon leaving Cadiz, brought a cricket on board the vessel so that he could hear it sing during the voyage; to the great annoyance of its owner, the cricket does not sing; suddenly, it does sing because it has sensed the proximity of land; from that moment "every night the cricket would give us his music." Hernández is amenable; he colors his descriptions and knows how to narrate.

In Paraguay's Asunción we will also find a Spanish woman, Doña Isabel de Guevara, who had arrived at the Río de la Plata with the expedition of Pedro de Mendoza. Her letter of 1556, addressed to the governing princess Doña Juana, is the first literary document that protests the unjust neglect of women. Isabel had been one of the co-founders of Buenos Aires; twenty years later she describes the hunger, calamities, burdensome tasks, and even the war efforts carried out shoulder to shoulder with the men: "The men became so enervated that the poor women were laden with all of the work, like washing clothes, curing the men, preparing what little food they had, cleaning them, acting as sentinels, stoking the fires, manning the crossbows whenever the Indians carried on an attack, even taking care of the ships, helping those men to stand by their posts who were still able to, shouting and fighting on the battlefield, taking command and putting order in the ranks of the soldiers, because since women are able to subsist on less food, we had not fallen into such a weakened state as the men."

Let us here close our review of the chronicles. They are so numerous (we have only mentioned a few) that already in those years an attempt to list them was made by ALONSO DE ZORITA (1512–1566?), *Catalog of the Authors Who Have Written Histories of the Indies* (*Catálogo de los autores que han escrito historias de Indias*).

The Theater

We have said that there were two kinds of artistic activities which, upon initial contact with the new American reality, acquired creative power although retaining an archaic, medieval appearance—the chronicle and the theater. We have examined the chronicle. On the theater there are only indirect references. The conquistadors celebrated their holidays in their own way with mystery plays, preludes, interludes, mummeries, etc.

It is recorded that during these years religious plays were composed by Friar Andrés de Olmos, Friar Juan de Torquemada, Luis de Fuensalida and others. Micael de Carvajal (1490?) visited Santo Domingo in 1534: it is possible that by then he was writing *Tragedy of Josephine* (*Tragedia josefina*, 1535), a religious play remarkable in the theater before Lope de Vega. In his miracle play *The Court of Death* (*Auto de las Cortes de la Muerte*, 1557)—whose ending was written by Luis Hurtado de Toledo—Carvajal presented some Indians who complain of the abuses inflicted by the Spaniards. Many pieces originated in Spain.

31

To have catechized the Indians so spectacularly, the missionary theater must have been quite original. With the aim of propagating the Christian faith, the missionaries adapted to the theatrical forms of the Middle Ages the incipient dramatic art of the Indians—floral fiestas or *mitotes,* ritual ceremonies, songfests, dances, pantomimes, and comical improvisations that aped the movements of animals or deformed humans, etc. The Church lent theological meaning to those spectacles which at times were prepared in the native languages. The Spanish chronicles abound in allusions to this theater from 1535 onward; Motolinía has left us a gracious description of the mystery play about the fall of Adam and Eve presented by the Indians in their own language (Tlaxcala, 1538). The combination of nature and scenery is impressive. At times the participants are so many that the stage collapses. The spectacle ordinarily ends with the baptism of great masses of Indians. In Mexico the needs of this type of representation influenced the architecture of the "open chapels," a kind of open-air theater capable of accommodating an immense audience. These spectacles were so well attended that the crowds overflowed the churchyard and moved into the streets. They were scenes of sacred history or of sacred allegories, interspersed with comic moments and even military parades.

The Inca regions all had their fiestas of this type. In Lima from 1546 and in Potosí from 1555, theatrical pieces were presented, some in Quechua, some in Castilian. The Inca Garcilaso describes several. In 1550 under the direction of the chief magistrates and the military, plays were presented in Guayaquil as rehearsals for the battles against Indians and pirates; and they utilized scenes from the *Cid,* the *Amadís* and the *Exploits of Esplandián* (*Sergas de Esplandián*).

Hence, the intermingling of Indian and Spanish elements produced an original dramatic type. It will seem a retrogression to medieval performances if we only fix our attention on the progress of the Renaissance theater in Spain; but, on the other hand, if we focus on the new American reality, we will understand that this dramatic type was innovational and open to many possibilities. The participation of masses of people in open-air scenes, for example, could have evolved toward theatrical forms not dependent on the Church. The audience was not just audience; it participated in the performances with sham battles and dances. Unfortunately the missionary theater languished and disappeared in the second half of the sixteenth century. The Church itself drowned the theater, in cleansing it of its initial secularity. (An example of this purging is the one imposed by the Third Mexican Council in 1585.)

Renaissance Literature

If the chronicles and the missionary theater maintained medieval traits, there were other activities that accentuated Renaissance elements. Even when these activities were not literary they were at least inspired by books, like the Utopia attempted by Vasco de Quiroga

(1470–1565) in Mexico, a reflection of Thomas More's *Utopia*. Erasmism, which affected the thinking of a few men in the New World, was to a certain degree Utopian.

P. Carlos de Aragón who arrived in America in 1512 delivered sermons which, according to Las Casas, showed that "he did not esteem the doctrine of St. Thomas." Even more anti-scholastic was FRIAR JUAN DE ZUMÁRRAGA (arrived in America in 1527; d. 1548), first bishop and first archbishop of New Spain, who had printed in Mexico a *Brief Doctrine* (*Doctrina breve*, 1544) with passages from Erasmus scarcely retouched, and a *Christian Doctrine* (*Doctrina cristiana*, 1545 or 1546) with echoes from Juan de Valdés. Also an Erasmist was LÁZARO BEJARANO (Spain; b. beginning of the sixteenth century; lived at least until 1574). In Seville he had written poetry between 1531 and 1534. He belonged to a circle of poets, intimates of Gutierre de Cetina. About 1541 he lived in the city of Santo Domingo in Hispaniola where he wrote satires against priests, politicians, and private persons. In 1558 he was accused before the Inquisition of mocking scholastic theology and of exalting Erasmus. Lost is his *Apologetic Dialog* (*Diálogo apologético*) in which he defended the dignity of the aboriginal population of America, not as a priest (from whom charity is expected) but as an administrator and master of Indians. Juan Méndez Nieto (1531–*ca.* 1617), a doctor with an inclination for literature, relates that because of an anonymous satire by Lázaro Bejarano, "they arrested all the poets" so that they might apprehend the author. The fact is there were many poets. No matter how little education they had, it was considered sufficient for trying one's hand at writing. It was a collective impulse. Names of writers are preserved even if almost all of what they wrote is lost. Lázaro Bejarano, who had already written poetry in Gutierre de Cetina's circle, as we have said, must have been the first to bring to America, in 1535, verses in the Italian manner. Before this time verses in octosyllables, hexameters, and in *arte mayor* were composed. Juan de Castellanos, of whom we shall speak immediately, blames the inability to crush Enriquillo's rebellion (1519–1533) in Santo Domingo on the softness of the muses. And he was generous in saying that many of the poets of Santo Domingo, like FRANCISCO DE LIENDO (1527–1584), for example, could "well polish this that I polish / and be laughing at my verses; / would that I had them to lend support / in this work that I here compose."

JUAN DE CASTELLANOS (1522–1607) arrived in America still a youth, and in America he became a humanist and a writer. From America he knew about Garcilaso's work and, imbued with the spirit of the Renaissance, in his discussions with Jíménez de Quesada on Castilian versification he sided with the new meters derived from the Italian school. His not-at-all-elegiac *Elegies of Illustrious Men of the Indies* (*Elegías de varones ilustres de Indias,* 1589) constitute one of the longest poems written in the world; and, of course, the longest in the Spanish language. He started off with Columbus (consequently, his verses are the first dedicated to Columbus). Castellanos was rich in experience. He wrote with a sure memory in his old age about all he had lived through from Puerto Rico to Colombia, giving us the different highlights of his life as an acolyte, a pearl fisherman, a soldier, an adventurer, an enjoyer of Indian women, and a parish priest. If one were to read these verses like one who listens to the rain, it might occur to him that if all the rhetorical scaffolding were taken down an enlivened and variegated narrative mass of innumerable episodes would appear.

The reader may also notice in Castellanos a love for the American land, a Creole's and realist's attitude that merits our sympathy. He considered himself an American Spaniard, different from and superior to the newly arrived Spaniards, of whom he made fun. Among those chroniclers who first used indigenous words, he was one of those who took most pleasure in doing so. *Bohíos*, "Indian huts," *macanas*, "clubs," *jagüeyes*, "cisterns" are imprinted with all their color and descriptive strength in evocative passages. His syntax is clumsy; his tone of voice, like that used in everyday conversation, is fluid and natural; his view of the conquest is clear in its heroic as well as in its daily aspects. He was sincere, passionate, and facetious. A good example of his irony (even having some elements of mock-heroic stylization and of parodying the eclogue) is the passage that refers to the Spanish peasants brought over by Las Casas to colonize the coast of Cumaná. These were peasants armed like knights, with red crosses on their breastplates, accompanied by their shepherdesses (after all, there was the question of "populating"), inept for fighting and, in effect, ultimately destroyed by the Indians. (Castellanos respected Las Casas, but he repeated the legend of the "knights in brown" caricatured by Oviedo.)

Castellanos knew that his language was shabby; he used to say "a simple language of truth and exactness," but he trusted that the things of America are so noteworthy that "by themselves they elevate the style." He was not a poet, but his verses are stirring when they tell a story, especially if it is about something painful or tragic. He embroiders his *Elegies* with differently colored threads taken from literature, history, and classical mythology. He had read Vergil, Ovid, Horace, Seneca, Terence. And, during a time when curiosity for things exclusively Greek was exceptional, he reveals having read Xenophon and others in the original. He did not re-create the classics as Garcilaso did; rather than assimilating, the plots of his chronicles were interwoven with the texts. From the Spanish literature he made use of Juan de Mena, Garcilaso, Ercilla, and perhaps *El Cartujano*. The chronicles of Oviedo and of López de Gómara were among his sources for the historical part of the poem. He wanted to keep to the facts, but because he believed in the supernatural, an imaginative and romancing light occasionally crept into his paintings. Because of his realist's attitude, he used the word *novela,* "romance," disparagingly; for example, it seemed to him that all that talk about Amazon Indians was "light-headed romance." But, after rejecting all the deception, he reserved the right to embellish his tales with comparisons taken from literary tradition: Indians like nymphs and naiads "such as those that appear in poems," so beautiful that "Jupiter would desire to be their husband"; Indian women, for their part, looking upon the Spaniards as "lascivious and lusty fauns"; monsters in the form of hermaphroditic giants or of two-headed dwarfs a foot high; bewitchments out of books of chivalry; there is, in a word, a flux and reflux of real life and literary life.

While some Spaniards (Núñez Cabeza de Vaca, for example) went around nude like Indians, others carried on a refined cultural life. Mexico already had a university, and one of its professorial chairs was held by Francisco Cervantes de Salazar (b. before 1515; d. after 1575). He arrived in Mexico in 1551 with a humanistic culture already demonstrated in his Latin works. He continued writing in Latin. His various dialogs, in the manner of Vives, described the university, its streets, buildings, and the environs of Mexico City; made rapid comparisons of the same things in Spain; and contained quick philosophical reflections, notes on the education of the mestizo, and a certain relativism in comprehending the native culture. Already there were mestizos who knew Latin, and even some who were teaching it. For his *Chronicle of New Spain* (*Crónica de la Nueva España*), which he wrote in Spanish, he profited from the *Letters* of Cortés (whom he knew personally) and from many other written sources (Motolinía, Herrera, etc.). He was a man of vitality. Archbishop Moya de Contreras, in a report of 1575 to the King, described him thusly: "He likes to talk and is susceptible to flattery, [he is] frivolous, fickle, and dishonest, and so convinced that he is going to be Bishop that some people have already made fun of him. After twelve years of being a prebendary [a clergyman] he has not shown traces of ecclesiastical spirit and is unreliable." What matters, however, is that Cervantes de Salazar knew how to see with his own eyes the conquistadors, the things of America, and the grandeur of the city of Mexico. Before he arrived in Mexico, he flattered Hernán Cortés by attributing to him, in an Epistle of 1546, a noble but imaginary Italian genealogy. Furthermore, he invented the legend of Cortés' burning his ships in order to compare him with the Greco-Roman heroes. But, after having arrived in Mexico, his words on Cortés, in his *Chronicle,* were objective.

Other Spanish writers, such as Gutierre de Cetina, arrived in Mexico. His contributions to America are insignificant—he barely alluded twice to the new lands. If, as they say, he wrote a theatrical piece in Mexico, it has been lost; and if he left any trace, it was the importation of the Italianate hendecasyllable. Perhaps it was Gutierre de Cetina, a guest in Mexico, who lullabied the Mexican FRANCISCO DE TERRAZAS (1525?–1600?) with Italian melodies. Terrazas wrote good sonnets "in the Italian style," an amatory epistle in tercets, and an unfinished poem on the *New World and Conquest* (*Nuevo Mundo y conquista*), which is too mild for its epic theme. This is an epic poem that opens the Cortés cycle on the conquest of Mexico.

Fantasy and the New World

Fantasies, born and developed for centuries, were transplanted to the New World—paradise, the fountain of youth, the seven enchanted cities, the eleven thousand virgins, giants, pigmies, dragons, children with hoary hair, men with tails, bearded women, headless monsters with eyes in their stomachs or in their chests, monkeys that go about playing the cornet. It is natural that this combination of man, beast, and myth would sharpen the preoccupation over the problem of how the New World had become populated, who the people were, whence they had come, and what were the abilities of these people whom the Spaniards found enveloped in the light of fantastic cosmogonies and zoological systems. We see, side by side, the speculations made by the medieval mind and also by the Renaissance mentality, which wrought an attitude we would call scientific today. Disengaged from the traditions that weighed upon them while in Spain, some Spaniards felt an awakening of intellectual curiosity for the strange reality that surrounded them. This is the conflict between the theological and the scientific which will become more marked with the passage of time, as we shall see in the succeeding chapters.

II. 1556-1598

Authors born between 1530 and 1570

Historical framework: Colonization under Philip II. Spanish imperial power is broken and the momentum of the conquest begins to lose its vitality. Social institutions, meanwhile, are consolidated.

Cultural tendencies: Second renaissance and counter reformation. Chronicles tend toward verse forms. Traditional and Italianate poetry. European-patterned theater. First writers born in America.

Spain closes in upon itself, incorporates poetic forms it once imported, and seeks national formulas—the second renaissance and counter reformation are upon her. In the colonies the writers live by borrowing. This is natural. And the borrowings are profuse. Much more than has been believed because, despite the publicized prohibitions of kings and inquisitors, all sorts of fiction—Latin, Italian, and Spanish poetry; pastoral, picaresque, and sentimental novels; books of chivalry; plays; Erasmistic writings; histories, legends, allegories, didactic pleasantries—circulated throughout America in amazing abundance. One must not expect this literature, derived from the mother country, to engender a colonial literature of equal vigor. The circumstances were quite different. In Spain, literature was the manifestation of a numerous populace, unified, steeped in tradition, fond of full-breathed and sustained dialog, sure of itself, vital and powerful; in the colonies, literature was practiced by a limited number of cultured nuclei mustered about small institutions, human islands amidst illiterate masses, dilettantes feeling incapable of persistent efforts in literary apprenticeship, timidly imitative, devoid of the legal, commercial, and technical apparatus of the book-printing trade, discouraged by material difficulties. Nonetheless, the colonies did remain in the company of the mother country, but always a step behind.

In the preceding chapter the writers we studied were almost all Spaniards. There were those who came to the new land already possessing literary training, and others in whom the vocation for writing developed after their arrival in America, but they all had a Spanish soul attuned to European cultural forms. In this chapter we shall see how the descendants of the Spaniards start writing. These are "children of the earth," Creoles like Terrazas or mestizos like the Inca Garcilaso, who are to transform colonial society. Mestizos' souls, enriched by the double vision of two historic worlds, begin to reveal a new society, unknown in Europe—a society in an occidental frame but with vigorous indigenous traditions. Some write in their native tongues and therefore escape beyond the boundaries of this history. There are, among those who write in Spanish, overtones of protest or of love of their own native traditions. Nevertheless, the literary penchant of mestizos and Indians sprang from the example set by Europeans, because the indigenous population did not have a literature of its own.

Chroniclers

If in the early period Spain had shown itself remiss in appreciating the value of the conquest of America, and the chroniclers wrote on their own initiative, now the king will look with favor upon the history of New World affairs (in 1596 Philip II appointed Antonio de Herrera y Tordesillas "Chief Chronicler of the Indies," who responded in 1601 by publishing the first part of the *Decádes* and in 1615 the second).

A new group of conquistadors and missionaries produced a new group of chronicles. Some chroniclers repeated things already recorded or, at best, added recent happenings to what was already known; others described for the first time regions recently conquered. Some chronicles are composed in a poor style, useful only to the historian; others are composed in a more elevated style. More often than not there was artistic awareness, or better still, literary awareness; indeed, some chronicles, such as those of the Inca Garcilaso, in prose, and those of Alonso de Ercilla, in verse, form part of the best literature of the period.

Because these chronicles sprang up along the travel routes of the New World, we shall conduct our examination by following the same routes: Mexico, Peru, Río de la Plata, Chile. But first let us deal separately with Father José DE ACOSTA (1539–1616) who, because of location and character, cannot be classified with the rest of the chroniclers. "I must let myself be guided by the thread of reason, even though it may be a thin one, until it completely disappears before my eyes," he used to say. It is gratifying to find, in a Jesuit of the counter reformation, so much curiosity for the causes of creation, and above all, so much independent judgment vis-à-vis the authorities. He holds Aristotle lightly, and he even is ready to dispute the Bible, which he does, in his desire to understand the problems of the new American environment. In 1590, at the end of the century of discovery, his *Natural and Moral History of the Indies* (*Historia natural y moral de las Indias*) is published. In the first section (the first four books) he studies what we would call today the physical and natural sciences, and in the second section (the rest of the books) he studies problems of culture: religion, history, politics, education, etc. These two perspectives, natural and moral, comprise his vision of a world, which, for the Catholic and Aristotelian Acosta, was organized hierarchically in a unit. It is not the historical element of his *History* that is most valuable. Acosta dealt with sources, and whoever searches for historical materials can gather them from these sources. On the contrary, what is interesting in Acosta's *History* is his anti-historical attitude. By meditating over what he has seen, Acosta no longer is amazed at man's diversity in the New World. The Indian was not so different from the European. In the former, one could see the spiritual light of universal man and even customs preserved from a distant common cradle. Furthermore, he adds: "It is well-known that even in Spain and Italy there are herds of men, who except for their gestures and shapes, have little in common with man."

The year following the appearance of Acosta's *Natural History,* another description of nature appeared in Mexico: Juan de Cárdenas' *Problems and Marvelous Secrets of the Indies* (*Problemas y secretos maravillosos de las Indias,* 1591). It is interesting that Cárdenas, an Andalusian, already sees differences between the Spaniards born in the Indies and the Spaniards of Spain, the former appearing to him to be more refined, discreet, and polished.

During this period no great original chronicles are written in Mexico. The one by Friar Juan de Torquemada (*ca.* 1563–1624) *Indian Monarchy* (*Monarquía indiana,* 1615) is a second-hand work, dull, and interesting only for the documents it includes—he copied Friar Jerónimo de Mendieta's *Ecclesiastical History of the Indies* (*Historia eclesiástica indiana*) at that time, unedited. On the other hand, the *History of the Indies of New Spain* (*Historia de las Indias de Nueva España*) by Friar Diego Durán (b. before 1538–1588), written on the basis of Náhuatl documents and first-hand data, is delightful.

Of the Mexican chroniclers born during these years the most notable is Juan Suárez de Peralta (b. between 1537 and 1545; d. after 1590). One can discern in him the softness of the young man of means who profits by his inherited advantages. This Creole, who used to say of himself that he only possessed "a little grammar, but a great yen for reading histories and associating with learned persons," was one of the first to write in Mexico. His *Treatise on Horsemanship* (*Tratado de la caballería de jineta y brida*, 1580) was the first book published by an Hispanic-American author on a secular subject. He followed with a *Book on Veterinary Art* (*Libro de alveitería*) still unedited. Toward 1589 he wrote *Treatise on the Discovery of the Indies* (*Tratado del descubrimiento de las Indias*) which is one of the best pictures of Creole life in sixteenth-century New Spain. Of the forty-four chapters, the first seventeen refer to the "origin and beginnings of the Indies and Indians" and to the conquest of Mexico. His concept of the indigenous past, which is not original since he is following Sahagún, Durán, Motolinía and others, is interesting as an indication of what the first Creoles believed to be their own historical background. The remaining twenty-seven chapters deal with the years in which his family established itself in Mexico. His father, who was a brother-in-law of Hernán Cortés, had been a conquistador. Suárez' style becomes visual and vivid as he relates what he saw and what he lived through. For example, the series of episodes that end with the execution of Avila are not wanting in novelistic vigor. After the arrival of Martín Cortés, Hernán's son, the gentlemen landowners squandered their estates on feasts, games, extravagances, bullfights, hunting parties, banquets, parades, etc. Philip II decided to put an end to so much festivity by depriving the landowners of their economic privileges: the *encomiendas*. It is the gaiety of the years of the viceroyalty that Suárez de Peralta evokes with nostalgia. He delighted in telling anecdotes and liked to spice them with irony. One can observe how the spirit of the conquistador's son is different from that of the conquistador; even more, how the spirit of the Creole is different from that of the Spaniard. There is, here and there, a glimmer of sympathy for the "Lutheran corsairs" of England. He speaks to us with pity and even with sympathy for several soldiers, somewhat intoxicated, who said jokingly that the people should kill all the Spanish authorities and "rise up with the land." They were hanged, he says, "guiltless." Suárez de Peralta is proud that there has not been nor can there be until the day of judgment "another land like Mexico." Since this was his fatherland, he wanted to keep it forever in a festive mood.

The chronicler of Colombia and Venezuela was FRIAR PEDRO DE AGUADO (d. after 1589), whose literarily colorless *History of Saint Martha and the New Kingdom of Granada* (*Historia de Santa Marta y Nuevo Reino de Granada*) relates "things that I have seen and touched with my hands."

For Peru we could add new names to the list given in the preceding chapter, both Spaniards and Creoles. Of interest is the *History of Peru* (*Historia del Perú*) by DIEGO FERNÁNDEZ of Palencia, Spain, an unpolished soldier, who arrived in Peru after the conquest. The details of events he witnessed are well-worded in the second part, but in the first part he copied previous reports. PEDRO GUTIÉRREZ DE SANTA CLARA, although born in Mexico (*ca.* 1570) wrote a *History of the Civil Wars in Peru* (*Historia de las guerras civiles del Perú*) and of other events in the Indies. FRIAR REGINALDO DE LIZÁRRAGA (Peru, *ca.* 1539–1609) in *Description and Population of the Indies* (*Descripción y población de las Indias*) gives an account of what he saw in his travels through Peru, Tucumán, Río de la Plata, and Chile. It is a type of traveler's guide, full of advice and practical information, but written with perception, detail, simplicity and variety. His point of view is that of the Spaniard—as he speaks of Creoles, mestizos, and Indians his scorn increases in degree. But Lizárraga, the son of a conquistador, feels the difference between the "old conquistadors" who founded a new nobility by dint of sacrifices and the "settlers who came after the land was cleared," is that the latter benefited from the efforts of others and took possession of what did not belong to them. He complains that the descendants of the old conquistadors are spurned and replaced by newcomers who "don't even know how to blow their noses, nor have they once in their lives reached for their swords." His book represents the post-conquest society with the wounds of the civil war not yet healed. The Indian and mestizo chroniclers, on their part, give us another interpretation of things. Two are FATHER BLAS VALERA (Peru, *ca.* 1538–1598) and FELIPE GUAMÁN POMA DE AYALA (Peru, 1526?–d. after 1613). The latter, in *The First New Chronicle and Good Government* (*El primer Nueva Corónica y Buen Gobierno*), recounts the greatness of the Inca period and the sufferings of the Indians during the colonization. He is well informed and scrutinizes conquerors and conquered from within. He does not conceal his resentment toward the Church. Because he transcribed Quechua poems that were sung or recited, he performed a service that neither Valera nor the Inca Garcilaso attempted.

The Inca Garcilaso de la Vega / The most gifted of the mestizo writers is the INCA GARCILASO DE LA VEGA (Peru, 1539–1616). He descended from Inca and Castilian nobility and moreover, on his father's side, from a family illustrious in the history of letters. The fusion of these diverse racial and cultural worlds in his person was the point of departure in his career as a writer. At twenty-one years of age he went to Spain; he was destined not to return. In 1590 he published a new translation of the *Dialoghi d'amore* by the Neoplatonist, Leon Hebreo, which he undertook for the delight of feeling penetrated by the Renaissance spirit of order and harmony. He decided to put into writing what he heard from a friend of his, a veteran of the Hernando de Soto expedition to Florida (1539–1542). The result was: *Florida* (*La Florida del Inca*, 1605). He could not help coloring the accounts of his friend because his own literary tastes intervened, and one can discern influences of everything he had read. He had read Greek, Latin, and Renaissance historians, and with these examples in mind, he proposed to save heroic deeds from oblivion, to teach the truth, to enthuse readers with his artistic resources, and finally, to convert history into "a teacher of life" whose concrete program was conquest and Christianization. The Inca, who had read the "portraits" written by his relative Pérez de Guzmán, imagines the psychological traits of his characters. He adorns the action, in the classic fashion, with imaginary speeches. And in fact, a good deal of imagination enters into his history. Since Aristotle, it had been repeated that poetry surpassed history because it recorded not only how things had happened but also how they should have happened. The Inca also believes in the dignity of fantasy. Of course, fictional events must approach truth and shy away from falsehood. And since the humanist of the Renaissance considered novels of chivalry false, the Inca will also declare himself an enemy of them. The only legitimate stand was to believe in novels having an historical basis or in histories that incorporated novelistic elements. Yet, in his *Florida*, not only do influences from the epic poems of Ariosto, Boiardo, and Ercilla appear, but also episodes similar to those in Byzantine and Italian novels and in books of chivalry; hence, his pages take on the brilliance of imagined adventure, with shipwrecks, long-lost people, sudden encounters, singular combats, the exploits of one hero against a prodigious host, Indians cut in two with one blow of a sword, imitations from classical antiquity, strange cities, exotic landscapes, sumptuous feasts, storms and misfortunes, descriptions of treasures, queens, palaces, arsenals and scenes which, in a false feudal framework, introduce Indians as "noble savages," eloquent in their feelings of honor. The written sources—chronicles, histories, poems—and the oral source of the friend who had participated in the expedition, gave him the facts; then he would embellish them. "I wrote the history of Florida, which indeed is florid, not with my own dry style but with the flower of Spanish prose," he said. While he was "tidying up" his *Florida* he was writing the *Royal Commentaries* (*Comentarios reales*), his most outstanding work. The first part was published in 1609; the second, finished four years later, was destined to be published after his death with the title *General History of Peru* (*Historia general del Perú*, 1617).

We have already said that in the chroniclers of the Indies what is of interest is the value of their personal perspectives, not the objective value of their historical reconstruction. However, in dealing with a chronicler of the standing of the Inca Garcilaso, we should be aware of the problem of his historical accuracy, even if only to dispense with it and, with a free mind, to study his imagination and his style. The Inca has been the target of three different critical fusillades, though the bullets join in flight and strike the bull's-eye. Those who disbelieve in the possibility of a great non-European civilization declare that the *Royal Commentaries* are "fairy tales," "a Utopian novel," not an historical text. Other historiographers of hypercritical heuristics and hermeneutics tear apart the mass of facts in the Inca's work with an analytical but uncomprehending attitude. A third group, in defense of the Spanish conquest and colonization, decides to discredit what they consider, erroneously, the Inca's Indian outlook. Also mistaken are those who, through their sympathy for the Inca Garcilaso, presume him to be an incarnation of the native soil, immune to everything Hispanic, grieved over the pride of Quechua traditions, enemy of the Spanish conquest, nationalistic in the defense of his Peruvian homeland, and a mestizo so inclined toward his Indian shading that he lived the life of a resentful man and an embittered writer. The truth is that the Inca used to say he was writing for both Indians and Spaniards "because I have been endowed by both nations"; "to say that I write endearingly of my nation because I am an Indian, is certainly misleading."

The Inca was hurt that the Spaniards misunderstood the Indian culture because of their ignorance of the Quechua language. This idea that a language is a way of thinking and that only he who can speak it may delve into the country's "customs, rites and ceremonies" led him to write a cultural history: he may do it—he says—because he had learned Quechua from his "mother's breast." Even more, he proposed that Quechua should be taught in order to maintain the unity of the Indians. But this must be a part of a bilingual education. As a matter of fact, he never doubted the virtues of the Castilian language, which he enriched with his own prose precisely because he desired that it thrive in the New World. The historiographic part of the Inca's writings is true to fact. Recent investigations are wont to corroborate Garcilaso in the order of events of the Inca conquests and in his geographic and historical exactness. Many of the legendary elements he uses were pointed out critically by the Inca himself: "and if some of the above-mentioned matters and others to be recorded seem fabulous, I bethought it proper that I not fail to write them down, so as not to remove the foundation upon which the Indians base the best and most grandiose events they relate concerning their empire." Be that as it may, one must not forget that Garcilaso was a reader of works of historical content and became accustomed to a Renaissance type of novelized historiography. Garcilaso was a humanist, who, being intimate with Inca culture, would project upon it the very Renaissance trait of yearning for the Golden Age. He yields to the Utopian aspirations of his time without losing sight of his direct knowledge of Peruvian reality. Some of his idealizations of the Inca realm were common to the thinking of Spanish humanists: communal property, indoctrination of non-Europeans, benevolent patriarchalism of philosophic princes. The theme of the just war and evangelization, theoretical axis of his work, runs through the entire literary apparatus of those years. Garcilaso considered the conquest and colonization beneficial, criticizing Las Casas' point of view. His is a Christian concept of life—the moral dignity of man in harmony with God and the world. In his serenity there was something of the Stoics whom he also read. He had need of Stoicism undoubtedly, to overcome his sadness. He had suffered because of the civil wars in Peru; he had traveled the road from opulence to poverty, from high esteem to scorn. Perhaps he felt a certain indigenous fatalism. But his sadness (which rises like a tide to inundate many pages of the second part of his *Commentaries*) had much to do with his conception of history. He saw something tragic in history. But his disillusionment was not negative; he knew how to discover the enchantment of adverse destinies. He insisted on his being a mestizo: "for being an epithet imposed by our parents and because of its meaning, I speak it out and I am honored by it." But don't think that his being a mestizo limits him racially. In those years, and in Spain, the physical differences between mestizos and Spaniards did not add nor subtract from a person's worth. The Inca enjoyed privileges as the son of an *encomendero;* he was intimately entwined in Spanish life and lived without engaging in manual labor. The tone of humility in the introduction to his works was the custom among contemporary writers and he knew it. He says: "in prefaces . . . I have noted that . . . authors excuse themselves." His disillusionments are not those of a resentful mestizo but those of any Spaniard who sought compensation in vain or who felt his aspiration to military glory frustrated. In chapter XV of Book I of the first part he tells how he used to hear about Inca cosmogony from his mother, relatives, and elders. This passage is famous for its emotional evocation and for the vivacity of its prose in which, not only does one hear the dialog, but one sees the gestures of those who speak.

The Inca recounts with pleasure. Instead of giving us quick summaries, he enjoys dawdling in the successive scenes of his story. His syntactical equilibrium corresponds to the equilibrium of a thought process which clearly proceeds with symmetry and ordered constructions. In the to-and-fro of the pendulum from simple to complicated language, the style of the Inca swings to the simple side. Furthermore, he followed the example of stylistic simplicity set by the chroniclers he had read: Cieza de León, Acosta, Gómara, Zárate, and Blas Valera. His completely natural syntax is without loose or ill-articulated components. He says: "My maternal language, which is that of the Incas; . . . my alien language, which is Castilian." Yet Castilian was his language, as much or more (we believe more) than the language of his Indian mother. What an admirable prose. What order and what care in the logical and clear presentation of his memoirs. He contemplated his work as an artistic object. And he felt the pleasure of being a man who dominated a rich cultural landscape from the vantage point of the mestizo who looks out from two historical slopes—the Indian and the European. The artistic importance of his *Commentaries* is enhanced because it draws attention to this privileged personal perspective. He wants to indulge in artistic play for the reader—so that a particular chapter "not be too short" he includes the story of Serrano (chapter VIII) which is so similar to that of Robinson Crusoe. That it is a Spanish public to whom he is directing himself and to whom he must make a new world intelligible explains his constant shifting of Indian categories to European categories.

Prosperous and Poor Lands / Prosperity was not a condition equally shared in every colony. There was a rapid flowering in Mexico and in Peru and by the beginning of the seventeenth century these colonies offer a fairly rich cultural background, as we have seen. In other parts there is a decline, as in Santo Domingo; in others, as in Paraguay and the Río de la Plata, life is arduous. From this latter region a chronicler emerges somewhat belatedly who depicts the coarseness of life in those early times, the mestizo, RUIZ DÍAZ DE GUZMÁN (Paraguay, 1554?–1629). Unfortunately he did not leave us the chronicle of his own days as a conquistador. The work known as *Argentina in Manuscript (La Argentina manuscrita)* and finished by 1612 has come to us incomplete in several manuscripts (none of which is the original) with textual variants. Its contents concern the discovery and conquest of Río Plata provinces and are interrupted precisely in the years that the author intermingles with the men whose history he had written. He collects legends because he believes in them; and because he does believe, he tends to stamp a certain fabulous quality even on very real episodes. Is the episode of the woman Maldonada and the lioness, for example, a legend told as reality or reality told as a legend? This is a theme, reminiscent of Androcles and the Lion, whose first Castilian version comes from *The Book of Exemplary Tales (El libro de los ejemplos)* by Sánchez de Vercial written at the beginning of the fifteenth century.

Another episode, the one of Lucia Miranda, the captive, was to have great vogue in the literature of the Río Plata. The Spaniards would take women from the Indians. The Indians did the same occasionally with Spanish women. This went on well up into the nineteenth century, and these scandals entered into poetry, theater, and the novel (Lavardén, Echeverría, Ascasubi, Hernández, Mansilla, Zorrilla de San Martín, etc.). Ruiz Díaz de Guzmán tells about pygmies, Amazons, miraculous interventions by saints. His sources are hearsay and his prose reflects the conversational style. Although a mestizo, his viewpoint is always that of the European side of his family.

Epic Literature: Ercilla

Some chronicles became literature. And there was literature that had value as chronicle, for example, ALONSO DE ERCILLA Y ZÚÑIGA's (1534–1594). The bloodiest episodes in Peru were not beween Spaniard and Indian, but between Spaniard and Spaniard. A group of men who descended from Peru to Chile clashed with the warrior tribes of the Araucanians; whence emerged the first epic poem of America, Ercilla's *La Araucana*. Ercilla, one of Philip II's courtiers, already possessed a good literary education when he arrived in America at the age of twenty-one. "I have passed many climes, I have moved under many constellations," he says. And what he saw and imagined in Chile he glorified in the octaves of his epic poem *La Araucana*. It is a chronicle no doubt, but quite different from all those mentioned up to now, since what is of most value in it is its esthetic nature. In *Apollo's Laurel* (*Laurel de Apolo*) Lope de Vega pegged him well: "Don Alonso de Ercilla / such rich [tales of the] Indies his faculties bear / that he arrives from Chile here / in order to enrich the muse of Castilla."

That is to say, his value rests on the fact that the Indies belong to the creative faculties of Ercilla, not that Ercilla belongs to the reality that is the Indies. The Indies are a mental, ideal process in the writer. The Indies are born in Ercilla and not Ercilla in the Indies. *La Araucana* emerged in the evolution of the epic genre as a specimen of rare plumage. It was the first work in which the author appears as an actor in the epic he describes; it was the first work that lent epic dignity to events still in process; it was the first work that immortalized with an epic the founding of a modern nation; it was the first work of real poetic quality that centered around America; it was also the first work in which the author, caught in the midst of a conflict between ideals of truth and ideals of poetry, laments the poverty of the Indian theme and the monotony of the warrior theme, revealing at the same time the intimate process of his artistic creation. It may be that *La Araucana* will not soar with the *Orlando Furioso, Jerusalem Liberated,* and *The Lusiades,* but it did fly high on its own wings. This epic fluttering in Hispanic skies—Lope de Vega's *Jerusalem Conquered* (*Jerusalém conquistada*), Valbuena's *Bernardo,* Hojeda's *Cristiada*—was certainly magnificent in the case of *La Araucana.* Ercilla arrived from Spain with a mind already formed by Renaissance literature, by theology, and by juridical discussions on the conquest of the New World. While he fought, he wrote. But his poetry was not dictated by what transpired. Proof of this lies in the fact that the twenty-two cantos relating events he had lived through are not better than the fifteen that refer to happenings prior to his arrival. The poetry flowed from his Renaissance Spanish soul—reader of Vergil and Ariosto, soldier of the Catholic kingdom of Philip II, and enemy of the Indian (not because of greed, but because the Indian was an enemy of his faith). Yet America was poetized with extraordinary descriptive precision in the narration of epic episodes, in character sketches, in metaphors of new and surprising perceptions. More memorable than the combats in Lope's *Jerusalem* or Valbuena's *Bernardo* are those of Lautaro, Tucapel, and Rengo. He narrates with a clear and sustained breath. He gives character to his Indians (the generous Lautaro, the savages Tucapel and Rengo, the heroic Galvarino, the courageous Caupolicán). As Homer admired Hector, Tasso Saladin, and Boiardo Agricane, in like manner does Ercilla admire his enemies. This is a literary trait, a Spanish trait; nevertheless, the Chileans are free to consider *La Araucana* a national poem. When Ercilla tired of the New World he would escape into love scenes, supernatural apparitions, prophecies, lyrical dreams, embellished mythological stories, imaginary voyages. This weakens the unity of epic construction on the one hand, but on the other, it converts *La Araucana* into one of the most complex poems of Golden Age literature. Following Lucan's example, Ercilla gave the most immediate events epic proportions, and the scenes of wizardry and marvels do not break the line of historical truthfulness because, after all, they formed part of the folklore and literature of the sixteenth century. "A true history"—yes; only that Ercilla was a poet and a reader of all that the Spaniards read in his day, not only the authors already mentioned, but dozens more (the Italians from Dante to Sannazzaro, the Spaniards from Juan de Mena to Garcilaso de la Vega) and his poetry has all the Renaissance grace. The three parts of *La Araucana* appeared successively in 1569, 1578, and 1589; and for the first time Spain felt that America had a literature.

La Araucana's Sequels / There were continuations, imitations, and emulations, and *La Araucana* became part of the body of great literature of all times. The influence of the poem, especially in America, was deep and long-lasting, and not confined to epic poetry. In the way of epic poems having New World themes, there sprouted *Arauco Tamed* (*El arauco domado,* 1596) by the Chilean PEDRO DE OÑA; *Purén Untamed* (*Purén indómito*) by HERNANDO ALVAREZ DE TOLEDO (b. 1550); *Elegies of Illustrious Men of the Indies* (*Elegías de varones ilustres de Indias*) by JUAN DE CASTELLANOS; *Antarctic Wars* (*Armas antárticas,* written between 1608 and 1615) by JUAN DE MIRAMONTES Y ZUÁZOLA, a soldier who took part in the struggle against the pirate Cavendish and recounted episodes of the history of Peru with the dash and imagination of a poet who has trained himself in the golden century epic techniques; *Wars of Chile* (*Guerras de Chile,* 1610) attributed to JUAN DE MENDOZA MONTEAGUDO; and those poems inspired by the conquest of New Spain: *The New World and Its Conquest* (*Nuevo mundo y conquista, ca.* 1580) by FRANCISCO DE TERRAZAS; *Intrepid Cortés* (*Cortés valeroso,* 1588) and *Mexicana* (1594) by GABRIEL LOBO LASSO DE LA VEGA; *History of the New Mexico* (*Historia de la nueva Mexico,* 1610) by GASPAR GUZMÁN (b. before 1570).

When we think of *La Araucana* all the other poems seem mediocre (with the exception of Oña's). With *La Araucana* at the top of the epic ladder, we place on a very low rung the *Argentina* by MARTÍN DEL BARCO CENTENERA (1544–1605). He follows models of medieval didactic poetry more than Ercilla does, and hence there is an archaic air even in his versification, which is irregular. Without a breath of poetry he versifies his recollections of adversities and failures suffered in the region of the Río de la Plata. He is a realist in certain episodes, but his attitude is not critical. He prefers truculent exaggeration, accentuated violence. What remained alive of his mediocre poem was its name, *Argentina,* an imitation of names like *Araucana, Aeneid, Iliad.* He did not invent it, but his insistence on the poetic adjective "argentine" and its noun form "the Argentine" as a name of the river and country was the origin of the modern name of the Republic. As easily as these poems submit to "true history," they just as easily escape into the novelistic, the fantastic, and even the allegoric, following the manner of Boiardo and Ariosto.

The State of Literature

Those who advanced literature in America knew very well that their voices were being lost in its echoless deserts. Some Spaniards who never came here generously praised the intellectual life of the Indies. It was a kind of courtesy, of building credit for the future, of desiring to improve matters. Francisco Sánchez in *That Nothing Is Known* (*Quod nihil scitur,* 1581) said: "How much ignorance prevailed up to now in the Indies! Now little by little they are becoming more religious, more keen, more cultured than ourselves." And years later Cervantes in *Voyage of Parnassus* (*Viaje del Parnaso,* 1614) and Lope in *Apollo's Laurel* (1630) will also make generous references to Hispanic-American writers. But, could the Spaniards imagine what was happening in the minds of their colleagues in the colonies? Could they measure the determination that the colonial writers needed in order to overcome so much discouragement? Their solitude, their timidity in taking the initiative, the lack of stimulus, the material obstacles in printing and marketing books, made them look humbly upon the great literary production of Spain. When Nebrija wrote his *Grammar* he believed that the Castilian language had reached its fullest development. It was the years of the *Celestina* and of the discovery of America. But the Spaniards who came to America and their children, either Creoles or mestizos, realized that in Spain literature continued its evolution. In 1492 the speech of the expelled Spanish Jews remained isolated and in its pre-classical mold, but the speech of the Spaniards who came to America that very year continued its historic life. Hispanic-America did not persist as a pre-classical linguistic province because the conquest and colonization were realized in the epoch of Garcilaso and Fray Luis, of Cervantes, Lope, and Quevedo. From 1520 to 1600 Hispanic-American society established itself. Yet the steady flow of Spanish population (which is to continue in the seventeenth and eighteenth centuries) continuously displayed the horizon of literary glories of Spain. There was undoubtedly some Creole resentment against the Spaniard. A satiric sonnet of the last half of the sixteenth century cited by Baltasar Dorantes de Carranza in *Brief Report of New Spain* (*Sumaria relación de las cosas de la Nueva España,* 1604) protested against the new arrival who "comes from Spain over the briny sea / to our Mexican homeland / an unsponsored boor / wanting in health and deficient in money," and who "afterwards deprecates the place where he acquired esteem, good taste and property."

However, in spite of this resentment, the colonial writers found Spain's literature seductive. For this reason, alongside the ballads, folk songs, and carols, a pretentious literature emerged: Latin verses and dialogs (like those of Francisco Cervantes de Salazar); Italianate and Petrarchan sonnets in the manner of Garcilaso and Gutierre de Cetina (like those of Francisco de Terrazas, already famous in 1577); epic poems (like those of Ercilla and his descendants); and a kind of fifteenth-century verses in the manner of Jorge Manrique (like those of Pedro de Trejo, who practised all genres and styles and even innovated meters and strophes). There were so many poetry competitions that González de Eslava says in one of his *Colloquies:* "There are more poets than manure." Indeed not even Vergil could have extracted one verse of gold from that manure—"*de estercore Ennii.*" The gold was in Spain, and prosists and versifiers, feeling literarily poor, were dazzled by the distant glitter. An anonymous Latinist, upon dedicating his version of *Brief Meditations* (*Meditatiunculae*) to Cortés' second wife, said to her: "I willingly did what I could in the translation of this book; if my vernacular is not as polished as that weaved by some Castilian rhetori-

49

cians, one should not marvel; after so many years of roaming about these barbaric nations and lands, where one deals more in the language of the Indians than in Spanish, and where one who is not a barbarian among barbarians is considered a barbarian, it is not surprising that I should forget the elegance of the Castilian tongue." When they could, they went to Spain and there they would write and publish their works.

The manuscript *Flower of Sundry Poetry* (*Flores de varia Poesía*) compiled in Mexico, is dated 1577. It is anonymous, although it is believed that Juan de la Cueva was one of its compilers or that it was he who took it to Spain. Here is a mixture of verse written by peninsular Spaniards, by Spaniards living in America, and even by Creoles (Terrazas, Carlos de Sámano, Martín Cortés, Juan de la Cueva, Gutierre de Cetina, Juan Luis de Ribera, González de Eslava, etc.). There were writers then, by the carload, albeit they were insignificant. Rosas de Oquendo, in his "*Soneto a Lima*," satirizes "Poets by the thousands, of scanty wit." We have already said that to write was an irresistible collective yearning. Not only did writers write, but they wrote about writers. Juan de Castellanos, about whom we have already spoken, left a gallery of illustrious men of the pen. A very incomplete list of Peruvian writers may be found in DIEGO DE AGUILAR Y CÓRDOBA's *The Marañón River* (*El Marañón*, 1538) and in the anonymous *Discourse in Praise of Poesy* (*Discurso en loor de la poesía*). EUGENIO DE SALAZAR Y ALARCÓN (1530?–1608?), a poet from Madrid who described Mexican landscapes in verse form, collected data on the intellectual life of Santo Domingo in his *Miscellany of Poetry* (*Silva de poesía*). Thanks to him there are preserved five sonnets and some blank verse by the earliest known poetess of the New World—the religious LEONOR DE OVANDO (d. after 1609), who possessed this intense vision of the "divine Spouse of my soul": "who suffered only to give me life; / And I know that for me alone he would suffer / And that he would redeem only me / if in this world he created me alone."

In a history of church oratory FRIAR ALONSO DE CABRERA (*ca.* 1549–1606) would have to stand out. Because of the artistic force of his words he also belongs to the history of literature. As a preacher his attitude was original, and the prose of his sermons is equally original. Instead of shackling his sentences, as was customary in his age, he wrote brief, simple phrases, constructing them with clarity and enriching them with anecdotes of popular customs.

Satire

The times were just right for satire. It was carried on many lips, especially those of MATEO ROSAS DE OQUENDO (Seville?, 1559?; he probably came to America in 1585; in 1621 he was still living in Lima). An untiring traveler—from Argentina to Mexico—he belittled everything he saw. In his long "Satire of Things that Occur in Peru in 1598" ("*Sátira a las cosas que pasan en el Perú, año de 1598*") he described a small segment of colonial society; his most violent verses veered toward women of doubtful morals and imposters. He despised the poor who, upon arriving in America, gave themselves airs of nobility while in reality they were offsprings of ordinary laborers. His having indulged in the very vices that he ridicules gives his autobiographical passages a picaresque tone not lacking in overtones of "baroque naturalism." He also wrote satires during his Mexican period. In his "A Gallant's Satire to a Creole Lady who Praised Mexico to Him" (*"Sátira que hizo un galán a una dama criolla que le alababa mucho a México"*) he gives vent to his ever-growing Spanish resentment against Creole life. Nevertheless, one can notice that after living many years in the colonies, his animosity against the Creole and his initial European arrogance slackened. In Mexico he managed to express some enthusiasm. With the passing years it seems the New World endeared itself to him.

The Theater

As they conquered or founded cities, the Spaniards transplanted European cultural organization. The Spaniards carried their institutions to all the conquered lands, and everywhere chroniclers and even writers emerged. But the capitals of the first two viceroyalties, Mexico and Lima, were the centers of an alert, complete, and continuous civilization. They even possessed a theater. As Agustín de Rojas observed in *Pleasant Journey* (*Viaje entretenido*, 1603) Juan del Encina began to write plays "during the days that Columbus discovered the great wealth of the Indies and the New World." In reality Juan del Encina was not "the father of the Spanish drama"; rather, with the presentation of the double eclogue during the Christmas of 1492, he became its secularizer. And the theater came to America.

We have already said that the first missionary theater was disappearing in the second half of the sixteenth century. The expurgation of its profane elements made by the Church, the change in customs, the growth of the cities, university and humanistic tastes, all contributed to opening the road to a European-patterned theater. The Latinist tradition of the Church colleges—allegorical dialogs on sacred themes, plays and tragedies in Latin or partly in Latin represented by the collegers in cloisters—was brought to Mexico and Lima by the Jesuits. Little has remained of this scholastic theater, an example being the inferior five-act tragedy, *Triumph of the Saints* (*Triunfo de los santos*, Mexico, 1578), attributed to Father Juan Sánchez Baquero and Father Vincencio Lanucci. The theme of Diocletian's persecution of the Church and the triumph under Constantine is versified in the Renaissance and Italianate manner, but it has little value. In addition to the missionary and scholastic theater, there was another type available to Spaniards and Creoles. The latter attended ecclesiastical ceremonies, processions,

51

entertainments, receptions for viceroys, pageantries, dances, and liturgical pieces—skits, interludes, preludes, mysteries, and even plays and tragedies with Biblical or allegorical themes—presented on stages that were becoming more and more secular. This theater suffered from the competition of the Renaissance Spanish theater, not only because of the repertory but also from the presence of theatrical companies from Spain. In 1565 publishing houses in Spain began producing collections of plays that were quickly sent to America, and it is possible that the Spanish play enacted in 1568 in Guayaquil was taken from one of these volumes. In 1599 the first Lope de Vega play was presented in Lima. Local plays were also written. The little that has been saved of this Creole theater is a prose interlude by CRISTÓBAL DE LLERENA (Santo Domingo, 1540—dead by 1627) presented in Santo Domingo in 1588. This satire of the public administration earned Llerena's expulsion from the island.

We are more familiar with the activities in Mexico of HERNÁN GONZÁLEZ DE ESLAVA (1534–1601), author of sixteen colloquies, eight preludes, four interludes, and some miscellaneous poetry. It is a pity that his earthy pieces have been lost, because the one extant, the *Interlude between Two Ruffians* (*Entremés entre dos rufianes*), which is more short story than theater—in the form of two successive soliloquies connected by a few gestures—reveals a certain humor. He was a good versifier, at times excellent, ingenious, facile, but stifled by the many compromises with viceroyal and ecclesiastical authorities. The blame was not exclusively his. All those who wrote for the festivals of the Corpus Christi and for the court feasts had to submit to an established set of theological and political rules. Furthermore, the Inquisition read all plays prior to their performance. González de Eslava condescended and, consequently, his colloquies move in a void, like the movement of a loom on which nothing is woven. He tended toward realism (that is why it is lamentable that his non-ecclesiastical pieces have been lost), but he translated his vision of reality in allegories having no dramatic force. It was a sort of journalism in which the outstanding events of colonial life were reported with an empty and pretentious language. The viceroy ordered the construction of seven forts as a defense against the attacks of the Chichimeca Indians? González de Eslava writes a colloquy converting the forts into the seven sacraments and the voyage of merchants from Mexico to Zacatecas into the voyage from earth to heaven. A textile factory for woolens is established? He has Penance spinning the wool of the Divine Lamb in the mill-church. At times, as in the *Colloquy of the Count of Coruña* (*Coloquio del Conde de la Coruña,* composed in 1580 upon the viceroy's arrival to Mexico), the allegorization is insincere, art-less, and without austerity. The Count's entrance into Mexico symbolizes the entrance of God into the Soul. God equals King, and Count Coruña equals Christ because (and notice to what levels this pseudoreligious palace theater descends!) Count signifies companion which is what Christ means, and Coruña is made up of *"Cor,"* heart, and *"uña,"* claw, which pulls us away from sin. Because of its Hispanic-American linguistic medium and its observations on history and customs, this theater is of more interest to philologists than to theater-lovers. Even its clear and well-constructed verses tell us little. In the *Colloquy of the Four Doctors of the Church (Coloquio de los cuatro doctores de la Iglesia),* for example, the following lessons in Church doctrine are given to two shepherds: The Eucharist, the virginity of Mary, Christ's redemption of man, and the reason for the irredeemable fallen angels, together with the usual inquisitorial threats of burning, torturing, knifing, and persecuting whoever does not believe to the last word the lessons of the four theologians. From a theatrical point of view it is pure conceptual interplay. The verses play in the void without having anything new to say and without being able to say anything new.

González de Eslava was a Mexican by naturalization. The first Mexican by birth in theater history was JUAN PÉREZ RAMÍREZ (1545?), author of the allegorical play in verse form, *Spiritual Marriage between the Shepherd Peter and the Mexican Church (Desposorio espiritual entre el Pastor Pedro y la Iglesia Mexicana,* 1574). It has been said the Spaniard, Juan de la Cueva, who lived in Mexico (1574–77), learned a few things from this Ramírez before returning to Spain to open the scenic road that led to Lope de Vega. We need not concern ourselves with Juan de la Cueva here. The only thing in his work that we can classify as American is a view of the Mexican landscape in his epistles.

III. 1598-1701

Authors born between 1570 and 1675

Historical framework: The colonies under the decadence of the last Hapsburgs: Philip III, Philip IV, and Charles II. Loss of American possessions.

Cultural tendencies: From the Renaissance to the Baroque. Literary plenitude.

Despite political and economic decadence, Spanish literature was extraordinarily enriched by a new vigor. In the first years of the seventeenth century, with the genial work of Cervantes and Lope de Vega, the apogee of the Renaissance is reached. Both authors' lives begin in a period of splendor, but in their last years they experience the Spanish decadence. The national crisis is revealed in what is called the Baroque style and which, if not new, is now consolidated and dominant.

The Spanish Baroque

Born during the last years of the Council of Trent or shortly thereafter, these Baroque authors found themselves in possession of a great literature that had run its course, and at the same time they were facing a void, since Spain had turned its back on the ebullient and vital culture of the rest of Europe. There was bitterness, anguish, resentment, disillusionment, fear, pessimism, and at the same time national pride; there was resignation to not living and thinking in step with the world, yet, a desire to astonish the world with a language of great affectation. Hence, the equilibrium of the soul is broken, and literary endeavor grotesquely cultivates the ugliness of things (as in Mateo Alemán) or gives itself over to forms that are obscure for the uninitiated, difficult even for the cultured few. Although Góngora profits by classical erudition, he rejects classical clarity and wishes to complicate his

54

language so that, like Latin, it be "worthy of persons capable of understanding it," that it be a cultist art for the elite who take pleasure in solving intricate stylistic difficulties. Quevedo, although in another direction, took on with the same expenditure of ingeniousness a style called "conceptist," in which logic takes delight in its own agility rather than in its movement to a conclusion. In Gracián, philosophy also is an activity in a linguistic zone outside the reach of the masses, where subtleness is more valuable for being subtle than for being true.

Alongside the great prosists—to whom we should add Saavedra Fajardo—the seventeenth century gave us the great poetic theater. Lope has already been mentioned. We may add Tirso, Mira de Amescua, Alarcón, and finally Calderón de la Barca, the last great figure of the "golden age." After the death of Calderón in 1680, only a few spent coals remain kindled, more ash than fire.

The Baroque Comes to America / In this period the colonies, as always, received all that Spain gave them. Immediately after being published, the *Quijote* and the *Guzmán de Alfarache* embarked for America. The plays of Lope also arrived. And on occasion the writers themselves arrived: Mateo Alemán in Mexico (1608) and Tirso de Molina in Santo Domingo (1616). Alemán writes *Events in the Life of Friar García Guerra, Archbishop of Mexico* (*Sucesos de Fray García Guerra, Arzobispo de Mexico,* 1613) and a treatise on orthography to which, it seems, he gave more importance than to his *Guzmán de Alfarache.* Catalogs, libraries, and bookstores yield a surprising quantity of poetry, fiction, theater, and history. In the private library of a single obscure Mexican there were, in 1620, Latin authors (Vergil, Cicero); Italian (Boccaccio, Aretino, Boza Candioto, Sannazaro, Ariosto, Tasso); Portuguese (Camoens); and, naturally, Spanish (Ercilla, *La Celestina,* López de Enciso, Antonio de Guevara, Lorenzo Palmireno, and poetic anthologies like López de Ubeda's *Garden of Divine Flowers* (*Vergel de Flores Divinas,* 1582), and Pedro Espinosa's *Flower of Illustrious Poets of Spain* (*Flores de poetas ilustres de España,* 1605). Another Mexican, Pérez de Soto, born in 1608, who was brought out of obscurity by an inquisitorial trial, had in his library 1,663 volumes in various languages, one-fifth of which was in *belles lettres*—two dozen pastoral, chivalric, and picaresque novels, collections of short stories (for example, those of *Conde Lucanor*), writings of Erasmus, *La Celestina,* epic and lyrical poetry by Greek, Roman, Renaissance, and Baroque (Góngora, of course) writers. A list of books being sold by a Mexican shop in 1683 is equally informative: among the 276 titles are found Góngora, Lope, Calderón, Rojas Zorrilla,

Cervantes, Quevedo, Pedro Mexía, Pérez de Montalbán, *el Lazarillo,* and Gonzalo de Céspedes.

Literature was also forming part of the happy open-air fiestas. In a "game of rings" (*juego de sortijas*) celebrated in Peru in 1607 (in the manner described by Luis Gálvez de Montalvo in *The Shepherd of Fílida—El Pastor de Fílida*) several horsemen costumed as Don Quijote and other knights-errant marched out in review. In 1621 in Mexico, in a "*mascarada,*" or street procession on foot or on horseback, where persons parade by symbolizing figures from mythology, history, and theology, there were famous knights-errant from novels, like Amadís, Palmerín, Don Quijote, as well as Sancho, Dulcinea, and other personages.

In general, the colonies were even more conservative than the metropolis. Europe had become divided between the Reformation and the Counter Reformation, and Spain was the center of orthodoxy. Great changes were occurring, especially in the countries of the North; in the course of a few decades constellations of non-Hispanic minds were to revolutionize the image of the world with a philosophy based on the free exercise of reason and on the experimental study of nature. Meanwhile Spain, wedded to scholasticism, its eyes glued to revelation and authority, will be deceived by the dream of a stable world; and in order that the colonies remain static as well, Spain reinforces its intransigence there. Although the colonies were very far from Europe and only a handful of Spaniards and Creoles could read or write, being as they were, lost in immense expanses of land or surrounded by masses of Indians, there were those who broke out of the encirclement and became familiar with the contemporary ideas of Descartes and others. These Creoles, like Sigüenza y Góngora and Sor Juana, who were anxious for the new science, were exceptions to the scholastic verbalism that dominated the seminaries and the universities. The feudal society in which they lived obligated the Creoles to hide their resentment and adulate the ruling-class Spaniards with ceremonies, verses, triumphal arches, lavish shows, and literary competitions of "conceptist" skill. We find progressive and retrogressive movements; conflicts between the beliefs of the Middle Ages and new facts; insecurity, fear, daring, and timidity; illusion and deceit; impulse to action and a withdrawing into the soul; lust for life and obsession for death; dryness of style and astonishing florescence of ornamentation, all moving to and fro in the lands of America—modes of life to which today the historian, in order to orient himself, places road signs at the two extremities of this period: Renaissance and Baroque.

Plan

It is significant that this century is so cleanly cut by two literary geniuses, both born in America: the Renaissance prose writer, Inca Garcilaso de la Vega and the Baroque poetess, Sor Juana Inés de la Cruz. We studied the former, because of his age, in the previous chapter; although, considering the dates of his writing, he would fit well here. Sor Juana will be studied at the end of this chapter.

How can the subject matter of this chapter be organized? By styles, from Renaissance to Baroque? By birthdates of the authors? By nations, from Mexico to Argentina? By a scale of excellence, descending from Alarcón and Sor Juana? By prose and verse forms? None of these criteria would manage to unravel the disorder of so much uneven and scattered literary activity. Even the groupings by genres, which is what we will attempt, will be unsatisfactory, because there are writers who cultivate more than one, and there are cases of hybrid genres.

Chronicles, Treatises, and Didactic Books

The first chronicles of the conquest were like a series of intaglios from which we made a bas-relief of the New World recently discovered. They were not literature, but we were able to read them with the attitude of the reader of literature. In the seventeenth century the struggles, conquests, and the founding of cities continue—and the chronicles keep coming. But these chronicles, unlike those of the early conquistadors, are not amazed at the newness of things, for they were written by the children or grandchildren, or by those who had come to tread on land already cleared. Nevertheless, a new narrative theme appears in the seventeenth century—the struggles with the Dutch and English corsairs. One may wonder whether the chronicles of the seventeenth century in general are less interesting than those of the two previous periods. If we lose interest, perhaps it is because we no longer see the chronicles outlined against the background of nature and ethnography, but against the brilliance of a literature which is being cultivated now as a luxury. A comparison between the chronicles and the purely literary works of the same period dims the luster of the chronicles, to the point that we can barely see the great transition from Renaissance to Baroque. Since chronicles appear together with religious and didactic treatises (at times the same author indulges in all these activities; at times all these activities appear in a single volume), it does not matter if the subgenres are mixed. The writing of clergymen, jurists, travelers,

57

frizzed with Baroque curlicues, is wont to cross over the threshold of literature.

For having been written in Náhuatl, the chronicle of FERNANDO DE ALVA IXTLILXÓCHITL (1568–1648) does not enter into this history; nevertheless, it is a valuable work, not only for its historical data, based on pictographs and information gathered directly from old Indians, but above all for its literary substance: legends, poetic songs, and elegiac poems.

Four chroniclers of real merit stand out. Bishop CASPAR DE VILLA-RROEL (Ecuador, 1587?–1665) is a pleasant chronicler to read. He initiated his studies in Quito, was ordained in Lima, went to Spain (for about ten years he traveled between Lisbon, Madrid, and Seville), returned to America, first as a Bishop in Santiago de Chile and then in Arequipa. "To write has been a continuous temptation for me ever since a tender age," he said. And he added, with a candid smile: "I composed several booklets judging that each would be another step to the top." At the same time he also ascended toward literary recognition, thanks to his anecdotal and gossipy prose. His attitude was that of the conversationalist; and, in spite of handling the material of sacred literature (and also profane), he always found the occasion to relate something, if not lived, at least vivid: parables, events, recollections. When he narrates bookish episodes, he animates them with humor and applies them to contemporary situations. Of his prolific work we mention *Comments and Discourses on Lent* (*Comentarios y Discursos sobre la Cuaresma*), *Sacred and Ecclesiastical Moral Histories* (*Historias sagradas y eclesiásticas morales*), and, above all, *Pacific-Ecclesiastical Government or Union of Two Powers Pontifical and Royal* (*Gobierno eclesiástico-pacífico o Unión de los dos cuchillos pontificio y regio*, 1656–1657). The latter title refers to the canonical and pontifical rights. In the Indies the ecclesiastical authorities are confronted with the civil and military authorities, and Villarroel wishes to reconcile both powers by using his knowledge of human vanities, his talent for getting along with people, and his friendly and sometimes ironic intelligence. He admired Spain but defended the Creoles against the incomprehension, ignorance, impertinence, and injustice of the Spaniards in the viceregal court, and he even demanded that the government of the colonies be vested in those born there.

The Jesuit ALONSO DE OVALLE (Chile, 1601–1651) wrote a *Historic Account of the Dominion of Chile* (*Histórica relación del reino de Chile*, 1646) in a prose excellent for its sensitivity to the beauties of the landscape. His greatest merit lies in the lingering descriptions of natural scenery. Besides describing the countryside, he also described the city and some Chilean customs. His inventory of beautiful sights smacks of touristic advertising; he wanted to attract missionaries from Europe, so he tells them that everything resembles Europe, except that in Chile there are no bedbugs. His pages, then, are addressed to Europeans, and in his eulogy of Chile, he followed European models, like the eulogy of Spain composed by Isadore of Seville. However, he does install Chile, and the Andes, in the realm of literature. He describes passages where rocks take on marvelous colors, the rivers reflect unsuspected images, and the sea loses itself in the infinite. His prose is not Baroque; on the contrary, it is almost colloquial in its slowness, repetitions, and long periods. But it assumes a poetic tint and imaginative dash whenever he is enthused. The contrast between his good passages and the rest of his prose indicates that Ovalle did not lack talent, but rather time or artistic will. He is a naturalist with imagination. In the chapter about the mountain range, for example, he becomes ecstatic and his fantasy adds impressions of light. He imagines himself on the top of an Andean peak. From there, he tells us that, while his head is in the blue and serene air, he sees the rain falling from the clouds at his feet upon the people below. Or he tells us that "the rainbow that we see from the land crossing the sky is seen from these heights extended along the earth as a footstool at our feet, while those who are on the ground see it above their heads . . ." The first part, descriptive and historic, is superior to the second which deals with the company of Jesus.

Bishop LUCAS FERNANDEZ DE PIEDRAHITA (Colombia, 1624–1688), like the Inca Garcilaso and Alva Ixtlilxóchitl, had in his veins royal indigenous blood. Though not as novelistic as the Peruvian nor as objective as the Mexican, Piedrahita, nevertheless, is one of the important chroniclers of America; and, like these two, he exalted the pre-Hispanic cultures, especially that of the Chibchas. He documented his work as best he could, searching archives in Spain, corresponding with other historians, and reading carefully the chronicles of others. He put Juan de Castellanos in prose and utilized the manuscripts (later lost) of Jiménez de Quesada; and he not only gave us descriptions of indigenous customs and historical events but he also interpreted them philosophically and morally. His own value, he used to say, consisted "of putting in less ancient language" what others had written about the conquest. Pure modesty. His *General History of the Conquest of the New Realm of Granada* (*Historia general de las conquistas del Nuevo Reino de Granada*, 1688), although uneven, is well written; and, when he is not dismayed, he manages to be graceful. Because of his preacher's attitude he tended to have sententious and oratorical moments.

Moving into the eighteenth century we find JOSÉ DE OVIEDO Y BAÑOS (Colombia-Venezuela, 1671–1738). He resided in Caracas almost all his life and wrote a pleasant and at times beautiful *History of the Conquest and Population of the Province of Venezuela* (*Historia de la conquista y población de la provincia de Venezuela*, 1723), from its discovery to the end of the sixteenth century. He worked hard in composing it, benefiting from other chroniclers and unearthing forgotten materials from the archives. He narrated heroic and singular deeds with art and eloquence. He wanted to be accurate, and he was, but with the accuracy of a literary style—pictorial prose, even musical prose stirred by Baroque forms. In addition to an occasional flight of verbosity, he was also Baroque in his inclination toward violent spectacle like the tyrant, Lope de Aguirre, assassinating his daughter.

These four chroniclers are interspersed throughout the period under discussion. There were others that should also be mentioned. Friar PEDRO SIMÓN (Spain, 1574–ca. 1630) arrived in America in 1604 and left some *Historical Notes* (*Noticias historiales*) on the realm of New Granada that harbored so many imaginary things they struck the fantasy of his readers. He speaks of Indians who drag their ears along the ground, who sleep under water, and who feed themselves by smelling fruit since they have "no ordinary way of expelling excrement from their bodies." He was, nevertheless, a slow, lengthy, and tedious writer. Friar BERNABÉ COBO (Spain, 1582–1657) ranged over the Antilles, Venezuela, Peru, and Mexico and in his *History of the New World* (*Historia del Nuevo Mundo*, 1636) he described the natural and especially the botanical geography of these areas more than the history. In order to counteract the false and exaggerated notions that were being propagated throughout Europe, he adjusted accordingly the phenomena he saw. Friar ANTONIO DE LA CALANCHA (Bolivia, 1584–1654) was a chronicler of religious orders. In his *Moralized Chronicle* (*Crónica moralizada*, 1638) he described the skies and the lands of Peru and Bolivia with an abundance of detail on colonial life. DIEGO DE LEÓN PINELO (*ca.* 1590), author of *Paradise in the New World* (*El Paraíso en el Nuevo Mundo*); PERO MEXÍA DE OVANDO, author of *The Woman from Ovando* (*La Ovandina*, 1621); DIEGO DE ROSALES (1603–1677), who is more realist than Ovalle, wrote *General History of the Realm of Chile* (*Historia general del reino de Chile*); Friar AGUSTÍN DE VETANCOURT (Mexico, 1620–1700?); and Father MANUEL RODRÍGUEZ (Colombia, 1638–1684) wrote *The Amazon and the Marañón Rivers* (*El Marañón y Amazonas*) with a prose of relative literary merit, clear but capable of dramatic effects and of rhetorical gleanings, as in the description of the eruption of the Pichincha. Friar DIEGO DE CÓRDOVA SALINAS, after the *Life of Saint Francis Solano* (*Vida de S. Francisco Solano*, Lima, 1630), published a well-written *Franciscan Chronicle of the Provinces of Peru* (*Crónica Franciscana de las Provincias del Perú*, 1651), replete with details on almost half a century of religious life in Peru and other parts, together with a description of viceroyal Lima (shaken at the moment by earthquakes and piratical assaults) and observations on geography and ethnography. Father ALONSO DE ZAMORA (Colombia, 1645–1717)—another mestizo—was the chronicler of his own religious order. Inferior to Piedrahita in style, he was nevertheless a good observer of nature, although he did lack the imagination of a landscapist. José de Buendía (1644–1727), is the author of *The Star of Lima Converted into a Sun on Its Three Crowns* (*La estrella de Lima convertida en Sol sobre sus tres coronas,* 1680). Father Francisco de Figueroa (Colombia, fl. middle seventeenth century), authored *Account of the Missions of the Company of Jesus in the Land of the Maynas* (*Relación de las misiones de la compañía de Jesús en el país de los Maynas*), with details on Indians and customs. Friar Francisco Vázquez (Guatemala, 1647–1713); Friar Pedro Tobar y Buendía (Colombia, 1648–1713), was chronicler of the miracles of the local Virgin. José Ortiz y Morales (Colombia, 1658) has shown us colonial society in his *Curious and Doctrinal Observations* (*Observaciones curiosas y doctrinales,* 1713). Father Francisco Ximénez (Spain-Guatemala, 1666–1729) was a historian. Father Juan Antonio Oviedo (Colombia-Mexico, 1670–1757) was one of the precursors of the great Jesuit humanists. Francisco Antonio Fuentes y Guzmán (Guatemala, fl. 1689) was author of *Historical Precepts* (*Preceptos historiales*). Juan Bautista de Toro (Colombia, d. in 1734) authored *The Religious Layman* (*El secular religioso,* 1721), wherein one observes Creole versus Spanish arrogance.

Novelistic Sketches

The royal decrees that from 1531 prohibited the circulation of novels were not totally obeyed. The few and poorly equipped presses of the New World, kept under the constant vigil of the authorities, of course, had to abide by the law; and, in fact, in the colonies no novels were published (or, as they were then called, "feigned stories," "books of romance that deal with profane and fabulous matters"). The printing in Mexico of Bramón's *The Goldfinches of the Virgin* is explained by the religious nature of the book, as shall be seen immediately. On the other hand, however, those decrees that restricted the circulation of novels printed in Spain were not complied with. They circulated, obviously. Once they reached the colonies there were attempts to destroy them, but neither is it known whether the Church mandates ordering the burning of "vain books . . . that are entitled *Dianas,* of any author whatsoever, and . . . the *Celestina,* and the books of chivalry" (First Synod in Santiago, Argentina in 1597) were carried out. To write a novel was a long undertaking, planned for a particular public, and one must imagine what went through the minds of the Hispanic-American writers. Besides the legal ones, other physical and psychological impediments must have discouraged possible colonial novelists. The manuscript had to be sent to the authorities in Spain for the printing permit with the risk that it might be lost, not to mention the years of waiting involved. Even though the permit might be granted, the Spanish monopoly of printers was another barrier. In America the presses were devoted to the clergy. Furthermore, the cost of printing was prohibitive. Nor could one count on a reader market in America. Perhaps there was inertia in the construction of organic works. Whatever might have been the case, the fact is there were no novels written in the New World. But why should this cause amazement, if in the Old World the novel still did not have proper esteem? The novel was to acquire standing only in the nineteenth century under the bourgeois political regimes. From the modern point of view of the "large public," the insignificance of the novel in the seventeenth century seems lamentable; but it is only natural that no one should feel at that time "obliged" to write novels as they were to write poetry, theater, or didactic prose and sacred orations. It was Cervantes who created, with his *Don Quijote,* the modern novel, but this type of novel was better understood outside of Spain. The moral exigencies that falsified reality and the cultivation of an overwrought prose which lends itself little to narration and dialog, were responsible for Spain's not profiting from the lesson inherent in Cervantes and in the picaresque novels. The novel declines rapidly. From the middle of the seventeenth century we can scarcely find one that is really a novel. The novels of chivalry and the pastoral novels, so popular in the earlier period, extinguish themselves in the seventeenth century. (Bernardo de Valbuena published his pastoral novel *The Golden Age in the Forest of Eriphyle* [*El Siglo de Oro en las selvas de Erifile*] in 1608, but he had written it twenty years earlier.) Now the taste for fantasy finds satisfaction not in the novel but in the theater. There was, then, no novel in the colonies. We can only speak of novelistic qualities in the chronicle and colonial histories.

JUAN RODRÍGUEZ FREILE (Colombia, 1566–1640?), a Creole from Bogotá and son of a conquistador, composed the chronicle of the "conquest and discovery of the new realm of Granada" up to the year 1636, the last in which he wrote. The book was known by the title *The Ram* (*El Carnero*); no one knows why. Was "Ram" the name given to manuscript folios? In example nineteen of the *Book of Cats* (*Libro de los gatos,* 1400–1420) a wolf takes on the habit of a monk but instead of saying "Our Father" he says "ram"; consequently, many monks, instead of learning the rules of their order, preoccupy themselves with the "ram," that is, the meals, wine, and mundane vices. Is this the meaning of the title of the chronicle under study? Or does the title refer metaphorically, in view of the many lives and honors interred in it, to the common grave of hospitals and churches, called "*carneros,*" in which they buried the dead? The *Carnero* is in effect a graveyard of war notices, changes in government, customs, psychological portraits, adventures, scandals, crimes, historical data, and legends. Rodríguez Freile attempted to be accurate, and he described evil in order to moralize upon it. But, fortunately, he was imaginative. "If it is true that painters and poets have the same kind of power, then the chroniclers must keep up with them," he used to say. Whatever he writes is not false like "those who write books of chivalry." But his own work, which he calls "orphan damsel," he will adorn with "borrowed clothes and jewels," and with "the most graceful flowers." These adornments in the composition of *The Ram* are the most pleasant: anecdotes, jokes, digressions, reflections, allusions to literary works, sermons, rascally tales, adventures, love affairs and adulteries, crimes and vengeance, intrigues, ambushes, and witchcraft. Thus, in this scandalous chronicle the risqué and bustling life of Bogotá passes before us as on a stage. He makes use of the literary and dramatic devices of the literature of his day. His unpolished yet appealing style bristles at times, thanks to Baroque technique, with a great use of secret doors, intercepted letters, handkerchief messages, disguises, escapes, and duels. He possessed a sense of humor, a narrative dynamism, and the ability to create a lively dialog. He profited from picaresque literature. He also read—and one can discern it—the Greco-Latin writers and Fray Luis de Granada. He was writing at the age of seventy and was still obsessed with the beauty of women, whom he describes untiringly, although he tells us that their beauty is the temptation of the devil: "Oh beauty, cause of so many evils! Oh women! I don't wish to speak bad of them, nor of men; but I favor saying that men and women are the worst vermin God created." *The Ram,* an original book, gives us, in a bold and unadorned prose, passages of novelistic value. In spite of his manifest misogyny and moralizing mind, Rodríguez Freile enjoys the scandals and improprieties as he follows the currents of his narrative art. The narrative tradition that he is following is that of the novels and the chronicles. He utilizes authors like Pero Mexía, Antonio de Guevara, and especially Fernando de Rojas, whose *Celestina* he cites from memory. In turn, *The Ram* became a source for the depictions of customs and historical literature of the nineteenth century.

DIEGO DÁVALOS Y FIGUEROA is the author of *The Austral Miscellany* (*Miscelánea Austral,* Lima, 1602), a curious work in which there is an admixture of fact and fiction, heroic deeds and spiritual evocations. His neat language has been laundered with the use of numerous citations and translations of Renaissance authors. The plot revolves around the author, who, fleeing from an unfortunate love affair, ends up in the lands of America where the marvels of the New World overwhelm and dazzle him.

Several works having elements of the pastoral novel were written in Mexico. The genre had been initiated in Spain with the *Diana* (1559?) of Jorge Montemayor. In a short time a whole family of similar novels appeared which were immediately passed on to America and there imitated. Balbuena's *The Golden Age* will be studied below. Right now we would like to dwell on a pastoral novel dealing with the Divine, *The Goldfinches of the Immaculate Virgin* (*Los sirgueros de la Virgen sin original pecado*, 1620) by FRANCISCO BRAMÓN (Mexico, d. after 1654). With this genre Bramón builds his own road, albeit a short and narrow one. The similarities to his models are external: braiding prose and verse, the stylization of nature by means of an aristocratic selection of exquisite objects, embellishing metaphors, allusions to classical myths, sentimental effusion, lyrical imagination, and dialogs between shepherds who are simply fur-clad embodiments of Platonic ideas. But with these pastoral trappings Bramón is to construct another class of narration. His goal is religious—to defend the purity of the Virgin Mary. All the action—parleys, promenades, processions, dances, songs, Masses, games, incision of Marian symbols on tree barks, theological discourses, architecture of arches, musical orchestrations, bullfights, and theatrical presentations—is an apologia of the mystery of the Immaculate Conception of Mary. (The goldfinches symbolize the shepherds who sing to the Virgin.) The central narrative thread links the immediate reality, especially space and time. Geography, nature, and ethnography are clearly situated: "in these Mexican gardens," "the Cathedral of Mexico," American plants, indigenous instruments, and Aztec dances. History is also well-delineated—it alludes to King Philip III and contemporary events. Allusions to a non-pastoral reality, such as religious, university, and artistic activities of the city, give *The Goldfinches* an air of the autobiographical novel. There is a curious metamorphosis of a genre—the pastoral novel becomes sacropastoral and pastoral-academic. *The Goldfinches* is the history of how the poet Francisco Bramón (who under the name of Anfriso becomes a shepherd only to rest from a competitive examination he has just undergone at the University of Mexico) conceives, writes, and represents the "Mystery of the Triumph of the Virgin and Mexican Couplets in Her Praise" (*"Auto del triunfo de la Virgen y Gozo mexicano"*) in order to return at once to the University where he will triumph in an academic way "with the green laurel of the Faculty of Canons." Two undulating lines, fiction and reality, crisscross here and there, with fiction readily reducing itself to reality or reality rising to the level of fiction. The protagonist is real and unreal, and the "mystery" he writes is also real and unreal; in this way the work in which they appear is simultaneously art and life. Genres within genres, real-author within protagonist-author, the reader feels himself a spectator in a literary workshop. As in Velázquez' Baroque painting, "Las Meninas," the desire for immortality makes Bramón paint himself within the painting in the very act of painting. Yet, despite this interesting form of the interior duplication of the novel—a real author slips into his own fiction and there we see him in the process of writing a theatrical piece —*The Goldfinches of the Virgin* is a tiresome work, written in an inflated, pompous, and unbearable manneristic prose.

CATALINA DE ERAUSO (Spain, 1592?–1650?) wrote, it seems, about her travels and adventures through Peru and other parts, always disguised as a man and living like a man. Copies of "reports" of 1625 and of 1646, whose originals are attributed to her, are preserved. These brief, simple reports written in the third person are similar to those submitted by conquistadors and soldiers to the king in order to win recognition for their services. The scandalous theme of the man-woman invited all kinds of fantasies, among them the legend of the nun Alférez, already treated by playwrights in the seventeenth century (e.g., Pérez de Montalbán). In 1829 Joaquín María de Ferrer published a picaresque *History of the Nun Alférez* which, according to him, was an authentic autobiography; if this were the case (and we believe not) the colony would have its novelette.

BISHOP JUAN DE PALAFOX Y MENDOZA (Spain–Mexico, 1600–1659) wrote verses, religious works, even a treatise on spelling. Because of their narrative interest, we shall speak of only two of his works. In *On the Nature of the Indians* (*De la naturaleza del indio*), in order to praise the virtues and merits of those "most useful and most faithful vassals of the Indies," he had recourse to anecdotes which not only are worthwhile as pleasant stories, but also allow us to hear the intelligent and cultured reflections of some of the Indians. *The Christmas Shepherd* (*El pastor de Nochebuena*, 1644), tending toward Baroque tastes, is the allegory of a devout shepherd who, accompanied by angels, recounts his travels and adventures through the regions of good and evil populated by personifications of vices and virtues. Hundreds of figures, drawn from fantasy and theology, move about in tiresome artistic harness—descriptions, dialogs, subtleties, mystic language. The background and ideas are traditional. Symbols and parables surge from sacred literature, although the influence of profane literature is also noticeable.

FRANCISCO NÚÑEZ DE PINEDA Y BASCUÑÁN (Chile, 1607–1682) in *My Happy Captivity or the Reason for the Protracted Wars in Chile* (*El cautiverio feliz or razón de las guerras dilatadas de Chile*) tells us of his own experiences of his seven months as a prisoner of the *Araucanians.* Between this experience of 1629 and the moment of relating it, 1650 or thereabouts, he interposes the desire to make literature, to present his father don Álvaro as a great conquistador, to insist on his own virtues as captain and good Christian, to serve the Church, to denounce the oppression of bad Christian Spaniards in the Indies, to describe strange customs. His recollections are almost novelistic. In fact, this was the first chronicle in which an essentially novelistic element appears—the building up of suspense in the action. The chieftain Maulicán took in Pineda from the field of battle, wounded. It was a great honor to have in captivity no less than the son of the feared don Álvaro. Maulicán attempts to convince the other chieftains to spare the life of the prisoner whom he has promised freedom. Will Maulicán succeed in saving Pineda from the bloodthirsty Indians lurking around? Will he keep his promise to free him? The Indians grant the custody of the illustrious captive to Maulicán. Furthermore, must Maulicán return his captive? If he does, Pineda will be executed. Maulicán, the protector of Pineda, takes him on a trip to Repocura. Intrigues. Skirmishes. In every town, dancing and feasting, drunken brawls, adventures. They arrive at Repocura, and Maulicán refuses to relinquish his captive to the other chieftains. He hides him, takes him from one place to another. Finally, Pineda returns to the arms of his father—Maulicán kept his word! Pineda's psychological observations are also worthwhile, novelistically speaking. And even the doctrines he wishes to promulgate —the truth of Christianity, the goodness of the Indians when they are evangelized properly by the Christians, the damage caused by the bad Spaniards—are expressed novelistically: in the form of dialogs, the Indians denounce in eloquent discourses the cruelty of Spanish men and women as "the reason for the protracted wars in Chile." Pineda has read humanistic and religious literature. He has also read picaresque, chivalric, and pastoral novels. And it is not always possible to distinguish between the literary embellishments of real-life scenes and pure episodic invention. At any rate, the impulses which advance the narration do not always come from actual recollections, but sometimes from books. Thus, literature is embroidered on the narrative cloth. Pineda, who is so punctilious in pointing out good and evil, the just and unjust, virtue and sin, illustrates his table of values with fictional episodes. For example, his surprising scruples vis-à-vis women. From the outset of the conquest, the Spaniard fell upon the nude and seminude women of America. Columbus, on his very first voyage, tells us how he had to intervene. And the chronicles reveal, more or less freely, the sexual frenzy of the Spaniards. Núñez Pineda is the one Spaniard who shuns Indian women. They pursue him; they want to give themselves to him. Even the beautiful and nubile daughter of Maulicán provokes him. And the chieftains themselves wish that he would give pleasure to the enraptured Indian maidens. But Pineda hides, sneaks away, prays to be liberated from the temptation of the flesh. It is not that he is insensitive to beauty. "Let us contemplate for a moment the most difficult temptation put before me by the spirit of evil on this occasion: a nude woman, white and clean, with great, black eyes, long eyelashes, eyebrows in the shape of a bow from which they flung god Cupid's arrows, her hair so long and so thick that it could serve as a coverlet, fell down her body to her legs, and other particulars that were sufficient at that moment to carry away my senses and my spirit." He tends to choke the narrative with religious, moral, and political reflections; but fortunately for the hedonist reader, the narration recovers its fire and gives us the quick rising flame of descriptions that are among the best in Hispanic-American chronicles. Remember, for example, the return of the captive, safe and sound, to the arms of his old father. His ethnographic descriptions are interesting. In his landscapes—stormy landscapes, with clouds of squally winds and torrential rains—efforts to use ornamental, aristocratic expressions appear: "we arrived as night drew its curtains," "the splendors of dawn began to dispel the confused mists of the night," "daybreak arrived with signs that the pregnant clouds again would discharge their icy offspring." Baroque, surely, but not too much so. He was familiar with the obscure and difficult style of conceptists, and he even tells us that it was practised by the Indians: "because also among the barbarians there are learned preachers who value themselves for not being understood by anyone." In general, Pineda was a plain writer. The verses he interpolated amidst his prose were translations or paraphrases from the classics and also inventions of his own. He preferred the quiet, simple ballads of sober but sincere tones.

Friar JUAN DE BARRENECHEA Y ALBIS (Chile, d. 1707) wrote the *Restoration of the Empire* (*Restauración de la Imperial*, 1693), a history containing a novelistic embryo. We will refer later to Sigüenza y Góngora's novelesque *Misfortunes of Alonso Ramírez* (*Infortunios de Alonso Ramírez*).

Spanish Writers in America
and Hispanic-American Writers in Spain

Occasionally great talented men of Spain visited the colonies. Cervantes was not permitted to come, but among the famous ones who did were Gutierre de Cetina, Juan de la Cueva, Mateo Alemán, Tirso de

Molina. (Luis Belmonte Bermúdez wrote his twenty-five plays after his return to Spain; Francisco de Lugo y Dávila, governor of Chiapas in the viceroyalty of New Spain, published in Madrid his *Popular Theater*, 1622, one of the "moral novels" of the Cervantine school.) They were only visits, and their influence is vague at best. There were visitors who wrote about America, but their place is in the literary history of Spain. On the other hand, one Hispanic-American writer, Juan Ruiz de Alarcón, made a long visit to Spain and, without saying one word about America, as if he had forgotten it, gave himself to the mother country, where he left the imprint of his genius.

Juan Ruiz de Alarcón / (Mexico, 1580–1639) was thirty-three years old when he established himself definitely in Spain (at twenty he left Mexico; he returned at twenty-seven; and lived six more years in Mexico). One does not live his entire youth in his native country in vain. Personal experience is attuned to the frequencies of the local environment. And although the artist may later change his locale and aspire to a more universal expression, the vibrations of that existence, tuned to earlier experiences, can always be heard in his works in a very subtle way. Alarcón's contemporary Spaniards soon detected a certain strangeness in his plays, and later critics have analyzed their non-typical, non-Spanish traits. They have a colonial Mexican character. Although his plays are constructed in the manner of Lope de Vega, they reflect the originality of a new society that is less vivacious and less extroverted than that of the metropolis. Alarcón's characters remain more in their houses than in the street; duels are avoidable; there is a prudent, reserved, and courteous tone (the Indian gave colonial society a tinge of sobriety); the *graciosos* or comic servants are not as scurrilous, perhaps because the Indian servants in Mexico were not permitted the familiarities of the servants in Spain. This search for external Mexican elements in Alarcón's theater is difficult and even sterile. The most obvious is a commentary on the water drainage system of Mexico City in *The Man Who Resembles Himself* (*El semejante de sí mismo*). And might it not be that his most apparent Mexican trait is his not wishing to speak of Mexico? One does not live the many years that Alarcón lived in Hispanic-America without being an Hispanic-American; however, at the end of the sixteenth century and beginning of the seventeenth century Alarcón, having decided to triumph in the Spanish theater, did so without having in mind any notions of patriotism. Alarcón had seen some theater in Mexico before going to Spain. From 1597 Mexico had a playhouse, that is, a permanent theater, with building, companies of actors, and a theater-going public. In this period Alarcón must have had a rough draft of *The Cave of Salamanca* (*La cueva de Salamanca*). But once in Spain he wanted to be a Spanish writer. The Inca Garcilaso, because of the nature of his subject, the Inca civilization, had insisted on his status as a mestizo. Alarcón did not have to speak of his status as a Mexican to fit better in the Lope circle of theatrical activity. It is possible, furthermore, that in the aggressive social life of Spain in that epoch, it would have been risky to introduce Mexican themes in his plays—the Spaniards would have mocked such esthetic deformity with the same cruelty that they had mocked his physical deformity. Alarcón was hunchbacked; and it has been said that his bitterness over this defect (more terrible in a time in history when physical beauty was overly esteemed) created a resentment that finds moral expression in his plays. There is, in effect, an ethical attitude in Alarcón. He ponders the values that orient or should orient human conduct. This moralizing preoccupation was undoubtedly tense in Alarcón's soul, but it was also one of the resonant chords of the Spanish theater of his time. One had to moralize in the theater. And they all moralize: Tirso, later Calderón. Even though Alarcón, in moralizing, followed his own ethical impulses rather than social conventions, the truth is, he did not go very far as a reformer. His morality is the traditional one: honor, loyalty, gratitude, love of one's neighbor. And even the value of his moral characters, both negative and positive, depends more on Alarcón's ability to move the characters dramatically than on the depth of the ideas presented. The liar, the slanderer, the ingrate, etc., have value as artistic characters. They are more complicated than would be necessary for a simple moral lesson. It is the action that pulls along all the characters of the Spanish play; Alarcón's characters, nevertheless, manage to stay awhile so that we can hear their reasoning. They speak directly to the mind. They are not lyrical. When they become lyrical, it is with moderation. Alarcón constructs his plays with care. Lope and Tirso wrote plays by the hundreds; he, only two dozen. Plays of intrigue, heroic plays. His best productions, character plays like *Walls Have Ears* (*Las paredes oyen*), *The Winning of Friends* (*Ganar amigos*), *Suspect Truth* (*La verdad sospechosa*)—Corneille adapted it in *Le Menteur*—give him an intelligent and modern air. The plays of character development at times take place under marvelous circumstances, such as, *Proof of Promises* (*La prueba de las promesas*); at times they unfold in sparkling dialectics as in *It Is an Ill Wind That Blows No Good* (*No hay mal que por bien no venga*, 1623?). With this play Alarcón closed his dramatic career. The main character—not type—Don Domingo de Don Blas, is one of the few in all of the plays of the Golden Age, who addresses himself directly to the intelligence of the modern reader. Don Blas is so anti-conventional that the sharpness of his dialectics converts this play into the least conventional one of its time. The good sense of the comfort-loving Don Blas surprises and entertains us—at least in the first two acts—because it is not part of a moral lesson, but of a psychological picture.

Theater

More space should be given to Alarcón, but his theater, after all, belongs to Spain. In truth, Spain is the center of all theatrical activity. It is the century of Lope de Vega, of Tirso, of Calderón. Their plays reach the colonies. Companies of Spanish actors bring the latest successes. They present them in palaces and in public enclosures. The audiences applaud. And they read the collections of plays which, from the time of Lope's first one in 1605, are imported from Spain. Plays of the Lope school first, and later those of the Calderón school, influence customs, habits of dress, and manners of speech. The Creoles seldom write for the theater, and when they do, they limit themselves to interludes to fill in the time between the acts of Spanish plays. What colonial writer will dare compete with the masters of Spain. The conformity of court life and of religious life, the lack of stimulus and, naturally, of talent impoverish the theater. Be that as it may, the productions in Spain and in America move along at different tempos. During almost all of the seventeenth century (at least until the death of Calderón) Spain is at its theatrical apogee while the colonies are scarcely producing little occasional pieces; from 1681 onward, the Spanish theater declines while the colonies begin to advance their theater with ambitious plays. In Mexico, prior to Alarcón, we had González de Eslava, already studied in the previous chapter, and after Alarcón, Sor Juana Inéz de la Cruz, whom we will study in another section of the present chapter. But if it did not produce outstanding figures, the Mexican theater did produce an outstanding number of plays. Seldom did one author write more than one play. The normal procedure was for someone to write a playlet to celebrate some event or to honor a particular person, and then he would retire from the theater, never to return to the profession. In reality neither drama nor comedy was cultivated, but rather little exercises in cajolery that were called preludes, dances, interludes, windups, mystery plays, and farces. The most fertile genre was the *loa*, or short panegyric prelude, in which four or six characters presented symbolically either mythological beings or qualities or places.

When they represented real men they were usually called "Indians" if they came from America, "gentlemen" if they were from Spain. These *loas* generally celebrated the proclamation of a new king or the welcoming of a viceroy or archbishop.

In Mexico they were composed by Francisco Robledo, Miguel Pérez de Gálvez, Jerónimo Becerra, Alonso Ramírez de Vargas, Antonio Medina Solís, and others. *The Colloquy of the New Conversion and Baptism of the Last Four Kings of Tlaxcala in New Spain* (*Coloquio de la nueva conversión y bautismo de los cuatro últimos reyes de Tlaxcala en la Nueva España*), attributed to Cristóbal Gutiérrez de Luna, seems to date from 1619. From 1684 is the unbelievable staging of the life of St. Francis of Assisi, *The Preacher of God and Patriarch of the Poor* (*El Pregonero de Dios y Patriarca de los pobres*) by Francisco de Acevedo. It has already been noted that Bramón included in his *The Goldfinches of the Virgin* a well-structured, well-versified mystery play that made notable use of indigenous scenery and choreography. MATÍAS DE BOCANEGRA (Mexico, 1512–1668), the poet of the famous "Song at the Sight of a Disillusion" (*"Canción a la vista de un desengaño"*), composed in 1640 the three acts of his *St. Francis of Borja* (*Comedia de San Francisco de Borja*). In it he has some *décimas* or ten-verse stanzas that recall Segismundo's first soliloquy in Calderón's *Life Is a Dream*, published four years earlier. On the other hand, he introduces native dances and songs. (AGUSTÍN DE SALAZAR Y TORRES, 1642–1675, returned to Spain when he was eighteen years old and there he wrote his plays—like Alarcón he belongs to the dramatic literature of Spain.)

Peru followed Mexico with the same type of theater. The first company of players was constituted in 1599 in Lima, and in the first years of the seventeenth century the *Casa de Comedias* (*Playhouse*) was established. The theater was enjoyed equally by the general public as well as by the aristocratic and ecclesiastical segments. (Friar Gaspar de Villarroel has recorded for us his youthful fancy for plays.) Although in general the works presented came from Spain, there were those by Creole playwrights having local themes; Núñez de Pineda Bascuñán, in *The Happy Captivity*, recounts with special care the episode of his relations with Maulicán's daughter in order to clarify matters, because in Peru, he says, a play had been written and staged that was "quite contrary to the facts, representing these love affairs in a very poetic way." The major figures in this period were Peralta Barnuevo (who, because of the dates of his plays, will be treated in the next chapter) and LORENZO DE LAS LLAMOSAS (1665?–d. after 1705). The latter composed two musical comedies: *The Gods Also Avenge Themselves* (*También se vengan los dioses*, 1698), with an elaborate stage populated by gods, nymphs and shepherds, and *Destinies Conquer Kindnesses* (*Destinos vencen finezas*, 1698), on the love of Dido and Aeneas. DIEGO MEXÍA DE FERNANGIL, of Seville, author of *Antarctic Parnassus* (*Parnaso antártico*), also wrote *The God Pan* (*El Dios Pan*, between 1608 and 1630), a kind of pastoral eclogue treating divine subjects in one act and in verse. Espinosa Medrano and Valle Caviedes, as shall be seen when they are discussed, also wrote for the theater.

To the Colombian theater belongs FERNANDO FERNÁNDEZ DE VALENZUELA (1616–last quarter of the seventeenth century), whose interlude *Laurea Criticizes* (*Laurea crítica*) caricatures various psychological and social types. A caricature of a man of letters who speaks in the language of Góngora is amusing and, in addition, has value as a document in the polemical history of that style. Of more importance in the Colombian theater is Juan de Cueto y Mena (Spain, 1602?– d. after 1669). In his writings he profited from Lope de Vega, Góngora, Quevedo, and Calderón. It would indeed be a curiosity if the conjecture were true that Cueto, as he versified his theatrical "colloquy," *Competition Among Nobles and Discord Reconciled* (*La competencia en los nobles y discordia concordada*, 1662) had taken into account the mystery plays or *autos sacramentales* of Calderón, and that the latter, in turn, on writing *Life Is a Dream* (1673), took into account Cueto's colloquy. If he made an impression on Calderón it must have been only in the idea of converting the four elements, fire, air, water and land, into the main characters of an allegory that takes Greek philosophic notions and interprets them in the light of scholastic philosophy. Cueto's universe was that of Ptolemy; his literature, that of the Baroque. In his "Song Describing Popa Hill" (*"Canción describiendo el Cerro de la Popa"*) he discolored in a Baroque style the outline of a Colombian landscape. He had his colloquy, *Paraphrasis Panegirica*, performed. A friend celebrated the verses of this colloquy in the courteous, overwrought, and adulatory language of the epoch thusly: "thou shalt no longer be Juan de Cueto / for thou shalt be Juan de Mena." Not so—he was and shall be Juan de Cueto y Mena, one of the many obscure poets who, in cleaving to Baroque techniques, managed with difficulty to come away with one or two happy images.

Poetry

Some of the chroniclers already reviewed used to interpolate verses in their chronicles or would scribble them in the margin. Meanderings of poetry in a sea of prose. The theater also may be considered poetry since it was written in verse. This section, then, cannot be rigidly considered as the only storehouse of poetry. Yet, we shall see the great poets of this period. However, in order to see them in their proper perspective, we shall have to mention many versifiers who left little poetic deposit. And since these poets are also prosists, how can we avoid speaking of prose again? The literary historian tries to part the waters, but they insist on joining again.

Bernardo de Balbuena / (Spain–Mexico, 1561 or 1562–1627) lived during exactly the same years as Góngora; and like Góngora, he felt the necessity of inventing an affected, ornamental, and aristocratic expression. But, although he Gongorized at times (in 1604 he said: "in what part of the world have poets been known as worthy of veneration as the poignant don Luis de Góngora?") Balbuena's Baroque style was independent; at least it ran unbridled, now this way, now that, along the wide stylistic course which at the end of the sixteenth and at the beginning of the seventeenth century opens out on Spanish letters where virtuosos of the language display themselves. For here is the discovery of the Baroque writers: language is a sovereign body that can contort itself, leap, immobilize in an enigmatic gesture, suddenly open its arms and give forth metaphors, then draw itself in to assume obscure conceptual attitudes, always replete with adornment, always proud of not being commonplace language. The very first octave Balbuena offered a lady as a description of the city of Mexico were the eight seeds from which the chapters of the *Grandeur of Mexico* (*Grandeza mexicana*, 1604) grew. Each verse would serve as a heading to a chapter. In this way, the *Grandeur of Mexico* emerged as though in a nursery, not with large forest trees, but rather with delicate garden plants. Balbuena wishes to please—in the first place, the lady to whom he dedicates the poem, and then also the powerful persons in Mexico. He has been living as a humble village priest for many years; in this moment of his life, perhaps unhappy about his own obscurity, he begins to praise the city in which he would like to occupy a better position. Descriptions of Mexico already existed in the current prose of the chroniclers, in the incidental verses of minor poets, and in the Latin dialogs of Cervantes de Salazar. Now Balbuena gives us a description in the Baroque manner, "ciphered," he says, that is, constructed intelligently in one small poetic unity. He had the poetic gift, as proven by the *Bernardo* (1624), a Baroque variation on a theme by Ariosto, but in the *Grandeur of Mexico* he will avoid the epic of the conquest. It is more garden than forest, but a garden with tall plants or, rather, a greenhouse garden that seems immense because we see it through the magnifying glasses of Baroque style. We are not given the poetry of the minuscule, of the humble, of the simple, but rather a view of court luxury, of the "grandeur of Mexico," which was only the exterior aspect of the Mexican reality. The structure of that "grandeur" is clear: there are not as many turns of expression, conceits or images as we find in Góngora and in Quevedo; but although his imagination does not twist the axis of reality, he covers them with embellishments. His inventive style is found in these embellishments; at times it is so energetic that the embellishment acquires a complete and autonomous beauty, ceases to be an embellishment functioning for an underlying phrase, and becomes pure poetry in and of itself. The clarity of construction is a Renaissance trait. Balbuena writes his epistle in hendecasyllabic tercets with quatrains at the end of each part, following the Italian tradition of poems of chivalry. In that way Balbuena's clarity makes the value of those isolated moments of artistic invention more visible. In his esthetic ideals he followed the Italians more than the Spaniards. When he wrote a pastoral novel, *The Golden Age in the Forest of Eriphyle* (*Siglo de Oro en las selvas de Erífile*, 1608) he leaped over the Spanish Dianas and Galateas to dive happily into the Italian source: Sannazaro's *Arcadia*. In Balbuena's eyes the pastoral world is already an empty one. Its myths and symbols have lost their content, their intellectual force. On the other hand, they remain as artistic forms. He imitated Sannazaro precisely because he saw him from a great distance, in an esthetic perspective. As in Sannazaro, his descriptive elements prevail over the narrative. The shepherds, after singing their joys and sorrows, with all their thoughts devoted to the absent shepherdesses, withdraw inconspicuously to one side. While the action calms down, the landscapes come into view dressed with all the luxuriance of a Baroque-colored fantasy. It is classical literary tradition that moves Balbuena, but his vitality lies in the filigree. He is attracted by the unreal, the contrived, the artful. He described the city of Mexico, but within a dream and guided magically by a nymph. Hills, plains, woods, caves, and rivers all belong to an ideal of geography. It is a fugue in which verse pursues prose and the supernatural the natural. The language of metaphors, mythological allusions, allegories, dreams, and incredible dialogs end up by evading reality, scarcely leaving in its wake an indication of art.

Heroic and Religious Epics / While still bishop of Puerto Rico, Bernardo de Balbuena had to flee, in 1625, before the incursions of Dutch pirates. Another bishop, Friar Juan de la Cabezas Altamirano, suffered more: he was kidnapped in 1604 by the French buccaneer, Gilbert Giron. And this episode is the theme of the first Cuban poem, *Mirror of Patience* (*Espejo de paciencia*, 1608) by SILVESTRE DE BALBOA (b. between 1564 and 1574; d. between 1634 and 1644). It is surprising that this poem, in two cantos having 145 epic octaves that flow clearly, simply, and with narrative force, should sprout suddenly in the midst of the cultural desert that was Cuba. It is a rhymed chronicle—perhaps Balboa was writing beneath the shade of the Ercilla tree—but here is not an account of the struggles of Spaniard against Indian, nor of Spaniards against Spaniards, but of Spaniards against "Lutheran" pirates, as Balboa calls them. In his prolog to the reader, Balboa confesses his imitation of Horace; and in the poem, reminiscences of Ariosto and Tasso are recognized, perhaps not directly, but through Italianate Spanish poets like Luis Barahona de Soto, who himself had imitated the *Orlando Furioso* in his *The Tears of Angelica* (*Las lágrimas de Angélica*). The influence that goes unnoticed is that of Góngora. There is no Baroque in *Mirror of Patience*. On the contrary, the stupefaction before the heresy of the French, the admiration for the patience with which the bishop suffers all, and the final heroic vengeance are conveyed in plain hendecasyllabic lines, sententious but without conceits, with mythological adornments but without cultist forms, almost always prosaic, although with an occasional poetic sparkle, especially in the narrative. All this equilibrium—although keeping the logical axis too much in view—makes Balboa a minor poet outside the literary frame that dominated in his time. In view of the fact that it was the novelist and poet, José Antonio Echeverría, who left us in his own handwriting the two extant versions of *Mirror of Patience* (with insignificant variants), it was believed at one time that the entire poem, and even the existence of Balboa himself, could have been a hoax. It is possible that Echeverría, while copying, may have modified and modernized the missing original. What is certain is that the *Mirror of Patience* is a work apart, singular even for its Creole, Cuban, and national feeling. "O happy island of Cuba!" it says. It is a "little Creole Negro" who will deceive the pirate into putting into land; it is an Indian who becomes the only victim of the French in the final battle; it is a Negro—"O, Creole savior, honorable Negro"—who thrusts the lance into the chest of Gilbert Giron and kills him. And when the bishop returns to Cuba, a freed man, the mythological gods come out laden with flowers and fruit of the American landscape to receive him. In this way indigenous words enter into the Horatian literary phraseology. The religious theme intertwines with the heroic: in the first canto, the suffering of the bishop; in the second, the vengeance against the heretic. But what dominates this second part is the color of the blood. This interlacing of themes of Christian humility and bellicose furor is very significant. Balboa lies between two traditions. Epic poetry had acquired such prestige in Spain that poets emerged intent on singing not only about the deeds of the conquistadors, but also of the saints. Even more: alongside the epics of princes, the epic of Christ. Poems on the passion and death of the religious hero already begin to appear by the fifteenth century. But it is after the Council of Trent that the epical-religious genre is filled with the squalls of the Counter Reformation. Furthermore, Tasso changed the meaning of heroic verse. Balboa restricted himself to a comparison of the bishop with Christ.

During these very years, another poet, DIEGO DE HOJEDA (1571–1615) in a monastery in Lima, wrote a vast poem on Christ himself. In Hojeda's *Christiada* there is but one theme: "I sing to the Son of God, Human and Dead." His doctrinal sources were the writings of the Church Fathers, the Gospel, Castilian sermons, religious treatises, lives of saints, the ideas of St. Augustine, St. Thomas Aquinas, and even Suárez; but literature came to the aid of his pen: Homer, Vergil, Dante, Girolamo Vida, Tasso, Du Bartas, Hernández Blasco, Ariosto, Boiardo, and the Spanish poets from the end of the sixteenth century and the Baroque poets of the beginning of the seventeenth. Despite its Baroque digressions, the work—divided into twelve books—follows a much more rigorous plan than other epics. Nevertheless, it is not this plan, nor the eloquence of the preachings, nor much less the theocratic rapture, that saves the *Christiada* for today's reader. Naturally, in a poem of such length having such a universal theme and dedicated to such a diverse public, we will find many modes, many styles, many reminiscences from different cultural sources. It is like a museum where everyone can admire what he pleases—the biblical phrase, the sacred oratory, the Renaissance tenderness. But there are, here and there, indications of an ornate, colored, metaphoric style, with a taste for contrasts, enumerations and overrefined detail; and perhaps it is these Baroque dynamics that strike our fancy. Hojeda amplifies passages from the Gospel, loading them with adornments. He takes episodes from the Classical period and modifies them by using them allegorically: thus Aeneas' and Achilles' shields are converted into the complicated vestments of Christ. Theology itself is poetized with post-Renaissance language, as in the beautiful Oration personified in Book II. Even his love for Christ is personal, concrete, rich in imagination and in sensorial experiences. This living love gave many of his octaves a lyrical and luxuriant brilliance. In the scene where Christ washes the feet of his disciples, the beauty of his hands is transferred to the light, to the water, to the flowers, in a joyous tremor. And when he describes the handsomeness of his unclothed body, the way in which he is whipped and jeered, Hojeda's love inspires one of the most poetic moments in all the literature of this cycle. His friend in Lima, Diego Mexía de Fernangil, dedicated 200 sonnets to the life of Christ. And, regarding Mexican literature, Corchero y Carreño's *The Vindication of Christ* (*Desagravios de Cristo*), the anonymous *Passion Poem* (*Poema de la Pasión*), and the *Eighth Wonder* (*Octava maravilla*) by Francisco de Castro should be cited here.

That the epic was now no longer up to its previous mettle is apparent in the *Arauca Tamed* (*Arauco domado*) of PEDRO DE OÑA (Chile, 1570–1643?). This Creole, born amidst the landscape and Indians that Ercilla had taken as the subject of his poem, also decided to imitate Ercilla, but he deviated from that reality even more than his model did. Oña was born almost the same year in which the first part of *La Araucana* appeared; he was eight when the second part appeared, and nineteen when the third was published. By the time *Arauco Tamed* was published in 1596—the first book in verse by an Hispanic-American author —a lot of literature had flowed beneath the *Araucana*. Oña turned to the epic, but discouraged by the conviction that that art form was "so refined and so perfectly developed," that, to continue after Ercilla, "would not be perfection but corruption." He related, therefore, the same heroic material (above all, that which Ercilla had given from Canto XIII of the second part on), but forcing his style in the less heroic sections. The Ercilla elements of the *Arauco Tamed* do not have the value of the voluptuous, mellow, and picturesque passages that Oña esteemed as true poetry. His battles, his portraits of Spanish soldiers or Indian warriors, his chronicle, his rhetorical technique of having past events enter into his poem (Oña's "prophecies" follow those that Ercilla puts in the mouths of Belona and Fitón), show him up as being inferior to Ercilla. On the other hand, Oña brought to the Araucanian epic a new spirit, lax in determination, Baroque in language. There were also embellishments and idealizations in Ercilla, but the procedure becomes more dense in Oña (after all the most outstanding example of Baroque poetics, Góngora, is this: an intensification of recognized artifices). Even the octave is modified in his poem—*ABBAABCC* instead of *ABABABCC*—making it more gracious and light, "with more softness," as the poet himself said. The tone of his voice is more lyrical; at least it is more personal. The perception of things, especially their hues, indicates that Oña's eyes are attentive to the miniature images that form in his consciousness and which he illumines further. It is a reflexive attitude in the search of images as well as concept that led him to a type of description which is at once intellectual and colorful. "The green surface of the earth / seemed white, with white bones, / and the spilled blood reddened / the clear streams of the sierra." Oña had one poetic advantage over Ercilla: his thought did not center on the great abstractions of theology, but by illustrating his thinking with minute observations of daily life, he achieved that force of expression that the discovery of new objects gives. Oña is richer in metaphors than Ercilla, not only because he has more of them, but also because they are newer and more surprising. In addition to the classical images— with animals, plants, and minerals—Oña invents metaphors in which one of the meanings points to commonplace things. He is so observant of objects that, although inanimate, they become animate; although immovable, they move, all in an explosion of impulses. The pennants that stream in the wind try to break loose from their staffs and fly off in the air; the light struggles with the branches of the trees; the water approaches with joy to receive the naked body of Fresia. They were not always American objects, and for this he has been reproached. But, after all, no poet is obliged to document the reality of his country with typical descriptions. Oña shied away from truthful representation because that was the impulse of the Baroque imagination: mythology, wealth of exotic names, bookish idyls, aristocratic movements. Oña's epic, like the body of a gymnast, relaxes certain muscles and flexes others; the flexed ones are those already described by Ovid's elegant bucolic art. It is a musculature in motion, nevertheless, because of the violent contrasts. Toward the end of his life Oña compressed the Baroque language that was spread throughout the *Arauco Tamed* and gave us another historical poem, *El vasauro* (1635) which, indeed, is interwoven almost strophe by strophe [with] all the conceptist and cultist threads of the epoch, especially of Góngora's. *El vasauro* related, without unity, the deeds of the Catholic monarchs and of the ancestors of the Viceroy of Peru from 1465 to 1492. (The *"vasaro"* is the *áureo vaso* or golden vessel that the monarchs presented to Andrés de Cabrera.) Ercilla still has his influence on Oña, as does the whole Italian and Spanish Renaissance. But, it must be repeated, Góngora still dominates even the poets who most resist him; and although Oña spoke ill of Góngora, he uses Gongoresque metaphors, syntax, and cultisms in *El vasauro* as well as in *Ignatius of Cantabria* (1639), the last thing he produced.

Other Baroque Poets in South America / Within the space available, we will dwell only on a few other Baroque poets. JACINTO DE EVIA (Ecuador, b. 1620) published in Spain a *Bouquet of Sundry Poetical Flowers Gathered and Cultivated in the Early Springtime of His Life* (*Ramillete de varias flores poéticas recogidas y cultivadas en los primeros abriles de sus años,* 1676), in which were collected compositions from his own garden and from those of his contemporaries, the Ecuadorian Father Antonio Bastidas and the Colombian Hernando Domínguez Camargo. There were all types of verses: lyrical, sacred, heroic, panegyric, epigrammatic. At times Evia submerged himself in Baroque obscurity and at times emerged above the clear surface. HERNANDO DOMÍNGUEZ DE CAMARGO (Colombia, 1606–1659) is one of the poets of quality. He did not squander the precious materials left him by Góngora. Without impairment they are there for us to see: alliteration, mythological allusions, Greek constructions, hyperbaton. Not only did he inherit Góngora, but he also fused these materials in a crucible, poured them in new molds, and gave them his individual stamp.

Domínguez Camargo's poems that appear in Jacinto de Evia's *Bouquet* are clearer, easier, and indeed more anthological than his unfinished *Heroic Poem of Saint Ignatius of Loyola* (1666). This poem, however, was his most full-blown work, where the syntax, the vocabulary, the metaphors, and the learned references of Baroque style press around the biography of the saint of his affection. (He was a Jesuit, but later abandoned the order and became a secular priest.) The theme of saint-hood is not treated ascetically. On the contrary, the poet escapes to the sumptuous and vivacious realm of pure form and there begins his decorations. The Baroque handled religious symbols esthetically. The poems about St. Ignatius' life primarily are meant to defend Spanish Catholicism against the heresies that were spreading throughout the rest of the world. It has already been noted that the military epic was succeeded by the religious epic; and the biographies of St. Ignatius (by Rivadeneyra and by Nieremberg) inspired heroic poems. In order to better awaken the piety of the masses, Jesuitism resorted to anec-dotes, ornamentation, hyperbole, convoluted images, pompous sym-bols. It was with this Baroque rhetoric that the hagiographic poems appeared in America.

The first, by the Andalusian Luis de Belmonte y Bermúdez (b. before 1587 and d. in 1630?), was published in Mexico in 1609. Then, the already-mentioned *Ignatius of Cantabria* (1639) by Pedro de Oña, and the *Heroic Poem to Saint Ignatius of Loyola* by Domínguez Camargo. Even after the Ignatian theme had lost its initial vigor, we find in the eighteenth century another *Heroic Poem to Saint Ignatius of Loyola* by Father Aguirre. We continue the list of Baroque poets. Francisco Alvarez de Velasco y Zorrilla (Colombia, 1647–d. after 1703) admired Quevedo (in the same way Domínguez Camargo admired Góngora), but he intended to concern himself "more with the simplicity rather than the elegance of style." He revealed himself a poet in his "Elegies to the Virgin" at the open-ing of his *Sacred, Moral and Laudatory Rhythmics* (*Rítmica sacra, moral y lauda-toria,* 1703?). Luis de Tejeda (Argentina, 1604–1680) left rough drafts of manu-scripts, also late copies of doubtful fidelity. Out of all his production he left some successful verses. They are not sufficient to give him weight, but he was the first worthwhile poet to appear in what today is Argentina. Almost all of what we preserve is of his later life when he withdrew to the Dominican cloisters, repentant of his stormy conduct, to weave autobiographical verses ("Ballad of His Life"), sacred verses, and, of less importance, explicative prose. Tejeda conceived, with-out finishing it, a plan for *Lyrical Crowns* (this is the title of a modern edition) in the form of a rosary: the prayers are distributed on three crowns, and on each crown appear the autobiographical and the sacred. On this structure he arranged his compositions which were of every type then cultivated. His style is generally Baroque in vocabulary, syntax, and interplay of conceits. He had learned this stylistic affectation in Spanish books. Góngora was among his many readings, and he occasionally Gongorized on the surface of the language. The introducer of Baroque style in Peru seems to have been Friar Juan de Ayllón (Peru, 1604), author of a euphuistic and soporific *Poem to the Canonization of the Twenty Three Martyrs* (*Poema a la canonización de los veintitrés mártires*). Góngora, Quevedo, and Calderón are present in Luis Antonio de Oviedo Herrera, Count of La Granja (1636–1717), Spaniard by birth, Peruvian by virtue of his work, author of the poetical composition *Life of Saint Rose of Lima* (*Vida de Santa Rosa de Lima,* 1711) and of the *Sacred Poem of the Passion of Christ* (*Poema sacro de la pasión de Cristo*), in addition to ballads, sonnets and plays. Another voice of religious literature is Juan de Peralta (Peru, 1663–1747), whose *Three Journeys in Heaven* (*Tres jornadas del cielo*) is also inspired by the Bible, more by the Psalms than by the Song of Songs. |

The one we must dwell on in Peru is Juan de Espinosa Medrano (b. after 1632–d. 1688). This mestizo used to be called *"El Lunarejo"* because of the *lunares* or moles on his face. He wrote at least the *Mystery Play of the Prodigal Son* in Quechua. Other Quechua pieces have been attributed to him; it has even been presumed (without foundation) that it was he who wrote *Ollantay,* the drama with Spanish structure and Quechua language and whose origin is still in dispute. In Spanish he composed the biblical drama, *To Love One's Own Death* (*Amar su propria muerte*), with plots *à la* Lope and verses *à la* Calderón. His sermons were noteworthy. He was at his best when writing cultist prose. He had studied at the University of Cuzco, and his discourses, collected in *The Ninth Wonder* (*La novena maravilla,* 1695) reveal a terse and elegant wisdom. He was a Góngora enthusiast, and his greatest glory rests in his *Apologetics in Defense of Don Luis de Góngora* (*Apologético en favor de don Luis de Góngora,* 1662). When *"El Lunarejo"* was born, not only had Góngora been dead ten years, but also important critical battles had been waged in Spain between Gongorists and non-Gongorists. But literary life was not as intense in the colonies, and the movement of literary tastes was much slower. Góngora was not in need of defenders in America—even those who reproved his poetical language imitated him, like Oña. For this reason the *Apologetics* is of value as an American reply to the rejections of Góngora in Spain. A copy of the anti-Góngora commentaries of the Portuguese Manuel de Faria e Souza came into the hands of Espinosa Medrano. "It seems that I am late in starting this task," says the latter, "but we Creoles live very far away; furthermore, when Manuel de Faria pronounced his censure Góngora was dead, and I not yet born." There is, then, no new contribution to the debate. On the other hand, there is in this belated Baroque poetics an understanding of the stylistic value of Góngora that is much more subtle, alert, appropriate, prudent, and brilliant than in the earlier Spanish apologias. "No one ever spoke ill of don Luis de Góngora except those who envied him or did not understand him; if he is to blame for this incomprehension, then blind men have cause to quarrel with the sun." What Espinosa Medrano is assessing in Góngora is the latter's verbal inventiveness, the energy with which he gives old literary treatment a new and surprising slant of beauty, his expansion of the Spanish language in order to insert the fresh tendencies of Latin. It is the lyrical brilliance, the lucid logic, the aristocratic bearing, that make him exclaim: "Long live the very learned and flowery Góngora, may he live long in spite of all the envies."

Satire

The fish net of literary history, however closely woven it may be, cannot hold all the schools of ballads and popular, festive, satiric, improvised, and burlesque poems which are so small that they escape through the mesh. It is sufficient to mention the most important of the satirists of this epoch, JUAN DEL VALLE CAVIEDES (1652?–1697?). An Andalusian by birth, he arrived at the mountain plains of Peru as a child, later moved to Lima, dissipated his life between gambling and women, fell into the hands of doctors; and against his doctors he wrote quatrains, ten-verse stanzas and ballads in which not only each epigram but also every adjective has a terrible aggressive power of its own. He attacked them for their ignorance, vices, and false prestige. The verses of his *Parnassus' Tooth* (*Diente del Parnaso*)—an allusion to his biting style: "chunks from my bite," he used to say—were not published during his lifetime, nor immediately after his death, but they were well known. He wrote dramatic exercises constructed allegorically: *Interlude of Mayor-Love* (*Entremés del Amor Alcalde*), *Dance of Doctor-Love* (*Baile del Amor Médico*), and *Dance of Gambler-Love* (*Baile de Amor Tahur*). This comic vein, with Quevedo-like witticisms, continued for some time; but in his later years, he acquired a mature, reflective attitude, and he wrote sonnets and other compositions with religious emotion and in a tone of repentance and melancholy. He had not been a futile imitator of the Spanish Baroque writers. He was acquainted with them and knew the writers from whom the Baroque writers had profited; but he possessed intellectual independence, individual inspiration, and a concise and gleeful style. In his *Letter* to Sor Juana he was proud that his only university had been his own spirit and that he had studied men more than books. His good sense, not in conformity with the superstitions of his time, is impressive. His poetry, satiric as well as religious and lyrical, is the freshest in colonial Peru.

Gongorism in Mexico / Góngora's influence in Mexico was earlier, better, and greater than anywhere else in Hispanic-America. It is possible that manuscript copies of *Polifemo* and the *Soledades* may have circulated in Mexico before they were published in Spain. Be that as it may, Góngora entered Mexico around 1600, in the shipments of *Romanceros* and *Flower of Illustrious Poets* (*Flores de poetas ilustres*). We have already seen how in Balbuena there were manifestations of Gongorism, although they were tenuous, since his cultism was personal and independent. As the seventeenth century wears on, the Mexican Gongorists multiply: Miguel de Guevara, Salazar y Torres, Arias de Villalobos, Francisco de Castro, Ramírez de Vargas, De la Llana, and hundreds more. We have already mentioned the anthological and very intimate "Song at the Sight of a Disillusion" by Matías de Bocanegra. Of the work of Luis de Sandoval y Zapata (fl. 1645) only vestiges remain, but among these fragments are splendid poetic flowers like the sonnet "Wingèd Eternity of the Wind" (*"Alada eternidad del viento"*). In him, more than in anyone else, lovely fantasy and rigorous geometry combine in resourceful forms. The recent re-evaluation of Góngora has wrought changes in the judgment on numerous Hispanic-American Gongorists. Undoubtedly most of them amused themselves by constructing formal complicated works, where one could not expect to find a beautiful surprise at the end of each of their poetic labyrinths as one could in Góngora. The poets wanted to display ingenuity in their concepts and culture in their images. They held hollowness in horror, and they tried to fill the hollowness of their times (in which energies were in tension but repressed) with Baroque deceptions. Once minds became excited by the interplay of pure forms, they no longer could stop, and at times did not even attempt poetry. Instead they constructed rebuses, riddles, conundrums, and feats of letter combinations. Retrogressive poems to be read up and down, and down and up; the same letters arranged in different words; disconnected letters which acquired meaning through their sounds; systematic display of all the letters of the alphabet; puns and other plays on words; compositions in which every word begins with the same letter; *centos* composed of unrelated fragments; echoes and double echoes; compositions, which, losing neither meaning nor rhyme, could be read three ways, in their totality and, also, split into two independent series; quatrains glossed, verse by verse, with four successive ten-line stanzas; acrostics further complicated by the use of glosses, and so on. However, in this literature of misguided effort there are also polished verses in which the human, social, and historic landscape of Mexico is reflected; verses which by themselves are literary landscapes against which greater figures, like Sor Juana, will be outlined. Furthermore, it was not only Góngora who was ven-

erated as a "prince of lyricists." They also read Garcilaso, the Argen-
solas, Lope de Vega, Fray Luis de León, San Juan de la Cruz, Herrera,
Calderón, and Quevedo. In fact, it was Góngora who sang loudest in
the midst of a multitude of poets. And it was poetry that raised its
voice in the Baroque era. There were surprising cases of variety and
innovation in metrics and strophes, as in the Mexican Juan de la Anun-
ciación. The Hispanic-Americans imitated or composed *centos* for the
numerous poetry contests that were celebrated on religious or civil
holidays. Some contests demanded an emulation of Góngora. In general,
these contests document the fact that there were groups of poets who
read each other; they write for each other and so become their own
public. This is the activity of humanists and erudites who pride themselves in belonging to an aristocracy where one gains admittance only
through the use of certain intricate passwords. The genre is the least
—it can be a simple carol or a full-blown epic poem. The only thing
that matters is that the symbols be pushed to their extreme. It is curious that this poetry, cut out of a learned pattern, should emit indigenous and even Afro-Spanish expressions. However, in Baroque literature popular elements are not spontaneous, but contrived. Negroes are
referred to as "jet with a soul." The poetry competitions were the
noisiest, most colorful and exciting events in the literary life of the
New World. Hundreds of poets participated in them, all anxious for
public recognition. (Bernardo de Balbuena remembered with pride
that in 1585 he had triumphed over three hundred rivals.) The city
dressed itself in all solemnity for the occasion, and there were sumptuous
processions along the specially decorated streets. All the arts collaborated in the festivities. Those poets who received awards had the satisfaction of earning the plaudits of the crowd as they read their compositions aloud, and, in addition, had the hope of gaining the plaudits
of posterity, because it was the custom to publish the best poems and
an account of the competition in a deluxe volume.

The Parthenic Triumph (*Triunfo parténico*) of CARLOS DE SIGÜENZA
Y GÓNGORA (Mexico, 1645–1700) is a description and collection of the
competitions of 1682 and 1683. Sigüenza y Góngora would be more
outstanding in a list of illustrious personalities in the colonies than in
a history of literature. He was an illustrious personality because, in
spite of being an obedient Catholic, his intellectual curiosity set him
apart from scholasticism and opened his eyes to the advantages of reason and experiment. His *Astronomical and Philosophical Terms* (*Libra
astronómica y filosófica*) is important in the history of ideas in Mexico in this sense: it implies a will to investigate new truths instead of

leaning on the erudition of authorized truths. He wrote, then, on un-
literary themes like archeology and history, mathematics and applied sciences, astronomy, geography, ethnography. And when he wrote verses,
he gave us the dregs of the Baroque. He was a relative of Luis de
Góngora y Argote, and perhaps because of this distant relation some
critics have wanted to study whether the Mexican Góngora also withdrew from Gongorism. There is no question about it. What he withdrew from was poetry. As we read him we are so depressed that when,
in the middle of all the verbiage, a few words of poetic transparency
arise, it seems that finally we will witness the miracle of an oasis. Nevertheless, it turns out to be a mirage. In these poetic odds and ends—
the language ground up by the cultist and conceptist machine—we can
find a good verse, at times a revealing word, but rarely a stanza, and
never a poem that is really worthwhile. In *Indian Spring* (*Primavera
indiana,* 1662), his first book, there is more poetic achievement than
in those that follow (if the strophes xxx, xxxi, xxxiv, xlvi, lviii, lx, lxiv,
lxvi and lxxviii could be considered good expressions). As a historian
he wrote longer-lasting pages, and perhaps in a history of literature his
place is that of chronicler of minor events. The prose of these chronicles was conversational, unlike the empty and gnarled prose with which
he larded up his little poetical works; and his narrative art at times
becomes so effective (in "Letter to Admiral Andrés de Pez," for example) that one reads with pleasure. These pages on the mutiny of the
Indians in June of 1692 are most interesting. One sees, hears, and smells
everything, such is the force of the details. His storytelling virtues are
best noticed in the *Misfortunes That Alonso Ramírez Suffered at the
Hands of English Pirates* (*Infortunios que Alonso Ramírez padeció en
poder de ingleses piratas,* 1690), which has the vivid movement of a
novel. By writing about the adventures of others in the first person,
the author gained the freedom to dramatize scenes objectively selected.
Alonso Ramírez is one of those long-suffering, staminal, virile Creoles
who carried on the drive of the Spanish conquistadors. But he is now
living in other times. Ramírez was born in Puerto Rico in 1662 and,
without realizing it, was living deep in the political decadence of Spain.
Exactly one century after the defeat of the Spanish Armada he is captured by the English "heretical pirates"; he undergoes terrible humiliations—the least of which was to hear the English call the Spaniards
"cowards and chickens." Once he gains his liberty, he and his men
sail in terror because they feel that all the seas are full of Englishmen.
Spain has lost its enterprising vigor, and in America the Creole suffers
from the impairment of his honor. Sigüenza y Góngora speaks of the

heresies of France and England; while Spain, having withdrawn more and more from the creative centers of Europe, now bases its pride on its Catholicity. Because of the cultural decline of the Spanish-speaking peoples, it is very surprising to see the rising strength of Sor Juana. Among the writings of Sigüenza y Góngora that have been lost is a "Funereal Eulogy of the Celebrated Mexican Poetess Sor Juana Inés de la Cruz" (*"Elogio fúnebre de la célebre poetisa mexicana Sor Juana Inés de la Cruz"*). They had been friends, and in one of her sonnets the little nun calls him "sweet, canorous Mexican swan." It seems incredible that Sor Juana should really admire Don Carlos' poetry—she was so far above it.

Sor Juana Inés de la Cruz / The most harmonious, gracious, and modulated voice of the Baroque period in Hispanic-America was that of Sor Juana Ines de la Cruz (Mexico, 1648–1695). It is difficult to evaluate it, in part because the Baroque style is difficult to evaluate, but mainly because the fascinating life of the little Mexican nun predisposes us to judge sympathetically anything she wrote. The entire Mexican court was convinced of her genius, and the Church was also, so much so that it became alarmed at her fame. In 1650 the Portuguese Jesuit Antonio de Vieyra had delivered a sermon disputing with St. Augustine and St. Thomas on which was Christ's greatest expression of love at the end of His life. Forty years later Sor Juana commented on it in a letter, "Crisis of a Sermon," which the bishop of Puebla decided to publish with the title *Athenagoric Letter* (*Carta athenogórica*, 1690), that is, "letter worthy of the wisdom of Athena." The bishop preceded it with a missive to Sor Juana, which bore the pseudonym *"Filotea de la Cruz."* In it the bishop advised Sor Juana to select subjects more carefully, to read the Gospel more, and to employ her talents on religious matters. Sor Juana wrote her *Reply to Sor Filotea de la Cruz* (*Respuesta a Sor Filotea de la Cruz,* 1691), one of the most admirable autobiographical essays in the Spanish language. Here she tells of her early desire for learning, her incoercible intellectual curiosity, the disadvantages of being a woman, her efforts to free herself of the impertinences, prejudices, incomprehension, and stupidities with which people trammel their betters. The prose is as fine and flexible as a fencer's foil, and above all, of an extraordinary efficacy in the defense of her spiritual calling. Her beliefs are orthodox. There is no doubt. But she has almost a rationalist's vigor and many of her protestations of humility have an ironic ring, sometimes hidden, other times not. After she asks herself, "Am I perchance more than a poor nun, the most insignificant creature of the universe, and the least worthy of your attention?", she adds that recognizing this "is not affected modesty." Indeed it is. Sor Juana knows she is right and expounds her case with agile dialectics. She is admonished to apply her industry to the Sacred Books and not to the secular. But, replies Sor Juana, "My not having written much on sacred subjects has not been out of distaste for them, nor out of lack of application, but because of excessive fear and reverence for those Sacred Scriptures, for whose understanding I recognize myself as incapable and for whose handling I am so unworthy . . ." She prefers verses and plays, "because a heresy against art is not punished by the Holy Office, but with laughter by the discreet and with censure by the critics." What authority does she hold for sacred matters? "Let's leave these to those who can understand them, for I want no truck with the Holy Office." "What is true, and which I shall not deny (first, because it is known to everyone; and then, although it operates against me, because God has given me the grace of desiring the greatest love of truth), is that since the first ray of reason struck me, the inclination to letters has been so vehement and powerful that neither the reprimands of others (of which I have had many) nor my own reflections (of which I have made not a few) have sufficed to dissuade me from following this natural impulse that God placed in me: He knows why and wherefore." There are those who believe—she says—that knowledge is superfluous and even damaging in woman. In view of "the total denial of a matrimonial life" her only recourse was to become a nun—this was "the most decent course I could elect by way of securing the salvation I desired." Therefore, "all the little impertinences of my nature: the desire to live alone, the desire of not having compulsory obligations that would interfere with the liberty of my studies, nor the noise of people that might break the reposed silence of my books, had to yield and be repressed." She wanted to flee from herself—"but, wretched me! I brought myself with me [to the convent] and I brought in this addiction to study, my greatest enemy, that I cannot determine whether the Heavens gave me as a natural gift or as a punishment, for to extinguish or hinder it by the duties that Religion demands, would make me explode like gunpowder . . ." "I returned (not really, for I never ceased), I persisted, I say, at the studious task . . . of reading, and rereading, of studying and restudying, with no other teacher than the books themselves." She complains of "the great labor not only for the lack of a teacher but of classmates with whom to confer and to apply what was studied, having for a teacher only a mute book and for a classmate an insensitive inkwell, and instead of explications and exercise, many disturbances, not only of my religious obligations . . . but of those chores inherent in community life . . . I cannot express with what envy I hear others say that knowledge has cost them no anxiety. Happy they! As for myself, not knowledge (which I still do not possess), but the desire for knowledge has cost me so much . . . My poor studies have navigated (or better said, have foundered) against the currents." She suffered persecutions, ill will, and hatred from those who believe that ignorance is saintly and abhor the loftiness of the spirit. What! Isn't an angel more than a man because it understands more? Is it not in his understanding that man is superior to the brute? "They have come to request that study be prohibited to me. One time they succeeded with a very saintly and very guileless mother superior who believed that study was something reserved for the Holy Office, and she ordered that I not study: I obeyed (for about three months while her authority prevailed) insofar as not taking up a book, but insofar as not studying in absolute I could not oblige, for although I did not study in books, I studied in all the things that God created, His universal machinery serving me as literature and as books." Should a woman be ashamed perhaps of such inclinations? She follows with examples of illustrious women who are cited so often in human as well as divine letters. Sor Juana mentions them in a long list, and she smiles with irony at the notion that women are considered inept while men, "just by virtue of being so, consider themselves sages." She proposes education for women administered by women. Concerning her criticism of Father Vieyra—in her *Athenagoric Letter*—is she not as free as he? "As I was free to disagree with Vieyra so is any person free to disagree with my opinion." The *Athenagoric Letter* and the *Reply to Sor Filotea* are the two greatest prose works of Sor Juana, which are followed in importance by *Incarnation Exercises* (*Ejercicios de la Encarnación*) and *Offerings of the Rosary* (*Ofrecimientos del Rosario*). In order to appreciate the intellectual liberty of Sor Juana one must refer to the ecclesiastical milieu of her times. Within the Catholic society there is a duplicate of the total society with the submissive and the rebel element. Sor Juana's behavior was not an outside rebellion—we have already said that she was an orthodox Catholic, fearful of heresies and scandals. But, within the bosom of the Church, she had the impulse to liberty, perhaps stimulated by the restlessness of the seventeenth century, an intellectual restlessness of which Descartes' *Discourse on Method* had been one of the sources. (In addition to this restlessness, she was tormented by an inmost irritating longing that we cannot explain and which yet is apparent in her work—she never found innermost peace, and her final ascetism in renouncing learning definitively, in order to dedicate herself to pious deeds, was perhaps less religious than is believed.) Her flight from the world and from her condition as a woman, her intellectual narcissism, the manner of treating amorous themes, seem to contain a certain mark of neurosis. It is as if Sor Juana, deep in the dregs of her subconscious, were to feel a conflict between her feminine nature and the yearning for masculine authority. The autobiography of her thirst for knowledge that Sor Juana offers in her *Reply* already had a poetic counterpart in *First Dream* (*Primero sueño*), a *silva* (that is, an irregular metrical form) of extreme Baroque style after the manner of Góngora's *Solitudes,* where Sor Juana relates the flight of her soul toward learning. The *Reply* and the *Dream* elucidate each other. Through the *Reply* we become aware of certain aspects of the genesis of the *Dream.* "For I have never written anything (in verse) through my own desire," she says, "but rather on the beseeching and behest of others; so that I remember having written nought for my pleasure except a little paper they call the *Dream.*" And on a prior occasion, "not even my dreams were free from this continuous movement of my imagination; rather it is wont to operate in them with more freedom and disencumberments, imparting with greater clarity and serenity the daily affairs that they preserve; disputing matters, making verses, of which I could make a long catalog, and of arguments and subtleties, that I have arrived at in a state of sleep better than awake." The *Dream*—a *silva* of almost a thousand verses—is constructed with systematic thinking: the soul, by virtue of nocturnal dreams, climbs to the heights in order to reach, in a single moment of rapture, the vision of all things created and, having failed, returns now with more humility to undertake the methodic and conceptual understanding of the simple to the complex, not without doubts, contradictions, scruples, and fears, until Sor Juana awakens and opens her eyes to a world enlightened by the rays of a new day. The sincerity with which Sor Juana lived her theme of life charges her verses with energy. She Gongorizes: neologisms, Latinisms, syntactical dislocations, tropes and metaphors, mythological allusions, and cultisms from all literature, chromatic ornaments, musical effects, difficult charades, and deliberate obscurities. However, occasional beauties scintillate with originality in this period style. Even more—in a certain sense *First Dream* is the poem that best represents not only Sor Juana, but her epoch. There were many Baroque poems, but in *First Dream* there is a sincere identification between a personal life and a collective style. The deceptive stratagems of the Baroque served as a hiding place for Sor Juana. Feeling the absence of love, she renounced the world—"rouged deceit"—and in solitude she withdrew into the innermost reaches of her being; there, her intellignce became her consolation and her joy. But she had to silence her intelligence, for it would have seemed impertinent and even heretical in a woman. The hermetic quality of the Baroque came to her aid. The *Dream*, through its theme and through its cultist style, was an autobiography with a secret cipher. The world is unreal: what is real is one's inner life. Through dreams she absents herself from the world, and she awakens contemplating the truth which is her intellectual activity as a solitary person. The rest of her poetry was circumstantial. If we separate the mishmash of pure versification—with allegories, commemorations and court gossipings—there remains a nucleus of great poetry in the form of sonnets, ballads, *décimas* (ten octosyllabic verses), and quatrains. In some of her carols she captured with impishness and agility the popular soul of Mexico. The poetry reflects her life in the country, in the city, and in the convent. Nevertheless, her personal experiences cannot be distinguished from her literary ones. At times she speaks not of what she has lived but of what she has learned in the lives of others. Therefore, her themes are not to be taken as her own. Hers is a poetry rich in intelligence—intelligence of life, but always intelligence. If she loved, or was loved, we know not, but in her excellent lyric poetry the amatory ones are enchanting. More than that, her lyric verse, especially the amorous type, is what really made her famous. With masterliness—and femininity—Sor Juana examines the love theme: separation, jealousy, neglect, rancor, abandonment, death. Of course the reader must be overcautious and not confuse love with mere rhetoric. The quatrains directed to the viceroy's wife (Amarilís, Filis, and Lisi in the verses) are protestations of affection very common in courtly poetry. From Medieval Provence to Renaissance Italy, and thence to Baroque Spain, the dithyrambic convention of singing to the noble and the powerful continued. The merits of the eulogized lord and the love offered by the poet were celebrated in hyperbolic fashion. The neoplatonic theories had just reinformed the convention that gave no more significance to the quatrains of Sor Juana, a woman, to another woman of the court, than to the sonnets of Shakespeare, a man, to another man of the court.

She was not only mistress of this chord, but of all those she struck: religious and secular, hermetical and popular, in conceits, emotions and customs. Since Garcilaso, hers was the school of great Spanish poetry; however, she emulated the Baroque poets of the seventeenth century. She gave unexpected lights to a style that in Spain was receding into the dusk. The eagerness for intellectual knowledge sharpened her mind, and in that joyful and enthused state of mental sharpness, the little nun renovated the vitality of poetic inventiveness. What was a withering in others in her was a blooming. To play with her intelligence was a thrilling adventure. To feel intelligent was disquieting. The movement of concepts—in highly varied correlations—was like the fluttering of the wings of a bird escaping from its cage. As soon as an event in her life offered itself to her verse, it was immediately amplified by a complicated reasoning. This reasoning was as vital as the event that occasioned it, so that the Baroque interplay did not disturb the lyrical uplifting. (Remember, for example, the sonnets "Divine rose that in gentle culture," "Stay, shadow of my elusive good.") The best she wrote was in the Baroque style (to the above we add the sonnets: "This that thou seest, rouged deceit," "Diuturnal infirmity of hope," "Green enravishment of human life," "Inés, when they scold thee for being roguish," "This evening, my beloved, when I spake to thee," "That Fabian may not love me, on being loved," "He who leaves me, ungrateful one, I seek as lover," "Silvio, I abhor thee and yet condemn," "Love begins because of disquietude"; the *redondillas*: "Foolish men who accuse," "This amorous torment"; the ballads: "Let us feign that I am happy," "If to give ye the good years," "There it goes, although it ought not to," "When, divine Deities," the *ovillejo* "Painting the beauty of Lisarda," etc.).

Her theater, sacred and profane, was Baroque and swung in Calderón's orbit. In addition to eighteen preludes, *"loas,"* two farces, *"sainetes,"* and one *"sarao"* or afterpiece, she wrote three mystery plays, *"autos":* the most admirable, *Divine Narcissus* (*El Dwino Narciso*, 1698), and then *The Martyr of the Sacrament* (*El Mártir del sacramento*) and *Joseph's Scepter* (*El cetro de José*). Because of its value as a spectacle, its lyrical songs, the rigor of its intellectual construction, the intertwining of biblical and Greco-Latin themes, the originality in the handling of poetic ideas and intuitions, and the vigorous parallelism of Indian and Christian rites, *Divine Narcissus* is one of the better mysteries in all Castilian literature. Sor Juana was acquainted with and profited by Calderón's play *Echo and Narcissus*. However, she surpassed it with an allegory with which she ambitiously intended, not necessarily to educate the Indians—in spite of the Indian personages in the *loa*, which was joined to the *auto*—but to please the cultured Spaniards of Madrid. Using the reports of the chroniclers for her base—especially those of Juan de Torquemada—she presented in the *loa* the Aztec rite in which Huitzilopochtli, God of Seeds, is eaten in a kind of host kneaded with flour and blood, showing the Devil's astuteness in deception by imitating Christian communion. For the purpose of demonstrating to "Occident" and "America"—two personages that symbolize the indigenous pre-Cortés culture—that the God of the Catholics and the Eucharist are true, "Religion" presents for them a mystery play, the *auto* of *Divine Narcissus*. Reworking Ovid's version of the Narcissus myth, Sor Juana puts on the stage a Christ-Narcissus, who looks into a spring of water and there sees reflected Human Nature. Since the latter was created in the image and likeness of God, Christ "seeing His image in the man, fell in love with Himself," dies for love and leaves the host, white flower of the Eucharist, as a remembrance and as an admonishment. Of her two plays, *The Obligations of a Home* (*Los empeños de una casa*, 1683), a cloak-and-sword comedy, and *Love Is a Labyrinth* (*Amor es más laberinto*, 1869), a mythological-courtly play, whose second act was written by Juan de Guevara. The first play is the better of the two. The play *The Obligations of a Home* (Calderón had written one entitled *The Obligations of a Chance Occurrence—Los empeños de un acaso*) is very entertaining. It develops from deception to deception, from misunderstanding to misunderstanding, with scenes in the darkness or semi-darkness, concealments, disguises, cloaked figures. The action, of a few hours' duration, takes place in Toledo, and its twists and turns are so vertiginous that it takes flight. Even the characters suffer from vertigo. They do not know whether they dream or are awake; they do not understand what is happening around them and are unaware that they have been thrown in the midst of some stage trickery. One of them invokes the Mexican rogue, Martín Garatuza: "inspire some scheme for me that seems of Calderón's design." Calderón, in fact, is the master who taught Sor Juana how to enmesh human destinies. Nevertheless, like a kaleidoscope, this Baroque interplay of mirrors and illusions has its geometry.

One can imagine Sor Juana smiling mockingly at the foolishness of men and women who believe it possible to impose love. Don Pedro loves Doña Leonor, but Doña Leonor loves Don Carlos. Don Juan loves Doña Ana, but Doña Ana loves Don Carlos. At the end, the only happy couple is the sincere lovers—the good Don Carlos and the discreet and beautiful Doña Leonor, in whom Sor Juana seems to have portrayed herself. In spite of the affectation and conventionality of the dramatic situations, the dialog goes on revealing a keen understanding of the secrets of the heart and the motives for human conduct. In the *sainete* interposed between the second and third acts, someone, speaking of plays, affirms "those of Spain are always better," and that no one in Mexico would dare boo "a play of Calderón, Moreto or Rojas." It may be for this reason that *The Obligations of a Home,* taking the path to the greatest prestige, places its action in Spain (there is, however, one Mexican character, the *gracioso* or comic servant, Castaño). Now that this *sainete* has been mentioned, we can say that it has one exceptional value—while the interlocutors wait for the third act of *The Obligations of a Home,* they poke fun at the first two acts; it is a case of interior duplication: Sor Juana converts into theatrical spectacle the ordinary conversation which goes on during the intermission of a performance and creates in this way an interpenetration, quite modern, of public and stage, of critics and actors. This procedure, which breaks the frontier between fiction and reality, is used surprisingly in the third act when Castaño, disguised as a woman, suddenly directs himself to the audience and consults the women on intimate items of apparel. Sor Juana synthesized all the currents valued and practiced in the first half of the century: traditional, Renaissance, and Baroque; popular, cultured and low-bred; here a stanza after the fashion of San Juan de la Cruz, there a *silva* after Góngora, or a *décima* after Calderón, or a ballad after Lope, or a folk song after Quevedo. She had us hear the voice of the Negro in her poetry. The Negro theme already existed in the literature of Hispanic-America. Negroes arrived in 1502, in the fleet of Nicolás de Ovando, and they appear in the chronicles. The poets of the Renaissance (Castellanos, Ercilla) presented them as inferior people. But Sor Juana, with the open curiosity of the Baroque, poetizes the Negro and uses him to give color and rhythm to her poetry. Later on the Negro will interbreed into the population of America and will participate in our literature until he will succeed in reaching a splendid expression in the twentieth century.

Mysticism

Other women were noteworthy in this period: in Ecuador, Jerónima de Velasco; in Peru, Santa Rosa de Lima (1586–1617); and two poetesses who are known as Clarinda, author of a "Discourse in Praise of Poesy," in tercets; and Amarilis, who sent to Lope de Vega an epistle in the form of a *silva*. But the woman who, after Sor Juana, reached the highest poetic expression in this century is the eloquent nun from New Granada Sor FRANCISCA JOSEFA DEL CASTILLO Y GUEVARA, called MOTHER CASTILLO (Colombia, 1671–1742). By poetic expression we are not referring solely to her verses (some of those attributed to her belonged to Sor Juana) but to certain revelations of her ascetic and mystic prose. She had read from mixed sources: alongside religious books—the Bible,

Santa Theresa, St. Ignatius, Father Osuna, and so forth—she read novels and sets of plays which she called "plague of the soul." She composed her literature from themes and forms of religious and Baroque letters, not as a vocation, but under orders from her confessors. One notices a slow progress in her prose, from mannerism and disorderliness in her first pages to the simplicity of her last. She wrote a kind of diary of her intimate devotions—publishers have called it *Spiritual Affections* (*Afectos espirituales*). She was twenty-two years of age when she began it—her prose was unsure, affected, exuberant, obscure, laden with rhetorical figures, defective in its expansive moments. Twenty years later she was still writing her diary but the prose was now more moderate. By then she had begun an autobiography that went from her infancy until she gave up the directorship of the convent—the publishers have called it *Her Life* (*Su Vida*). Since it is a work of maturity, the *Life* differs from the *Affections*, not only because she gives us anecdotes and episodes of good and bad convent habits, but also because it is composed with a less luxuriant, less confused prose. Putting to one side the virtues of her prose—which were never excellent—Mother Castillo is of interest to us because her religious sincerity pierced her heavy words like a ray of light. Her religious calling was so intense that she does not resemble anyone in her epoch. In a flight of oratory Mother Castillo comes to rest at the height of the greatest of Christian themes. She is disorderly, digressive, without doctrinal rigor. But the metaphors shine out from her pages, and as they shine they light up the sentiments of a soul stirred by the joy and the panic of her visions of God. She was *the* mystic of our letters.

IV. 1701-1759

Authors born between 1675 and 1735

Historical Framework: The Bourbons take over the Spanish throne. Under Philip V and Fernando VI the Spanish Empire begins its efforts to retain the colonies.

Cultural Tendencies: The end of the Baroque. The Rococo. Neoclassicism.

From the end of the seventeenth century, France exerted a cultural hegemony over all Europe. Spain received this influence even before the Bourbons entered to govern the country. Undoubtedly the change in dynasties favored such influence. However, more than being Gallicized, Spain was being Europeanized—alongside French influences there were those of Italy and England. But the cultural level between Spain and the rest of Europe was so uneven that Spain's cultural ascension was very slow. In just one generation—let us say from 1680 to 1715— the Enlightenment was imposed upon Europe. In Spain, on the other hand, the new spirit, rationalist in philosophy and classical in literature, begins to manifest itself in the third decade of the century. Until then the dominant literature was the Baroque. It was natural that the rise of Hispanic-American culture was even slower. The currents of the Enlightenment passed from Spain into America and influenced ideas and customs, but they did not inspire a neoclassical literature until the end of the eighteenth century. On the literary road, then, the colonies lagged behind the mother country. The Baroque style continued to be cultivated when already in Spain it was forgotten or transformed into rococo or remembered mockingly. Lacking great figures—one can scarcely mention Peralta Barnuevo, Juan Bautista Aguirre, Paz Salgado, Santiago Pita—we must attempt the depiction of a broad cultural tapestry. Compared with that of Europe, and even with that of Spain, it is meager. Nevertheless, we cannot dispense with it if we wish to understand the slow awakening of the spirit of the 1700's. New lights begin to temper the skies. From the point of view of ideas, the first radiations of the Enlightenment filter through the clouds of scholasticism. From the point of view of *belles lettres,* the warm colors of the Baroque are softened by rococo pinks and cooled by neoclassical blues. The order of ideas and the order of letters are not as disparate in reality as they seem to be from the two sentences describing them. Each time a classification is attempted we stumble against obstacles: treatises with literary touches and literature for didactic ends, and the continuation of the Baroque throughout the century, in spite of the attempts of neoclassicism to block its path. With this word of caution—that there are no fixed demarcations—we shall first speak of the writers of discursive prose and then of those, either in verse or prose, who would enter into the field of literature.

From Scholasticism to the Enlightenment

The center of ideas now lies outside of Hispanic culture. What is happening in Europe (and Spain is the last to find out) is nothing less than the liquidation of Christian cosmology, as it was organized by the churches, and on the other hand the triumph of a new cosmology founded on reason and experience. From a bird's-eye view (that is, a philosopher-bird) the slow and complex process of the decomposition of the authority of the Apostolic Roman Catholic Church occurred at the same time as the exploration, conquest, and colonization of the New World: between the fifteenth and eighteenth centuries. The corrosive agents of this decomposition in Europe were Protestantism, Humanism, and Rationalism. Thanks to the dissolvent action of these three forces, occidental culture renews itself radically—the culture of the eighteenth century is called the Enlightenment. The European Enlightenment consists of the belief that men, here, in this real world, can attain a perfection that for Scholasticism was only possible to Christians in a state of grace, after death. Newton (nature can be explained rationally) and Locke (we can apply natural solutions to human things) are integrated into the Enlightenment (nature, reason) and replace such previous principles as grace, salvation, and predestination. The Englishmen Newton and Locke did not go as far as their French disciples. The French became the disseminators. In the first half of the eighteenth century—the setting of this chapter—men of the Enlightenment like Voltaire and Montesquieu constitute a moderated generation. They are deists who mock all that displeases them. Only in the second half of the century—the setting of the next chapters—does there appear a generation of radicals. Their displeasure no longer permits them to laugh. Years of atheism, years of mechanism. And there will be a third generation (classical rationalists who follow Holbach; sentimental romanticists who follow Rousseau, whose ideal man is a rational and sensitive man, intelligent and good-natured, sound of heart and head) which brought about the American Revolution of 1776 and the French Revolution of 1789 and which will influence the revolutionaries of the Independence of Hispanic-America. But let us not hasten. We are in the period 1701–1759. In Europe, we repeat, there has been a change: life comes down from the Christian, supernatural Heaven, after death, to a land where at any moment natural happiness will be attained. A change which implies the doctrine of progress through the radiation of the light of reason. The Roman Catholic Church had always taught; now it had to be taught. And the Church, in fact, cannot help but learn. Reason has us understand the laws of Nature. In a Universe-watch, created by a God-watchmaker, men live who are capable of reading the movements of its hands. God exists for Voltaire, the deist. But there is no reason to beg Him for miracles—all that is necessary is to understand the watch. (From 1750 onward God will be dispensable— He will be replaced by the Goddess of Reason.) Ethics will be autonomous. For Christians, Man is born in sin; evil is explained by human greed, and the salvation brought by Christ does not imply a cultural policy of environmental betterment. For the men of the Enlightenment, the environment is decisive. That is why one must arrange rationally the external circumstances of life so that man can orient himself toward good. Christianity, obviously, does not disappear. It resists, and continues to appeal to the masses. But nowhere has the Church preserved its power as it has in Spain. The philosophers of the eighteenth century in Europe used to protest because there existed many things that offended reason: all of the medieval past that survived in arbitrary institutions. Moreover, reason—after Descartes, Newton, Locke—claimed the power of organizing human and social affairs. In Spain the new spirit did not go beyond the limits of the Church. The humanitarian spirit prevailed within the Church, in one sector of the clergy and of the flock, a sector not visible nor differentiated. Between the mystical heaven of Christianity and the terrestrial heaven that the men of the Enlightenment fixed in the future, there is in Spain an intermediate heaven, namely, that if society must be improved, it should be done by Christians within the Catholic church. Of the three agents of dissolution in Europe that changed the conception of the world, Protestantism had no effect in Spain, and Humanism and Rationalism operated from within the sphere of the Church. Spain was not ready for the leap that Europe had taken, and even the natural and physical sciences continue into the eighteenth century tied to ecclesiastical authority. One must think, in this period, of the labors of a Feijóo, who reconciles religion and philosophy. In Hispanic-America orthodoxy was even more marked —at least here only orthodoxy is manifest. Up to the beginning of the eighteenth century, modern thought, in philosophy and in religion, had not sifted into the Hispanic-American colonies. (Scholasticism will predominate even up to the last decades of the century.) Theology was based on revelation and attempted to demonstrate it rationally. Scholastic rationalism prevailed: the Cartesian type of rationalism was not known, except in very few instances. The sciences depended on theology, and reason on faith. There are only intra-ecclesiastical disputes. Polemics and satires give an illusory appearance of intellectual liberty. It is fundamentally a three-sided family squabble: the Dominican order and its Thomist school; the Franciscan and its Scotist school; the Jesuit and its Suarist school. The Thomists dominated the field of education, and it is natural that some religious orders would be resentful. With so much tension within the Church, it is easy to imagine the resistance to what was openly heterodox. Scholasticism, at first, rejects absolutely all enlightened tendencies; then, it fortifies itself by taking cognizance of its own nature and protecting its weaknesses; finally, several solitary voices, within the Church, are raised against Scholasticism. The Inquisition alone cannot be blamed for this misoneism (hatred for the new). Hispanic-American inquisitions did not need to censure Spanish thought because it arrived in the New World already censured by the inquisitions of Spain. The censuring of French and English thought revealed a more spontaneous "holy horror" for novelties rather than a fixed inquisitorial policy. The Inquisition operated on a practical basis, not a speculative one. It prohibited; it did not discuss. Its doctrine was that the great truths had already been discovered and, therefore, there was no progress possible. Hence, the annals of the Inquisition offer no interest for a history of ideas—they only give us data on prohibited ideas. Another repressive force against new ideas was the apologetic literature in defense of the Church and against anything modern. To be a Catholic, it is said, one need not be a philosopher; but if one is a Catholic and a philosopher, he has to be an Aristotelian.

Chronicles, Treatises, and Didactic Books / Useful to a historian of Hispanic-American culture, but not interesting to a reader eager for ideas, are the chronicles, histories, memoranda, critical, theological, scientific, and philosophic treatises that appear in the first half of the eighteenth century. A history of culture has to be constructed from facts: but at times, in order to understand the philosophic renovation of this eighteenth century, one must imagine that there were men whose beliefs fell outside the Aristotelian-Scholastic currents, only they could not express them. So the historian finds himself in a difficult position: he must minimize the importance of many of the writings of that century because they are belated echoes; on the other hand, he must lend importance to the void of the non-written, because there, in that silence, new voices are breeding that are to erupt at any moment. In Europe there were new movements; in Hispanic America, only a few men who, to make matters worse, did not express themselves. In Europe there were new movements because the changes had borne fruit. It has been said that the seventeenth century was "an age of geniuses." Galileo and Descartes had student experimenters, like Torricelli and many more. In Hispanic-America experimentation was most inferior—Sor Juana makes us laugh with pity when she speaks of her experiments in the kitchen. Nor did Hispanic-America in the seventeenth century have any philosophic geniuses. Thus, the Hispanic world in the eighteenth century was not prepared to take the leap from Nature to Reason as the Enlightenment had done. Our science remained attached to the authority of the Church; and when it broke loose, it did so, not like a ripe fruit falling from the tree, but like a branch cut by a European axe. In Europe the Enlightenment felt that Greeks and Romans first, and then the men of the Renaissance and Reformation, had contributed to the exaltation of reason. The Catholic church, medieval and obscurantist, was for the men of the Enlightenment evil. The Enlightenment, like every new religion, needed a devil and the Church was that devil. But in Hispanic America this was not possible. Everything in Hispanic-American culture was different. Greeks and Romans were known through Church versions; humanists and reformers had not drawn away from the Church. And in comparison, the Hispanic Enlightenment did not break with the Church.

We said that, in view of the dearth of great personalities, we would paint a cultural atmosphere. Atmospheres are painted with large brush strokes as in the synthesis given in the pages above, or with a pointillist technique of light touches, which will constitute the catalog of names we are about to give below. In general, these names mean nought in the history of literature, but since they are here drawn together they will give the reader the sensation of seeing a laborious group of humans.

Because the majority of the authors were priests, most of them wrote about religion or excelled in sacred oratory. Oratory is the art of using oral language for the practical purpose of persuading the listener. Therefore, it documents not only ideas, but also tastes. And one must study it because it usually slips its linguistic structures into literature. Cultism eventually reached oratory. America also had preachers as bombastic as the one cudgeled by Padre Isla in *Fray Gerundio de Campazas*. However, there were brilliant religious orators like Father Francisco Javier Conde Oquendo (Cuba, 1733–1799). And theoreticians of oratory like Joaquín Díaz Betancourt (Mexico, fl. 1752) and Martín de Velasco (Mexico, fl. 1726). Among the clergy who wrote on ecclesiastical themes let us mention Ortiz y Morales (Colombia, n. 1658); José J. Parreño (Cuba, 1728–1785); Vergara y Azcárate (Colombia, d. 1761). Of special interest to us is the Jesuit MANUEL LACUNZA (Chile, 1731–1801). He was a "millenarian" or one who believed in the very ancient prophecy that the world would close out its account before the sixth millenium was up. Because the creation of the world, according to Genesis, had taken six days, after six thousand years human history would come to its end—then justice and goodness would prevail over the earth in the seventh millenium. In order to defend the millenarians Lacunza wrote *The Coming of the Messiah in Glory and Majesty (La venida del Mesías en gloria y majestad)*, with a great apparatus of Biblical erudition and a great display of talent. The redaction was finished toward 1790; it was published in 1811, and many editions followed. Josaphat Ben-Ezra, the "Christian Hebrew," was presented as the author. The Church put it on the Index, not for its beliefs (which were "defensible" for a Catholic) but for minor deviations; for example, the idea that the Church would also fall into the betrayal in the days of the Antichrist. The prophecy of a kingdom of Jesus Christ on earth lasting a thousand years in a Utopian community with one language, with no discord, and with Hell closed up cannot help but have an aura of poetic charm.

Of the chroniclers and historians, we mention a few: FRIAR DOMINGO DE NEYRA (Argentina, 1684–1757), with one or two good descriptions of his country; the bishop PEDRO AGUSTÍN MORELL DE SANTA CRUZ (Santo Domingo–Cuba, 1694–1768), passable writer in his *History of the Island and Cathedral of Cuba* (*Historia de la Isla y Catedral de Cuba*); BASILIO VICENTE OVIEDO (Colombia, 1699–1780) who with his *Qualities and Riches of the New Realm of Granada* (*Cualidades y riquezas del Nuevo Reino de Granada*) forms a treasure-trove of things that he not only admires but also tries to put to practical use. JOSÉ MARTÍN FÉLIX DE ARRATE Y ACOSTA (Cuba, 1701–1765) left an apparently disordered and jumbled history, yet with a plan, or at least having a consistent direction—his love of Cuba and his pride in being a Creole of pure Spanish forebears. His *Key to the New World* (*Llave del Nuevo Mundo*, 1761) begins to turn from the Discovery itself, but he only opens up on something when he feels the pulse of his own times. The aristocrat Arrate, hurt because certain Spaniards disparage Cuba, reminds them that they too are disparaged by Europeans for being "backward." In some of the pages he speaks with pleasure of the beauty of the landscape, of fiestas in the country, of court etiquette, the bright life of the city, fashions, refinements and luxuries—an ideal of elegance, of license, of frivolity, ostentation and festivities which, when it becomes more vivid later on, will inspire a rococo style.

Father JUAN DE VELASCO (Ecuador, 1727–1792) is one of the important figures in his country. His *History of the Realm of Quito* (*Historia del reino de Quito*, 1789), although rich in observations and data, is full of legend, fable, and imagination. In it there are giants and amazons. The Andes are the result of the Diluvium. Plants and rocks have virtues and vices. As in a novel of chivalry, the Emperor Huaina-Cápac falls in love with Queen Shiri Paccha, and peace is made between two warring nations. The child begotten of this love, Atahualpa, will conquer his stepbrother, Huáscar, an offspring, not of love, but of "reasons of State" between the Inca and the imperial Coya.

FRANCISCO XAVIER ALEGRE (Mexico, 1729–1788) left a copy of the "History of the Company of Jesus in New Spain" almost completed when he was caught up in the expulsion of the Jesuits; in Bologna, Italy, he drew up, "almost from memory," a compendium of the same work. FRANCISCO XAVIER CLAVIGERO (Mexico, 1731–1787) published his history of Mexico in Italian—the Spanish original remains unedited. He idealized the pre-Cortés Mexico with a modern sentimentalism; although he had read writers of critical thought—Feijóo, Descartes, Newton, Leibnitz—modern preoccupations seem to be absent in his comments on miracles.

There were those who wrote of jurisprudence (MELÉNDEZ BAZÁN, Santo Domingo, d. in 1741) or of science (SÁNCHEZ VALVERDE, Santo Domingo, 1720–1790; FRANCISCO XAVIER GAMBOA, Mexico, 1717–1794; PEDRO VICENTE MALDONADO, Ecuador, 1710–1748) or of philosophy (JOSÉ ANTONIO ALZATE, Mexico, 1729–1799). There were Latinists (JOAQUÍN AYLLÓN, Ecuador, d. in 1712; JUAN B. TORO, Colombia, 1670–1734). JUAN JOSÉ DE EGUIARA Y EGUREN (Mexico, 1695–1763) formulated his very important *Bibliotheca Mexicana* in order to destroy the "black legend" that Europeans had fabricated against America—confronted with the prejudice that the nature of the New World impedes the development of the spirit, he is going to demonstrate the brilliant and precocious productiveness of Mexican letters.

In the midst of religious literature—mysticism, hagiography, and so forth—the thought of the epoch falls back on old explanations, even though it has a presentiment of the change in philosophy. Religion, morals, and law traveled together in Scholasticism, and now they continue on together in their attempts to explain America. What is the origin of America? How is one to understand these lands—unknown to the ancients—within the cosmology and chronology of Scholasticism? Even toward the end of the Colonial period, picturesque hypotheses are proposed; for example, those of FRANCISCO XAVIER ALEJO ORRIO (1763), *Solution of the Great Problem of the Population of America Where on the Basis of the Holy Scriptures Is Found an Easy Way to Explain the Transmigration of Men from One Continent to the Other* (*Solución del gran Problema acerca de la población de América*

*en que sobre el fundamento de los libros santos se descubre fácil camino a la trans-
migración de los hombres del uno al otro continente*); or those of ORDÓÑEZ Y
AGUIAR, *History of the Creation of Heaven and Earth in Conformity with the System of American Heathenism* (*Historia de la creación del cielo y la tierra conforme
al sistema de la gentilidad americana*). And one might add the extraordinary
explanations of PEDRO LOZANO (Spain–Paraguay, 1697–1752), author of the *Description of the Great Chaco* (*Descripción del Gran Chaco*); JOSÉ GUEVARA (Spain–
Argentina, 1719–1806), author of the *History of Paraguay, Río de la Plata and
Tucumán* (*Historia del Paraguay, Río de la Plata y Tucumán*). Instead of discovering the distinctive qualities of America, it was customary to sheathe them
with European notions. To know America was to interpret it in the light of the
Bible and Greco-Latin-Medieval culture. Between the creation of the world and
the Diluvium—a period of 1656 years, no more nor less—the earth was a single,
solid continental mass throughout which men were distributed. After the Diluvium,
Noah's Ark arrived at the great island Atlantis, port of call to the New World.
Or perhaps the Hellenic god Poseidon was the first inhabitant of Atlantis, and
his descendants populated the American lands. The Mayan or Aztec civilizations
offer up archeological and folkloric riches that those Spaniards of the first half of
the eighteenth century do not know how to value—they wish to force them into
a biblical framework of universal history. Nevertheless, within a few years this
Scholastic vision of the world will suffer such a severe blow that it will crumble
to the ground, and in its place a rationalist interpretation will be erected. The
cleric who best saw the threat, the blow, and the fall, and who most energetically
defended the Church, was JOSÉ MARIANO VALLARTA Y PALMA (Mexico, 1719–
1790). He denounced those hidden roads down which that impious philosophy
was moving and, in doing so, he may have been the first Hispanic-American
Scholasticist who expounded a history of ideas. Only, for him, it was the history
of Evil. He began writing in Mexico. Having been expelled, together with the
other Jesuits, he went to Italy and there he saw triumphant what had been in
Hispanic-America only a menace. That is, the modern philosophy seen from the
American side was a storm in bloom, and seen from Europe the storm had already
destroyed Christendom. Descartes, Gassendi, Copernicus, Newton are the per-
petrators of all those infamous, anti-religious principles. He considered Newton
the most dangerous because of his theory that bodies had been created from the
very beginning by particles of prime matter put into motion. The laws of attraction
and repulsion did harm—Vallarta used to say—to the Church's explanation in the
Genesis. All experimentation is a scandalous departure from theology. And even
poetry, when it sings in the name of liberty instead of submission to divine law,
is denying Christ's faith. There were more modern trends of thought, but unlike
those in the rest of Europe, they did not work loose from the mother Church's
apron strings. Yet conceptual thought was becoming more up to date in the colonies. Already under the rule of Philip V and Fernando VI, a change is noticeable.
In emulation of France and England, Spain organizes scientific expeditions. In
1736, La Condamine commission, which included French scientists, arrived in
Ecuador to measure the degree of earth's meridian. Among the participants were
JORGE JUAN (Spain, 1713–1773) and ANTONIO DE ULLOA (Spain, 1716–1795),
whose geographical, nautical, cultural, and social observations pass into his *Historic Report on the Voyage to South America* (*Relación histórica del viaje a la
América meridional*, 1748) and into the almost revolutionary *Secret Reports*

(*Noticias secretas*) whose authenticity has been challenged. The *Historic Report* illustrates that kind of scientific literature in which Alexander von Humboldt would, later on, excel with his *Voyage aux regions équinoxiales du Nouveau Continent*. Ulloa set down in numerous records and reports his experiences of many years in America, in his administrative functions in many locales. His overall view is revealed in the *American Reports* (*Noticias Americanas*, 1772). They were received with praise. A well-ordered and readable global description of the American environment was lacking. Here he gives abundant data on the physio-natural characteristics of America and on the many possibilities open to man's labor.

These foreign scientists leave traces: orientation toward intellectual clarity against Baroque erudition. Thus, erudition acquired critical sense and slowly converted itself into an anti-Scholastic movement. European philosophy was its nerve center. Even the clergy had to renovate the content of its teachings. Interest in all that was new continued to increase during the second half of the century. For this reason we will study the work of Pablo de Olavide in the next chapter although we might be expected to place him here, since he was born before 1735 (as was José C. Mutis). On the other hand, we bring forth another writer who, since he was born before 1675, should have been examined in the previous chapter, except that he helps us illustrate the cultural orientation of those years, namely, Peralta Barnuevo. And since he created literature, he will serve to head the following section.

From the Baroque to the Rococo

We have said that the predominance of Scholastic philosophy over all intellectual life since the Counter Reformation made the penetration of rationalist principles and experimental methods difficult. Even those spirits most avid for knowledge—like the Peruvian PEDRO DE PERALTA BARNUEVO, 1663–1743—vacillate between truth and faith, sallying out to face the ideas of European philosophy and science but then withdrawing without daring to take the field as all nations, except Spain, had done from the Renaissance to the present. Not only can Peralta Barnuevo be studied under two political regimes (the first half of his life under the Hapsburg viceroys; the second, under the Bourbon viceroys), but his work, although dominated by the characteristics of Baroque culture of the seventeenth century, also offers the first fruits of neoclassical "Frenchification" in Hispanic America. His broad base of knowledge—he was a historian, jurist, theologian, mathematician, engineer, astronomer, dramatist, and poet, apt in several languages—belongs to that type of cultured man whom we have already studied in Sigüenza y Góngora. However, he tends more to the school of the

Scholasticists rather than to the Encyclopedists, but he also anticipated the Encyclopedist ideal of the eighteenth century. If for a moment he seems to be a precursor of the latter, it is because of a mimetic phenomenon: as the Scholastic traditions with their taste for great syntheses come to rest in the eighteenth century, they resemble illuminist rationalism, like certain butterflies that simulate the leaves they light upon.

Peralta adheres to mysticism in spite of his scientific knowledge— cosmography, mathematics—and in spite of his technical knowledge— he directed the work on the fortifications of Lima. His book, *Passion and Triumph of Christ* (*Pasión y triunfo de Cristo*, 1738), is an expression of a philosophy anterior to that of the Enlightenment. Having been disillusioned beforehand by a science of which he saw only the beginnings, Peralta affirms that true wisdom is inscrutable, as inscrutable as God himself. The universe cannot be reduced to human laws. The least forgettable of his literary works are the poem *The Founding of Lima* (*Lima fundada*, 1732) with a few Gongoristic touches; the operetta *Triumph of Love and Power* (*Triunfos de amor y poder*, 1711?), with mythological gods partaking of human love and with a setting more to the Italian taste than that of Lope's time; the play *Affection Conquers Kindness* (*Afectos vencen finezas*, 1720); and a tragedy *Rodoguna* copied from Corneille's *Rodogune*. The influence of Molière's *Les Femmes savantes* and *Le Malade imaginaire* can be discerned in two afterpieces he wrote; this was an early influence since at least one of these was written in 1711.

In addition, he wrote interludes and dances. His most ambitious play was *Affection Conquers Kindness*, a plot in Lope de Vega's style but lacking his poetry, in Calderón's manner but lacking his philosophy. The reader is distracted and loses the threads of this story of love between princes and princesses in a pseudo-Greek world where everyone always speaks pompously. There is not a single scene of real artistic merit. And only a few verses sound well—one admires the variety of metrics rather than of images. All is toned down to crepuscular grays: the lover is not as passionate, the villain is not as depraved; the *gracioso* or comic is not as funny. And though Olimpia, on hearing Roxana's anguish in song, gives the formula of the esthetic catharsis: "After all, evil is not so ugly / when it sings so well; / for groans are other things / when dressed in warbler's clothes"—what is certain is that the play's sentiments are not purified until they attain poetic stature. One of the most vivid passages, Lisímaco's relating his fight with the lion, is entertaining but not moving. There are situations which are pleasant in themselves. Lisímaco and Orondates are walking through a little woods sighing for the love of two princesses who they believe to be dead; upon seeing the princesses they believe them to be visions of a dream; later they see carved on the bark of trees initials that remind them of the names of their loved ones; they decide to follow these markings. Meanwhile, one of the princesses, Estatira, has made her way to a little stream that symbolizes with its crystalline current "the purity of my love, / the constancy of my tear." "Learn from it [Cleone answers her]: don't you see that the stream would punish, with a flood, him who would impede its course?" The two heroes find her there, asleep; the scenes end with intense movement: recognitions, knife duels, abduction in a carriage, pursuit. Songs and dances raise somewhat the lyrical tone of the play.

Theater

Since we are on the subject of the theater, let us pause a moment before a curious phenomenon: the abundance of theatrical production in all the colonies, an idea of which can be gathered by this register of authors.

In Mexico, José Mariano Abarca, Pedro José Rodríguez de Arizpe, Felipe Rodríguez de Ledesma y Cornejo, José Antonio Rodríguez Manzo, Manuel Urrutia de Vergara, Manuel Zumaya; in Colombia, Jacinto de Buenaventura; in Peru, Félix de Alarcón, Pedro Bermúdez de la Torre, Manuel Oms, Marqués de Castell-dos-Rius, Vicente Palomino, Domingo Prieto; in Bolivia, Salvador de Vega; in Argentina, Antonio Fuentes del Arco.

Of all of these there is none whose vocation is really the theater. Generally they are authors of a single little play (preludes, interludes, dances, farces, afterpieces, colloquies, etc.) or, at best, four or five. Dramas and full-length plays are extremely rare. The preludes were written in verse on the occasion of the installation of a new king, viceroy, or archbishop. Customarily they had symbolic personages (from mythology, like Phoebus Apollo; or of certain qualities, like goodness and wealth) and also "Indians" and "gentlemen" according to whether America or Spain was represented. The taste for theater was shared by all levels of society: aristocratic theater in palaces; popular theater in *corrales* or courtyards; theater for general entertainment in the *Casa de Comedias* or Playhouse; religious theater in monasteries and nunneries. Already one can notice in the theater a *costumbrista* trend, *i.e.*, the depiction of local customs and manners, which will be so significant in the years to come. In 1774, for example, an anonymous *Prelude on the Scholar (Loa del Licenciado)*—in whose preface Indian speech is imitated—is performed in Lima, at the Viceroy's court. Also in these years, Negro and popular dialects are phonetically transcribed. This cult of the popular and plebeian speech, which we find in the theater as well as in the satire, proves to be the antecedent of the *costumbrista* literature—a literature that will reach its peak during the Romantic period (for instance, in the Gaucho literature of the Río de la Plata).

We shall point up only a few of the twenty or so who dedicated themselves to the theater. FRIAR FRANCISCO DEL CASTILLO ANDRACA Y TAMAYO (Peru, 1716–1770) wrote plays, dramas, preludes, farces, allegorical pieces and an *Interlude of Judge and Litigants* (*Entremés del Justicia y litigantes*), quite entertaining in its free dialog and in its real-life characters. In his "Couplets of the Blind Man of Mercy" he shows himself as a very popular, bold, and quick satirist. JERÓNIMO DE MONFORTE Y VERA (Peru) left a very entertaining and worthwhile farce, *Love, the Sprite* (*El amor duende*, 1725), with character types such as the Spanish lover, "cloaked" coquettes, a naive Negro maid; with much action; droll dialog; and with narrow Lima streets as a setting. EUSEBIO VELA (Spain–Mexico, 1688–1737), a continuator of the Calderón school, put on plays in the viceregal palaces. Three have been edited: *If Love Exceeds Art, Neither Art Nor Love Exceed Moderation* (*Si el amor excede al arte, ni amor ni arte a prudencia*), *The Loss of Spain Over a Woman* (*La pérdida de España por una mujer*), *The Apostolate of the Indies and Martyrdom of a Chieftain* (*El apostolado en Indias y martirio de un cacique*). The first portrays the adventures of Telemachus on the isle of Calypso, with great visual apparatus and scenes of magic and enchantment; the second portrays the traditional theme of Rodrigo; the third is an apology on behalf of Franciscan missionaries, Hernán Cortés and his soldiers. Vela does not deal in little things. He lays hold of the most spectacular techniques possible in the theater: fires, collapsing buildings, all exaggerated to the limit. JOSÉ AGUSTÍN DE CASTRO (Mexico, 1730–1814), a poet of Calderonian tastes, author of preludes and mystery plays, is esteemed for his *The Cobblers* (*Los remendones*), a "new farcette" and *El Charro*, a "new playlet." In the Mexican Castro, as well as in the Peruvian Castillo Andraca y Tamayo, popular characters speak with local idioms and slang, a phenomenon which, we insist, will be of major importance when it later becomes a source of a new literature.

One of the most elegant and lyrical plays of this period was *The Gardener Prince and Cloridano Feigned* (*Príncipe jardinero y fingido Cloridano*), written between 1730 and 1733, by SANTIAGO DE PITA (Cuba, d. in 1755). Perhaps his theme may derive from the "scenic opera" of the Florentine Giacinto Andrea Cicognini (1606–1660), *Il principe giardiniero*. However, Santiago de Pita embroidered his plots on the backdrop of the Spanish theater as developed by the Golden Age playwrights. There are echoes of Lope's lyricism, but even more one hears the formalist Baroque interplay of Calderón and Moreto in every scene. Conceptist and cultist images, twists and turns in versification, situations, conventions, and the like, bring to mind the theater of the seventeenth century. That century, seen from the eighteenth, is now a literary background, beautiful in itself but also embellished by distance. With artistic nostalgia, Santiago de Pita has the idealized figures of his poetic plays stand out against that gilded background. He makes literature then, by profiting from an already venerable literature; for example, the comic Lamparón's comparing himself to Sancho Panza and describing his master Fadrique as another insane Don Quijote. Santiago de Pita's Baroqueness is academic, serene, elegant, sentimental, and sprouts preferences that later will be characteristic of the rococo: intimacies in a garden, in a Utopian Thrace, with poetic refinements, aristocracy, women boldly declaring their passions, exaltation of pleasure, action imitating the geometry of a dance, artful scenery yet taken from nature, and so on. Within the eighteenth century this play moves along an emotional current and not along the rationalist one of neoclassicism. Theatrical functions in palaces tended to be so luxuriant in staging, in adornments, and in music that by themselves, leaving aside what was being enacted, they record a new spirit.

JERÓNIMO FERNÁNDEZ DE CASTRO Y BOCÁNGEL (Peru, 1689–1737), himself an author of a prelude-operetta, described in *Peruvian Elysium* (*Eliseo peruano*, 1725) a pompous show by Antonio de Zamora: "the orchestra began to ring out the sonorous symphony of violins, oboes and other instruments . . . After a very sweet bass, it ended in the festive happy air of a minuet which serves as a cue to raise the curtain. The stage revealed a luxurious forest and delightful grove . . . One cannot esteem too much the happy shower of lights which, at the soft sounding of a whistle, were thrust down from the backdrop; for it was a veritable inundation of diamonds that drowned our sight in each one of the illustrious actors . . . The rich material of the exquisite and fine apparel, all of sheer fabric, seemed to wish to hide, ashamed at not being able to express more behind the many jewels that covered it. The tufts of feathers and down that filled the air gave off a vague and rich quality of spring . . ."

Prose

We have alluded to a mass of prose writings in the first part of this chapter. In this section, however—a section more concerned with literary values—very little of the afore-mentioned prose can be included. And whatever is mentioned has to be Baroque. In fact, it would seem that what is not Baroque is not literature at all.

One must not expect to find the novel here, for the reasons stated in the preceding chapter. In France and in England the novel has to arise amidst the sluggishness and scorn of the erudite and the preceptists, and on arising it does so with the movements taught by *Don Quijote* and the picaresque novels. But despite the fact that the best elements of the European novel will have a Spanish look (like *Gil Blas* by the Frenchman Le Sage and the stories of the Englishmen Smollett and Fielding), Spain does not figure in the shaping of the modern novel. What is certain is that everywhere the novel fared poorly. Philosophers and satirists take possession. When they wish to rehabilitate the novel, they push it toward genrés that are considered more noble, so that they speak of the novel as a "poem in prose"; a heroic-comic poem, for example (this is how they classified *Don Quijote*); or a poem in serious prose, in the manner of Fénélon's *Télémaque*, which had an extraordinary acceptance and was imitated and read everywhere. The first years of the eighteenth century were bleak ones in Spain. No one knew what was happening in the world. Only during the epoch of Charles III will there be a quickened intellectual throb, but still not for the novel. Consequently, it would be too much to expect that there would be novelizing in the colonies.

The lawyer ANTONIO DE PAZ Y SALGADO (Guatemala, end of the seventeenth century–1757) interests us for two works in which satire and anecdote are combined with jocular narrative forms. In *Instruction for Litigants* (*Instrucción de litigantes,* 1742) he attempts to reveal to the general public the secrets of the legal profession. The festive tone, the autobiographical touches, the legal cases, and a certain Quevedo-like glow lend the book a relative legibility. Even more Quevedo-like was *The Flyflap* (*El Mosqueador,* 1742), "to put to flight . . . every kind of fool." The biting description of dullards and the manner of defending oneself against them is witty and expressive. A spiritual autobiography—*The Pilgrim with Guide and the Universal Medicine of the Soul* (*El peregrino con guía y medicina universal del alma,* 1750–1761), by the Mexican friar, Miguel de Santa María, that is, MARCOS REYNEL HERNÁNDEZ—can be placed here.

Poetry

Baroque Poetry / As we move on to poetry we must first recognize the vitality of the Baroque movement. That it is not a style of decadence is proved by the fact that in America, at least, it exalts the imagination, although poetry does decay in the eighteenth century.

It is true that there were other types of poetry, for example, popular and Latin poetry. In popular, satiric poetry we have already mentioned Castillo Andraca y Tamayo and his "Couplets of the Blind Man of Mercy" (*"Coplas del Ciego de la Merced"*) and we could couple him off with JUAN BAUTISTA MAZIEL (Argentina, 1727–1788), a mediocre and obscure poet (albeit a renowned jurist) who composed one of the first attempts at Gaucho poetry: "A Cowhand Sings in Prairie Style about the Triumphs of His Most Excellent Lord Don Pedro Cevallos" (*"Canta un guaso en estilo campestre los triunfos del Excelentísimo Señor Don Pedro Cevallos"*). We shall see the fortune that this kind of verse, along with eighteenth-century theater and satire, will meet in the nineteenth-century romantic surge of the Gaucho literature. Churchmen produced Latin poetry, for they felt a cordial kinship to this style. The Jesuits DIEGO JOSÉ ABAD (Mexico, 1727–1779), the above-mentioned Francisco Xaxier Alegre, and RAFAEL LANDÍVAR (Guatemala, 1731–1793)—especially the latter who authored the very important *Mexican Country Sojourn* (Rusticatio Mexicana)—wrote Latin poetry of marked value; yet it lies beyond the pale of this history which is concerned only with poetry written in Spanish.

Leaving to one side, then, the Latin and popular poets, we come to the Jesuit father JUAN BAUTISTA DE AGUIRRE (Ecuador, 1725–1786). In the middle of the century, a full century and a quarter after the death of Góngora and a quarter of a century from Luzán's *Poética*, Aguirre presents us with a beautiful Baroque flower. He left us scarcely a score of poems. And it is amazing that in such a small number there should be such variety of tone: moral, theological, amatory, satirical, lyrical, polemical, descriptive compositions. And such a variety of metrics: sonnets, rhymed octaves, *silvas* (verses of seven and eleven syllables), *canciones, liras* (five-line stanzas), ballads, *décimas* (ten octosyllabic verses), and quatrains. And, finally, such a variety of influences is apparent: Góngora, Quevedo, Calderón, Rioja, and Polo de Medina. For Aguirre, poetry must have been a formal type of entertainment; and perhaps because of this attitude, the Baroque poems, in which his playful disposition and extreme formal style coincided, are his best. A syllogistic logic runs through his syntax forcing it to bob and weave striking hyperbaton, ellipsis, constructions based on symmetries and contrasts, and so on. But his logic has exchanged abstractions for metaphors so that a reality rich in colors, sounds, plastic beauty, and fragrance appears. At first sight it looks like dynamic poetry. Then one notices that nothing moves—the author has violently discharged a metaphoric light upon an immobile concept (like someone who, in the darkness of a cemetery, suddenly casts a light upon a gravestone). But if what matters to us is not the logical meaning of the verses, nor their function within the allegory, nor the philosophy of the poet, but the very movement of the metaphor as a meteoric fragment, then we must indeed recognize a certain dynamism in Father Aguirre. Some of his images are wrought with all the intensity of authentic poetic vision: metaphors of a good poet in mediocre poems.

A fellow student of Aguirre was IGNACIO ESCANDÓN (1719), an Ecuadorian by birth although he lived and wrote in Lima. He was a passable poet and his most interesting aspect was his eulogy of Father Feijóo and his plans—unfulfilled—to write a history of Hispanic-American literature. "Southern America," he used to say, "was more abundant in minds than in mines and being a land of men of letters it became a sepulcher in their memory."

A list of Baroque poets would be very long. It suffices to mention FRANCISCO

RUIZ DE LEÓN (Mexico, 1683), who is still Gongorizing in his religious poem *Sweet Myrrh for the Encouragement of Sinners* (*Mirra dulce*) and in *Exploits of Hernán Cortés* (*La Hernandía*, 1755), an account in verse form of Cortés' deeds; JOSÉ SURÍ Y ÁGUILA (Cuba, 1696–1762), a poet of religious timbre, improviser for religious ceremonies and holidays, an eager gleaner of Baroque words; LORENZO MARTÍNEZ DE AVILEIRA (Cuba, 1722–1782), also a religious poet, with one or two satirical compositions. The historian Juan de Velasco, of whom we have already spoken, left us a *Collection of Sundry Poetry, Composed by a Man of Leisure in the City of Faenza* (*Colección de poesías varias, hecha por un ocioso en la ciudad de Faenza en 1790*), the first to include Ecuadorian writers. In it are RAMÓN VIESCAS, author of a "Dream at Dante's Tomb" ("*Sueño sobre el sepulcro del Dante*"); JOSÉ OROZCO (1733–1786), author of the heroic poem "The Conquest of Menorca" ("*La conquista de Menorca*"); the brothers AMBROSIO and JOAQUÍN LARREA; and the nostalgic MARIANO ANDRADE (1734). In this anthology of Ecuadorian poets there are satiric, elegiac, and heroic poems in Renaissance and Baroque styles. Among the Spaniards (who are also represented) Góngora stands out significantly.

Rococo Poetry / But the Baroque slowly becomes rococo. JOAQUÍN VELÁZQUEZ DE CÁRDENAS Y LEÓN (Mexico? 1732–1786) wrote sonnets with elegance and sensuality that were more rococo than Baroque. FRANCISCO ANTONIO VÉLEZ LADRÓN DE GUEVARA (Colombia, 1721–d. after 1781) was a court and society poet, who bequeathed his verses to viceroys and their wives. He has few Gongoristic traits, and in his verse there is a tone of gallantry. This tone has already become rococo. The attitude is new, as is his use of mythological themes. His quatrains on the "birthday of a lady" have rococo grace. In his descriptive ballad of a stroll by the Salto waterfall, there is a feeling for nature and a picture of liberal and mirthful customs of gentlemen and ladies who drink, ride horseback, lose themselves in the woods, etc. There is, indeed, the rococo, or rather, one sees in the background the viceregal society that participates in a refined European way, whose style in those days was the rococo.

The word "rococo" has been printed so often in this chapter that it is now time to define it. Rococo style came about in Europe during the first half of the eighteenth century. In Hispanic-America it appeared much later. The word itself, "rococo," was not used in Hispanic-America, but this need not be an obstacle to its use here. Everyone knows that first the changes in style appear, and after a goodly number of years have passed the changes are described and baptized. The truth is that the word "rococo" became current only after the style to which it alludes had been substituted by a new one: Neoclassicism. Rococo, as used in 1754 by the new critics of classical tastes, meant something already outmoded, something that should be ridiculed. But it is obvious that in the Europe of the first half of the eighteenth century, it was a fresh and vital phenomenon. An antecedent to the word "rococo" was "*rocalla*," which from the sixteenth century meant any outdoor construction or place of luxuriousness and enjoyment: gardens, fountains, grottos, bowers. These architectonic contrivances were elegant, but based on unhewn rock work, incrustations of shells, capricious forms of marine foam and floral boughs. From Italian, French, and German *rocalla* comes the rococo. In the eighteenth century the rococo, essentially a decorative style, softens the Baroque. The ostentatiousness, the magnificence, the heaviness, the tragic movement of great masses, the violence of the Baroque are converted into a style that is pleasing, playful, pinioned, dancing, dazzling, delicate, apparently frivolous and licentious, always discriminate, always refined, smooth in its undulations, and shimmering with gracefulness in its smallest detail. If the Baroque expressed a desperate vision of life, the rococo expressed a life of joy and voluptuousness. The sensual richness of rococo style indicates that men have decided to seek happiness freely. In this sense the rococo accompanies the movement of ideas outlined earlier. Are not libertinism and effeminate delicateness supported by the illuminist idea that, through reason, we discover the naturalness of the sex act, previously considered sinful? One of the rococo elements is the appetite for pleasure. We must remember that, in the eighteenth century, Christian eschatology had been substituted for another cosmology which promised heaven on earth; and more: it was believed that all men could reach happiness very shortly. Granted that within this idea of terrestrial bliss moral notions were inserted, but, at the same time, did not this idea release an effluvium of hedonism? Let us recall the scenes of delight in gardens abounding in flirtations, music, and perfumes, that is, Watteau, Fragonard, Boucher, *et al.* Are they not painting pieces of paradise achieved along the line of human progress? In Hispanic-America the rococo manifested itself, as was to be expected, in a mitigated degree—yet its erotic notes of dissipation and love affairs, of tenderness and perversity, of gentility and indiscretion; its landscape tones, in which nature appears as a refuge for gallantry; its moods of intimacy accentuated by proceedings that veil and unveil in ornamental interplay ironies and flights from reality, are found in poets, prosists, and playwrights. Let us not forget that luxury is no longer just a theme in Hispanic-America, but a real experience. The viceregal courts have created an atmosphere of sumptuousness, exquisiteness, and courtship. When the aforementioned Friar Antonio Vélez Ladrón de Guevara describes precious materials, he sees before him the pearl industry on the Colombian coast; and when he refers to the ladies as "madames" he reveals a courtly and Frenchified corner in his mind.

V. 1759-1788

Authors born between 1735 and 1760

Historical framework: Because of the social, political, and economic reforms of Charles III, the position of Spain and its colonies improves. Nevertheless, the dissatisfaction of the Creoles increases.

Cultural tendencies: Ideas of the Enlightenment. Neoclassicism.

The movement of ideas and styles described in the preceding chapter becomes more widespread in this period. The idea of progress begins to make inroads. In general, the Roman Catholic Church did not believe in this concept of progress because what was more evident to it was the idea of retrogression: we have retrogressed from paradise and any betterment on earth is only a preparation for supernatural salvation. The scant attention given to the idea of progress was concomitant with the slight material progress of the Hispanic-American colonies. That is to say, that in Europe, philosophy was elaborating an idea of progress in the face of concrete results of material progress. In Hispanic-America the reverse is true: first we speak abstractively about progress; material progress comes later.

Polemics on the Inferiority of the New World

In these years the polemics on the supposed inferiority of the New World break out all over Europe. In 1768 the Prussian abbot Cornelius De Pauw declared that the substance of America was weak and that the Indians were degenerate brutes. He concedes the possibility of some progress—"in three hundred years America will look as different from today as it looks today from the time of its discovery"—but that progress will presuppose the de-Americanization of America. Since De Pauw also railed at the Spanish conquistadors and the Catholic missionaries, the Roman Catholic Church was the first to react within the Hispanic sphere. In addition to the Spaniards (first the abbot, Juan

Nix, and mostly Father Feijóo, who exercised great influence in this matter and others), the Creoles also jumped to the defense of America.

The Jesuits, expelled in 1767, felt annoyed at the scorn that Europeans held for America, and at times aroused by nostalgia, were moved to defend their homelands, as in the case of the Mexican ANTONIO LÓPEZ DE PRIEGO (1730–1798). In some 280 *Décimas* (1784) he imagined an argument between an Italian who had been in Mexico and a Mexican who had been in Italy and ended with a sonnet censuring those who do not realize "that good and bad are found everywhere." Father Francisco Xavier Clavigero—with whom we have already dealt—wrote his *Ancient History of Mexico* (*Historia antigua de México*, 1780–81) with the intention of refuting the idea of a degenerate America. Father JUAN IGNACIO MOLINA (Chile, 1740–1829), in his *Compendium of the History of Chile* (*Compendio de la historia . . . del reino de Chile*, 1776), answers these European calumnies with pride in his native country and its inhabitants. Father BENITO MARÍA DE MOXÓ (Spain–Bolivia, 1763–1816) in his *Letters from Mexico* (*Cartas mexicanas*, 1805) puts forth his observations on the landscape in order to undercut the prejudices of De Pauw and his followers. Fury subsided with the years, but from time to time voices are raised against the "calumniator and imbecile De Pauw," in tune with the patriotism of the Independence and the romantic feeling for nature: the Argentinian FRANCISCO JAVIER ITURRI, 1738–1822; the Peruvians JOSÉ MANUEL DÁVALOS, HIPÓLITO UNANUE, 1755–1833, and Manuel Lorenzo Vidaurre; the Colombians DIEGO MARTÍN TANCO and Francisco José de Caldas; the Mexican Friar Servando Teresa de Mier; and the Honduran JOSÉ CECILIO DEL VALLE, 1780–1834.

Whether they may have been defending themselves against the vilifications of the Europeans or whether, along with the polemics, they were expressing confidence in the intelligence of the Creoles, it is certain that during these years one of the preoccupations of writers was with American progress.

Expulsion of the Jesuits / There were those who reacted against progress and there were those who supported progress. In this balance of forces the position of the Jesuits was a curious one. In 1767 Charles III ordered that the Jesuits in America be expelled. They departed in flocks. And perhaps because they wrote their works in exile, and at times in Italian or Latin, they have not been considered in the history of Hispanic-American letters. To be sure, their importance in a purely literary history is not great, but it is indeed in a cultural and political history. The humanistic culture of the Jesuits was like a bridge between the Baroque and the Neoclassical. As antiroyalists and cultural deforceors, the Jesuits gave a new direction to Spanish intellectual traditions. They came to a *rapprochement* with the Creole bourgeoisie; they sympathized surreptitiously with the cause of national autonomy and diffused some of the philosophical and scientific ideas of the Enlightenment.

We mentioned several of these Jesuits in the preceding chapter and at the beginning of this one: Francisco Xavier Clavigero, Francisco Xavier Alegre, Rafael Landívar, Manuel Lacunza, and others. Other writers born after 1735 could be added: PEDRO BERROETA (Ecuador, 1737), poet; ANDRÉS CAVO (Mexico, 1739–1803), historian; MANUEL FABRI (Mexico, 1737–1805), biographer of the brothers of his order; JUAN LUIS MANEIRO (Mexico, 1744–1802); PEDRO JOSÉ MÁRQUEZ (Mexico, 1741–1820), who combined his concern for archeology with esthetics; and many others. The expulsion of the Jesuits damaged literary culture but in the long run permitted the unobstructed expansion of the modern spirit. As anti-royalists and conservers of cultural life, the Jesuits formed the ideological root for the revolution of the colonies against the metropolis. Certainly, their modern spirit made the Church a more effective force, and without them there was more intellectual liberty.

Scientific and Didactic Activities / In sacred oratory the Church cried out with no restraint: Father JUAN BAUTISTA BAREA (Cuba, 1744–1789), Father RAFAEL DEL CASTILLO Y SUCRE (Cuba, 1741–1783). But modern voices were also heard. A defense of ideas—dedicated to "Mexican youth"—was undertaken by the Jesuit ANDRÉS DE GUEVARA Y BASOAZÁBAL (Mexico, 1748–1801). He extolled Descartes, Galileo, Bacon. FRANCISCO ANTONIO MORENO Y ESCANDÓN (Colombia, 1736–1792) was one of those who executed the order for the expulsion of the Jesuits. He proposed an important educational reform, promoting the study of the physical and natural sciences in order to correct "futile questions of Scholastic theology." He advised theologians to begin studying "in order to flee from the superstition and credulity into which the masses easily fall." In philosophy, he used to say, "eclecticism . . . experience and observation must prevail." JUAN BENITO DÍAZ DE GAMARRA (Mexico, 1745–1783), who was not a Jesuit, but who was far from Descartes, imported eclectic philosophies (or at least seventeenth- and eighteenth-century philosophies of which the eclectics partook). His *Errors of Human Understanding* (*Errores del entendimiento humano*, 1781) criticizes formal Scholasticism and proposes a practical logic. There was scientific activity. JOSÉ CELESTINO MUTIS (Colombia, 1732–1808) was one of the greatest naturalists of his time. He maintained an epistolary correspondence, in Latin, with his European colleagues, Linnaeus, Berguis, Willdenow. Linnaeus, in a letter dated 1774, called Mutis "immortal"; and when years later Alexander von Humboldt arrived in Colombia he is amazed at the library of Mutis, this "venerable 72 year old clergyman": "Outside of Banks' in London, I have not seen a botanical library as large as Mutis'." He fought against the intellectual lethargy of Spain and its colonies, expounding scandalous things like the Copernican system!

ANTONIO DE ALCEDO Y BEXARANO (Ecuador, 1735–1812) wrote a notable encyclopedia of Hispanic-American subjects—*Geographico-historical Dictionary of the West Indies or America* (*Diccionario geográfico-histórico de las Indias Occidentales o América*, 1786–1789). Physicists and mathematicians like JOSÉ IGNACIO BARTOLACHE (Mexico, 1739–1790); ethnographers and archeologists like JOSÉ DOMINGO DUQUESNE (Colombia, 1748–1822) and ANTONIO LEÓN Y GAMA (Mexico, 1735–1802) point to a new intellectual tension. The new critical, didactic, and constructive spirit of the Enlightenment first appeared in reforms of intellectual life: the founding of literary gazettes, greater participation in social affairs, care of libraries, translations, bibliographies. For now the beginnings of an argumentative, satirical, or pedantic epoch are seen which at least have a solid direction in historical scholarship. In history we might cite Ignacio José Urrutia y Montoya (Cuba, 1735–1795); the deacon Gregorio Funes (Argentina, 1749–1829); and Antonio del Campo y Rivas (Colombia, b. in 1750), of whom we have a local *History* charged with a humanitarian spirit that condemns the conquistadors as "destroyers of the human species" and denounces their cruelty for which "humanity is horrified" (notice the word "humanity").

Thought of the Enlightenment

The most fruitful changes during this period are found in the field of thought. These are the years of the intellectual beginnings of the autonomist movement. The Creoles travel to Europe and return with revolutionary pamphlets and ideas. Sailing ships arrive laden with seeds of the Enlightenment.

Encyclopedism, openly rooted in the philosophy of the French Enlightenment, was cultivated by Pablo de Olavide y Jáuregui (Peru, 1725–1804). Already noted for his intellectual brilliance and capacity for action, he went to Spain in 1752 to defend himself from accusations that dishonored him. He was incarcerated. Later he made a fortune and enjoyed the protection of the court. In France he thrust himself into the turbulent life of the salons, where he came to know artists, writers, and philosophers: in rococo art, Boucher; in Neoclassical literature, Marivaux, Marmontel; in ideas of the Enlightenment, Diderot. He struck up friendly relations with Diderot, D'Alembert, Voltaire. Back in Madrid he started a literary salon like those in Paris and constructed a private theater for which he translated and adapted Racine's *Phèdre*, Voltaire's *Zaïre*, Regnard's *Le Joueur*, Maffei's *Merope*, etc. He frequented Jovellanos' literary circle. In 1776 a satire directed at Olavide appeared: *The Enlightened Century: Life of Don Cherrytree Born, Reared, Educated, Exalted and Died in Accordance with the Lights of the Present Age. Published as a Model of Customs by Don Justo Vera de la Ventosa* (*El Siglo Ilustrado. Vida de Don Guindo Cerezo, nacido, educado, instruido, sublimado y muerto según las luces del presente siglo. Dado a luz por seguro modelo de las costumbres por Don Justo Vera de la Ventosa*). Following the form of the picaresque novel, the author, a Spaniard, invents a character through whom he mocks, episode after episode, the ideas of Olavide. Jailed, condemned, and harassed by the Inquisition, he fled to France in 1780. The revolution having broken out, he became one of the adopted citizens of the Republic. But in time he came to abhor the Republic. Experiencing an inner, personal crisis, Olavide, with bowed head, began to meditate over the frailty of human presumptuousness and to write poetry on sacred themes—about nine thousand verses of fiery religiosity. A little after 1794—the year he was taken prisoner in Orléans, a victim of the Jacobean Terror—he returned to the Catholic faith and wrote *The Gospel in Triumph or the History of a Philosopher Undeceived* (*El Evangelio en triunfo o Historia de un filósofo desengañado*, 1797). He wrought a novelesque plot interwoven with autobiographical episodes. A philosopher stops at a monastery by chance. Through the preachings and example of one of the monks he repents his wickedness. Upon rejoining society he readjusts his life and his family's in accordance with Christian norms. Letter-writing formed part of the literary mode of the epoch. Epistolary novels, like Samuel Richardson's *Pamela*, Rousseau's *La Nouvelle Héloïse*, Goethe's *Werther*, were being read. Consequently, Olavide takes recourse to this technique to illustrate the controversies of the philosopher in him, his moral crisis, and his conversion. Olavide's theological knowledge was weaker than his religious conviction. His prose is tinged with sentiment and fantasy; it is a prose that, despite his return to Spanish faith, preserved the twists and ways learned by having read so many French writers. His repentance extended itself to his verses—*The Spanish Psalter or Paraphrastic Version of the Psalms of David, the Canticles of Moses, Other Canticles and Some Prayers of the Church* (*El salterio español o Versión parafrástica de los Salmos de David, de los cánticos de Moisés, de otros cánticos y algunas oraciones de la Iglesia*) served the cause of faith, but not of poetry. In the same fashion the hendecasyllables of his *Christian Poems* (*Poemas cristianos*) will alienate the poet, but not the moralist. This was the last of his writings. And so ended, on the plains of conservatism, traditionalism, and Catholicism, the man who in his youth had been an eminent figure of the Enlightenment.

In secret meetings the Creoles air the equalitarian preachments of Rousseau. Philosophy and politics conspire to change the colonial order and even to overthrow it. One of the most outstanding personages of the Enlightenment was the mestizo FRANCISCO EUGENIO DE SANTA CRUZ Y ESPEJO (Ecuador, 1747–1795). He possessed encyclopedic knowledge. While in philosophy he was imitating some of the sensualist ideas, in politics, whether he knew it or not, he was preparing for American independence. Documents reveal that in Quito the revolutionaries of 1809 were accused of being "inheritors of the seditious plans of an old inhabitant named Espejo who died years ago in that capital." The writings of Espejo moved from hand to hand. He would accuse colonial education of being "a slave's education." Neoclassicism like sixteenth-century Erasmism was an attempt to Europeanize the Hispanic world. And it is strange that now, as in the sixteenth century, the satirical dialogs in the manner of Lucian would be the genre preferred by the new spirit. Espejo wrote the *New Lucian or Awakener of Minds* (*Nuevo Luciano o Despertador de ingenios*). It consists of nine conversations between the characters Murillo and Mera (the latter is the spokesman for Espejo) on such topics as rhetoric and poetry, philosophy, plans of study, and theology. The purpose of the work is to examine and criticize ideas and institutions. It is the best exposition of colonial culture of the eighteenth century. In it he reviewed the colonial poets. He wrote other works which continue the *New Lucian.* He directed, and wrote in its entirety, the first Ecuadorian newspaper *First Fruits of the Culture of Quito* (*Primicias de la Cultura de Quito*). Also in a mocking vein (although different from that of Espejo) is the *Guide for Blind Wayfarers . . . Taken from the Memoirs of Don Alonso Carrió de la Vandera . . . By Don Calixto Bustamante Carlos Inca, alias Concolorcorvo* (*Lazarillo de ciegos caminantes . . . sacado de las memorias que hizo don Alonso Carrió de la Vandera . . . por Don Calixto Bustamante Carlos Inca, alias Concolorcorvo*). Although Concolorcorvo really existed and did accompany Carrió de la Vandera, he had nothing to do with the composition of the book. It was all a hoax. ALONSO CARRIÓ DE LA VANDERA (Spain, *ca.* 1715–d. after 1778) printed it clandestinely in Lima, in 1775 or 1776, put down Gijón as the place of printing, moved the date up to 1773, and pretended that Concolorcorvo had taken it from the reports of voyages that he dictated to him. Why? Carrió de la Vandera, who had been settled in Lima since 1746, was commissioned in 1771 to inspect and reorganize the stage posts between Buenos Aires and Lima. Involved in some sort of misunderstanding with a postal administrator, he may have decided to guard himself against a direct attack by publishing his observations as if someone else were doing it. Carrió gave this explanation in one of his letters: "I disguised my name so as not to see myself in the necessity of giving away all the copies. Your grace knows how dry a diary may be, particularly in sparsely populated areas, so that it behoved me dress it up according to local tastes so that wayfarers might amuse themselves during their stopovers and that their travels become less rigorous." The *Guide,* in fact, is conceived as a traveler's manual, including some documentation, chronicle, popular traditions, local customs, jokes, anecdotes and dialogs, all with a certain novelistic flavor. One picaresque element is that of having Concolorcorvo speak in the first person: "I am Indian through and through, although I shall not vouch for my mother's tricks. Two princess cousins of mine preserve their virginity, much to their regret, in a convent in Cuzco where they are maintained by the King, our lord. I find myself resolved to solicit the job of dog beadle for the Cathedral of Cuzco in order to enjoy ecclesiastical immunity." His intention was to educate, to reform. Carrió is familiar with Greco-Roman and Castilian literature (Cervantes, Quevedo, Gracián, Feijóo), but he is not bookish. On the contrary, he describes directly the American reality he sees around him. He is a very Americanized Spaniard who critically overcomes all provincialism—superiority lies in civilization, not in this or that nation. His criticism at times runs against Spanish administration; sometimes he is anticlerical. With smiles and irony he chastises Spaniards, Creoles, mestizos, and Indians. There is sympathy for the well-bred man, be he Spaniard or Creole. From here he runs rapidly down the scale: Gauchos, mestizos, Indians, Negroes. The *Guide,* for the most part, is a very lively description of the trip from Montevideo to Lima, passing through Buenos Aires, Córdoba, Salta, and Cuzco. The picaresque tone, the rhythm of the action, the description of customs, and the art of surprising the reader in an unexpected situation makes the reading entertaining at times. In this travel diary (for this is what the *Guide* is) the eye picks out singular things: the couplets sung by the *gauderios* or gauchos, the sale of Negroes, the differences in customs from one locality to another.

Among these travelogs (although it must be noted that their purpose was scientific) one should mention those of FELIX DE AZARA (Spain–Argentina, 1746–1821), who looked at nature and man in the light of the progressivist ideas of the Enlightenment as revealed in his very interesting *Report on the Rural State of the Río de la Plata in 1801* (*Memoria sobre el estado rural del Río de la Plata en 1801*).

In the last twenty years of the eighteenth century the intellectuals and the cultured urban citizenry—like Espejo, Nariño, Rojas y Salas, Gual y España—realized that they had better take advantage of the times and control the new social changes. More significant than literary activity (which bore the Neoclassic stamp on it and which was channeled into typical Neoclassical genres) was the intellectual life in the universities, in the press, in literary clubs, in French books, in polemics between the Jansenists and sensualists. The active philosophy of the French Revolution was more influential than written philosophy. Literary history at times tends to appropriate great political figures that in reality do not belong to it, but because they were "men of letters" (in the broad sense that this term has in Spanish America) the inclusion is permitted and justified. This is the case of FRANCISCO MIRANDA (Venezuela, 1750–1816). His importance is political because the historical events of the movement of independence rise from his intrigues and struggles, but it is proper to consider his writings in that they expose an original spirit. Without having any literary ambitions he recorded here and there what he saw, thought, heard, and read. His keen and concise comments are as excellent as his documentation of those years of crisis.

The Theater

Because of its social character, the theater is an index of the refinement with which the customs of the capital cities of Spain and of Europe are imitated. Pablo de Olavide had been charged with the construction of a new playhouse (the old Colosseum had been destroyed in an earthquake), and he built such a sumptuous one that it reflected all the brilliance of the rococo age. Here, the celebrated Creole actress Micaela Villegas, known as Perricholi, reigned from 1760 onwards. She was the mistress of the Viceroy Manuel de Amat y Junient; and her bearing, her coquettishness, her rakish elegance gave the colonies the same tone of beauty and pleasure that Europeans enjoyed in their courts. In the second half of this century a new kind of description of customs is wrought by the interludes and farces. The slackening of the mining industries in Mexico and Lima, the centers of court theater, coincides with the establishment of theaters and opera houses financed by landowners and businessmen who were fond of entertainment, in cities showing economic growth: Havana in 1776, Buenos Aires in 1783, Caracas in 1784, Montevideo in 1793, Bogotá in 1793, Guatemala in 1794, La Paz in 1796. Works in pretentious Neoclassic fashion are produced; however the Creole farcists multiply and instead of putting *majas* and the Madrilenians of the Spaniard Ramón de la Cruz on the stage, they present the popular types from the different regions of Hispanic-America, for example, *The Love of the Farmer's Daughter* (*El amor de la estanciera*), an anonymous farce in verse, composed between 1780 and 1795. It lacks literary worth, and its value as a picture of customs is marred because the author could not have chosen more vulgar expressions even had he wished to mock Argentine country life and people. The practical joke played on the Portuguese is not worse than that played on the two gauchos and their wives. The girl is also a vulgar type. The historian, however, must be alert to this literary activity which devoted itself to depicting popular types, ways of life, slang expressions, and dialogs among humble people: alert, because from this will spring what will later be called Gaucho literature. It is this literary activity, and not the songs of mythical minstrels, that becomes the source of the "singing gaucho" image as created by Hidalgo, Ascasubi, Hernández, and other poets of the people.

Journalism

A note or two on journalism, an activity typical of the eighteenth century, is in order here. In the sixteenth century printed sheets carrying European news appeared. In the seventeenth there are journals, issued irregularly, for example, the first *Gaceta de México* is of 1667. But it is in the eighteenth century, when periodicals emerge everywhere and change intellectual life. Of those dedicated to literature and to the sciences, the ones edited in Mexico by José Antonio Alzate (1729–1799) and José Ignacio Batorlache (1739–1790) are noteworthy. In Colombia Francisco Javier Caro (1750–1822) published a pleasant *Diario* (1783) in which bureaucratic life is ridiculed.

Novelistic Prose

There is nothing to say about the novel. As we have pointed out in preceding chapters, the novel, such as had been created by Cervantes, was forgotten in Spain. Father Isla, in his *Friar Gerundio,* revealed narrative talent, but unlike Cervantes, he allowed his satire to smother his novel. Since the Spaniards could no longer create a novel in the tradition of Cervantes, they attempted to take possession of Le Sage's *Gil Blas* (and Father Isla, on translating it, said he was restoring to Spain what France had stolen from it). In truth, literary tastes in Spain did not esteem novelists like Cervantes so much as novelists like Marmontel and Florian. The country that had seen the birth of the modern novel, thanks to Cervantes' *Don Quijote,* valued Cervantes for two services alien to art: the ridiculing to death of a literary genre and the defense of the language against translators of French. They did not know what to do with the novel, a genre discredited because it lacked classical antecedents. It was a degeneration of the epic, was not morally edifying, or was a frivolous fabrication of falsehoods. What can one say, then, of the novel in Hispanic-America? In Mexico there is Friar Joaquín Bolanos' *Death's Prodigious Life* (*La portentosa vida de la muerte,* 1792) in a verbose, truculent, rhetorical prose, padded with sermons, illustrations from religious literature, and symmetrical and contrasting enumerations. With the omnipresence of the "empress of the sepulchers," Bolaños' allegory intended to strike the consciences of contemporary Mexicans, who were, according to him, diverted by trivial pastimes and entertainments. The medieval theme of death, elaborated by the Baroque, was being offered to readers living in a rococo age who felt "well situated in the world." So it is not strange if readers did not appreciate Bolaños' work—they found it in bad taste. Even clergymen like Father José Antonio de Alzate Ramírez criticized it as being "prejudicial to dogma and good customs" because Death, after all, appears as a burlesque figure and the author seems to adhere to the doctrine of probabilism. Furthermore, he adds, it is "an ill-devised novel." It has little of the quality of a novel. The personification of lady Death does not manage to take on life; her visits to men in all walks of life are wanting in adventure. We know, as a certainty, that novels were written (several historians have had the manuscripts in their possession), but those manuscripts of novels only prove narrative avocations, since they never made the printing presses: *Fabiano and Aurelia* (1760) by Father José GONZÁLEZ SÁNCHEZ.

Poetry

Poetry drags along, its wings clipped. The Baroque, after it is sweetened into the rococo, must bow down before Neoclassicism.

MANUEL DEL SOCORRO RODRÍGUEZ (Cuba–Colombia, 1758–1818), writes mannerist poetry in the Baroque manner. DIEGO PADILLA (Colombia, 1754–1829) is the author of a funeral oration to Charles III. Father José M. SARTORIO (Mexico, 1746–1828) poured his best into poems to the Virgin (and his worst, into verses on current events). He cultivated the fable, a genre typically eighteenth century. If he imitated Iriarte, as did many fabulists of the time, it was for his genre and not for his doctrine. The Argentinian MANUEL JOSÉ DE LAVARDÉN (1754–1809) is the author of "Ode to the Majestic River Paraná" (*"Oda al majestuoso río Paraná,"* 1801), the best poetical composition written in his country prior to 1810. It is a didactic allegory in which the river, a fluvial god, appears described in terms of the local landscape; the river symbolizes the cultural and economic prosperity of the Río de la Plata people. All that is preserved of Lavardén is this "Ode," a "Satire" (1786) against Lima and in defense of Buenos Aires, and a "Philosophical Oration" that he delivered in 1778 at the Royal College of San Carlos. Lavardén's theatrical production has been lost; all we have are works attributed to him but unconfirmed. His tragedy *Siripo* was performed in 1789; there is extant a second act that is said to belong to it. This is doubtful—this second act may belong to a later *Siripo* by another author. The plot, revolving around the chieftain Siripo and Lucía Miranda, is legendary; it was treated by Del Barco Centenera, Ruy Díaz de Guzmán, and other chroniclers. Lavardén remained silent during the English invasions and reconquest of Buenos Aires while many other poets celebrated the victory. Among those who are to be recorded here because of their dates of birth is the cultured JOSÉ PREGO DE OLIVER, whose hendecasyllables sang praise to the heroes of the Reconquest, and the popular PANTALEÓN RIVAROLA (1754–1821) whose octosyllables sang praise to the heroic action of the masses.

Satire / Satiric poetry, especially that directed against the new spirit by the traditionalists, documents the existence in Hispanic-America of a licentious and frivolous society, with court *soirées* and Versaillesque parties, with gallantry and refinements in love and in art. In 1786 there are some anonymous "Venus' Rules for Flighty Girls and Ladies" (*"Ordenanzas de Venus para las majas y chinas de volatería"*) in which there is a caricature of the rococo: frothy goddesses, pleasurable art, saucy witticisms, strutting women, impudent conversation, "much laughing, hand gestures, manipulation of the fan," transparent clothes, dances, music and theater, and walks in the gardens.

VI. 1788-1808

Authors born between 1760 and 1780

Historical framework: Under the inept rule of Charles IV Spain takes a purely defensive position and begins losing her colonies. Because of the Napoleonic invasions, Charles IV abdicates in favor of his son Fernando VII: the days of the Spanish empire in America are over.

Cultural tendencies: Literature carries a Gallicized, Neoclassical stamp. Rationalism is colored by subjectivism.

A history of literature intent on adjusting itself to its own material—the record of man's effort to express himself in beautiful words—should close its eyes to what was the most important element of this last period of the eighteenth century, which was not literature, but the movement of philosophic ideas and the preparation for political independence. At any rate, to point out what most approximated literature, let us begin by glancing at these ideas and thus come closer to literature.

Religious, Philosophic, and Political Ideas

Sacred oratory, even though it may soar esthetically, continues to be bound by the mental attitude of the clergy: e.g., Father José POLICARPO SANAME Y DOMÍNGUEZ (Cuba, 1760–1806), famous for his "sermon of the cloud," given in Santo Domingo. There is abundant religious literature, reverently leaning toward its own traditions and dogmas, like *Spiritual Watering for New Plants (Riego espiritual para nuevas plantas)* by Mother MARÍA PETRONILA CUÉLLAR (Colombia, 1761–1814). In a simple and spontaneous prose she attempts to direct novices and nuns. However, in general, the most significant pages, within religious themes, were those that carried on the discussion of the new ideas. JOSÉ AGUSTÍN CABALLERO (Cuba, 1762–1835) was a man of the Church, except that he attacked Scholasticism and expounded on Locke and Condillac. Further, his *Elective Philosophy (Philosophia electiva)* was a systematic formulation of anti-Scholastic thought. In the face of the advances of this modern philosophy, Scholasticism, though ever resisting, withdrew. An illustrative case is the course on ethics given in Buenos Aires between 1793 and 1795 by MARIANO MEDRANO. His method was still Scholastical, though not strictly so, and the doctrine professed follows that of Aristotle and Thomas Aquinas, though not to the letter. Medrano, as a Catholic and monarchist, resists the thought of Hobbes, Locke, Rousseau, and others, but while resisting it he does not fail to receive its blows and retreat from his own dogmatic line; and in this way the new ideas advance on the classrooms of San Carlos. In reality Scholastic philosophy (which was decadent toward the end of the eighteenth century, especially in the Río de la Plata area) was counterproductive. In 1793 when the flames of the French Revolution were lighting up the American colonies and Miranda had launched his campaigns of emancipation, Medrano wished to convince his Creole students of the absolutist rights of the Spanish monarchy. He defamed Las Casas; he cloaked the theological thought of Vitoria; in short, he cut the only emotional ties that the Creoles could have felt for their Spanish past. A few years later these Creoles would be the leaders of the move for independence. There were friars who, already undermined by some encyclopedist ideas, accepted independence as inevitable and even worked together with the patriots. In Colombia the enlightened CAMILO TORRES (1766–1816), author of *Record of Grievances* (*Memorial de agravios*, 1809), had a clear idea of the importance of Hispanic-America in the world economy and knew that the anti-liberal errors of Spain were going to incite independence. JOSÉ FÉLIX DE RESTREPO (Colombia, 1760–1832) was a supporter of the educational reforms of Moreno and Escandón. He was not an Encyclopedist, but rather a "Christian philosopher" who abandoned Aristotelian methods and adopted experimental ones. For him, the sciences were not enemies of religion. He fought for the abolition of slavery, was in favor of the Independence and against Spanish "despotism" and "tyranny." TOMÁS ROMAY (Cuba, 1764–1849) was a progressive, scientific, and constructive soul, but with a good literary education. FRANCISCO ANTONIO ZEA (Colombia, 1766) was a mind possessing literary sensitivity (some verses have been attributed to him) and even in his descriptions of the "endowments" and "bewitchment" of botany there is a loving view of nature, related to that of the rococo. The fact is that the pages of studious and thinking men are saturated with the sentimentalism of the age, as in the *American Letters on Politics and Morals* (*Cartas americanas políticas y morales*, 1823) by MANUEL LORENZO DE VIDAURRE (Peru, 1773–1841) and in one of the greatest scientific spirits of his time, FRANCISCO JOSÉ DE CALDAS (Colombia, 1771–1811). The eighteenth-century style of the "sensitive man," quick to tears, is seen in Caldas' letter to his teacher Mutis, concerning Humboldt's rebuff to him, or in the letters to his sweetheart. It is the influence of the exclamatory letters in Rousseau's *La Nouvelle Héloïse*, a literary novelty. Caldas was a naturalist with literary talent and his descriptions of nature, e.g., that of Tequendama, have the value of art. His prose is akin to that of Feijóo, Jovellanos, and Quintana, although that terrible landscape through which he moved apprehensively is wont to inspire in him expressions of powerful pathos. "Reason, experience are my light," he would say; but he also received light from his heart. Light is the key word. He published his *New Granada Weekly* (*Semanario de la Nueva Granada*, 1808–1809) to "promote incessantly the Enlightenment and the happiness of its peoples." When the Independence failed he was shot by Enribe, the one made famous by the phrase: "Spain does not need learned men." Nor does the figure of ANTONIO NARIÑO (Colombia, 1765–1823) belong to literary history, because he produced no literature. Nevertheless, he lived the literature of others, and he should be mentioned here, if only as an example of an Hispanic-American intellectual during the last years of the colony. Nariño's private library was the richest in the Viceroyalty of New Granada. He discussed these books, many of them prohibited, with his friends; and he used to print on a hand press selections of his readings to give to his friends. He translated the *Déclaration des droits de l'homme* (1794), which had great repercussions since it prepared for the uprising of the colonies.

JUAN EGAÑA (Peru–Chile, 1768–1836) left us a book of memoirs, *The Chilean Consoled in Prisons* (*El chileno consolado en los presidios*, 1826). He was one of the Creole encyclopedists, author of a dramatic poem and also a jocular one, but when Marcó del Pont deported him to the island of Juan Fernández he wrote his memoirs in prison.

Without belonging entirely to the world of letters, the figure who ornamented the literature of this period with the most original coloration is FRIAR SERVANDO TERESA DE MIER (Mexico, 1763–1827). The great event of his life, the cause of his misfortunes and indirectly of his autobiographical pages, and even of his political thought, dates from 1794, and it occurs within the cultural life of the Church. We refer to his sermon denying the popular tradition of the Virgin of Guadalupe and affirming the preaching of the Gospel in America by no less than Apostle St. Thomas himself, before the arrival of the Spaniards. Mier lamented the preference given to Spaniards. He loved his native land. In the way Spain invented its Apostle St. James, he decided (after hearing Borunda and not being quite convinced) to invent a St. Thomas Apostle for Mexico. Here his misfortunes are born: if Mier were right, we Spanish-Americans would not even owe our faith to Spain. Mier is not in disagreement with the Church, but with Spain. Had he persisted in this thinking, Mier would be one of many ecclesiastical minds who still insisted on an extravagant view of the world even after the triumph of the Enlightenment. But he grew in human stature because of the cruel persecutions he suffered, and as he grew more and more aware of the world, he embraced political causes that placed him in the historic line of the Independence. Nevertheless, one must not lose sight of the fact that Mier had his head filled with ideas from the past, that he defended Catholic faith against the heretics (Jansenists, deists, atheists) and, in the final instance, although he may associate himself with the efforts of the Independence, he justifies his action not with the principles of the political philosophy of the Enlightenment, but with the myth that St. Thomas had preached in America: "in the same way that St. Thomas prophesied the coming of the Spaniards, he also predicted the end of their domination, and this more or less is the moment." This myth (like the one about the Apostle St. James in Spain which, incidentally, he links with his own) sets Mier apart from the new intellectual movement. But he was not a misoneist, and at times he criticized friars for their narrow views. He had the cosmic vision of a priest, although not the temperament of a priest. He lacked humility, meekness, and serenity. And this psychological conflict will give birth to his originality as a person and to the contradictions of his literature. Literarily Mier exists through his memoirs which belong to the eighteenth-century cycle. His autobiographical pages, which have been collected by editors under the generic term *Memoirs,* make our acquaintance with Mier in his grievous contacts with ecclesiastical life. But his work gains literary interest when he raises his sight and looks at the reality of the countries in which he lives. The *Accounts* (*Relación*), for example, give a good description of France, Italy, and Spain. Here is Mier the writer. Mier said that the translation of *Atala* which appeared under the name of S. Robinson, pseudonym of Simón Rodríguez, was his. Be this as it may, there are no Chateaubriand traits in his literature or in his make-up. He did not create artistic prose. Nor did he try to describe natural landscapes nor artistic monuments. Either he speaks of his own misfortunes (insisting always that he is persecuted because, as an Hispanic-American, his intellectual superiority is intolerable to the Spaniards) or he describes the most immediate social circumstances, those involving his travels. He generally reflects on differences in customs; in so doing, his attitude is influenced by eighteenth-century traits (criticism, didacticism, reform), not by nineteenth-century traits (the understanding of things regional, popular, and unique). His prose runs rapidly but with dignity. From time to time, there is a happy epigram. At times, with a stroke or two, he paints a character that deserves to live in a story. There is wit, occasionally sarcasm, and, at times, violent polemics. Whether his memoirs are novelistic or not could be argued—no one will argue that he, Friar Servando, was not a novelistic hero.

Journalism

Journalism becomes more intense and intervenes more effectively in the ideological and social transformation of the epoch. Occasionally these periodicals opened their pages to literature and even to literary criticism, as when Manuel del Socorro Rodríguez came to the defense of the literary activities of New Granada by answering a reader who believed that verses should not be published in New Granada because it was literarily inferior to Mexico and Peru.

The Theater

During these years, 1789 to 1808, the establishment of theaters continues—details have already been given. A greater index of the growing interest in theater, however, is what is happening in cities where it had existed many years earlier. The score of plays that were presented each month in Mexico and in Lima were by Spanish authors—the Hispanic-Americans devoted themselves more to farces and short pieces. In truth the men of the theater of those days were more play-adapters than playwrights. For their adaptations they preferred successful authors. The repertory of the Mexico City and Lima theaters was almost the same as that of Madrid. It seems that as the theaters began to sustain themselves as public entertainment, the most recent authors became the leading ones. Calderón, inevitably, was the god—he headed all the repertories. Others from the Golden Age appear repeatedly: Moreto, Rojas Zorrilla, Mira de Amescua, Vélez de Guevara. On the other hand, Lope, Tirso, Alarcón were not considered because their school seemed too remote. The taste for the modern element oriented itself around the recent authors of the eighteenth century: Iriarte, Jovellanos, Ramón de la Cruz, García de la Huerta, Moratín, Moncín, Valladares, Cañizares, Bances Candamo, Arellano, Zamora. The works of non-Spanish authors that were given were the Frenchmen Racine, Molière, Beaumarchais, Jean Baptiste Rousseau, and the Italians Goldoni, Metastasio, Apostolo Zeno. In a history of theatrical tastes throughout the eighteenth century, in its transition from Baroque to Neoclassicism, minor and obscure figures are of special interest. These are figures of little significance when seen from the highest perspectives of literary history (history should move from peak to peak), but yet they reveal a process of modernization and even Americanization of the theater.

In this sense certain little works that were performed on occasion are of interest, such as *The Mexican Lady in England* (*La Mexicana en Inglaterra*, 1792), *La Morbella* (1792), and *American Loyalty* (*La lealtad americana*, 1796) by FERNANDO GAVILA, an actor in the company at the New Colosseum in Mexico. Other Mexicans were: JUAN DE MEDINA (fl. 1796), MANUEL QUIRÓS Y CAMPO SAGRADO (fl. 1792), DIEGO BENEDICTO VALVERDE (fl. 1790), JOSÉ MARÍA VILLASEÑOR CERVANTES (fl. 1809), and JUAN WENCESLAO BARQUERA (1779–1840). In 1791 the *Peruvian Mercury* (*Mercurio peruano*) of Lima was urging "a little modern taste in the preference for pieces" and above all, that sensible people not join the applause that the "low-class plebeians" gave to the interludes. But that is the way one of the most successful playwrights, the actor RAFAEL GARCÍA ("Chicho"), entertained with his scurrilous farces and interludes. There was also theater in other parts of Hispanic-America: FRANCISCO COVARRUBIAS (Cuba, 1774–1856), JUAN FRANCISCO MARTÍNEZ (Uruguay, fl. 1807), JUAN ANTONIO TRIS Y DOYAGUE (Chile, fl. 1792). The most outstanding figure was that of CAMILO HENRÍQUEZ (Chile, 1769–1825), a boisterous patriot, who, having rooted himself in Buenos Aires, wrote politico-sentimental dramas. One is *Camille or the Patriot of South America* (*Camila o la patriota en Sudamérica*), an example of bad theater, where there is an attempt to teach the people tolerance and liberty. This Chilean friar was a liberal. He used to say, "Voltaire, Rousseau, Montesquieu are the apostles of reason." He took part, as a journalist and as a versifier, in the political propaganda favoring the Independence.

Imaginative Prose

There are no novels, and what follows now is a continuation of the history of a genre absent in Hispanic-America, which was begun in previous chapters. A type of realist narration nourished by national traditions was cultivated in Spain throughout the eighteenth century. But it did not have literary quality. It was merely a picture of customs, satirical or ironic. Everyday reality did not seem worthy of artistic seriousness. The best Spanish writers had no wish to write novels, and the public had no wish to read books that reflected trivial circumstances of Spanish life. They translated more than they wrote. The translations, to select the best among the dregs, were of Swift, Fielding, Goldsmith, and Richardson (if not Richardson at least one of his continuators, Frances Sheridan, whose *Memoirs of Miss Sidney Bidulph* was translated by JACOBO DE VILLAURRUTIA, 1757–1833, only he did it from a French version and entitled it *Memoirs for the History of Virtue* [*Memorias para la historia de la virtud*]); those of the German Campe and Goethe's *Werther;* those of the Frenchmen Marmontel, Florian, Mme de Genlis, Ducrai-Duminil, Saint-Pierre's *Paul et Virginie* and Chateaubriand's *Atala* (the latter by the Mexican Friar Servando Teresa de Mier in 1801); those of the Italians Della Croce (*Bertoldo*) and Count Zaccharia Serinam. All this translation activity was carried on despite the animosity of the literati, the court circles, and the Inquisition (in 1799 an order from the Council prohibited the printing of novels). Of course, the cultured minorities read in the original those novels not translated, like those of Ann Radcliffe, Defoe, Rousseau, Voltaire, Diderot. Within her borders, then, Spain was moving in a void and those who wished to breathe the air of the novel had to turn to foreign sources. European narrative currents placed more emphasis on emotion, morals, psychological analysis, conversation, the monolog, the epistle, and philosophy. There is an eruption of sentiment, tearful virtue, feminine themes, exoticism, travails, fantasy, the supernatural, literary trickery, deism, and pantheism. In this climate the new Spanish novelists, Montengón, Martínez Colomer, Mor de Fuentes become weary and falter. All this arrives in the colonies much later, much confused, much weakened. Consequently, one must not expect in Hispanic-America a novelistic production in tune with the times.

Novelistic traits are barely found in the priest, JOSÉ MARIANO ACOSTA ENRÍQUEZ (Mexico; his literary works are from 1779 to 1816). He included Cervantes, Quevedo, and Torres Villarroel in the plot of his

Dream of Dreams (*Sueño de sueños*) and with them he undertook a voyage to the netherworld, presenting death in an allegorical form. Acosta Enríquez narrates in the first person, and with his three admired writers he converses about the changes in fashions and speech, about old age, medicine, and death. Retinues of people of every class appear and personifications of popular sayings and moral symbols pass by in review. There is no narrative skill in them. Even the theme of *Dream of Dreams* is not new. Quevedo had written "Dreams" and Torres Villarroel had imagined a dialog with Quevedo. To this company Acosta now adds Cervantes—he was not the first in gathering this group, because in 1728 Nicolás de Molani Nogui had published a *Plaint Made by Don Quijote de la Mancha at the Court of Death Against Don Francisco de Quevedo on the First and Second Part of the Visions and Visitations of Don Diego de Torres.* (*Querella que Don Quijote de la Mancha da en el tribunal de la muerte contra Don Francisco de Quevedo sobre la primera y segunda parte de las visiones y visitas de Don Diego de Torres*). But, despite all, this little work is interesting for its information on the literary tastes of the eighteenth century. He must have written it around 1800: he speaks of "the end of the century just over, called the century of light," and the most recent book he mentions is the translation of Richardson's *Clara Harlowe,* of 1798 (and it may even be possible that the *Robinson* he speaks of is the translation of Campe's *The New Robinson,* in which case the date is 1800). From his 1800 position he glances back at the history of Spanish narrative and points out the literary fortunes of Cervantes, Quevedo, and Torres Villarroel, adding interesting notes on the dominant tastes of the eighteenth century. He informs us that the many translations from the French are changing the language of the writers. Among the books that are "running through Mexico similarly to yours"—he tells the three Spaniards—he lists those of the Frenchmen Bottens, Fénélon, Le Sage, Mme de Genlis; of the Englishmen Fielding (Henry as well as Sarah), Richardson; of the German Campe; and the Italian Serinam. Among the Spanish novels, Acosta mentions Montengón's and *The Town's Entanglements* (*Los enredos de un lugar,* 1778) by Fernando Gutiérrez de Vegas, which he feels is the best. Acosta tells us that the hero of this novel, the licentiate Tarugo, resembles Don Quijote.

Poetry

During the last thirty years of the colony, Mexico was a thriving humanistic center. Classicism, even though of reflected light, had warmth. At least it heated the heart of many versifiers. Horace, Vergil, Ovid,

Catullus, Martial, and even the Greeks were translated, imitated, and commented on copiously. The only person from the epoch of Charles IV who was a writer by vocation if not by talent was FRIAR MANUEL DE NAVARETTE (Mexico, 1768–1809), a poet of Mexican landscapes who was more refined in his Neoclassic culture than he was perceptive in his observations. He began publishing his verses in 1806. He encouraged the Mexican Arcadia (one of the many academies of the period), whose members assumed the names of shepherds in imitation of the anacreontics of Meléndez Valdés. The latter taught him how to sweeten his erotic verses, and also to read Young, whose *Night Thoughts* he imitated in "Night of Sorrow" (*"Noches tristes"*) and in "Moments of Sorrow" (*"Ratos tristes"*). In this way he moved from the soft pastoral poetry of his youth to the elegiac poetry of the disenchantment of his later years. In "Eucharistic Poem of Divine Providence" (*"Poema eucarístico de la Divina Providencia"*) there are reminiscences of Fray Luis de León. Similar to him is MANUEL JUSTO DE RUBALCAVA (Cuba, 1769–1805), classic poet, moderate, decorous. In his *silvas* he sang to Cuban fruit, in imitation of Vergil ("Eclogue") and the Spanish poet José Iglesia de la Casa. His sonnet "To Nise Embellishing a Flower-piece" (*"A Nise bordando un ramillete"*) is among the best he did. MANUEL DE ZEQUEIRA Y ARANGO (Cuba, 1764–1846), like other Neo-classical poets, wrote didactic, heroic, and satiric poems. He succeeded, however, in his bucolic meters (we are referring to his ode "To the Pineapple" (*"A la piña"*) where he sings to the pleasures of the tropics. With trappings taken from mythology he composes a kind of fantastic biography of the pineapple, from its birth to when it is adorned on earth by Poma and Ceres, to when it is borne by Ganymede to Olympus where it triumphs among nectars and aromas and is celebrated by the gods. This artfulness, so typically Neoclassical, acquires a native, Creole emotion when the poet boasts with pride about the pineapple, "splendor of my country." He followed in the steps of Meléndez, Cienfuegos, Quintana. One of his most poetic inventions occurred not in his poetry but in his life when, having gone insane, he believed that his hat made him invisible. GRACILIANO AFONSO (Canarias–Puerto Rico, 1775–1861) translated Anacreon from the Greek and composed more or less original anacreontics.

The fable, that old moralizing and practical genre, was transformed in the eighteenth century into ideological discussion. Animals spoke like philosophers in the manner of the Spaniards, Iriarte and Samaniego. In Hispanic-America the genre and not the philosophy was imitated by JOSÉ NÚÑEZ DE CÁCERES (Santo Domingo, 1772–1846); DOMINGO DE

AZCUÉNAGA (Argentina, 1758–1821), skeptical spectator of the society in which he lived, who introduced animals and local matters in his fables; FRIAR MATÍAS DE CÓRDOVA (Guatemala, 1768–1828), the author of a notable fable, "The Attempt of the Lion and the Success of His Undertaking" (*"La tentativa del león y el éxito de su empresa"*); and RAFAEL GARCÍA GOYENA (Ecuador–Guatemala, 1766–1823), in whose thirty or so fables one glimpses certain ideas that were new in the Hispanic-American continent.

In the last years of the eighteenth century, satiric poetry, the anonymous as well as the known, is charged with the stormy air of social and political questions. Poetry acts as a barometer of the great changes that are impending. Satiric aggression was used principally by the defenders of traditionalism, who were losing ground against the advances of Modernism. But satire was also a channel of revolutionary unrest. The poems of derision were generally anonymous, but some names are preserved: MARIANO JOSÉ DE ALVA Y MONTEAGUDO (Cuba, 1761–1800) and his festive glosses; Father ÁLVARO MONTES DE OCA (Cuba, 1768–1848). The great influence on satiric poetry in America was Quevedo: his themes, his formulas, his language, his moments of appetite and glut for the world. A Quevedo disciple was ESTEBAN DE TERRALLA Y LANDA, an Andalusian who lived in Mexico and later in Peru where he satirized local customs in his ballads, *Lima Inside and Out* (*Lima por dentro y fuera*, 1797), a bitter work, showing disorder and displeasure. In *The Life of Many or a Week Well Employed by a Lima Dandy* (*Vida de muchos o sea una semana bien empleada por un currutaco de Lima*) he noted down day after day the emptiness of life. But whose? That of a typical fop? We suspect it was his own life. He was an egocentric who blamed the Creoles for his economic and social failures. He felt persecuted. What was happening was that he could not learn to adapt. He joined the Spaniards in their anti-Creole attitudes. He was not very intelligent and was blind to the great historic changes of his time. Let us finish now with occasional poetry (after all, poetry loses life when it becomes mere commentary on external and ordinary events; for instance, the enormous number of verse compositions to which the English invasions of Buenos Aires gave rise).

On the Threshold of Independence

Hispanic-American readers, with patriotic impatience, may wish that the distinctiveness and originality of their respective countries be presented and if that be the case, we may be reproached for the attention given to European styles and ideas up to now in these pages. But the study of literature, in order that it aspire to universal norms, does not need to pay too much attention to those characteristics of American society which might just as well be found in books on ethnography. The Europeans brought to the New World their wealth of culture; and though they adapted themselves to the environment and their children, and grandchildren, and great-great-grandchildren were Americans, European culture did prevail. Granted they live in a different historic setting from the European, but European influences never cease. The ties between the metropolis and the colonies are close. The lack of direct communication is compensated for by the idealization of the European culture which is not known first-hand, and by the desire to belong to the best-known culture. In the eighteenth century, for example, just when a more original expression of American experiences was to be expected (because the colonies now seemed distant from the first Spanish settlers and from the initial founding of cities and institutions) a new Europeanizing wave comes again to conceal the undeveloped indigenous culture. Constant waves of immigration, technical and administrative progress, commercial activity, movements of armies and navies, and the like, continue the cultural contacts initiated in the early years.

PART TWO

VII. 1808-1824

Authors born between 1780 and 1800

Historical framework: Wars of Independence, which end in the triumph of Creole arms.

Cultural tendencies: Neoclassicism and the first indications of English Romanticism.

Since history is pure flux, each of its periods is one of transition. In the period 1808 to 1824 the transition referred to in the previous chapters continues on: within the Enlightenment ideas become more liberal, literary forms more varied, and individual styles more emotive, but the Enlightenment itself is moving along new roads and, when least expected, it will be seen conversing with voices that are already romantic. Since shortly we will leave the Enlightenment and come face to face with Romanticism, it is fitting that we should do justice to the former. In the realm of action, the culture of the Enlightenment made noble efforts to regenerate Spain and its colonies. In the realm of ideas, it helped in getting out of the Scholastic quagmires and affirmed humanitarianism, liberty, progress, reason, and the study of nature. In the realm of literature, it achieved the virtues of clarity, order, equilibrium, and universality.

Neoclassical Liberalism

Neoclassicism was the literary face of the Enlightenment. But in Neoclassical themes, like that of Nature, for example, one notices that the writers go beyond rational limits and give us emotional vistas. Nature (once held suspect by traditional Christianity) is venerated more and more and is not looked upon as sheer mechanism (as by the rationalists), but as an organism with purpose. Another theme of Neoclassical literature was politics. From the old Latin word *liberalis* (befitting a man of free birth) comes the adjective "liberal," and precisely in these years the Spaniards and Hispanic-Americans, convened in the Parliament of Cádiz, hypostatize that adjective into a political concept. From here the slogan "liberalism" (already used by 1814) is coined to characterize the system of beliefs opposing the absolute power of State and Church. The political themes of Neoclassical literature were, then, those of liberalism. Liberalism was the political expression of the will to dignify man, which at bottom, implied the faith that man was capable of being dignified. Liberty and Progress were, therefore, the keys to the epoch. Liberalism vivified literature. Literature had often been a mere academic, rhetorical exercise for frivolous entertainment. Now the cultured minorities made literature a vital act. Neoclassicism, in this way, acquired new impetus. The intellectuals felt responsible for the liberty and progress of American society. Thanks to liberalism the poets, teachers, writers, and orators were able to give philosophic meaning to a revolution and a declaration of independence which broke out before the colonies were prepared for them. Though it is true that there were economic, social, and political forces that moved in that direction, it is also true that the Napoleonic invasions of Spain precipitated events and forced the colonies to improvise the emancipation. When the insurrectional movement begins in 1808 many of the intellectuals we have studied in the Colonial period are still living and writing. And there are also old or middle-aged men who first begin to write. But we turn our attention here to the literary contributions of the younger men.

Poetry

Neoclassical Poetry / José Joaquín de Olmedo (Ecuador, 1780–1847) wrote some ninety poetic compositions, few of which could be saved by a demanding reader. They cover a long period, from 1802 to 1847, with long intervals because his poetical capacity and even his calling would fail him. He was always a Neoclassical poet, imitator of the Greeks and Romans, and in his enraptured moments he was close to Meléndez Valdés, Cienfuegos, and Chateaubriand (whose *Atala* he versified in "Indian Song" [*"Canción indiana"*]); generally, he was in line with Quintana and Gallego. There are two of Olmedo's poems that rise above the level of his times, even beyond America. "The Victory at Junín: Song to Bolívar" (*"La victoria de Junín. Canto a Bolívar,"* 1825), and "To General Flores, Victor of Miñarica" (*"Al general Flores, vencedor en Miñarica,"* 1835). The historic importance of both events shook the poet Olmedo and impelled him to work with all the strength

of his art, a grandiloquent art not only for the deliberate imitation of
the eloquence of his great models but also because his soul tended to
the emphatic; and so we have the case of a poet composing coldly,
astutely, slowly, with much care and retouching, who achieves fiery and
stormy effects. Because of these odes Olmedo passes as an ardent and
vehement person while down deep he was sober, moderate, pensive,
sensible. Thanks to the correspondence between Olmedo and Bolívar
and the variants between editions, the genesis of the "Victory at Junín"
is known. It seems that Bolívar asked him to sing the praises "of our
latest triumphs" (although he urged that his name not appear). Olmedo
began to conceive of his poem when he was apprised of the battle of
Junín (August of 1824); but it was the victory at Ayacucho (December 9 of the same year) that inspired a grandiose ode, with Bolívar as
the hero, of course, but constructed in such a way that not only Junín
(where Bolívar fought) figures in, but also Ayacucho (where Bolívar
was not present). In order to unite the two battles in the same tale,
he turned to an old page in the epic book—a supernatural apparition
that prophesied, after the victory at Junín, the more decisive victory at
Ayacucho. It is Huayna-Cápac, the last Inca to rule over the undivided
Empire. The discourse that Olmedo puts in the mouth of the Indian
is typical of the humanitarian philosophy of the epoch. Olmedo did
not advocate the restoration of the Incas, far from it. But the men of
his generation (both Creoles and Spaniards) had worked up a sentimental Indianism which served to condemn the cruelties of the conquest and, while they were at it, agitate against political absolutism.
Basically, the chant of independence follows the liberal thinking of the
Spaniards themselves who, on the other hand, were sanctioning Las
Casas and writing historical novels and dramas with indigenous themes.

Another political characteristic of those years was that Olmedo (or
better, Huayna-Cápac) speaks of the peoples of America as "of one
family and a single people." The genuine feat—he says—is not in de-
feating Spain, but in creating an Hispanic-American federation of hard-
working and free provinces. Olmedo demanded so much of himself
that he became discouraged with the imperfections of his verses and
came to believe that he had failed. Nevertheless, "The Victory at Junín"
is one of the best odes in our literary history. His verses flow like
powerful waves of music, and the reader yields to the enchantment of
his interplay of sounds—resonant in verses like "the horrendous thunder
that in clamor explodes," soft like "in sonorous murmur and niveous
foam," always vivacious, light and sinuous. His was not empty eloquence. He unfolded his verse with solemnity and one fears that this

might end in mere pomposity, flatulence, and wordiness, but the surprise comes in the conciseness with which he has selected each word, each rhythm, each image. His is a verbal economy in a genre and style that tend toward extravagance. Olmedo expressed his feeling for landscape and thus the poem, epic in its inspiration, didactic in its purpose, quivers with lyricism. This lyrical accent was what was newest and what was most American. Once his fantasy was struck by a ray of color from the landscape, the poet would begin to elaborate his impressions, animate and personify things so as to convert them into storybook personages. Olmedo was the poet not only of the last wars of independence but also ten years later he was to poetize the civil wars. "To General Flores, Victor at Miñarica" is an even more accomplished ode than that offered to Bolívar because of its delicate sounds, its evolved and original images, the spontaneity with which the verses run and the feelings that are laid bare—feelings of horror at the anarchy and fratricide that were beginning to dismember the great and united Hispanic-America of which he had sung earlier.

Andrés Bello / Higher yet in literary rank was ANDRÉS BELLO (Venezuela, 1781–1865). His early education was religious though tempered by the tastes of the Enlightenment. He read the Latin classics with relish (at the age of fifteen he was translating one of the books of *The Aeneid*); he enjoyed Cervantes and Calderón; his knowledge of French and English opened before him a panorama of the great social and cultural movements of Europe. He stood out early because of his broad intellectual curiosity and his literary proclivities. His first poetical exercises are sheer probing. Traits from Horace and Vergil and from the Italo-Spanish school of the sixteenth century join the Neoclassical esthetics—prosaic, didactic, scientific—of the eighteenth century.

Poetry, urged by the ardor for construction, attempts to rectify the intellectual backwardness of the Spanish-speaking nations. And this patriotic, progressivist ideal takes all activities in tow, so that lyricism, too, drags along. His sonnet "To the Victory of Bailén" ("*A la victoria de Bailén*," 1809)—which Bello always valued among his better poems—closes the first period of his life. Then in 1810 he is off to England as an aide to Bolívar and López Meléndez, both delegates of the Caracas revolutionary junta; and he will pass his second period, until 1829, in London (the third will be his Chilean period, from 1829 to 1865). Bello had never been a revolutionary. He was more in sympathy with an enlightened monarchy. From 1810 to 1829 he was alone in London, in the midst of the splendor of European culture, and began the study of languages, literature, philosophy, history, sciences, law. It was the most fertile period of his life. In his *American Library* (*Biblioteca Americana*) he published the "Address to Poetry" ("*Alocución a la Poesía*," 1823), fragments of a poem that Bello intended to entitle "America." It is a Neoclassical *silva*, but within this tradition the poet sings with a new spirit. He invokes Poetry to leave the courts of Europe and to come to the nascent nations of America where nature and history will be more propitious to it. In the midst of the wars of Independence, therefore, the poet launches a program for literary independence. There is here an American feeling of nostalgia and love—above all, the feeling for an epoch just beginning.

The Hispanic-American armies were fighting in the name of liberty and progress against the despotism and the inquisition of Fernando VII horrifying wars like all wars (Bello was never a bellicose poet), but which opened the way for the creative forces of history. Humanity was shaking off the yoke of the past, and the battles in America were "instances of the great struggle for liberty, that was beginning." The universal triumph of that historic urge, although certain, was still far off. Enlightened in this way by the resplendence of liberty, America uncovered its beauty and was becoming worthy of poetry, a poetry whose voice, though educated in Europe, would sing of native themes. The "Address" of 1823 set an original course in literary history, not only of Hispanic America, but of Spain, urging poets that they not be led astray by rhetorical imitations. Bello profited by his classics and continued his study of them, but his purposes were new. Even his invocations to the Muses—so rhetorical—took on the value of an esthetic manifesto. Three years later he published in the *American Repertory* (*Repertorio Americano*) his *silva* "To Agriculture in the Torrid Zone" ("*A la agricultura de la Zona Tórrida*," 1826). It was conceived in the same plan as the "Address," but the poet could not fuse both *silvas* because basically they were of different poetic stress. The battles of Junín and of Ayacucho had ended the wars of Independence, and Olmedo had just poetized the events. Reconstruction had to take place. Let the people put down their arms and take up their plows. The theme of the glorification of country life as opposed to city life was a classical one; and the reminiscences of Vergil, Lucretius, and Horace are evident. But Bello has affection for the country, because it is the home*land* he loves most. His preachings, aimed at dignifying the populace, become dissolved in a genuine feeling for the tropical landscape. The Bello of the *silva* "To Agriculture" penetrated the road leading to the expression of an original America which he understood because it was his. His poetic language, nevertheless, resembled the traditional one. There was a descriptive-didactic school derived from the Romans, continued by the humanists of the Renaissance, cultivated by those Jesuits who versified in Latin, and enlivened by the naturalism of men like Humboldt whom Bello met in Caracas. The ideas of the Enlightenment also urged upon him prosaic and moralizing verses: peace, work, virtue, reconciliation with Spain, political unity of Spanish-America. It is to "agriculture," a practical activity, and not to "nature" as landscape, that he dedicates his poem. This is Neoclassical. But that abundance of images, that impetuous enthusiasm for description, that pride in American fruit and its indigenous names, that nostalgia saturating the entire poem, overflowing its moral and intellectual molds and rising in a lyrical tide, isn't this new to our literature? For this reason the images on American plants, which in the "Address" were dispersed, but in the *silva* "To Agriculture" are developed, enriched, brought into play with one another, acquire not only more beauty but also more meaning. This is where the poet crystallizes his rich vein of sentiment. As he pressed on to his own intimate and American world, Bello was approaching the Romantics. However, let us beware. If what moves us most in the "American *silvas*" is their lyricism, it is because this lyricism is closer to present-day tastes. But Bello remained true to his Neoclassical poetics and from that esthetic position corrected his own impulses. There are other poems that belong to this period: among the best, the "Letter Written From London to Paris From One Hispano-American to Another" (*"Carta escrita desde Londres a París por un americano a otro"*), a moral epistle to Olmedo in which Bello feels exiled not only from America but from the world; and in tercets rich in patriotic feeling, he laments what would become obvious in the years to come—that Independence had brought neither virtue, nor the dream of happiness. In London Bello cultivated the friendship of Blanco-White, Puigblanch, José Joaquín de Mora, and other Spanish liberals. Blanco-White, the leader, tried to have his friends break away from Neoclassical rhetoric. The example of English poetry, fresh, sincere, inspired by the beauties of nature, by folklore, by the simple life and by the immediate reality, had its effects. The first romantic budding in Spanish literature appeared, as a consequence, in *London*, but being a literature written by *émigrés* (and sometimes in English) it had no influence in Spain; therefore, it is not registered in literary histories. In any case, it was a Romanticism so different from that which prevailed after 1834 (when the *émigrés* educated in France returned to Spain) that it is not generally referred to as such. Bello could not be an exception to the change in literary tastes of the London *émigrés*. Romanticism in the English pattern must have influenced his description of the beauties of his land. Still, during his years in London he did not write Romantic poetry. Once he became established in Chile, in 1829, he published posthaste an article on the poetry of Fernández Madrid (fellow expatriate in London) and in it he referred to the new literary movement, that of the Spanish *émigrés* of 1823–a movement far removed from Meléndez Valdés and Quintana. But the Romanticism that caught fire in Spain was that imported from France. The liberals who had discovered in London the value of original poetry, devoid of imitations from French classicism, were displeased over this new Gallicization of Spanish letters. Their reaction seemed anti-Romantic, but in reality it opposed what was insincere in the new fashion. Bello understood the ideals of Romanticism, but he was prepared to resist the new mode. He denounced the fancy dress of the Gallicized Romantics. He translated Victor Hugo (as he had translated Byron earlier) and he even profited by the translation of the *"Prière pour tous"* (1830) in order to pour into it his own intimate feelings–the "Prayer for All" (*"Oración por todos,"* 1843) is an adaptation more than a version. Is it the old Bello translating the young Hugo, or is it the Classicist Bello paring down the imagination of the romantic Hugo? At any rate, in it one sees Bello in the midst of the Romantic current, but resisting. The same could be said of his translation of *"Les Djinns"* (1828) in "The Jinn" (*"Los duendes,"* 1843).

The arrival in Chile of the Argentinians Sarmiento, Alberdi, López –above all, Sarmiento–shook literary life violently. These Argentinians had learned their Romanticism in French books; and a polemic was kindled in which Bello appeared as a Classicist. Nevertheless, in his famous inaugural address at the University of Chile in 1843, Bello demonstrated that he was the most understanding of all. He had known Romanticism at its English sources–he was just questioning the superficiality of the improvisators. Mischievously (he had a fine sense of irony) he unmounted the Romantic springs and mechanisms of the machine and then mounted them again, demonstrating in this way that he understood its functioning. In 1846 (more or less) he fancied the Romantic fashion in a composition he called "The Fashion" (*"La Moda"*) revealing all its secrets. It is a poetics in reverse, noteworthy because Bello ridicules not from the outside but from the inside and understands completely. When Mitre went astray in his composition "To the Chilean Condor" (*"Al cóndor de Chile,"* 1849), Bello ridiculed the lack of logic in its Romantic style in his own "The Condor and the Poet" (*"El cóndor y el poeta"*). Proper construction was his law and for this reason his greatest achievements were in this line. He wrote legends (at least one, "The Outlaw" [*"Proscripto"*]) in the Romantic fashion. But this was not his forte. He was a civilizer, a master builder of nations. He was also a thinker and his last work, *Philosophy of Knowledge* (*Filosofía del entendimiento*), gives him a unique place in the philosophic panorama of Hispanic-America. Although in it Bello refers only to psychology and logic, it is sufficiently systematic to be incorporated in the history of ideas. Bello's thinking no doubt reflected European tendencies. He sought a deviation from what he considered the dominating philosophies of his time: the Scotch schools (Reid, Dugald, Stewart, Brown) and the eclectic (Cousin, Jouffroi). For this he profited from the lessons learned in the English philosophy that preceded the Scotch (from Hobbes to Hume, especially Berkeley). He gathered from eclecticism elements of Kant, and with the indications of positivism that was rising before him he proposed reducing the "powers of the soul" to intellect and will. He divided the study of the intellect between Psychology and Logic (he did not complete his system with the study of the will in two disciplines, moral psychology and its practice in ethics). All he said had already been thought before, but he thought about it again. And the energies which he exerted on these already-discussed ideas created a very personal shade of meaning especially visible when it is the philologist and writer Bello who is communicating his experiences. *Philosophy of Knowledge* is, in short, an exceptional Spanish book of those days.

More Neoclassical Poets / In Buenos Aires—as in other cities of Spanish America —the revolution of 1810 against Spain was carried on with Spanish political formulas (Jovellanos provided some of them); and in the first poems sung to liberty, resounded the Neoclassical ideals in vogue in Spain. There undoubtedly existed the will to create a new nation and to give that nation its own literary expression. But the truth is that when the themes of the war of independence were discussed in literary circles, these themes did not inspire a new poetry, but seeped into traditional poetic forms. A part of the great abundance of patriotic versification, beginning in 1810, was collected into two books: *The Argentine Lyre* (*La Lira argentina*) and the *Collection of Patriotic Poetry* (*Colección de poesía patriótica*). An examination of the verse production of these fifteen years barely saves several names from oblivion. VICENTE LÓPEZ Y PLANES (1787–1856), who had already documented in more than a thousand hendecasyllables "The Argentine Triumph" (*"El triunfo argentino"*)—triumph over the English invaders—now wrote a "Patriotic March" (*"Marcha patriótica"*), one of many that circulated in those days, and which was later converted into a national anthem. ESTEBAN DE LUCA (1786– 1824) also wrote a patriotic march, odes to Creole victories and to liberty in America, and elegies to the death of our heroes. His "Song to the Victory of Maipú"

(*"Canto a la victoria de Maipú"*) and his "Lyric Song to the Liberty of Lima" (*"Canto lírico a la libertad de Lima"*), though his best, are spirited only in their civic intentions. Neoclassical rhetoric had clipped their wings.

The man who raises himself above all this drabness and reaches a level close to the great Neoclassical poets of Hispanic-America (Bello, Olmedo) is JUAN CRUZ VARELA (1794–1839). His youthful poem "Elvira" gives him kinship with the erotic poets Cadalso, Meléndez Valdés, and Arriaza. Although in his early years as a poet Varela believed he would consecrate himself not to themes of blood, carnage, and wars, but to "tenderness, laughter, and amusement," he joined before long the chorus of patriots, and sang to the triumph of Maipú (1818), to the death of Belgrano, to the freedom of Lima, and so on. Rather than poetry, it was declamation; not even impassioned declamation but the cold academic type, typical of the Neoclassical period. From 1820 on Rivadavia, first as government minister and then as president, gave unity and impetus to the enlightened culture of his epoch, and Cruz Varela was to become the official poet. Whoever looks back to these brief years of the Rivadavia epoch will perceive a Utopian luster that was soon to be dulled by civil wars and barbarism. There was trust in reason as an instrument of public welfare. The life of the people had to be regulated and, in keeping with rational norms, progressive institutions of universal value had to be founded. Cruz Varela became the poet of Rivadavia's administration. Like all Neoclassicists he was a reader of Vergil (later he was to translate fragments of *The Aeneid*), and from the episode of Aeneas and Dido he wrote a three-act tragedy; or rather, an elegy, because what stands out in *Dido* (1823) is the sadness and death of the abandoned queen. Years later he wrote another tragedy, *Argia,* inspired by Alfieri and, like Alfieri, he disguised his hatred of tyrants in the old clothing of classical antiquity. The theater in the Río de la Plata area was then "a practical school of morals." The Society of Good Taste in the Theater (founded in 1817) intended to protect the public from the "corruptions" and the "absurdities" of Lope de Vega and Calderón. Cruz Varela's two tragedies lifted the Río de la Plata theater, but in truth contributed nothing that had not been done before in Spain. With his "Song to Ituzaingó (*"Canto a Ituzaingó"*) he returned to the war theme. But now the battle was against Brazil, not Spain. The poets of the war against Spain had become muted. Cruz Varela was the solitary figure; he wrote of the new enemy emulating Olmedo's "Victory at Junín." In 1827 Rivadavia fell; Dorrego was shot in 1828; and in 1829 a dictator who was to dominate the country until 1852 entered the scene: Juan Manuel de Rosas. Cruz Varela fled to Montevideo and there he died. A few months before his death he let his "swan song" be heard: "The 25th of May of 1838 in Buenos Aires." His political, civic poetry was vehement in its invective against Rosas. For the vigor of its images and for the repudiation of the sham Neoclassicists it is among the most original and moving that he wrote. His tercets run to the rhythm of the beat of his soul: nostalgia, contempt for Rosas, and the dignity of the defeated. He does not fling improprieties; he takes his leave melancholically.

Everywhere there is cultured poetry in Neoclassic form, of themes taken from the philosophy of the Enlightenment, at times mocking and satiric in tone, but always moralizing. Examples are: SIMÓN BERGANO Y VILLEGAS (Guatemala, 1781–1828), who was condemned by the Inquisition for being an "agitator of pernicious and seditious ideas," wrote fables, rondels, a "song to vaccine" and a *"silva* to political economy"; Father JOSÉ TRINIDAD REYES (Honduras, 1797–1855), the first poet to appear in his country, wrote some political satires called "whens" because "when" was the first word of each refrain. His patriotic poetry follows the line of Quintana. His best efforts were "Pastorals," versified theatrical pieces of popular inspiration. And JOSÉ MARÍA SALAZAR (Colombia, 1785–1828), a Neoclassical lyricist but author of an *Ode to the Death of Lord Byron* (*Oda a la muerte de Lord Byron*).

Popular Poetry / Alongside this urbane, cultured, academic poetry there was another one, closer to the common people.

MARIANO MELGAR (Peru, 1791–1815) was without doubt an educated mestizo. He had scarcely time to express his own erotic inspiration because he died at an early age; furthermore, part of his poetry was destroyed precisely because it dealt with love. Of what remained we can recognize the Neoclassical preferences: fables, translations and imitations of Vergil, and translations of Ovid. But, on the most sentimental side of the Neoclassic style, Melgar succeeded in two things: first, in singing to a love he actually experienced; and second, in molding that song into the short meters of the Quechua ballads. Melgar's "*Yaravíes*" are not poetically important, but that indigenous melody, which is both emotive and stanzaic, was something new. He launched a mestizo poetry which the Romantic poets later will carry through as they return to nature and native themes. Melgar, because of his vernacular tone—remember his *palomitas*, "doves"—is outstanding among other Peruvian writers of his time: e.g., the satiric poet JOSÉ JOAQUÍN DE LARRIVA (1780–1832), who, after having made fun of Spain, will make fun of the new republics.

Origin of the Gaucho Literature / The most significant outcome of the popular poetry written during the wars of Independence was the emergence of what has been called "gauchesque poetry" (*poesía gauchesca*).

The word "gaucho" appeared in the Río de la Plata region toward the end of the eighteenth century with a derogatory meaning: the gaucho was, among other things, the vagabond, knife-wielder, outlaw, and rustler. No doubt the term "gaucho" abstracted from the entire nomadic population of the plains those human traits which, because of their hostile resistance to civilization, alarmed the law-abiding citizenry. But before long the word took on a more favorable meaning. First of all the gaucho masses began to take an active part in the historic life of the nation, and from 1806, at the time of the English invasions, they demonstrated a sense of abnegation and patriotism; they understood the political meaning of the 1810 revolution and even came to the defense of the ideals of independence and democracy when some Buenos Aires groups were vacillating. During the military siege of Montevideo (1812) the Spaniards degraded the patriotic army by calling it "gaucho." Right then and there the word "gaucho" was adopted by the patriots in a new affirmative and defiant sense, as in the case of "Güemes' gauchos." The noun "gaucho" appeared incidentally in an occasional song or farce, but as yet it did not really exist in literature. The one who intentionally created that figure which will constitute a genre, the Gaucho literature, is BARTOLOMÉ HIDALGO (Uruguay, 1788–1822).

Hidalgo was not a gaucho himself, but both rural and urban characteristics coexisted within him as in all the inhabitants of the Río de la Plata region. He knew the man of the fields and was familiar with his idioms. Continuing the cult of the plebeian expression which came from the eighteenth century—something we have already pointed out in previous chapters, in our study of the sketch of customs, dialectal dialogs of the theater, and popular satire—Hidalgo decided to use the gaucho song as a form of political propaganda in favor of the independence wars. This is what had been done in Spain, as a national reaction against the Napoleonic invaders and their Spanish sympathizers, the only difference being that in Río de la Plata the figure was, naturally, the peasant and rustic man. It is not, thus, that anonymous songs of minstrels spread throughout the pampas and reached literature. In fact, what artistic value the genuine songs of the gauchos had is a matter of folklore, not of literary history. Concolorcorvo, around 1776, heard them and said "horrid ballads." Therefore, literature does not gather the poetry of the gauchos, but incorporates a tradition which has been artistically elaborated by cultured men who sympathize with the gaucho and sometimes address themselves to him, trying to speak his language.

What Hidalgo did was to create, with traditional literary elements, a literary gaucho. Hidalgo's importance lies in his being, if not the first, at least one of the first to discover in poetry the value of the rural Argentinian population. He brought into being a new literary form by using the melody of a popular dance—the *"cielito"* or "heaven"—the rural dialect, the dialogs of regional theater, and the social and political themes of his time. He succeeded in expressing the tone of gauchesque improvisation in his "heavens" (*cielos*) and "dialogs" (*diálogos*). In the verses of Hidalgo the gaucho is not a mythical minstrel, but a countryman who comments on the political realities of the wars against the Spaniards in a spontaneous, plebeian, and awkward style, which is new in the literary framework of Neoclassicism.

Assuming the attitude of the gaucho, Hidalgo poetizes the feelings of the country population in the wars of Independence and the struggles for liberty. In his "heavens" he sings of the militant ideals of the strife from 1811 to 1816 against Spanish power. Love for the fatherland, hatred for the tyrants; he encourages the gauchos to struggle against the partisans of Fernando VII. In his "dialogs" he does not delimit himself. They have as a background the years 1821–1822. Hidalgo contemplates the conflicts in his land and evokes the glories of the Independence with which he wishes to exalt the Creoles with the vision of their patriotic deeds. And because of this serious intent the "dialogs" offer us the best of Hidalgo. Note especially the "Report Made by the Gaucho Ramón Contreras" (*"Relación que hace el gaucho Ramón Contreras"*): part of its originality springs from the fact that we see the city and the independence celebration of May from the point of view of the gaucho Contreras—"costumbrism" but now complicated with the mirror-like conscience of the protagonist. Hidalgo immediately won the acclaim of the populace, both in the city and in the country. Two of his gauchesque works were published in *The Argentinian Lyre* (*La lira argentina*, 1824). In this first collection of patriotic poetry from the Río de la Plata, he introduced what appeared to be a humble invention, but which proved to be a revolutionary one, because it opened the way to an original American expression. We shall see how Hidalgo will have disciples and how his humble creation will be transformed curiously during the Romantic period.

The Novel

From the Mexican group of the period of Independence—ANDRÉS QUINTANA ROO (1787–1851), FRANCISCO MANUEL SÁNCHEZ DE TAGLE (1782–1847), FRANCISCO LUIS ORTEGA (1793–1849), JOAQUÍN MARÍA DEL CASTILLO Y LANZAS (1781–1878) and others—we will project the oldest and the best: JOSÉ JOAQUÍN FERNÁNDEZ DE LIZARDI (1776–1827). He started by writing plebeian verses (in general, satiric), which he printed in pamphlets to be sold in the streets. However, from 1812 on, he wrote prose works, wherein his talents came to the fore. He had been educated within the currents of the liberal thinking of the Enlightenment. He seemed to have been indifferent to the Independence, but his liberalism was authentic—the evil did not lay in the fact that the colonies belonged to Spain, but that its institutions transgressed against reason and liberty. He accused the Church for the ignorance of the people, he welcomed the abolition of the Inquisition, he attacked the vices of the powerful, and he insisted on the necessity for a radical social reform. The triumph of the absolutist reaction in Spain restored the Inquisition and Lizardi had to conceal his ideas, but he did not acquiesce. When the censor condemned his newspaper articles Lizardi decided to take refuge in a new type of literature. It was a fortunate decision. Thanks to it the first novel in Hispanic America appeared: *The Itching Parrot* (*El Periquillo Sarniento*), published in 1816 in three successive volumes (because of official prohibition, the fourth volume appeared posthumously). Why were no novels produced during the three-hundred-year Colonial period? We have already answered this. The fact is that suddenly the genre is born in Mexico, with the cries of a healthy and original child. It was born resembling its mother—the picaresque novel. There is a striking resemblance in its outward appearance: narrative in the first person, descriptive realism, a preference for everything sordid, successive adventures in which the hero goes from master to master and from trade to trade, sermons to make it easier to swallow the bitter pill. But the soul of the new offspring was different. Lizardi continues the optimism of eighteenth-century Rationalism; thus, in spite of appearing to be a picaresque writer in his descriptions of the bad customs of the city of Mexico, he did not create a *pícaro* or rogue. Periquillo is not a *pícaro*, but a weak character thrown among bad influences. Lizardi's achievement was to fill the emptiness of the hero's will with the social seaweed and rubbish left by the undertow of his time. Lizardi's affiliations are with the eighteenth century; therefore, his novel shows more kinship to the picaresque genre of Le Sage, Father Isla, Torres Villarroel than to that of the Baroque. Where can we place *The Itching Parrot* within the tradition of the Spanish novel? The national, satiric, and realist novel continues to be written in Spain from 1700 to 1808; however, from 1785 the new European novels of Richardson, Goethe, Mme de Genlis, and others were being read. But this modern, sentimental, and pre-Romantic novel would bear fruit in the following period, from 1824 onward. In *The Itching Parrot* there are sentimental episodes of this type, with the persecution of virtuous men, unfortunate women, sex accepted as a normal force, and so on. We should recall the story of Don Antonio (Vol. I, chaps. xix–xxi), or that of the ragpicker (Vol. II, chap. iv). From an overall point of view, however, *The Itching Parrot* lies within the realist tradition. It is a realism that does not take its themes seriously, but rather reduces them to the stylistic plane of the comic. The misfortunes that befall our protagonist are due to his incapacity to live in accordance with rational and virtuous norms. Periquillo is the sandwich man who moves about in Mexican society calling attention to the evils of that society. That is, he moves along the avenues of the ideas that Lizardi had on social life. Each chapter is a step in the development of a philosophy. The intention is to demonstrate that when a boy, weak in character and badly reared because of his mother's snobbery, falls, he falls into the miseries of a cave of thieves, a hospital, prison, the travails of a scribe, barber, apothecary. Lizardi aspired to something more than a description of society—he wanted to improve it. He was not one of the "enlightened philosophers" (those who broke with the Church), but a "Christian philosopher" (those who proposed reconciling Catholicism and liberalism). Unfortunately he was more of a moralizer than an artist and sacrificed narrative freedom. Even leaving aside his moral sermons, his aim at reform is so obvious that it appears in the very construction of the episodes. Let us recall in the early chapters the three schools Periquillo attended in succession: the first, with a good but ineffective teacher; the second, with an effective but bad teacher; and the third, a synthesis of all the pedagogical virtues that the author offers as a solution. This means that Lizardi does not deny that there may be paths open to good; but he does wish to show the grossness, the typical, the ordinary in the life of his time. This is the attitude of a depicter of customs, not a detractor of values as in the picaresque. We have given *The Itching Parrot* some consideration because of its historical importance, but Lizardi's masterpiece was *Mr. Dandy the Showoff* (*Don Catrín de la Fachenda*). Here he has learned the art of storytelling without being distracted by digressions. It does not have the color variegation of the vignettes of *The Itching Parrot*, but it has more of the novel—the action runs more gracefully from episode to episode, and is conceived in more proportioned equilibrium. He tells his story like Cervantes, whom he imitates—the end of chapter III where he abruptly cuts the scene leaving Tremendo and Modesto with their sabers raised, to take it up again at the beginning of chapter IV when they furiously discharge their blows, is a parody of the fight between Don Quijote and the Biscayan, also interrupted by the changing of chapters (a parody, in turn, of the *Araucana*). It looks back then to a picaresque past. But what is certain is that *Don Catrín* is of value for its novelty. Its theme is the life of a Mexican youth, well-groomed and of good family, who because of his ancestry, disdains honest work and as a consequence falls to the depths with the speed of a suicide falling from a tower. In his falls the poses he strikes are these: soldier, swindler, gambler, comedian, servant in a brothel, assailant, and beggar. The adventures are entertaining, and the irony with which they are narrated is among the finest in Hispanic-American literature of the day. The didactic intention is evident: the characters have symbolic names; the dialog is generally channeled along typical notions of good and evil, of intelligence and stupidity, of maliciousness and virtuousness; the threads of the plot, in their depiction of the reformist philosophy of the author, are interwoven in symmetries and in contrasts. In spite of all this, Don Catrín takes on life as a character. We see him; we hear him. We would recognize him if we saw him in the street. He exists. He is a type, we admit, but sufficiently concrete and individualistic for us to feel his presence as if he were a neighbor. In his death throes, with gaping mouth, Catrín remains faithful to his way of being.

It is possible that the reader of today may become annoyed at the constant intervention of Lizardi's irony in Catrín's autobiography. Although the story is told in the first person, the reader is aware of two narrative focuses: one is the protagonist's point of view, the other is Lizardi's, also seen through the protagonist, thus making for an ironic, squint-eyed view. This novel is also notable for its style which moves at the tempo of a yesteryear's nobleman but is, nevertheless, agile and youthful. Witticisms sound like phrases we have read in good Spanish literature; but they were not just added, they were born on the lips of the characters created by Lizardi. Artistically inferior are his other two novels: *Little Miss Quijote and Her Cousin* (*La Quijotita y su prima,* 1818) and *Sad Nights and Happy Days* (*Noches tristes,* 1818). In addition he wrote fables and theatrical pieces. His novels are the most original produced in America during the years that the colonies were struggling for their independence.

Also autobiographical, picaresque, and depicting social customs was *The Wandering Christian* (*El cristiano errante,* 1847) by ANTONIO JOSÉ DE IRISARRI (Guatemala, 1786–1868). He published another rough copy of a picaresque novel, *History of the Heroic Epaminondas of Cauca* (*Historia del perínclito Epaminondas del Cauca,* 1864?). He was a brilliant polemicist, conservative, monarchist, antiliberal, restless, untiring traveler, a rancorous personality, and a man of great human interest. He is also the author of *Satiric and Burlesque Poetry* (*Poesías satíricas y burlescas,* 1867).

The Hispanic-American novel anticipated the Spanish one in another direction —the historical novel. In 1826 *Jicoténcal* appeared in Philadelphia, by an anonymous author. It was the first historical novel written in Castilian in the nineteenth century. Its subject matter was American (the conquest of Mexico) and it preceded by two years the first historical novel by a known Spanish author. Is it legitimate to include *Jicoténcal* in a history of Hispanic-American literature? It has been said that its author was a Mexican. This is difficult to prove. His censure of Hernán Cortés is not inspired by Mexican patriotism, nor much less, by a pro-Indian spirit, but by the rationalist, humanitarian, and liberal ideas of the Enlightenment. The author, whoever he was, selected Tlaxcala as his setting and Jicoténcal as his hero, because this reality lent itself better than any other to his Francophile ideology. Tlaxcala becomes the Republic; Cortés and Moctezuma the despots; the young and the old Jicoténcals symbolize liberty, virtue, and reason; Teutila, innocence. Even American color is lacking in *Jicoténcal*—conventional landscapes, few indigenous words, barely a trace or two of local customs in the marriage ceremony of Jicoténcal and Teutila. It is a discursive not a descriptive novel, and the discussions interpret the events of the Mexican conquest in European terms. The author is more liberal than patriotic, more rationalist than Indianist. It is not a Romantic novel.

Offhand, there are no traits of Walter Scott. There is no storytelling; there is ser-monizing. Its sentimentalism derives rather from the pre-Romantic historical novels of France: Marmontel, Mme de Genlis, Mme Cottin, Chateaubriand. Sentiments are always directed by reason, more rococo than Romantic.

Sundry Prose

In the form of marginal activity several grandees wrote good prose, like José CECILIO DEL VALLE (Honduras, 1780–1834), framer of the declaration of inde-pendence for Central America and author of beautiful descriptions of nature; VICENTE ROCAFUERTE (Ecuador, 1783–1847), President of the Republic, who con-tinued writing while in office; and General José María PAZ (Argentina, 1782–1854), author of some excellent *Memoirs* (*Memorias*), written in a manly, plain, objective style, that were true to the military facts, and novelistic in the expression of strong sentiments of disillusion.

The liberal ideas of the Encyclopedia had wrought their influence since the eighteenth century, but the violence of the French Revolution, Jacobinism, and the general excitement, gave way to an irrational, sentimental, and therefore, almost Romantic element. Rousseau—one of the sources of French Romanticism—inspired the men of the independence. Miranda had read him; Simón Rodríguez, Bolívar's teacher, taught him; and SIMÓN BOLÍVAR himself (Venezuela, 1783–1830) was nourished so much by Rousseau that, without having been a writer, he is one of those who best represented him. Some of Bolívar's pages approach literature, like "My delirium in Chimborazo" ("*Mi delirio en el Chimborazo,*" 1824) or the pen-etrating glances of the "Letter from Jamaica" ("*Carta de Jamaica*"), or his pre-amble to the constitution of Angostura, his proclamations and letters. His genius for action bridled his Utopian imagination, and his prose trotted, spirited and checked, with beautiful gambols. But Bolívar was more a theme than an author, because the wars of independence were described in poetry; and Bolívar was the hero.

The Theater

The struggle for independence during these years particularly harmed the de-velopment of the theater. Let us focus our attention on MANUEL EDUARDO DE GOROSTIZA (Mexico, 1789–1851), a talented Neoclassical playwright of the Moratín school. Absent from Mexico since childhood, his work belongs to the Spanish thea-ter. Already he had produced his best works when, in 1833, he returned to Mexico. But his plays—for example, *With You, No Matter What* (*Contigo, pan y cebolia*) —which were performed in Mexico since 1833, without a doubt opened a new epoch of the theater. ANASTASIO M. DE OCHOA Y ACUÑA (Mexico, 1783–1833) who left the manuscript to a novel of sorts—*Alexander and Myra's Letters* (*Cartas de Odalmira y Elisandro*)—was a jocose poet and wrote two plays.

√ Pre-Romanticism

In this period we have seen the first Romantic sparks flying in the Hispanic cultural skies, wafted by winds from Spain. The words "ro-mantic," "romanticism" were already known as synonyms for picturesque, extravagant, absurd. What is important in literary history is the use of these words to designate a new esthetic current. And naturally this defining or characterizing use of the term is posterior to the existence of the new literary current. The word "romanticism," in this sense, belongs to the nineteenth century, but the literature to which it refers comes from the eighteenth. The concept "romanticism" as opposed to "classicism" is used, with complete awareness of its importance, in Germany from 1802, in France from 1816, in Italy and Spain from 1818, in England from 1823. These definitions were disseminated thanks to the efforts of August Wilhelm Schlegel. As we said when studying Bello, there were curious contacts between the liberal Spanish and Hispanic-American *émigrés* in England and English Romanticism. The English writers whom now we call Romantics constituted a group possessing a coherent vision of poetry, imagination, nature, and spirit. Their style, rich in metaphors, symbols, myths, at times obscure, mysterious and even mystical, was new. The mechanical conception of the universe is rejected in favor of the creative power of fantasy. The simplest and most humble aspects of the world are saturated with metaphorical light. With his songs the poet participates in the infinite and eternal forces of the universe. Nature appears as an animated, organic, living totality in such a way that the poet, as he celebrates its purpose, identifies beauty with truth. One notices how this Romanticism, seen in England and quickly felt by all other European literatures, awakens a new sensibility even in minor Hispanic-American figures.

JOSÉ FERNÁNDEZ MADRID (Colombia, 1789–1830), who was called "the Sensitive One," was one of the first to cultivate a poetry with themes of home, with overtones of meditation, and with feelings for nature which he must have read in England, because in France it appeared at a later date. He also was a reader of Chateaubriand. He had *Atala* staged in the form of a tragedy. With the landscapes of *Atala* in mind, he composed "The Mountain Rose" (*"La rosa de la montaña"*). English poetry not only was to the liking of the *émigrés* in England, but also to those living in the United States. JOSÉ ANTONIO MIRALLA (Argentina, 1789–1825), translator of Thomas Gray's "Elegy," had lived in both countries. Young and the false Ossian were other influences that arrived from England, directly and indirectly. It affected not only verse but also a type of poetic prose: ruins, tears, remembrances, solitude, melancholy, a nature convulsed by the anguish of men, become manifest even in discursive prose. In a university discourse JOSÉ MARÍA GRUESSO (Colombia, 1779–1835) gave definitions like this: "The murmuring of a fountain is the sweet smile of a nymph; the trills of little birds, the weeping of Philomela; the dew that humidifies the fields, the tears of Endymion; and the rustling of the trees, the sighs of the god of woods." He wrote poetry. "The Nights of Geussor" (*"Las noches de Geussor"*), in which he speaks of little "romantic" woods, derives from the *Nights* of Young. And, in fact, his friend Ulloa called him "the Hispanic-American Young." Francisco Antonio Ulloa (Colombia, b. 1783) wrote in an artistic prose in which the reading of Fénélon, Ossian, Saint-Pierre, and Chateaubriand can be detected. His sentimental letters were in keeping with the times: tears, tender friendship, kisses. He translated "A Night" from Ossian's poetry, and in a sugary letter he dedicated to Gruesso "those beauties worthy of sensible hearts and of sad melancholy that have drawn from your soul such tender and pathetic sighs." The literary phenomena just alluded to are not openly Romantic, but they prepare us for the coming of the new style.

VIII. 1824-1860

Authors born between 1800 and 1835

Historical framework: Dismemberment of the colonies into national segments; anarchy, rule of the petty dictator; struggles between absolutism and liberalism.

Cultural tendencies: Romanticism in two forward movements. From *costumbrism* (the depiction of local customs) to realism.

Following the example of all Europe, Hispanic-American literature became Romantic. Yet the conversion to the new trend was not as simple as one might expect. We have already seen how some earlier Neoclassicists ended by accepting the stimulation of the new esthetics (Bello). Now we shall see that the contrary happened: some young men went about still hanging on to Neoclassical skirts as if unaware of the change (Baralt). Along with these there were those who vacillated, now toward academic traditions, now toward artistic liberty, resisting the advance of Romanticism by feigning indifference, or by going along almost without realizing it (Heredia). But those who gave equilibrium to the period are those writers who were fully conscious of the new concepts of life, art, and history.

In the preceding chapter some allusions were made to the first indications of Romanticism: the propagation of Schlegel's definitions in Spain; the emigration of Spaniards and Hispanic-Americans to London, where they were witnesses to the new mode; the influence wrought by France. In this chapter France's influence will be affirmed. In effect, the first Hispanic-American generation of Romantics, who knows what it wants and acts in a polemical program, abandons its mother Spain and adopts France as its stepmother. This occurs especially in the more aggressive countries like Argentina toward the middle of the century. Later the Hispanic-American will realize that France was not a mother, but a good aunt, and will embrace Spanish Romanticism.

This is why Romanticism, speaking neither French nor English, but Spanish, arrived late to the slow-paced countries. European Romantic literature entered America already Hispanicized. It was not so much that French influence had diminished, since this was not to happen until the twentieth century, but that Spanish influence had increased.

We have then, two Romantic generations: the first is the one that gives significant works prior to 1850, such as Sarmiento's *Facundo;* the second is that which begins to produce after 1850, for example, the serial stories with which Alberto Blest Gana initiates himself into the genre of the novel. If, roughly speaking, we date the first generation according to the writers born between 1800 and 1825, and the second generation according to the writers born between 1825 and 1850, it will be evident that not all of the second generation will fall within the confines of this chapter. Here we will study a few of the writers of the second generation; and the rest, because of their long lives or because of their impact on literary development, will be placed in the next chapter. Because it was a vital, changing, expansive, and long-lasting movement, Romanticism cannot be easily enclosed within chronological limits. One could even outline more than two Romantic generations—doesn't Romanticism reach our own times, in continual transformations?

On the Threshold of Romanticism / The golden key that opens this chapter is JOSÉ MARÍA HEREDIA Y HEREDIA (Cuba, 1803–1839). As a child Heredia was already translating Latin writers, studying in them his first lessons on literary composition, and was imitating French and Spanish Neoclassicists. His elders were doing the same thing—translating and imitating. When he arrived in Mexico at the age of sixteen, the Humanism he found there had lost its spiritual force and had reduced itself to prescribing norms for art and to paraphrasing, without art, a past from which no one could receive inspiration. Heredia never forgot his apprenticeship in Latin letters—even in his poetry written at full maturity, in moments of great sincerity and lyricism, his verses contain classical reminiscences; hence, the reader will recognize in "my sepulcher shall not contain me completely" from "Poetry" the *"Non omnis moriar"* of Horace. He received his Neoclassical influence from the poets who revived the old school of Salamanca: Meléndez Valdés, the best lyricist of his time, Cienfuegos, Jovellanos, Quintana. He began writing in a literary gamut that extended from sweet and melancholy eroticism to social and philosophical poetry. Examples from English and French literature marked the right direction for him; and by translating and imitating Ossianic poetry, Chateaubriand, Byron, Ugo Foscolo,

Lamartine, and perhaps Victor Hugo (whom he never cited, yet whose works he possessed) he was able to tinge his own verses with imagination, melancholy, and Romantic anguish. This dolorous tone in his poetry is what is most valuable in it. His was the humanitarian philosophy of the Enlightenment: peace, liberty, justice, rational order, progress. He would meditate on and exalt these themes using the declamatory gestures of a Quintana.

When he returned to Cuba he conspired in favor of its independence and became an heroic poet. Nevertheless, his originality does not rest on his patriotic fervor, but on nostalgia—a more intense form of love of country. In him, nostalgia manifests itself in the evocation of landscapes and loves. His soul had the scar of Cuba on it. He had lived only for a short time on the island and for this reason idealized it. A feeling of absence and of being far away constitute the leitmotiv of his literature. He created innumerable verses to "the day of departure" from Cuba which was like one of those mental traumas from which one never fully recuperates. He suffered exile more as a lyricist than as a citizen. He did not feel "at home" anywhere, neither in Mexico nor the United States. The truth is that even in Cuba he was not happy. He loved his country, but he had no roots. Nothing could console him because he carried his unhappiness in his heart. The greatest impetus (if not in his life at least in his poetry) was love. His first love is a Cuban one, to be sure. He will never forget. It is a constant theme in his expression. It refracts and gives iridescence to conventional literary language, but one recognizes the force of that insistent ray of light: to love and not to be loved in return, jealousy, preference of love to fame, the desire not to harm one's beloved by tying her to one's own unfortunate life. The Cuban landscape is remembered by an enamored soul and, therefore, at a distance, the poet in exile evokes it as part of a tender love. Later circumstances were to bring him to write about the necessity of war against the Spanish oppressor (it has been mentioned that Heredia was a civic-minded, patriotic poet). But more powerful in his lyricism than that abstract notion of a free fatherland is his sense of nostalgia. Heredia was unadaptable but in his unadaptability he yearned for quietude. At times his theme of peace, developed as a civic virtue, uncovers in its harmonics the real feeling of the poet: peace, yes, but above all, that he be left in peace. This ideal of the tranquil life is as obsessive in him as is the love of women and the recollection of the beauties of his homeland; all this rises together before him like a mirage before a man lost in a desert, like the dream of a sad and solitary man.

Of all the poets of Neoclassical background, Heredia is the one who speaks most about himself. He was the most lyrical of all. After the critics had defined Bello as the poet of "Address to Poetry" and of the *silva* "To Agriculture," and Olmedo as the poet of "The Victory at Junín" and of "Victor of Miñarica," in order to maintain the symmetry, they had to present Heredia as the poet of "In the Temple of Cholula" (*"En el teocalli de Cholula,"* 1820) and of "Niagara" (1824). But an anthology of Heredia would be more extensive than that of Bello or Olmedo—he hit the lyrical mark more often and left several compositions as good (and even better?) than the two mentioned above. The poem that best situates Heredia in literary history is "In the Temple of Cholula," of which there are two versions, one from the 1825 edition and the more polished and augmented one of the 1832 edition. The melancholy, the sight of ruins, the comparison of the monument to the volcano, the musing over nature, history, and the feeling of time, point to a fresh imagination. The perception of each shade of color, of the outline of each thing, appears with extraordinary clearness; and yet, such precise description, which makes us feel as though we were endowed with another pair of eyes, is not physical: there is no exterior reality except that of the soul in anguish, which contemplates, feels itself alive, and meditates. Dusk is a movement of shadows in the intimacy of a consciousness that has escaped from its own time.

In his song to "Niagara" nature again allows itself to be penetrated with lyricism; the poet is astonished before that natural wonder, and of others even greater: God, Time. And in this expansion of the self, the desire for his beloved and the nostalgia for Cuba increases. Behold with what force Heredia breaks the Neoclassical framework of this poetry and gives vent to his (romantic?) emotions in "Misanthropy" (*"Misantropía"*), "Lovelessness" (*"El desamor"*), "On My Birthday" (*"En mi cumpleaños"*), "To the Star of Venus" (*"A la estrella de Venus"*), "Return to the South" (*"Vuelta al sur"*), "Deceits" (*"Desengaños"*), "Pleasures of Melancholy" (*"Placeres de la melancolía"*), "Hymn to the Sun" (*"Himno al sol"*), and "Hymn of the Exile" (*"Himno del desterrado"*)! When we say that he broke the Neoclassical framework of his poetry we refer to the rationalistic, didactic inner form of classicism because, insofar as it relates to the standards of versification, he maintains those of his epoch. If we expand the concept of Romanticism Heredia falls within it, because of the overtones of sensibility to nature, to ruins, to exile, to suffering. Heredia also wrote drama, criticism, and short stories. The best story is "History of an Italian Highwayman" (*"Historia de un salteador italiano,"* 1841). Even with a style of prose that trots under tight reins, it has Romantic force: the setting is in the Abruzzi, exotic to a Cuban; the theme, the Italian youth who becomes a bandit in despair of love; the angelic woman; the contrast between the purity of Rosa and the brutality of the bandit captain; the passion of the young man (who does the narrating), and the final act of wishing to be her first executioner since he had not been her first lover (symbol: the captain possesses her in life, deflowering her; the young man possesses her in death, planting a dagger in her heart; love and death).

José Joaquín Pesado (Mexico, 1801–1861) was a mediocre poet who never rose to great heights; yet he never wrote a poem that was really bad. There is dignity in his measured, slow, sure, correct movements. He knew a good deal of literature (he read Latin, Italian, French) and before setting up a verse he must have rapidly reviewed his readings. At every step we find reminiscences of the Bible, of the Greeks and Romans, of Dante and Petrarch, of Tasso, of Fray Luis de León. This is without counting the translations and imitations that he himself indicated. He was more meditative than lyrical, but his abstractions move so well within each strophe that they seem like cold children of his fantasy. Better than his love poems, "To My Loved One at Early Mass" ("A mi amada en la misa del alba"), are his sacred ones; and better than these are the sonnets and descriptive ballads, "Places and Scenes of Orizaba and Córdoba" ("Sitios y escenas de Orizaba y Córdoba"). Better yet, and of more significance to our literary history, was his collection The Aztecs (Los aztecas, 1854). Here he attempted to revive indigenous Mexican poetry. An Indian translated old poetical traditions of Nezahualcóyotl for him which Pesado transformed into Spanish verse. It represents the efforts of a cultured poet; for example, in his poem on the "Vanity of Human Glory" ("Vanidad de la gloria humana") one recognizes the Medieval notion "Ubi sunt qui ante nos in mundo fuere." But the will to poetize the Indian soul will appear more and more in Hispanic-American literature. In the cultivation of Neoclassical Mexican poetry, one might mention Manuel Carpio (1791–1860) together with Pesado. He was his elder in years, although his poetry came later. Other names will appear further on, at the point in our history where Neoclassicists and Romanticists encounter one another.

Of the three poets that Venezuela offers in the first years of the independence, Fermín Toro, Juan Vicente González and Rafael María Baralt (1810–1860), the one most addicted to Neoclassical tradition was the latter. His cold precepts, his cold verses, his cold historical depictions, his cold disdain of cosmopolitan culture, and his cold academic knowledge take the spice out of his work, and today no one is disposed to read it. His thinking was liberal; his literature, conservative. On the other hand, the other two poets harmonize the classical tastes of the classroom with the new taste for history, local color, emotions, and intuition and, therefore, are the forerunners for the younger Venezuelan Romantics, José Antonio Maitín and Abigaíl Lozano. Juan Vicente González (Venezuela, 1811–1866) cultivated the poetic prose that was being stylized in the eighteenth century; and in fact, his Messenianas are adaptations of the elegiac Messenianas of the abbot Jean-Jacques Barthélemy. He was also a historiographer of passionate prose, similar to his contemporary, the Argentinian Sarmiento, who had the ability to feel the turbulence of the masses. His *Biography of José Félix Ribas* (*Biografía de José Félix Ribas*) evokes, with violent depictions, the beginnings of Venezuelan independence. González skirts history and enters Romantic literature as an arm of the sea invades the land. FERMÍN TORO (Venezuela, 1807–1865) esteems Neoclassical literature enough to continue it in his anacreontic verses "To the Nymph of Anauco" ("*A la ninfa de Anauco*"). But his feeling for history, developed through his reading of men like Chateaubriand, brought him close to Romanticism. He was the first Venezuelan to approach the new esthetics so closely, while maintaining an equilibrium with traditional forms. He wrote an "Ode to the Torrid Zone" ("*Oda a la zona tórrida*") which was reminiscent of Bello's *silva* in more than just the title and had a greater capacity for wonderment before the legend and nature of America. In his "Song to the Conquest" ("*Canto a la conquista*"), also of classical form, the Indian is not only a spectacle but also a spectator, for Toro imagines him in the act of watching those who in turn are describing him. Unfortunately, his poem "Hecatonphony" ("*Hecatonfonía*") remained unfinished, but the cantos we have breathe the mystery of the Mayan ruins: "Each sign is a mystery, a problem, each ruin." "There is horror, sublime horror / in this region of awe." He carried this very Romantic feeling for the past to the historical novel. In *The Widow of Corinth* (*La viuda de Corinto*) he presented the struggle between Mussulman and Christian, although the tragic love he is relating is independent of the historical framework. In *Sibyl of the Andes* (*Sibila de los Andes*, 1849) he wished to exploit the American theme, but his efforts did not reach completion. Another novel was *The Martyrs* (*Los mártires*). He wrote "sketches of local customs" because it was the fashion—*Customs of Barullópolis* (*Costumbres de Barullópolis*). This genre descended from the eighteenth century carrying its rationalistic and didactic philosophy with it, but the moment comes when it sheds this burden and turns Romantic. Fermín Toro wrote a humoristic article, "A Romantic" ("*Un romántico*"), in which one can see that Romanticism was new to him. In describing a madman who recites evil and incestuous verses at midnight, Toro has him say: "I am a Romantic!" and then adds: "I was amazed; never had I heard that word"; "from that moment I tremble whenever I hear the word Romantic." Writers interested in the customs of different countries have left jocular portraits of this new human type, with his manners, gestures, and words. Romanticism, then, was a theme in the "sketches of local customs." Later, the sketches themselves will be Romantic.

Many of the patriots who had fought in favor of independence, or those who had expected great forward strides after the battles of Junín and Ayacucho, became quickly disillusioned. Hence, a critical, mocking, bitter, though not reactionary, literature emerged. Certainly reactionary was the implacable FELIPE PARDO Y ALIAGA (Peru, 1806–1868). His family, monarchist and haughtily aristocratic, had emigrated to Spain after the realization of Peruvian independence. There Felipe was educated, during the dark years of the despotism of Fernando VII. On his return to Peru, Felipe Pardo was displeased by republican institutions and liberal principles and attacked them furiously in the name of a decrepit order. He did not understand the meaning of the social changes of his time, and consequently his satiric verses, his famous rondels, his plays, his sketches of local customs have lost all of their vital significance, despite the skill with which he wrote them. He was against equality of races, against social justice, against political liberty. It was shocking to him that instead of a hereditary king—a Spanish one, naturally—

there should be as ruler a "czar of three tinctures, Indian, white, and black, / who governs the American continent, / and who calls himself the Sovereign People." He laments the law that sees as equals a white man of good family and "the black man who yokes up your oxen / and the one who irrigates your cornfields." In his satiric poem, "Political Constitution" (*"Constitución política,"* 1859) he ridiculed democratic citizenship. His education was Neoclassical: that of the "enlightened despot," that of rhetorical authorities. He began writing odes of an academic cut. He admired Quintana; on the other hand, he found sentimental "pastoral or bucolic" poetry annoying. His soul was devoid of lyricism. That is why he succeeded in his satire ("The Snout" ["*La Jeta*," 1834]) in didactic plays (*Fruits of Education* [*Frutos de la educación*, 1829], *An Orphan Girl in Chorrillos* [*Una huérfana en Chorrillos*], and *Don Leocadio*) and in his articles on customs ("The Mirror of My Land" ["*El espejo de mi tierra*," 1840]). He wanted to be caustic: "If my truths burn, so do cauteries, but they cure." But Pardo did not have remedies to cure the ills of an independent America—he believed in the colonial past. Instead of cauteries he applied vinegar to the wounds. His scorn at least permitted him to see the defects of the first republican period with clarity. These defects, it may be said in passing, were inherited from the Colonial period. His moralizing intentions are evident. His talent is evident. But he is lacking in the tenderness which gave greatness to the style of other writers of customs. He imitated the Romantic Béranger; he cited Byron; he paid tribute to Zorrilla in "a homage of admiration to the new characters of the Castillian poetry of this young priest of the Muses." But he was not a Romantic—his articles on local customs, "A Voyage" (*"Un viaje"*), "The Promenade of Amancaes" (*"El paseo de Amancaes"*), do not feel the fascination of the original landscape, nor the historical movement of the life of the people.

Of the same literary stature as Pardo, and in the same satiric vein, was MANUEL ASCENCIO SEGURA (Peru, 1805–1871) who wrote another type of sketches of customs, satires, and comedies. They were adversaries. Before all else, Segura felt the Peruvian reality as his own: "In spite of my misfortunes," he says, "I have not yet lost my attachment to the things of my land." With his mocking but understanding smile, Segura joins the historic march of his country: hence, the "national" quality of his literature. The dialecticism, which coming from Pardo's derisive pen was used to humiliate the Peruvians, in Segura fulfills the function of creating sympathy for the Creole. He is full of life, clear-minded, witty, fond of meandering and prying. While he is describing the customs of his time, he is constantly talking about himself, because although he may be laughing, he is part of what he is describing. He identifies himself with the people; he *is* the people. One of his themes is his own career as a writer—he tells us how and why he writes. He does not take himself seriously; although half-jokingly, he asserts that his writings follow "the spirit and tendencies of his age." His tone is conversational and thus enriches his prose with lively and capricious expressions. His epigrams do not become brittle. In his festive verse—certainly he was more festive than satiric— Segura showed facility in giving fluidity to his witticisms and in making them run in a variety of meters. "*La Pelimuertada*" (1851) was his best poem. But his theatrical pieces in verse give him importance in our literary history. One of the first was *Sergeant Canuto* (*El sargento Canuto*) of 1829. He wrote a total of fifteen plays, of disparate value. He is esthetically attuned to a range of plays from the farces of Ramón de la Cruz to the works of Bretón de los Herreros. *The*

Resigned Man (*El Resignado,* 1855), *Ña Catita* (1856), *A Toy* (*Un juguete,* 1858), *Episodes of Amancaes* (*Lances de Amancaes,* 1862), *The Three Widows* (*Las tres viudas,* 1862) laid the foundation for the Creole theater of Lima. To ask for deep dramatic conflict, new theatrical situations, fine psychological analyses would be asking too much. But the dialog incessantly crackles with mirth and imagination. In spite of a conventional verse and a conventional theater—monologs, asides, mechanical entrances and exits, and traditional intrigues—the characters are real. They are real as social types, not as individual characters, but at any rate, real. His works contain a popular realism, at times uncouth, like Ña Catita's intestinal discomposure, and at times they are written with the touching power of folklore, as Ña Catita squats to separate two straws that have fallen to the ground in the form of a cross: "Nothing . . . just that there's a cross here. / Don't step on it." Themes treated are marriage, the political shenanigans of Lima, the abuses of newspapers, factious military personnel, and the mania to enter the civil service.

In tranquil, correct, and elegant epic octaves JOSÉ BATRES MONTÚFAR (Guatemala, 1809–1844) released a throng of dynamic images at full speed. He knew how to tell a story, and the best he wrote were three spicy tales, "False Appearances," "Don Pablo," and "The Clock," grouped together under the curious title *Traditions of Guatemala* (*Tradiciones de Guatemala*). The plot is disclosed quickly and deftly; that his talent was primarily narrative is proved by the fact that the best passages are those in which the poet entangles his plot, and keeps us waiting, filled with curiosity, until the final disentanglement. But he was dynamic in other respects; for instance, in his imagination, which infuses even inanimate objects with movement, life, scope, and gestures. In "Don Pablo," for example, the dialog between the moon and the lamppost ("Now all reigned in peacefulness and repose, / now the moon was submerging in the West / and in the tremulous light that it cast / the dying lamppost bid it its last") is one of the innumerable lyrical notes in his poetry. The lyricism is in step with the narrative; it whets its voice on the jocular tone of the situations and characters described. Therefrom derives one of the effects (may we be permitted to say "*à la* Heine"?) of José Batres' verses; it seems as though the poet were ashamed of having uncovered his lyrical tenderness and, quickly interrupting himself, makes a wry face and laughs. This may cripple his expression. No doubt. But remember that the minor genre in which he wrote—humorous short stories in verse—was a crippling free-for-all in literature. Batres Montúfar was a solitary, timid, cultured, skeptical, ironic man. His good humor does not sound like a jester's jingle bells—it is silent, like an intelligent smile. The false values of the mealy-mouthed atmosphere in which he lived wounded him profoundly and painfully; but his heart bled honey. He criticized the hypocrisy, the ignorance, the violence, and the stupidity of the men and institutions of his time. His most woeful sentiments were expressed in poems like "I think of you" ("*Yo pienso en ti*"), an anthological gem. Also from Guatemala was the good poet JUAN DIÉGUEZ OLAVERRI (1813–1865). Although GABRIEL GARCÍA MORENO (Ecuador, 1821–1875), scarcely belongs to literary history, his political importance threw a sidelight on his belligerent activity both as a prose writer and as a satirical poet.

✳ Romanticism

Before presenting the different literary groups, let us take note of their general characteristics. Romanticism chose the closest wellspring, which was the ego and its circumstances. From this spring, flowing in a definite place and at a definite time, emerges a literature that wishes to free itself from the authorities of the past. More attentive to the voices of his individual life than to the counsels of universal reason, the Romantic writer feels himself to be the center of the world, but at the same time, a creature of that world. It is a vague feeling of harmony between the subjective and the objective that expresses itself in undefined effusions. Romanticism affirms free and spontaneous inspiration, emotional impulses, historical conditioning in lives of men and people, literature as an evocation of a nationalistic past and also as propaganda for a liberal future. In the Americas we will recognize in the children the faces of their European fathers. In America, however, cultural phenomena will arrange themselves in peculiar series. In the first place, the Creole Romantics lacked a great domestic literature. They did what they could to safeguard the few literary monuments they remembered, and when they battled for a new style it was because they had put themselves, mentally, in the old world. They joined the ranks of distant armies. At home there were no enemies: colonial works and writers could not impose norms nor dominate literary creativity. Everything, then, had to start from scratch.

Creole Romanticism was more a civilizing activity than a school of *belles lettres*. The weapons, no matter how literary they may have appeared, were used outside of literature, in the war between tradition and progress, Hispanicism and Europeanism, masses and minorities. In general, the Atlantic coast of the continent was more belligerent in its Romanticism than the Pacific coast. In the region of the Río de la Plata the colonial past was poor indeed and, as Bello observed in a letter to Mier in 1821, Buenos Aires was the city where the least reading was done. For that very reason they were not as conservative there as in Peru or Mexico: literature surged forth with the same impetus as the desire for national independence. Violence was evident in polemics and doctrinaire manifestoes that were lacking in other countries. While the Río de la Plata generation was more cosmopolitan than traditional, the Romantic models of the other countries were generally those of traditional Spain. Some of the Spaniards who visited or settled in America were promoters of their national literature: José Joaquín de Mora, Fernando Velarde, Sebastián Lorente, Juan Bautista Arriaza, García Gutiérrez, Zorrilla. Nor were the Hispanic roots weakened in those colonies that did not become independent, like Cuba and Puerto Rico, in spite of the growing prestige of French and English literature. A map of European influences in Hispanic America would show these names with frequency: the Spaniards Larra, Espronceda, Zorilla; the Frenchmen Hugo, Lamartine, Chateaubriand; the Englishmen Byron, Walter Scott; the Germans Goethe and Schiller (who were known indirectly); and the Italians, scarcely Manzoni and Foscolo. Not all Romantics knew they were Romantics. In order not to be confused with the traditionalist Romantics who looked to the Middle Ages in religion, legend, and egotism, there were many who militated within a social, democratic, progressive, prophetic, liberal, collectivist Romanticism and denied they were Romantics. Thus burlesque parodies by Romantics against Romanticism arose. These were quarrels between brothers and some of them renounced the family name.

The social Romantics, especially in the Río de la Plata, were shunning their Spanish past, defending the right to an American language, and promising a national literature, based above all on the new landscape and on the new way of life. Linguistic nationalism was more radical in Argentina than anywhere else. The Romantics of the ego as well as the Romantics of society imposed their terminology: meditative, horrible, fatidic, nefarious, somber, deliriums, ruins, or proscripts, lights, progress, socialism; and naturally, American words that designated native things of the land: neologisms, archaisms, indigenisms. The indifference to things Spanish and the admiration for things of other European countries and, above all, the penchant for improvisation had as a consequence the acceptance of many foreign words, especially French, into the language. The emphasis on emotion, the inaccuracies of thought, and the carelessness in writing left their mark on Romantic syntax. The preferred forms in verse were the sonnet and the ballad: in general, the ballad was preferred in regions where the cultured minorities were proud of their Spanish past: Mexico, Cuba, Colombia. Metric forms were enriched, especially in strophic combinations. In order to give variety to a composition and in order to diversify the movements of a theme, the Romantic poets mixed measures with notable frequency. Together with this polymetrics there were renovating attempts at unearthing or inventing meters. These attempts, if they were not far from those wrought by the Modernists at the end of the century, in some cases anticipated Rubén Darío, for example, in Gertrudis Gómez de Avellaneda, José Eusebio Caro, and others. With these varied meters poetry now can keep time with the off-beat palpitations of life rather than with the beat of ideas. Literary genres acquire new meaning. Many theatrical pieces were written but few were performed—nor were they of much value. On the other hand, prose displayed all its strength. "Beautiful prose thrusts itself into the future / and verse in obscurity lies dethroned!" exclaimed the Peruvian Salaverry in his sonnet "Verse and Prose' (*"Verso y prosa"*). He exaggerated, but certainly with Romanticism prose becomes literarily dignified in novels, short stories, newspaper serials, sketches of social customs, essays, memoirs, travelogs, and even prose poems. The sketch of customs, a reforming genre in the eighteenth century though in the nineteenth century it is in sympathy with local color, becomes dynamic and is converted into the short story. The local customs of these "sketches" enter into the composition of realist novels. Historical and romantic narratives were more abundant. Political novels were not lacking, nor were curious allegorical novels.

Within the vast repertory of themes in the world of Romanticism, the most typical ones in Hispanic-America were the natural landscape, human types, ways of living under different social circumstances, and history. In those countries having large indigenous masses there was an idealization of the Indian: an evocation of a distant Indian, of the pre-Columbian age, of the conquest, and of the colony. In Argentina, on the contrary, literature was hostile to the Indian. The treatment of the close-at-hand, real, contemporary Indian was not very romantic. In the nineteenth century there are few writers (González Prada will be one of the first) who see him as a social problem. History was cultivated with profusion in novels, dramas, and in prose and verse legends. Even a genre was invented—the "tradition," with Ricardo Palma heading a school of forty imitators. A strange aspect of Romantic historicism was the works—in their majority theatrical, although there were narratives as well—that presented episodes of literary life about characters who were real writers, e.g., Cervantes.

Argentinian Romanticism / We pause in Argentina because, unlike other Hispanic-American countries, it had a clearly Romantic generation. 1830 is the delimiting year. Until this year the educated men of Buenos Aires lived in the rationalistic and humanitarian "Age of Reason." The May revolution, the Independence and the first political and cultural organization of the Republic from Moreno to Rivadavia were carried on under the sign of the Enlightenment. From 1830 on, Buenos Aires received the influences of French Romanticism, and the generation of Echeverría, Alberdi, Gutiérrez, López, Sarmiento and Mitre is formed and is in agreement in justifying the total break with Spain, in expressing the original emotions that the American landscape will arouse, and in putting a liberal political system to the test.

Of the young men who had not become involved in the civil wars between Federalists and Centralists (known as *Unitarios*), but whom the tyrant Rosas had forced into exile, ESTEBAN ECHEVERRÍA (Argentina, 1805–1851) was the standard-bearer. In 1825 Echeverría left for France. At the time, he was twenty years old and had lived tempestuously, without having been ensnared in the rationalist nets that his teachers at the School of Moral Sciences of Buenos Aires had stretched out for him. Through what he revealed later in his writings, and from the information left by his friends, we infer that Echeverría attentively observed, during the four years in Paris, the synthesis of Romanticism and liberalism that was being produced precisely at that time. But of the rich canvas that France presented, Echeverría profited only from a few aspects. Between 1826 and 1830 important books appeared by Vigny, Hugo, Lamartine, Musset, Sainte-Beuve, Dumas. But more than these Frenchmen, it was the English and German who had influenced them, who oriented Echeverría's tastes. He studied the philosophy of history and society which, evolving from the German historical school from Herder to Savigny, lent new accents to the French thought of Leroux, Guizot, Lerminier, Cousin, and others. Echeverría left Paris, if not educated by Romanticism, at least with his mind sharpened by his Romantic readings. By then he had projected two Romantic formulas upon the Argentinian reality: political liberalism, which came to justify the break of the American colonies with Spain and advocated the continuance of the revolutionary line of May, 1810, and artistic sympathy toward the way of life of the people, which exposed him to the possibilities of an autochthonous literature based on the historical and geographical peculiarities of the pampas. Although the first formula was the more significant in the history of political ideas of Argentina, in a literary history we are obliged to refer only to the second. He had no calling nor genius for poetry. He fulfilled, nevertheless, the function of a forerunner in the external history of our literature. *Elvira, or the Argentine Bride* (*Elvira, o la novia del Plata,* 1832) was the first seedling transplanted directly from France, independent of Spanish Romanticism; *The Consolations* (*Los consuelos,* 1834) was the first volume of verses edited in Argentina; "The Captive," one of the compositions in *Rhymes* (*Las rimas,* 1837) was the first work that displayed with skill the aim of a poetry that looked to the landscape, tradition, local color, the people, and history. The young set, dissatisfied with academic "good taste," became enthused with Echeverría. They believed that with "The Captive" ("*La cautiva*") national literature had been established. Its simplicity sounded like sincerity to them; its emotional abundance, poetical richness. This consecration no doubt flattered Echeverría. His life had been difficult—it would be so to the very end. He was poor, sickly, tormented. These were his misanthropic years; and the literary reputation he earned from 1832 to 1837 must have alleviated his sadness. But, as his friend Gutiérrez noted, he felt more like the "hero of a novel," and reputation was not enough—glory, glory, and nothing else! "I renounce reputation," he wrote to Gutiérrez in 1836, "glory, yes, I would want if it were given me . . ." Today Echeverría is one of the glories of Argentine history, not because of his verses, but because he put his reputation as a versifier—that reputation that he renounced—to the service of the political regeneration of his country. Because of his literary reputation, young men followed the battle standard that he had once raised. From then on his prose works would surpass his poetry. He was, indeed, a better prosist than a poet; for this reason, *The Slaughter-House* (*El matadero*, 1837–40) takes a place of honor in literary history. It is a sketch of customs of extraordinary realist vigor, differing from what had been written earlier because of the intensity of its pathos and climax. As a sketch of customs it has a political and reformist purpose: to expose the despicable rabble that supported Rosas. But suddenly certain figures take on life and the sketch becomes a story. Then, in spite of the muckiness of the description, the Romantic outlines become clear: the contrast between the horrifying note of the child whose throat is cut and the humoristic note of the Englishman knocked down in the mud; a feeling for the "picturesque" and the "grotesque"; an aura of misfortune, fatality, death; the literary beautifying of the ugliness of the riffraff by comparing it with extreme ugliness; the curious spectacle of hundreds of "African" Negroes; the presentation of the young "Centralist," the gallant hero who loudly hurls challenges at society, in counterpoint as in a melodrama with musical background of guitars and popular song, and who, before he can be assaulted, dies of indignation, bursting into "rivers of blood." In other, more serene prose writings, Echeverría left his lucid road signs that led out of the mire in which "federals" and "centralists" were having their disputes. Echeverría had a serious plan. Aware of the respect in which he was held, he decided to rally all youths around a clear doctrine. Thus was constituted in 1838 the Young Argentina or the May Association which branched out quickly throughout the remotest corners of the country. Thanks to Echeverría and his May Association, Argentine Romanticism distinguished itself within Hispanic-American literature, in the form of a well-rounded generation. Romantic voices made themselves heard here and there through all Hispanic-America; only in Argentina however, in the decade of 1830, did a generation of young Romantics, educated by the same books, tied together by the same vital attitude toward historical reality, arise. Witnesses to the calamities of their fatherland, they were friends who, in their assiduous personal associations, concurred in fundamental points of view, worked and talked together in clubs and newspapers, and while sounding the death knell of past norms, expressed the repertory of their own yearnings in a new style. Echeverría imposed upon them their initial discipline. The work they accomplished is amazing. Argentina has never again had such a group of men thinking in great concepts.

In addition to Echeverría, some of the most important authors in Hispanic-American literature came from this group: Sarmiento, Mitre, Alberdi, Gutiérrez, López. To these names can be added the best lyrical poet of those years: Mármol, another exile from Rosas, unattached to the Association but personally associated with the members. Furthermore, Argentinian exiles brought their Romantic ideals to Uruguay and to Chile, and from there launched forceful literary movements. As important as was the purely literary contribution of this generation—novels, dramas, poems, essays, sketches of customs, history—it cannot be abstracted from political action. That philosophic thought be applied to social reality and literature be employed in the service of justice is characteristic of Hispanic-American culture. These Argentinian writers who banded together in 1838 will formulate the Constitution, will become members of Parliament and ministers and, at least two, Mitre and Sarmiento, will become presidents of the Republic.

When Echeverría returned from Paris laden with novel ideas, JUAN BAUTISTA ALBERDI (Argentina, 1810–1884) was among those who understood the Romantic writers most lucidly. The capacity to understand was his forte. He was more or less cold, reflexive, observant, careful, adaptable, and more understanding toward Romanticism than enthusiastic. He signed articles on local customs with the pseudonym of Figarillo. The truth is that Fígaro [Larra] had an influence on all Argentinian Romantics. Perhaps Larra is the only Spanish writer who figures in the spiritual formation of this group, otherwise so attentive to France. Once in Montevideo, Alberdi continued to cultivate this type of critical, mordant, and moralizing literature: not only sketches of customs, but also theatrical pieces, which are valuable not for their art, but as documents of his political activity. In reality, the figure of Alberdi was growing in political and not literary stature, and his most important writing, *Bases* (*Las bases*), which had a decisive influence on the spirit of the framers of the Constitution of 1853, for example, does not belong in this history. More interesting, literarily, is what Alberdi wrote when he became enmeshed in a merciless polemic with Sarmiento. Alberdi's *Letters from Quillota* (*Cartas Quillotanas*) and Sarmiento's *One Hundred and One* (*Ciento y una*) barely clarify their respective points of view on national organization—basically they were in agreement. But in their personal antipathies they expressed themselves with such vehemence that at times their letters took on literary value: above all, those of Alberdi—who never was as good a writer as Sarmiento—because they displayed his fencing skill in polemics. His long absence, since 1838, had weakened his grip. From Europe his thrusts were no longer hitting the mark. He was only successful in theoretical works. But the work written in those years that most merits attention here is his *Daylight's Pilgrimage* (*Peregrinación de Luz del Día*), an allegorical novel on Argentine politics. Truth (i.e., Daylight) escapes from the horrors of Europe in 1870 and expects to find honor, tranquility, and decorum in the New World. Daylight scarcely disembarks in Buenos Aires when he comes across his old enemies, who also had fled Europe in order to settle in South America: the hypocrite Tartuffe (Molière), the intriguing Basilio, and cynical Figaro (Beaumarchais), the rogue Gil Blas (Le Sage), the seducer Don Juan (Tirso). He will also meet Don Quijote, Sancho, etc. While arguing with them, Daylight, chagrined, discovers that the Argentina of Sarmiento, who was president at the time, had betrayed the ideals of liberalism. This allegorical novel, showing signs of improvisation and defects of a writer who had not cultivated himself as such, but containing a few aphoristic phrases of great strength, can amuse one who is interested in the clues and can recognize the allusions to the political scene of those days; as pure literature, it will put one to sleep. In it Alberdi lost his coldness and, disillusioned by the liberals, expressed with original images and ingenious phrases his morose feeling as an exile. Unfortunately, he did not sufficiently elaborate his allegory, which even lacks unity. Rather than a novel, it is the outline of a novel. It is read painfully, or at least with yawns, because one keeps stumbling over masses of rubbish. But it has the merit of not resembling anything written during this period.

Alberdi's most intimate friend was JUAN MARÍA GUTIÉRREZ (Argentina, 1809–1878), a student of literature more than a writer. When he wrote his poems, sketches of customs, and novels, he put more care in his expression and this immediately set him aside from the disorderliness of his colleagues. His attitude was one of respect for the literary past, an attitude which was to change him eventually into a historian and critic of literature, as can be seen in the stamp of Neoclassicism which still marks him. The volume of his *Poems* (*Poesías*, 1869) leaves no doubt that its author was addressing himself to a cultivated public—he was aiming high. He wrote sketches of customs; his best known, "The Ant Man" ("*El hombre hormiga*," 1838), is not noteworthy. But noteworthy was *The Captain of the Patricians* (*El capitán de patricios*), an idyllic novelette written with all the Romantic formulas of a tearful literature: an ideal love in a paradisiacal San Isidro, the summer-resort town near Buenos Aires, between an angelic lady and an archangelic patriot, interrupted tragically by the wars of independence. Yet, Gutiérrez' imagination does cut a swath in all that borrowed material and does manage some lyrical raptures that are surprising for having been written in those days. Although published in 1874, it had been written in 1843. Amidst the alluvium of sketches of customs that covered Hispanic-America, the majority of which were coarse and unpolished and always realistic in style, the poetic prose of *The Captain of the Patricians* had the merit of putting forth an aristocratic ideal of expression. The fact that poetic language ages quickly does not subtract from its merit: whoever has sufficient literary education can salvage sincere lyrical expressions from outmoded styles. Gutiérrez was a man of exceptional intelligence, but one who consumed himself in an obscure task: to present and study the then immature

Hispanic-American literature. There can be no great critic without a great literature. And Gutiérrez, who had an extraordinary aptitude for criticism, could not surpass the stature of the literature to which he dedicated himself.

BARTOLOMÉ MITRE (1821–1906) is another of those Argentinians of this same generation who exalted the country through his great deeds, but who sacrificed his literary talent to action. His youthful *Rhymes* (*Rimas,* 1854), his drama, *Four Eras* (*Cuatro épocas,* 1840), his novel, *Solitude* (*Soledad,* 1848), and his essays on literary criticism give evidence of Mitre's multiform talents. Nevertheless, his best contribution to the field of letters is his historical works.

Domingo Faustino Sarmiento / When in 1838 some of the young men who had studied in Buenos Aires returned to San Juan with the books in fashion—books by Lerminier, Leroux, Cousin, Sismondi, Saint-Simon, Jouffroi, Quinet, Guizot—DOMINGO FAUSTINO SARMIENTO (Argentina, 1811–1888) allowed himself to be infused with the new current of ideas. But Sarmiento's originality rests in his having intimately fused the Romantic philosophy of history with the intuition of his own life as part of that history. He felt that he and the nation were one and the same creature, compromised to an historic mission within the process of civilization. Owing to this, his writings, since they are always political acts, have a peculiar autobiographical tone. In his first autobiography, *My Defense* (*Mi defensa,* 1843), forged in Chile like a weapon, Sarmiento shows himself fighting with all his might against poverty, backwardness, ignorance, violence, injustice, and anarchy. His phrases are refracted into two beams: one that illuminates the impulse of creative will, and the other the inertia of adverse circumstances. The reader will quickly notice that this polarization has a philosophic meaning: it alludes to the conflict between spirit and matter, liberty and need, history and nature, progress and tradition. And, in fact, when Sarmiento passed from feeling his own personal life to interpreting the public life of Argentina, the confidential material of *My Defense* was converted into a political formula: "civilization and barbarism." *Civilization and Barbarism: Life of Juan Facundo Quiroga* (*Civilización y barbarie: Vida de Juan Facundo Quiroga,* 1845) is not history, nor biography, nor novel, nor sociology—it is the vision of a country by a young man anxious to act as a transforming force from within. "The evil that afflicts the Argentine Republic is its extension," he says. The cities are islets of civilization; the pampa envelops them and engulfs them like a sea of barbarism. From the countryside come the gauchos, knife in hand: they are simply savage manifestations of nature, without any historic initiative. The men of the city are those who promote progressive phases in the operation of civilization. In this setting, and with these actors, the political drama from 1810 has taken place in two acts: (1) the May Revolution and Independence stood for the struggle of European and liberal ideas that settled in the cities against the absolutism of a Spain that no longer created spiritual values but ruled with the weight of tradition; (2) then anarchy takes over because, from the immense plains of the country, resentful hordes are loosed upon the cultured cities. Argentina, says Sarmiento, is dominated by such somber figures as Juan Facundo Quiroga and Juan Manuel de Rosas. With Facundo dead, Rosas must be overthrown. But that would not be sufficient. After all Rosas is only an incarnation of this barbaric reality. It is reality itself that must be transformed. Now the author turns to the public and proposes a political program of national reconstruction: public education, European immigration, and technical-economic progress. This dialectic was so simple that Sarmiento himself found it insufficient, and as he went along in the book, he had to complicate it with paradoxes, omissions, and reservations that come to contradict his thesis. The countryside was not so barbaric; the cities were not so civilized. Furthermore, Sarmiento sympathized esthetically with the gaucho customs that in the name of political principles he disdained. "Facundo and I have affinity," he once exclaimed. And the intellectual gaucho that was Sarmiento— "I am Doctor Montonero, the mobster Doctor," he said on another occasion—deep down commiserated with the other real gaucho, Facundo, his brother Cain. Within the dynamic scheme with which Sarmiento gave meaning to his perception of the country—civilization against barbarism —the terrible shadow of Facundo took on a powerful artistic reality because he was not simply a rhetorical theme, but a pathetic presence in Sarmiento's bosom. In this sense Facundo is an imaginary creation of Sarmiento. He impresses us as a living personage precisely because what gives him life is the fantasy of the author. And the exaggerated strokes with which Sarmiento paints the criminality, lasciviousness, courage, and primitivism of Facundo do not come just from the political intention of denigrating him, but also because, for the Romantic Sarmiento, all of nature, including Facundo, was shaken by something tremendous, fascinating, and catastrophic; and as Sarmiento became apprehensive before this horrendous mystery of barbarism he gave his piece a tremolo of melodrama. Nevertheless, his Facundo, with all the fantastic and exaggerated elements that one could wish for, was real.

Subsequent investigations have rectified some of the details of the picture; even Sarmiento corrected himself several times. But it is essentially what he saw in 1845. In *Facundo*, Sarmiento revealed his literary talent. This was even more apparent in the epistolary book that followed, *Travels* (*Viajes,* 1845–47), because here the pleasure of narrating was greater than political motivation. These letters are so imaginative that they are considered among the best prose of the time. At each step they take us by surprise with their sharpness of observation: they have merit as sketches of customs and landscapes of France, Spain, Africa, Italy, and the United States. Even more surprising than the observations made is the observer who is making them. In no other book does Sarmiento's soul open so widely and deeply, with his enthusiasms and depressions, his solemnity as a prophet, and his humor. He feels like an actor in the world he is describing; his letters, then, are the fragments of a virtual novel. Further, they carry an implicit philosophy of history. Not only did he have the gift for metaphor, which rendered his intimate self into concrete images, but also for abstraction, which elevated minutiae to universal categories. On the road of civilization, Sarmiento tells us, nations run, become tired, sit in the shade to doze, or else strike out with a desire to arrive before the others. They are like people. And what matters is not what they have been in the past, but the impulse they carry. Sarmiento becomes disillusioned with Europe, which is too quiet, and proposes as a model the civilization of the United States, which advances with the strides of a giant and promises political liberty and economic well-being. His memoirs in *Provincial Memories* (*Recuerdos de provincia,* 1850) continue those in *My Defense.* But eight very intensive years have transpired. His rovings through Europe and the United States have given him a favorable perspective from which to understand Spanish America. Now he is more man, more writer. He is conscious of his mission and addresses a public that will survive him. His style is more personal. He writes his memories not only from the political need to answer Rosas' calumnies with a self-portrait that reveals him superior to Rosas, but also to abandon himself to the sweetness of the evocative tone. He looks around him and sees a procession on the march—it is the march of civilization on Argentinian soil. He mixes with the multitude. And what a pleasure it is for him as he recognizes his own family in that great dispersion of people driven on by the good spiritual wind! In his rich, full, and colorful experience of an "I" excited by the commotions that come down from the past, there is also the consciousness of a providential mission to fulfill. He lived not only his own individual life, but also the life of the people, of mankind, and even of God, inasmuch as from Sarmiento's point of view history was the development of a divine plan and he felt himself an agent of history. In 1851 Sarmiento left Chile to join Urquiza's army, which in the Battle of Caseros

(1852) defeated Rosas, and thus began a new cycle in Argentine history—that of organization. Disillusioned with Urquiza whom he only partly understood, Sarmiento left Argentina. Once in Chile he wrote the *Campaign of the Grand Army* (*Campaña en el Ejército Grande*, 1852), another of his good books, which is pleasant as the intimate diary of a novelist, despite the disorderly mixture of documents, anecdotes and personal effusions. What he wrote later—discourses, commentaries, proposals, and pamphlets which fill several volumes of his works—is less valuable. It is understandable. From 1862, which is the date of the unification of Argentina, to 1880, which is the date on which the city of Buenos Aires becomes the federal capital, Sarmiento is seen in the role of governor. His judiciousness as a governor was less inspiring than his passion as an expatriate.

A new group, the "men of 1880," is beginning to receive the influence of new cultural ideas. They are reading Darwin, Spencer, Taine. Now it is believed that the methods of the natural sciences can explain even spiritual phenomena. Sarmiento had always been a fancier of the spiritual goals of history. But, from having insisted so much on practical results, his Romantic way of thinking was becoming more and more empirical and arrived at a meeting ground with positivism which offered a mechanization of the concept of historical evolution. When at the height of his life Sarmiento wanted to organize his ideas on history in a systematic way, he wrote the outline of a positivist book: *Conflicts and Harmonies of the Races of America* (*Conflictos y armonías de las razas en América*, 1883). It is the last and the worst of his sociological works, because of the scientific pretentiousness of its disconnected verbiage. The thesis—if there is one—is the racial inferiority of Hispanic-American society. Intuitive ardor was his forte, not science. He would set upon reality, enraptured, and attack it from within with such a will to possess it, to personalize it, to change it, that when he sought to describe it, he realized that he was both subject and object. For this reason his style is autobiographical and his autobiographies are national histories. Sarmiento only used to write when he had something to say. His habits were those of the journalist and not the writer. Occupied with many tasks simultaneously, his manipulation of words was another way of working. They struck like waves. And if they seemed to withdraw somewhat abated, it is as the undertow of the sea, which quickly returns and with greater impetus. He reaches expressive fullness effortlessly; and even in his moments of carelessness his creative genius spills over.

The Historical Novel in Argentina

Another important person in the group exiled by Rosas was VICENTE FIDEL LÓPEZ (1815–1903). In his *Autobiography* (*Autobiografía*) he tells how, as of 1830, there was in Buenos Aires "a torrential ingress of books and authors that had never been heard of before. The works of Cousin, of Villemain, of Quinet, Michelet, Jules Janin, Merimée, Nisard, moved among us producing a fantastic following of new ideas and preachments about Romantic, classical, eclectic, Saint-Simonist schools and writers . . ." López gave himself, body and soul, to the study of the philosophy of history. With this preparation he wrote a historical novel on the effects in Lima of Francis Drake's piratical expedition of 1578 and 1579: *The Heretic's Bride* (*La novia del hereje*). In his epistolary prolog of 1884 he says he wrote the novel at the age of twenty-five (that is, in 1840) and that he published it later as a serial in a Chilean newspaper. In the same epistolary prolog he expounded the Romantic conception of the historical novel better than anyone of his Hispanic-American generation. Its point of departure was a profound understanding of the historical nature of man. Our existences are fixed in the framework of time: a past clings to our backs, and with it we move out into the future. In addition to existing, we coexist with our society. If one human action affects the collective development, we call it historical. But certainly every action, no matter how private it seems, is historical, since we are at every moment subjects of history, agents of a spiritual process. What we know from documentary evidence of the past helps us to imagine that which we cannot know, but which we can intuit vividly—all human drama being one. The novel, containing what we know and what we can imagine, saves the past. There is, therefore, no conflict between actual deeds and the atmosphere with which our fantasy envelops them. With this theory, López wrote one of the most interesting historical novels of Hispanic-American Romanticism. He puts into motion the pendulum of Spain in the sixteenth-century world and describes her colonizing enterprise in Lima: rivalries between the Church and State and between the various religious orders, the Inquisition, customs of the middle class and of the aristocracy, the attitude of the Spaniards toward the English Protestants, peculiarities of the coastal seamen and of the homosexuals of Lima. His point of view is that of a liberal nineteenth-century Creole who makes use of colonial literature, like Centenera's poem, but who has respect for the apologias furnished by English letters on behalf of Drake and other pirates. López conceded more attention to the novelistic than to the historical. His interest lies in the narrative, integrated in the historical; the narrative is not the rear guard or the appendix to history, but has a dignity of its own. Oxenham's raid is historical, but its purpose—the seizing of two women—is novelistic. As in Walter Scott, the historical personages (Drake, Oxenham, the Viceroy Toledo, the archbishop Mogrovejo, Sarmiento de Gamboa) remain in the background, and the principals (Henderson, María, Father Andrés, Mercedes) are fictitious. The tone is always Romantic: opposed loves between the heretic Henderson and the Catholic María, contrasts in black and white between hero and villain, deaths of atonement; nocturnal encounters, intrigues and vengeance, naval battles, inquisitorial trials, limpid idyllic scenes and scenes of local color, heroic sacrifices, espionage, secrets pathetically revealed, yearnings for freedom, and nature in solidarity with the human drama, as in the scene of the earthquake. Finally, Henderson and María escape from the claws of the Inquisition, reach England, and live happily ever after. The marriage between Drake and Juana (the daughter of a Spanish priest and a Peruvian descendant of the Incas) is a fiction that brings to the fore López' interest in showing the good relations between English pirates and Hispanic-Americans. The blackness of the novel is not in the pirates, but in the diabolical Father Andrés, the character of greatest strength because, precisely through him, López discharged the frightening darkness that he imagined. The evocative vignettes of colonial Lima and the speed of the action maintain the reader's interest despite the ponderousness of the prose. Inferior were his "historical short stories," *The Insane Woman of the Guard* (*La loca de la guardia*), that move along the road of San Martín's liberating army, and his epistolary novel, *The Great Week of 1810* (*La gran semana de 1810*). The name of López is best defended in his work as a historian.

Parenthetical Remarks on the Theme of the Pirate / If we have spoken more about López' historical novel, *The Heretic's Bride*, than of his admirable *History of the Argentine Republic* (*Historia de la República Argentina*), it is because our obligation is literary. But even in his novel, what is interesting is its philosophy of history, so typical of Romantic liberalism. One way of proving this is to compare the judgment on piracy formulated by López with that put forth by the colonial writers. The French pirates during the Franco-Spanish war of Charles V and Philip II against France (1520–1559); the English corsairs during the struggles of Philip II against England (1568–1596); the Dutch freebooters during the hostilities of the Low Countries against Spain until the Peace of Westphalia (1648) and, finally, the buccaneers and sea-robbers, who up to 1750 were masters of strategic points in the Caribbean, all undermined Spain's power in the New World. Our writers painted them in narrative poems, theatrical works, and chronicles as Protestant heretics, agents of the devil, the scourge of God, enemies of truth, justice, religion, property, commerce, social order, monsters of infamy and cruelty. Cristóbal de Llerena, Juan de Castellanos, Silvestre de Balboa, Martín del Barco Centenera, Miramontes y Zuázola, Rodríguez Freile, Oviedo Herrera, Sigüenza y Góngora, Bishop Lizárraga, and scores of others let the pen fly when they described the depredations of the "Lutheran" pirates. The most respected for his exploits was Drake (about whom Rodríguez Freile will say, that for having been a page in the court of Charles V, he was very "Hispanicized"). At times they express admiration for the pirates; at times they put the blame for piratical successes on the ineptitude of the Spaniards; but in general, the tone is always one of horror and condemnation for the heresies and ravages of the pirates. In passing they record unwillingly that Negroes, Indians, and certain Creole groups sympathized with the pirates expecting that "the English" might bring freedom to colonial life. This identification of piracy with freedom will encounter its true place in Romanticism. Like Byron, like Espronceda, the Romantics exalt the titanic life of the pirate and convert him into a hero of liberty: the pirate had been the first to challenge the religious, political, and economic absolutism of Spain, from which the Romantic liberals had just emancipated themselves. And so, in the historical novels of the nineteenth century, a series of idealizations of the pirate emerges. The series is opened by López' *The Heretic's Bride*. Among others, it is followed by Justo Sierra O'Reilly's *The Freebooter* (*El filibustero*, 1841), Coriolano Márquez Coronel's *The Pirate* (*El pirata*, 1863), Eligio Ancona's *The Freebooter* (*El filibustero*, 1866), Vicente Riva Palacio's *The Gulf Pirates* (*Los piratas del golfo*, 1869),

Alejandro Tapia y Rivera's *Cofresí*, 1876, Francisco Añez Gabaldón's *Carlo Paoli*, 1877, Soledad Acosta de Samper's *The Pirates in Cartagena* (*Los piratas en Cartagena*, 1885), Francisco Ortea's *The Treasure of Cofresí* (*El tesoro de Cofresí*, 1889), Carlos Sáenz Echeverría's *The Pirates* (*Los piratas*, 1891), Santiago Cuevas Puga's *Shackles and Hangman, Other Pirates in Penco* (*Esposa y verdugo, otros piratas en Penco*, 1897).

Other Argentinian Romantics / Among the enemies of Rosas—called the "banished ones"—there were only two important poets, Ascasubi and Mármol, each of whom was different. HILARIO ASCASUBI (Argentina, 1807–1875) was the one who dug deepest into the popular vein. He was a man of the city, but of all his rich experiences, early trips to Europe, revolutions, wars, newspaper campaigns, he elected as the theme of his satiric poetry the experience of the countryside and its people. He has been compared with Jasmin, the Gascon dialectical poet, celebrated by the French Romantics. But Ascasubi was versifying the language of the gauchos after the example of Hidalgo. In *Paulino Lucero* the gauchos are Centralists, enemies of Rosas. They chant their love of liberty, their hatred for tyranny. The tone is somber and horrified in the face of so much crime. In *Aniceto the Rooster* (*Aniceto el Gallo*) his attitude is soothed and festive. Rosas had been deposed, and Ascasubi, who stood on the side of Buenos Aires against the Confederation, now derides the political inconsistencies of Urquiza. (He had used the titles, *Paulino Lucero* and *Aniceto el Gallo* as pseudonyms.) His most important work, reflexive and not burlesque, was *Santos Vega or The Best Twins* (*Santos Vega o Los mellizos de la flor*), whose action takes place in the last thirty years of colonial life, although the reality described belongs to the country and city of the middle of the nineteenth century. Anachronisms break the historical illusion that the poet wished to create. In 1851 he published a few fragments, then interrupted the composition. Twenty years later he took it up again; it was published, complete, in 1872. Santos Vega narrates the history of two brothers, Luis, the bad one, and Jacinto, the good one, but deals particularly with the bad one. The theme of the "bad 'un" was common in ballads and pseudo-historical serials on bandit exploits. The author moralizes and wishes to amaze and move the reader. There is a poetization of the customs and landscape of the pampas. Ascasubi looks at a reality that has disappeared, detail by detail. Nevertheless, his spirit is not nostalgic. He describes everything as if it lay before his eyes. The dawn, the dance, the advance of the Indians are all scenes of precise contours and colors. He felt the adventures of men of action; he felt the dangers of the frontier; but he did not know how to construct a novel in verse. The composition is defective. Yet the voice of the gaucho is heard. It is oral poetry to be recited by a *payador* or gaucho songster, rather than poetry written to be read in a book.

JOSÉ MÁRMOL (Argentina, 1817–1871) wrote his first verses on the wall of the cell where Rosas had shackled him in 1839: the emphasis with which he related this circumstance over and over was typically Romantic. Everything he wrote was typically Romantic: verses, dramas, novels. And the circumstance was always the same—the tyranny of Rosas. When Rosas fell, the poet became mute. The poems that Mármol presented at the poetry competition of 1841 in Montevideo carried an epigraph by Byron; and Byron's *Childe Harold's Pilgrimage* inspires his first important work—the twelve *Songs of the Pilgrim* (*Cantos del peregrino*). Naturally, this was not the only influence. There is that of Lamartine, Zorrilla, and Espronceda. But Byron was for Mármol the last great poet that Europe had given: "Song died with Byron," he says in the first verses of his poem. However, one must not forget the influence of his friends, Alberdi and Gutiérrez, who had composed a type of poetical diary on their voyage to Europe, "Eden" (*"El Edén"*). On remembering the poems inspired by the sea, Mármol cited *Childe Harold,* although it is possible, as Gutiérrez suspected, that "Eden" (a Byronian work, anyway) might be a closer source. Mármol began writing the *Songs of the Pilgrim* during his trip to Chile in 1844. The ship left Rio de Janeiro and descended to Cape Horn but, drawn to the Polar Zone, it could not reach the Pacific and had to return to its point of departure without making any stopovers. In the *Songs,* the poet duplicates himself—both he and his character, Carlos, recite. They are one and the same lyrical person, but each song by the pilgrim Carlos is preceded by a narrative prolog. While the songs strictly maintain the same elegiac tone, the prologs tend to change to a festive one. Mármol would rebel Romantically against the classical tradition of pure genres. All in all, the poem has "system," as Mármol himself says. Nothing happens in the *Songs:* the poet, alone, in mid-ocean, meditates on man and on the lot of his country, evoking American landscapes and contemplating the beauty of the sea, of the night, and of the clouds. But there is order: "decrepit Europe" is compared to an America open to the future; he remembers his youth, his first love; he describes the tropical landscape he sees before him, and that of Argentina which he sees in nostalgic visions; as they sail along the Argentinian coast he thinks of the horrors of the tyranny. And so the *Songs,* which are a miscellany of evocations, develop like a travel diary. Furthermore, there is a lyrical sequence of thought. In his round-trip voyage, from the tropics to the South Pole, there is no soul other than Mármol's which sings to the exterior landscapes (skies, coasts, sea) and to the interior ones (nostalgia, indignation, rapture in the face of beauty): the soul lifts all themes to a high point of imagination. No doubt Mármol is verbose. Owing to the excessive facility of his improvisation, he is incorrect in his extremely varied versification. At times he is prosaic, at times declamatory; but his undisciplined lyricism is of value because his imagination was extraordinary.

Another collection of his verses was *Harmonies* (*Armonías,* 1851–1854). With some of these he gained his greatest popularity because of their violent disdain of Rosas. Disdain more than hatred. In any event, the hatred of one who disdains deep in his bosom. Rosas was belittled forever; in fact, a man who could be disdained in this fashion could not possess any greatness. The drums of Mármol's poetic damnation of Rosas deafened his readers so that they did not hear the lyrical, more intimate strings that also formed part of his orchestra. Mármol was not less important in the history of the novel than in that of poetry: his *Amalia* (1851–55) was a serial based on truculent adventures occurring in Buenos Aires during the abominable years of the Rosas tyranny. It is therefore a political novel; and, as Mármol had lived and suffered under the Rosas regime, it is an autobiographical novel too. He seems to have taken on a double identity in the two characters, Daniel and Eduardo, some of whose adventures Mármol had lived. In spite of the exaggerated tints, of the overwrought contrasts, of the belligerently feverish fictional elements, *Amalia* succeeded in the truthfulness of the political picture it presented. He intended, as he explained in his prolog, "to describe in retrospect personages who live in the present." Ten years separated the narrator from what he narrated, but he created such an illusion of greater distance that some critics consider *Amalia* a "historical novel." Nevertheless, the past was recent; in fact, it was not a past. The author viewed matters, not from an historical perspective, but from a political one; he objectified contemporary reality into historical form, not because it was actually "history" but because, deep in his heart, he felt it was decrepit. The dialog has extraordinary vivacity; the characters live; and although many of the novelistic situations bear the mark of the Romantic serial, they do succeed each other dynamically. And the reader, no matter how much he smiles, does not put down the book. Mármol was less fortunate with his dramas of 1842: *The Poet* (*El poeta*) and *The Crusader* (*El cruzado*).

Uruguay and Chile / When they went into exile, the Argentinian Romantics took their ideals and their libraries with them. In Montevideo, Argentinians and Uruguayans identified with the same cause. It would be idle to differentiate them into national groups: nationality was not felt as today. Alongside the Argentinians, the Uruguayans also sought Creole expression. None of them left an estimable work: neither the critic ANDRÉS LAMAS (1820–1891) nor the poets ADOLFO BERRO (1819–1841) and JUAN CARLOS GÓMEZ (1820–1884).

The Argentine *émigrés* also initiated the Romantic movement in Chile. Sarmiento and López had arrived with new ideas; they were the agitators. We have already studied Andrés Bello, who, for his superior culture, was above all the polemics on the language and on Romanticism that took place in 1842. From this date the so-called generation of '42 derives its name, a group formed by Bello's sons, Carlos (1815–1854), Francisco (1817–1845), Juan (1825–1860), and Emilio

(1845–1875) and by his spiritual children. Some Chileans satirically resisted the ideas of Argentine Romanticism: Jotabeche, Sanfuentes. Others, Lastarria, for example, and also the liberals who were closer to Mora than to Bello, sympathized with the new mode. J. J. Vallejo, known by the pseudonym JOTABECHE (1809–1858), wrote such animated sketches of customs that they seem like stories. SALVADOR SANFUENTES (1817–1860), as a disciple of Bello, read a good deal of the classicists and even translated Racine. His verse legends are also in classical style. Yet, there is a feeling for the Hispanic-American past, an idealization of the Indian, a taste for violent, passionate contrasts, an art of narrating adventures that, if it were not for the author's academic attitude, could be associated with the beginnings of Chilean Romanticism. His best legend is "The Carillon" (*"El campanario,"* 1842), on tragic loves in the colony. He published other stories in verse, and one drama. The Indianist theme that he dealt with in some of these legends, *"Inami," "Huentemagu,"* have a Chateaubriandesque stamp. JOSÉ V. LASTARRIA (1817–1888) did not surpass Jotabeche as a painter of customs, but he was the superior storyteller: "The Beggar" (*"El mendigo,"* 1843). In his "Speech on Literature" (*"Discurso literario,"* 1842) Lastarria advised the young writers to observe the immediate Chilean reality. Then, he proceeded to follow this advice. His narratives tend to be loaded with political intentions—e.g., his *Don Guillermo,* 1860, is more libel than novel—or in any case, with observations of the historical and popular life of Chile. In his old age he gathered up his narrative works in *Yesteryear and This Year: Novels and Stories of Hispanic-American Life (Antaño y ogaño. Novelas y cuentos de la vida hispanoamericana,* 1885). In one of his first stories, *The Lieutenant Alonso Díaz de Guzmán* (1848), there appeared the figure of Catalina de Erauso, the Lieutenant Nun. In his last years Lastarria yet published one good story, "A Daughter" (*"Una hija,"* 1881), where he showed sympathy for the Negro in his clash with the white man. One of the books of this generation most read today is that of VICENTE PÉREZ ROSALES (Chile, 1807–1886) —*Memories of the Past (Recuerdos del pasado,* definitive edition 1886). Written with amenity and in a good prose, these memories, with the passage of time, have been converted into history, and the book, into one of the masterpieces of Chilean literature.

Bolivia / Four minor poets make up the frame of Bolivian Romanticism: MARÍA JOSEFA MUJÍA (1813–1888), of a sorrowful muse; RICARDO JOSÉ BUSTAMANTE (1821–1886), poet of the hearth, of homeland, of nature; MANUEL JOSÉ TOVAR (1831–1869), who attempted the biblical theme of the Genesis in the poem *The Creation (La creación)*; and NÉSTOR GALINDO (1830–1865), a bard of melancholy intonation.

Mexico and Cuba / Independent of the Romantic movement that had been projected from Buenos Aires into Montevideo and Santiago de Chile, more Romantics sprang up in other parts of America. In a short time the wave covered all the countries of Spanish speech.

In Mexico, the Romanticism of FERNANDO CALDERÓN (1809–1845) moved in great noisy strides across the boards of the stage, yet fell over its feet whenever it wished to go over to lyrical poetry. His dramas, in verse, were inspired in a remote past of exotic lands—a typically Romantic genre which was propagated all over Hispanic America (one instance among many: in 1842, when Calderón produces *Herman or the Return of the Crusader* (*Herman o la vuelta del cruzado*) in Mexico, Mármol, at the other end of the continent, in Argentina, produces another drama on the same theme, *The Crusader* (*El cruzado*). His play *None of the Three* (*A ninguna de las tres*), in which he presents Mexican characters and criticizes the excesses of Romanticism, was exceptional. Of course, even in his tragedies there is a love of country and an aversion to tyranny that, although dissimulated under European disguises, reflect his Mexican attitude toward the dictator Santa Ana. In this libertarian nationalism he is following Alfieri, whose *Virginia* is present in Calderón's *Death of Virginia* (*Muerte de Virginia*). IGNACIO RODRÍGUEZ GALVÁN (1816–1842), inferior to Calderón as a dramatist—he too cultivated historical dramas—surpassed him as a lyricist. Effusive, wailing, he swells like a river, and the waves of desperation, anger, complaints, and consternation pound and abuse the great themes.

There was resistance against Romanticism, not only on the part of conservatives, traditionalists, and Catholics, but also on the part of an atheist and liberal reformer with classical tastes—IGNACIO RAMÍREZ (1818–1879) whose pseudonym was *The Necromancer* (*El Nigromante*). He was one of the noble figures in the struggles known as the Reform, but the work that bears on literary history is of little note. Nevertheless, in his humanist and scholarly poetry suddenly there is a blaze of passion, hatred, and sarcasm, whereupon one recognizes the intimate life of the author, much more Romantic than his verses, in its titanic negation of God, of Spanish traditions, and of the ruling political order. Honorable and reformist like Ramírez, but without culture, without spirituality, and Romantic in his negligence of style, if not in his sensibility, was GUILLERMO PRIETO (1818–1897), poet of the masses, robust and picturesque, author of *The Holy Mondays of Fidel* (*Los San Lunes de Fidel*), a collection of interesting sketches of customs. As in all Hispanic-America, the Romantic novel of Mexico preferred historical subjects (JUSTO SIERRA O'REILLY, 1814–1861; JUAN A. MATEOS, 1831–1913); and adventures and love episodes (FERNANDO OROZCO Y BERRA, 1822–1851; FLORENCIO M. DEL CASTILLO, 1828–1863). The robustness with which the genre of the novel had been born in Lizardi was in part inherited by the hair-raising and scurrilous MANUEL PAYNO (1810–1894). He wrote the type of novel called "serials" with no other purpose than to amuse his readers. He had the defects of the pulp narrator: glibness, truculence. But from *The Devil's Tiepin* (*El fistol del diablo*, 1845–46) to *The Bandits of Río Frío* (*Los bandidos de Río Frío*), his best book, he composed a lively canvas of local customs. His observations were penetrating, but his documentary material was constructed following Romantic conventions. Because of his feeling for adventure and his observations on contemporary life, sometimes ironic, he can still be read with pleasure.

Another of the Lizardi heirs was José Tomás de Cuéllar (1830–1894). In the light of his lantern—*The Magic Lantern* (*La linterna mágica*) is the title of his collection of novels—Cuéllar roguishly projects Mexican types and customs. Luis G. Inclán (1816–1875), who knew Mexican country, life better than anyone else, uses this knowledge to build a novel of adventure, *Astucia, Chief of the Fraternal Order of the Leaf, or the Cowboy Smugglers of the Bough* (*Astucia, el jefe de los Hermanos de la Hoja, o Los Charros contrabandistas de la rama*, 1865–66). The reader who, with piqued curiosity, is able to follow the successive episodes without tiring, can be grateful to Inclán's basic art of narrating. To bring to a close the Mexican Romantic scene, one must observe that one of the themes was its Indian past. After the serious efforts to gather up the traditions of Nahuatl culture, undertaken by Olmos, Sahagún, and others, interest fell off. If the Baroque writers of the seventeenth century, such as Sigüenza y Góngora, turn their attention to the indigenous past, it is to pause before the picturesque or to create fantasy from history. Clavigero, Veytia, Boturini, writers of the Enlightenment, profit in the eighteenth century from what already had been said in the sixteenth century without adding new views. It is with Romanticism that literature opens up to the old indigenous culture: granted, that through that open door, fantasy, improvisation, and facile enthusiasm go in and out. Bustamante, Roa Bárcena, José Joaquín Pesado, Rodríguez Galván, Peón Contreras, Calderón, Chavero, for example, reelaborated the most popular chronicles without coming into contact with the primitive texts.

In Cuba, Diego Gabriel de la Concepción Valdés, known as Plácido (1809–1844), was not far in his precepts from those writers born in the eighteenth century, for example, Quintana and Martínez de la Rosa, whom he admired. He was an obscure figure lacking the enlightenment of a literary education and, what is more serious, an original imaginative style. He versified with facility: ballads like the "*Jicoténcal*"; erotic sonnets like "The Flower of the Cane" ("*La flor de la caña*"); anacreontic, legendary, civic, epigrammatic compositions. In nothing was he able to go beyond his mediocrity, although occasionally he touched certain zones of his inner self, as in this image from his sonnet "Fatality" ("*La fatalidad*"): "Devoid of any clemency of pity / thou hast with spines encircled me, blind Deity, / As a font whose marge displays for its array / the thorny, pungent cacti and wild maguey." His compatriot José Jacinto Milanés y Fuentes (1814–1863), on the other hand, sounded the two characteristic notes of Romanticism: rebellion and the resurrection of the Golden Age theater. His best years as a poet were those from 1835 to 1843, after which he became hopelessly insane. But even during those years of mental lucidity, the poetic light was intermittent. Many of his compositions—festive, of local color, descriptive, social, amatory—diverted him into the shadows of other poets. He wanted to think and to be: to think, in the sense that the Victor Hugo or Espronceda type of Romantic gave to this vague elocution; to be, "the bard who illumines the people." It is possible that Milanés may have reached the crowds through these paths. His most worthy attribute, however, was his lyricism: the tenderness, the ingenuity, the complaint of his unwilling solitude, the delicate amorous sentiment. He also wrote for the theater. His most serious effort was the drama in verse *Count Alarcos* (*El Conde Alarcos*, 1838), whose theme comes from a sixteenth-century ballad already dramatized by Mira de Amescua, Lope de Vega, and Pérez de Montalbán.

More lyrical and powerful than the voices that had been heard in Cuba—Plácido and Milanés—was that of GERTRUDIS GÓMEZ DE AVELLANEDA (1814–1873). Educated in the personal though still Neoclassical poetry of Meléndez Valdés and Quintana, she never untied herself from those bonds and, at her height, continued to admire Gallego and Lista. Her Romanticism, therefore, was eclectic. The veil with which women cover their most ardent feelings and the veils that grandiloquence placed about the nakedness of her soul never succeed in veiling her sincerity. Her lyricism is not the serene jet from a garden spout, but a force of nature in freedom. She loved with a daring vigor, so intense that she could not be happy. The loves of Avellaneda, turbulent in her and in the Spanish society of her time, for she had lovers as well as husbands, usually were soothed in pure religious devotion. And she was even at the point of becoming a nun. She wrote poems on faith. This was a passionate, vehement woman, carried away by pleasure, depressed by sadness, and at times serenely peaceful. She always felt urged by a necessity for expression that caused her to meditate carefully on the workings of art, and in this way to reach a clear esthetic conception. We refer not only to those poems in which she sings to art, but also to those in which she sings to the virtues of clarity, formal perfection, and a careful style. At times, she was too careful retouching the re-editions of her lyrical verses (the first in 1841; the second 1850; the third 1869–71) and this academic touch-up de-petaled the rose. Nevertheless, because of her awareness to art, all of the sentimental outbursts did not become maudlin but were converted into elegant stylization. Though her heart is rent, Avellaneda does not disfigure her own image. Even if she is a Romantic, she preserves something of the academic "good taste" in which she was educated during the waning years of its vogue. The Spaniards consider her among their Parnassians. And they are justified, for it was in Spain that she lived, published her poetry, and triumphed. But she also belongs to the literary history of Hispanic-America, not for the mere accident of her birth, but because she had already written poems before leaving Cuba and always felt nostalgic ties and love for Cuba. One of her noteworthy sonnets is precisely one in which she records her sorrow on leaving her homeland—"On Departing" (*"Al partir"*). And Cuba, which on her lips was always "my homeland," is present in many of her compositions. She wrote dramas (*Baltasar*) and novels (*Guatimozín*). Generally, they transpire in times and places unknown to her. On the other hand, her novel *Sab* (1841) is based on things she saw in Cuba. Its theme is slavery—a mulatto slave, Sab, falls in love with the daughter of his master—and the novel, though Romantic, has excellent descriptions of Cuban reality.

After having mentioned Avellaneda's fiction, let us pass on to the Cuban novel, whose chief promoter during these years was DOMINGO DELMONTE (Venezuela–Cuba, 1804–1853), although he himself did not write novels, only Creole ballads (*Romances*). Young Cubans who read Romantic authors (from Walter Scott to Victor Hugo and Honoré de Balzac) met in Delmonte's house. And from these meetings came the first narrations. The themes were the Indian, Negro slavery, local customs, and the historical past. RAMÓN DE PALMA (1812–1860) published a short Indian story, *Matanzas y Yumurú* (1837) and two other short novels, of which *Cholera in Havana* (*El cólera en la Habana*, 1838) was the better. The fashionable historical novel, put in vogue by Walter Scott, prompted JOSÉ ANTONIO ECHEVERRÍA (1815–1855) to publish *Antonelli* (1838). His protagonist is the Italian architect Antonelli, whom we see in Havana in the year 1560, constructing the Morro castle by special request of Philip II. With these very thin threads of history the novelist, in a most Romantic fashion, weaves his tragedy. Antonelli woos in vain the angelic Casilda, Lupercio's betrothed. His soul is agitated and possessed by contradictory passions: love and hate, pride and despair, generosity and jealousy. The night of the feast in the Morro castle, Casilda and Lupercio fall victims to an Indian's vengeance. Antonelli, who has prompted the Indian to commit the crime, now collapses to the ground, overcome by remorse. The tale includes all the Romantic themes, such as the ominous bird, the solitary, nocturnal walks, the battle between angel and demon which rages within each man's soul, mysterious shadows, secret amorous rendezvous, serenades by moonlight, duels, violence, tears, fainting spells and tender dialog, conflict between the nobility and the commoner, condemnation of the superstitious fanaticism of Philip II, readings from Dante . . . Aside from those moments when Echeverría interrupts the thematic flow of the novel with explanations, reflections, or conversations with the reader, the prose style is also Romantic by virtue of its sentimentality.

Notable in the history of the novel was CIRILO VILLAVERDE (Cuba, 1812–1894). In ten years of continuous literary activity, he wrote almost a score of Romantic narratives that do not amount to very much: incestuous love affairs between brother and sister or between father and daughter, deaths, disasters, superstitions, violent passions, sketches of customs, melodrama. His best work *Cecilia Valdés or The Angel's Hillock* (*Cecilia Valdés o la loma del angel*) [an English translation has appeared under the title *The Quadroon*] was published in its first part in 1839 and revised and completed in 1879; the version of 1882 should be considered as definitive. It is a pulp novel with a coarse plot: the loves of the beautiful mulatto Cecilia and the young master, Leonardo, who do not know that they are brother and sister; when he is about to marry another woman, Cecilia incites an admirer of hers to kill him. Villaverde made a plot of stew, with real persons, with customs obvious to all, with observations on different social classes and races, from domineering Spaniards to Negro slaves, with dialog where different manners of speech are heard, with reflections on the most somber aspects of Cuban life. Realist art? That is what the author boastingly declared. His readings had been from the Romantics (Chateaubriand, Saint-Pierre, Scott, Manzoni, James Fenimore Cooper, Dickens), but he leaned toward realism. It was not so much that he was a realist; rather, one might say, that with the failure of the novel as art, what is of interest to the readers is the crude reality, without novelistic refinement, that was left. What most attracts our attention are the sketches of local customs dispersed here and there. Villaverde, because of his interest in describing the customs of colonial Cuba in the 1830's, painted a convincing, if a bit painful, picture.

One of the problems which preoccupied the young writers of Delmonte's group was slavery. In spite of the legal abolition of slave trade (1815 and 1817), it was still practiced. Thus, there arose in protest the abolitionist literature: *Petrona y Rosalía* (1838) by FÉLIX MANUEL TANCO Y BOSMENIEL (Colombia–Cuba, 1797–1871) and *Francisco* (written in 1839; published posthumously) by ANSELMO SUÁREZ Y ROMERO (1818–1878). The latter, which Delmonte ironically subtitled "the sugar plantation or the joys of the fields," records the ugliness and ignominies of slavery, life in sugar refineries, and the customs of the peasant; and his intensity in documenting has given realist energy to the still-Romantic prose of the author. *Francisco* began a cycle of anti-slavery novels: we have already mentioned Avellaneda's *Sab* and we could add ANTONIO ZAMBRANO's *The Negro Francisco* (*El negro Francisco*).

Regional novels full of social criticism and moralizing intentions, but far below the standards of Cirilo Villaverde, were those of JOSÉ RAMÓN DE BETANCOURT (1823–1890), *A Charity Bazaar in 183 . . .* (*Una feria de la caridad en 183 . . .*, 1841). ESTEBAN PICHARDO Y TAPIA (1799–1879), *The Fatalist* (*El Fatalista*, 1856), RAMÓN PIÑA (1819–1861), *Honest Jerome* (*Gerónimo el Honrado*, 1859).

Custom sketches were the most abundant; and in Cuba, along with the aforementioned writers, JOSÉ VICTORIANO BETANCOURT (1813–1875) and, better yet, JOSÉ MARÍA DE CÁRDENAS Y RODRÍGUEZ (1812–1882) did the honors.

Venezuela and Colombia / No doubt, Cuban Romanticism casts its line and reaches Venezuela. Among the most renowned Venezuelans of the first generation, the one who stands out is JOSÉ ANTONIO MAITÍN (1814–1874), famous for the "Funeral Chant" (*"Canto Fúnebre"*) in memory of his wife. During these years there is not an elegy that outshines this one in sincerity, sweetness, circumspection, and simplicity. Then ABIGAÍL LOZANO (1821–1866), skillful in words best forgotten, and CECILIO ACOSTA (1818–1881), esteemed as a thinker but estimable for his poem "The Little White House" (*"La casita blanca"*).

Passing from Venezuela to Colombia we meet a select group of writers. In poetry, JOSÉ JOAQUÍN ORTIZ (1814–1892) wrote Neoclassical patriotic odes and JULIO ARBOLEDA (1817–1861) composed an epic-legendary poem on colonial subject matter—*Gonzalo de Oyón*. It was lost: all we have is an unfinished version.

Along with these men stands a superior poet—JOSÉ EUSEBIO CARO (1817–1853). His life was a short-lived flame, but intense and brilliant. This flame was fed by the culture of his time and by his own combustible and violent temperament. Although he was not a philosopher, the ideas of his time are emblazoned on his works. He began as a skeptic, a rationalist, a utilitarian, through his readings of Voltaire and the Encyclopedists, Bentham and Destutt de Tracy. Then he returned to the Catholic faith, impressed by Balmes, José de Maistre and Bonald, only to turn to Comte's positivism and, in turn, to Christian tradition once again. In these changes one can see a search for a moral, worthy, and decent position. Each one of his poems was a moral act, either because of its civil theme, or because of his urge to achieve sincerity. As a lyrical poet he figures in the purest and happiest vein of Romanticism. He had formed his style following the lead of the Spanish authors from all ages, and also of the classic writers of Italy and France. The Romantics, above all the French and English, helped him to discover his lyrical path. Caro's lyre lacked none of its strings, not even the political and philosophical. Themes that usually invite an impersonal treatment, in him sounded personal. He is always at the center of emotion; he always draws from his own interior. Political invective, moral meditation, landscape description, and didactic purpose do not deflect him from his lyrical sway. Here, as well as in his intimate themes of love and family, we recognize the sincere and fiery temper of a soul that wishes to be alone and to express something original. Because even though Caro was a fighter in the political anarchy of his day, he always felt deeply the rumble of his own personality. He was an exile, and the exiles of Hispanic-America were banished because they had a living interest in their society. It was society that exiled them and not the Romantic yearning for solitude, as in the case of many Europeans. In Caro we have both conditions: exiled of necessity, and exiled for being a solitary type. He began by clothing himself as a poet in loose, free, and flowing meters, somewhat after the manner of Quintana, Gallego, and Martínez de la Rosa, thus moving comfortably, as in the *silva* "The Cypress" (*"El ciprés"*), in a slightly declamatory posture, to be sure, but with that attitude of yielding himself to the reader that characterized all his works. Later on, following the English more than the Latins, he imitated the classical hexameter, combining it at times with the hendecasyllable. Evidently, he was seeking his own rhythms; and in this third manner of versification, he punished each line with unusual accents, perhaps stiffening the flow of the words, but enriching the poetic language.

In prose, the most abused genre was the sketch of customs which, in certain cases, became short story and even novel. JOSÉ MANUEL GROOT (1800–1878) was one of the first to cultivate it. Pages of memorable descriptive achievements are contained in *Bunkhouse Notes* (*Apuntes de ranchería*) by JOSÉ CAICEDO ROJAS (1816–1897). EUGENIO DÍAZ (1804–1865) author of sketches of customs and historical narrations, also wrote novels; one of these, *Manuela*, is more effective in its realist description of country life than in the emotional description of love.

Other Countries / In Guatemala the best prose writer was SALOMÉ JIL (1822–1882), anagram of José Milla. He evoked the colonial past in a series of historical novels: *The Nazarene Trees* (*Los nazarenos*), *The Governor's Daughter* (*La hija del adelantado*), *The Inspector* (*El visitador*). The real and fictitious characters converse convincingly. This idealization of the past is of least interest today; on the other hand, we esteem his activity as a painter of his time more and more. His *Sketches of Customs* (*Cuadros de costumbres*), more good-natured than satirical, animate the society in which he lived, save it from oblivion, illumine it with the grace of art. They have, at moments, the movements of a short story, and they have even created a popular character, Juan Chapín.

Romanticism comes to the Dominican Republic with MANUEL MARÍA VALENCIA (1810–1870). But the Dominican poets of this generation never reach full vigor: FÉLIX MARÍA DEL MONTE (1819–1899), NICOLÁS UREÑA DE MENDOZA (1823–1875), JOSÉ MARÍA GONZÁLEZ (1830–1863), FELIPE DÁVILA FERNÁNDEZ DE CASTRO 1806–1879), JAVIER ANGULO GURIDI (1816–1884), FÉLIX MOTA (1829–1861), MANUEL DE JESÚS DE PEÑA Y REINOSO (1834–1915) and JOSEFA ANTONIO PERDOMO (1834–1896).

The Second Romantic Generation

We have seen how the first shoots of Romanticism, transplanted from Europe, took root in various countries. Now we shall study the writers who began to write after Hispanic-America had cultivated its own Romanticism. In certain areas like Peru, Ecuador, Puerto Rico there was no Romanticism other than that of this second generation.

Verse / From the cluster of Peruvian poets—JOSÉ ARNALDO MÁRQUEZ (1830–1903), MANUEL ATANASIO FUENTES (1820), MANUEL NICOLÁS CORPANCHO (1830–1863), CLEMENTE ALTHAUS (1835–1881), LUIS BENJAMÍN CISNEROS (1837–1904)—we shall pick only one: CARLOS AUGUSTO SALAVERRY (1830–1891). He wrote about a score of dramatic works, in verse and in the Romantic manner, but he was a poet, not a dramatist. His lyricism was irascible, for that was the mode, but in his most sincere moments he succeeds in expressing himself in correct verses. From Ecuador's vintage we collect NUMA POMPILIO LLONA (1832–1907), modern in his sorrow, traditional in his sonnet form; and JULIO ZALDUMBIDE (1833–1887), meditative, contemplative, elegiac, religious.

In Puerto Rico MANUEL A. ALONSO (1823–1889) initiates interest in local customs and things Creole: he collected popularly inspired verses and prose in *The Rustic* (*El Gíbaro*, 1849). He was, then, the first chronicler of the national character. His attitude is gay, but moralistic. From his recollections (he was in Spain at the time) he reconstructed typical pictures of local customs: weddings, dances, cockfights, horse races. Because even his poetry resorts to phonetic orthography in order to imitate the speech of the Puerto Rican peasant or *jíbaro*, his work is also a linguistic document. ALEJANDRO TAPIA Y RIVERA (1826–1882) poured his Romantic wine into poetry, novels, and dramas. He was a propagator of uncomfortable ideas, like the heretical one of *The Sataniad, Grandiose Epic Dedicated to the Prince of Darkness* (*La Sataniada, grandiosa epopeya dedicada al Príncipe de las Tinieblas*). He would rewrite history artistically in his dramas and novels. His themes were not always on Hispanic-America, although two certainly were:

The Quadroon Woman (*La cuarterona,* 1867) which deals with racial prejudices, and his novel *Cofresí* (1876) on the Puerto Rican pirate of the same name. He wrote curious allegorical and philosophical novels. What is read today with pleasure is *My Memoirs* (*Mis memorias*). Two other Puerto Rican poets were José Gualberto Padilla (1829–1896), patriotic, classical in his tastes; and Santiago Vidarte (1827–1848), Romantic versifier, Espronceda disciple of melancholy and pessimistic tone, dealing in themes of love, religion, and nature.

All of the writers about whom we will now speak were aware of their Romantic antecedents in their own countries, and their works represent in some a continuation, in others, a reaction to this past, and in still others, a leap forward. We shall see those who leaped farthest in the next chapter.

In poetry, there were the slow-paced young Mexicans Alejandro Arango y Escandón (1821–1883) and José María Roa Bárcena (1827–1908). The latter, who as a lyrical poet is barely passable, was inspired by indigenous legends in the colorful life of the people, in Mexican landscapes, and even in the fantastic ballads in prose of Nordic literature which made such an impression on our Romantics. His short stories should be studied. The Venezuelans twist Romanticism so that we see them early stretching toward English, German, and Italian poetry (Jose Antonio Calcaño, 1827–1894, and Juan Vicente Camacho, 1829–1872) and toward the native landscape (José Ramón Yepes, 1822–1881). The Cuban Juan Clemente Zenea (1832–1871) finds his way into anthologies by way of his elegiac "*Fidelia.*"

In Colombia Gregorio Gutiérrez González (1826–1872), like others of his compatriots, was formed in the school of the Spaniards Zorrilla and Espronceda, and of the Venezuelans Maitín and Lozano. Above all, it was in Zorrilla's, though not in all of Zorrilla's poetry, but in the "Zorrilla-ization" is most obvious, Gutiérrez González achieved such simplicity of style and such sobriety of emotion that his sin of imitation is attenuated. Moreover, he seems to have been so aware that his lugubrious and vexing poems were the artificial fruits of the fashion of the day that at the same time he wrote them he censured and even ridiculed them. The truth is he preferred the sober verse of a more sentimental vein, sincerely felt. That is why, though he followed in Zorrilla's wake, he digressed for moments toward a more intimate expression which years later Bécquer would cultivate with genius. Let us say that his preference was "realist," a condition which made him reach greater poetic heights, and which assured him a place of honor in our literary history. I am referring to his *Memoir on the Cultivation of Maize in Antioquia* (*Memoria sobre el cultivo del maíz en Antioquia,* 1866). Gutiérrez González retires from the literary society of his day and takes refuge in one of the primitive woods of his country to compose, not only his most extensive poem, but also the strangest and most original of his generation. With a humoristic wink he pretends to present to the School of Sciences and Arts a *Scientific Memoir* (*Memoria científica*). Since he wishes to be understood by the people, he declares that his instructions will be precise, clear, and methodical: "The not-too-Spanish words I use / in my writing will not be underscored / for since I write only for Antioquia / I do not write Spanish but Antioquian." And in fact, the poetic language of the *Memoir* is so rich in indigenous and dialectal words that even the Colombians of Bogotá must have recourse to the linguistic notes that two friends of the poet added to the edition of his complete works. Yet, the *Memoir* is not a poem that lives exclusively in one province of America. True, its theme is regional: Gutiérrez González describes how thirty peons and the landowner search in a woods for terrain adequate for the cultivation of maize; how they fell trees and burn the ground; how they build their huts, sow, irrigate, and defend the seed from the birds; how maize grows; how it is harvested and cooked. But the art of looking at and idealizing every detail in a lyrical image, the emotion felt for the customs of a simple people and the contrast between life in the open and life in the city were the refinements of a very cultured poet. In this picture of agricultural labors we do not see the *Georgics* of Vergil—as we did in Andrés Bello—but the direct observation of nature by an imaginative writer. The narration moves in a clear line; and undoubtedly many of its hendecasyllables are incorrect, heavy, and even prosaic. Nevertheless, how remarkably stylizing is Gutiérrez González' attitude! He looks down from above, as if he were visiting the earth from another planet; and from this distance (not with the eyes of the peon) he is astonished at the strange beauty of each movement below.

In Chile there was a group of poets: EUSEBIO LILLO (1826–1910), GUILLERMO MATTA (1829–1899) and, the best, GUILLERMO BLEST GANA (1829–1904). He was Romantic from beginning to end. In *Poems* (*Poesías*, 1854) he weeps over an amorous disillusionment. Of course there is much mournful art in his weeping. He is a lad who has read many lines of lachrymose literature. And with the passing of years, he himself will laugh ironically at the youthful poetry of suffering. He had translated Musset; and, like Musset, he considered himself to be suffering from the *mal de siècle*. Later he became more tranquil and abandoned the pose. If earlier he had written in an exalted state an anthological piece, "No, All Does Not Perish" (*"No, todo no perece"*), now he writes a compassionate one, equally anthological, "The First Kiss" (*"El primer beso"*). Blest Gana, in his period of maturity and sincerity, gave proof that his melancholy was his own and not that of the Europeans he had read. That is to say, in his last years of poetic production he gave expression to the disenchantment and sadness which as a youth he had seen imperfectly in his own depths. As a good Romantic, he wrote a Chilean historical drama in verse on *Almagro's Conspiracy* (*La conjuración de Almagro*). Difficult to classify is the Argentinian CARLOS GUIDO Y SPANO. He lived from 1827 to 1918. He covered, thereby, a great stretch of literary history. He stayed on the surface of a mitigated but elegant Attic, refined, sober Romanticism. His first book, *Leaves in the Wind* (*Hojas al viento*, 1871) is a collection of compositions dating from 1854: tender, candid, with sentiments of kinship, containing reflections more or less philosophical, or civic themes lyrically treated, as in his famous *"Nenia"* dedicated to Paraguay and written on the occasion of its devastation by war. Many of his poems, like "Myrta at the Baths" (*"Mirta en el baño"*), "In the Cherry Trees" (*"En los guindos"*), "Marble" (*"Mármol"*), have plastic qualities. His precise mention of the color of things underscores this poetic plasticity. Because of his cold polish, his visual sensitivity, and the reminiscences of the *Greek Anthology* (*Antología griega*)—which he translated in part—Guido y Spano has been associated with the Parnassian ideals of the Modernists. In his second book of verses, *Distant Echoes* (*Ecos lejanos*, 1895), verses on current events abound.

Prose / The ideas of interesting men like the Chileans FRANCISCO BILBAO (1823–1865) and BENJAMÍN VICUÑA MACKENNA (1831–1886) and the Venezuelan ARTÍSTIDES ROJAS (1826–1894) were naturally put in prose. It is the art of prose that interests us here, even though that art, as in the depicters of local customs, may be rudimentary. Juan de Dios Restrepo, better known as EMIRO KASTOS (1827–1897), believed that his sketches of customs lacked brilliance because, above all, one had "to respect the truth" (as if truth could not be brilliant!). What happened is that, being more the observer than the man of imagination, Kastos, although possessed of a dry humor, was not inspired by the desire to color his pages. He was a spirit so disillusioned with man that his derision proffered no hope for correction. The local colorist, JOSÉ MARÍA SAMPER (1828–1888), had a certain but not too notable flair. JOSÉ MARÍA VERGARA Y VERGARA (1831–1872), enlivener of the literary movement in Bogotá, was a sentimentalist whose sentimentalism learned its mode of speech in the books of Chateaubriand. In his letter "A little handful of grass" (*"Un manojito de hierba"*)—pulled from Chateaubriand's grave during his trip to Europe—Vergara y Vergara wrote with lyrical tension or with essay-like delivery. In legion with other writers—and this is one of the unfortunate phenomena of our literature—Vergara y Vergara put his greatest effort into writing on non-American themes; when he wrote about America, on the other hand, he scribbled in haste. It is to be lamented that his sketches of customs do not have the artistic dignity he could have given them. For example, in "The Three Cups" (*"Las tres tazas"*) —each cup serves to recall the fashions, ridiculous to his way of thinking, of the social gatherings in Bogotá: chocolate in 1813, coffee in 1848, tea in 1865—the theme is more interesting than the literary solution. The fact is that, aside from Chateaubriand, his tastes descended toward Fernán Caballero and Trueba: and his depictions of customs place him even below this level. JOSÉ MANUEL MARROQUÍN (1827–1908), who tried his art of versifying in "The Puppy" (*"La perrilla"*), earned his fame as a narrator in *The Moor* (*El moro*, 1897), the story of a horse narrated by the horse: an equine autobiography in the manner of Anna Sewell's *Black Beauty,* rich in observations of local customs.

The novel put a definitive frame around the subject matter of the sketches of customs. The local customs in these sketches were shreds from the picaresque novels of Spain which had influenced the English

(Addison, Steele), the French (Jouy, Mercier), and Spanish (Larra) prosists; transformed in this way, these sketches on customs had their effect on the Hispanic-Americans. But within the novel there is a clear-cut difference between eighteenth-century sketches of customs—let us say, *A Town's Intrigues* (*Los enredos de un lugar*) by Gutiérrez de la Vega—and the nineteenth-century ones—let us say, *The Devil Loads the Weapons* (*El diablo las carga*) by the Venezuelan Ros de Olano, 1802–1887—because in the nineteenth century, the writer becomes more interested in the plot of the novel than in the atmosphere. Moreover, the plot and the environment interest him more than social satire. The serial-type novels (in France, e.g., those of Sue, Dumas, Ponson du Terrail, Paul Féval) accustomed readers the world over to absurd episodes, to the most complicated and unending plots, contrasts between angelic and sinister persons, passions, violence, and exaggeration. Although in Hispanic America they were not always written in serial form, this type of novel was also cultivated.

Sue's *The Mysteries of Paris* (*Los misterios de París*) was followed by *The Mysteries of Santiago* (*Los misterios de Santiago*, 1858) by José Antonio Torres (Chile, 1828–1864). A little novel of adventure, with a complete string of Romantic traits, is the one by Mariano Ricardo Terrazas (Bolivia, 1833–1878): *Mysteries of the Heart* (*Misterios del corazón*, 1869). In these novels there is a mixture of historical, erotic and, with curious frequency, anti-clerical adventures as in *Father Horán: Scenes of Cuzco Life* (*El Padre Horán. Escenas de la vida cuzqueña*, 1848), in which Narciso Aréstegui (Peru, 1826–1869) narrates the murder of a Catholic penitent by his father confessor. Romanticism shows two of its facets in Aréstegui's pulp-magazine story: the feeling for nature and liberal thought. Another of the Romantic genres, as we have seen, was the historical novel: Juana Manuela Gorriti (Argentina, 1819–1892); Soledad Acosta de Samper (Colombia, 1833–1913); Nepomuceno J. Navarro (Colombia, 1834–1890); Daniel Barros Grez (Chile, 1834–1904); Francisco Mariano Quiñones (Puerto Rico, 1830–1908). Of the army of novelists of these years, we shall pause before but a few of them, if only to give an idea of what was being novelized, and in what way. There was only one outstanding novelist, Alberto Blest Gana, and he will be reserved for the end of the list.

One who attracts attention in this genre is Vicente Riva Palacio (Mexico, 1832–1896). He was a man who studied the archives. He knew the colony like the palm of his hand, and especially what happened behind the closed doors of the Inquisition. Nevertheless, more than lucid evocations, his novels are more like serial adventures: *Martín Garatuza* (1868) is perhaps better than *Nun and Wife, Virgin and Martyr* (*Monja y casada, virgen y mártir*); *The Pirates of the Gulf* (*Los piratas del Golfo*); *The Return of the Dead* (*La vuelta de los muertos*) and the rest of his works, although not much better. He displayed his humor and talent writing on the past traditions of Mexico; these were better constructed than Palma's Peruvian traditions since they were closer to being short stories—his posthumous collection was called *The General's Stories* (*Los cuentos del general,* 1896). However, his best stories are not those that gave wings to the massive colonial chronicles, but those that relate happenings and events that he knew from more immediate sources. His years in Madrid left a mark on his style. He was, after Roa Bárcena, the founder of the Mexican short story. It is possible that posterity will keep his short stories and not his novels. EUSTAQUIO PALACIOS (Colombia, 1830–1898) is the author of *The Royal Ensign: Chronicle of Eighteenth-Century Cali* (*El Alférez Real. Crónica de Cali en el siglo xviii*), a Romantic novel, not so much for its historical evocation, after all, that past was quiet recent—1789 —and Palacios gathered it without effort, nor for its descriptions of local color, although from here emanates most of the interest the novel may have today, but for the melodramatic and maudlin mark impressed on it by the nineteenth-century novelistic tradition. A gush of sentimentalism covers the thick, heavy dialog. It lacks subtlety; it lacks shading. For this reason the situations are sentimental, but sentiment is missing. The novelistic construction is naive and predictable. The author displays his materials with such candor that the novel becomes so translucent as to permit the reader to see through to its denouement. The love of the orphans, the villain, the foreboding of a mystery in Daniel's life, and the revelation of the secret marriage of his parents, the parallelism between the tender loves of Inés-Daniel, on one hand, and Andrea-Fermín, on the other, the happiness that is showered on all at the end, must have enchanted the contemporary reader: today we are disillusioned by the psychological superficiality of those characters who nonetheless speak eloquently.

The old Romantic sentimentalism inspired many idyllic and historical elaborations, like *Cumandá* (1879) by JUAN LEÓN DE MERA (Ecuador, 1832–1894). Of the Romantic novels of this epoch, it is the one that can least defend itself from the changes in taste. It has become irremediably old.' Even when it was conceived in 1871 this type of novel was outdated; it was derived from the *"poèmes en prose,"* a genre that from Fénélon to Chateaubriand had included in its narrative the language, and even the subject matter from poetry (Homer, Milton, Gassner, Ossian, etc.). The poetic vein remains fresh in *Cumandá*: it moistens with lyrical metaphors the description of the jungles, mountains, and rivers of eastern Ecuador and the sketches of customs of savage natives. No doubt the settings and scenes of this virgin America are what Europeans admired and what made them consider *Cumandá* as one of our principal works. But, when all is said and done, it is a novel; and judging it as such, it is false from its very first line. The action occurs in 1808, but it stems from the uprising of the Guamote and Columbe Indians in 1790. The reader immediately guesses that the lovers Cumandá and Carlos are sister and brother, separated in infancy by the tragic events of the rebellion. In one blow the interest of *Cumandá* as a novel of adventure is destroyed. But Mera's worst miscue as a narrator is his overflowing sentimentalism, at once conventional and swollen. Instead of inviting the reader to enter imaginatively into those unfortunate loves, thus creating the condition that will involve him emotionally, he weighs the reader down with heavy sentimental bundles, prepared, condensed, and wrapped with the trademarked ribbon of twaddling Romanticism. Hence, there is not a single moving character, a single convincing episode, a single dialog that records the living speech of the people. Everything is absurd, even ridiculous. Mera's attitude toward the Indians of his own country—European in literature, Spanish in politics, and Catholic in metaphysics—also falsified what has been called, for some reason, "Indianism," in *Cumandá*.

The Romantic novel idealized the Indian by presenting him as a poetic, exotic, legendary, or historical personage. Anselmo Suárez, Gertrudis Gómez de Avellaneda, Rosa Guerra, José Ramón Yepes, José María Lafragua, Eligio Ancona, Ireneo Paz, J. R. Hernández, Manuel de Jesús Galván, Ramón de Palma y Romay, Alejandro Tapia y Rivera, and others wrote romances with Indian characters. Mera perhaps approaches the more recent Indianist novel because of one particular: when he alluded to the violent protest by the Indians against the injustice and abuse that the despotic landowners subjected them to, he implanted a social theme that in time was to be the most important within this genre. We repeat then, *Cumandá* is worthwhile as a poetic exercise on an American theme, that is, as a point of contact of the novel with the Indianist poems that Mera himself had written. *The Virgin of the Sun* (*La virgen del sol*, written in 1856, published in 1861) is a verse legend in which the historical facts dealing with the crumbling of the Inca empire before the advance of the Spaniards serve as a framework for the novelistic embroidering of loves and vengeances. In "Indigenous Melodies" ("*Melodías indígenas*," 1858) he also harks back to the Indian past. "I have also tried to make myself Indian," he tells us in the prolog. Rather, he has disguised himself as an Indian. Down deep, he had no feeling for the Indian. At most it was a pretext for his European-styled texts. Mera tried his hand at sketches of customs. His *Ecuadorian Novelettes* (*Novelitas ecuatorianas*) especially "Between Two Aunts and an Uncle" ("*Entre dos tías y un tío*") describe an Ecuadorian scene which we are able to recognize.

José Modesto Espinosa (Ecuador, 1833–1915), author of *Miscellany* (*Miscelánea*) and *Sketches of Customs* (*Artículos de costumbres*), was an accomplished narrator of local scenes.

In Uruguay, if any writer is to be mentioned, it must be Alejandro Magariños Cervantes (1825–1893). His lyrical poetry is trivial. No better, but at least more typical, was his verse legend *Celiar* about tragic loves that are placed at the end of the eighteenth century. In *Caramurú* (1848) a snarled-up novel about a gaucho during the period of Portuguese domination in 1823, a coarse and pulp-serial Romanticism wastes even what might have been worthwhile: customs and local color.

In Chile MANUEL BILBAO (1829–1895), in order to propagate his liberal, anti-clerical ideas, used the technique of the serial novel. In *The Elder Inquisitor* (*El inquisidor mayor*, 1852) he painted the colonial atmosphere of Lima, the city in which Bilbao initiated his literary career. Another novel, one of adventure but quite historical, was *The Pirate of Guayas* (*El pirata de Guayas*, 1865).

The best novelist of this generation was another Chilean, ALBERTO BLEST GANA (1830–1920). He lived in France between 1847 and 1851; there he read Balzac and began his vocation as a novelist. He wrote several novels in which, not unlike Balzac, he presented a cycle of Chilean life from the Independence to the beginning of the twentieth century, with the social movements of the middle class, political marriages, the customs of Santiago, the power of money, the conflicts between "status seekers" and the oligarchy, the political tumults. Balzac was not his only model; he even cites Stendhal, when the latter was scarcely known in the Hispanic world. He was one of the first realists in Spanish letters: Galdós was to write shortly thereafter. His work as a novelist might be divided into two periods. From 1853 to 1863 he wrote ten novels; he then produced, in addition, a drama and various articles of customs and chronicles. Between 1864 and 1897, a long silence. And from 1897 to 1912 only four novels. The important ones from the first period are *The Arithmetic of Love* (*La aritmética del amor*, 1860), *Martín Rivas* (1862) and *The Ideal of a Profligate* (*El ideal de una calavera*, 1863). Blest Gana himself gave the formula for his realism: "The painting of verisimilar incidents, provided there is nothing extraordinary and if the coloring is alive and true, can be of as much interest to the reader as the uncommon events with which many modern novelists have corrupted the tastes of the unlettered" (1861). With this condemnation of the pseudo-Romantic serial writers Blest Gana laid out a new course for the Hispanic-American novel. He was strongly determined to be a novelist addressing himself to Chilean readers. His purpose was to novelize ordinary life, and in order to accomplish this, he had to restrain his own feelings. Blest Gana, who was not championing a cause, understood and sympathized with his fellow citizens. And his characters, who are grouped according to their affluence, show no real conscious class struggle. In *The Arithmetic of Love*, the protagonist is a young man who wishes to live well, but who does not have the money to finance such a life. He wavers between cynicism and virtue and after many misfortunes ends up by marrying his first sweetheart, the poor but loyal Amelia. *Martín Rivas* was better. But Blest Gana still makes up his characters by insisting that they retain his ways of being and speaking. The procedure is mechanical, so that he mechanizes all of his figures, which move without acquiring the dimensions of real characters. The interest in *Martín Rivas* lies in the changing situations, in the weaving of the plot, where Martín, Rafael, Leonor, Edelmira, Chilean society, and the mutiny of 1851 are drawn in filaments of vivid color. Realism? Yes, because the Romantic way of relating now disdains excessive sentimental effusion—"without any affectation of sentimentality," says Blest Gana—and, on the contrary, describes bourgeois life more effectively, cooling down into humorous scenes. But this is still not the realism of those novels with which he will break his long silence. *The Ideal of a Profligate* continues the procedure referred to, although improving it. The same combination of novelistic episodes with historical episodes—the protagonist is shot after the mutiny of Quillota. The same picture of youths from an impoverished middle class, having ambitions and promiscuous loves. But Abelardo Manríquez is now different from Martín Rivas, not only in his moral conduct but in that, as a character, he has more life, more novelistic authenticity and complexity. In his second period Blest Gana wrote *During the Reconquest* (*Durante la Reconquista*, 1897), *The Migrants* (*Los trasplantados*, 1904), *Crazy Estero* (*El loco Estero*, 1909) and *Gladys Fairfield* (1912). With the exception of the last, these are Blest Gana's best. For its theme and its art, *During the Reconquest* is above all the best. Earlier, Blest Gana had used historical episodes in order to accelerate the denouement of his novels; now the whole novel is made of history. It is one of the best historical novels of Hispanic-America and, according to some, if not his masterpiece, at least it is his most ambitious undertaking. It harks back to the years 1814–17, from the eve of the battle of Rancagua to that of Chacabuco. He interweaves many novelistic intrigues in a rigorous historical tapestry which he copies from Barros Arana's *General History of Chile* (*Historia general de Chile*) and colors it with his own observations on Chilean society which had not changed much in the few decades that had passed. In *The Migrants* he illuminated in a crude light, sometimes derisive, sometimes tragic, the family life of some rich Hispanic-Americans living in Paris. Dazzled by false lights, they look down upon their native lands and, in turn, are looked down upon by the European aristocracy. *Crazy Estero* is perhaps the most gracious, delicate, entertaining, and refined of Blest Gana's novels. It consists of adventures and loves—back in the Santiago of 1839—tinted by the nostalgia with which the aging Blest Gana evokes the years of his childhood and youth.

The autobiographical talent of LUCIO VICTORIO MANSILLA (Argentina, 1831–1913) assures him of a higher place than many of those writers with less talent who consecrated themselves to the more sacred genres: poetry, drama, novel. This does not mean he did not work in literature: he translated a novel by Vigny and another by Balzac; he translated, with Dominguito Sarmiento, Laboulaye's *Paris in America* (*París en América*); he wrote a play about local customs, *An Aunt* (*Una tía*, 1864); a Romantic drama, *Atar Gull*, 1864; a collection of maxims, *Moral Studies* (*Estudios morales*, 1864); a pretentious historico-psychological essay, *Rozas*, 1898, and others. But his natural gift was autobiographical; it is dispersed throughout pages which remain fragmentary despite the author's having bound them in volumes: *Between Us: Thursday Chats* (*Entre nos. Causeries del jueves*, 1889–90), *Portraits and Recollections* (*Retratos y recuerdos*, 1894), *My Memoirs* (*Mis memorias*, 1911), *Brief Pages* (*Páginas breves*). Of all this literature, the most important book, and one of the most original in America, was *An Excursion Among the Ranquel Indians* (*Una excursión a los indios ranqueles*, 1870). He had been named frontier commander of Río Cuarto, Córdoba by President Sarmiento in 1868. It meant the continuation of the conquest of the desert from the Ranquel Indians. Mansilla signed a treaty with them but since the Indians were distrustful of the good faith of the Christians, and with reason, he decided, courageously, to visit the encampment of the Indians, unarmed, in order to convince the Indian chieftain. He lived among the Indians, and the chronicle of those days does not have an equal in our literature. In this book there is political intent: to mock the institutions of our civilization by contrasting them with the forms of sociability in the wigwam village of the Ranquel Indians. "Like Gulliver in his travels to Lilliput," Mansilla says, "I have seen in my travels to the land of the Ranquels the world such as it is." But his political thought which was against "strong governments," against a "civilization having no clemency" for the Indians, against the corruptive barbarism of the Christians, did not take a Utopian form as in Swift nor an allegorical one as in *Daylight's Pilgrimage*, which Alberdi was publishing that very year in order to rail against similar evils. Rather, it was embodied in his descriptions of the life of the Indians. In time, the political allusions weakened, but as a result, Mansilla's value as a narrator increased. The human groups he describes are complex: Indians, mestizos, renegades, white adventurers or outlaws, captured women. Mansilla looks upon them as a portion of Argentina, a portion in which the evils from the city operate: many of the whites are worse than the Indians. Each life is a drama. Mansilla presents it dramatically. And the pampa setting, which Echeverría had idealized and which Sarmiento had described without having seen, in Mansilla is real. His air of naturalness, which at times becomes a disregard for literary form, had the virtue of avoiding oratorical style.

IX. 1860-1880

Authors born between 1835 and 1855

Historical framework: Just as we can define the previous period as anarchic, in spite of the efforts of the people to give themselves a Constitution, we can define this period as one of achievement in the field of organization, although anarchy continues to gnaw at the insides of Hispanic-America.

Cultural tendencies: Second Romantic generation. Intellectual, scholarly, critical attitude. Early fruits of the Parnassians and the naturalists.

The authors whom we studied in the previous chapter had kindled their torches in the great Romantic bonfire of 1830; then they passed them on to younger men; and in this way, while Romanticism remained in the past, Romantic torches were still burning in many hands at the beginning of the second half of the century. In some instances they were extinguished: it was clear that several writers turned toward the light of humanistic literature. The truth is that Romanticism no longer has its earlier theoretical splendors. Now it is nothing more than a calm practical exercise. It becomes Romantic literature without the belligerent display of its esthetic formulas. Since authors had to write with more discipline, with more scholarship, they seek the manner of the classicists and the philologists. The themes of this second generation of Romantics are the usual ones: the sadness of defeated titans, popular speech and habits, indigenous legends of extinct peoples, history. Occasionally perhaps, in the form of a new theme, the nostalgia for home, inspired by many years of exile or of civil war, appears. Romanticism's sketches of customs end by becoming realist in technique. At the end of this period there will be writers who will cultivate letters for their own sake and begin to bring to America the first indications of the new literary movements of Europe, such as Parnassianism and naturalism. We will attempt to harmonize the literary development by grouping writers like musical chords, and by combining these chords according to their national key. Of course, there will be dissonances. Let the first strain be that of the gaucho poets of Argentina.

The Gauchesque Poets

Before commencing the study of the works which culminated the gaucho poetry movement, the reader should reread what has been stated in preceding chapters about the *costumbrism* movement, a movement which had been paving the way for the arrival of Bartolomé Hidalgo since the eighteenth century. Thanks to Hidalgo, the gaucho was transformed into a symbol for the rustic, Creole classes which opposed not only the foreigner but also the sophisticated elite of the city. Both partisans and adversaries of Juan Manuel de Rosas edited newspapers and pamphlets where they imitated the rustic speech. Even the most cultured writers, who were moved by a moral passion amidst the civil wars, attracted by the crude spectacle of the fields, and, above all, convinced by the Romantic ideals of a literature founded in local color and popular expression, began to mythicize the gaucho. We have already seen that Hidalgo's gaucho was not the transposition of an alleged wandering minstrel of the pampas, but a conscientious artistic creation with a regional literature for a parent. But the Romantics began to convert the gaucho figure, a somewhat uncouth figure as presented by the political verse, into a noble myth. Sarmiento, in *Facundo*, gives us the characterization of the singing gaucho. Mitre, in his *Rhymes*, re-elaborated upon the legend of Santo Vega, "the uncultured bard of the pampas." Ascasubi, very aware of the importance of gaucho poetry, set about writing a work in that style, and thus arose his *Santos Vega*. And finally from this glorification of the gaucho, two remarkable poems will emerge: *Fausto* and, above all, *Martín Fierro*. Afterwards, the gaucho theme shall so extend into all genres that it is not here possible to follow, step by step, its development and course: in the novel *Don Segundo Sombra* by Güiraldes, it will dissolve into pure idea.

ESTANISLAO DEL CAMPO (Argentina, 1834–1880) was a cultured city man, who knew how to write lyrical poetry in the Romantic manner of his time. Nevertheless, his place is among the gauchesque poets. We have seen already how, first Hidalgo, and later Ascasubi, although both city men, had lived in the country and were able to imitate rustic speech in composing their poems. Ascasubi was primarily a teacher. And despite the lack of experience in things rural, Del Campo started his literary life by writing gauchesque verses in imitation of Ascasubi. Del Campo responded to the satires published by Ascasubi under the pseu-

donym Aniceto el Gallo (Aniceto the Rooster) with others written under the pseudonym Anastasio el Pollo (Anastasio the Chicken). This
went on from 1847. The compositions of Anastasio el Pollo, of a political
or purely jocular nature, did not conceal their Ascasubian ancestry. Del
Campo would not have gone very far had it not been for a chance occurrence. On August 24, 1866, Gounod's *Faust* was performed at the
Theater Colón in Buenos Aires. Five days later, Del Campo sent the
manuscript of his own Creole version of *Faust* to Ricardo Gutiérrez
with a dedication to the latter. It was a masterful work of epigrammatic humor, of imaginative liveliness, of fluid versification, of sympathy for the inner feelings of its rural characters. The world of the
gauchos was alien to Del Campo; therefore, he could not imitate it.
Ascasubi had imitated the gauchos and Del Campo imitated Ascasubi.
In the use of the dialect—pronunciation, vocabulary, syntax—Del Campo
fell short. Being the good city Creole that he was, Del Campo was
close to rustic Argentine speech, but it required an effort for him to
learn the type he wished to imitate. A study of the variants between
the manuscript and the first edition of *Faust* shows his desire to adjust
to the country language. However, there was something more worthwhile than the imitation itself. Del Campo achieved the style of traditional poetry, that is, the one that the people feel to be their own,
transmitted by word of mouth, and from generation to generation without anyone's being interested in knowing who the author might have
been. But in his march toward a popular, or rather traditional, poetical
style, Del Campo appropriated a style of life not his own and light-
heartedly created individual personages such as Anastasio el Pollo and
Laguna, who look out onto a cultured world with their own way of
feeling, of thinking, and of being.

Anastasio el Pollo goes to Buenos Aires, by chance enters one of the
more elegant theaters, is overwhelmed by the scenes of Gounod's opera,
and once he returns to his "country," he relates point by point all he
saw and the way he saw it to his friend Laguna. The story of Faust,
Marguerite, and Mephistopheles appears interpreted, translated, re-
created through the impressions of these simple souls. The contrast between the reality of the gaucho and the artistic world of the European
is a happy one; but this contrast takes place in the spirit of the reader
of the poem. Del Campo and his cultured public enjoy the dialog between el Pollo and Laguna from without; within, the poem has sincere
emotional unity. Artistically, Del Campo was superior to his model,
Ascasubi. Nevertheless, he would be surpassed later by another Gauchesque poet: Hernández. By virtue of the publication of *Faust* (1866)

the question of whether there existed a "national literature" was revived in Buenos Aires. A balance sheet is drawn up and there are those who, in 1870, say that such a literature does not exist. Might *Fausto* perhaps be "national literature"? Is the external description of language, clothing, customs, folklore, sufficient to consider a literary work "national"?

José Hernández (Argentina, 1834–1886) lived in the midst of these discussions. He was a man of letters who sympathized with the cause of the gauchos and distrusted the Europeanist spirit of the statesmen of his day. He must heve been fed up hearing the same remarks: gaucho literature did not have literary merit, it was only enjoyable in works like *Fausto*. And he probably felt resentful since his own preferences did not figure in the table of values of his time. What is certain is that he decided to join the gaucho series by writing a poem also: *Martín Fierro* (the "Departure," 1872; the "Return," 1879). His intentions were serious. In the depths of his verses there is a muted polemic against the Europeanist group that is indifferent to the gaucho world, or against Europeanists who believed that *Fausto* was the measure of what gaucho literature could produce. Hernández breaks out in song, fully aware of his sober mission, and above all, quite cognizant that there are those who do not believe in him or in the gaucho literature of which he was capable. He reproaches the gauchesque poets for a task half done. Hernández realizes that he himself is bringing something new and more complete. And in order to record it, he imitates with more talent than the others the authentic voice of the gaucho. *Martín Fierro* then, has a twofold public—cultured readers and gauchos. With the same words he will offer two distinct messages. Before the cultured readers, he demands justice for the gaucho. Before the gauchos, he attempts to give them moral lessons to better their condition. In other words, *Martín Fierro* was a political poem when read in the city and a pedagogical poem when read in the country. However, upon miming the gauchos with the intention of bettering them morally, Hernández achieved something ingenious: an emotional and imaginative identification with the world of the gaucho. His *Martín Fierro* became an outstanding example of an individual poet who allies himself with popular poetry, re-elaborates its material, exalts it poetically, and allows the profound voice of an entire society to be heard in his own voice. *Martín Fierro* is not an epic poem. It is a popular poem in which the poet, with all deliberation, puts his song in the service of an oral tradition. The impulse is individual; the source is popular. Hernández does not adapt the poems of others—he invents everything, but in the spiritual attitude of a legendary *payador* or gaucho ballader. For this reason, his *Martín Fierro* seems to derive from an anonymous people. For this reason the gauchos read it as their own. For this reason the traditional elements are not brought from the outside, but felt and conceived by an Hernández transformed into an ordinary inhabitant of the pampas.

He was, then, a cultured poet with a traditional manner. The cultured poet is easily recognized in the skilled construction of the poem and in his intentions toward social reform which give coherence of plot to the adventures and value to the protagonist as a type and as a symbol. The traditional manner is that of improvisation. Hernández had observed the country men with keen attention. He lived with them and imitated them. Saturated with the gaucho spirit, Hernández makes believe he is improvising: "the couplets spring from me / like water from a fountain." It's not true—the emendation of the manuscripts and the study of the systematic lines in *Martín Fierro* reveal the arduous task involved in its composition. One of *Martín Fierro's* stylistic traits is that Hernández writes containing himself, attuning his voice to that of the gaucho he carried in him. He knows that his cultured voice would cripple the poem, that it is the voice of the gaucho that will give it its quality. He does not write in a prevalent gaucho dialect, but rather in a normal Spanish language to which he gives interior form with a gaucho perspective. It is an individual, energetic, creative language, rich in folklore but with no frontiers between what he gathered and what he invented.

The seven years between the "Departure" and the "Return" accentuate the poem's intention to promote reform. The conduct of the gaucho Fierro is motivated by different reasons. In the "Departure" Hernández raises a series of sociological frames within which he moves the anarchic, proud, and maltreated figure of the gaucho. The point of departure, then, is logical and constructive, and belongs to one who has studied social reality and proposes to disseminate his political message. There are allusions to the doctors of Buenos Aires, to Sarmiento's politics, to the government's abuses. Allegorically, Fierro flees with no other hope than that offered by the Indians who live beyond the pale of civilization. In the "Return," Fierro reappears, but with a European and progressivist vision of work: "for the land gives no fruit / if not watered by sweat." "Vandalism is ended." Now he avoids fights and explains why earlier he had killed; they are legal justifications which show that Hernández, down deep, was a conservative who respected the law, the reason being that, by 1879—Avellaneda is the new president, Sarmiento no longer holding the reins—Hernández recognizes "society" as legitimate, which earlier he had condemned in the "Departure." There are two moralities in the "Return": the one that Hernández proposes and one that the cynicism of the old man Vizcacha documents as a reality. The first morality having ideal goals and the second, opportunistic ones. Hernández' idealism and Vizcacha's realism. An Argentina with a program and an Argentina without a moral. Lights and shadows. Civilization versus Barbarism: here is where Hernández, the enemy of Sarmiento, in the end agrees with him. *Martín Fierro* is one of the most original poems emanating from Hispanic Romanticism. Its strophe, keeping within Romantic metrics, indicated that it desired to avoid classical rigor without allowing itself to be dragged under by traditional currents: octosyllabic verses organized in sextets, with the initial verse free of rhyme. The poem had the traits of the "Romantic school": literature as an expression of society; local color; nationalism; sympathy for the people; the exotic theme of Indian customs; the exiled and doleful hero as the victim of society; Fierro's noble friendship with Cruz; the novelistic episodes of violent contrasts as in the death of Vizcacha, the fight between the Indian and Fierro in front of the woman, the child whose throat is cut, and the happy meetings of Fierro with his children and with those of Cruz.

Other Argentinian Poets / OLEGARIO ANDRADE (Argentina, 1839–1882) clings more to the forms of Romanticism than Hernández did. Of Andrade's two epochs —that of Entre Ríos, 1855–75, and that of Buenos Aires, 1876–81—the second is of more weight for being the period of his best poetry. "The Condor's Nest" (*"El nido de cóndores"*), "The Lost Harp" (*"El arpa perdida"*), "San Martín" and others, possess the mark of "titanism," a characteristic of Romanticism; and in fact, the symbol of Titan appears in "Prometheus," his "song to the human spirit." Andrade's creative imagination was more epic than lyrical. He prefers to relate what took place in the world to that which takes place in his soul. Nevertheless, what Andrade objectifies best are metaphors, that is, lyrical visions: visions with amplifying crystals that magnify everything beyond measure. Robust, sensational metaphors constructed with such a desire for clarity that they generally appear in the form of comparisons and similes with the structural links "like" and "as" in plain sight. They are the metaphors of a visual poet who pours his inner world into a mold of things that lay before the eyes of everyone—plastic metaphors. Although one may recognize their kinship to the metaphoric language of Romanticism (Victor Hugo's, especially), Andrade's metaphors are not adopted children, but the natural children of his fantasy. They have the same features, like the members of one family, but each one lives its own life. Andrade writes from the position of one ready to leap. He is obsessed with space, with heights. He leaps upon great themes—progress, homeland, the future, liberty, human destiny—from hyperbole to hyperbole. Resonant poetry, round but not hollow, or at least no hollower than the breast from whence the strength of song emanates; always affected, partly because art is affectation; grandiose for its grandiloquence, but not great; because in spite of everything Andrade was not a great poet. He lived bewildered by the peal of his own declamations and the declamations typical of the journalism of his age: Andrade paid dearly for not knowing how to forget that he was a journalist when he wrote poetry.

The terminal date for this chapter is 1880. And it happens that in Argentina those who were between thirty and forty years of age were called "men of the '80's": 1880 was the year of the federalization of Buenos Aires which gave the country its definitive organization. Because of its political significance, historians have chosen the eighties as a literary landmark. The only trouble is that during this period of time—ten years before, ten years after—writers of different generations converge. Men like Vicent F. López, Bartolomé Mitre, and Lucio V. Mansilla are still influential figures. Yet the representatives of the eighties are O. Andrade, E. Cambacérès, E. Wilde, L. V. López, M. Cané, R. Obligado, J. A. García. The common features which bind them are the feeling of belonging to families which had helped to build the nation or which deserved to govern the republic; coupled with the awareness that the social and political transformation of Argentina was thwarting their ambition and forcing them to fail; and a skepticism and sterility, which sought a mode of expression in a fragmentary literature of ironic and autobiographical tone. Here we shall deal only with the poets; of the prose writers we shall have more to say later on in the chapter.

The lyricists who had the best reputation at this historical juncture were Guido y Spano, Andrade, and Rɪcardo Gutiérrez (1836–1896). To these were added the new poets Obligado and Almafuerte. The poetic work of Rafael Obligado (1851–1920) is very scarce; he wrote only one book, *Poems* (*Poesías,* 1885) augmented in the second edition of 1906, and even in it, moments of excellence are scarce. But in Argentina he was considered "the national poet," in part because he insisted on themes and attitudes along the Echeverría-Ascasubi-Hernández line, at a time when the country was putting a cosmopolitan mask on its Creole face. Having taken refuge in a simple poetry—nature, the past, affection for regional types, folklore—he seemed original to his friends and readers. What was original, nevertheless, was his poetizing in this manner in the face of the waves of immigration, of technical-economic progress, of the imitation of European styles, ideas, and customs, of the ambition for material wealth. The exaltation of nationalism was what gave fame to Obligado. Of his poems, some legendary, others historical, others intimate, time has saved his *Santos Vega,* the *payador.* First Bartolomé Mitre, then Ascasubi, and later Eduardo Gutiérrez in a novel, had already written about this *payador.* Obligado had heard his peons tell how Santos Vega had been outsung by the Devil, and from that time on had wandered over the countryside like a soul in purgatory. With material taken from literature and folklore he wrote his poem: not in a Creole dialect but in very precise, very lyrical language, made subtle with shimmering images of mystery and, within the scope of Romanticism, disciplined through a great deal of literary study. The poem is not pure poetry, nevertheless, for it contains moral preoccupations, patriotic lessons, and even an allegory: in the section "The Death of the *Payador*" Ragged John, the stranger, symbol of progress, industry, science, and European imagination, diabolically triumphs over Santos Vega, symbol of moribund Creole tradition. In adding a new canto in 1887 ("The Hymn of the *Payador*)" to the three in the first edition, he accentuated his patriotic intent.

Among the "men of the '80's," Cané, Obligado, Oyuela, *et al.,* we cannot include Pedro B. Palacios, better known by his pen name Almafuerte (Argentina, 1854–1917). The former were cultured, rich, sober, influential, elegant, satisfied, conventional, Europeanized. Almafuerte was swimming against the current. And later, when the "men of the '80's" were succeeded by those "Modernists" clustered about Rubén Darío, Almafuerte remained once again outside the group: on one occasion he asked for recompense "in the name of Hispanic-American letters, which I have saved from decadentism and effeminacy." Indeed, he could not be a "decadent," that is, one of the new poets who admired Verlaine, for the simple reason that what he was poetizing was another decadence—Romanticism. Literarily speaking, he was ill-mannered; in order to enrage the estheticians he made believe he was worse than he was. The first impression that one receives on reading him is that of the deformity of his verses. But he who perseveres in reading him will discover a poet of vigor, even more, a poet of spiritual complexity. Defective and unequal, his poetry reflects the character of a very singular person. He was a blasphemer. He was misanthropic, misogynous, megalomaniacal and Messianic; eccentric through and through, with misguided aspirations toward being a prophet and philosopher, stentorian in voice, delirious, furious, haughty, rude, and grotesque. But he was a lyricist with a new voice in our literature. That voice resounded, augmented by continuous hyperboles. He directed himself to the rabble, to the "vile sweaty multitude." He was not a poet of the masses, despite the fact that his popularity came from the lower classes, but an aggressive individual. At first glance his style seems to be popular claptrap, vulgar expression, related to the tango dives and the low-life toughs of the slums; but if the style is carefully observed it reveals a desire to renovate poetic language, to adopt new meters, to invent words, to seek a certain perfection in an incessant correction of the work itself. He had bad taste, but was individualistic in the brazen sincerity with which he renounced the conventions of his time, and dared to confess his anguished vision of life. Everything for him was a failure: himself, man, the Universe, God. His pessimism, his disdain, his anger are deep-rooted. And for having discovered failure in the very root of existence, no one has poetized better than he the ugly, the obscure, the poverty-ridden, the aborted, the sordid, and even the repugnant. He expressed his somber humor in generally epigrammatical prose: *Evangelics* (*Evangélicas*). Since it is the function of prose, more than verse, to articulate thoughts with rigorous logic, it is in his prose that the contradictions in Almafuerte's logic appear. He believed and disbelieved in the dignity of man; he believed and disbelieved in God and in a universal order; he believed and disbelieved in a universal truth; he believed and disbelieved in moral progress; and on and on. The robustness of his thought was in its onslaught; the direction did not matter. It was badly articulated thought, but rich in insight into the wickedness of man and the falsehoods of society. He is one of the few Argentinian poets of the nineteenth century esteemed by those of the twentieth: Lugones admired him and some of the young writers of today still admire him.

Colombia / In Colombian Romanticism, which generally played in the octave that goes from Chateaubriand to Victor Hugo, RAFAEL POMBO (1833–1912) sounded with personal impetus. He lived the longest of the Colombian poets—seventy nine years—and was the most fecund—over four hundred poems without counting translations, fables, and stories in verse. Many years, many works, in which one naturally can point out several stages. From 1851 to 1853, in the first onrush that smacks of Zorrilla and Byron, his poems are more sentimentalist than sentimental, although the plaintive notes are usually subdued owing to the moral complexion of the man. In his second phase, during his residence in the United States, he reaches his fullness. His travels, the experience of a foreign culture, his relations with distinguished people, his friendship with Longfellow and Bryant, the study of classics and moderns which contributed to his skill as a translator, and the maturity of his years, all gave flexibility and strength to his verse, from the ode to the epigram, from love elegies to philosophic meditations, from landscape description to civil and jocular themes. His third phase goes up to 1912. It is after his return to Colombia and the decadence of old age that his poetry tends to reasoning, and the modes of versification become fixed: the sonnet was the preferred form of his later years. But these phases run entirely in the Romantic orbit, without a tinge of Neoclassicism, without an indication of the Modernism to come. One theme dominates his poetry: love, which inspires him from his youthful "The Glass of Wine" (*"La copa de vino"*) to the senile "Avisag." The love of a bachelor for all women and not for one; the love of real and ideal women, angelic and sensual women, women of all races and ages, and in "Elvira Tracy" even dead women. It was eroticism of the flesh and of the imagination that tormented him just as easily with the vision of beauty as with the vision of his own failure. He even indulged in false feminine poems (*"Mi amor"*) that deceived readers into believing that hidden in Colombia, was an ardent Sappho: Edda la Bogotana. Later Pombo confessed his fraud by writing "Edda," one of his better known poems. His sentiment for women went hand in hand with his sentiment for landscape—after all, woman and landscape were for him spectacles of nature. He would move on to the landscape not as a gardener who arranges it in pretty shapes, but as one restrained and distrustful of the force of art: "Put up your lyre, poet, / put up, painter, your palette, / and your chisel, sculptor; / nature is better / than the sign that interprets it." In "Prelude to Spring" (*"Preludio de primavera"*) it is nature that is worthwhile: at its feet, the life of man is small and only inspires melancholy. This meditation on our destiny as men, whenever he contemplated nature, tended to overwhelm his spirit.

Since Heredia, Niagara Falls has always been an obsession in Hispanic-American poetry; when Pombo in "At Niagara" (*"En el Niágara"*) began to describe that "museum of cataracts," "factory of clouds," "a sea staved in by the weight of its waves," he showed a visual strength more powerful than had anyone else. What he saw is here in his verse: the reader sees Niagara again because it lies before his eyes. Torrential poetry, like Niagara itself. He did not adhere to the graphic element only, and one might add that this is the least important in Pombo's poetry. Misanthropy is pleased to depreciate man as it exalts nature. Why fear nature?: "the gravest evil it does is a good: it offers us a grave, a bed for the tired." Man: "there is the monster," "there is the asp whose contact I shudder," "atrocious grafting of angel and devil." "For me," he ends by saying, "life is a sarcasm." There was within Pombo a Leopardi, and he gave us his desperate note. At twenty-four years of age, he wrote sixty-one *décimas* "The Hours of Darkness" (*"La hora de tinieblas,"* 1864) which, for the sincerity of its doubts, is blasphemous to one of religious conscience, profound and anguished to all. Pombo, on the strength of his Catholicism, recanted in old age, but what he had said remained, and his work is a high point in the history of our literature. He was one of the best lyricists of his generation; but the waters are so boisterous that the undulation of his verse becomes rough, turbulent, and broken, and so our ears at times suffer from the noise. Because of his achievements we must forgive him his failings.

With DIEGO FALLÓN (1834–1905), EPIFANIO MEJÍA (1838–1913) and RAFAEL NÚÑEZ (1835–1894) we could close the list of Colombian poets of the second Romantic generation. Fallón had his idealistic feeling for nature, Mejía, his realist verses in traditional form, and Núñez, his poetry of ideas. After them came others, disciplined through their contacts with the classicists and philologists. In Colombia, a conservative and traditionalist country, pedagogical norms have always been overbearing. The Spaniards had not participated in the march of modern linguistic history, which was primarily German, with French and Italians bringing up the rear. After el Brocense (Francisco Sánchez de las Brozas) there was a long interruption, until the Colombian RUFINO J. CUERVO (1844–1911) became the great linguistic leader—the Spaniard Menéndez Pidal would come later. Inclined also toward the study of language—although more a grammarian than a philologist—

was another illustrious Colombian, MIGUEL ANTONIO CARO (1843–1909) who brought his seriousness as a scholar to literature. He was an excellent representative of the humanistic flourishing in Colombia in those days. His closeness to Horace, Propertius, Catullus, and, above all, to Vergil—he translated *The Aeneid* admirably—left its mark and·countermark in every verse. His verses were born with wisdom and are technically irreproachable, but they are cold, as if born in the damp basement of literary history. They lack flair and feeling. The poet goes about on his knees because his religion is not the defiant titanism of the Romantics, but a humble and resigned Catholicism. His sonnet "To Himself" (*"A sí mismo"*) is propped on Caro's two knees, one classical, the other Catholic. His thought was academic, not critical; or in other words, he succeeded as a critic when his materials were academic, but he did not understand the new values. In time, his constant rejection of what he did not understand separated him from the literature of his time. He remained like a classical statue: in a statuesque style he wrote one of the best poems of his age—"To the Statue of the Liberator" (*"A la estatua del Libertador"*).

Mexico / We have yet to play the Mexican strains. As elsewhere, we find in Mexico during these years poets who stuck to tradition. In *Murmurs of the Forest* (*Murmurios de la selva*) by Monsignor JOAQUÍN ARCADIO PAGAZA (1839–1918) the tradition was classical, of Vergilian breath. The tradition of the productive JUAN DE DIOS PEZA (1852–1910) was Spanish Romanticism, grandiloquent in public themes and eloquent in his domestic affections: *Songs of the Home* (*Cantos del hogar*, 1884). Also Romantic in the Spanish manner, though more lyrical, was MANUEL ACUÑA (1849–1873), author of "Nocturne" (*"Nocturno"*), which was inspired by an amorous sentiment and written on the eve of suicide as a farewell to life and love. Acuña was a poet of liberal ideas in politics and a positivist in philosophy. "Before a Cadaver" (*"Ante un cadáver"*) is a curious example of how Romantic lyricism makes its way through the themes of scientific materialism, in those years new and' provocative. Another Romantic in the Spanish manner was MANUEL M. FLORES (1840–1885) the erotic poet of *Passion-flowers* (*Pasionarias*). On the other hand, AGUSTÍN F. CUENCA (1850–1884) looked to the side from where, years later, the innovators were to appear.

Other Countries / And now the final arpeggio. DOMINGO ESTRADA (Guatemala, 1850–1901) was a Romantic of modern tastes, an admirer of Martí, a translator of Poe. MANUEL MOLINA VIGIL (Honduras, 1853–1883) sang romantically to liberty, love, and death. LUISA PÉREZ DE ZAMBRANA (Cuba, 1835–1922) was the author of the best elegies of her generation. In the Dominican Republic the first lyrical voices of quality are heard: those of JOSÉ JOAQUÍN PÉREZ (1845–1900), author of *Indigenous Fantasies* (*Fantasías indígenas*), SALOMÉ UREÑA DE HENRÍQUEZ (1850–1897) with civil and civilizing intentions, and the emphatic FEDERICO HENRÍQUEZ Y CARVAJAL (1848–1951). The patriot MANUEL RODRÍGUEZ OBJÍO (1838–1871) could also be listed. In Puerto Rico, there are two Romantics: one of French education, JOSÉ DE JESÚS DOMÍNGUEZ (1843–1898), author of *Elegiac Odes* (*Odas elegiacas*) and *The White Houris* (*Las huríes blancas*); and the other, more important, a Romantic in the Spanish manner, JOSÉ GAUTIER BENÍTEZ (1850–1880), serene, melancholic, Becquerian, with his themes of love and country; and we might even add the name of LOLA RODRÍGUEZ DE TÍO (1843–1924).

The Venezuelans were JACINTO GUTIÉRREZ COLL (1836–1903), who knew the Parnassians in France, and ANTONIO PÉREZ BONALDE (1846–1892). What unknown affinities made Pérez Bonalde translate Heine and Poe? We don't know. So unknown were they that they did not reveal themselves in his original poetry. Nevertheless, his having translated Heine and Poe, who a few years later would be rediscovered by the "Modernist" generation, has occasioned the belief that the elegiac Pérez Bonalde was a precursor of that poetic tone, rich in shades and exquisiteness, that prevailed from 1890 on. A precursor? Perhaps. But why not say he was a straggler? Poe and Heine had entered Spanish literature before Pérez Bonalde was born. The preference for the Germanic, with its predilection for things mysterious, legendary, supernatural, is noticeable already in the decade of 1840. Bécquer himself, who manifested this better than anyone else, came later. Because of his Nordic, misty Romanticism, Pérez Bonalde was considered a "strange one," a modern, almost a Modernist. But his books of poetry, *Strophes* (*Estrofas*, 1877) and *Rhythms* (*Ritmos*, 1880) do not belong to the cycle that Darío's *Azure* opens. His best tone was the nostalgic one. His "Return to the Homeland" (*"Vuelta a la patria"*) is a beautiful Romantic evocation of his town and family. The Ecuadorian CÉSAR BORJA (1852–1910) was somber in his sentiments, luminous in his images. The Chilean JOSÉ ANTONIO SOFFIA (1843–1886) was one of those poets of minor key, moderate, simple, acceptable to good families. His *Lyrical Poems* (*Poesías líricas*) date from 1875. Bécquer was giving the softest notes to Spanish Romanticism. Soffia preferred that softness. Softly he sang of love—above all, of his wife—of nature, loneliness, mystery, death, virtue, his native place, God.

Prose Writers

Certain names are lacking in our panorama of poetry. It is not that they have been forgotten, but they stand out as writers of prose and, as such, they will be studied farther on: Isaacs, Palma, González Prada, Varona, and Sierra. The prose of this generation is extraordinary; if, in addition to those names, we add Montalvo, Hostos, and others to come, it will be evident that we stand before the best prosists of the nineteenth century.

Juan Montalvo / In order of merit, the best prosist is JUAN MONTALVO (Ecuador, 1832–1889), one of the best in the Spanish language. A great many of his works derive from the struggle against the evils of Ecuador, which are the evils that prevail in our America: anarchy, military bossism, the fanatical desire of the clergy for power, the ignorance of the masses, despotism, administrative corruption, rudeness, injustice, poverty. But Montalvo's political literature does not have the turbulence that could be expected from such a combative life. He made literature out of politics; and his literature was made with skillful language. Attentive to language, Montalvo would even become distracted from the theme upon which he was writing. His interest was not so much on the ideas, but on the musical and plastic richness of the language. He thought more with words than with ideas. Although it was the essay that gave him best results, Montalvo vacillated in his literary career by writing poetry, short stories, and dramas. He never valued his own verses. On the contrary, he came to believe that he was gifted for narrative. He wrote a few short stories that had unity. They do not have the quality of the illustrative "episodes" (cf., *Seven Treatises—Siete tratados*), of the anecdotes at the service of his discourses (cf., *Orations Against Catiline—Las catilinarias*), of his allegories and parables (cf., *Moral Geometry—Geometría moral*), of the stories on Ossianic poems or Greek legends, and so on. These pages are more like unrelated exercises of narrative ability which never developd completely. What is certain is that Montalvo was not interested in giving accounts of actions, but in delivering discourses. Even in *Chapters that Cervantes Forgot (Capítulos que se le olvidaron a Cervantes)*, which constitute a novel, what can be salvaged are the interpolated essays, or those put in Cervantes' mouth. Upon writing the book Montalvo's attitude was that of the essayist and not that of the narrator. Instead of telling us about the adventures of Don Quijote, he substitutes for them essays on insanity as a source of adventure, on the virtue of water, tears, decorum, and poverty, the value of action, his respect for trees. His tale breaks off and disappears. What remains alive and warm in the book are the essay fragments, alien to the environment of Don Quijote. The same can be said of his dramas, which do not exist in themselves, except as vehicles for pieces of discursive prose. And since what we are hearing is the voice of the author-ventriloquist that apparently comes from the mouth of each puppet, stage dialog is not dialog at all, but a monolog in various voices. The poet, the narrator, the dramatist are shadows of the essayist.

The best of Montalvo's literature, then, is his essays. But to point out which are his best is difficult. There are essays which, as brief discursive units, are quite good. Notice, for example, many of those in *The Spectator (El espectador)*. They are short, simple, effective, agile. But it seems that this type of minimal essay did not satisfy him. He strove for more ample and complicated compositions, opulent architecture, "treatises." Montalvo wrote articles spontaneously, but he considered them of little consequence and regarded them only as elements of larger "works." Thus the miniaturist leaped into the composition of the vast mosaics of his *Seven Treatises*. The more literary airs he put on to capture imaginary readers, the more precious his style became, the more his composition went out of control. He would improve the fragments and cripple the totality. In the *Seven Treatises* there are many moments of brilliance, many rhythms, much wealth of metaphor and aphorism, many techniques, and a greater frequency of felicitous poetic devices; but each treatise is not a fluent unit, created from within, but a scaffolding—at times clumsily erected—upon which are placed paintings barely connected to each other. On the other hand, in the short essays of *The Spectator,* these paintings appear in isolation. But his having left them in that state indicates that Montalvo had not much interest in them and did not "work them out" for us artistically; and, in fact, they are simple and wanting in thought and in imagination.

When he looked out on his own life, Montalvo generally focused his esthetic eye on experiences that lent themselves to romantic adornment, on experiences of resentment, displeasure, indignation, horror, hatred, and on experiences stimulated by literature. Consequently, there is in his prose a principle of differentiation between the modal qualities of what is beautiful, truculent, and traditional. When the solitary Montalvo—that Montalvo who is aware of the exquisiteness of his sensibilities—started to express his intimate emotions, he tended to give us a poematic prose. However, a romantic prose, oriented toward the "poem in prose," approached the "Modernism" of the following generation. His yearning for solitude, and within that solitude, the desire to enjoy the landscape and his own melancholy, was a retractable, timid, nervous moment of his soul. Except that that soul did not find peace in withdrawal: it felt permanently offended by the world, and at the slightest humiliation, sometimes without any humiliations, it leaped into the arena ready to fight. In the same way that he found the esthetic formula for his exquisiteness, which was that of the poem in prose, he found for his defamation of men and things, for his fits of tragic, pessimistic, disillusioned or sarcastic humor, the esthetic formula of the insult. The resentment that burned in his viscera swirled in the air like smoke until it entered the spotlight of defamatory literature and became diatribe. In his seclusion as well as in his exasperation Montalvo took pleasure in remembering glorious scenes and in visualizing himself as a person of fantasy. Thusly, his experiences were shaped into patterns, themes, models, ideals, and reminiscences of certain forms of artistic expression that had already been consecrated by history. When he related anecdotes of his own life, he usually enriched them with recollections gathered from books; or the opposite, he projected an autobiographical intention on his bookish recollections. It would be interminable to enumerate the literary traditions that find a place in many of his pages. The past constantly oozes from every word. Montalvo's prose is one of the richest in nineteenth-century Spanish.

Perhaps Montalvo's greatest expression of energy, and the most amazing, is his having invented, in a little corner of America, a personal language: a language kneaded with the clay of many centuries of literature and kneaded for the love of the language itself. He had the extraordinary gift of coining phrases, of avoiding the well-trodden path, and of finding marvelous expression, of evoking a reality with the slightest touches of imaginative prose. From this need to twist and complicate his expression, he achieved, with more frequency than his Spanish-speaking contemporaries, stylistic fragments of the first order.

Ricardo Palma / Ricardo Palma (1833–1919) was the great figure of lagging Peruvian Romanticism. He wrote dramas in verse which he condemned later as "abominable monstrosities" and many verses (four volumes) which he called, with manifest disinterest, "rhymed lines of writing." In the entertaining, confidential notes of *The Bohemian Life of My Time* (*La bòhemia de mi tiempo*, 1887) Palma tells of the Romantic literary excesses of the years 1848 to 1860. Disappointed and mocking, Palma withdrew from Romanticism; but only after he had lighted one of his torches to illumine romantically the Peruvian past. The romantic sympathy for the past took possession of certain literary genres. A born narrator, Palma must have felt the attraction for all of them: the historical novel, the sketch of customs, the legend, the short story. He did not submit to any of them, but taking a little from here and a little from there, he created his own genre—the "tradition." Already in 1852 he was writing stories on traditions; ten years later these "traditions" were taking on definitive configurations, and from 1872, the long series of *Peruvian Traditions* (*Tradiciones peruanas*), in perfect form, are published. From 1872 to 1883 there were six series which were followed by others with different titles: *Old Clothing* (*Ropa vieja*, 1889); *Moth-eaten Clothing* (*Ropa apolillada*, 1891); *Knick-knacks and Traditions and Historical Articles* (*Cachivaches y Tradiciones y artículos históricos*, 1899–1900); *Appendix to My Latest Traditions* (*Apéndice a mis últimas tradiciones*) already in print in 1911. (We have read the manuscript of "Off-Color Sauce" (*"Tradiciones en salsa verde,"* 1901), still unprinted, and scarcely printable because of its pornography.) With the years, Palma became aware of his originality and recorded the formula of his invention in several places: in his letter to Pastor S. Obligado, in the prolog to Clorinda Matto de Turner's *Traditions*, in the introduction to his *Old Clothing*, in the frequent allusions to his theory and to the method of the traditionalist, diffused in the *Traditions* themselves. From these we extract one: "A dash or two of lies, and an equal dose of truth, no matter how infinitesimal or homeopathic it may be, a good deal of nicety and polish in the language, and there you have the recipe for writing Traditions . . ." The socio-geographical-historical-psychological tapestry he offers us in his *Traditions* is quite extensive: from the beggar to the viceroy; from Tucumán to Guayaquil; from the time of the Incas to contemporary events in which Palma himself had a role; from the idiot to the genius.

But in the center of the tapestry, and woven with a fine thread, is the resourceful viceregal society of eighteenth-century Lima. The sources are numberless and at times unrecognizable: edited and unedited chronicles, histories, lives of saints, books on travel, pasquinades, wills and testaments, tales by missionaries, convent registries, verses, and, in addition to the written word, the oral one of the proverb, the cliché, the couplet, superstition, legend, popular stories. The structure of the *Traditions* is also complex. The combination of historical documentation and narrative action is disarranged, shifting, free. At times there is no structure at all; the events moulder and smother the narrative. Or, in one tradition, there are many other minor traditions inserted one into the other. The granary of plots, situations, and interesting characters is so abundant that a whole family of short story writers could feed there. One sentence might be the kernel of a possible story. Even Palma's spirit unfolds on two planes. He was in Herderian sympathy with the voices of the people, but also indulged in Voltairian mockery of them. But the person who influenced his humor was not so much Voltaire as Balzac and his *Contes drolatique*. He has the multiplicity of perspectives of the bantering skeptic, and even his protestations of impartiality—"I don't subtract or add anything"—are ironic needlings at the absolutism of the Church and State.

He was a liberal, and only took seriously the right to a free conscience, and the sovereignty of the people and the moral values of good, honor, and justice. His dominant tone is one of mischievous, picaresque jesting. And he even keeps the smile on his lips when he relates the poetical miracle of "The Scorpion of Friar Gómez" (*"El alacrán de Fray Gómez"*) or the dramatic sacrifice of "Mother Love" (*"Amor de madre"*). This latter "tradition," one of his best, enthused Benito Pérez Galdós so much that, according to what he tells in a letter, it gave him the desire to write a drama "like *El abuelo*." Nevertheless, because of that semi-mocking, semi-compassionate smile of Palma, "Mother Love," more than drama in the Galdós manner, would lend itself to the grotesque theater of the Italians Chiarelli and Pirandello. Tragi-comic farces, and not tragedies, would be found in Palma's vein. Despite his carelessness, he was a good narrator. He knows how to make us wait for the denouement. There is not a single virtue of the short story writer that Palma did not have. He presented his characters gracefully, especially the women; he selected strange conflicts, tangled them, and then untangled them. But there is not a single "tradition" that is really a short story. His joy at being an antiquarian causes him to collect facts; and to make room for them, he interrupts, deviates, and constantly alters the course of the story. His handling of historical facts keeps his hands so occupied that he cannot give the action that final tweak for a surprising wind-up. He is attracted not only by the action, but also by the historical atmosphere in which it occurs; and that atmosphere is composed of particles of archival dust. The facts float in the air, loosely and wildly. As with Montalvo, Palma's prose is something of a linguistic museum in which words and tropes are squeezed into the smallest spaces. However, in contrast to Montalvo, Palma's language is more American and more popular. In this instance Palma, who as a member of the Peruvian Academy, corresponding to the Spanish, had worked in lexicography, responded to a linguistic theory: that the vocabulary enriches itself by allowing free entry to Americanisms, archaisms, neologisms, cultured and popular words; but that one must conform to the syntax studiously and zealously. In the *Traditions* the oral and written language, the Spanish and Hispanic-American language, the popular and cultured language constantly interchange their thrusts, movements, cadences, words, and syntax. Since these undulating ideals of expression had joined, separated, and then joined again in literary history, even Palma's artistry has a good deal of the colloquial, and in turn, his manner of conversing, a good deal of literature. On the whole, his prose is enchanting for the way it vitalizes hackneyed expressions and for raising popular expressions to the category of artistic monuments.

The Novelists

JORGE ISAACS (Colombia, 1837–1895) was born exactly one hundred years after Bernardin de Saint-Pierre; but his *María* (1867) belongs to that literary family that was founded by the novel *Paul et Virginie* at the end of the eighteenth century. In *Paul et Virginie*, Saint-Pierre had created the idyl of innocent creatures who, in the midst of a nature equally innocent, love each other with a love that death will seal with absolute purity. Years later Chateaubriand, with that same sentimental tendency to idealize love and to discover a new geography, wrote *Atala*: again the purity of first love, in the lonely regions of the forests of

America, between two youths whom death consecrates as virgins. So in writing "that dialog of immortal love impelled by hope and interrupted by death," Isaacs was following an erotic star that had guided an entire caravan before. But it was Chateaubriand who taught Isaacs to orchestrate his vague eroticism esthetically. For this reason, when Efraín reads the novel *Atala* to María, he records very significantly that María "was as beautiful as the creation of the poet, and I loved her with the love he had imagined." Even more—the reading of Chateaubriand harbingers for Efraín and María the sad unravelling of the idyl they were living, as if *Atala*, in a subtle way, were the libretto of a drama that they were performing. As he Chateaubriandized, there was one thing that Isaacs felt sure about—his outlook on landscape. Chateaubriand had written about an ideal America; Isaacs describes a concrete America in which he loved, worked, and struggled. For a Frenchman, the American setting of *Atala* was exotic; for Isaacs that America was his own land. Consequently, *María* has a national significance that is lacking in *Atala*. In *María* the colorful image of our American life is given back to us—Americanism, not exoticism. But exoticism was such a typically Romantic trait that Isaacs refused to renounce it and hence gave us the story of Nay and Sinar in an African frame. Africa was for Isaacs what America was for Chateaubriand. Isaacs' descriptions were not realist: he looked upon the landscape with eyes already accustomed to the Romantic mode. Just enjoying nature was, in itself, a Romantic disposition. Isaacs knew, therefore, that the landscape was a great literary theme. And he developed it as a mood, in the Romantic manner. "If happiness caresses us," says Efraín, "nature smiles upon us." Contrasted with the garden landscape where María strolls, Isaacs describes nature without María as disarrayed, terrible, foe-like. Paradise and purgatory. When the novel of hell, of the green hell of the jungle, emerges in America later, men are worth, esthetically, less than the serpents.

Another of the discoveries of Romanticism that influenced Isaacs was local color. When Isaacs began writing, all Colombians, some more, some less, were writing or reading recollections of city, country, and family life. Isaacs gave in to the vogue. But the depiction of customs, which, when written as separate articles have a bitter taste, once incorporated in novels, is sweetened by the prestige of things sentimental. In *María*, even mocking touches are affectionate. The novel was weakened somewhat by these dissonances between the idyllic notes and the notes on customs. Yet, there are appealing scenes in the evocation of José's highland farm, the tiger hunt, the loves of the young girls,

Tránsito's wedding and Feliciana's burial, and, above all, the rustic picture of delicious Salomé, painted in the center like a mulatto nymph, innocent, playful, and sensual. This happy feudal society in which masters, peons, and slaves live together without sordidness is as idealized as the loves of the two young masters. The Romantics had falsified the idea of Man; and Isaacs describes the feelings of María and Efraín in the false fog of these notions. María was born as an abstraction, but the sincerity of the author began humanizing her. This María was a lyrical synthesis of Isaacs' love experiences, the ideal of his early years, the imaginative focal point where that great diffused light of real remembrances and longings would be concentrated. Although Isaacs worked his eroticism to the point of molding it into the literary category of the woman-seraphim, he had a surfeit of rich amatory experience—experience that was real, diversified, concrete in its details—that saved him his idyl.

He liked women and knew how to differentiate them. It is obvious that he feels strongly attracted to all the women of the Cauca. Isaacs transferred his virility to Efraín. In spite of the delicacy of his love, Efraín was completely tense, completely attentive to all of María's little exposures of flesh. María also feels the attraction for Efraín: it is not always literature that joins them, but love. If Efraín's arm brushes against her body, a blush reddens her face. Kisses flutter timidly, without ever alighting, but always seeking each other. The idyl between María and Efraín repeated old vignettes, but the sincerity of tenderness created the miracle of such fresh expression that it seemed original. The rites of an amorous fetishism—the exchanging of flowers, of locks of hair—the coquettishness and innocence with which María hides or abandons her hand to the caresses of Efraín, the using of the child John as a household cupid, the landscape as confidant, the pre-enjoyment of sadness while enjoying happiness are moments sincerely lived, sincerely expressed. The first letter that María writes to Efraín is so authentic that one is surprised to find it in a book; and the last pages are to be remembered always as among the best in the Spanish literature of its time. The stream of poetry that runs through the work is not continuous, but it lasts long enough to count in the history of our artistic prose. On the other hand, in his verses which treat of narratives, remembrances of childhood, patriotic songs, moral reflections, and landscapes, a profound lyric vision very seldom appears.

MANUEL DE JESÚS GALVÁN (Dominican Republic, 1834–1910) novelized history in *Enriquillo*. He had been educated in the tradition of academic classicism and his cultural limits were Jovellanos and Quintana, Scott and Chateaubriand. In evoking the Spanish colony of Santo Domingo (1502–1533) Galván subjected the march of his novel to norms of historical accuracy; he sacrificed the artistic value of the narrative each time he had to choose between his imagination and his documentation. Even in those cases where he found no documents, instead of inventing, he interrupted the narrative. He substantiated historical truth on original documents, even to the point of transcribing entire pages of Las Casas and of explaining episodes with lessons in history. It is amazing that Galván should succeed in achieving a novel of such literary quality, in spite of the difficulties of his complicated historical theme and of his academic method. The Indian had become extinct in Santo Domingo as a consequence of Spanish political action, so that the Dominicans, standing up to Spain, invoked the Indian as a symbol of the spirit of liberty. National restoration motivated the support of indigenous elements. Galván, in the midst of this indigenist flowering —José Joaquín Pérez had just published *Indigenous Fantasies* (*Fantasías indígenas*, 1877)—began his novel by also idealizing the Indians. The first part of *Enriquillo* was published in 1878, the completed edition in 1882. However, although Galván feels the pull of the Romantic sympathy for the Indian, he does not allow himself to be dominated by it. He notifies us explicitly that he is on the side of European civilization: "We beg the reader to believe that we are not attached to the Indiophilic mania. We shall never overpass the limits of just compassion . . ." There is, then, a difference in attitude between Galván and the other indigenist writers of his time. Galván converted Father Las Casas into the doctrinal axis of his novel, following his writings to the letter of the word, at times textually. But Galván did not interpret Las Casas' preachings as proof of the moral turpitude of Spain, but as a noble example offered to the world by Spain. After all, Las Casas was a Spaniard; and the strength of his invectives redeems Spain. Galván called his novel a "legend." A Romantic title. But his prose, rather than resembling that of other writers of "legends," such as the Romantics Zorrilla and Bécquer, resembles that of the Neoclassicists Jovellanos and Quintana. This is why in *Enriquillo* there dominates a framework of logical, clear, ample, serene phrase, with a minimum of regionalisms and indigenisms reluctant to leave the norms of "good taste." Nevertheless, typically Romantic embroideries abound on this classical canvas. Above all, the embellishments on the theme of love: impossible loves like that of Grijalva and María de Cuéllar who both die of sadness, and the constantly interrupted idyl of Enriquillo and Mencía. With these pages the readers of 1880 must have refreshed the emotions

experienced from previous Romantics. And, as in all Romantic literature, they must have felt the contrast at Valenzuela's lustful out-
rage of Mencía's honor. These contrasts of Romantic mores between
heroes and villains that Galván loves to etch until he succeeds in por-
traying Pedro de Mojica are perhaps the best study of perversity in all
Hispanic-American Romanticism.

Another Romantic touch was the animation of Nature as a confidant
of human passions. Also Romantic was the heroic ideal—liberty or
death—which appears with typical emphasis; living for fame and posterity; the technique of weaving the threads of the action into a plot
rich in coincidences, disguises, sudden sentimental outbursts, rendezvous at night, with repentances and final atonements. The characters
live original lives, with the exception of Las Casas. This is understandable: Las Casas is not a novelistic personage but a dedicated historical
figure, and Galván preferred to show his known characteristics, without re-creating him imaginatively. Enriquillo, on the other hand, lent
himself to unrestricted psychological elaboration. He is not a symbolic
hero but a mestizo of flesh and blood, and soul. We see him in his
youth, grieved by his orphanhood, respectful of the Spaniards who are
rearing him, always compassionate for the maltreated Indians. He tol-
erates jokes and even impertinences because he seeks the good side of
things. As he grows, his idea of justice grows within him, and once,
upon seeing the Spaniards beat the Indians with rods, he feels the first
throb of a new calling: to defend those of his race. We see how Enriquillo learns more each time by looking within himself. The evil of
others whets the conscience of his own virtue and of his duties as an
Indian; a few steps more and Enriquillo discovers that "death is preferable to the humiliation of the soul." This discovery beats him down:
he knows that the great tests will begin now, precisely because he has
discovered his moral law; now he believes only in rebellion, and he
rebels. Even in minor characters, Galván indicates subtle psychological
changes. The life that Galván was able to infuse into his characters is
so great that the dialogs acquire a real dramatic quality.

Another of the best novelists of this generation is IGNACIO MANUEL
ALTAMIRANO (Mexico, 1834–1893). As in others, political agitation often
took Altamirano away from literature. He was a worthy poet—*Rhymes*
(*Rimas*, 1880)—and he had a novelist's grasp. He started to write
Christmas in the Highlands (*La navidad en las montañas*, 1871) with
a "sketch of customs" in mind; but it did not end up as such. It is,
rather, a little sentimental novel, with landscapes, action, and types
embellished with the artificial light of literature—of literature and not of

folklore. When a child recites a Lope de Vega ballad, the priest expresses his satisfaction that children are learning poetic Spanish compositions and not "the very bad verses" of popular ballads. These complaints against the debasing of good poetic Spanish tradition in the poor couplets of the people were heard in many Romantic writers: Tapia y Rivera, in his *Cofresí*, laments that verses by Calderón had wound up deformed in the mouths of the popular balladeers. The Indians become "real shepherds similar to those who appear in the idyls of Theocritus and in the eclogues of Virgil and Carcilas." The loves of Carmen and Pablo follow Romantic conventions. The technique of the narrative—one narrator introduces a character, who in turn relates another episode, and on and on—is not that of the "sketch of customs." Altamirano militated in favor of the Mexican Reformation; and he created as a protagonist a perfect priest, exceptional, unique, an ideal image who, because of the clearly delineated contrast with the clerics of those days, must have flattered the liberals more than the Catholics. But Altamirano's importance in the history of the novel rests on *Clemencia* (1869) and, above all, on *The Blue-Eyed Fellow* (*El Zarco*). The first is a sentimental, Romantic novel, psychologically false, in no way set off from the great mass of novels of a similar type that is produced in those years. Set in the last weeks of 1863 and the beginning of 1864, when Maximilian's French army was forcing the Mexican patriots into constant retreat, *Clemencia* relates the unfortunate loves of four youths in Guadalajara: the blond Flores and the brunette Valle, the blond Isabel and the brunette Clemencia. The two women, one angelic, the other ardent, both love Flores, who is physically handsome though morally base. Valle, on the other hand, is physically repulsive, but morally superior. Flores betrays the patriotic cause and is about to be shot; but Valle, who loves Clemencia, sacrifices himself, helps his rival to freedom, and dies in his place. Only then does Clemencia realize that she should have loved Valle. She withdraws from the world and enters a convent.

In *The Blue-Eyed Fellow* the imperfections of a posthumous manuscript are scarcely noticed, even though it did not receive the benefit of the final retouches that the author, who was so careful in his style, could have given it. *The Blue-Eyed Fellow* is an episode of Mexican life in 1861–63 when, at the end of the civil war between liberals of the Reformation and the pro-clerics, groups of cold-blooded bandits terrorized the tropical zone. Several characters are taken from real life: the blue-eyed fellow, Salomé, Martín Sánchez, the great Benito Juárez. In the composition we note Romantic concessions: the play of symmetry and contrast between the good Pilar and Nicolás, and the evil Manuela and the blue-eyed fellow; the ominous owl that chants on the branch where the blue-eyed fellow will be hanged. But it is a realistic novel. When he describes the landscape, and he does it beautifully, he does not associate it with the moods of the characters. "An indifferent Nature followed its normal course," he comments during one of the most dramatic moments. He describes the bandits' den in full color, but it is not the "local color" of the Romantics. Further, Manuela's love for the bandits—nourished by Romantic books—is presented with ironic observations. There are allusions also to the inverisimilitude of *Atala* and *Paul et Virginie*. Altamirano's attitude is that of the moralist. At times his feelings intervene too peremptorily, and the novelist defines a character before he has presented him, and judges him without giving us time to see him live. Nevertheless, Altamirano's desire to understand and explain good and evil made him one of the most penetrating novelists of this generation. His psychological analyses are complex, precise, cogent. *The Blue-Eyed Fellow* is noteworthy for the attention focused on the souls of its characters—one sees them in intimate conflicts with pros and cons. And in these souls changes take place; they are souls that mature, and the transitions are there to be seen. Furthermore, he knows how to tell a story. The episodes are well linked: the thread of the action runs rapidly and the reader's attention does not wane.

One of Altamirano's friends was JUAN DÍAZ COVARRUBIAS (Mexico, 1837–1859), and like him, a Romantic and a liberal. He dedicated to Zorrilla his somber and sepulchral poetry. He wrote several novels: *Gil Gómez the Insurgent or The Physician's Daughter* (*Gil Gómez el insurgento o La hija del Médico*), set amidst the wars of Independence; *The Middle Class* (*La clase media*), in which he exalts the virtues of the bourgeoisie and criticizes aristocratic groups; *The Sensitive One* (*La sensitiva*); and *The Devil in Mexico* (*El diablo en México*), "sketches of customs." This latter work is a good literary exercise. The breakup of the theme—the disillusionment of love—into Romantic, ironic, and realist planes is varied and apt: narratives, local customs, letters, intimate diaries, little homespun philosophies. The author describes the landscapes, and even the moods, in Romantic rhetoric, but is capable of subtleties. His characters read Byron and George Sand, but the author is aware that Romanticism is a style, that is, a way of life in the past, and in the midst of his sugary poetic effusions, he laughs mockingly on seeing the triumph of what he calls "positivism." In the wind-up, the "devil," an anti-Romantic devil, mocks the lovers by separating them and coupling them in unexpected pairs.

The Thinkers

Among the writers of essays and treatises in Puerto Rico—CAYETANO COLL Y TOSTE, 1850–1930), and SALVADOR BRAU, 1842–1912—one stands at the peak: EUGENIO MARÍA DE HOSTOS (Puerto Rico, 1839–1903). Similar to other civilizers that we have mentioned and will mention,

Hostos preferred action to art. In caring for his conduct, he was careless with his literature. We cannot grant him the same place in literary history that he would deserve in a gallery of great American teachers. He differs from Bello, Sarmiento, Montalvo, Varona, González Prada, Martí—all builders of nations—in having renounced his literary vocation abhoringly. In *Social Morals* (*Moral social,* 1888), his most important work, he wrote three chapters against literature. He used to say that he disdained it in the name of morality and logic. His attitude is strangely incomprehensive, narrow, and dogmatic. Is there in his rancor against novels, dramas, and even poetry, a wounded vanity, a feeling of failure, the haughtiness of an apostate? In his youth, Hostos had ambitions of literary glory; except that a "crisis of character"— to use his own words—came to enrich his life in generous struggles and to impoverish his pen in didactic functions. In Spain, where he was to live from 1851 to 1869, he wrote brief lyrical tales, prose ballads that followed the fashion of imitating Hoffmann, Gessner, Ossian. And uppermost, he produced a poetic novel, *The Peregrination of Bayoán* (*La peregrinación de Bayoán,* 1863). Considering its merits in style, imagination, and sincerity, it is really lamentable that Hostos did not persist in this genre. It is a strange novel. According to one of its first readers, the Spanish novelist Nombela, the style was of an "absolute newness" in Hispanic letters; and, in truth, it was not the current prose. In the prolog to the second edition of 1873, Hostos tells us of the process of creation, the circumstances in which he composed it, and his moral and political intentions. One need not dwell, however, on what Hostos says: in 1873 he opined that "letters are the vocation of the indolent or of those who have already finished their life's labor," and he exaggerated the value of *The Peregrination of Bayoán* as a doctrinaire work that combated Spanish despotism in the Antilles. Undoubtedly, it contains some serious thinking: the liberty of his fatherland, the unity of Puerto Rico, Cuba, the Dominican Republic, and Haiti, duty before happiness, the claims of justice and truth. But the message is diluted in an intimate diary of extraordinary lyricism, because that is what *The Peregrination of Bayoán* is, an intimate diary. Unfortunately, its didactic purpose, the allegories, and the novelistic episodes cripple the artistic quality of this intimate diary. It is the diary of Bayoán; and Hostos, who appears as the editor of these intimate pages, reconstructs the novelistic action when the diary is interrupted, and even intervenes in the plot. All of the characters have symbolic names: Bayoán is the name of the first aborigine of Borinquen, that is, of Puerto Rico, who doubted the immortality of the Spaniards; Darién, the loved woman, is the indigenous name of the most beautiful region of Cuba; her father

Guarionex bears the name of a powerful Haitian chieftain at the time Columbus reached the island. And Hostos informs us that the three characters "represent in this book the union of the three great Antilles." The value of *The Peregrination of Bayoán* lies, in spite of the author, in his poetic vision of the landscape and of life, and in the new aspects of his prose. His outlook was typically Romantic. By way of proposing sources, if it is necessary, those that would have gratified Hostos might be Goethe (*Werther*), Foscolo (*Jacopo Ortis*), Byron (*Childe Harold*). Many of the situations in the novel (Darién's illness and death), many of the themes (solitude, exile, dolorous love, the titanism of the hero who challenges his times, the feeling for nature), many of the procedures (emotions, characters, and deeds drawn in clear-cut contrasts of black and white) are of the Romantic school.

But Hostos is original because, through self-contemplation, he discovers very personal nuances in the depths of his soul. From these depths, touched thusly by the spirit, there arose impetuously an exclamatory, intermittent, vivid, voluptuous, passionate, variegated, morbid, rich, and imaginative style. It does not succeed as a novel: it is foggy in its symbols, broken in its narrative, disproportionate, in any case. *The Peregrination* would have been more worthy had Hostos given us the intimate diary in its nudeness. But no doubt there are pages that begin to shine vigorously. He never wrote like that again. It is strange that Hostos, who was so effusive in *The Peregrination,* so sentimental in the story of his loves, *Inda* (1878), so bland in his *Stories for My Son* (*Cuentos a mi hijo,* 1878), should believe that the most important thing was to be a "logical man." He sacrificed his intimate self, which was rich and complex, to a logical activity that did not carry him very far. He was not a philosopher, despite his yearning to be a systematic thinker. He managed to construct an abstract prose, hardened by symmetries and oppositions in the manner of the Krausists and the positivists. But he had no aptitude for theory, and his thought, although noble, had a short radius. His first contacts with philosophy had been his knowledge of Krausism. The influence of the German Krause on the generation of 1868 in Spain: Sanz de Río, Salmerón, etc., is now well known. But Hostos followed one of the currents added to the repertory of ideas of the Spanish Krausists: positivism, with its trust in reason and the experimental sciences.

We have just seen, in regard to Hostos, that, on treating the scholarly and critical intellectuals, we have profiled some aspects of their literary creation, even though this was not where they gave their greatest efforts. The less lyrical intellectuals do not lend themselves to such treatment. These are: ALEJANDRO DÉUSTUA (Peru, 1849–1945), early influenced by Krause and later one of those who introduced

Bergson in America, whose *Esthetics* (*Estética*) was founded on the metaphysical principle of liberty; and GABRIEL RENÉ-MORENO (Bolivia, 1836–1908), the greatest glory of Bolivian letters. His lively, variegated, and frisky prose is among the best of his time; but the labor of this person, withdrawn into his Bolivian themes and, inside Bolivia, withdrawn into his intellectual aristocracy, was rather that of an historian. Our outlook is esthetic; and, therefore, it will not be surprising if we also dwell on the literary work of three of the most serious thinkers of these years: González Prada, Justo Sierra, and Enrique José Varona.

Although he had written verses when he was twenty, MANUEL GONZÁLEZ PRADA (Peru, 1848–1918) did not bulldoze his way completely into literature until after 1880. Until his death he will be the most gifted writer of his country, feared and hated by many, surrounded by a few disciples. After his death his stature gradually assumed giant-like proportions: his books continue to win disciples. He broke, violently, not only with the little lies of our civilization, but also with the large ones. He rejected Spanish absolutist tradition, he denounced the responsibility of the Catholic church for iniquities in the world, he condemned unjust privileges—Property, State, Military—he ridiculed literary academies and priggish pens, he chastised the optimism of fools, he cursed cowardice and carnality. Our literature had had tremendous polemicists: Sarmiento, Montalvo. But González Prada's protest was even more terrible because it dealt blows not against persons and parties, but against the whole of the ruling order. He was an atheist, an anarchist, a naturalist, a partisan of the Indian and the worker. His only conservative impulse was that of the nationalist: so long as frontiers exist, he used to say, we must hate the enemy who crosses them. This was purely an emotional impulse, if one remembers that the frontiers in Hispanic-America were not definitely fixed and that conflicts were between brothers of the same language. His intellectual make-up had been formed in reading the men of the Enlightenment, some Hegel, Schopenhauer and Nietzsche, a little Guyau and Renan, and a good many, almost all, of the positivists: Comte, Spencer, Darwin, Claude Bernard. He spurned metaphysics and embraced the natural sciences, which influence is noted by his preference for biological and physical metaphors. He differed from other supporters of science, however, in placing liberty and equality above order and hierarchy, and disputed with positivist sociologists who spoke of the racial inferiority of the Indians and the inevitable failure of the Hispanic-American countries. He ended by exalting anarchist ideology more than the belief in science. In Marx he saw "one of the greatest social agitators of the nineteenth century," but he felt closer to Proudhon, Tolstoy, and Kropotkin. His sincerity constructed a new style for him: there is not, in these years, either in Spain or America, a prose as sharp and incisive as that of González Prada. He scorned the limp language of the type of Castelar and Valera, and parting from them, he discovered areas in our language that could still be made erectile. The importance of González Prada in Hispanic-American literature is due more to his prose than to his verse, which does not mean that his verses were bad, but that his prose was the vehicle for what interested him most—critical thought.

His verses are distributed in nine volumes: *Minúsculas* (1901), *Presbiterianas* (1909), *Exóticas* (1911) written between 1869 and 1900. The other volumes are posthumous and include poetry from 1866 to 1918: *Peruvian Ballads* (*Baladas peruanas*), *Graphites* (*Grafitos*), *Ballads* (*Baladas*), *Adoration* (*Adoración*), *Libertarians* (*Libertarias*), and *Fragments of Life* (*Trozos de vida*). In his work we see him changing his posture: now González Prada, the thinker, puts his foot forward, now González Prada, the lyricist or the technician of the verse. He believed that poetry should give rhythm to intelligence and images to the communication of knowledge. Part of his poetry was, thereby, intellectual and didactic. *Graphites* are epigrams on man and his activity. *Presbiterianas* is anti-clerical satire. In *Libertarians* the theme is social and political. His own life, sentimental, amorous, intimate, is expressed in *Adoration* and *Fragments of Life*. But in the same manner in which he renewed ideas in his prose, he renewed forms in his verse. His protestations became lyrical, exalted; his scholarly spirit led him to experiment with the rhythmic structure of verse. Before Modernism, the variety of verses offered by González Prada is not found in the Spanish language. In *Ballads* one sees his familiarity with the poetry of all languages (Spanish, French, Italian, German, English, Scandinavian) and his having profited from imitation, adaptation, and translation. *Minúsculas* and *Exóticas* were the books of poems that put him on the road to Modernism. He had lived in Paris. He had read Parnassians and symbolists. With the refinement of a virtuoso he plays with imaginative and formal novelties. He adapts the French rondel, triolet, villanelle, pantoum; the English Spenserian; the Italian *laude, ballata, stornello, rispetto;* the Persian quartets. And he invents the polyrhythm without rhyme: "White Horses" (*"Los caballos blancos"*). In the manner of Baudelaire he cultivated the "correspondences" between senses, the "synesthesia" so preferred by the impressionists: "In a Strange Country" (*"En país extraño"*). Although he was aware of the new movement in poetry, he did not proffer any judgment on the

Modernists. In fact he wrote little on Hispanic-American poetry. Leaving aside his rhythmic experiments, his most original contribution was his *Peruvian Ballads* in which the Indian theme appeared viewed from a different angle; the Indian was no longer idealized for decorative purposes as the Romantics had done, but was presented as a real Indian, with all of his anguish, understood within history and the Peruvian land.

Of the two major figures that Cuba offers in the last third of the nineteenth century, MANUEL SANGUILY, 1848–1925 and Varona, we shall dwell only on the latter. As a thinker ENRIQUE JOSÉ VARONA (1849–1933) felt comfortable astride French positivism and English empiricism. Although delimited by the dominant ideas of the nineteenth century, the fact that Varona was skeptical about the welfare achieved by man, and yet energetically directed his own conduct toward superior moral values, gives a personal tone to his philosophy. Basically, he was confident that man, when he let himself be carried away by the illusion of liberty, could better the world. It was an illusion of liberty, because Varona was a determinist, an agnostic inclined toward the sciences; and man appeared to him as a creature capable of redeeming himself within the evolution of nature. Cuba had had its philosophic careerists: Félix Varela, José de la Luz y Caballero, José Manuel Mestre; but Varona was the first Cuban to convert philosophy into rigorous discipline. Notwithstanding, he was more successful in his fragmentary reflections than in his systematic works, such as the three volumes of *Philosophic Lectures* (*Conferencias filosóficas*), for example. The aphorism is the best vehicle for a relativist. And those in *Linked Aphorism* (*Con el eslabón*) offer pages of great penetration and beauty. His brief essays, collected in *From My Belvedere* (*Desde mi Belvedere*) and *Violets and Nettles* (*Violetas y ortigas,* 1917), must count among the best in our literature. One could extract from them integral theories (for example, his relativist esthetic theory), but his charm is in the sprightliness with which he goes from subject to subject. His poetry was youthful. He began with patriotic verses—his "Ode at the Death of Gaspar Betancourt Cisneros" (*"Oda a la muerte de Gaspar Betancourt Cisneros"*) is of 1867—and ended the bulk of his poetic activity with *Poems* (*Poesías,* 1878) and *Cuban Landscapes and Narrations in Verse* (*Paisajes cubanos y narraciones en verso,* 1879). He was a prosaic poet, with the prosaic quality of Campoamor, although "Wings" (*"Alas"*) and "Berceuse" show such a restlessness for wandering, for achieving impossible perspectives, for yearning to be something else, and for living away yonder where one dreams, that they are equivalent to poetry. "Wings" belongs to his *Poems* and

"Berceuse" to *Of My Recollections* (*De mis recuerdos*) which he published in 1919 under the pseudonym of Luis del Valle. It was a theme he felt vividly, and it would reappear in *Little Poems in Prose* (*Poemetas en prosa,* 1921). He valued the Parnassians and the symbolists; but he referred to the "Modernists," and also to the "futurists" and "cubists" who came after them, with irony because, in his opinion, "they go on wishing to say what they never finish saying."

Justo Sierra (Mexico, 1848–1912), a disciple of Altamirano, became, in his turn, a teacher. Such is history, a relay of torches from generation to generation. Sierra was, above all, a maker of men, and today his written work is of less importance than his tutelage. He labors as an historian, essayist, educator, orator, politician, storyteller, poet. Here we look at his minor side: that of the man of letters. Minor because it did not grow commensurate with his public stature. He went into letters drawn by Romantic voices, the robust one of Victor Hugo, the muted one of Musset, and from Spain, the intimate voice of Bécquer. His poetry, collected posthumously, has gracefulness, freshness, elegance, and it is not uncommon that some of it (*"Playeras,"* for example) is judged as anticipating Modernism; there is also (in "The Bucolic Funeral" [*"El funeral bucólico"*]) the perfect art of picking up classical themes and inviting them to walk down the avenue of fashion. Justo Sierra's poetry became prose in the double sense that, for one, it fell into prosaic forms and, secondly, it rose toward the Bécquer-like *Romantic Stories* (*Cuentos románticos*) collected in 1896. He knew European literature: the French Parnassians, D'Annunzio, Nietzsche. And he approached the new Hispanic-American poets with a greeting of sympathy and recognition. His prolog to the poetry of Gutiérrez Nájera is a landmark in our literary criticism. At the same time, it is luxuriant prose, imaginative, lyrical, and charming. He did not always write in this fashion. He was not an esthete, but a servant of practical programs and ideas akin to "positivism."

The Men of 1880, in Argentina

There was a group of prose writers who knew, and some of them practised, at least two of the current French styles: Parnassianism and naturalism. This is the "men of '80" group, in Argentina. They had the air of dilettantes, as if intellectual curiosity were a luxury. They were generally distinguished for their fragmentary, sundry, opinionated prose. They also contributed to the more imaginative genres: the novel, the short story, the drama, and poetry. Santiago Estrada (1841–1891), although his talent was that of chronicler and critic, wrote several "fantasies" with poetical intention. Lucio Vicente López (1848–1894), author of various titillating stories in the manner of Daudet or Dickens, left in *The Great Village* (*La gran aldea,* 1884) a novelistic description of "Buenos Aires customs." Badly constructed, carelessly styled, it nevertheless has a certain enchantment because during the twenty years in which the action occurs the Argentinian capital had grown and changed dizzily, and López was its best chronicler. MIGUEL CANÉ (1851–1905) defined his own literature in the titles of his books: *Light Prose* (*Prosa ligera*), *Literary Chats* (*Charlas literarias*), *Notes and Impressions* (*Notes e impresiones*). Capriciously he lighted on many themes with agile intelligence, and his entertaining autobiography, *Juvenilia* (1884), is noteworthy precisely because it is the record of life in a boarding school, suffered and enjoyed by an intelligent lad. He had a deep Romantic fund of pessimism, sadness, egocentrism, desires for adventure, and preoccupations with time. EDUARDO WILDE (1844–1933) gave a finer expression to the ironic, humoristic attitude of the "men of the '80's." His intellectual work is so abundant and his jocular tone is so persistent that the more fantastic, imaginative, intuitive portion of his work—his stories, poematic prose, and autobiographical pages—remained in the shadows. He was an improviser; and defects in style are more anoying in him than in his contemporaries, because in Wilde they interrupt an admirable capacity for original phrasing. He had a rare sensibility and knew how to express it in images so audacious for his time that they remind us of the influence the Parnassians were exerting in Buenos Aires in the decade of the eighties. Read in *Prometheus and Co.* (*Prometeo y Cía.*) the stories: "The Rain" ("*La lluvia*"), "Tini," "The First Night in the Cemetery" ("*La primera noche del cementerio*") and you will discover the potentiality of a great writer. His autobiography *Downstream* (*Aguas abajo*) is one of the finest in this generation of Argentinian autobiographers. Ironically enough, the best of all these Gallicized Argentinian writers was a Frenchman: PAUL GROUSSAC (1848–1929). He had come to Argentina when he was eighteen, and there learned Spanish, which he used admirably. He was a teacher of critical severity, of disciplined study, of intellectual sternness. From 1880 Buenos Aires is reading poems and stories of the French Parnassians; furthermore, these Parnassian writers—Banville, Mendès, Silvestre, Coppée, France —are contributing directly to Buenos Aires newspapers. And Paul Groussac will be one of the first to study them in America. In a series of articles, "*Medallions*" ("*Medallones,*" 1884) he commented on the work of Leconte de Lisle. Other Argentinians were also doing so—Domingo Martinto, Martín García Merou—but since they are younger we shall refer to them later. Although one can find in Groussac an occasional touch of Parnassian beauty, he sought in the novel—*Forbidden Fruit* (*Fruto vedado*)—in short stories—*Argentinian Tales* (*Relatos argentinos*)—and in the drama—*The Crimson Banner* (*La divisa punzó*)—a vigorous, human, and personal expression. He was not a "Modernist"; yet Rubén Darío will later recognize him as one of his masters of "Modernist" prose. When Groussac published *Forbidden Fruit* (1884) he had lived in Argentina for eighteen years, which was precisely his age when he arrived in Argentina; and because he wanted to master Spanish, although the Argentinians of his generation were slipping toward French, he, a Frenchman, developed a purer, more Hispanic, more correct prose than the native Argentinians. His novel is divided into two parts. The first in Buenos Aires, in the northern country, and in Tucumán; the second, aboard ship, with a stopover in Rio de Janeiro, and the finale in Paris. It is an autobiographical story of an adulterous love affair. Marcel Renault, the protagonist, repeats some of the real-life events of Groussac himself. And he put forth the psychological problem of double nationality. Groussac also showed a preference for complicated psychological cases in his *Argentinian Tales:* "Crazy Wheel" ("*La rueda loca*"), "The Inheritance" ("*La herencia*"), "The Nun" ("*La monja*"), "The Deserted Home"

(*"El hogar desierto"*), and the best of them all, "Number 9090" (*"El número 9090"*). The Crimson Banner (1923) is a drama in three acts with Rosas and his daughter as the key characters. At the end Manuelita sacrifices her love for Thomson and remains with her father, who needs her and profits from her. The contrast between Rosas and Manuelita is adroit: Rosas is barbaric, intuitive, cunning, crafty, energetic; and Manuelita the incarnation of nobleness, docility, pride, and tenderness. Groussac does not intervene in the work; he does not take sides. He is a dramatist who can impersonalize himself in order to create persons.

The most talented novelist of this Argentinian group was EUGENIO CAMBACÉRÈS (1843–1888). Like many of his colleagues—Cané, Wilde, López—he was a man of the world, of vast reading knowledge (especially in French), skeptic, scoffer, conservative, with all of the refinement that his trip to Paris and the leisure of the aristocratic clubs of Buenos Aires offered him; and together with this, he enjoyed the direct experience of country life. Amidst demure circles, his four novels caused as many scandals; and it seems that at his death he left a fifth novel unpublished, which his wife hastened to burn at the behest of her father confessor. They were naturalist novels, in the manner of Zola. Nevertheless, Cambacérès was not overpowered by his model; he profited from Zola not so much from the technique of the experimental novel, as from the example that it was legitimate in art to unveil the sordid conditions of human life. Candid, intelligent, free, agnostic, daring, he had no illusions about how little man was worth. His moral sense—shown in the cynical and brutal behavior of his principal characters—challenged the conventional lies of society, but with a tired, grumbling gesture he throws up his arms, recognizing that the power of nature lowers us to the level of animals. With bitterness, almost in anger, he describes human indignities. And so that it hurts the more, he chooses wickedness, sickness, corruption, vice, adultery, failure, death. The repugnant description of Paul's syphilis, in *Sentimental Music* (*Música sentimental*), was a proof that the novelist was not ready to let himself by frightened by bad taste; and, in fact, his vigorous naturalism subjects us to sexual scenes that were new to our literature. Its theme is not love; it is the tedium that comes after the orgasm. Not only was he truculent in his novelistic situations, but his prose also violently trampled the reader: his was the graphic, evocative, conversational language of Buenos Aires where Creole idioms, Italian and French expressions, and metaphoric innovations tumble together as in a gutter. *Without Direction* (*Sin rumbo*), his best novel, documents the complexity of the Argentinian reality of those years: there are shacks where the red paint of Rosas' epoch could still be seen; there is an old man who fought against Rosas; there are contrasts between the refinement, the culture, the art, the gay adventures, the nightclub life in the capital, and the hard country labor in the province of Buenos Aires. The character Andrés is one of the best delineated psychological studies in the Argentine novel.

Other Novelists / From Uruguay comes EDUARDO ACEVEDO DÍAZ (1851–1921) who novelizes the Independence and the civil wars in *Ismael* (1888), *Nativa* (1890), *Cry of Glory* (*Grito de gloria*, 1893) and *Lance and Sabre* (*Lanza y sable*, 1914). The first three form a triptych and place Acevedo Díaz among the most energetic novelists of America. Of this triptych of novels, the first is the principal one, still Romantic in its heroic and mythical exaltation of the gaucho formation of the country, but written with a powerful, observant, realist art. Life in the city, and above all, in the midst of nature, the sufferings, the violence and the aspirations of an unpolished people, the onslaught with which men act on reality and create history, the colorful customs, the highlights of the soul, carry Acevedo Díaz' mark of narrative ability. *Ismael* takes place in the time of Artigas, from the preparations of the Creole uprising against the Spaniards to the battle of Las Piedras and the expulsion of the patriotic friars from Montevideo in 1811; *Nativa* skips the period that goes from Artigas' rise up to his fall and brings us to a minor episode during the Brazilian domination in 1824; in *Cry of Glory* he tells of the liberating crusade of the *Treinta y Tres Orientales* up to the gaucho battle of Sarandí in 1825. *Lance and Sabre* is not linked with the others, but it completes the historical picture with the first civil wars. He wrote other novels: *Solitude* (*Soledad*) is the one of most literary value, the one with the best prose, the one most in tune with the artistic tendencies of the European novel of his day.

As has been seen, some of the writers already examined cultivated the historical novel. There were many others who also did so. In the majority, these novels fell beyond the pale of literature—they were wild, truculent, coarse serials, even less artistic than the serial novels of the Spaniard Fernández y González. In the last decades of the century one notices the tendency to apply the techniques of realism to the evocation of the past. As in Europe, after Walter Scott and Manzoni come the realists Flaubert and Georg Ebers, so in Spanish America the novelists promised themselves, above all, to be faithful to the truth, at least the truth as they came to know it in the books at hand. To fix the details of the transition from the Romantic novel to the realist is impossible. Nevertheless, it is clear that the scrupulous insistence on being faithful to historical reality was restraining the flights of fancy more and more. The Romantic philosophy of history was succeeded by positivism.

Now we will play a little chess and put all our men on the table. We shall try not to repeat names that have appeared elsewhere. From Mexico ELIGIO ANCONA (1836–1893), IRENEO PAZ (1836–1924), EULOGIO PALMA Y PALMA (b. 1851),

CRESCENCIO CARRILLO Y ANCONA (1836–1897), JUAN LUIS TERCERO (1837–1905). From Cuba RAIMUNDO CABRERA (1852–1923) and EMILIO BACARDÍ (1844–1922). From Venezuela EDUARDO BLANCO (b. 1838), JULIO CALCAÑO (1840–1919), JOSÉ MARÍA MANRIQUE (1846–1907). From Colombia FELIPE PÉREZ (1836–1891), MARCO ANTONIO JARAMILLO (1849–1904), JESÚS' SILVESTRE ROZO (1835–1895), FRANCISCO DE PAULA CORTÉS (b. 1850), TEMÍSTOCLES AVELLA MENDOZA (1841–1914), CONSTANCIO FRANCO VARGAS (b. 1842). From Ecuador CARLOS R. TOBAR (1854–1920). From Chile LIBORIO E. BRIEBA (1841–1897). From Argentina EDUARDA MANSILLA DE GARCÍA (1838–1892). From Bolivia SANTIAGO VACA GUZMÁN (1847–1896), whose best novel, *His Excellence and His Worship* (*Su excelencia y su Ilustrísima,* 1889), not only records, historically, the enmity between the governor and the bishop in sixteenth-century Paraguay, but also, philologically, resorts to the prose of that epoch. But one of the best novelizers of history in Bolivia, and one of the best in all Hispanic-America, was NATANIEL AGUIRRE (1843–1888), whose novel, *Juan de la Rosa* (1885) evokes episodes of the history of Cochabamba between 1810 and 1812. The subtitle reads: "Memoirs of the Last Soldier of the Independence." In reality the narrator is relating his childhood, so that the struggles for Independence appear as seen through the eyes of a twelve-year-old. Since Aguirre's object seems to have been to fill in the missing knowledge about the heroic resistance of Cochabamba against Goyeneche, he stuffs the story with didactic pages and puts excessively conventional discourses in the mouths of his characters. As a novel, it hits false notes. Aguirre writes an adorned, academic, and careful prose. But he composes carelessly. Some of his techniques of composition are those of the Romantic or serial novel; for example, the mystery of the identity of the narrator's father, the contrasts between villainy and virtue, the beauty of the women. Aguirre's liberalism and patriotism are obvious; still, in *Juan de la Rosa* there is not a vivid description of the Bolivian people. The Indians are scarcely pointed out in the distance, although in the most sentimental passages one always hears the singing of the *yarvíes* and *huaiños.* Not only historical novels, but also different types were undertaken by the novelists already mentioned and by others.

We add more names. FRANCISCO GREGORIO BILLINI (Dominican Republic, 1844–1898) novelized the social life of his island in *Baní or Engracia and Antoñita,* although with a honeyed sentimentalism. He was a poet and dramatist, but today his depictions of customs are what interest one most. MERCEDES CABELLO DE CARBONERA (Peru, 1845–1909), a solitary and radical figure, studied Zola and was a naturalist in several city novels, feeding on the corruption and ruin of the upper classes—*Blanca Sol, Consequences* (*Las consecuencias*). NICOLÁS HEREDIA (Cuba, 1849–1901) was a realist in *The Businessman* (*Un hombre de negocios*). LUIS SEGUNDO DE SILVESTRE (Colombia, 1838–1887), who, before his novel *Journey* (*Tránsito*), evidently had journeyed through Isaacs' *María.* Chilean themes, similar to those of Blest Gana with even more love incidents and with the same recognition of the power of money, tempted other novelists. None of them bested the master. Along a mediocre line—Valderrama, Rodríguez, Murillo, Vargas, Enrique del Solar Marín—only one stood out: VICENTE GREZ (Chile, 1847–1909), who was also a poet and dramatist. Of all his novels, *A Wife's Ideal* (*El ideal de una esposa,* 1887) is notable for the analysis of the jealous passions of a married woman. MANUEL FERNÁNDEZ JUNCOS (Spain–Puerto Rico, 1846–1928) gave us descriptions and stories of the island, in an elemental realism. In Mexico the realist novel, seasoned to the Spanish taste and not in the raw realism of the French, had good representatives. JOSÉ LÓPEZ PORTILLO Y ROJAS (1850–1923), author of poetry, drama, essay, excelled in his short stories which were recently gathered—*Complete Stories* (*Cuentos completos,* 1952). In one of them, "In a Stagecoach" (*"En diligencia"*), he judges the state of literature as it appeared to him: two young men decide to win over a woman through literature, one considering Zola and naturalism to be in the vanguard as the only school worthy of the century, and the other defending the Romanticism of sentiment and tears. López Portillo y Rojas, of course, left Romanticism, but did not go into naturalism. His purpose was to be a nationalist—to create Mexican literature. What he did was follow the footsteps of the Spanish regionalist. Nevertheless, he felt a genuine sympathy for the more destitute social classes of Mexico, and this is preserved in his novels *The Parcel of Land* (*La parcela,* 1898), *The Forerunners* (*Los precursores,* 1909) and *The Weak and the Strong* (*Fuertes y débiles,* 1919). The first of these is the best.

In EMILIO RABASA (1856–1930) the sketches of customs of the Romantic years now unfold more ambitiously and give us functional characters and problems within a social and political reality which is then studied. Of his five narrations, the novel *The Uprising* (*La bola,* 1887) and the novelette *The Three Years' War* (*La guerra de tres años,* 1891) are the best. He denounces the afflictions of our countries—bossism, militarism, clericalism, bureaucracy, corruption, politicking, and so on—and he does it mordantly. Alongside those named we must cite RAFAEL DELGADO (1853–1914) who, when he wanted to be a realist, was impeded by his excessive sentimentalism. In the *Woodlark* (*La calandria,* 1891), *Angelina* (1895), *The Rich Relatives* (*Los parientes ricos,* 1903), and *Ordinary History* (*Historia vulgar,* 1904) a Romantic gust keeps the description of regional customs fresh. He was also a short story writer, poet, and theatrical author.

The Theater

Plays were written by the same authors we studied in other genres. Therefore, it would be necessary to repeat a few names, Daniel Barros Grez, for example, who was Chile's principal dramatist. New names would be those of JOSÉ PEÓN CONTRERAS (Mexico, 1843–1907), DANIEL CALDERA (Chile, 1852–1896), OROSMAN MORATORIO (Uruguay, 1852–1898), and MARTÍN CORONADO (Argentina, 1850–1919).

X. 1880-1895

Authors born between 1855 and 1870

Historical framework: New economic and social forces. Prosperity, immigration, technical advances, capitalism. Greater political stability. The oligarchies and the democratic opposition.

Cultural tendencies: The cult of European innovations. French Parnassianism. Naturalism. The first generation of "Modernists."

The Hispanic-Americans who came into public life around 1880 (that is, when their countries had already passed through the worst of anarchism) still admired, romantically, the heroes of political action; but they had a presentiment that, were the circumstances to change, their role would not be an heroic one. With a gesture of bitterness, irony, or deception, depending on the particular case, they withdrew from the fight and dedicated themselves to literature. And even within literature they withdrew into nostalgic moods, toward humanistic studies, toward ideals of formal perfection, either clearly seen or half seen in European writers, especially the French. In this period the writers are varied; but what they had in common seems to be the resentment toward the immediate conditions of social life and the boastful air of being the first to cultivate letters for letters' sake. The humanists of classical tastes, as well as the Romantics, the realists, the Parnassians, and, finally, those who later will be called Modernists all felt irritated by society, and this irritation (as in oysters) makes them secrete pearls of literature. From Rubén Darío on, Modernism will be a movement with an unmistakable direction (therefore, we will study it in the following chapter); but until Rubén Darío, the different directions of those interested exclusively in literature will be confused. In this sense, the list of the "precursors of Modernism" must be much longer than is believed. Long before Modernism, for example, poets who had not been considered as precursors had achieved, nevertheless, extremely varied combinations of new verses. Let us enter this period through its poetry and come out by its prose; and when we deal with the poets, let us leave to the end those who will prevail when Modernism triumphs.

A. MAINLY VERSE

1. The Last Academicians, Romantics, and Traditionalists

It has been said already that various poets were sleeping in an academic position, in a Neoclassical convalescence. For this reason, when a new poetry emerges during these years, in a certain way equivalent to the renovation realized in Europe by the French Parnassians and the English pre-Raphaelites, it is a reaction, not against Romanticism, but against the supine Neoclassicism. The fascination for the unknown German and English languages (Heine, Poe), lyricism shimmering in mystery (Bécquer), the art of perfect ornamentation (Gautier), the pure beauty of French Parnassus (the masters Gautier, Leconte de Lisle, Banville, Baudelaire and their disciples Sully-Prudhomme, Heredia, Coppée, and Mendès) made their heads giddy as if they were sailing on a swelling sea; but they were all anxious to reach a port, they did not know which, where "things modern" awaited them. In this sense they are "forerunners." But, of course, forerunners do not know what they are forerunning. The critic then must be overly cautious, or he may fall into confusion. We shall go from (1) those poets who value tradition most to (2) those who value innovation most.

Central America: In Honduras, José Antonio Domínguez (1869–1903) was a melancholic and patriotic Romantic, deeply attached to the rules. In El Salvador, Vicente Acosta (1867–1908) versified on vernacular themes. In Costa Rica, Justo A. Facio (1859–1931) and José María Alfaro Cooper (1861–1931) preferred old molds. But the best of the Costa Rican poets was the regionalist Aquileo J. Echeverría (1866–1909), who versified the customs of rural life in short meters with a language rich in dialecticisms, in descriptions of types, landscapes, events, and in the nature and folklore of his region. He was a Romantic in his sentimental keynotes and a realist in his desire to reproduce things as they appeared to the eyes of everyone. "Concho" is the rural inhabitant of Costa Rica; *"concherías"* are his actions and expressions. Echeverría's country folk are not poor nor rich: they are of the comfortable middle class. So authentic are his scenes that one could study in his verses the social reality of the Costa Rica of his day. The lucidity of his observations has given him renown. But his renown is greater than his value as a poet. Echeverría's Costa Rica is not the same today, so that *Concherías* (1905) has acquired another virtue with the passage of time: that of awakening in its readers patriotic nostalgias and emotions. A capable versifier within the poverty òf traditional rhythms, Echeverría is not a poet who surprises his readers with new findings. One fears that each verse will be followed by a commonplace, and this is what happens. The *Ballads* (*Romances*, 1903) are Romantic in the fashion of Spain and all Hispanic-America—familiar, erotic sentiments, wrought with cultural images and even with Greek myths.

Antilles: The Puerto Ricans LUIS MUÑOZ RIVERA (1859–1916), JOSÉ DE DIEGO (1868–1918), and FRANCISCO GONZALO MARÍN (1863–1897) were straggling cultivators of a civic and political poetry still Romantic in form.

Venezuela: FRANCISCO LAZO MARTÍ (1864–1909) versified native themes.

Colombia: JULIO FLÓREZ (1867–1923) interpreted, without complications, popular feelings. Instead of stumped and shaded tones, he worked in jets of colors; but this ardent, this passionate, this spontaneous man had a gloomy outlook on life. JOSÉ JOAQUÍN CASAS (1865–1951) was a versifier of classical precepts, popular themes, and religious moods. DIEGO URIBE (1867–1921), popular in his inspiration and in his direction, was a sincere elegist.

Ecuador: REMIGIO CRESPO TORAL (1860–1939) was careful in his form, but without modernity.

Chile: JULIO VICUÑA CIFUENTES (1865–1936), as a poet, was a formal humanist.

Uruguay: At the time JOSÉ ALONSO Y TRELLES, "Old Pancho" (1857–1924), belatedly began as a poet (1899), Romanticism *à la* Zorrilla de San Martín was in its death throes and the Modernism of Herrera y Reissig was being born. Old Pancho, unattached to either group, poetized. He poetized within the popular gaucho current. In 1915 he collected his poetry in his only significant book *Wild Weeds* (*Paja brava*)—sentimentalism that seemed worthwhile precisely because it was not touched by art.

Argentina: Standing in the doorway, looking into the streets of the past is CALIXTO OYUELA (1857–1935), of classical and Hispanic tastes, disciplined in his respect for the academies, preserver of dry lyrical forms.

We could continue like this, in an unending list, but it would be better to describe two grades of this non-Modernist poetry: Othón's and Zorrilla de San Martín's.

MANUEL JOSÉ OTHÓN (Mexico, 1858–1906), one of the best describers of nature in our literature, was of classical formation. His formation came from so far away (Horace, Vergil, Garcilaso and Fray Luis de León) that he looked like a solitary figure. He had more recent antecedents: in Spain, Núñez de Arce; in Mexico, Monsignor Arcadio Pagaza. But Othón's communication with nature was personal and direct, and in this sense, has no need of an explanation of his sources. "We should not express anything that we have not seen," was his formula for artistic sincerity. And no one expressed better than he what he saw in the valleys, forests, rivers, mountains, and deserts of Mexico. On describing what he sees, he places his own spiritual tremor into each thing, in a kind of pan-Othonism. He was a religious spirit, and his constant intervention in rustic landscapes tends to have metaphysical force or the tonality of a prayer. He did not insist on bucolic themes;

but in the context of pastoral life, he gave us the totality of his personal feeling for life. The identification of soul with nature is in itself Romantic, but versified with a classical technique. He did not innovate forms; on the contrary, he was content with those of the Golden Age. His musty literary lineage did not allow him to sympathize with the style that would be called Modernist. Further, his traditionalism changed to rancor. He thought Modernism was the enemy of poetry. The notion to write *Hymn to the Forests* (*Himno de los bosques*, 1891) came to him while reading a critic who lamented that Gutiérrez Nájera's "*Tristissima Nox*" (1884) did not understand, love, nor describe the Mexican landscape. This polemic attitude did not detract from the greatness of his poetry, but it enclosed it within the history of styles. Despite the fact that his decisive book *Rustic Poems* (*Poemas rústicos*) dates from 1902, the significance of his total works is clearer in the period that we are now studying, 1880–1895. He published in this period his first two books of verses: the first in 1880 and the second in 1888. But his echo will be heard among the Modernists; and at the height of Modernism, his "Savage Idyll" (*"Idilio salvaje"*) will stun us with its powerful voice. This poem is the one that best measures Othón's stature, and in the poetry prior to Darío, his stature is one of the most imposing. An ardent and sudden passion for a young woman inspired his "Savage Idyll." Artemio de Valle-Arizpe, in his *Book of Anecdotes on Manuel José Othón* (*Anecdotario de Manuel José Othón*) relates that the poet, fearing that his wife would find out about his other woman, took on an air of innocence and attributed the love affair to the historian, Alfonso Toro, to whom he dedicated the first sonnet. In spite of this first introductory sonnet which the reader should forget for being unworthy of the poem, "Savage Idyll" is a heart-rending confession. In order to understand it better, one must read others of his compositions of the same year, 1905; for example, "Fervent" (*"Urente"*), in which he describes his beloved mistress, and "From a Poem," in which he questions her with allusions to Canto III of Dante's *Inferno*.

We do not wish to explain "Savage Idyll" with a biographical anecdote: the setting of the poem, the poet's frame of mind, and even his images and words had already been tried much earlier, over and over, in sundry compositions. As in all sincere poets, there is in Othón a certain monotony. The landscape as a space wherein the blows of his spirit resound was an image already used by Othón. It is possible, then, that that biographical episode about Othón does not explain anything: what is certain is that Othón felt the necessity to poetize the conflict between religious virtue and carnal ardor in a fierce setting.

In "Savage Idyll" one sees, clearly, that when he describes nature it is to integrate it with his spirit. The landscape is interiorized; it folds back upon the broken fragments of love and sin. The mountain and its precipices, the desert, the gray sunset, the eagles, the horizons, and the plains are converted into symbols of his own passion, in his solitude and old age. Descriptive, of course, but examined in the mirror of spiritual remorse: "And in me, what a deep and prodigious cataclysm! / What shadows and fear in my conscience, / and what a horrible distaste of my own self!" Othón also wrote short stories and short novels in which the landscape and the sentiments of the country people prevail, and theatrical pieces bearing the telltale mark of Echegaray. It has been said that his best dramatic composition is *The Last Chapter* (*El último capítulo*, 1905) in one act and in prose, a judgment which, if it were true, would condemn the others irredeemably, since this one has no theatrical value. The theme is interesting: Cervantes is writing the last chapter of the second part of *Don Quijote* when he receives a visit from the author of the apocryphal Quijote (Avellaneda). Had he had theatrical talent, Othón would have made of Cervantes what Tamayo y Baus made of Shakespeare: a dramatic character. But the work, in spite of being one act, has no unity—the episode between Cervantes and Avellaneda loses its power because the reader has been distracted already by other unconnected episodes. The dialog is emphatic, oratorical, wholly inflated with words that are not emitted from a mouth on stage but from the Romantic conception that the author had of Cervantes' genius, and of his interpretation of Don Quijote.

Juan Zorrilla de San Martín (Uruguay, 1855–1931) began to work out his poem *Tabaré* in 1879; finished it in 1886; corrected it in 1887; published it in 1888; republished it—on each occasion with new variants—in 1892 and 1918; and gave the definitive text in the "edition corrected by its author" in Montevideo in 1923. Certain critics have read it with a rhetorical preoccupation: to what genre does it belong? Versified novel? Epic poem? They have tended to detract from its merits because it does not fit their rhetorical notions. Zorrilla gave no importance to the novelistic theme, which is quite ingenuous: Tabaré, a mestizo born of a Charrúa chief and a captive Spanish woman, receives, from early childhood, the grace of baptism; as a youth, he sees Blanca, sister of the conquistador Don Gonzalo, and he feels intensely attracted to her because she recalls to his mind the memory of his dead mother; his baptized soul and his warrior inclinations struggle inside him; he saves Blanca from the arms of an Indian, but Don Gonzalo, believing Tabaré to be the rapist, kills him. In considering *Tabaré* an epic poem the author warns us that he gave the word "epic" a personal connotation: the demonstration of the laws of God in human happenings. *Tabaré* is a Catholic poem, and, therefore, it is vulgar to interpret it, as has been done, in the light of naturalist verisimilitude. When Zorrilla describes the Indians he is not proceeding from an ethnographic attitude, but from a metaphysical one. His theme, the destiny of the Charrúa race, is conceived theologically—what supernatural will condemned this race? The poems intuits, poetically, the Charrúa race at a moment when it is about to disappear: it is darkness, meaninglessness. Thanks to Tabaré, the mestizo with the blue eyes, Zorrilla looks out upon the abyss and sees the sparks of the vanished race. Tabaré, then, appears on the edge of two creations: the Charrúa race, which is nature, and the Spanish race, which is spirit. The death of Tabaré condemns the Charrúa race to eternal silence; with its physical disappearance, the possibility of its being understood also disappears. In spite of its exterior make-up, legendary, novelistic, epic, *Tabaré* is a lyrical poem.

Zorrilla de San Martín, as many other poets of his day, came out of the Spanish Romantic school of José Zorrilla, Núñez de Arce, and Bécquer. But it was Bécquer who taught him how to control his voice. Zorrilla de San Martín "Becquerized" with such delicateness—images suggested by mystery, descriptive impressionism, melancholy contemplation of life and death, vague fluctuations between reality and dream —that he placed himself in the lyrical vanguard. He succeeded with a type of suggestive verse, because his lyricism originated from a vision of life as mystery, and a pictorial verse, because the poet intended to be lucid and perfect in his descriptive forms. Bécquer was not an accidental source, but a kindred spirit who showed him the road to style. Other poets remained as prisoners within the Romantic enclosure. Not Zorrilla. From Romanticism two specialized buds emerged, one of plastic perfection (*Parnasse*), the other of musical suggestion (Symbolism). Zorrilla goes from Romanticism to Symbolism, but independently of French literature. His passage was opened by Bécquer's Nordic vagueness. Zorrilla's poetry is clear and, even more than Bécquer, he tried every possibility of expression: idea, fiction, passion, sound, suggestion, descriptive plasticity. But he trod where Bécquer had already trod: the allusion to states of soul that vacillate between wakefulness and dream; the suspicion of a mystery which at once envelops us and lies within us; the trust in the revealing power of the metaphor and the confided secret. Zorrilla's attitude is similar to that which, later on, the initiates to Symbolism will have, except that his poetry, deliberately vague, is rich in visual substance. He is always successful with the visual image, which improves the narration and distinguishes it. His images run the gamut of impressionistic language: animation of nature, empathy, synesthesia, etc. From Bécquer he borrowed, together with his delicateness, the simplicity of the verse. Such simplicity is achieved, however, with a rich variety of musical suggestions: the leitmotiv ("to the river fell the flower . . ."), the sudden shift of accent from the penult to the ultimate syllable, the unfolding of hendecasyllables and heptasyllables. The choice of this versification responded to a vague, persuasive mood, more interested in the fluid and subdued communication of metaphors than in a strong and articulated sonority. This tendency in Zorrilla toward a poetry of allusions makes him one of the purest and freshest lyrical poets in America; if we set aside the naive novelistic architecture of *Tabaré,* many of his verses will be modern. His prose works—essays, travelogs, discourses, history—are less renovating.

We have said that a displeased Othón had turned his face away from those who were ushering in a new poetry. Among those who certainly felt the deliciousness of the new breeze on their brows, those who were the heralds of the new esthetics that was to take the name Modernist, one must include, from Mexico, Agustín F. Cuenca and especially, Justo Sierra, with whom we have already dealt.

2. The First Modernists

Difficult to place in this zigzagging march of poets is SALVADOR DÍAZ MIRÓN (1853–1928). He rests between Justo Sierra, who announces the arrival of Modernism, and Gutiérrez Nájera, who opens up the door. Or better, Díaz Mirón is the one who enters through the window. From 1886, the year in which Díaz Mirón published a notebook of poetry, his voice touched all our America; in 1889 Darío pays tribute to his libertarian spirit; and in 1890 he dedicates a "Medallion" to him in his new edition of *Azul.* Later Díaz Mirón deserts his past and recognizes only *Stone Chips (Lascas,* 1901). The poet himself points to the year 1892, when he was imprisoned for having killed a man, as the beginning of a new "artistic criterion." Prior to 1892 he was a Victor-Hugoesque and Byronian poet, grandiloquent in thought and metaphor. "*Sursum,*" "To Glory" ("*A gloria*"), "Interior Voices" ("*Voces interiores*") illustrate this manner, his most temperamental. The poet intends to be a tribune, a prophet, a revolutionary. "To sing to Filis for her sweet name / when the clarion calls: 'awaken, steel!' / that is not a poet, nor a man." He scorns "the muse of tinsel and ermine" and prefers, on the contrary, to sing to "human suffering," "the city with its beehive noises," truth, justice, virtue . . . (*"Sursum"*). However, Díaz Mirón, in spite of his social art, his clamorous hyperboles, and his aphoristic reflections, managed not to blemish his standing as an artist. He was bombastic but elegant. And the cultural breeze that blew through his verses—citations from mythology and history, the selection of words and effects that ran against the grain—pleased even the Modernists who did not share his disdain for ivory towers. In his second period, that of *Stone Chips*, Díaz Mirón becomes serene. He who had prophesied political revolutions, carried out the only revolution possible for a poet—revolution within himself. However, it was not a great revolution. Basically he did not change: in the same way that earlier he had revealed modern flashes in his rhymed oratory, now we will also encounter rhetorical declamations in his verses, so beaten and worked over that they fall away like sparkling "stone chips." He is the same old Díaz Mirón, but in *Stone Chips* he passes away his solitude with interplays of accents and rhythms. There is more delicateness. He feels the pleasure of overcoming technical difficulties that he himself creates. One should read "Pepilla," "Vigil or Sleep" (*"Vigilia y sueño"*), "Exemplar" (*"Ejemplo"*), *"Nox"* and it will be seen that he sacrificed his volcanic energy for the perfections of a miniaturist—a great sacrifice for him, because of the eruptive force which he had to contain in himself. The Parnassian decorousness of his strophes often congealed his emotions. Despite all chastisement, his emotions reappear, converted into an heroic volition for the betterment of the art of verse. With manly constraint, he refused to fall into the use of easy rhymes and rhythms. His musical effects were so rigorous that no one has been able to imitate his difficult verses. He Latinized his sentences, suppressed unaccented grammatical particles, enriched the rhyme, brought out with his accentuation the chorus of the five vowels, magnified each detail in the crystal ball of a metaphor, and fused sensations in synesthesic impressions. In addition to word-sound, he offered a psychic interior and a suggestive musicality. In *Stone Chips* he was a Modernist, although a Modernist who remained alone, rebellious and menacing. His last period is that from 1902 to 1928: these poems, in which he sharpened his technical talent, were collected by Antonio Castro Leal into the volume, *Complete Poems* (*Poesías completas*).

In our literary history, Martí, Gutiérrez Nájera, Casal, and Silva seem to form part of the first group of Modernists. The death of all of these, prior to 1896, has influenced historians in rounding out this group. But we must resist the temptation of embellishing history with geometric schemes. Other schemes have been proposed: for example, that this Modernist group has a meridian in time—1882, the date of Martí's *Ismaelillo*, or 1888, the date of Darío's *Azul*—and a latitude in space— to the north of Ecuador lived the Colombian Silva, the Mexican Gutié- rrez Nájera, the Cubans Martí and Casal, the Nicaraguan Darío. It is not easy to delimit this "first Modernism." González Prada, Zorrilla de San Martín, Almafuerte, each of whom contributed to the poetic reno- vation in his own way, were older than those considered Modernists; and they lived to the south of Ecuador. If these are withdrawn, then Silva and even Martí should be withdrawn because they do not fit comfortably within Modernism either.

On the other hand, the great figure, Rubén Darío, fills not only the first Modernist period, but also the second, which began in the year 1896; and we prefer to study him in the next chapter when it is possible to speak of Modernism as a well-defined esthetic movement. One must not expect a clear division between Romanticism and Modernism. They are not opposite categories. They could not be because, in spite of their differences, both stand partially on common ground. It was, after all, those who were unsatisfied with Romanticism who left it, seeking modernities. So-called Modernist literature adds, to the discovery of emotional life made by the Romantics, the almost professional aware- ness of what literature and its latest fashions are, a feeling for the more prestigious forms, the aristocratic effort to excel in a high sphere of culture, the industry of combining diverse styles, the conviction that it was, by itself, a new art, and the pride of belonging to an Hispanic- American generation which, for the first time, was able to specialize in art. Let us leave for the moment, the definition of Modernism. This is not a history of "isms" but of creative personalities, and, remaining faithful to our chronological approach, we will pause now before the authors of the period which ends in 1895: Martí, Gutiérrez Nájera, Casal, and Silva.

José Martí / (Cuba, 1853–1895) is the most gigantic figure of all this period. The Cubans do well in revering his memory; he lived and died heroically in the service of Cuba's liberty. But Martí belongs even to those of us who are not Cubans. He is too big for Cuba; he is too big for America: he is one of those luxuries that the Spanish language can offer a universal public. He scarcely had time, however, to devote himself to letters. He left a few organized works, though these are not among his best. He was an essayist, a chronicler, a public speaker; that is to say, he was fragmentary, and his fragments often reach poetic heights. With him culminates the Romantic effort toward an esthetically elaborated prose. In the history of prose, Martí stands between two other giants: Montalvo and Rubén Darío. He still seems close to Montalvo for the prevalence of syntactical structures that could be found in any author of the Golden Age; and he seems close to Darío for his references to an aristocratic, cosmopolitan, and estheticist culture. His greatest literary heritage was Hispanic—Renaissance and Baroque writers—not French. However slightly Gallicized he may have been, certainly the poetic air of many of his pages becomes clear if we keep in mind that Martí esteemed the French writers who had created a pictorial prose (Gautier, Flaubert) and an impressionist prose (Daudet, the Goncourt brothers). He complained of the linguistic inertia of the Spaniards, and in seeking elegant forms in others' languages, he preferred French literature to English. He was not an esthete. He did not conceive of literature as the activity of a special esthetic organ. Writing for him was a way of serving. He revered letters for their practical virtues: the sincerity with which they unbosomed the generous emotions of man, the usefulness with which they helped to better society, the patriotism with which they shaped a Creole conscience. For this reason, even in his evaluation of artistic prose, there were moral overtones. In this sense, the pages he wrote in 1882 on Oscar Wilde are very significant. He valued "the noble and judicious things" that Wilde had said in propagating his faith in the cult of beauty and art for art's sake; but he corrected them with reflections on "the moral power and transcendental purpose of beauty."

Martí's ideas on art changed in the course of his career, and if some of them were not contradictory, at least they were accentuated contradictorily. It is as if the will to artistic perfection and the will to exemplary conduct were struggling within Martí. He always restrained his taste for pure art—a repudiation which in him was more energetic than in others because he was splendidly gifted for pure artistic expression—but in his later years he pulled on the reins so hard that his impulse to art was held back also. Roughly around 1887, as his impatience for action grew, Martí began to reject the quintessence of literature and the profit derived from the European Modernists, especially the French. There are in his works two periods: one more esthetic and the other more moral. The first crystallized in a novel, the only one he wrote: *Ill-Omened Friendship* (*Amistad funesta*, 1885). The plot, with the story of a tragic love, interweaves Romantic threads. But on this

Romantic canvas Martí will embroider a few garlands that have no
equal in the Hispanic-American novel of those years. Martí was the
first to contribute to the novelistic genre within the literary renovation
we call Modernism. He describes a bucolic, Arcadian, pastoral, rococo,
"literatized" nature. He also embellishes his characters with a twofold
procedure: the first, that of artistic *composition,* wherein the movement of the bodies strikes supreme attitudes in the manner of live pictures, and the second, that of artistic *transposition,* wherein the human
figures become more impressive because they are compared with masterpieces in museums. In the use of paintings, sculptures, precious stones,
objects of luxury—becoming more frequent in literature from Gautier to
the Goncourts—Martí succeeded more than anyone else in the Modernist literature of the Spanish language. As in Gutiérrez Nájera, Rubén
Darío, Casal, and all the others who are to come, Paris is the ideal avenue of escape from the immediate reality to more beautiful horizons.
Ill-Omened Friendship is the first book of artistic atmosphere, of sophis-
tication, of snobbism, of softness and intellectual preciosity in Hispanic-
American literature—others of this type will come later, those of José
María Rivas Groot, Vargas Vila, Díaz Rodríguez, Angel de Estrada, etc.
Within the narrative genre, Martí will continue his estheticism in children's stories for the magazine *La Edad de Oro* (1889). Yet his prose
is not as French as that of Darío, who is already writing. Martí was an
orator and he used all the little whiplashes of persuasion of which the
Spanish language is capable. As he wrote, excited by the practical needs
of the public speaker or shaken by the declamatory urge, he tended to
give his prose the structure of the sermon, the discourse, the proclamation, the oration. It is not the classical architecture of our preachers
of the Golden Age, nor that of Donoso Cortés, nor that of Castelar.
He overloads, complicates, amplifies, subordinates, and disproportions
excessively. He looses a storm of ideas, thunderclaps of emotion, and
lightning strokes of metaphors that cause his perorations to explode.
His sincerity is torrential; it demolishes dikes and cuts new river beds.

But behind his eloquence is a hard-working architect. His prose is
not a museum of classical tropes as was Montalvo's during those same
years; all told, he still preserves some of the harness in which classical
elocution moved. That these schemes of oratorical prose are old in our
literature was no obstacle to Martí in fortifying them. In Martí the
schemes are used as frames for his impressionistic paintings. His oratorical moments are replete with descriptions, reflections, and lyrical
images. No doubt he is an emphatic writer, but frequently his emphasis
is not eloquent, but expressive. He is rich in melodic variety, unmeas-

ured phrases, and, on the other extreme of the rhythmic scale, concise, elliptical, exclamatory sentences. Martí gave suppleness to his prose in order to better convey his impressionistic experiences. As a poet he was no less excellent. *Ismaelillo* (1882) was, for its time, a strange book: in meters of popular appearance, and with a popular theme—remembrances of home and the faraway son—Martí elaborated a brief, pictorial poetry of unexpected rhymes, of complex syntax, of archaisms and verbal riches, of condensation and detailed art. The language and metrics are regular: the new subtleties rest in the images of a tender, yet virile, sensibility. Martí continues to be preoccupied with his involvement in civil and political fights: in the midst of these stormy waters, he settles down like a serene lake. It is an enchanting, crepuscular lake where all is tenuously veiled and vanishes in a beautiful unreality. With the years, Romanticism had become overloaded with much rhetoric; when Martí lay bare his tenderness in *Ismaelillo*, that bareness, although Romantic, seemed new, and the Modernists considered it to be an inauguration of new forms. They had also considered Bécquer in this light. His posthumous *Free Verses* (*Versos libres*), written about the same date, were quite different. His violence occasionally emits smoke, like the burning of green wood. On other occasions—"Sky Flowers" (*"Flores del cielo"*)—it burns in flame, the last great blazing of the Romantic Titans: "Pallid with love, standing in the shadows, in my garden, / the sky enveloped in gigantic raiments / of astral light, / I'll make a magnificent bouquet of stars. / My hand will not tremble at seizing light!" And Romantic love, as in "Winged Cup" (*"Copa con alas"*): "I felt, embracing thee, that all of life embraced me!" "Thou alone, only thou, knowest the way / to reduce the Universe to just one kiss!" Since they were published many years after the death of Martí, the *Free Verses* had no influence in Modernism, which can also be said of another posthumous collection—*Flowers of Exile* (*Flores del destierro*). In *Simple Verses* (*Versos sencillos*, 1891) Martí was original because he fathomed deeper zones of himself and he apprised us of them in compact symbols. These verses, "playfully" written, are octosyllables, some are monorhymes, which was a novelty, and others are written with a capricious use of rhyme, repeating the same word, or having it reverberate in the interior of a line. But with all this, the simplicity is apparent. "I love simplicity, and I believe in the necessity of putting sentiment in plain and simple forms," he announced in the prolog; but it was the simplicity of a sincere and ingenious man. From this trait derives his power of seduction over the not-very-simple Modernists.

Occasionally one notices the preciosities that enter into the current definitions of Modernism: impressionistic traits, cultured exquisiteness (for example, compositions X, "The Tremulous and Lonely Soul"; XVI, "At the Fretted Embrasure"; XXII, "I Am at the Strange Ball"; XLII, "At the Strange Bazaar"). Even in poem IX the serious theme of "the child from Guatemala / she who died of love" is converted gracefully into a plastic and melodic playing: in contrapuntal form Martí harmonizes, in quatrains that pursue one another, the description of a death in the present (the cadaver, the burial, the funeral procession) and the evocation of a love in the past (the leave-taking, the return of the lover with his new spouse, the suicide in the river of the forgotten one). It is not a biographical episode; it is an esthetic exercise, with artful vignettes and musical accompaniment, very much to the Modernist taste. He was a poet of double accent, Romantic and Modernist, always very personal, quick in his leaps from intuition to intuition, capable of dressing the most abstract idea in a concrete image: "and time flew by and an eagle / flew over the sea" is his dynamic way of counting the minutes.

3. The Other Modernists

MANUEL GUTIÉRREZ NÁJERA (Mexico, 1859–1895) was not a renovator of metrics: he felt comfortable in the tradition of the octosyllable and the hendecasyllable. But he was, to be sure, a renovator of the mood of the poetic image. He overcame the doubts that tormented him, coincidental with the irreligious crisis of his time, and sounded, for the first time, the elegant, graceful, refined, light notes that Rubén Darío will continue to orchestrate. With romantically preferred sentiments—above all, those preferred by Musset and Bécquer: sadness, impossible love, mystery and death, grief—Gutiérrez Nájera sets himself before his mirror and dresses elegantly. In this self-contemplation, the poet takes pleasure, not so much in his own sentiments, but in the images in which he clothes them. Because of this attitude even elegiac themes take on a brilliance, a coloring, a pleasant array, as in his "Elegy" on the death of his friend Alvarez del Castillo, where Death is a beautiful, enamored lady. There was a "before" in which Gutiérrez Nájera was melancholy, depressed, anguished; but now, as he looks at himself in the mirror of art, he primps himself, ready to go out, and smiles. "Are you suffering? Seek the gentle lover, / the immobile and immortal beauty," he says in *"Pax anima";* and here he gives us an idea on how to convert ethics into esthetics: "While there are flowers, gather them; / forgive the rose its thorns. / When anguish overshadows my spirit /

I seek clarity and calm in the heights / and an infinite compassion whitens / on the frozen crests of my soul!" This is estheticism, neither frigid nor frivolous, at least not as frigid nor as frivolous as will be seen in other poets to follow, but which plays with life until it gives it a figure of pure beauty: "and make, artist, with thine anguish, / lofty sepulchral monuments." Life becomes an artistic monument. There are plastic images, well contoured so that we can see them; but other images also suggest visions without showing us the concrete things that those visions see, in a kind of vague musical language. In his verses to "Schubert's Serenade" he exclaims in envy: "Thus would my soul speak . . . if only it could!" He envies music for its ability to insinuate—a new attitude in our literature. In *"Non omnis moriar"* Gutiérrez Nájera takes Horace's theme, dear to estheticism, and re-elaborates it with the opposition, Man-Poet: the poet expresses the ineffable in man. Through this road Hispanic-American Romanticism, as was the case earlier in Europe, begins to withdraw from the public and the poet ends up by believing himself to be a tortured person through God's choice. Gutiérrez Nájera—*el Duque Job* (Duke Job) was his most famous pseudonym—does not feel chosen, but he does feel aristocratic; he was more duke than Job.

Justo Sierra, who wrote the prolog of the posthumous edition of his *Poetry* (*Poesía*, 1896) attributed to him, "French thoughts in Spanish verses" (as Valera would attribute to Darío a "mental Gallicism"). Not only did Gutiérrez Nájera read the French writers in French (in poetry, from Lamartine to Baudelaire and especially Musset, who was most like him; in prose, from Chateaubriand to Flaubert and Mendès), but also literature in translation—he had no connections with earlier Mexican writers. Seen from America he was a solitary figure who, along the road, would meet others like himself, and all together they would constitute a group: that of the so-called first Modernist generation. In Spain there was no poetry of this kind, with such gracefulness, distinction, and refinement, and for this reason Gutiérrez Nájera will amaze the Spaniards (Villaespesa, less of a poet, will be one of those amazed). His images, discomposing to the readers of the day, were themselves composed in a melody of perfect unity: images arranged like a panorama that unfolds, each time in deeper planes, enriching itself with the discovery of new beauty; images which, in spite of the coherent composition, file by like agile, individual bodies. Of admirable rhythmic mastery is "To the Corregidor's Wife" ("A la corregidora"): the soul in each object seems to speak in an insinuating and onomatopoeic voice. The words that Gutiérrez Nájera's ears choose, the harmonious

242

ones, those that are best entwined in rhythms and rhymes, coincide with those chosen by his eyes, the most luxuriant objects, the prettiest, the most exquisite. He was also able to make out another reality, that of "the dark, / silent currents of my soul" (read "Dead Waves" ["*Ondas muertas*"] and "*Tristissima Nox*"), and this is the dimension we most value. The poetry of Gutiérrez Nájera has lost its power to excite the reader of today—when Mexican youths look for the sources of modern poetry they find them in González Martínez, Tablada, and López Velarde. A few steps more and they would find Gutiérrez Nájera as a pristine source.

Excellent is Gutiérrez Nájera's prose and more significant than his poetry, at least in the history of Modernism. A tireless journalist—he was editor of the *Revista Azul*—he devoted himself to displaying his French trimmings. His chronicles were masterpieces. They alighted capriciously on the most frivolous happenings of the week, and in this way they created the illusion of an ironic and beautifying veil of fantasy. The impressionistic description, the good humor, the notations of his Mexican travels, the ingenious commentary sounded frivolous but they were responding to a premeditated theory of prose. There was in him also the literary critic. His fiction has not lost all of its freshness. *Fragile Stories* (*Cuentos frágiles*, 1883) and the posthumous *Smoke-Colored Stories* (*Cuentos color de humo*) gathered together a few of them—today, thanks to the *Complete Stories* (*Cuentos completos*, 1958 edition), we can appreciate in its total value the transformation of narrative prose in the hands of a poet. Samples of his storytelling art are: "History of a Counterfeit Coin" and "The Novel of the Trolley." He was aware of the dangers of poetic prose: one, keeping in the coffer—he used to say—loose pearls, instead of stringing them into a necklace of action; another, the breaking of Spanish grammar by forcing the intercalation of French forms. The remedy—he noted—is to read Jovellanos, good administrator of the language.

JULIÁN DEL CASAL (Cuba, 1863–1893) published two books of poetry, *Leaves to the Wind* (*Hojas al viento*, 1890) and *Snow* (*Nieve*, 1892); and another, posthumously, *Busts and Rhymes* (*Bustos y rimas*, 1893), in prose and verse. Recently collected were his short stories, poems in prose and chronicles: pages of artistic aspirations, interesting as guides for the study of Casal's poetry, not as substitutes for them. His three books of poems have an elegiac intonation. In the first, Casal has not completely disentangled himself from the Spaniards Zorrilla, Bartrina, Bécquer, and Campoamor, although his Romanticism convulses with expressions in the manner of Heine and Leopardi, and already there are reflections of the French lyrics of Gautier, Heredia, Coppée and Baudelaire. In the second book, the transcendental pessimism, the aristocratic vocabulary, the metric renovation, the search for perfect forms, and the cultivation of the descriptive-pictorial poem are already Modernist. Not only does he pay tribute to the Frenchmen Baudelaire, Gautier, Banville, Mendès, Leconte, Heredia, Richepin, Verlaine and Moreàs, but also to the Hispanic-Americans Gutiérrez Nájera and Darío. At this point he is a Parnassian, and his greatest god, Gautier. No one less than Verlaine himself commented on *Snow*, and reproached Casal for his Parnassian addiction. "I believe," he said, "that present-day mysticism will reach him and when the terrible Faith has bathed his young soul, poems shall bud from his lips like sacred flowers." He was right: the Parnassian ideal of cold and objective forms impelled Casal to neglect the quiverings of his melancholy. In the third book of poems, he reveals himself to be more somber, personal, audacious and innovating. Now on the altar, next to Gautier, are Verlaine and Baudelaire. The yearning for a supreme form, the flexibility of the verse, the cult of morbid sensations, the artistic transpositions, the taste for Hellenistic, rococo, and Japanese cultures, the mastery in the arrangement of radiant words, symbols and objects, all insert Casal into the orbit of Modernism. Seen in its better moments, his poetry is intimate. It fills the brief life of the poet to the brim, but it does not spill over. Absent from it are civic chants, descriptions of the homeland, and erotic tales. Or, better said, the few verses of topical themes are insignificant. He did not feel the natural beauty of the Cuban landscape. In an island of sun, greenery, joy, bustle, he preferred to shut his doors and remain in the darkness, alone, in his sickly confinement. His poetry, then, is poured completely within his sad soul. The exclamations of sadness were repeated so often in European and American Romanticism that at times it is difficult to distinguish between the voice and the echo; but there is no doubt that Casal's verse "Why, O Lord, hast thou made my soul so sad?" was an authentic voice. It may well resemble other Romantic voices, but it is so revealing of Casal's being that were a similar verse found in an earlier poet (in Vigny there are two like it) Casal's would still be original.

He was taciturn, not so much because he had a pessimistic conception of life, nor simply because he was poor, timid and ill, but because, besides all that, he was not constitutionally made for participating in the joyful enticements of the world. He does not judge this world: his theme is his own sadness that arises from a hidden source. He feels displeasure with life, that is all. But he does not complain; the world is indifferent to him, and when he declares that it is mud and morass, he is giving us an impression, not a philosophy. He feels dead in life; and there is in him a joyful expectancy of the finite death which, at least in certain verses that were lost in newspapers, made him think of suicide: "And in the distance, toasting consolation / to my bitterness, only the pistol's mouth / smiles at me." If one read "Nihilism," it can be seen how sincere was his desire to be dead: "I feel only the urge to consume myself / or to live in my eternal poverty / with my faithful companion, discontentment, / and my pallid lover, sadness." It is a tragic beat that is heard in all his poetry. In "Autobiography" one sees that the poet is not doing poetic exercises on the Romantic theme of anguish, but is expressing himself sincerely. What is most moving in Casal is, precisely, his not wishing to play with forms, which he could have since he was gifted in exhibiting artifices, but his preferring to give simple form to one obsession: that of dying. Art was for him a refuge. He had no illusions about his poetry: he thought it would be dispersed in "the bitter waves of oblivion." But he abandoned himself to his art, as one does to opium, and submerged ever deeper into his dreams. His early Romanticism had been superficial: his soul drifted on the conventions of his day, his verses floated emptily. But in his best compositions Casal sinks like a deep-sea diver. At times his diver's gear is the plastic, colorful, refined poetry that Casal admired in Gautier and Heredia; at times, it is the crepuscular and insinuating poetry that Casal admired in Baudelaire. The first type of poetry, because it was similar to the poetic language of French Parnassianism, took on a kinship with that of other Hispanic-Americans who were reading the same authors. There are verses of Casal which bear a notable resemblance to others of Gutiérrez Nájera and Rubén Darío. He would compose live pictures as if he were inspired by paintings: like those of Gustave Moreau. Huysmans, in *A Rebours*, had likewise described paintings by Moreau.

Objects are not embellished by Casal; they were already beautiful in art and the poet carries them like adornments. It is an aristocratic, cosmopolitan, exotic atmosphere, with the luster of Paris and of Tokyo, with swans, eighteenth-century courtesans, precious stones. The titles, "medallions," "chromos," "cameos," "old ivory," "sketches," "Ideal Museum," declare his intent to be an artisan of forms and colors. Turning to the other direction of his poetry, toward the most secret penumbra of his inner life, Casal (dazzled by Baudelaire) expressed his "sanguinary vision of neurosis," his voyage "toward the glacial land of insanity"; his synesthesia "the dormant body perceives / through my magic sopor, / sounds in color, / color in sounds." See *"Post Umbra,"* "The Song of Morphine" (*"La canción de la morfina"*), "Horridum somnium," "Body and Soul" (*"Cuerpo y alma"*).

José Asunción Silva (Colombia, 1865–1896) walked the path of a Romantic garden that had already withered; and no sooner do we see him following the footsteps of the prosaic Campoamor and Bartrina (*"Gotas amargas"*) than he veers toward the places preferred by Bécquer (*"Crisálides"* and *"Notas perdidas"*), On his return from Paris and from London he brought a library of contemporary writers and initiated his friends in the spirit of the new literature. Nevertheless, the affected mannerisms of the "Rubendarians," as he used to call them, annoyed him, and under the signature of Benjamín Bibelot Ramírez, he dedicated a satire called "Strawberry-Colored Symphony with Cream" (*"Sinfonía color de fresa con leche"*) to the "decadent humming birds." All his work was done in his youth, this must be kept in mind; and it was achieved as an aspiration, almost as though he had divined his early death. This is without counting the loss in a shipwreck of manuscripts representing five years of poetic work. According to the testimonies of those who had seen those manuscripts, they were his best poetry. Silva neglected his public relations; since the favor of his readers did not interest him, he did not help them by arranging his own work which, for its confused mixture, produces a false impression of immaturity. His little volume of poetry lacked unity, and the diversity of his patriotic, festive, folkloric, narrative, erotic, and philosophic compositions obscures his merit. Now that we have his *Complete Works* (*Obra completa*, 1956), gathered by Rafael Maya, the critic can turn away from trodden paths and follow Silva when he enters the mysterious, intimate, quivering, lyrical path which will take him to the poetic renovation that other poets had ventured on.

His literary culture was up to date with the latest French and English quotations. He had read Poe and Baudelaire, and in his prose page "Me, a Poet?" he cites Rossetti, Verlaine and Swinburne. He had spiritual affinity with Poe, above all. The influence of Poe has been pointed out in the rhythms of "All Souls Day" and of the third "Nocturne," two compositions in the new metric technique. More than an influence, it was an affinity between the shadows and mysteries of Poe and the nocturnal quality of Silva: cf. "Tell Me," "Ronde," "Nocturne," "Midnight Dreams," "Moon Light," "Serenade," "All Souls Day." Is the influence of Poe present in the procedure of changing meters? Doubtful. Silva, in reality, followed his own pleasure in displacing rhythms. His versification becomes sweeter as it travels the road to free verse.

In "A Poem" he gave us his esthetics: "I dreamed, in those days of forging a poem /of rare and nervous art, supreme and audacious work." He was not always faithful to that idea of esthetics. When he was, the moments that count, he left us tremulous poems of morbid sentiments, suggestive of enigmas, with accents of tenderness and melancholy. Silva's pessimism had its roots in his body, in his soul, in his philosophy, in the philosophy of the day. His best poems, a good example of them is "Ebbing of Life" (*"Vejeces"*), are those that evoke time gone by, the voice of things outworn, the visions of childhood, the shadows, the noises, and forgotten fragrances, and all this in a poetic language that was vague, evanescent, musical. What is deserving of his fame are his "Nocturnes," especially the third, the one of the "long shadow." With a faltering voice whose silent moments are like tremors, with a kind of poetic stammering as though the poet were bewildered by a supernatural apparition, and in his stupor, could only manage to move his lips or to bite them in order to contain his weeping, this "Nocturne," written, as they say, at the death of his sister Elvira, is one of the loftiest expressions of lyricism of the epoch; it is new in timbre, in tone, in musical structure, in its phantasmal, elegiac theme, in its rhythmic imitation of sobbing. This Silva of the nocturnes is the one closest to us. He is, of all the Colombian poets of the nineteenth century, the only one who speaks to the poetic sensibilities of today. While other Modernists were discerning the world, Silva discerned himself. His melancholy lyricism made him disdain Romantic grandiloquence and Modernist sumptuousness, and it is his poems of obscure mysteries that save him for us. His novel *After Dinner* (*De Sobremesa*) analyzes the character's hypersensitive psychology in a Paul Bourget fashion.

In every country there were poets, and national pride will take us to task if we omit them.

Mexico: FRANCISCO ASÍS DE ICAZA (1863–1925), JOSÉ MARÍA BUSTILLOS (1866–1899) and BALBINO DÁVALOS (1866–1951).

Antilles: There were other Cubans who took the first steps of Modernism with Casal, but so timidly, that alongside him, they seem to be taking another direction. ANICETO VALDIVIA, Count Kostia (1859–1927) carried on the taste for French novelty, but in Castilian he preferred not to innovate. BONIFACIO BYRNE (1861–1936), hailed by Casal as a poet of new accents, did not do his tour of service under Modernism. He was, rather, a poet of patriotic emotion. EMILIO BOBADILLA (1862–1920), better known for his mordant criticism under the pseudonym Fray Candil, worked in Spain. Though he attacked Modernism, his verses profited by the metric reforms of the Modernists. The Dominican Republic had given two poets: José Joaquín Pérez and Salomé Ureña de Henríquez. Not unlike them in quality, we may add GASTÓN FERNANDO DELIGNE (1861–1913), author of *Galaripsos*. He excelled in the brief poem, somewhat in the manner of Campoamor.

Because of his power of observation and of the depth of his thought, he almost converted the psychological poem into a new genre, in which the intimate life of a person is illumined in a critical instant—"Woes," (*"Angustias"*), "Secrets of Cristina" (*"Confidencias de Cristina"*). He also wrote philosophical poems— "Annihilation" (*"Aniquilamiento"*)—and political ones—*"Ololoi."* Deligne derided Modernism: he was in truth a realist, and even a naturalist, with lapses into prosaic discourses. He practised metric innovations. It must be said that Modernism taught the Dominicans the art of varying versification, but it did not uproot them from the Romantic and realist orbit. ENRIQUE HENRÍQUEZ (1859–1940), the one of the nocturnes, was a Romantic. And even FABIO FIALLO (1866–1942), in spite of his participation in Modernist literary life, Romanticized anguished love, like Heine and Bécquer, as can be seen in *A Life's Song* (*La canción de una vida*, 1926), in which he collected a great deal of his work. We shall not go into the lesser poets: EMILIO PRUDHOMME (1856–1932), CÉSAR NICOLÁS PENSON (1855–1901), PABLO PUMAROL (1857–1889), RAFAEL DELIGNE (1863–1902) and ARTURO BAUTISTA PELLERANO CASTRO (1865–1916), author of the popular *Creoles* (*Criollas*). In Puerto Rico JESÚS MARÍA LAGO (1860–1929) was a Modernist in his belated *Sandalwood Coffer* (*Cofre sándalo*, 1927).

Venezuela: Here too Modernism arrived late and manifested itself more in prose. One can scarcely mention, as Modernist poets, the names of MANUEL PIMENTEL CORONEL (1863–1907), and GABRIEL MUÑÓZ (1864–1908).

Colombia: ISMAEL ENRIQUE ARCINIEGAS (1865–1937), in his early years a follower of Bécquer, later exchanged his spontaneity for Parnassian jewels.

Bolivia: ROSENDO VILLALOBOS (1860–1939), translator of Parnassians and symbolists.

Chile: The rebel Bohemian PEDRO ANTONIO GONZÁLEZ (1863–1903) became a character in two novels, Marcial Cabrera Guerra's *The White Feather* (*La pluma blanca*) and Luis Enrique Délano's *The Laurel on the Lyre* (*El laurel sobre la lira*), rather than a figure in literary history. His role was that of the poet coming from the past with his head bent down, who all of a sudden stumbles upon the first Modernist poets, is amazed at their brilliance and begins immediately to cultivate the superficial and external aspects of the new poetic language.

Argentina: There are various writers who break the tradition and create a movement that in 1893 will recognize Rubén Darío as the greatest poet of the language: we will list the most important one, LEOPOLDO DÍAZ (1862–1947). He was one of the first frequenters of the French *Parnasse.* In his *Sonnets* (*Sonetos,* 1888) there already is a searching for Greek myths, a transferring of figures from the plastic arts to poetry, a relishing in pagan pleasures, a polishing of perfect forms—actions common to all Modernists. His Parnassian *Bas Reliefs* (*Bajorrelieves*) are from 1895. Darío was already in Buenos Aires and he eulogized it with brotherly affection. In his later work—*The Shadows of Hellas* (*Las sombras de Hellas,* 1902), *Atlantis Conquered* (*Atlántida conquistada,* 1906), *Amphoras and Urns* (*Las ánforas y las urnas,* 1923)—Díaz continued to gyrate in the center of his Parnassian esthetics, always golden but ever more frigid.

Rubén Darío, because of his birth date, should be studied here. But Rubén Darío was younger than Gutiérrez Nájera and Casal; he published *Profane Prose* (*Prosas profanas*) when they, and Martí, and Silva had already died, and it was with this book of 1896 that estheticism reaches its fulness, becomes conscious of its revolutionary program, is given a name, "Modernism," and its influence reaches Spain. Therefore, we will find Rubén Darío in the next chapter.

B. MAINLY PROSE

1. Novel and Short Story

(*1*) *MEXICO* / Among the Mexicans who enriched the realist art of narration, several of whom we mentioned in the preceding chapter and others whom we will mention in the following, two come to the fore during these years: Micrós and Gamboa. ANGEL DE CAMPO, who used the pen name MICRÓS (1868–1908), printed in the newspapers sketches of customs. From his impressions of society came short stories and a short novel, *The Rumba* (*La rumba*), in which he poured heaps and heaps of naturalist detail onto a woeful story. *Things Seen* (*Cosas vistas*) is the title of one of his books, a title that declares an objectivity that Micrós did not possess. When he was not caricaturizing or displaying his irony, he appeared as a sentimentalist. He felt tenderness and pity for all humble, poor, unprotected, and infirm life. In his compassion, he included animals, who he imagined suffer as humans. From his sympathy for all who suffered grew his moral criticism, which at times became inflamed. FEDERICO GAMBOA (1864–1939) is the Mexican novelist who approached the closest to what was then considered the modern novel, that is to say, the experimental novel that proposed studying Mexican society. He documented the customs of the people in the naturalist method, and preferred erotic themes. *Supreme Law* (*Suprema ley*, 1896), the story of a consumptive who is ruined by love, is set before a vast background of Mexican society. In *Santa* (1903) he achieved a greater equilibrium between his naturalism, his eroticism, and his depictions of customs. Is Santa, the prostitute, a literary first cousin to Zola's Nana or to the Goncourts' Elisa? Gamboa recovered his Catholic faith, already effective in *Reconquest* (*Reconquista*) and in *The Wound* (*La llaga*), and became a reactionary. He was an intense dramatist; perhaps his best constructed drama was *Between Brothers* (*Entre hermanos*).

(*2*) *CENTRAL AMERICA* / *Honduras:* The first novel, *Angelina*, belonged to CARLOS F. GUTIÉRREZ (1861–1899).

Nicaragua: SALVADOR CALDERÓN RAMÍREZ (1868–1940) cultivated the fantastic in *Stories for My Carmencita* (*Cuentos a mi Carmencita*).

Costa Rica: The tradition of the sketch of customs lasted longer in America than anywhere else. Many writers, wanting to adhere to reality, scarcely managed to express themselves literarily. They would emerge from the mucky depths, and look about; they were part of the nature they described. It is not worthwhile listing names. In Costa Rica the depiction of customs, an old form in other places, surged forth at the end of the century with a new vigor, as if it were revolutionary. From the land mass of America comes a nation, Costa Rica, but it comes without a literature. For almost four centuries that land did not produce writers, either significant or insignificant—they did not even have a press until 1830. When writers finally appeared they split into two groups, one, the cosmopolitan estheticists, the other, regional realists. It was the realist group which was more esteemed for being closer to things. After PÍO VÍQUEZ (1848–1899), a rich temperament although a poor writer, after MANUEL ARGÜELLO MORA (1845–1902), the first notable narrator, and after JUAN GARITA (1859–1914), depicter of customs, rises the important—important in Costa Rica—figure of MANUEL GONZÁLEZ ZELEDÓN (1864–1936), better known by the pen name MAGÓN. He described the city of San José, a city that was barely a city; he described it inside and outside, home life, school life, life of the bureaucracy, of social clubs, and of cafes, of the plains, of the valleys and of the coffee plantations; he described poverty, feast days, love, popular types, everyday things, things he saw and, in the country, things he thought he saw. He did all this with the rapidity of the conversationalist, with dialectic colloquialisms, without worrying about creating situations or of drawing characters. He was an observer of details, preferring indelicate subjects since he was a naturalist. Literature of the people, by the people, and for the people: a democratic formula of slight esthetic value but well documented. To be sure, there is no corny sentimentality in Magón. This is a negative value. Nor is there brashness: another negative value. It is not that Magón is forward and natural in manner, but that in his sketches of customs there is no room for mawkishness nor for brashness because neither is there room for literature. His mood is one of joyfulness, irony, and mischievousness. His sketches of customs rarely acquire the architecture of the short story. One built-up story is "Eclipse of the Sun" (*"El clis de sol"*); and another, "One's Own" (*"La propia"*). The former has antecedents in *"Por qué era rubia?"* by P. A. Alarcón. González Zeledón enumerated, described, but did not construct a story. He is entertaining, like coarse conversation; and he is worthwhile because he has understood a people who, for having a place under the sun, deserve to be placed before a literary mirror so their reflection can be seen. Magón did in prose what his cousin Aquileo Echeverría used to do in verse. Other writers of customs copied him, such as MANUEL DE JESÚS JIMÉNEZ (1854–1916), CLAUDIO GONZÁLEZ RUCAVADO (1865–1925), CARLOS CAGINI (1865–1925), RICARDO FERNÁNDEZ GUARDIA (1867–1950). The realist novelist of most substance in Costa Rica in these years was JENARO CARDONA (1863–1930), author of *The Cousin* (*El primo*, 1905), a novel of the city about middle-class people, and *The Sphinx of the Path* (*La esfinge del sendero*, 1914), even more removed from the depiction of customs because of the analysis of the struggle of conscience in a priest.

(3) *ANTILLES* / In the Antilles the narrative genre did not have luster.

Cuba: RAMÓN MEZA (1861–1911) authored the satiric novel, *My Uncle, the Civil Servant* (*Mi tío el empleado*, 1886). The first part is a satire against bureaucracy. Its episodes appear to be disfigured by a mocking fantasy; and in this weird and senseless labyrinth, with snatches from picaresque literature and the atmosphere of a nightmare, constant peals of laughter are heard. In the second part, which takes place seven years later, his satire is directed toward the upper levels of Cuban society in the Colony. The narrative moves at a slower pace, although some of his best impressionist effects are in this part.

Dominican Republic: FABIO FIALLO (1866–1942) went from poetry to prose, to the point where some of his poems were actually paraphrased into short stories. We have already placed him as a poet elsewhere. The motif of his *Fragile Stories* (*Cuentos frágiles*, 1908) is the female figure as an object of artistic contemplation. He is also the author of *Mefisto's Apples* (*Las manzanas de Mefisto*, 1934) and of a dramatic work. He remained impervious to vernacular themes. On the other hand, FEDERICO GARCÍA GODOY (1857–1924), essayist and critic, wrote a novelistic trilogy with episodes of national history. The first novel was the best, *Rufinito* (1908), whose protagonist is a political boss. This was followed by *Dominican Soul* (*Alma dominicana*, 1911) and *Guanuma* (1914). Others: CÉSAR NICOLÁS PENSON (1855–1901) collected in his *Old Things* (*Cosas añejas*), traditions of the end of the eighteenth and of the nineteenth century in the manner of Ricardo Palma. José Ramón López (1866–1922), whose *Stories of Puerto Plata* (*Cuentos puertoplateños*, 1904), although clumsy and not very original, do have some attraction. Pedro María Archambault (1862–1944), in *Pine Groves* (*Pinares adentro*, 1929) gave us an eclogue description of highlands. Jaime Colson (1862–1952) was a depicter of customs in *General Babieca, Patricio Flaquenco*, and *Corporal Chepe* (*El cabo Chepe*). Virginia Elena Ortea (1866–1903), a devoted and cultured narrator, author of a mythological story "The Diamonds," also wrote realist works.

Puerto Rico: Matías González García (1866–1938) crudely novelized the life of Creole workers in *Things* (*Cosas*, 1893) and *Ernest* (*Ernesto*, 1894). But the most important novelist, within this Creole naturalism, was Manuel Zeno Gandía (1855–1930). He was a physician and with a clinical eye wrote his "chronicles of a sick world," *The Pond* (*La charca*, 1895), *Garduña* (1896), *Business* (*El negocio*, 1922) and the posthumous *Redeemers* (*Redentores*). They are studies of wretchedness, hunger, vice, and the anguish of the Puerto Rican colony. As a good naturalist Zeno Gandía intervened in the make-up of his novels with his doctrines. Thus, his personages remained types rather than characters; furthermore, the environment, which is what the author wanted above all to describe, made the characters flat. He wished to regenerate the physical and spiritual life of the fields, and of the villages and cities, to correct materialist egoism, to dignify man. Although more observant than imaginative, Zeno Gandía managed to imbue human and social conflicts with enough substance so as to merit a place in the history of the Hispanic-American novel.

(4) Venezuela: Manuel Vicente Romero García (1865–1917) was effective with *Peonage* (*Peonía*, 1890), a "novel of Venezuelan customs." The author (or rather, the style) is dry, unappetizing, cynical, sarcastic. It is not that his admittedly materialist conception of life is to blame for his hardness as a writer, because other positivists of his time were more compassionate and human; and it is his materialism that reveals the best of him as a person, which is the spirit of social reform, his criticism of evil Venezuelan traditions. If Romero García does not draw his readers' sympathy, it is because earlier, on creating his novels, he felt no sympathy for his character creations. Or, said in another way, he lacked novelizing power. Although written under the aegis of Isaacs, *Peonage* has nothing of *María*. Even similar scenes are viewed with different eyes. He tells us in an interesting digression on Venezuelan literature that he esteems Romantic poetry, but he is not a Romantic, rather, a depicter of customs, a realist, even a naturalist. The novel, in itself, does not have much value: it is the story of a love, cut short by exile and death, in the midst of a degraded Venezuelan family. The moral and political reflections add nothing to the story; on the contrary, they prejudice the novel's action. The description of customs remains, though. This is what Romero García believed to be most worthwhile, and he advocated an art derived from nature and society. Gonzalo Picón-Febres (1860–1918) is celebrated for *Sergeant Felipe* (*El sargento Felipe*, 1889). In its historical background—the fratricidal war between Matías Salazar and Guzmán Blanco—this novel describes country life and tells of tragic loves and vengeances. Realism? Not much. At any rate it is a realism softened by many Romantic tears; when this realism, softened in this way, does become hardened, it is in phrases, cut like jewels, in a poetic style.

Some of the metaphors are more intuitions than ornaments. The mood is sentimental. At times the moral judgments on the cruel and stupid civil wars give the prose a declamatory leavening, and the phrasing swells in wide rhythms. His descriptive pages are the best: beautiful landscapes, beautiful portraits like that of Encarnación (on one occasion it says that the girl "resembles a figure from Mistral, the candorous poet of Provence"). But there is not one character that really lives —Sergeant Felipe least of all. Picón-Febres always keeps them in his potter's' hands and will not release them so they can live. MIGUEL EDUARDO PARDO (1868– 1905) a novelist's apprentice, wrote with an abundance of verbiage and a scarcity of vivid expression. *A Whole People* (*Todo un pueblo*) is a novel without unity. A young lad, Julián, the descendant of a destitute Indian family, but who now comes from a good family, wishes to reform society. Anarchist? Socialist? His mother, a widow, gives herself to a scoundrel, the father of Julián's sweetheart. In the end, Julián kills the scoundrel. Balzac, Flaubert, and Zola are mentioned as models for a possible novel on the defects of the society he is describing, but *A Whole People* does not follow those models. JOSÉ GIL FORTOUL (1852–1943) is preferable as a historian rather than as a novelist, although with his *Julián* (1888) he was one of the forerunners of naturalism in the French style.

(5) *Colombia* / Some of the narrators of this generation—Vargas Vila, J. M. Rivas Groot—because of their connection with Modernism, will be shifted to the next chapter. Other narrators—LORENZO MARROQUÍN (1885–1918) and FRANCISCO DE PAULA RENDÓN (1855–1917)—will be only mentioned here, so that we may devote all the available space to the great novelist of these years, TOMÁS CARRASQUILLA (1858–1940). His production came late in life; and because of the contrast between his realism and the cosmopolitan tastes of the Modernists there were those who believed his novels, written between 1896 and 1935, were outmoded stragglers. Carrasquilla, in fact, complained of the Modernist fashion, and in his "homilies" to Max Grillo and other young esthetes he recommended a realist program—"to describe man in his medium"—that would reveal the national character spontaneously. The realism of Carrasquilla, nevertheless, was closer to the artistic novels of the twentieth century than to the pedestrian sketches of customs of the nineteenth, although certain of the narrations were pedestrian. He was an original man. He had writing talent to spare; and he also dominated a language rich in Antioquian idioms, pure Spanish, and golden down to its last roots, lithe and agile in its daring moves. But he did not take the career of novelist seriously. He would scribble down copy without thinking of his reader; he did not even intend to publish. Almost as if he had taken a bet that Antioquia would lend itself as a setting for a novel, he came to write *Fruits from My Land* (*Frutos de mi tierra*, 1896), "taken directly from Nature," says Carrasquilla himself, "without idealizing at all, the reality of life." His having written in a void, with-

out regard for a reading public, and without aspirations of producing a book, damaged the skeletal frame of his stories. They are of varied structure, of varied themes—the novels: *Grandeur* (*Grandeza,* 1910); *The Marquise of Yolombó* (*La Marquesa de Yolombó,* 1926); *A Long Time Ago: Memoirs of Eloy Gamboa* (*Hace tiempo. Memorias de Eloy Gamboa,* 1935–36); novelettes: *Little Luther* (*Luterito*), later entitled "Father Casafús" ("*El padre Casafús,*" 1899); *Salve, Regina,* 1903; *Child's Affection* (*Entrañas de niño,* 1906); *Ligia Cruz,* 1920; *The Blue-Eyed Fellow* (*El zarco,* 1922); and folkloric, fantastic, psychological, and symbolic short stories: *At the Right Hand of God, the Father* (*En la diestra de Dios Padre,* 1897); *The Lonely Soul* (*El ánima sola,* 1898); *The Rifle* (*El rifle,* 1915); *Palonegro,* 1919. Carrasquilla's narrative is characterized as a whole by the numerous characters it presents, all taken from the mines, the fields, the highlands, the villages, the Colombian roads, and intertwined in ordinary circumstances; these characters do not show their inner selves directly ("Father Casafús" is an exceptional example of interest in things psychological), but rather live outgoing lives constantly compelled to create dialog. In his pages there is talking and talking: idle chatter, anecdotes, gossiping, with the genuine mischievousness of the people. But the conversation of these characters is not "put" in their mouths mechanically, as the writers of customs used to do; Carrasquilla first listened to popular conversation, assimilated it, and then created characters who speak with natural and expressive vigor. This means that Carrasquilla identified popular speech with his own style and in this way anticipated the manner of the regionalist novelists of today. Even so, although the setting, the customs, the situations and the characters are taken from the people, Carrasquilla does not rub elbows with the crowd, making believe he sees things at their level, as the realists used to coldly feign, but he sincerely surveys all from his solitary lookout. He looks so intently that his eyes probably hurt. Even his humor hurts, because it discovers human weakness. He is more observant of the movement of the masses than of individual actions. His attitude is one of love for his region and for the humble, but with philosophic aloofness. For this reason, he has created deep and complex characters—women, children— for this reason, personal recollections have such power in his stories. He does not offer theses, he does not protest, he does not preach, he does not moralize, but he does have a philosophy—naturalism—which brings him to compare human quality with the animal. In order that the comparison may be better defended, Carrasquilla shows syphilitics, suicides, and ignoramuses, steeped in the "garbage cans" of nature—cf.

"Money Mad" ("*A la plata!*"). Carrasquilla preferred *Salve, Regina* and *The Marquise of Yolombó*. With only a few alterations, the history of the beautiful Regina—consumed by the fever of doubt, by purity, faith, love, scruples—could have gained in tragic power. *The Marquise of Yolombó* could be called the possibility of a great novel. It is a historical novel, since the action takes place from the middle of the eighteenth century to the post-Independence war days. However, the novel is more ethnographic than historical. It tells us the story of the Creole woman, Barbara, who, from age sixteen until she becomes wealthy, wishes to become a miner. However, she obtains the title of Marquise from Charles IV, falls victim to a scoundrel who weds her in order to rob her of her reserves of gold, loses her mind and regains it in her old age, when Hispanic America has become a cocoon of republics. If it is not history, at least it is chronicle. And the best part is not the thin novelistic line, but the large daubs of color with which the mining customs of Yolombó are described—customs of the rich Spanish families and customs of the poor Negro families, with artistic sympathy for both. Folklore and human masses are what one sees on the primary plane. From there, receding into the background, are a few, very few, clearcut episodes: the grotesque idyl between Don Chepe and Silverita, the cruel scene between Martín and the crucified Negro, Orellana's baseness. And, even more blurry, a few, very few, attempts at drawing characters: Barbosa, Don Chepe, Martín, María de la Luz. On the whole *The Marquise of Yolombó* is badly constructed—digressions, anachronistic reflections, lessons in history or in ethnography that rupture the story's integrity.

On the other hand, the prose is spiced with regionalisms and neologisms. Carrasquilla has placed himself within the Antioquian language, and from there speaks with liberty. The effect is surprising. We cannot place this prose in the history of Spanish realism, with Galdós, for example. Carrasquilla lived isolated from current literary tastes, although in *The Marquise of Yolombó* he cites Balzac and Flaubert. He was not only isolated in his Antioquia, but between him and Antioquia he placed an esthetic glass plate. Through this glass, he deformed regional matters. He described with sharpness and irony. He scrutinized minute detail and captured it with stunning words. It is obvious that for him writing was a solitary game. For this reason he was not, nor could he be, popular. If we call him a realist it is for lack of a better word. He made reality crystallize in an apparently rich and colloquial language, but it was really an artistic language. Reality and language, crystallized in this way, are a new creation, like those systematically deformed creations known as *esperpentos*. In fact, Carrasquilla speaks to us of characters who "enter in the form of *esperpentos*." These are esperpentic scarecrows that Valle-Inclán will tackle later. Carrasquilla coldly laughs at the material he elaborates. There is an atmosphere of farce, as in chapters II and III where the old man Don Chepe wants the hand of the young marriageable Silverita. The figures are stretched out or made squat, as in a caricature. The pleasure derived from this distortion is not that of the realist novel of the nineteenth century, but that of the artistic prose of the twentieth. In his best moments Carrasquilla does not document his reality; he subjects it to the refractions of aberrant lenses and mirrors. His reality may be humble—ignorant Spaniards, Creoles lost within the American landscape, Negroes adhering to their African traditions, receding Indian shadows—but his optics is aristocratic. This is so only in his better moments (had Valle-Inclán known them, he would have enjoyed them and even profited from them for his *Tirano Banderas*), because otherwise, judged in its totality, *The Marquise of Yolombó* is a failure. As an example of popular short stories the reader should consult *At the Right Hand of God, the Father* where he can admire the humor and irony with which old folklore themes are dressed in the costumes of Antioquia.

(6) *Ecuador* / We have the novelist ALFREDO BAQUERIZO MORENO (1859–1950), tidy and cultured in *Sonata in Prose* (*Sonata en prosa*), but capable of picking out characters from the crowd of ordinary people as he does in *El Señor Penco*, 1895. The writer who masterfully opened a series of realist Ecuadorian novels of social content was LUIS A. MARTÍNEZ (1868–1909). *On the Coast* (*A la costa*) is a landmark novel with its almost scientific eagerness for truth. It records changes in the life of Ecuador: its old social customs, its new hopes for transformation. The prose is lively and clearcut, although capable of crudities. It was Martínez who made forward strides in Ecuadorian realism. There were others of less momentum: everything considered, the most important of these were JOSÉ RAFAEL BUSTAMANTE, whose novel *To Kill the Worm* (*Para matar el gusano*, 1912) rotates around the figure of a drunkard from the middle class of Quito; and JOSÉ ANTONIO CAMPOS, with his more or less humorous narrations, tending in general, toward lessons in liberal politicking—*Cathodic Rays* (*Rayos catódicos*), *Will-o'-the-Wisps* (*Fuegos fátuos*), *Things of My Land* (*Cosas de mi tierra*).

(7) *Peru* / There were women novelists beginning with the first group of Romantics, and women also made their contribution to realism. The Peruvian CLORINDA MATTO DE TURNER (1854–1909) is remembered for her boldness in bringing to the novel the formulas of Indian liberation put forth by González Prada. *Birds Without Nests* (*Aves sin nido*, 1889) refers to two lovers, Manuel and Margarita, who turn out to be half-brother and -sister, begotten by two Indian women and the parish priest. The novel affirmed the principle that the Peruvian nation was formed by the multitudes of Indians disseminated on the Eastern side of the Andes range and it also denounced the tyranny of the governor, the clergy,

and the landowners. The book brought scandals. There were protests and persecutions. The author had put her finger on the wound—the clerics and oligarchs felt the pain. The novels that followed, *The Nature of Men* (*Índole*), *Heritage* (*Herencia*), do not broaden the place in literary history that *Birds Without Nests* gave the author; but that place is already broad since it belongs to one who originates a tendency; and, in fact, after Matto de Turner will come the revolutionary posing of Indian problems. Her *Cuzco Traditions* (*Tradiciones cuzqueñas,* 1884–86) lack the variety, imagination, and mischievousness of the "Peruvian traditions" of Palma, whom she called "my teacher."

(8) *Bolivia* / The first important group of narrators will be seen in the next chapter.

(9) *Chile* / After Alberto Blest Gana, the first important narrators that come forth in Chile, in the order of our preference, are Lillo and Orrego Luco, and perhaps we should also mention Gana. These are the ones who will open a breach for a legion to come. In the next chapter we shall examine the novelists and short story writers who continue to explore Chile's social reality: Prado, D'Halmar, Santiván, Edwards Bello, and others.

BALDOMERO LILLO (1867–1923) stands out, not only for his original talent, but also for the newness of his themes. He worked in a mining town of southern Chile, and from his first-hand observations of the misery and suffering there, his short stories emerged. From first-hand observation, to be sure, although it was from the literature of the French naturalists, especially from Zola's *Germinal,* he learned to relate and denounce at the same time. In the stories of *Sub Terra* (1904) the prose, in spite of an occasional stumbling over the grammar, and an occasional falling into artistic mannerisms, advances effectively with measured steps. With a vigorous realism it shows the hardships of the coal miners. He cries in protest, but his protest does not remain an outcry; it becomes literature. From the same recesses of his soul where the protest echoed, came his understanding for the underdog, the ragged, the Indian: it was this understanding, more than the protest, that made Lillo one of the most effective writers of his time. He seldom wrote stories with humorous intent; his mood is one of pathos. He showed his emotions without any pretense and he sought the sympathy of his readers, as in "Compartment Number 12," "Repayment," "The Screwloose Devil," "Juan Fariña." The stories in *Sub Sole* (1907) were more ambitious, but not thereby better. In this collection, he barely relates scenes at the mines; rather, he writes stories of local color set in the countryside or at the seaside. There is less sentimentalism and, in compensation, much better humor. Above all, he cultivates a type of parable, allegory, and legend related to the poetic prose of the Modernists. In his posthumous collections, *Popular Stories (Relatos populares), The Find and Other Stories of the Sea (El hallazgo y otros cuentos del mar)*, the variety of moods and themes is more visible.

The Chilean realists devoted themselves almost entirely to country themes; if they dealt with the city it was in relation to the country. Nevertheless, the first novelist of this inclination, LUIS ORREGO LUCO (1866–1949) excelled in city themes and, within the city, in social themes of the distinguished and privileged class. He was the novelist of Chile's rapid social and economic growth. With some French naturalism, and somewhat more Spanish naturalism, he observed the life of the upper bourgeoisie. He does not record healthy life, but rather moral sicknesses. He intended to paint a vast series of "scenes on the life of Chile." The first was *A New Idyll (Un idilio nuevo, 1900)*, which took place in the city of Santiago, in the contemporary epoch, in high society; its theme is the importance of love, and of righteousness in the face of the power of money. In *Big House (Casa grande, 1908)*—the most famous of his novels—he exposes matrimonial discord in a disintiguished house, in a world of business dealings, parties, luxury, neurosis and immoralities that end with the husband's murdering his wife. It is a novel of parlor customs and of gossiping, the first in which the way of thinking, acting, and feeling of the opulent class of Chile is analyzed. *In the Family (En familia, 1912), Wounded Tree Trunk (Tronco herido, 1929), Black Beach (Playa negra, 1947)* are several more incisions into the flesh of Chilean society. His novels make up a monochord cycle which is stylistically out of tune; but they are valuable as chronicles of Chilean life. At times his chronicle becomes history, as in *Memoirs of a Volunteer of the Old Fatherland (Memorias de un voluntario de la Patria Vieja, 1905)* and *Through the Storm (Al través de la tempestad, 1914)*.

FEDERICO GANA (1868–1926) did not limit himself to the description of customs, but enriched them with feeling, psychological sharpness, and even poetry. His stories *Days in the Field (Días de campo, 1916)*—the most celebrated is "The Señora"—is a collection of capably done sketches. This author, who goes out hunting, gallops over the countryside conversing with the country folk and making observations on them, was at bottom a timid, languid, saddened man. Gana revealed his melancholy, more than in his stories, in brief poems in prose which he called "daubs of color." Other Chileans: the depicter of customs DANIEL RIQUELME (1857–1912), MANUEL J. ORTIZ (1870–1945), successful with his *Letters From the Village (Cartas de la aldea, 1908)* and ALBERTO DEL SOLAR (1860–1921) who, although he left his country, published an Indianist novel, *Huincahual*, in 1888. In 1890 he published a realist one, *Rastaquouère*, on the disillusionments of South Americans in Paris.

(*10*) *Paraguay* / Barrett will be seen in the next chapter.

(*11*) *Uruguay* / Of the Uruguayan generation that yielded its best fruits between 1895 and 1910 (Rodó, Carlos and María Eugenia Vaz Ferreira, Herrera y Reissig, Florencio Sánchez, Horacio Quiroga) we will carry here two realist narrators: Viana and Reyles.

JAVIER DE VIANA (1868–1926) wrote a forgettable novel, *Gaucha*, 1899, whose burden of defects outweighs the virtues of its composition. He was a forceful writer. And so prolific that he conceived four stories in three hours, or so he tells us. The first collections indicate a greater effort at composition: *Countryside* (*Campo*, 1896), *Gurí and Other Stories* (*Gurí y otras novelas*, 1901). Later his narrations develop more rapidly: *Macachines* (1910), *Dry Kindling* (*Leña seca*, 1911), *Yuyos* (1912). At the end of his career, Viana was proceeding mechanically and produced several volumes in which he rarely added anything new. He admits that he had learned to tell a story from Zola, Maupassant, Turgenev and Sacher-Masoch. Nevertheless, his art was spontaneous, so typically conversational that to cite these masters was just coquettishness. His theme was life in the country, and he destroyed the Romantic image of the gaucho by presenting him as an animal. Men and women are products of the soil: this naturalist conception of life of his is so apparent that he brings to light every image, every adjective. He tends toward the anecdote—a passion, a crime, a deceit, a civil war scene or one of country life. But at times he wraps the anecdote in literature— generally landscape literature—and it is clear then that in his library, in addition to the Romantics and realists, there is no dearth of Modernists. That is, he had learned some techniques from them. But he was inclined toward the ordinary: regional language, the sensationalism of violence and sordidness, the complacency in forms of life that the author, as well as the readers, feel are below them. He cultivated the unexpected development, not always by reversing a situation, but sometimes through a psychological change in the characters.

CARLOS REYLES (1868–1938) is the best novelist that Uruguay offers in this generation. His technique is realism, and the reality he novelized with least vacillation was that of the Uruguayan countryside. He treated other themes: life of the city in Uruguay (*The Race of Cain* [*La raza de Caín*, 1900]) and in Spain (*The Bewitchment of Seville* [*El embrujo de Sevilla*, 1922]). But it was the landowner in Reyles who, definitively, took up the pen to write, if not the best pages from a stylistic point of view, at least the most enduring. This rich landowner had no sympathy for the poor people who worked his lands, but he knew what it was to work in the fields. His *Beba* (1894) at times sounds like a manual on agronomy and cattle breeding, but ably describes peasant types and customs. *Gaucho Florido* (1932) is a novel of the Uruguayan ranch with "uncouth gauchos." It has intense episodes, but the novel as a whole tends to extend itself and weaken its virtue. Reyles' novels are also psychological—morbid psychologies, a little in the manner of Huysmans' *The Race of Cain,* and perhaps even taken from Proust, as in the scene where Pepe spies on the erotic games of the two women in *To Love Battles . . . Fields of Feathers (A batallas de amor . . . campos de pluma).*

Although inferior to Viana and Reyles, but still within the literature of country themes, we could cite MANUEL BERNÁRDEZ (Spain–Uruguay, 1868), author of *Narrations (Narraciones)* wherein the descriptive is passable and the declamatory is to be rejected.

(12) *Argentina /* In Argentina a group of writers appeared who made the novel their profession. The theme, predominantly social, documents the upheavals in a country that saw at least the optimism of the great presidencies of Mitre, Sarmiento, and Avellaneda crumble away. Their procedure was realist and, in some cases, contained abstract theses and problems, in the manner of the naturalists. The group: MANUEL T. PODESTÁ (1853–1920), FRANCISCO A. SICARDI (1856–1927), JOSÉ SEFERINO ÁLVAREZ, *"Fray Mocho"* (1858–1903), CARLOS MARÍA OCANTOS (1860–1949), MARTÍN GARCÍA MEROU (1862–1905), SEGUNDO I. VILLAFAÑE (1859–1937). With the impossibility of studying them all (many are not listed) we will pick out a few. MARTINIANO LEGUIZAMÓN (1858–1935) lagged behind, with his historical subject matter and with the still Romantic tone of his regional novel, *Montaraz.* The action is placed in Entre Ríos, in 1820. We are shown political bossism, gaucho mobs, and a sentimental plot: the heroic conduct of the outlaw Silva who defends two loves, his woman and his land, until he dies in an epic struggle, a victim of the outrages of the invaders, amidst the horrors of conflagration and destruction. The idyl is weak; the description of peasant life, strong.

If Leguizamón walks at an old man's pace, Miró steps forth at a youthful gait. JOSÉ MIRÓ (1867–1896) wrote his only novel, *The Stock Exchange (La Bolsa,* 1891), under the pseudonym of "Julián Martel." He was a business reporter for *La Nación* and, although a young man of twenty-four, he knew the world of stock-jobbing and its shady operators. He had before his eyes a tense, excited society: false cosmopolitanism and the subversion of old Creole values as a consequence of the immigrant inundation, the desire for luxury and ostentation, the parasitism of the ambitious, the opportunism of the politicians, the contrast between quickly amassed fortunes and the chronic poverty of the poor, embezzlement, and vice. His descriptions strive to be realist and even naturalist, but the technique is primitive, immature, coarse in construction. Hand in hand with the direct observations of the atmosphere of the Buenos Aires stock exchange (in the novelty of this theme lies the greatest merit, perhaps the only merit, of the novel) there are second-hand observations, like those that inspire in him an anti-Semitism apparently of European origin, since in Argentina this type of "problem" did not exist at that time. The declamations of moral judgments and the political reflections damage the novel. The life of Dr. Glow is the novelistic axis, but the workings of business deals are clearer than human conflicts. He did not emboss either his characters or his prose.

The novelist who is winning more and more respect with the years is ROBERTO J. PAYRÓ (1867–1928). His patient, understanding, honest, tolerant, and hopeful conception of an Argentina in transition is scattered throughout his chronicles, stories, and dramas. After clearing away twenty or so volumes, we are left with *Laucha's Marriage* (*El casamiento de Laucha*, 1906), *Pago Chico* (1908), which could be fused with the posthumous "stories of Pago Chico," and the *Entertaining Adventures of the Grandson of Juan Moreira* (*Divertidas aventuras del nieto de Juan Moreira*, 1910)—three works built on a common theme: the rogue in Argentine life. They have a family air about them; as a matter of fact, they are neighbors who know each other. But the three novels presuppose three different focal points, dissimilar attitudes toward Argentina and, of course, they crystallize in different modes of style. Three books, three outlooks. That of the rogue, of the humorist, and of the sociologist. *Laucha's Marriage* is the history of an infamous, vile, and scoundrelly act. But Payró treats the roguery of Laucha's behavior with the roguery of the art of narrating, that is to say, that Payró, since he is as roguish in his art as Laucha is in his conduct, achieved a picaresque novel in which the vision of the author is not tinged with scruples. The world that oozes out of the novel is the world as a rogue intuits it; he assumes his role and rambles on, enjoying himself, confident that no other values exist which are more legitimate than his. The author does not even appear in the written word—the story takes on the appearance of a Laucha monolog. Payró masterfully solved this delicate problem: presenting Laucha chatting before a meeting of Creoles in such a way that the monolog might be psychologically truthful and artistically worthwhile. In this and in many other ways, he is an exemplary novelist. The stories in *Pago Chico* evoke once again, the same roguish reality as that of *Laucha's Marriage*, but with an important change in perspective: Laucha was relating an episode of his life, in his own words, and passing on his own judgments. In *Pago Chico,* on the other hand, the episodes are being related from the outside by a chronicler whom one supposes to be a jokester, an outsider writing from documents. In *Laucha's Marriage* there was no civic moral; only the voice of a blackguard without feelings of social solidarity was heard. But in *Pago Chico* a model citizen is describing social ills. However, when he began to recall the political banditry of Argentina, the understanding and reformist soul of Payró impregnated his pages with good humor. He gave us the humoristic vision of a world of rogues. In *Entertaining Adventures of the Grandson of Juan Moreira,* on the other hand, he created a rogue with an intent that was absolutely serious. It deals with the same social and human reality that we saw in the previous works. But now Payró constructs the outlines of this reality so that we may judge it. He has mounted the material of the novel on the axes of a theory of progress for the Argentine Republic. It is a novel with theoretical supports. A rogue is speaking—the novel is supposed to be the autobiography of Gómez Herrera—but this rogue moves along the paths of strength of Argentine politics. And following behind Gómez Herrera, Payró points out those paths of strength, because now, what interests him most is the form the country takes, rather than the anecdotes of his character, Gómez Herrera. Payró was less fortunate with his dramas, although because of the seriousness of the problems posed, they dignified the incipient Río de la Plata theater.

2. Essay

Of the thinkers of this epoch the most systematic was ALEJANDRO KORN (Argentina, 1860–1936). He criticized positivism but with historical understanding. Korn leaned preferentially toward Kant but supplemented him with Schopenhauer, Bergson, and others. In *Creative Liberty* (*La libertad creadora*, 1920) he formulated the philosophy which he developed later. His philosophy discarded metaphysics as a personal, irrational belief, and undertook an inquiry into the subjective world. He offered us a doctrine of values from which his ethics derive: an energetic exploration of conscience in its struggle for liberty. His prose was extraordinary, incisive, clear, ironic, elegant, and expressive.

In a group of essayists having the double vocation of thinkers and artists appear CARLOS ARTURO TORRES (Colombia, 1867–1911), author of *The Idols of the Forum* (*Los ídolos del foro*); CÉSAR ZUMETA (Venezuela, 1860–1955), who wasted his complex talent in newspaper work and, in spite of his being more capable than others, left fewer works; ALBERTO MASFERRER (El Salvador, 1868–1932) was a self-made intellectual who wrote prose poems and interesting sociological essays; MANUEL J. CALLE (Ecuador, 1866–1919), a liberal journalist, renowned in his own time for his sarcastic, skeptical, pessimistic but festive "chats." There were intellectuals of great influence in their countries who left no literary works, as in the case of the introducer of positivism in Paraguay: CECILIO BÁEZ (1862–1941).

The great journalists of Modernism were not always gilders of style, but in their pages, no matter how simple their language may have been, they gathered gold from the best literatures.

BALDOMERO SANÍN CANO (Colombia, 1861–1957) was one of these. His disquieted humanist soul unfolded like the pages of a great newspaper, where the themes and news of our time are recorded. It contains all of the sections, including the comics and international news, because he traveled in many countries, and brought back information and commentary on the remote Anglo-Saxon, Germanic, and Scandinavian literatures, not to mention his trips through libraries and through the broad mansions of his own spirit. He was friend and mentor to the first Modernists, from Silva to Valencia; and not only because he lived long, but because he understood new things that came across his path, he continued to be the friend and mentor of youth, and in his old age he discerned the face of surrealism, existentialism, and today's communism with a sharp eye. His skepticism consisted in being attentively alert to all points of view. For him, literary criticism was knowing how to listen to what each author was saying. His prose articulates his logical thought with the same controlled energy with which the artists of his generation articulated their own concept of beauty. Therefore, although it may appear otherwise, Sanín Cano's cold and elegant desire for preciseness is Modernist. He collected some essays in *Manual Civilization* (*La civilización manual*, 1925), *Inquiries and Images* (*Indagaciones e imágenes*, 1926), *Criticism and Art* (*Crítica y arte*, 1932), *Essays* (*Ensayos*, 1942). Not even his memoirs *From My Life and Other Lives* (*De mi vida y otras vidas*, 1949) form an organic whole. In *Humanism and the Progress of Man* (*El humanismo y el progreso del hombre*, 1955) he gathered essays from his last twenty-five years—the bulk of them written in his last ten years. His is a prose inhabited, not visited, by the epigram; that is, the epigram moves about spontaneously wherever it pleases and does not confine itself to the living room.

C. THE THEATER

The most preoccupied and occupied thinkers were poets. The poets were novelists. The novelists were playwrights. In reality, writers cultivate many genres simultaneously; for this reason, it is difficult to classify our history in terms of literary types, unless we dismember the authors and distribute the parts throughout different paragraphs, thereby sacrificing the living unity of each person to the clarity of the design. So in speaking of the theater, we should return to the authors we listed as novelists. In the Río de la Plata region, we have the interesting case of the theater growing out of the novel. The novels of EDUARDO GUTIÉRREZ (Argentina, 1853–1890) were not noteworthy, but they became noteworthy because of the role they played in the formation of the Río Plata theater. Gutiérrez was a truculent serial writer, of ordinary vintage, who scribbled pages with infallible popular success. In ten years he wrote some thirty novels of adventure, intrigue, violence, and murder. Some of them were gauchesque, along the line of *Martín Fierro,* and they fascinated the readers with their barroom brawls and their outlaws living on the wild frontier between barbarism and civilization. The most famous was *Juan*

Moreira (1879), the chronicle of a real bushwhacker who in 1870 or thereabouts, put his knife in the service of the local political bosses, but who was converted by Gutiérrez into a hero, the personification of courage and the protest against the abuses of law enforcers. In 1884 a Buenos Aires circus asked Gutiérrez to adapt his *Juan Moreira* to a pantomime with songs, guitars, dances, gauchos on horseback, and knife and gun duels. Two years later the actor Podestá, the same one who had organized the pontomime, decided to convert it into a spoken drama. With dialogs taken from Gutiérrez, and others of his own invention, Podestá was founding, in 1886 in the circus arena of Chivilcoy, a crude and uncouth theater, but an original one. In rapid succession new adaptations of other Gutiérrez novels followed; new works were written and *Juan Moreira's* offspring multiplied profusely. There had been theatrical antecedents, unrelated to one another, most of which never reached the stage, and which generally were of little significance. But the popular theater, conceived as a tight, stable world with continuity of plays, staging, actors, public, and critics, began in the Río de la Plata with the gauchesque drama. It is given the general designation of the Río de la Plata theater because Argentinian and Uruguayan writers became intermingled in a single movement, as shall be seen in another chapter.

XI. 1895-1910

Authors born between 1870 and 1885

Historical framework: Industrialization. Growth of international capitalism. Porfirio Díaz in Mexico. Liberal oligarchy in Argentina. Spain loses its last possessions in America.

Cultural tendencies: Height of Modernism.

The Characteristics of Modernism

In the preceding chapter it was seen how there appeared in all Hispanic-America clear indications of a change in Romantic tastes beginning in 1880. In literary history this change has been baptized with the name Modernism. We will attempt to give its general characteristics. The dominating trait was the pride that writers had in being part of a minority. The Modernists entertained an heroic concept of life; but since social and political circumstances of life in America had changed, they could no longer be heroes in action, instead they became heroes in art. The important thing was not to succumb to mediocrity. One had to turn away energetically from every middle path. Literary forms were cultivated as supreme values. Everything could be fitted into these forms, the new as well as the old, but the forms themselves had to be provocative, challenging, and surprising. Their program was a positive one: to build, word upon word, verbal skyscrapers. And in fact their polemics did not inveigh against the past (on the contrary, the past fascinated them) but against the present, against a bourgeois present filled with clichés, commonplaces, indolence, and petty satisfactions. The passion for form carried them to estheticism, and it is this aspect that generally critics have studied. However, with this same desire for new forms, the Modernists also created a naturalist, philosophic, political and Americanist literature. Any spiritual effort would enthuse them, so long as it had some distinction. To be distinguished meant using any kind of expression—even that given over to the common, the ugly, the abnormal, the coarse, the sickly, the plebeian—and therein manifest elite tastes, always displaying oneself as as artist. The acceptance by the Modernists of all new enticements, whether they were esthetic or not, confuses the panorama. For this reason, in order to mark the limits of Modernism, one must cut near to its esthetic center, and thus be certain of dealing only with Modernism. This is precisely what we propose to do. Nevertheless, we shall insist that part of what remains beyond those limits is also Modernist. A good deal of naturalist, Creole, indigenist literature is Modernist, and if not considered as such, it is because its themes have been grouped with non-Modernist realism. In other words, Modernism was a literary tone, not a theme.

The Modernists learned to write by observing in Romanticism what was elegant and not what was impassioned. But it was in the school of French Parnassianism where the Hispanic-Americans learned to yearn for perfection of form. When the Modernists were marching triumphantly through Hispanic-American letters with Rubén Darío at their head, they became aware of the triumph of symbolism in France during those very years, and on the march, they added to the rich visions of Parnassian manners, the rich musicality of symbolist manners. In verse as well as in prose they tried procedures that were quite new—above all, a prodigious rhythmic renovation. In addition to the rhythms of language they also tried those of sensibility and of thought. They cultivated interplays of synesthesia, Hellenistic evocations, eighteenth-century rococo, symbols of aristocracy such as the swan or the fleur-de-lis, collections of precious objets d'art, Japanese and Chinese curios, impressionistic chromatisms, nervous refinements, anti-bourgeois philosophies, moral crises, political rebellions, miniatures of poematic prose. Modernism ran through all of Hispanic-America, but to follow it step by step is difficult. Where and when was the first Modernist lamp lit? Along what national lines was all America lighted by Modernist esthetics? At times a very humble poet initiates a formal mutation, and though he is not worth serious study, one should note what he was able to do with it. It is well known that insignificant teachers tend to be obscured by their own students. In each country Modernism had its own peculiar rhythm, and a particular poet is not necessarily an indication of national tastes, either because he is a recluse or because he is a perpetual traveler. Perhaps Argentina and Mexico are the only countries where Modernism took hold in compact groups, in a sustained activity in every genre, from the very first hours (about 1880 and there-abouts) until its definite liquidation during the first years of World War I. The other countries participated in Modernism in an uneven and intermittent way.

Lacking a better plan, we shall proceed with this one: first we will study the Modernists who stood out more in verse than in prose, begin-ning with Rubén Darío, the most outstanding. Each time we illuminate one of the great figures, we will take the occasion, in passing, to glance at the other minor figures who hover around him. In this way we shall see the national groupings. Although we will limit ourselves to enu-merating poets without studying them individually, the reader must understand that this is not a simple catalog, but rather an atmosphere: these congeries of clouds belong, after all, to literary meteorology and do contribute to the landscape. Then we shall pass to the Modernists who distinguished themselves more in prose than in verse: however, before doing so, we shall have to complete the panorama of the verse by referring to the non-Modernist or barely Modernist poets. In like manner, when we finish reviewing the prose writers we shall dedicate the last pages of this chapter to the non-Modernists. The essay and the theater will bring it to an end.

A. MAINLY VERSE

1. Modernist Poets

Rubén Darío / And now RUBÉN DARÍO (Nicaragua, 1867–1916). In Spanish America, where European literary waves came successively to intermingle, young writers were reading the Parnassians, and later the decadents, without giving up Victor Hugo. Rubén Darío has admitted that his friendship with the Salvadorian Gavidia, beginning in 1882, brought him close to Hugo and to the Parnassians. This is the period of his study of French poetic inventions. He reads and imitates Gautier, Coppée and Mendès. Illumined by these lights, his compositions writ-ten while he was still in Central America acquire the brilliance of fore-runners. In mid-1886 Rubén Darío arrived in Chile and was dazzled by Valparaíso and Santiago, since they were the first important cities that he had seen which had an air of prosperity and certain European pretensions. The poets of the first and even of the second Romantic generation had not had a real, immediate experience of luxury, while Rubén Darío and his contemporaries were to have one. In Chile he continued to be informed of the contributions of French literature. But despite his preference for Parnassian poetry, he wrote *Thistles* (*Abro-*

jos), Rhymes (Rimas), and *Epic Song (Canto épico,* 1887) in the traditional manner. At the same time he wrote *Azure (Azul,* 1888) where he innovated more in the stories and poetic prose than in the verses. In prose he jumped to a high level; on the other hand, he walked slowly toward those exquisite verses he admired from a distance. And as he walked he looked from side to side, selecting friends. Feeling himself surrounded by a whole group on the move, he launched a second edition of *Azure* (1890), augmented with verse and prose. A comparison of the two editions will show Darío's advance toward nonconformity. His verses now are marked by the principles of artistic purity which earlier he dared express only in prose. He seemed to understand that his role was to precede others in the modernization of Spanish verse; and without renouncing his old ways, he no longer was distracted. All he needed now was to sound out the atmosphere in Spain, where he went in 1892. After a two-month glance at literary Spain he was convinced that reform was necessary.

Upon his arrival in Buenos Aires in 1893, Rubén Darío encountered a restlessness among the Parnassian and decadent literati. More talented than the young initiates in French Parnassianism, Darío became part of a circle of which he soon was proclaimed leader. It was then that he decided to explain himself through theoretical canons—his articles *The Strange Ones (Los raros),* the "preliminary words" of his *Profane Prose (Prosas profanas),* and "The Colors of the Banner" (*"Los colores del estandarte"*) are dated 1896. Ever since his days in Central America Rubén Darío had observed that new poets were making themselves heard. Now he suspected that these voices were raised above the chorus of Spanish poets; and he began to feel the pride of a young independent American generation: "the young writers have kindled today's revolution." But that revolution had no name. Little by little the term "modernism" began insinuating itself. Rimbaud had said: *"Il faut être absolument moderne."* The word "modern" is of Latin origin; even the word "modernism" had been used. But now the words "modern," "modernist" are in the air of America and Spain intermixing with "Parnassians," "symbolists," "decadents," "esthetes," "the new ones," "reformists," "ultra-reformists" . . . Darío decides in favor of the word "modernism" and converts it into the name of this young movement and of America's contribution to the artistic revolution in the Spanish language. One of Rubén Darío's highest merits was that of inciting each poet to grapple with his own formal problems and to resolve them artistically. He was not alone. But Rubén Darío surpassed them all, not only because of the greater strength of his genius, but also because he quickly propounded a program for himself. He sought inventions in the literature of his time; and he even sought them in old Spanish poetry. He was conscious of the craft of poetry; and he systematically proceeded to perfect all non-hackneyed techniques. This desire for verbal perfection is what gives permanence to his works. Therefore, in the final analysis, it is the will to forge a style that defines his Modernism, the smelting and alloy of all the "isms" of the epoch. On publishing his *Profane Prose* in 1896 he must have felt on his shoulders all the responsibility of the new movement. Martí, Gutiérrez Nájera, Casal, Silva, all had just died prematurely. Others, older than he, who were headed toward the same goal by a different road (Díaz Mirón, Leopoldo Díaz), changed direction in order to join him. But his contemporaries, the younger ones (Lugones, Nervo), grouped around him and formed the so-called second Modernist generation. Rubén Darío knew what was expected of him, and he began to alter the poetics of the Spanish language. *Profane Prose* sounded scandalous from its very title. With a perfect musical sense Darío tried every kind of verse type and rhythm. Regular versification predominated in his reforms (the torrent of ametrical verses is loosed in Hispanic-America after 1920); and he even was too timid to run risks with "the dangerous temptation of free verse." But his inventions and restorations—metric combinations, shifts in accentuation, interior rhymes, unexpected clashes and dislocations of sounds, free designs, asymetrical strophes, assonance, consonance and dissonance in rapid interplay, rhythmic prose, daring ruptures in the sonoro-semantic unity of the verse, etc.—exquisitely modulated the prosody of our language.

A considerable amount of all this technical ostentation was inspired by French tendencies toward free verse. Darío himself confessed to certain debts he owed for his versification. But on reading the sources pointed out by him or by his critics, one must admire his autonomy of procedure. *Profane Prose* is not just a collection of poems: it is a book of poetry with a soul, with gestures, with a countenance. The opening through which Darío escaped from America was Paris—an ideal Paris. Here he profited from a new world of objects: the France of Banville and of Verlaine, the France of the eighteenth century, the France of mythology and orientalisms, the France of the rococo. Even in his evocations of the Argentinian, Chilean, and Spanish landscape, there is a deformed mirror, made in France. In Rubén Darío an aristocratic feeling, disdainful of the reality of his time, is objectified in an exotic, cosmopolitan poetry, reminiscent of art and nostalgic for historic epochs. Some compositions are more perceptive of the exotic,

268

others of the cosmopolitan, others of the assets already accumulated in musical and plastic arts, others of the prestige of Greece, Rome, the Middle Ages, and eighteenth-century France, but in every composition all of these are heard. And this unity is expressed in different sentimental tonalities:

(1) The frivolous mood. The elegance, the playfulness, "the smiles and coyness," and the dances, are manifestations of a cult of pure art; but the estheticism that considers art as superior to life implies a serious, difficult, and almost religious will to honest expression. Frivolity is converted into an austere poetic ideal.

(2) The hedonist mood. Feasts, wines, strollings, kisses, flirtations, contemplation of beautiful forms and of graceful movements, all indicate that Darío, in a deliberate mental act, established pleasure as a goal of life.

(3) The erotic mood. Of all his pleasurable experiences, the erotic was the most powerful, organic, profound, and permanent.

(4) The reflexive mood. Although the poetry of *Profane Prose* skims along an estheticist culture, the poet tends to look within himself and to ask what life is. This reflexive mood will become more acute with the passing of time.

Years later, when a new generation emerged in Spain (they will call it the generation of '98), Rubén Darío knew that all its members, either coldly or fervently, admired his skill. Some move in cadence with him (Salvador Rueda); others do not join the procession but look upon it respectfully (Antonio Machado) or begrudgingly (Unamuno); there are the enthusiasts (Villaespesa, Valle-Inclán); and the younger ones who will carry the banner to a poetry of pure essence (Juan Ramón Jiménez). Certain of his importance in America and in Spain, Darío opens his eyes inwardly, deepens his poetry. There was a virtuoso in him who, in order to display himself, preferred to offer novelty instead of originality, and also an intuitive side capable of poetizing his direct visions. The virtuosity of *Profane Prose* was imitated because it could be imitated; it contained themes and procedures sufficiently intellectual to serve as a stimulus to a school of poetry. His trade had followers. However, after *Profane Prose*, Darío wrote poetry of an emotional strain that could no longer be developed as rhetorical exercises because they blossomed from a particular way of experiencing the world. The Rubén Darío of *Songs of Life and Hope* (*Cantos de vida y esperanza*, 1905) is the same as the one of *Profane Prose*—before all else, the same aristocratic demeanor. But in the *Songs of Life and Hope* we witness the esthetic crisis of *Profane Prose*. The lights of the precious lamps, lit in France, are lowered; the flames of an interior fire are raised. There is no break with the past, only a change in the scale of values. It is like a beginning of autumn. The aristocratic evasion of reality that we saw in *Profane Prose* is still evident. Another direction taken in the *Songs of Life and Hope* is the preoccupation over social problems. The attitudes of Darío prior to *Azure*—politics, the love of Spain, the awareness of Spanish America, apprehensions over the United States, moral norms—reappear, but with all the virtues of a haughty style. The third direction of the book, the most intact, is that which moves toward a knowledge of life: the poet leans reflexively on his own existence and asks what is art, what is pleasure, what is love, what is time, what is life, what is death, what is religion.

Art is an adventure into the absolute: it is almost a mystic way to knowledge. And the artist, a hero, a dolorous demigod in his solitude.

Pleasure is a pre-taste of death.

Love is painful because, seen in the light of a philosophy of life, it flees whilst we enjoy the flesh, and in its pursuit we grow old and die.

Time produces a duality in us and we contemplate the image of our own life as if, from the bark, we were waving good-by to it.

Life is a bitter mystery of failure and meaninglessness. He who questions life is lost: wanting to know what we are and why we live afflicts us in vain.

Death perhaps is the only answer to the secret of life: we live in the middle of the road of death.

Religion is the trembling before something terrible that overwhelms us with its power. It gives neither peace, nor consolation, nor security. It is only a light beyond this storm in which we agonize, and which we know not how to reach.

Songs of Life and Hope is Rubén Darío's best book. He will write better poems later, but, as a book, his other books will not surpass it: *Wandering Song* (*El canto errante*, 1907), *Poem of Autumn and Other Poems* (*Poema del otoño y otros poemas*, 1910), *Song to Argentina and Other Poems* (*Canto a la Argentina y otros poemas*, 1914). Many of the poems that remained dispersed in newspapers, in the tomes of others, or went unedited, deserved to have ascended to the Olympus of books arranged by Darío himself. Rubén Darío left poetry in a different state from which he found it: in this respect, he joins Garcilaso, Fray Luis de León, San Juan de la Cruz, Lope, Góngora, and Bécquer. His formal changes were immediately appreciated. Not only was he a master of rhythm, but also with incomparable elegance he poetized the pleasure of living and the terror of death. The transformations in

Castilian prose that Rubén Darío fostered were equivalent to those in verse, although less glittering. We have already spoken of the stories and prose poems in *Azure*. Rubén Darío surpassed them with other stories, and with other prose poems, gathered in various posthumous books. And it is, above all, in his non-narrative and unintentionally poetic prose where one finds his most vivid qualities as a prose writer: *The Strange Ones* (*Los raros*, 1896), *Peregrinations* (*Peregrinaciones*, 1901), *The Caravan Moves On* (*La caravana pasa*, 1902), *Sunny Lands* (*Tierras solares*, 1904). A fragmentary, casual prose, but nevertheless energetically victorious over the commonplace.

CENTRAL AMERICA / *Nicaragua:* Although Darío came from here, there was not in this country a select group that promoted Modernist tendencies. SANTIAGO ARGÜELLO (1872–1942) was the only poet worthy of mention: *Eye and Soul* (*Ojo y alma*, 1908). He was pedantic, with a penchant for the esoteric, although at times he poetized his native countryside and wrote civic songs. He wrote some theater and, in prose, left some pages useful for a history of Modernism. Keeping apart from the influence of Darío were JUAN DE DIOS VANEGAS (1873) and ANTONIO MEDRANO (1881–1928); and even more so, SALVADOR SACASA S. (1881–1937). In the first group of poets who saw the splendor of Rubén Darío—although they did not participate with him—we shall place JOSÉ ÁNGEL SALGADO (1884–1908), JOSÉ TEODORO OLIVARES (1880–1942) and SOLÓN ARGÜELLO (1880–1920).

El Salvador: In reality there were no Modernist groups of any value in the countries of Central America. We have already mentioned FRANCISCO GAVIDIA (1863–1955), who was Darío's teacher: with him the new accentuation of the Alexandrine and the adaptation of the Greek hexameter into Castilian are introduced. From his reading of French literature, from his translations, from his "The Idyll of the Woods (*"El idilio de la selva,"* 1882) and from his *Verses* (*Versos*, 1884) comes the urge for the reformation of metrics. However, the keynote in his poetry, as well as his verse dramas, was Romantic.

Guatemala: The Modernist poetry of MÁXIMO SOTO HALL (1871–1944) is less remembered than his novels.

Costa Rica: We can scarcely name genuine Modernists (LISÍMACO CHAVARRÍA, 1878–1913, was not one) except for ROBERTO BRENES MESÉN (1874–1947), the most militant personality of his country because of the restlessness he lent to the atmosphere. He began as a positivist and ended as a theosophist. And in a dozen books of verse, beginning with *In the Silence* (*En el silencio*, 1907), he charged his lyricism with ever greater intuitions of a philosophic nature. In addition to novels, literary and philosophic essays, and didactic treatises, he wrote poetic prose.

Honduras: JUAN RAMÓN MOLINA (1875–1908) was one of those born under the poetic sign of Rubén Darío. His themes and even his words were from the Modernist repertory. He was a tortured soul (his pessimism will drive him to suicide), and he infused his poetry with an unmistakable, personal mood. His lyricism was varied in its tones: rich, in "Fishing For Mermaids" (*"Pesca de sirenas"*), eloquent, in "The Eagle" (*"El águila"*), descriptive, in "Song to the Río Grande" (*"Canto al Río Grande"*), elegiac, in "To a Dead Woman" (*"A una muerta"*), anguished, in "Mother Melancholy" (*"Madre Melancolía"*). Although he stubbornly sought perfection of form, he was not a mere craftsman. He read a good deal in literature, philosophy, even sciences, and his vision of life was complex. He was an egotist, a bitter person wearied of life. When writing in prose he made an effort to achieve an elegant style, no matter how sordid the reality he was describing, as can be seen in the short story *"El chele."* Also Hondurian are Luis ANDRÉS ZÚÑIGA (1878), dramatist, fabulist, and a poet of pessimistic vein; JULIÁN LÓPEZ PINEDA (1882–1958), J. J. REINA (1876–1919) and AUGUSTO C. COELLO (1884–1941).

Panama: In this country (united to Colombia from 1823 to 1903, later an independent republic) the presence of Darío in 1892 encouraged a young group of writers: DARÍO HERRERA (1870–1914), whom we shall see below among the prosists, LEÓN A. SOTO (1874–1902), ADOLFO GARCÍA (1872–1900), SIMÓN RIVAS (1868–1915), GUILLERMO ANDREVE (1879–1940), and others.

Argentina: Lugones and Carriego / On leaving Central America, Rubén Darío, of course, left it a literary desert. On the other hand, on arriving in Buenos Aires, he found himself surrounded by a Modernist multitude. Argentina offers a different picture from that of its sister nations. Here there was a generation well-initiated into European modernities prior to Darío's arrival. We saw this in earlier chapters. And when other countries begin to become Modernist, it will be from Argentina —center of intense Modernism—that the first generation of writers who purify themselves in a new simplicity will emerge. We shall see this in the next chapter. In Buenos Aires Darío had his great school, and even those who did not belong to it were attentive to what was happening there. There were also cases of much older poets who had begun independently of Darío and who admired and emulated him. (Not only in Argentina: we already mentioned the case of the Mexican Díaz Mirón.) One of these cases, as will be remembered, was that of Leopoldo Díaz. Among the Argentine poets of this generation who clustered about Rubén Darío and formed a Modernist group were EUGENIO DÍAZ ROMERO (1877–1927), DIEGO FERNÁNDEZ ESPIRO (1870–1912), CARLOS ORTIZ (1870–1910), MARTÍN GOYCOECHEA MENÉNDEZ (1877–1906), PEDRO J. NAÓN and others who, for having stood out in other genres (Enrique Larreta, for example), will be treated further on.

But, of course, the poet whose contributions to poetry in America were no less valuable than those of Rubén Darío was LEOPOLDO LUGONES (1874–1938). Like Darío, he was an extraordinary verbal gymnast. He explored new territories; and his combative energy was such that even his own credos combated each other. At first, it was combat between his political credos and his esthetic credos; later, this combative energy brought him to other dilemmas, conflicts, and defections. The man who began as an anarchist, ended as a fascist. Yet in his versatility, which was considerable, one recognizes the depth of his character. He possessed, to express it in his own words, "the flexible unity of the current / which, as it runs, changes." Lugones gathered together and absorbed all influences. Later, the hand of Argentine poetry opens and the fingers point out the different directions to succeeding generations. Minor poets will specialize in several of these directions, at times advantageously; however, after Lugones no poet appears who, like him, is able to grasp all of poetry in his fist. He remains the most copious and renovating of poets, and it is difficult to evaluate him because each epoch selects the Lugones which suits it best. His *Gilded Mountains* (*Montañas del oro*) were too difficult for imitators, but *Garden Twilights* (*Los crepúsculos del jardín*), *Sentimental Lunar Poems* (*Lunario sentimental*), and the *Ballads of Río Seco* (*Romances de Río Seco*) were three apprentice shops for three successive generations.

Nevertheless, in Lugones there is something unaccomplished. His zest for life, his richness of perception, the freshness of his poetic intuition—all of an exceptional intensity—yielded to the sporting vanity of displaying himself with words, forms, and techniques. He wanted to be astonishing. He astonished by exaggerating his virtuosity. He who had lived and felt so much preferred to be seen in the pose of the athlete. *Gilded Mountains* (1897), *Garden Twilights* (1905), and *Sentimental Lunar Poems* (1909) were ostentatious gymnastics. With *Secular Odes* (*Odas seculares*, 1910) it seems that he will find himself as an Argentine poet; and in fact, all that follows (*The Faithful Book* [*El libro fiel*, 1912], *The Book of Landscapes* [*El libro de los paisajes*, 1917], *The Golden Hours* [*Las horas doradas*, 1922], *Ballads* [*Romances*, 1924], *Manorial Poems* [*Poemas solariegos*, 1927], and *Ballads of Río Seco* [*Romances de Río Seco*, 1938]) depicts the spiral of his talent, one of the greatest in America.

We shall see how that spiral opens, in ascending and descending curves. The Lugones of *Gilded Mountains* stood to the left of Modernism. Compared to these sensations, metaphors, and ideas, convoluted in a tempest of syntactical complications, even the Rubén Darío of *Profane Prose* must have seemed very simple at that time. The lyricism of this book was less than its rhetorical spasms. Lugones furiously whipped the anarchic horses of poetry, now tired from so much running, from Hugo up to the recent "strange ones." In a pandemonium of beautiful but shocking images, he called for a revolution of styles. And further he claimed for himself the role of thinker and prophet. What he knew best were the sky and highlands of his province, but a poet sings of what his spiritual eyes select, and not what his physical eyes have seen. Lugones wished to orchestrate what he knew least: the decadent literature of Parnassians, foreign and local. In *Garden Twilights* his stentorian voice becomes honeyed. Lugones here dominates the art of dissociating metaphors delicately. In two or three poems he was bold enough to transfer Parisian free verse into Spanish; but on the whole what dominates are meters of classical control. Masterful verses, but lacking intimate resonance. Frivolous charm, cold exquisiteness, aristocratic ways of painting a landscape and refining a form. But not even the erotic theme is convincing as something really lived. His gallantries remain as a decorative imprint. Also in this, he was inferior to Darío. He moved from huge mountains to miniature gardens like one who changes instruments in order to prove how talented he is, and that he can compete with Samain and company. His lyricism was intellectual; his loves were feigned. They are poems that conform to the conventions of the colorist and to the impressionistic programs of Modernism. This much they do, and do well—as, for example, in "The Old Bachelor" (*"El solterón"*). His search for artifices carried him to selenography, an entire book dedicated to the moon, "a kind of vengeance that I have dreamed of ever since childhood, whenever I have been assailed by life." Thus came about the *Sentimental Lunar Poems,* a tree-nursery where he had transplanted, from the Symbolist grove, runners of Moréas, Samain, Laforgue, above all Laforgue! and, once they had taken root, all the new poetry of the continent was forested with them. It is the most influential of Lugones' books. His metaphors were reproduced at times verbatim by poets in America and Spain. He strove for far-fetched originality, acrobatics in concepts and rhythms, humorism that caricaturishly animates inanimate things with rapid strokes and, as it will be called after the first World War, a dehumanized art. His "Hymn to the Moon" (*"Himno a la luna"*) is a natural for anthologies. Never in our literature had festivities of such prodigious imagination been seen. Each metaphor, an eye. The young writers of the postwar avant-garde who had rejected Lugones' cult of rhyme followed him in his cult of metaphor. With these caprices, diversions, exploits, unwonted poetizations of the prosaic, subtleties, absurdities, clownishness with scientific, plebeian and invented words, the virtuosity cycle of Lugones' poetry is closed—although the *Sentimental Lunar Poems* remains somewhat apart, as a unique book.

Those readers who are always asking for a poet's credentials—autobiographical lyric verses or patriotic epic poems—will insist that the best Lugones is the one who opens the cycle with *Secular Odes* and, if these readers are nationalists, they will say that the *Odes* are Lugones' best book. Since the May Revolution for Independence was being celebrated during the writing of the book, Lugones wished to render homage to Argentina. He pushed his inspiration, and a good deal of his poetry failed. Still, the *Secular Odes* are happy, optimistic, and alive. Lugones came out of his interior chambers, which had been carpeted by the French, and jovially looked out upon the fields and towns. He abandoned the pyrotechnics of the *Sentimental Lunar Poems* and reclined on classical traditions from Vergil to Andrés Bello. With arrows of light he transfixed even the most ordinary objects of Argentine reality; and he gave his polyphonic song the dynamism of inceptive narratives and outlines of action such as that of the deputy and the immigrant's daughter in "Cattle and Crops" (*"A los ganados y las mieses"*). The emotion of feeling oneself the member of a large family, the remembrance of heroic deeds, the love of each thing, the expectations, the sowing of creative energy, sharpen his capacity for observation. Between the *preludium* of the *Secular Odes* and the *postludium* of the *Ballads of Río Seco*, there are the interludes of five books. In *The Faithful Book* love and nature are the dominant themes: in this instance, it is real love. Lugones, although an erotic man, was not an erotic poet. He sings of matrimony more than of love, the hearth more than of the flame. He refers to the incidental: the family; the essence would have been the enamored couple. Lugones possessed a certain hardness. He lacked tenderness, passion. Nevertheless, "White Solitude" (*"La blanca soledad"*) and "The Song of Anguish" (*"El canto de la angustia"*) are of a personal harmonious lyricism. The nature theme was more obvious in *The Book of Landscapes*. His poetic orthodoxy of traditional rhythms and strophes and of the subjection of poetry to rhyme, makes him monotonous, but his sincere, varying, lyrical emanations gush forth freely. The "Pluvial Psalm" (*"Salmo pluvial"*) would be sufficient to make us respect his imaginative power, and it must be noted that it is not the only one.

The elegance of the Parnassians and symbolists still enchants him; but Lugones, without ceasing to be elegant, begins to look directly at the movement of the natural realms of his land. In *The Golden Hours* lyricism is interweaved with reflection, the lyrical fibers being the most vivid (see "The Infinite"). But even this original lyricism appears less potent than his descriptive and epic talent. His vignettes, among which Japanese and rococo examples are not lacking, correspond to Modernist modes of 1900, but the thoughts on happiness, sorrow, morals, anxiety, and anguish are personal. The compositions in *Ballads* are not all ballads, but generally the traditional voice of Spain and Hispanic-

America is heard more than that of France. That which is popular, racy, deep and common in man appears. Lugones feels that his song is the echo of the song of other men. This coming out of oneself and addressing the reality of all is accentuated in *Manorial Poems.* Here the spiral, which will culminate in the *Ballads of Río Seco,* begins to ascend. Lugones drops the sham, deepens his own nostalgia, returns to the emotions of his adolescence in Córdoba, restricts his field in order to govern better his old impulse of evasion. His austerity, so terrestrial that it is almost dry, renounces all that is not traditional, national, or familiar. In one of his best compositions, "The Song" ("*El canto*"), he defines himself: "For I am no more than an echo / of the native song I bear within me." In the *Ballads of Río Seco* his will to depersonalize himself so that neither voice nor gesture is distinguishable, to fuse into an anonymous people, to despoil himself of all literary festive dress, and to afford himself an outlet for his collective themes of patriotism, faith, love and courage, reaches the farthest extreme. A little more and he would have gone beyond the realm of poetry. Lugones had a foreboding of his artistic exhaustion, of his failure, and there is a note of resentment as he guards himself against possible attacks: "Perhaps someone may scorn / my stories for being Creole. / This is not for outsiders, / city-slickers nor simpletons." These *Ballads of Río Seco* emanate nevertheless from a great interior tension—a tension contrary to that of the *Sentimental Lunar Poems* (his other great book), but no less ambitious.

His prose was not of the quality of his poetry. He was a great technician of prose, not a great prosist. His skill in the use of a language enriched by dint of study and reflection was not accompanied by skill in the use of ideas. For this reason we shall leave to one side, without denying its merits, what is not pure literature: biographical, historical, ethnographical, philosophic, didactic, political, and philological essays. What he did have was sensibility and imagination, effective above all in visual metaphors. That is to say, that on reading his prose one has a desire to return to his verses. Even in *The Gaucho War* (*La guerra gaucha,* 1905) we find the pyrotechnics of the poet. This work consists of twenty-two historical stories of the fight for independence, and introduces into Argentine literature the mountainous north. They deal with anonymous masses and not with leaders: Güemes is alluded to only at the end. It may be that his model was *La legende de l'aigle* by Georges d'Esparbès. Lugones, working with a language having some of the Baroque energy of Quevedo's, but in a literary workshop of preciosity and naturalism established by Modernism, created a brutal, overwrought, dense style that years later Valle-Inclán would call *"esper-péntico."* The descriptive portion mounts on the back of the narrative forcing it to move at a slow pace. Indeed, the descriptions, with great richness of impressionistic effects, have their own movement of sensations. When the episodic action seems to tarry, what begins to move along is the sensitiveness and the imagination of the poet who has climbed above the narrator. Let no one be mistaken: he was a talented narrator as proved by *Strange Forces* (*Las fuerzas extrañas,* 1906) and *Fatal Stories* (*Cuentos fatales,* 1924). The first is a book of brief stories, some of which are admirable—"Rain of Fire," "The Horses of Abdera," and "Izur." His fantastic stories are inspired by a vague oriental mysticism, by classical myths and by science fiction. In *Fatal Stories* there is also magic, superstition, truculence, metamorphosis. *The Angel of Shadows* (*El Ángel de la Sombra,* 1926), is a novel of an impossible passion, with characters who are moved not by life but by the springs of an anti-novelistic fatality. Up to his tragic end (he committed suicide) he sought new forms of expression.

With *Garden Twilights* in 1905 Lugones had marked the Modernist apogee in Argentina. Later, as will be seen in the next chapter, the poets of the generation of Fernández Moreno will be less defiant. But now that Lugones has led us to Argentina, let us surround his name with others that were born between 1870 and 1885. Many were still Romantic, preoccupied with social philosophies or given over to the sentimental: RICARDO ROJAS (1882–1957), ERNESTO MARIO BARREDA (1883–1958), MARIO BRAVO (1882–1944), and above all Carriego. One of the Argentine poets who went farthest in the anti-preciosity reaction was EVARISTO CARRIEGO (1883–1912), who drew his inspiration from the tender, sentimental, and trivial memories of his native suburb. After his *Heretic Mass* (*Misas herejes,* 1908) Carriego's muse abandoned pedantries, obscurities, neologisms, decadentisms and cultivated a poetry with a touch of tango lyrics, but with depth. *The Soul of the Suburbs* (*El alma del suburbio,* 1913) was the title of the posthumous book in which his compositions of this period were gathered. The family scenes, of simple, sincere, and penetrating emotion, are those that are most remembered: "The Little Seamstress Who Took That Bad Step," "The Chair That Now Nobody Occupies," "You Have Returned." He was a Creole from those outlying districts where the city loses itself in sparsely populated areas. For having written of life in the city outskirts, of workers, hoodlums, and enamored girls, for having written with much sentiment and even with tears, Carriego pleased his readers and has remained in the memory of the people. He also remained in the memory of younger poets, such as Raúl González Tuñón and Nicolás Olivari. One who placed himself completely beyond Modernism was MIGUEL A. CAMINO (1877–1949). With his *Chacayaleras* (1921) he initiated a regional poetry (his region was Neuquén, in the southern mountain range) where one hears rustic voices and sees scenes of the life of the people. The theme of his poetry has been well defined by the title he gave to the compendium of his works: *The Landscape, Man and His Song* (*El paisaje, el hombre y su canción,* 1938).

Bolivia / RICARDO JAIMES FREYRE (Bolivia, 1868–1933) was a friend of Rubén Darío and of Leopoldo Lugones and joined them in the condemnation of routine poetry and in the claim-staking of new poetic lodes. His first book, *Primeval Fountain* (*Castalia bárbara*, 1897) was an experimental laboratory for rhythm. Rhythm for rhythm's sake. He combined verses with such liberty that his name became associated with the introduction of "free verse" in the Castilian language. In reality, he introduced only one attempt at free verse, which was timid in comparison with the polymorphism that was to come later. But we must listen with the ears of the end-of-the-century poets. It was like a strange dance to which words had been invited purely for the beauty of their sonorous bodies: they held each other by the waist and whirled and tapped and interrupted each pose in order to begin over, again and again. No ideal music was heard: at least the spirit of the reader was not penetrated by vague and insinuating sensations. Of course, he watched the rhythmic feast, because the rhythms were forms of dancing words. In the midst of such an exaggeration of rhythms, the reader became distracted and lost the meaning of what he was reading. It was the coldness of Parnassian poets who erected their structures with unfeeling perfection. Since the initial themes of *Primeval Fountain* came from Scandinavian mythology, from Nordic and wintry landscapes (Richard Wagner's lyrical dramas had begun the vogue), the rhythmic beats struck everyone as something strangely savage. And, in fact, "The Song of Evil," "Strange Voice," "*Aeternum vale*," "Errant Venus," "The Nights" were astonishing. The adjective "barbaric" was appropriate to this poetry: it had the same geographic and religious exoticism as Leconte de Lisle's *Poèmes barbares*, and graftings of versification as in Giosuè Carducci's *Odi barbare*. In general this first book of Jaimes Freyre had a minimum of immediate impressions perceived directly from life. Although the poet tells us that he is "nostalgic, sad and dreamy unto death," this way of being does not reach us through the fibers of the verse, but comes down like the white light of an idea burning in some cerebral lamp. In his second book of poems, *Dreams Are Life* (*Los sueños son vida*, 1917), metric liberty is even greater, but the dance has now quieted and we can capture the meaning of the feast. Here is an album of Parnassian poetry in the collective style of Modernism. In "Times Gone By" ("*Tiempos idos . . .*") Jaimes Freyre gives us the key to his artistic transposition: "I have seen you on the enchanting canvases / where mundane feasts are immortalized / perhaps in the *Embarcation for Citeres . . .*" It is the same canvas of Watteau that had inspired in Darío some of the images of "It was a soft breeze" (*"Era un aire suave"*). "Subliminar," which is more intimate ("it is now time for interior orchestras to play"), is one of the best compositions of the book. Other themes concerning the universal suffering of the masses now emerge vigorously ("The Outcry" [*"El clamor"*], for example), and prophecy is not lacking in "Russia" (1906): "The blaze that will consume the remains of the past / will come from the heart of the country of snow . . ." His short stories—printed in magazines—are typically modernist ones (soaring to Byzantium, to China) although two of them do take place in the Andes and have Indian characters.

Bolivia gave Jaimes Freyre and that was all. Modernism will only enter this country at the beginning of the twentieth century, when two outstanding figures will be seen: Reynolds and Tamayo. This completes the triangle of the great Bolivian poets of Modernism. GREGORIO REYNOLDS (1882–1947) was a sentimentalist, attired in the vestments of Modernism. He expressed deep lyricism in *Psyche's Coffer* (*El cofre de Psiquis*), *Turbid Hours* (*Horas turbias*), *Prisms* (*Prismas*), without counting his epic essay *Redemption* (*Rendención*) and his scenic poem *Chimeras* (*Quimeras*). FRANZ TAMAYO (1880–1956), who in his *Odes* (*Odas*, 1898) was more Victor-Hugoesque than Rubén-Darían, later became a Modernist and cultivated rare and very fascinating interplays of sounds. Devoutly he studied Greco-Latin classicism and, hence, the inspiration for his lyrical tragedies *Prometheid or Oceanides* (*La Prometheida o Las Oceánides*, 1917), *Scopas* (1939) and others. He is also the author of some *Greek Epigrams* (*Epigramas griegos*, 1945). Sometimes he supersaturates his pages with bookish and pedantic elements. Other Modernists: JUAN FRANCISCO BEDREGAL (1883–1944), a Romantic with Modernist manners; MANUEL MARÍA PINTO (1871–1942), who lived in Argentina and scarcely had any influence on his native country; EDUARDO DÍEZ DE MEDINA (1881).

Uruguay: Herrera y Reissig / In Uruguay (another of Argentina's neighbors) Modernism manifested itself first in prose rather than verse, but there were notable poets. If we leave to one side the more *outré* writers, such as ROBERTO DE LAS CARRERAS (1875), the nucleus of Uruguayan poetry of this period is Vasseur, Frugoni, María Eugenia Vaz Ferreira and Herrera y Reissig. ÁLVARO ARMANDO VASSEUR (1878) and EMILIO FRUGONI (1880) struck the combative, optimistic, and confident note of an approaching social justice. MARÍA EUGENIA VAZ FERREIRA (1875–1924)—*The Island of Canticles* (*La isla de los cánticos*)—was a solitary voice, solemnly religious, although capable of creating sharp images on a high level.

The ten years of poetic production of JULIO HERRERA Y REISSIG (1875–1910) is like a round mirror in which the figure of Modernism is reflected from head to foot. He was not a great poet, but he wrote with an imagination so excited by symbolist literature that his language has a rare anthological quality. Here we will find cemeteries, drugs, satanisms, loathings, exoticisms, synesthesias, violet shades, idealizations of the countryside, a good deal of eroticism, and some magic. It is difficult to point out a precise source; yet, on reading, one has the indefinable impression of witnessing an epoch. He did not reach the mass of readers; but those who read· him in Spain and throughout Hispanic-America were poets, and in this way he influenced the course of lyricism. For many years he was a landmark in Uruguayan poetry. Even today, when poetry moves along other paths and Herrera y Reissig is no longer a master, his poems are read with pleasure and admiration. The echoes most easily recognized are those from the European continent—Baudelaire, Verlaine, Mallarmé, Laforgue, Samain, and those from the American continent—Poe and Rubén Darío. He breathed poetry, he fed on poetry, he walked in poetry. In this way, his verses gave voice to a poetic style that was the air, substance, and spirit of his life. Like the symbolists, he was disinterested in practical reality and turned his nocturnal eyes toward the most irrational zones of his being. There he sought what, through his readings, he knew other poets had found. His point of departure was from a collective style; but his point of arrival was his own body, wherein he discovered a prodigious fountain of metaphors. There is not, in our poetry, another such example of a metaphoric machine gun. From *The Pentecosts of Time* (*Las pascuas del tiempo,* 1900) he stepped firmly into the home of Modernism; in a short time he traversed its large hall and in an obscure corner, complicated by a series of mirrors, attracted attention because of his eccentric figure. Even more than Darío, he was daring in his excessive and even grotesque images, with hermetic mythologies and quasi-expressionistic allegories. For this reason, ten years after his death, when young writers read *The Evening Matins* (*Los maitines de la noche,* 1902), *The Ecstasies of the Mountain* (*Los éxtasis de la montaña,* 1904–07) and the "Moon Gathering" (*"Tertulia lunática"*) in *The Tower of the Sphinxes* (*La Torre de las Esfinges,* 1909), they were dazzled by the compact treasure of images and considered him a precursor of the cult of metaphor to which they were giving themselves. Herrera y Reissig was a discontented person, disenchanted by the world in which he was born, who created for himself an imaginary world where he could better live: a mythical, hallucinated world of pure images, but which appears real because of its disorder and contradictions. The conflict between health and morbidity, innocence and sin, happiness and suffering gives his style the oscillating movement between plebeian and luxuriant words, between forms of culture and revery. His mood is also changing: ironic, misanthropic, sharp, trivial, playful, enraptured. He sought an inner equilibrium by trying to reconcile in a very personal expression what he saw with his poet's eyes, even the ugly, the base, the monotonous.

Peru: Chocano and Eguren / In spite of González Prada's early inno-vations, verses polished in cosmopolitan shops with Parnassian facets, symbolist lights, and polyrhythmic techniques, Peru accepted Mod-ernism quite late. But the two names that it offers are important: Chocano and Eguren.

Because his was the eloquence of words recited in the public squares, the wind has carried away almost all the work of José Santos Chocano (Peru, 1875–1934). He was closer to Díaz Mirón than to Rubén Darío; and if he is grouped with Darío and other Modernists it is because he was a visualist who had learned to paint in the language of the Par-nassians. What he saw, however, was different from the reality of the Modernists. Chocano dedicated himself to poetizing an external view of America: nature, legends and historical episodes, stories about In-dians, themes dealing with political activity. He was a minor poet, be-cause the cloth of poetry is not cut to the size of things seen but to that of the soul that sees. He took the lead in the Modernist movement of Peru, and he was equipped, for this purpose, with the egotism and torrential verbal power of the politician. Further, his control of new verse techniques served for easy and popular themes. A poet of the elite, but operating in the street. It was natural that he should be applauded. His most famous books, *Soul of America, Indo-Spanish Poems (Alma América, poemas indo-españoles,* 1906) and *Fiat Lux!* (1908) were an expression of the objective, visible, nationalist aspects of the poetry of those years.

Chocano continued to poetize when suddenly there appeared an anti-Chocano poet (anti-epic, anti-declamatory, anti-realist, anti-obvi-ous) who inaugurated a new poetic style—José María Eguren (Peru, 1874–1942). He was a "strange one" in the exquisite sense which the word had assumed ever since Darío's *The Strange Ones;* but his strange-ness was that which came later and was no longer that of Modernism. His first book of poems was called *Symbolics (Simbólicas,* 1911); but the title was foreign to the symbolism that the symbolists had exposed. In *The Song of the Figures (La canción de las figuras,* 1916) and in *Shadows and Rounds (Sombras y rondinelas),* both edited in 1929, to-gether with a collection of the early works bearing the title *Poetry (Poesías),* Eguren became even more introspective, as if he had closed his eyes and inwardly were looking at hallucinating phosphorescences. His poetry had the incoherence of dreams and nightmares. Figures appear and vanish like phantoms in clouds of opium. The incredible colors, skyblue blood, bluish gold, purple nights, green beards, glow for an instant and then feather out, fuse, and end up by dissolving into shadows. There is no action, at least action with meaning. Something moves in that unreal and misshapen atmosphere, but we do not understand it. It is as if men, walking in their sleep, had walked through certain magic mirrors and now slink as beautiful dehumanized silhouettes. Animals, plants, stars, things, landscapes also yield to marvelous metamorphoses. The poet mixes his sensations in disordered impressions, and seems to respect only two kinds of order: a very select artistic vocabulary and fixed musical schemes.

LEONIDAS N. YEROVI (1881–1917) versified rather than poetized Peruvian customs without the fine esthetic conscience of the Modernists, to whom he alluded ironically.

Colombia: Valencia / A few years after Silva's suicide there appeared in Colombia GUILLERMO VALENCIA (1873–1943) with his only book: *Rites* (*Ritos*, 1898). Only a few years intervened, yet it seems that poetry had advanced a good piece. In order to measure the distance one need only read Silva and, right after, the paired Alexandrines that Valencia shaped in "On Reading Silva" (*"Leyendo a Silva"*). Silva could only sense an esthetics of exquisite rarities; Valencia was as familiar with that same esthetics as he was with the palm of his hand. What had advanced, of course, was the awareness on the part of the Modernist poets of what they intended to do. When Valencia made the acquaintance of Darío in Paris he had already published *Rites;* but in *Rites* there is an indication of his having known Darío as a poet. Without any vacillation, without painful calculations, armed from head to foot on his first expedition, Valencia placed himself in the vanguard of those who were transforming poetry. He was not going to be a vociferous leader—he was an economical poet, scanty, compressed like a metal, who gave his great blow and then retired forever. Afterwards he turned to translation (his *Cathay* [*Catay*, 1938] are ancient Chinese poems). With Romantic heart, Parnassian eyes, and symbolist ears, Valencia offered a poetic world that was different from that of his colleagues. If we had to give him one label it would have to be the Parnassian, even though his social preoccupations, and his cerebration are not what we expect from a school given to pure formal perfection. Among his best poems are: "Job," "St. Anthony and the Centaur" (*"San Antonio y el centauro"*), "Palemón the Stylite" (*"Palemón el estilita"*), "The Two Heads" (*"Las dos cabezas"*). He had the gift of lyrical definition; that is, with a minimum of language he succeeded in reducing the image that had formed in his imagination to its very limits. The words are like grains of sand, which in one of his best poems, "The

Camels" (*"Los camellos"*), adhere to and clothe the form of an ideal camel. He selected his words with such economy that at times his definition, though intelligent, is not intelligible. Part of his obscureness was a result, then, of his conciseness; other areas of his poetry were obscure because the poet and his symbols slipped into a mysterious thicket. His Catholicism is not sufficient to decipher the mystery. In "White Storks" (*"Cigüeñas blancas"*) the daring of his metaphors, drawn as if sketched in India ink, is striking. Here he insinuates his esthetics which seems to consist of creating difficult problems to solve or, even more, of standing before them in absolute silence.

In spite of the Parnassian perfection of his descriptions, Valencia did not disregard his emotions. In this, he was closer to Leconte de Lisle than to Heredia. He enriches each verse with impressions always wishing to feel more, as he says in his translation of D'Annunzio's sonnet: "Ah, were I to be given other new senses!" ("Doleful Animal"— *"Animal triste"*). Even his spirit of protest against social inequities cut a path to his poetry, and in "Anarkos" he opposed bourgeois hypocrisy with the same force with which his spirit of poetic reform opposed the academies. What is curious is that Valencia was called "conservative" in Colombian politics. In a sense he was a conservative: while other Modernists were evolving toward vital expressions and even were indulging in youthful pirouettes during the years of the first World War, Valencia preferred to cultivate Modernist orthodoxy. His skill in the aristocratic and sober selection of forms was part of a ceremonial ritual. Today he seems too elegant and cold for the young writers, and he is read much less. Nevertheless, of all those who wrote prior to 1900, Valencia and Silva are the most respected of Colombian poets.

Other poets from this same batch should be placed farther down the scale. Víctor Manuel Londoño (1876–1936) was a Parnassian in the manner of Heredia. Ismael López, known by his pseudonym Cornelio Hispano (1880), is also a Parnassian but not phlegmatic, as his *Caucan Elegies* (*Elegías caucanas*) prove. And still another: Max Grillo (1868). (Isaías Gamboa, 1872–1904, was appreciated especially in Chile, where he spent a few years, for his melancholic poetry and a novel dealing with Chile.)

Mexico: Nervo, Urbina, Tablada, González Martínez / During these years Mexico became a principal center of Modernist production. Poets appeared in the *Revista Azul* (1894–96), founded by Gutiérrez Nájera and Carlos Díaz Dufoo (1861–1941), in the *Revista Moderna,* directed in 1898 by Amado Nervo and Jesús E. Valenzuela (1856–1911) and in the *Ateneo de la Juventud* (1909). We shall list some of them. Efrén Rebolledo (1877–1929) ran the gamut of all Modernist themes (eroticisms, Parnassianisms, Japanese-isms) working his verses with a careful chisel. Rubén M. Campos (1876–1945), Hellenist in the manner of Leconte and Heredia, later was sidetracked to prose. FRANCISCO MANUEL DE OLAGUÍBEL (1874–1924), a Romantic in feeling, a Modernist in form. MARÍA ENRIQUETA CAMARILLO DE PEREYRA (1875), sentimental, simple, whom we shall refer to below, among the narrators. The roster can be completed with RAFAEL LÓPEZ (1873–1943), ROBERTO ARGÜELLES BRINGAS (1875–1915), LUIS CASTILLO LEDÓN (1879–1944), EDUARDO COLÍN (1880–1945), MANUEL DE LA PARRA (1878–1930), RICARDO GÓMEZ ROBELO (1883–1924), ALFONSO CRAVIOTO (1884–1955). Now that we have glanced at the Modernist panorama, it is time to pull out the salient poets.

First of all, AMADO NERVO (1870–1919). Once upon a time the extensive work of Amado Nervo (more than thirty volumes of poetry, novels, short stories, criticism, chronicles, poems in prose, essays and even a theatrical piece) held the admiration of the entire Hispanic world. Today the portion still admired has shrunk to a fine bouquet of poems and half a dozen short stories. His poetry has ranged from opulence to simplicity, from sensuality to religion, from playfulness to sobriety. His poetry was born in an age of precious stones, tinsels, exoticisms, morbid sensation, exquisiteness, satanical affectations, voluptuousness, mysteries, and technical fineries. His first books of poetry, *Black Pearls* (*Perlas negras*, 1898), *Poems* (*Poemas*, 1901), *Interior Gardens* (*Jardines interiores*, 1905), belong to Modernism. Later, in *Whispering* (*En voz baja*, 1909), Nervo begins to denude his soul; and in *Serenity* (*Serenidad*, 1914) and *Elevation* (*Elevación*, 1917)—"from today on, let silence be my best poetry"—he denuded himself to such an extent that he seems diminished. "I seek a discreet tone, a medial shade, the coloring that does not explode," he confesses. Note the voluntary "I seek." The fact is that in his simplicity there is much gleaning and even a certain amount of rhetoric; after all, once the first period of verbal luxury and artificial themes had passed, Modernism responded to a new slogan: to appear candid and sincere. One system of esthetics was sacrificed with the hope of gaining the good graces of another. It has been said that it was a moral crisis rather than an esthetic change. After ten years of loving a woman (Ana, the "Constant Lover," who died in 1912) Nervo had tormented his eroticism to the point of converting it into spiritism: he had to believe "that my Anita still lives in some form and that she loves me and waits for me." He turned, then, toward the immortality of the soul and toward God. Certainly Nervo continued loving women until his own death. A man's life does not necessarily explain a poet's art. What matters, therefore, is the esthetic transition, not his more or less disconsolate seven years as a widower; and in these very years he wrote some of his best poems. Of posthumous publication were *The Constant Lover* (*La amada immóvil*) and *The*

Divine Archer (El arquero divino). The best in Nervo is the lyricist who expresses himself with artistic awareness choosing from his personal experience the most beautiful moments. When he gives up to the reader sentimental material not esthetically configured, his mood, which becomes more confiding than lyrical, languishes. And it languishes most when he changes theme and style and abuses the abstract, conceptual language that he believed to be philosophic. From his later years is the verse "I know nothing of literature" (*Serenity*) and his program of writing "without literature" (*Elevation*). He then gave himself charitably to console, preach, and even catechize with his notions of elevation and renunciation. The public was grateful for his good sentiments; the more demanding readers lamented the lyrical impurity of his moral purity.

In prose he traveled the same road toward simplification from "the extensive periods, the pompous turns, the fertile lexicon" (as he described his own procedures) to a more nervous and aphoristic style. Nevertheless, he did not excel as a writer of prose. He works to good advantage when his conversational narrative (because he was a conversational artist) dictates the movement of his pen, not when he wants to imitate the artistic prose he admired (*Plenitude* [*Plenitud*, 1918]). He wrote science fiction in the fashion of H. G. Wells, whom he read, or stories with metaphysical ideas, such as Nietzsche's "eternal return" or the Pythagorean transmigration of souls, or about strange extrasensory experiences, which he worked out himself or from reading oriental religions, spiritualist and irrational philosophies.

Luis G. Urbina (1868–1934) navigates his own skiff. A Modernist? Yes, in his serenity, elegance, and musical suggestiveness. But the sadness of his chant and the intimate tone are still Romantic. Urbina seems to have closed Mexican Romanticism; at least he purifies it and retains only the tenderness and the sincere confession of his torment. The inner unity of his work is admirable. It is as if he had succeeded with his first book and the others that followed were confirmations of the first, from *Verses* (*Versos*, 1890) to *The Last Birds* (*Los últimos pájaros*, 1924). As a technician of verse he was also admirable, though he hides the technique and it seems that his music develops directly from his melancholy without the help of words.

José Juan Tablada (1871–1945), born in Modernism, but disquieted by the promises that he caught sight of on the poetic horizon, tried new ways, renewed himself constantly and even fled toward Japanese-isms (he cultivated the *haikai*) and ultraisms. He was, then, a shifter, an adventurer, one who does not allow himself to be surprised by new fashions: he sees them coming from a distance and goes to meet them. Which is his best book? *Li Po and Other Poems* (*Li Po y otros poemas*), *The Pitcher of Flowers* (*El jarro de flores*), *The Market* (*La feria*). It depends on which of the many Tabladas we consider the best. Though not a great poet, his presence was very profitable for the young writers who wanted to risk other roads. Tablada tied the loose ends of poetry, from Gérard de Nerval, Aloysius Bertrand, Baudelaire and Gautier to Apollinaire and Max Jacob, and attaching himself to this long thread of many knots, traversed the labyrinth of twentieth-century literature. His verses were technically irreproachable. Tablada's images had the virtue of surprising the reader because he esteemed the value of surprise in literary language. He was always alert for new modes and, consequently, aware of the wearing away of old fashions which once had captivated him. In this way he rid himself of themes of sadness, of Parnassian insensitiveness, of estheticizing Bohemianism, when he saw them on the way to becoming outmoded. He was a cosmopolitan writer, or at least one who resisted all provincialism. He was an original spirit, or at least one who resisted established tastes.

Because of his age ENRIQUE GONZÁLEZ MARTÍNEZ (1871–1952) belonged to the group of Mexican poets formed by Nervo, Urbina and Tablada; or, outside of Mexico, to that of Lugones, Valencia, and Jaimes Freyre. In this sense, he deserves to be studied here. Yet, it is after 1910 that González Martínez achieves his best writing and becomes one of the great gods of literary circles. Just as Lugones, he was admired and followed even by the youths who, shortly after 1920, were stoning the Modernist lamps. His first two books (*Preludes* [*Preludios*, 1903] and *Lyricisms* [*Lirismos*, 1909]) were noble, serious, sincere. Although the author, withdrawn to his provincial corner, distrusted the Modernist sect that reigned in Mexico (in effect, he held up no one's banner, not even Rubén Darío's) his verses, as all others written in his generation, responded to the very Modernist desire to punish forms until they submitted to the artistic models that the French Parnassians recommended. But it was in two subsequent books (*Silenter,* 1909 and *The Hidden Paths* [*Los senderos ocultos,* 1911]) where González Martínez astonished everyone, and never stopped astonishing them, because of the limpid serenity of his self-interrogations. "Seek in all things a soul and a hidden / meaning; do not embrace vain appearances." His was lyrical, personal poetry; but the poet does not write of the external happenings of his daily life, but of a distilled autobiography, made of pure spirit, with the essence of his emotions and thoughts. With so much contemplation and so much introspection on what he had contemplated, one ends by envying not the music but the silence; however, poetry, which is a delicate body of sounds, cannot be silent; so González Martínez turns toward that portion of his poetry which is almost attached to silence: verbal exquisiteness. Not an estheticizing, extroverted, ornamental exquisiteness, but that of interiorization: "may all things affect thee like a mysterious / imprint intensely engraved . . . for I know not if I be diffused in all / or all penetrates me and abides in me." One of the poems in *The Hidden Paths,* the famous sonnet "Twist the neck of the swan" (*"Tuércele el cuello al cisne"*), indicates how, in González Martínez' scale of values, the direction of exquisiteness is reversed—it no longer leads to the swan of deceitful plumage "who sounds his white note at the blue of the fountain; / he only promenades his charm, but does not feel / the soul of things nor the voice of the landscape," but toward the wise owl: "he has not the charm of the swan, but his restless eye / which pierces the shadows interprets / the mysterious book of the nocturnal silence." Some critics observed in this sonnet certain intentions to express an esthetic manifesto; others, seduced by the image in the first verse ("Twist the neck of the swan of deceitful plumage") believed that that neck was in truth Rubén Darío's. Rubén Darío had certainly not only twisted the necks of swans before González Martínez, but also ever since *Songs of Life and Hope* (1905) no one could accuse him of frivolity and superficial estheticism.

In his memoirs, published under the titles, *The Man of the Owl* (*El hombre del buho,* 1944) and *Peaceful Madness* (*La apacible locura,* 1951) González Martínez clarified his views, for those who needed clarification, that he did not react against Rubén Darío, but against certain "Modernist" topics used by Darío's imitators. In his next book, *The Death of the Swan* (*La muerte del cisne,* 1915), the sonnet reappeared with the title "The Symbol" (*"El símbolo"*): another error on the part of those who supposed that González Martínez had liquidated his Modernist past and that he now moved toward another poetic sign. Not at all. In every book that followed, written in his maturity, in the autumn and winter of his life, González Martínez preserved his initial tone of nobility, of austerity, of fidelity to his esthetics. He is not among the poets who indulge in pirouettes when they are old in order to attract young writers to themselves. In his books (the last one: *The New Narcissus* [*El nuevo Narciso,* 1952]) there are no leaps over an abyss from one esthetics to another, but there is an ascension, within his own way of being, toward an art continually becoming more preoccupied with ultimate problems. Hopelessness, sobbing, doubts, smiles, the anguished feeling of life, of death and of time are purified in an admirable calm.

Other Countries / Up to now only those countries have filed past which have given at least one great Modernist poet: Darío, Lugones, Jaimes Freyre, Herrera y Reissig, Santos Chocano, Valencia, Nervo. Other countries were not as fortunate but since they also figure in the Hispanic-American Modernist process, we shall see what they have to offer.

Antilles: Cuba: Despite Cuba's being the cradle of Julián del Casal, there was no notable Modernist movement until the advent of the twentieth century. The sisters JUANA BORRERO (1877–1896), who only left a little tome of *Rhymes* (*Rimas,* 1895) and DULCE MARÍA BORRERO (1883–1945), intimate, personal, but not a Modernist. FRANCISCO JAVIER PICHARDO (1873–1941) approached Modernism through his admiration for the Parnassians. AUGUSTO DE ARMAS (1869–1893) went to Paris and wound up writing verses in French—he left us only a few compositions written in Castilian. Other names FERNANDO DE ZAYAS (1876–1932), JUAN GUERRA NÚÑEZ (1883–1943), JOSÉ MARÍA COLLANTES (1877–1943), JOSÉ MANUEL CARBONELL (1880). The brothers CARLOS PÍO UHRBACH (1872–1897) and FEDE- RICO UHRBACH (1873–1931) published a volume of poetry in 1894: *Twins* (*Gemelas*). Only the section "Ice Flowers" (*"Flores de hielo"*) belongs to Carlos Pío. Federico continued his poetic production which is marked by rich sensibility and precise control of expression. His best book: *Resurrection* (*Resurrección,* 1916). REGINO E. BOTI (1878–1958) flows beyond Modernism (*Mental Ara- besques* [*Arabescos mentales,* 1913]) and runs along the free verse river bed but without joining the one that young writers will open after 1920.

Dominican Republic: We still see no Modernist poets here. There were, of course, poets who learned from Modernism the art of rich, varied, and complex versification, like the erotic APOLINAR PERDOMO (1882–1918). Names are not lacking: BIENVENIDO SALVADOR NOUEL (1874–1934), BARTOLOMÉ OLEGARIO PÉREZ (1873–1900), ANDREJULIO AYBAR (1872). But, we repeat, the Modernists shall be reviewed in the next chapter. Nevertheless, because of his age, we must place here a "strange one," a verbose, pompous ultra-modernist. We refer to OTILIO VIGIL DÍAZ (1880). He organized "Vedhrinism," a movement of poetic restlessness which, in its desire to renovate, was the immediate antecedent of "posthumism" which we will study in the following chapter. He was the inventor of free and sonorous rhythms upon which surprising images float.

Puerto Rico: Modernism appeared in Puerto Rico after a delay of two or more decades, when it was already disappearing in other countries. And even then (1911, 1914) Puerto Rican Modernism wanted to renovate verse without renouncing either the sentimental Romantic ballast or the regional themes. It was, in truth, a short-lived fashion which produced no central figure. The most interesting was that of LUIS LLORÉNS TORRES (1878–1944), whose relations with Modernism were not very intimate. His books, *At the Foot of the Alhambra* (*Al pie de la Alhambra*), *Visions of My Muse* (*Visiones de mi musa*), *Symphonic Sonnets* (*Sonetos sin- fónicos*), *Voices of the Great Bell* (*Voces de la campana mayor*), *Heights of Amer- ica* (*Alturas de América*), reveal him as a conservative, popular poet, proud of his Hispanic traditions, nationalist in the love of his island, with a preference for historic, civil or Creole themes. His most personal tone was the erotic. He aspired to the formulation of new esthetic theories: *pancalism* (all is beauty), *panedism* (all is verse). These esthetic theories came from those of the German Krause. Lloréns Torres was, after Gautier Benítez, the next highest peak on the island. He began a poetic renovation, and in a new way captured the Puerto Rican landscape and its popular essences. On the lips of José de Jesús Esteves (1881–1918) Modernism still speaks Romantically in his use of Hispanic and Creole themes.

Venezuela: Modernism arrived here belatedly. Even in the latecomers it barely ignited Carlos Borges (1875–1932). In these years Arvelo Larriva and Arreaza Calatrava shine like twin stars. Alfredo Arvelo Larriva (1883–1934)—*Sounds and Songs (Sones y canciones,* 1909)—playful in his forms, of mischievous, free-wheeling and capricious poetic good humor, was the most Modernist. The sound of a fresh breath of Creolism, subjected to the rigors of a difficult music, was heard in his flute. During a time when Modernist esthetics was better represented by prose writers, he did what he could to have this esthetic current run through his verse. José Tadeo Arreaza Calatrava (1885)—*Song to Venezuela (Canto a Venezuela), Song to the Mining Engineer (Canto al ingeniero de minas), Sadness (Lo triste)*—was an epic poet on civic themes, tormented in his subjective moods and opulent in verbal treasure. In other Venezuelan poets Modernism is watered down with Romanticism. During years of great international influence and of cosmopolitan styles, these poets remained faithful to their native land: Sergio Medina (1882–1933), with his *Poems of Sun and Solitude (Poemas del sol y soledad)* and *Tropical Cicadas (Cigarras del Trópico)*; and Juan Santaella (1883–1927).

Ecuador: This country was not very hospitable to Modernist poetry. Francisco Fálquez Ampuero (1877–1947) continued on the road opened by César Borja. He is still a Romantic, although his admiration for the Parnassians, especially for the Heredia of *Les Trophées,* inspired him to sculpture verses and strophes. Alfonso Moscoso (1879–1952), in paintings which are almost Parnassian, seems to approach Modernism, but his metrics are still traditional. Luis Cordero Dávila (1876–1932) revered Rubén Darío but was not among his followers; in spite of his elegances and his polished verses there was in him a non-Modernist oratorical pomp. Luis F. Veloz (1884), of quick and epigrammatic wit, walked on the fringes of the garden where Silva and Valencia strolled, but he abandoned poetry prematurely. Manuel María Sánchez (1882–1935) at first civic, circumstantial, and declamatory, later turned elegiac and intimate. Another: Emilio Gallegos del Campo (1875?–1914). In reality, only in the following generation do Modernist fruits appear.

Chile: The Chilean republic, so important in the history of Modernism (that is where Darío published *Azure*) produced no great poet. Minor poets, yes: Francisco Contreras (1877–1933), enthused firstly with Modernism, tuned his poems to that tonic: *Coat of Arms (Toisón,* 1906). Later he propounded a new program: *The New Worldism (Mundonovismo,* 1917), attentive to native countryside scenes, customs, and speech. Manuel Magallanes Moure (1878–1924) was one of the most outstanding lyricists of Chile. His melancholy, elegant, tender, and at times erotic lyricism was always sensitive to Nature and it sought expression in simple verse of short meter: *The House by the Sea (La casa junto al mar,* 1919) is one of the good collections of poems of this era. Carlos R. Mondaca (1881–1928) was an intense poet of the elegy. Antonio Bórquez Solar (1874–1938) strove to be a modernist, but his talent lay in the evocation of Nature and History of his natal archipelago. Miguel Luis Rocuant (1877–1948) was a poet of forms sculptured in a Parnassian manner. Others: the oratorical Víctor Domingo Silva (1882–1960), Alfredo Mauret Caamano (1880–1934), and Jerónimo Lagos Lisboa (1883–1958).

Paraguay: It had no Modernists because, in reality, it had no literature. Modernism would arrive much later: the only names that can be intercalated here are those of FRANCISCO LUIS BARREIRO (1872–1929) and, above all, ALEJANDRO GUANES (1872–1925) whose posthumous collection is entitled *Passing Through Life* (*De paso por la vida*). Guanes sang of his country, home, and death. They are verses of minor tone, at times of Parnassian make—his most memorable are those of "The Legends" (*"Las leyendas"*). He was a theosophist and his philosophic-religious ideas are reflected in his poems. He and Fariña Núñez (whom we shall see farther on) are those who progress toward Modernism.

2. Non-Modernist Poets

Before going on to prose let us pay a courtesy call on those who lived beyond the pale of Modernism.

Among the non-Modernists there were, as we have seen, poets who did not reach the level of the new style and who were backward in respect to their times. But occasionally their opaqueness and their backwardness (negative values from the esthetic point of view) became, through the pull of circumstances, civic values. In Puerto Rico, for example, there were those who feared that after 1898 the Hispanic configuration of Creole culture might be marred by the assault of Anglo-American civilization. The need was felt to reinforce the work of writers vested in the reality of Puerto Rico, either those who adopted popular words (Alonso, Vassallo) or those who dealt with Creole themes in a cultured language (Tapia). These are poets, then, who patriotically exalted Hispanic and Puerto Rican traditions. VIRGILIO DÁVILA (1869–1943), in cultured verses, gave expression to the "hillbillyism" of the countryside (*Aromas of the Land* [*Aromas del terruño*, 1916]) and of the urban areas (*Town of Yesteryear* [*Pueblito de antes*, 1917]). In Central America, DEMETRIO FÁBREGA (Panama, 1881–1932). In Venezuela, ANDRÉS MATA (1870–1931). In Colombia, when the reader begins to feel annoyed by the declamatory sonority or the sweetish musicality of the poetry of these years, he becomes grateful to LUIS CARLOS LÓPEZ (1883–1950) for his elemental, schematic verses expressing Creole reaction to international pomp. López (*From My Hamlet* [*De mi villorio*, 1908]; *Mushrooms from Riba* [*Los hongos de la Riba*, 1909]; *By The Shortcut* [*Por el atajo*, 1938]) is at times coarse in his derision of types and customs of provincial life, but capable of keen irony and can even bring lyrical smiles to a sentimentalism that blushes and hides its face. In Chile CARLOS PEZOA VÉLIZ (1879–1908) wrote sketches of local customs in prose, amatory verses, and poems of social protest. For formalist critics there is too much deformity in his sentimentalism or in his realism; the sociologists, on the other hand, are grateful to him for having reflected, with a plebeian soul, the sufferings of the lower classes: the ragged, the down-and-out, the hobo, the rebel, the day laborer. Other non-Modernist or barely Modernist Chilean poets were DIEGO DUBLÉ URRUTIA (1877), JORGE GONZÁLEZ BASTÍAS (1879–1950) and SAMUEL A. LILLO (1870–1958). In Paraguay, IGNACIO A. PANE (1880–1920).

B. MAINLY PROSE

Although we have seen the authors of this period rotating around an axis of poetry, they were also, in many cases, excellent prose writers. In the same way, the prosists whom we are about to study were also poets. Frequently their prose was written with the same lyrical tension that informed their verse. One can see a whole gamut from poetry to poetic prose, and from this to an artistically elaborated prose. Even the realists and naturalists, even the narrators of regional and folkloric themes were sensitive to the new art of prose. But of course, realism was a dividing line between two proud attitudes: on one side, the pride with which the Modernists organized verses and prose in an esthetic and subjective world; on the other side, stories and novels were organized placing pride in objective description. Literature was no less a calling for the realists. Certain tendencies apparently contrary to estheticism, such as naturalism, were also modern attitudes and arose from the awareness of fashions and from the same desire to renew art.

1. Novel and Short Story

(a) *Estheticizing Narrators* / Modernist prose saw itself pressed when it had to novelize, because of the intimate conflict between the attention given to the pretty, bejeweled phrase and the attention given to the true development of the action. The equilibrium is difficult, and to care for one virtue generally supposes the lack of care for another. The "poem in prose" was one of the most fervid rites of Modernist cult. There were those who emasculated themselves in celebrating it, and, when we read them now, we feel pity for them. It was a lyrical miniaturism which, when in the service of a profound view of life, contributed in dignifying Castilian prose, but when it simmered down to empty verbalism became a childish epidemic.

For a history of artistic prose, in good and bad taste, these names should be recorded: ARTURO AMBROGI (El Salvador, 1875–1936), author of *Knick-knacks* (*Bibelots*); RAFAEL ÁNGEL TROYO (Costa Rica, 1875–1910), author of *Terracottas, Sunrise* (*Ortos*), *Topazes* (*Topacios*); ALEJANDRO FERNÁNDEZ GARCÍA (Venezuela, 1879–1939), author of *Alchemist Gold* (*Oro de alquimia*) and *Lilacs in Bloom* (*Búcaros en flor*); AMÉRICO LUGO (Dominican Republic, 1870–1952, author of *Heliotrope* (*Heliotropo*). Some of these prose poets also wrote novels and short stories—artistic, of course.

(1) *Mexico* / There scarcely was a Hispanic-American country that did not do some gardening in the narrative genre. The same gardens that one had become accustomed to seeing in verse now were also seen in prose. The poetess MARÍA ENRIQUETA CAMARILLO DE PEREYRA (Mexico, 1875) wrote stories and novels. *A Strip of the World* (*Jirón de mundo*, 1918) is a rose-tinted, lachrymose novel. It has no local color; rather it has a temporal color, but of the nineteenth century, with touches of the sentimental, Romantic, bourgeois, feminine novel of the type of Charlotte Brontë's *Jane Eyre*. Teresa, abandoned at a convent door, grows up

to become a governess in a rich home caring for a sickly girl. The father of the girl, Doctor Santiesteban, is a sad widower, also very ill, and a paragon of perfection. He has a good-natured son who falls in love with Teresa, and an ill-natured daughter who hates her. Teresa had been corresponding with an unknown friend who inevitably turns out to be Santiesteban. When they identify each other, the ill-natured daughter, Laura, screeches insults at them. The doctor dies on the spot, from a heart attack, and Teresa takes permanent refuge in a convent. Within its genre, the novel is well written, with a prose that tends to be poetic, and an action that holds interest. Along with other similar novels, it drifts to all parts of the world. ANTONIO MÉDIZ BOLIO (1884–1957), a poet and dramatist, whose best book is *The Land of the Pheasant and the Deer* (*La tierra del faisán y del venado*), in which he elaborates legends of the Mayas.

(2) *Central America / Guatemala:* The goldsmiths of prose (and "goldsmiths" is not always a eulogy, since not all are of good taste) even gilded the pages of newspapers. The first name to reach this juncture is that of ENRIQUE GÓMEZ CARRILLO (Guatemala, 1873–1927). He educated his tastes in Europe where he went for the first time in 1889. But there were so many literary, artistic, and philosophic tendencies that, more than his tastes, he educated an extraordinary skill in referring to all of them. In spite of the humbleness of his trade—commenting on the creations of others—his prose was one of the most agile of his time. His knowledge of all contemporary European literature was fabulous. He was an impressionist whose impressions, more than of life, were of literary life. We are indebted to him for having left well-written gossipy tales. He was not a critic in the true sense, not even of what he admired. Some of the writers he knew, Loti, for example, gave him the desire to go farther in his intellectual curiosity. He traveled a good deal, and from his travels he created such books as: *Present-Day Russia* (*La Rusia actual*), *Heroic and Gallant Japan* (*El Japón heroico y galante*), *The Smile of the Sphinx* (*La sonrisa de la Esfinge*), *Eternal Greece* (*La Grecia eterna*), *Jerusalem and the Holy Land* (*Jerusalén y la Tierra santa*), *From Marseille to Tokyo* (*De Marsella a Tokio*), *Views of Europe* (*Vistas de Europa*), *The Charm of Buenos Aires* (*El encanto de Buenos Aires*). These lands were provinces of his Gallicized soul (and naturally, his best chronicles came from his stay in France). He was a chronicler of genius. In part because he perceived that the "chronicle" was a worthy literary genre and he devoted himself to it with the strength of a lyrical vocation. He placed a magnificently orchestrated language at the service of everyday themes. He seems to be frivolous; but in reality it is because he is so comprehensive that he appears to be on the surface of everything. He wrote novels. The one he preferred was *The Gospel of Love* (*El evangelio del*

amor, 1922). It is made with the pap of many books, old ones (the Bible, Jacopo da Voragine's *The Golden Legend*) and new ones (France's *Thaïs*, Flaubert's *La tentation de Saint-Antoine*, Louÿs' *Aphrodite*). It takes place in the first quarter of the fourteenth century, in Byzantium. Teófilo, an ascetic, tortures his flesh to attain religious purity, until he hears that Jesus wants him to love a woman. He finds her, but learns that what Jesus wished was that he love completely and fully; hence, he goes to live with the anchorets, but this time to preach to them "the gospel of love." They stone him to death. It is a Modernist novel in preciosity of style: the theme is common to estheticism. For the same reason that estheticism was hedonist the Modernists fancied its opposite: asceticism. Pleasure was derived from the contrast between sensuality and the denial of the flesh, between the faun and the angel, as Darío would say. From the enjoyers of life, even in the most degrading forms, one passed to the torturers of the flesh through the mechanics of opposites. Gómez Carrillo exalts life, sensuality, love; and he even dares to dip into theology and to freely interpret the Bible, the lives of saints, and the writings of the Fathers of the Church. His novel is interesting as a variation on a theme of the times, but it lacks movement, vital reality, and psychological depth. It is too replete with conventional phrases and bookish passages. Gómez Carrillo touched upon the religious theme in other books. He called himself a Christian, but his novel, naturally, lies beyond any Christian church. One of his most palatable books is *Thirty Years of My Life* (*Treinta años de mi vida*), in three volumes.

Honduras: FROILÁN TURCIOS (1875–1943) began as a Modernist poet (see his anthology *Almond Flowers* [*Flores de almendro*]). He excelled nevertheless in his *Cruel Stories* (*Cuentos crueles*). Villiers de l'Isle-Adam had written stories with the same title; and there are resonances of Poe in two of his novels: *Annabel Lee* and *The Vampire* (*El vampiro*). He also wrote narrations in a tropical setting. He had great influence in the literary life of his country.

El Salvador: ARTURO AMBROGI (1875–1936), cited above, also wrote *Book of the Tropics* (*El libro del Trópico*), narrations that are among the first of a regionalist tendency in his country.

Costa Rica: Akin to the sketches of local customs, as a genre, were the Francophiles ALEJANDRO ALVARADO QUIRÓS (1876–1945) and RAFAEL ÁNGEL TROYO (1875–1910), the latter a miniaturist of the Modernist school and author of artistic prose. MARIA FERNÁNDEZ DE TINOCO (1877) carried her love of archeology to two novels, *Zulai* and *Yonta*, which re-create imaginatively the origin and the struggles of the American indigenous races.

Panama: Before his exile in 1898 DARÍO HERRERA (1870–1914) had been the initiator of Modernism in his country, in verse and prose. He left Parnassian verse

Spanish-American Literature: A History

to enlist as a short story writer, but kept his Parnassian desire for verbal perfection. *Distant Hours* (*Horas lejanas*, 1903), although stories in an American setting, have such a refined and learned spiritual elegance that they do not seem to have been written in America. The obsession for the unique, the precious, the right word, came from Flaubert. Another Panamanian narrator, GUILLERMO ANDREVE (1879–1940), distinguished himself more as a promoter of the works of others. He is the author of a novel about spiritualists, *A Corner of the Veil* (*Una punta del velo*, 1929).

(3) *Antilles* / MANUEL FLORENTINO CESTERO (Dominican Republic, 1879–1926) composed stories of Modernist art with a prose that oozed out into the titles: *Stories for Lila* (*Cuentos a Lila*), and a novel, *The Song of the Swan* (*El canto del cisne*).

(4) *Venezuela* / In Venezuela, a country of novelists, the artistic direction is indicated by Coll, Domínici, Urbaneja Achelpohl, and Díaz Rodríguez. In 1894 the first three launched their review *Cosmópolis*, a vent for "all the literary schools of all the countries."

PEDRO EMILIO COLL (1872–1947) wrote very little (among his best: *Words* [*Palabras*, 1896]; *The Castle of Elsinor* [*El castillo de Elsinor*, 1901]; *The Hidden Path* [*La escondida senda*, 1927]), but his chronicles and stories have us feel the presence of a "hospitable mind," (as he himself used to say) a keen, skeptical, merry and pessimistic spirit. Narrative did not interest him. He was rather a contemplative sort who glossed his own contemplations. He left, nevertheless, several stories that reveal his understanding of the spiritually poor ("The Broken Tooth" ["*El diente roto*"]), his curiosity for Baudelairean sensuality ("Opoponax") and even his exercises in naturalism with Modernist pen ("Drunken Creole" ["*Borracho criollo*"]). Like César Zumeta, Coll was capable but unproductive.

PEDRO CÉSAR DOMÍNICI (1872–1954) wrote mannerist novels—with the voluptuous and artificial manners of Pierre Louys or of D'Annunzio—which refused to be American even in theme; for example, *Dionysos* (1907) speaks to us of Alexandrian eroticisms. Others novels, *The Triumph of the Ideal* (*El triunfo del ideal*), *Voluptuous Sadness* (*La tristeza voluptuosa*), refuse contact with life (too vulgar!) and prefer contact with the expressions of an inner-chamber literature. In the prolog to *The Condor* (*El cóndor*, 1925) the author tells us that many years after his Greek novel *Dionysos,* he decided to attempt the "American novel," whose action would unfold in our hemisphere. The *Condor* is a novel that is a little Indianist, a little historical, a little poetic—in any case, not much novel. It relates the war deeds of Angol, the archer of one of the remotest tribes of the Inca Empire. It is set in the times of Atahualpa's "quarrel" with Huáscar and of the Spanish conquest of Peru. From the love of Angol for Guacolda are born twin daughters. One of the conquistadors, in turn, will love one of Angol's daughters, and from this love will be born the first mestizo in Peru; with Huáscar and Atahualpa dead, Angol carries on the struggle until he is killed. There is sympathy for the indigenous cause, but the novel is completely false. The excess of literature—"Modernist" literature, if we wish to calumniate Modernism—spoils the unraveling of the action.

LUIS MANUEL URBANEJA ACHELPOHL (1874–1937) is, of the three, the one who profits most from the land in which he lives. Like the rest, he is impregnated with Modernism, but he gives a Creole, native direction to his verbal art. His Modernism, let it be said in passing, contained naturalist ways. He resembles those painters who went to impressionism in a desire for truth and for faithfulness to a model. Be they as they may, his novels, *In This Country* (*En este país*, 1916); *The House of the Four Cowhides* (*La casa de las cuatro pencas*) and especially his excellent stories, managed to do without the esthetic ballast of their generation and thus gained in loftiness and in stature. He was one of those who knew how to look, artistically and with sincerity, at life and at the landscape of the villages, mountains and Venezuelan plains. He usually interrupts the action to marvel at nature. First the bucolic note, then, through the pretty trails of Modernism, he advanced toward a realism *à la* Zola or *à la* Bourget. With stories like *"Ovejón"* it can be said that Urbaneja Achelpohl initiates the history of the Venezuelan short story.

One of the great Venezuelans, and one of the greatest novelists in all Hispanic-America in this period, was MANUEL DÍAZ RODRÍGUEZ (1871–1927). His is an exemplary case of a prose style that, with discretion and measured movements, slips past the reefs of a preciosity which does not know how to novelize, and of a naturalism which novelizes without knowing how to write. His first books, *Secrets of Psyche* (*Confidencias de Psiquis*, 1896), *Sensations of Travel* (*Sensaciones de viaje*, 1896), *About My Pilgrimages* (*De mis romerías*, 1898), *Stories in Color* (*Cuentos de color*, 1899), take solace in European civilizations —he had lived in France, in Italy, and his views were those of Barrès, of D'Annunzio. His *Stories in Color* narrated myths and legends ("blue," "green"), allegories and parables on his artistic ideas ("golden," "pale red"), reflections on love ("pale blue," "red"). Significantly, Venezuela appears in the three stories without any color: "white," "gray," and "black." All is shading, sound, perfume, caresses, evocation, and even human suffering is phrased a little to Parnassian and a little to symbolist tastes. There are no heroes in his stories: impressionistic atmospheres are the motivating characters. In his second group of works (*Broken Idols* [*Idolos rotos*, 1901]; *Patrician Blood* [*Sangre patricia*, 1902]), Díaz Rodríguez clashes with Venezuelan reality and repudiates it esthetically. His ideal man was the "distinguished one" of Nietzsche; but his characters do not struggle. They are pessimists, defeatists, unadaptables who go into exile or to suicide. In *Broken Idols* he shows the aristocratic figure of Alberto Soria, the sculptor, in contrast with sordid and barbarous Venezuelan masses. He wanted to regenerate his country by means of his esthetic cult—the rabble harasses and breaks the icons. But Díaz Rodríguez persists in believing that a disinterested art, proud of the elaboration of beautiful forms, can at least save the liberty of intense souls; and he writes another estheticist novel, *Patrician Blood*. His novelistic scope is minimal: to present the social weakening of the upper-class Creole. What is worthy is the description of the states of soul; and this description is not that of a psychologist but of a symbolist writer. This is odd, because the theme would have lent itself to a psychological novel; after all, it is the novel of a neurosis. Metaphoric art insists more on esthetic impression than on psychological observations. The atmosphere is also estheticist: paintings by Botticelli, poetry by Swedenborg, music by Schumann and Wagner, discussions on Nietzsche, the affirmation of the supernatural over scientific reality, immersions into the subconscience, drugs, the theme of the submerged cathedral. It is not accidental that the novel begins with the description of the sailing of a transatlantic liner and that the uprooted Tulio Arcos does not reach the shores of Venezuela. In the last years of his life Díaz Rodríguez attempted a Creole narrative, *Pilgrim or The Enchanted Well* (*Peregrina o el pozo encantado*, 1922) and other stories, in which his artistic ideals worked well, in the land and in its men. It is as though he were disillusioned and had taken refuge in country life, in the direct emotional experience of nature. Withal, he continued to press the narrative material in order to coin spectacular phrases. In other words, what is spectacular in these latest works lies more in the expression of Díaz Rodríguez than in Venezuela. And he pressed with such ardor that not only the description remained jelled in metaphor, but he even gave the action itself incredible dramatic spasms: for example, in "Summer Eclogue" (*"Egloga de verano"*) when Justa decapitates Gaucharaco with a single axe-blow, the head, which was fully extended as the body "stretched in its effort to slip into the room, was cut off cleanly, and leaped, grasping the sheet of the cot with its teeth in its last convulsive moment. That is the way they found it, still hanging from the bedsheet . . ."

(5) *Colombia* / Many novels were written for colleagues and not for the ordinary reader. The relative popularity that the novels of JOSÉ MARÍA VARGAS VILA (Colombia, 1860–1933) enjoyed was exceptional, perhaps because his literary niceties—rhythmic prose, orthographic dislocations, artificial vocabulary and syntax, self-worshipping flights of fancy—were at the service of a morbid bad taste. Among the more than twenty novels he wrote are: *Ibis, Afternoon Roses* (*Rosas de la tarde*), *Swamp Flower* (*Flor de fango*), *The Seed* (*La simiente*). JOSÉ MARÍA RIVAS GROOT (1863–1923) did write good, little artistic novels. *Resurrection* (*Resurrección*), for example, will hardly please the general public, but will offer to the scholar the pleasure of recognizing, one by one, the composites of the refined European cultural world "in the aurora of the 20th century," as the author puts it. Several artist-characters are in love with a woman who possesses the beauty of mystery and death. They discuss Parnassianism, symbolism, and pre-Raphaelism in literature, impressionism in painting, Wagner in music. The positivism of the natural sciences is denied, and, on the other hand, a Catholicism beautified by artistic imagination is exalted. The irrational is cultivated: neurasthenias, rare

sensations, dreams, forebodings of the supernatural, and, crowning all of this, the esthetic aspects of the Catholic religion. His brother, EVARISTO RIVAS GROOT, 1864–1923, also wrote Modernist, though more realist, stories.

(6) *Ecuador* / We shall study the *Tragic Eclogue* (*Egloga trágica*) of Gonzalo Zaldumbide in the next chapter.

(7) *Peru* / CLEMENTE PALMA (Peru, 1872–1946) wrote fantastic, macabre, ir-reverent tales: *Evil Stories* (*Cuentos malévolos*, 1904); *Wicked Tales* (*Historietas malignas*, 1925). His last novel, *XYZ*, 1934, is science fiction: it tells of the invention of a process for projecting motion picture images on protoplasm, thus creating lives that repeat exactly those of Hollywood actresses.

(8) *Bolivia* / Although Arguedas fits here among the estheticizing narrators, we have placed him farther on.

(9) *Chile* / Augusto Geomine Thomson, better known as AUGUSTO D'HALMAR (Chile, 1882–1950), began as a naturalist with *Juana Lucero* (1902), a raw, hard novel about the fall, the movements, the prostitution, and the death of a woman of easy virtue. Then he changed esthetics. He veered toward motifs and modes that were less and less realist and more and more poetic. His short novels and stories usually force themselves to pursue a prose ideal of beautiful forms. They fall short of possessing it. In this pursuit, the novels and stories, in general addicted to personal reminiscences, forget the requirements of the narration. *Passion and Death of the Priest Deusto* (*Pasión y muerte del cura Deusto*, 1924) was a novel with a plot, although a simple one. It is set in the year 1913, in Seville—a Seville of tourists, a Seville still pagan in its religious holidays. And it tells us of a questionable, risqué, three-year friendship between a Basque priest and an adolescent. The psychological analysis is not as fine as the painting of a morbid, "decadent," atmosphere of the type that pleased the Modernists. The ecclesiastical life is not austere: the priest is surrounded by bullfighters, trapeze artists, painters, songsters, poets. Deusto himself is a musician; his beloved Pedro Miguel, a singer and dancer. There is more estheticism than "psychology," more Oscar Wildeism than Proustianism in the description of a love which, "having reached its extreme," can no longer be prolonged. Thus D'Halmar wrote narratives which reflect immediate things as easily as the most artificial fantasies. This fluctuation between naturalism and the ideals of the imagists was part of the era—even Barrios will produce *Lost One* (*Un perdido*), on the one hand, and on the other, *Brother Ass* (*Hermano asno*); and Prado, *Rural Judge* (*Un juez rural*) and *Alsino*. But if we situate D'Halmar, author of *Juana Lucero*, in this section of estheticizing prosists it is because his influence

over other writers was due precisely to his aerial prose which invited subtle lucubrations.

(10) *Paraguay* / RAFAEL BARRETT (1877–1910) is a writer of very complex prose, capable of irritating pamphlets (*Argentinian Terror* [*El terror argentino*], *The Truth About Plantations* [*Lo que son los yerbales*]) and of harmonious stories (*Short Tales* [*Cuentos breves*], *Dialogs* [*Diálogos*], and *Conversations* [*Conversaciones*]).

(11) *Uruguay* / With a curious admixture of estheticism and naturalism, the great narrator of abnormal themes was HORACIO QUIROGA (Uruguay, last day of 1878–1937). Though he occasionally wrote artistic verse and prose (*Coral Reefs* [*Los arrecifes de coral*, 1901]), novels (*History of a Turbulent Love* [*Historia de un amor turbio*, 1908], and *Past Love* [*Pasado amor*, 1929]), a novelette (*The Persecuted* [*Los perseguidos*, 1905]), drama (*The Sacrificed* [*Las sacrificadas*, 1920]), Horacio Quiroga excelled in the short story. He published several collections: *The Other's Crime* (*El crimen del otro*, 1904), *Tales of Love, Madness and Death* (*Cuentos de amor, de locura y de muerte*, 1917), *Jungle Tales* (*Cuentos de la selva*, 1918), *The Savage* (*El salvaje*, 1920), *Anaconda* (1921), *The Desert* (*El desierto*, 1924), *The Beheaded Chicken and Other Tales* (*La gallina degollada y otros cuentos*, 1925), *The Exiled* (*Los desterrados*, 1926) and *The Great Beyond* (*Más allá*, 1935). To these titles may be added stories scattered in newspapers, now collected in several posthumous editions. A chronological study of the stories, one by one, might permit us to group them in his first period of technical apprenticeship, a period of maturity, and the final period when Quiroga retired with ebbing strength from the art. But his books cannot be classified in stages, because, in general, they are comprised of stories written in very separate years. So that the date of the volume says nothing of the date of composition of the individual stories. Quiroga chose the stories in each book on a thematic and not a chronological criterion. He never achieved a book of perfect unity (the most integral was *The Exiled*) but at least he had intentions of doing so. In addition, Quiroga usually retouched and even recast his stories on transferring them from periodicals to books. Perhaps his best stories appeared between 1907 ("The Feather Pillow" ["*El almohadón de plumas*"]) and 1928 ("The Son" ["*El hijo*"]). It has been observed that in his later years Quiroga seemed to have shifted from the short story to newspaper writing: articles, news items, commentaries. Nevertheless, he wrote short stories up to the last moment, though not as good as those in the series that ends in "The Son." The action of a great portion of his stories takes place in an untamed nature; sometimes

his protagonists are animals; and, if men, they are usually undone by the forces of nature. It has been said, consequently, that Quiroga is typical of only one aspect of Hispanic-American literature, to wit, geography and zoology as more significant than history and anthropology. But neither jungles nor vipers write stories: it is a man who uses them in his writings, and it will always be the vision by this man, and not the things, that is significant in literature. This man Quiroga, for whom nature was a literary theme, had nothing primitive about him. He was an author of complex spirituality, refined in his culture, with a nervous and morbid organization. He had begun as a Modernist and never broke from this initiation. His prose became more and more clumsy, his narrative technique more and more realist. But he remained faithful to his initial esthetics: to express obscure, odd, personal perceptions. He had a theory of what a short story should be (see the "Decalogue for the Perfect Short Story Writer" ["*Decálogo del perfecto cuentista*"], "The Rhetoric of the Short Story" ["*La retórica del cuento*"], "Before the Tribunal" ["*Ante el tribunal*"]). And although he had not cited his masters one would have recognized their influence. But he did cite them: "Believe in one master—Poe, Maupassant, Kipling, Chekov—as in God Himself," he said; and he could have mentioned others, because he read a good deal. No, he was not a primitive; and even his view of the jungle was that of an exceptionally educated eye.

The moods of his stories are varied, even a humoristic one here and there. Nevertheless, a good anthology would be inclined toward his cruel stories in which he describes sickness, death, failure, hallucination, fear of the supernatural, alcoholism. We know of no perfect story of his; generally, he wrote too rapidly and committed errors, not only in style, but also in narrative technique. But the sum total of his stories reveals a writer of first magnitude in our literature. Let us recall the dynamic scheme of emotions in "The Beheaded Chicken," "Adrift," "The Son," "The Desert," "The Dead Man," and a dozen others. Sometimes Quiroga himself is the subject of his short stories. The autobiographical elements of his fiction are a very complex problem, and the critic must take care. In Quiroga Art and Life become confused. He felt that his own life was distorted by a cruel fate. His literature also wore a fatidical grimace. And Quiroga, as a man, went back and forth, from Life to Literature and from Literature to Life, always urged by a demon who made him love and then destroy the object of his affection, to yearn for success and, yet, to wish for death. He was an eccentric man, and one of his eccentricities was to plunge into reality as though reality were fiction and he himself played the role of a character, or to the contrary, to plunge into fiction as though fiction were a store of real events. The many anecdotes which describe Quiroga as a harsh and difficult man rather correspond to a novelistic character. And his short stories are full of characters drawn from everyday intercourse. Somehow his dedication to a life of manual labor and his writing sensitive literature with those same work-hardened hands were disharmonious. He cursed both work and literature. In the last analysis he was a maladjusted, lonesome man.

(12) *Argentina* / In the Modernist prose of Argentina the names of Estrada and Larreta are retained today.

ÁNGEL DE ESTRADA (1872–1923) was an aristocratic and solitary figure who wandered through real worlds, and worlds of dreams, of art, and of history. His novelistic pictures (the best, *Redemption* [*Redención*, 1905]) shine more as paintings than as novels. His heroes are phantoms who escape from the author and only live in phantom worlds, yearning for beauty, falling back on museums, on literature, and on histories of art. Perhaps his most poetic pages are his chronicles, such as *Color and Stone* (*El color y la piedra*) and *Forms and Spirits* (*Formas y espíritus*).

ENRIQUE LARRETA (1873–1961) is the best novelist that Argentina has produced within the elegant style of Modernism. *The Glory of Don Ramiro* (*La gloria de don Ramiro*, 1908), an historical novel of the epoch of Philip II, with a voyage to America by the protagonist linking the two Hispanic worlds, was a masterful coordination of the effort to evoke the past and the effort to evoke sensorial perceptions. His impressionistic style, the conversion of sensations into objects of art, was exceptional in our literature. *Zogoibi* (1926) brought a new value: that of stylizing with preciosity a tragic adventure in the Argentine plains. All occurs within a few months, from the beginning of summer of 1913 to the beginning of winter of 1914. Federico de Ahumada, who like Boabdil, the last king of Granada, is called "Zogoibi," the little unfortunate one, and the sweet and pure Lucía love each other idyllically. Lucía's aunts oppose this betrothal because Federico is an atheist. Federico then falls in the arms of Zita, a mysterious and sensual foreigner, married to an American industrialist, Mr. Wilburns. Federico struggles between love and lust; one evening in the country when he takes final leave of Zita, he sees someone in the shadows and, believing him to be an enemy, stabs him, but discovers that he has killed Lucía, dressed in gaucho clothing. Federico kills himself and falls at the body of his beloved. The novel is related in the third person by an author who entwines happenings that occur in different places with the simple thread of his story; in addition, he knows his characters inside and out. This author, however, is not a realist but an impressionist who records exquisite artistic intuitions. *Zogoibi* is a well-constructed novel whose tragic end, for example, is ably arranged with convolutions in the plot, suggestive details, coincidences and forebodings. The prose images, which are rich in sensibility and also in culture because of the frequent allusions to the plastic arts, music, and literature, are not in disharmony because Larreta has domiciled refined Argentinians or high-classed foreigners in his "ranches." His characters are "decadents" who have just returned from Paris or have been educated in European culture. There are even an opium eater and a countess. Federico himself feels like the hero of a French novel, and, effectively, he is playing the roles that he read in his books. The Europeanism and even the snobbism of the characters in *Zogoibi* do not falsify the novel. These are traits of Creole oligarchy and Larreta was writing from this aristocratic point of view. There is no superimposition of two conflicting social strata: the novel has a unity in its outlook on life. Although the members of the oligarchy imitated Europe, they had their feet planted in these lands and they governed them; for this reason, when Larreta and his characters listen to peons speaking or glance at rural customs and the rebellious actions of the incipient workers' movement, they document a real life that they knew quite well without any effort. The metaphors fuse the double experience of the Buenos Aires oligarchy: literary mannerism and the immediate knowledge of nature. One example: "it was a sad hut but at the same time smiling, all twisted to one side, like the cowhand when he speaks to the boss." *Zogoibi* reveals the mental process of some of the characters and, like every psychological novel, it forces the reader to participate vividly in the course of inner time; but a different time is also evoked, that of a Creole, patrician life prior to the first World War. The last novels of Larreta are: *Shores of the Ebro* (*Orillas del Ebro*, 1949), and *El Gerardo* (1956).

Stories and novels about abnormal realities, the abnormality being either in the circumstances or in the minds of the characters, had been written during the Romantic period. Now, in cultivating this abnormality, the writers did not conceal their pleasure in playing the esthetic role of eccentrics, decadents, and psychopaths.

ATILIO CHIAPPORI (Argentina, 1880) withdrew to the subtle frontier where morbidness is at one and the same time art and horror. *Borderland* (1907) is the title of his first book of stories. It was also the first book of short stories of this type to be produced in Argentina. Chiappori had studied mental disorders scientifically and knew how to sketch with a technical language. He did not fall into "experimental and scientistic" naturalism. He utilized, on the contrary, his psychological penetration to make Modernist literature. His characters are usually literary men and artists, or, in any case, victims of their rare perceptions, persons with manias for introspection, sick people who feel that mental aberration is aristocratic. Chiappori himself writes in an atmosphere charged with literary phantoms: D'Annunzio, Poe, Barbey d'Aurevilly. The stories explain these disturbances as clinical cases or describe them as mysterious adventures into the unknown. We no longer read them with the same pleasure as the "decadents." Not even "The Blue Tie" ("*La corbata azul*"), which is one of the best, will be saved for posterity. But they had the merit of having initiated a genre. Later Chiappori published a novel, *Eternal Anguish* (*La eterna angustia*, 1908) and other stories, *The Island of Red Roses* (*La isla de las rosas rojas*, 1925), where the morbid note is subdued.

Of this group of writers specializing in the abnormal, there was one who trod on the fringes of madness: MACEDONIO FERNÁNDEZ (1874–1952), the wandering comet. Because of his age he belongs to this chapter. Because he fascinated both the young writers who heard him (the Borges, Girondo, Marechal, González Lanuza generation) and the young writers who were not able to hear him but who read him with mouths agape (the generation of the '40's), Macedonio would belong to the following chapters. And because of his sparse literary achievements—although he did succeed with witty verbalism as an "oral writer" —he does not belong to any chapter of this *History*. But we shall include him because we knew him and, to be sure, the man was a peculiar person. His nonsensical book was *All Is Not Vigil When the Eyes Are Open* (*No toda es Vigilia la de los Ojos Abiertos*, 1928), a philosophy whose point of departure was epistemological idealism. The rest of his books published later were old pages pulled out, against his will, by frolicking friends: *A Newcomer's Papers* (*Papeles de Recienvenido*, 1930), *A Novel That Begins* (*Una novela que comienza*, 1941), *Continuation of Nothingness* (*Continuación de la Nada*, 1945), *Poems* (*Poemas*, 1953). The best Macedonio is the one in the letter to Borges —verbal magic, later published in *Proa*. The rest is unreadable digression, unless one is seeking among the ruins of this broken prose (of this broken reasoning), larvae of a surprising, ingenious, and even poetic, solipsism. He gave us a humoristic vision of the universe. A universe which, after the operations it underwent by Macedonio's imagination and sophistry, remains ridiculous together with all us men who inhabit it. Yet, there is in him a serious aspect, that of illustrating with his life, with his writings, with his conversations, the disintegration of contemporary letters. In the first place, the disintegration of literary genres, then, the disintegration of the writer himself who ends up by disappearing into nothingness. Macedonio scarcely wrote and never worried about organizing his thoughts or his pages. For this reason, on reading him we have the sensation of spying into the soul of a man at the moment of penning his thoughts. That is to say, we are only present at the first discomforts of a difficult pregnancy. But it is exactly these discomforts that interest the present-day readers who are accustomed to a literature that may also be spontaneous, disarticulate, elemental, arbitrary, capricious, and confused.

(*b*) *Realist Narrators* / Naturalism, with its psychiatry, its monstrous flowers of sordidness, and its strange esthetics of ugliness, occasionally made its way into the poetic literature of Modernism. But it followed its own course toward an objective description of reality. On their part, Modernist writers usually lowered their sights to the customs and landscapes of their region, diverting themselves in a kind of Creolism and Indianism. It would be too schematic to divide narrative prose into a Modernist half where what counts is the subject-contemplator, and a realist half where what counts is the object-contemplated. But now we shall lean slightly toward this latter half, as we descend from Mexico to Argentina.

(*1*) *Mexico* / Many figures squeeze into the picture of the realist novel of Mexico. We would rather analyze one: Azuela. But since his importance rests on being the founder of the novel of the Revolution, as a curiosity we would like to mention first HERIBERTO FRÍAS (1870–1925) who, in *Tomóchic* (1894) gave us the chronicle of an Indian rebellion against Porfirio Díaz, with sympathy for the rebels.

MARIANO AZUELA (1873–1952). His first stage as a novelist began with *María Luisa* (1907) and ended with *The Underdogs* (*Los de abajo*, 1916), his sixth novel. Those who judged it from a political and not a literary viewpoint believed that *The Underdogs* was an anti-revolutionary work. In truth, at first glance the novel does not seem to stand by the Revolution, but rather to criticize the brutal episodes from Madero's assassination to the defeat of Pancho Villa's partisans in the battle of Celaya. The men who surround Demetrio Macías did not take arms and hurl themselves into the Revolution on principle, but were impelled by personal motives and events. Demetrio Macías himself, as their leader, does not have a political awareness. When his wife asks him at the end why he continues fighting, Demetrio "distractedly picks up a little stone and hurls it down the canyon. He stands thoughtfully looking down the gorge, and says, 'Look at that little stone, how it doesn't come to rest.' " Inertia, not ideals. The brutality that moves them all is fierce in "Whitey" Margarito. Nor has the minor intellectual, Luis Cervantes, who wishes to supply Demetrio with an ideology, become a revolutionary through conviction; he is a resentful person, an opportunist, a charlatan. Solís is the only authentic revolutionary, and within the novel he reveals the secret of Azuela as a citizen and as a novelist. Solís is disillusioned, not by the Revolution, but by its failures. This disenchantment leads him to contemplate the Revolution at a distance, as an objective reality; and from this esthetic distance he envisages it "beautiful even in its barbarism." Azuela also is a disillusioned revolutionary: the lack of meaning in the struggle wounds him. But he feels its tragic beauty and, though he judges it on a moral plane, he describes it artistically. The Revolution as an object of contemplation: from this Azuela's realism is born. He will depict circumstances more than men. *The Underdogs* offers a continuous action: when the novelist skips an episode he will return to recoup in a retrospective evocation. The action closes in a perfect circumference—although in inverse position, Demetrio and his men will die in the last chapters on the same spot where they began their fighting in the first chapters. However, in this lineal action there is no intention of showing the psychological growth of the characters. The object, we repeat, is not the psychology of the characters but the reproduction of one phase of the Revolution. The characters and their vicissitudes are fragments of the composition of the painting. Azuela's objectivity is that of the naturalist: the circumstances are the determining factors, men, without liberty, without goals, are animals. And, with a naturalist technique, Azuela presents men and animals piled together, fused into a single mass.

By 1916, realism and naturalism had triumphed in the novel the world over. It was not necessary, as in the period from Stendhal and Balzac to the Goncourts and Zola, to prove that the literary treatment of sordid reality could reach serious dignity in art. Azuela had no need to wrestle with an enormous mass of details. Therefore, he efficiently used vigorous, novelistic outlines, rapid, flickering and suggestive prose, dialectical dialogs, impressionistic techniques, and contrasts between the iniquities of man and the beauties of the landscape. His impressionism was the visual one of the realists, not the synesthetic one of the Modernists. Azuela used to say that he only wrote to give vent to his emotions and that all his themes were real. His strength, certainly, seems to come from events, not from art. Nevertheless, the artistic in

Azuela is allowing himself to be permeated by events, giving us the illusion of seeing what the author saw. He possessed sobriety, nakedness, the capacity for synthesis, imagination to strike in one metaphor of powerful, illuminating violence the whole of a social situation or psychological conflict. In his second stage, from 1916 to 1932, Azuela decided to experiment with some of the tricks of the latest literature of the day. "I abandoned my usual manner, which consists of expressing myself with clarity and conciseness," he explained in some autobiographical notes; and he twisted phrases and proffered conundrums in *That Woman Malhora* (*La Malhora*), *Retaliation* (*El desquite*), and *The Firefly* (*La luciérnaga*). These were the postwar years of "stridentism" which we will define in the next chapter: "Dada" images, "futurist" objects, hermetism of contorted symbols, anti-logical style, expressionism, obscure monologs. Azuela became infected. Just a few blotches on his skin. He recovered his health and returned to his own, which was the chronicle and social criticism. The third stage goes from *Pedro Moreno the Insurgent* (*Pedro Moreno el insurgente*, 1933) to *Lost Paths* (*Sendas perdidas*, 1949) a novel on the working class of the city. He also wrote short stories and theater. But his novels remain the most substantial part of his literature. In it there is the Mexico of Porfirio Díaz, the Mexico of the Revolution, the Mexico that emerged after the Revolution. But as a novelist he succeeded more in the negative register of errors, crimes, corruption, treachery. He understood less the efforts at national regeneration. In short, he enriched the novel of Hispanic-America with at least two works, *The Underdogs* and *The Firefly*. His posthumous novels, *The Curse* (*La maldición*) and *That Blood* (*Esa sangre*), continued to denounce the social defects that remained in spite of the Revolution or that appeared because of the Revolution: crude novels, the first satiric, the other bitter, both born of Azuela's moralist background.

(2) *Central America / El Salvador:* JOSÉ MARÍA PERALTA LAGOS (1873–1944) was a jovial narrator of social customs.

Costa Rica: Estheticism (Alejandro Alvarado Quirós, Rafael Angel Troyo) and realism (Magón, Jenaro Cardona) emerged from nowhere, the first buds of a national expression amidst a people who had lived centuries without literature. We have already spoken of Magón. But the creator of the realist novel was JOAQUÍN GARCÍA MONGE (1881–1958). In *The Landmark* (*El Moto*, 1900), his first novel and furthermore, the first significant novel in Costa Rican letters, he weaved the adverse loves between peasants on a loom of social customs, with the joys and suffering of the people. Also dated 1900 is his novel *The Daughters of the Fields* (*Las hijas del campo*) which looks into the city and its problems. Dated 1917 are his short stories, *The Evil Shadow and Other Events* (*La mala sombra y otros*

Spanish-American Literature: A History

sucesos), perhaps his best work because of the reproduction, at times naturalistic, of social customs and language of the peasants.

Panama: SALOMÓN PONCE AGUILERA (1868–1945), situated between Spanish realism and French naturalism, left a collection of sketches of peasant customs: *The Clods* (*De la gleba*, 1914).

(3) *Antilles* / Without hesitation one could mention a dozen narrators in the Antilles. We shall pause only before those who did not exceed their quota of blunders.

Cuba: First, JESÚS CASTELLANOS (1879–1912). He published various stories under the title *The Conspiracy* (*La conjura*, 1909). The first proposes a thesis: there is a social "conspiracy" to destroy all superior, idealistic, noble individuals, here symbolized by the physician Augusto Román. The physician lives in Havana with a hospital nurse, a voluptuous girl, of animal sensuality. He would like a university chair in order to devote himself to scientific investigations. Social conventions bring pressure upon him to abandon his mistress. Augusto, out of goodness, refuses to do so. He is not given either the chair, or the position as director of the hospital. He also loses the opportunity to marry a rich girl. When he realizes his mistress is a prostitute, he decides to become a cynic and yield to social conventions. Quite superior to *The Conspiracy* is *The Heroine* (*La heroina*). Here there is no thesis on which to waste the story. With a careful prose, in which good images flash, and with a vivid and continuous narrative rhythm, he has drawn an intimate episode in the life of the well-to-do Cuban bourgeoisie. The ironic tone is the best in the novelette. Of naturalist parentage are Carrión and Loveira, both of them notable. MIGUEL DE CARRIÓN (1875–1929), with an attitude that emulated that of the scientistic psychologist, he dissects the personality of a woman in *The Honorable Woman* (*Las honradas*, 1918). CARLOS LOVEIRA (1882–1928) anarchical-unionist in his fight for labor, learned in literature what he could from Zola and diagnosed social ills in various novels: *The Immoral Ones* (*Los inmorales*, 1919), *Generals and Doctors* (*Generales y doctores*, 1920), *The Blind* (*Los ciegos*, 1923), *The Last Lesson* (*La última lección*, 1924) and the best, *John Doe* (*Juan Criollo*, 1928). In this way he documented the last years of the Colony and the first years of the Republic, but his capacity for observation was counteracted by his incapacity to compose well-structured stories with clearly drawn characters. In him the social material overrides the psychological creation. Others are ARTURO MONTORI (1878–1932), with scenes of social customs, and LUIS RODRÍGUEZ EMBIL (1880–1954), who was still writing historical novels.

Dominican Republic: TULIO MANUEL CESTERO (Dominican Republic, 1877–1954) learned to write so well in the Modernist school that he could have become a neat miniaturist. And, in effect, his preciosity (influenced by D'Annunzio's) was registered in several books. But fortunately he cultivated the short story and went from psychological analysis (*Blood of Spring* [*Sangre de primavera*, 1908]) to the description of Dominican life (*Romantic City* [*Ciudad romántica*, 1911]). His novel *Blood* (*La sangre*, 1915) is the best he wrote and, undoubtedly, one of the best novels of the period. He subtitled it "a life under tyranny." The life in question is that of a Quixotic teacher and journalist, Antonio Portocarrero; the tyranny, that of Ulises Heureaux, who was assassinated in 1899. The action runs from 1899 to 1905 in the chaotic period that followed Heureaux' assassination. The "life under tyranny" refers then, to the chapters in which Portocarrero, from his prison cell, evokes the days of his childhood and adolescence. Consequently, there are two temporal dimensions: the inspection of the present and the retrospection of the past. And it is in the examination of the present, from 1899 to 1905, that Portocarrero's characters come out in relief. This deliberate structure of the novel facilitates psychological analysis. In many other Hispanic-American novels this type of intellectual and political hero who fails because he does not know how or does not wish to come to an agreement with reality has been presented. But Cestero, though he sympathizes with his hero, humanizes him, permeates him, and describes him with shades and lights. He gives us, then, a double exposure: external, the Dominican Republic, and internal, the life of an unadaptable. The prose also shows Cestero's preoccupation with construction: he punches out his phrases in classical molds (seventeenth-century classical) and in modern molds (Modernism of the beginning of the twentieth century). Naturalism and estheticism scuffle along together.

MANUEL DE JESÚS TRONCOSO DE LA CONCHA (1878–1955) was the most fertile and spontaneous collector of the traditions and anecdotes of national life: *Dominican Narrations* (*Narraciones dominicanas,* 1946). RAFAEL DAMIRÓN (1882–1956), poet, playwright, depicter of customs, and novelist in a series of reconstructions of the conflicts in contemporary political history, beginning with *On Caesarism* (*Del cesarismo,* 1911) up to *The Political Boss's Wife* (*La cacica,* 1944). This last one is a psychological study of a strong and evil woman. HAIM LÓPEZ PENHA (1878) wrote *Renaissance* (*Renacimiento,* 1942), a novel on the customs of the contemporary city. ARTURO FREITES ROQUE (1874–1914), satirized political intrigues in *Relentless* (*Lo inexorable,* 1911).

Puerto Rico: Between Matías González García, of whom we have already spoken, and MIGUEL MELÉNDEZ MUÑÓZ (1884), a group of short story writers and novelists formed, which was alert to popular customs and to the social problems of the island. One of them was ANA ROQUÉ DE DUPREY (1883–1933).

(4) *Venezuela* / We have already alluded to the artistic currents of Venezuelan narrative. In the other current, the realist, we must place RUFINO BLANCO-FOMBONA (1874–1944). His first verses were produced at the Modernist still; but what attracted him to this style was only the exaltation of violent personalities, for that is what he was, a violent person. He used to say that he felt "closer to the Romantics, even when I never withdraw from the truth that I see." He reproached the Modernists for their softness, their exoticism, their ardor for imitation, their

blindness to things of America. It is certain that he occupied himself more with America than other Modernists in his work as a political and critical pamphleteer and as a historian; but his work of pure literary creation did not turn out as well as his program for an original American art had promised. His true merit rests on his *American Stories* (*Cuentos americanos,* 1904)—augmented in the edition entitled *Minimal Dramas* (*Dramas mínimas,* 1920)—and in novels such as *The Man of Iron* (*El hombre de oro,* 1915), *Mitre in Hand* (*La mitra en la mano,* 1927). Unfortunately, even here he only showed the knack for writing novels, and not the novels that can be achieved with this knack. He left caricatures, not characters. His political passions, his satirical intentions, his pride in being instinctive and barbaric, his journalistic techniques applied to art deteriorated his creative vision. If he is called a "realist" it is to contrast him with the preciosity of other narrators. In reality, Blanco-Fombona unbosomed his feelings too much to be an objective narrator. He was obsessed by the stupidity, the evilness, and sordidness of people (even he himself was not a man of exemplary morals) and when he was not deforming reality with his diatribes, he impoverished it with sex. *The Man of Gold,* for example, is not a good novel. The title refers to Irurtia, a miserly person and a usurer, who becomes the Venezuelan Minister of the Interior. It contains spry, sarcastic pages, but the novel, as a whole, is not spry. Its worst defect is its inverisimilitude. If it were a farce it would not matter, since a farce is based on a forced situation. But this is half a farce. Further, it intends, without achieving it, to be a novel of psychological analysis of the characters Irurtia, Rosaura, Olga, Andrés. The reader feels unsatisfied because neither the farcical tone nor the psychological tone is pure. There is in Blanco-Fombona a conflict between his psychological view of man and his moral-sociological judgment of man. He is better endowed to do the latter because his was a polemical, reforming, aggressive talent. But he did not succeed in the selection of the narrative genre. In the prolog to *Minimal Dramas* he confessed his philosophy (or his ill-humor): "I have discovered always and everywhere the same: an identical well of stupidity, evil and suffering." Unfortunately, his "minimal dramas" don't even express this misanthropy well, because as he arranged them, the material gives way in his hands. He wanted to inform the reader of what he had seen, heard, or lived, rather than surprise him with new situations and unexpected endings. In his later years he tried to renovate his narrative technique. *The Secret of Happiness* (*El secreto de la felicidad,* 1935) is, rather than a novel, the outline of a novel, with political schemes, and a schematic prose. But it does have innovating characteristics in the technical history of the genre. In short, though he did not leave any really powerful book, Blanco-Fombona left, on the whole, a fairly considerable work which interests us because of his human personality. In this sense, we enjoy the diary of his life, from 1906 to 1914, which he published in 1933 with the title *Road of Imperfection* (*Camino de imperfección*)—a diary which keeps uncovering an erotic, political, and literary mass of anecdotes, always vain, and at times brilliant. Another novelist: RAFAEL CABRERA MALO (1872–1936).

(5) *Colombia* / In Colombia the novel of national or regional atmosphere barely received any incentive from Modernism. It was born realist and continued being so. EMILIO CUERVO MÁRQUEZ (1873–1937), although he wrote *Phinées* (1913), a novel of the time of Christ (similar to Sienkiewicz' *Quo Vadis?*), left narrations of more significance. CLÍMACO SOTO BORDA (1870–1919) described the social milieu of his time with some naturalist touches: *Diana the Huntress* (*Diana Cazadora*). JESÚS DEL CORRAL (1871–1931) wrote *Stories and Chronicles* (*Cuentos y crónicas*) with a witty feeling for local anecdote, as can be seen in "Let the sawer go by" ("*Que pase el aserrador*"). But the narrator with most substance was Francisco Gómez Escobar, who signed his works EFE GÓMEZ (1873–1938). He stood out in the short story and the short novel: *My People* (*Mi gente*, 1936), *Crude Souls* (*Almas rudas*, posthumous) are titles that declare the theme of his literature, which was to paint—better than anyone else in his country had done—the life of farm workers, miners and the down-and-out. He was most interested in man, and for his plots he selected situations where man's failures were due to accidents, injustice, madness, and vice. His stories, collected in several volumes, were the first in Colombia to delve into the psychology of the characters. The linguistic naturalism of many of the regionalist writers of this generation was a bad habit; though not always. There is at least one good short story in this genre: "The Machete" by JULIO POSADA (1881–1947), a story told in the first person by a farm laborer who arrives, looking for work, at a farm. He relates how he found work, how he fell in love with Pachita, how he became friends with the Negro, how the Negro taught him to sport his machete, how the Negro was in love with the same girl, and how the Negro and peon fenced, progressively becoming better friends, while Pachita ran away with another man. In order to carry his linguistic naturalism to an extreme, Posada published the story, not in printer's type, but with manuscript plates, and in a phonetic orthography.

(6) *Ecuador* / To the antecedents of Ecuadorian realism already mentioned—Luis A. Martínez and Manuel J. Calle, who also wrote a novel, *Carlota*—we should add EDUARDO MERA (1871–1913), not so much for his travel book, *From Distant Lands* (*De lejanas tierras*), but for certain jocular stories.

(7) *Peru* / The most vigorous realist narrator was ENRIQUE LÓPEZ ALBUJAR (1872). More than short stories, his were notes on highland life, with a deep understanding of the indigenous soul, and a spirit of protest and reform against injustices: *Andean Stories* (*Cuentos andinos*, 1920), *New Andean Stories* (*Nuevos cuentos andinos*, 1937) and, less significant, those in *The Charitable Acts of Mrs.*

Tardoya (Las caridades de la Señora Tardoya). He also has a novel: *Matalaché,* a social criticism and documentation of the life of Negro slaves on the great planta- tions. He was not one of those indigenous narrators who, in their desire to defend the Indian, end up by reducing him to the skin of an abstraction. Rather, he was interested in the inner life, even the psychosis, of the Indian. ANGÉLICA PALMA (1883–1935) Clemente's sister, Ricardo's daughter, wrote novels in a minor key in a Spanish realist vein. *Romantic Colonial Days (Coloniaje romántico,* 1921), a "novel of historical evocations," takes place in Lima, from 1705 to 1729, though its central episode is in 1709 and deals with the awakening of a love affair that would have ended in adultery had it not been interrupted by the death of the Viceroy Castell-dos-Rius, at whose literary coteries the lovers used to meet. A little more interesting is the description of these literary parties. Literature within literature.

(8) *Bolivia* / ALCIDES ARGUEDAS (1879–1946) made his debut with an Indianist novel, *Wata-Wara,* 1904, later recast as *Race of Bronze (Raza de bronce),* and with a novel of the city, *Creole Life (Vida criolla,* 1905), but he incorporated himself into the roster of great Hispanic-American novelists with just one book: *Race of Bronze* (1919). This novel, divided into two parts, develops in a continuous time sequence. Its action, however, is broken into loose episodes: voyages, adventures, sketches of local customs, scenes of heavy work, struggles with nature, vices, illnesses, deaths, ethnographic notations with pagan and Christian ceremonies, a parade of multiple characters, reflections and discussions. The plot becomes more solid when he relates the loves of Agustín and Maruja, their suffering, the abuses heaped upon the Indians by the Creole landowners and their mestizo servants; and it is interweaved with threads of fire and blood when the brutal Pantoja kills Maruja, and Agustín and his family avenge the killing. Actually, there is no characterization: the indigenous community is the protagonist. The first part begins at a pastoral gait and with idyllic promises; but suddenly the novel veers toward an abominable reality, and the second part, after several pages of history and sociology, becomes an angry denunciation of the cruelty with which the "whites"—including the priest—vent their brutality on the Indians. Arguedas narrates from outside, in the third person. Constantly he intervenes with moralizing and political judgments—at times he puts his thoughts in the mouth of Suárez, a Modernist poet and reader of Gorki, who compares the misery of the natives with that of the Russian muzhiks. Less convincing, artistically speaking, is the oratory in the mouths of the Indians. The prose, always carefully wrought, tends to be poetic, above all in the beautiful passages. These poems in prose do not disharmonize the somber picture: Arguedas' Modernism is sufficiently ample to accept naturalist procedures.

JAIME MENDOZA (1874)–"the Bolivian Gorki," as Darío called him–threaded an album of loose scenes about the miserable life of the mines: *In the Lands of Potosí* (*En las tierras de Potosí*, 1911). And DEMETRIO CANELAS (1881), in *Stagnant Waters* (*Aguas estancadas*, 1911) made his characters live in well-sounding and well-produced dialogs. In contrast to both, the Bolivian ABEL ALARCÓN (1881) preferred the historical novel of Inca times (*In the Court of Yáhuar-Huácac* [*En la corte de Yáhuar-Huácac*, 1915]), or of colonial times (*Once Upon a Time* [*Era una vez*, 1935]).

(9) *Chile* / JOAQUÍN DÍAZ GARCÉS (1877–1921), known by his pseudonym "Angel Pino," was a short story writer with a preference for the humoristic aspect of the customs of peasants, laborers, soldiers, and bandits: his novel, *The Voice of the Torrent* (*La voz del torrente*), although disordered, has life. JANUARIO ESPINOSA (1879–1946) was a novelist of the middle class, though his best work, *Cecilia*, takes place in the country. GUILLERMO LABARCA HUBERTSON (1883–1954) continues to be read, because of the stories in *Watching the Ocean* (*Mirando al océano*, 1911). OLEGARIO LAZO BAEZA (1878) specialized in *Military Stories* (*Cuentos militares*) and was more interested in psychology than in the external situations; he wrote a novel, *The Last Gallop* (*El postrer galope*). TOMÁS GATICA MARTÍNEZ (1883–1943) novelized the "great world," his intent being one of social criticism. Others: VÍCTOR DOMINGO SILVA (1882–1960), TANCREDO PINOCHET (1880–1957).

(10) *Paraguay* and (11) *Uruguay* / Farther on we shall discuss the narrative of these countries.

(12) *Argentina* / Neither ALBERTO GHIRALDO (1874–1946) nor MANUEL UGARTE (1878–1951) was typical of the Argentinian realists of these years. Both were literarily in debt to Modernism; and when they approached reality it was more as politicians than as writers. The best of all in this realist category was Lynch.

BENITO LYNCH (1880–1951) was one of the few popular novelists. He cuts out a piece of land, populates it with men and women, invents a plot rich in human and psychological conflicts, and then makes us believe that what he is relating is real. The characters speak as Argentinians do in real life, in the dialect of the Río Plata region; and if they are Europeans, they speak their jargon. The landscape, the characters, and the situation that motivates their lives form a solid unity. At no time is one aspect overcharged at the expense of another. Lynch will not yield to the temptation of entertaining poetizations of nature, of dense studies of characters or of social theses. His virtues as a landscapist, as a psychologist, or as a connoisseur are manifested with notable conciseness: in evocative metaphors, in details that reveal the insides of souls, in rapid allusions to the ills of rural Argentine society. Minimum touches, in short, that invite the reader to collaborate imaginatively in the progression of the novel. The progression of the novel –this is what worries Lynch. Even descriptive passages (for example, the admirable description of the fire in *Rachel* [*Raquela*]) function

in the service of the story. The mental agitation of the characters
abets the action and creates surprising denouements, as in *Palo verde:*
a man kills another; the law protects him; with a single word in court
he could save himself; but, confused, he does not utter it and is condemned. Lynch reduces everything to dynamic lines. From here stems
his preference for truculent and brutal effects which accelerate the
action and leave the reader in suspense. He had the knack of country
novels, but when he attempted city novels the outcome was not as
happy. His definite appearance in letters dates back to *The Vultures
of the Florida Ranch* (*Los caranchos de la Florida,* 1916), a history of
violent hatreds and loves. *Rachel* (1918) showed another side of Lynch
—the comical. After *The Evasion* (*La evasión,* 1922) and *The Ill-Muted
Women* (*Las mal calladas,* 1923) Lynch wrote his masterpiece—*The
Englishman of the Bones* (*El inglés de los güesos,* 1924). It deals with
an English anthropologist who arrives on the pampa to excavate Indians' bones; he takes lodgings on the humble ranch of a peon; Balbina,
the peon's daughter, falls in love with him and, for a while, it seems
that the Englishman will also yield to love; but when his investigations
are over, the gentlemanly, kindly, cold, and selfish Mr. Gray says good-
by and leaves; the girl hangs herself. The plot, skeletonized in this
fashion, gives no idea of the interior complexity of the novel: the local
color, the well-delineated customs, the spicy rural language, and the
deft weaving of circumstances and events are at the service of the keen
observation of the awakening of love. In the two novelettes that followed (*The Mistress' Whim* [*El antojo de la patrona*] and *Palo verde,*
1925) Lynch created characters possessing more inner life and, consequently, was better able to display his talents as a psychologist. Thirteen short stories appeared in 1931 with the title *Buenos Aires Countryside* (*De los campos porteños*). Two years later Lynch brought all of
his works to a close with *The Romance of a Gaucho* (*El romance del
gaucho*). It does not have the narrative energy of *The Vultures of the
Florida Ranch* nor of *The Englishman of the Bones.* Notwithstanding,
it was his most ambitious novel. The story of a love between a gaucho
and a refined married woman lent itself to a slow, deep and ample
psychological treatment. Lynch let an authentic gaucho speak his own
language, and it is the story of the gaucho that we read. Only Lynch,
within the Argentine novel, has been capable of that linguistic deception: the vernacular dialect in which *The Romance of a Gaucho* is
related is somewhat genuine and yet it has esthetic dignity. The author,
in a transport of sympathy and imagination, makes himself a gaucho
and tells a story in his voice and in his dialect.

Another representative realist was MANUEL GÁLVEZ (1882–1962). The great quantity of writing he did with an eye turned toward commercial success lowered his quality as a writer, which was high in the realist novels: *The Normal School Teacher* (*La maestra normal,* 1914), *The Shadow of the Convent* (*La sombra del convento,* 1917), and *Nacha Regules* (1918). We prefer *Metaphysical Anguish* (*El mal Metafísico,* 1916). He surprised the literary life of Buenos Aires at the turn of the century. His portraits are so similar to the models that one recognizes them: they are no less than Almafuerte, Ingenieros, Florencio Sánchez, Ghiraldo, Gerchunoff, David Peña, and many, many others. Novels on bohemian life already existed: the newness of Gálvez was to describe Modernist circles with a non-Modernist technique. Hence, some dissonance: his protagonist Carlos Riga represents the Romantics' and the symbolists' idea of a poet. Riga's calling is almost religious. He is dreamy, disdainful of the masses, unadaptable, sick, distraught over the social incomprehension of a young and materialistic country. Gálvez, who sympathizes with the "metaphysical anguish" of purely esthetic contemplation, writes, however, without zeal. There is dissonance, then, between the aristocratic ideal of Riga and the ideal of a democratic novel of Gálvez. Between 1914 and 1938, the dates of *The Normal School Teacher* and *Men in Solitude* (*Hombres en soledad*), respectively, he published seventeen novels. After ten years of wandering through history and memoirs, he returned to his career as a novelist with works on the Rosas epoch (a cycle of five novels) and on contemporary life, including the last days of Perón (*Tránsito Gúzman,* 1956). Whoever is interested in the theme of the autonomous characters and in the form of the interior duplication of the story (with illustrious Spanish antecedents: Galdós, Unamuno, etc.) may enjoy perhaps *The Two Lives of Poor Napoleon* (*Las dos vidas del pobre Napoleón,* 1954). The more Gálvez insisted on his Catholicism the more watered-down his art became. In his best novels he knows how to overcome his major defect, namely, the weaving of episodes, details, and useless digressions into the story; but his characters are not in good relief because he does not emboss well. Others: the regionalist EDUARDO ACEVEDO DÍAZ, JR. (1882), author of *Ramón Hazaña;* and MATEO BOOZ (1881–1943).

2. Essay

Due to positivism, philosophical interest became generalized, and in this respect we have already seen the work of Varona, Hostos, and others. Now we shall study the emergence of the refuters of positivism.

Nevertheless, this philosophical movement, imported from Europe but well accommodated to the social needs of Hispanic-American countries, continued its domination everywhere for some time. Spencer and Stuart Mill were the most frequent sources; somewhat less, Comte. Positivism made us respect the sciences, extricated psychology from metaphysics, promoted sociology, gave experimental solidity to investigative studies, systematized observations, applauded clear reasoning, invited progress, affirmed an autonomous ethics, practiced liberalism. Later, when it reached its exhaustion in Europe, positivism became incarnated in one of the most talented thinkers of this generation: José INGENIEROS (Argentina, 1877–1925). He is more important in a history of philosophic ideas than in a history of literature, but he has the right to be studied here as well, because of his influence on literary groups and for the occasionally Modernist adornment of his prose. He was the staunchest exponent of a philosophy founded on science. His outlook was more scientistic than positivist, since he admitted the possibility of a Metaphysic, though only as a transitory hypothesis constantly corrected by the progress of empirical knowledge. Despite the fact that for him biology was at the base of psychology, and that upon the latter all cultural disciplines were constituted, José Ingenieros raised an inspiring ethics, the reason being that at the bottom of positivism, even after it had fallen into disuse as a theory, there was an honest desire for investigation, for betterment, for justice, for truth, for faith in the rationality of man.

In Hispanic-America the animators of worthy liberal and socialist movements were positivists. In contrast, many of their adversaries profited by anti-positivist polemics in order to deny the achievements of free examination and even the liberal and non-ecclesiastical history of our countries. In the name of a spiritualism which, were it to be lightly scratched, would reveal the old dogmatic color under the varnish, those so-called anti-positivists were preparing the absolutist Catholic reaction which later was to threaten political freedom. Some of the first reactions against positivism in the field of philosophy have already been mentioned: Deústua, Korn. But, outside the field of philosophy, others had reacted earlier. Modernism spiritualized discursive prose, and one can even say that it initiated a spiritualist philosophical movement.

As we have said already, in the second half of the nineteenth century the natural sciences had imposed themselves as a model of all knowledge, but in the later years determinism ceded ground before heavy polemical attacks. Its basis was scientific systematization: epistemology yanked its base away. As the books on European positivism arrived late in America, so did the books on European anti-positivism. What dominated in Hispanic-America was positivism in action, diffused, evolved from the practical necessities of our social life. The classical positivism that was known was that of Comte and Spencer, with some Stuart Mill and a lot of reading of Renan and Taine.

The attempts at a new positivist epistemology in Europe—Avenarius, Mach, Vaihinger—had no echo here; the ideas of Nietzsche and of William James would arrive later. It is not at all strange, then, that the first sign of the crisis of positivism would appear in Hispanic-American letters before it appeared in university classrooms. The esthetics of Modernism implied a repudiation of the mechanical theory of life. Art was a refuge, a faith, a liberation where nothing was repeated, where nothing was explainable with the logic of the physicist. Alejandro Korn, whose idealistic philosophy of a creative freedom has already been alluded to, has related how the reading of Darío's *Azure* led him, from idea to idea, to a new philosophic current that put the accent on the spirit.

José Enrique Rodó / The thinker who best fused the literature of Modernism with spiritualism was JOSÉ ENRIQUE RODÓ (Uruguay, 1871–1917). The culture of his adolescence and youth was that of a humanist: classical Greeks, Romans, and moderns (Plato, Marcus Aurelius, Montaigne, Renan). This humanism made him restless, anxious for spiritual exaltation, so that on receiving the influence of the positivists of the nineteenth century he did not carry the naturalism implicit in them to an extreme. Comte and Spencer as a basis, and later, Taine, Renan, and Guyau, constituted his positivist readings. But from them he only borrowed material with which to cement his conception of the spirit: at the pinnacle of his building he kept a banner that fluttered to the anti-positivist winds of Main de Biran, Renouvier, Boutroux, and Bergson. His anti-positivism was not polemical, nevertheless. He always respected rational and experimental knowledge of reality, except that he adjusted it with an active idealism. Rodó's idealism was neither metaphysical nor epistemological, but axiological. That is, he saw man raising himself from nature and striving toward certain ideals, toward the values of good, truth, justice, and beauty. And these ideals and values derived from the dynamic and creative life. The world was real, man was real, and human ideals were real. Rodó believed in reason, but as a function of life. Non-vital reason, he used to say, falsifies our knowledge of reality: only vital reason reveals the meaning of the world. He was not, then, an irrationalist, although he admitted, especially in artistic creation, intuition—intuition which for Rodó was "the occult, constructive power of nature, which operates in the mind without the interference of reflection." His conception of the world harmonized the complex interior unity of man with the complex exterior unity of the universe; and in the depth of that harmony he felt the strength of a powerful love for form.

The universe for him had one purpose. The omission of Rodó in the histories and anthologies of ideas, prepared by professors of philosophy, is unjust. Read the essay, "New Directions," in *Próspero's Watchtower* (*El mirador de Próspero*), which he dedicated to Carlos Arturo Torres' *Idola Fori* in 1910, and you will discover one of the earliest and most lucid analyses that has been written in the Spanish language on the crisis of positivism. His first important work was *Ariel* (1900). After the war of 1898 between the United States and Spain, Rodó became apprehensive of American imperialism. Preoccupied over the growth of the United States at the expense of Spanish America but without limiting himself to the political theme, Rodó wrote *Ariel*, which won him international prestige and gave him extraordinary influence in the moral formation of the youth of Hispanic America. Unfortunately some readers reduced *Ariel* to a scheme that discredits its purpose: for these readers Ariel versus Calibán symbolizes Hispanic-America versus Anglo-America, spirit versus technics. Reducing the book to such a scheme does not make it appear to be a call for mental, spiritual, and physical effort, but rather a school for conformists. If our countries, backward, ignorant, underfed, subjected to foreign capital, barren, stunted, traditionalist and anarchical had, in spite of this, a spirituality superior to that of the United States, we could consider ourselves satisfied. There is nothing of this sort in *Ariel*. From the point of view of the call to work, *Ariel* continues the series of other books favorable to the United States—those of Sarmiento, for example. The United States theme is only an accident, an illustration for a thesis on the spirit. To contrast the two Americas and to launch a political manifesto were so far from Rodó's intention that *Ariel* was not an anti-imperialist work. He makes allusion only to moral imperialism not so much exercised by the United States as by the desire of imitation on the part of Spanish America. He was criticized precisely for having neglected the problem of economic imperialism, contrary to Manuel Ugarte, Blanco-Fombona, Alfredo L. Palacios. But Rodó did not intend to treat this subject.

The United States is an example, not a theme of the essay. What he wanted was to contrast spirit and matter. It was a moral, idealistic essay which anticipated his masterpiece, *The Motifs of Proteus* (*Motivos de Proteo*), written from 1904 to 1907 and published in 1909. In this work also, Rodó proposes to describe the soul in its essential unity and to point out the dangers of mutilating it by excessive specialization. What theory of the mind did Rodó have? What was his metaphysics of the spirit? Above all one notices a veering (even more: a reaction) away from the atomistic, mechanistic, explicative psychology that had been dominant during positivism. Rodó, with or without Bergson's influence, affirmed the temporality of psychic life. We participate, he says, in the universal process; but, in addition, we have our own individual time. From this double temporality of our lives he draws his dynamic "ethics of becoming" (*"ética del devenir"*): "This continuous transformation is imposed upon us as a necessity; but it serves as a frame in which free and rational energy is evident." If we do not take the initiative at each change in ourselves, our personality will vanish into the world of matter. Our personality is programmatic, prospective, teleological. Its meaning is revealed to us in our vocations. And in this way Rodó continues his admirable airing of the theme. The outside appearance of the *Motifs* is fragmentary. The variety of forms used—the parable, the poem in prose, the analysis, the theoretical speculation, the anecdote—contributes also to this mosaic appearance. There is in it, nevertheless, a dialectics. The perspective of *The Motifs of Proteus* is so broad, so open, that it gives unity even to the pages that were left scattered and collected afterwards: *The Road to Paros* (*El camino de Paros*, 1918); *New Motifs of Proteus* (*Nuevos motivos de Proteo*, 1927); and *The Last Motifs of Proteus* (*Los últimos motivos de Proteo*, 1932). Moreover, his ideas were coming to completion in his essays on apparently non-philosophic themes, for example, the admirable *Próspero's Watchtower*, 1913. He was a thinker; he was also an artist. His prose benefited from both talents. The sentences are juxtaposed, coordinated, and subordinated to a dignified, serene, noble, and highly finished architecture. All is harmonious and beautiful. A cold prose, of course, the coldness of marble—or better, the coldness of Parnassian forms—but perfect. He was very imaginative, though his imagination accepted discipline. No one, during the Modernist period, has described the process of creative writing better than he. As an acute literary critic, he did it on behalf of other writers, but he also spoke to us of his own passion for the beauty of style in "The Genesis of Form" (in *Próspero's Watchtower*) and in "A Single Force in the Depths of the Universe" (in *The Last Motifs of Proteus*). In a list of the ten best writers of Hispanic-America the name of Rodó would be indispensable.

Other Essayists / Mexican positivism had a solid doctrinaire consistency and was prevalent from 1860 to the beginning of the twentieth century, until the *Ateneo de la Juventud* rallies to its standard with William James, Boutroux, and Bergson and declares war on it. In this *Ateneo* the voices of José Vasconcelos, Antonio Caso, and Pedro Henríquez Ureña were heard. José Vasconcelos (1881–1959) has written short stories—*The Citation* (*La cita*, 1945)—theater—*Prometheus, the Victor* (*Prometeo vencedor*, 1920); *The Kidnappers* (*Los robachicos*, 1946)—memoirs—*Creole Ulysses* (*Ulises criollo*, 1935); *The Storm* (*La tormenta*, 1936); *The Proconsul* (*El proconsulado*, 1939); *The Disaster* (*El desastre*, 1946); *The Flame* (*La flama*, posthumously). These would suffice to give him fame. He was outstanding, however, as a thinker, in a series of massive volumes. *Study of Everything* (*Todología*, 1952) is the recasting of a philosophic system. The philosophic figure that influenced him most in his philosophizing was Schopenhauer. His subsequent conversion to Catholicism did not seal off this source, which continued to nourish him. Vasconcelos is an irrationalist. Human life is here for action. The world is also a product of an active principle that goes on achieving qualitative changes, from matter to spirit. But man organizes his life along the lines of an ethical conduct. Except that this ethics is transfigured into esthetics, because in acting man creates his own personality emotionally. Vasconcelos wishes to possess the reality of the world itself, in the individual and particular beings; and his organ of possession is esthetics and mystics.

ANTONIO CASO (1883–1946) took, as a point of departure, human existence in its most singular forms: life, which is basically biological and subject to a selfish economic principle, "maximum income with minimum effort," in man, is capable of enthusiasm and is exalted by an impartial art and a self-denying charity. Charitable sacrifice opens our eyes to a supernatural order: through the path of moral action we arrive at metaphysics and religion. Caso's Christian philosophy of existence is in no way affiliated with the Church. We will refer to Pedro Henríquez Ureña in the following chapter.

In Cuba, FERNANDO ORTIZ (1881).

In Puerto Rico: NEMESIO P. CANALES (1878–1923), the author of *Chit-chat* (*Paliques*, 1923).

In Venezuela: EDUARDO CARREÑO (1880–1956) and, above all, SANTIAGO KEY AYALA (1874–1959) who always distinguished himself for the refinement of his prose, although in contrast with the cosmopolitan Modernists, his preferred themes were those of his native city.

In Peru: FRANCISCO GARCÍA CALDERÓN (1880–1953).

In Paraguay: MANUEL GONDRA (1871–1927) and JUAN E. O'LEARY (1879).

Uruguay gave, in addition to Rodó, another great refuter of positivism and its fallacies, a professional philosopher: CARLOS VAZ FERREIRA (1873–1958). One of the most original and analytical minds of America, Vaz dealt with every theme —epistemology, logic, ethics, esthetics, pedagogy, politics—and in every case knew how to fuse theory and life as they exist in reality, with a rigorous investigation into the roots of problems. He was initiated as a thinker in positivism (closer to Stuart Mill than to Comte or Spencer), but the obvious rigor of systems did not satisfy him and he preferred fragmentary expression as in his amazing *Fermentario* (1938).

RICARDO ROJAS (Argentina, 1882–1951), a poet, short story writer, dramatist, essayist, historian, is one of the personalities of Argentine culture: this means that more importance is shown to his person than to his books. In 1923 he put together his *Poems* (*Poesías*), generally Romantic and belatedly visited by Modernism. His stories in *The Country of Jungles* (*El país de la selva*) describe myths and customs. In the theater he has presented *The Colonial House* (*La casa colonial*), *Elelín, the Salamander* (*La Salamandra*). His most monumental labors, however, are in the fields of the essay, criticism, and literary history.

C. THEATER

Now let us step into the theater. The Río de la Plata theater, first. The rustic drama, having jumped from the circus ring to the theater stage with Gutiérrez-Podestá's *Juan Moreira*, attracted new authors, and before long the initial theme—gaucho versus legal authority—formed with others a Creole braided lasso. Buenos Aires is now an active theatrical center. Spanish, French, and Italian companies bring in an international repertory. And thus the Río de la Plata theater begins to embellish itself with artistic intent. The gauchesque way continues (ELÍAS REGULES, OROSMÁN MORATORIO, VÍCTOR PÉREZ PETIT) and acquires a certain literary value with *Calandria* (1896) by MARTINIANO LEGUIZAMÓN and *Jesús Nazareno* (1902) by ENRIQUE GARCÍA VELLOSO (1881–1938). Neither *Calandria* nor *Jesús Nazareno* retraces the model of the sanguinary gaucho—the first character redeems himself through his work, the second one is a hero with a "message" in the manner of Echegaray's heavy dramas. Another deviation from the initial theme was that which, leaving behind the gauchesque drama in open plains, barbaric and violent, arrived at the domestic drama of the peasants. MARTÍN CORONADO (1850–1919) effected it in verse with *The Stone of Scandal* (*La piedra del escándalo*, 1902) and the second part, *Don Lorenzo's Farm* (*La chacra de don Lorenzo*, 1918). NICOLÁS GRANADA (1840–1915), in prose, gave a new twist to the rural theme: in *To the Fields!* (*¡Al campo!*, 1902) he showed a married couple (of farmers) living in Buenos Aires, and not until the third act did the pampa appear. Granada also cultivated the historical drama (*Atahualpa*, 1897), a genre in which DAVID PEÑA (1865–1928) excelled with *Facundo* (1906) and many others. The farce, which later will be the unending preference of the Río de la Plata theater public, lifted its head due to the efforts of CARLOS MAURICIO PACHECO (d. 1924) and ALBERTO NOVIÓN (1881–1937). The plays of the middle class came forth almost perfectly from the hands of GREGORIO DE LAFERRÈRE (1867–1913), with a vivid comic sense and sureness in the characterization of popular, saloon types. His first piece, *Jinx* (*Jettatore . . . !*, 1940), was elemental—he wanted to produce laughter through the exhibition of a mania. *The Crackpots* (*Locos de verano*, 1905) was more complex. Not one mania, but many, one for each character—and each character, introspective, comically hermetic, isolated from the others. The theme of *In Their Clutches* (*Bajo la garra*, 1906) was the ravages of calumny. Unfortunately Laferrère jumped suddenly from his satiric acts to the dramatically intense final act. His best work was *The Women of Barranco* (*Las de Barranco*, 1908), a play about shameful poverty, well constructed, well conceived, well described, with two literary creations, Doña María and Carmen, together with other vivid characters. With the example of serious theater offered to the Buenos Aires public by foreign companies, there were those who became oriented toward a theater of conflicts, problems, and theses—EMILIO BERISSO (1878–1922). We spoke of Payró elsewhere because he was essentially a narrator, not a dramatist, despite the fact that his *Tragic Song* (*Canción trágica*, 1902) was, along with the plays of Sánchez and Laferrère, one of the cornerstones of the Río de la Plata theater. We must stop for Sánchez, the greatest Hispanic-American theatrical author of this generation.

FLORENCIO SÁNCHEZ (Uruguay, 1875–1910) had seen the best theater of his time: above all the Italian companies—Novelli, Zacconi, Eleonora Duse—who brought to the Río de la Plata the dramatic repertory of Ibsen, Björnson, Sudermann, Bracco, Giacosa, Hauptmann, Tolstoi. Though not a scholar, he read authors of "advanced ideas," generally anarchists and socialists who influenced his conception of social life. His literary preference was the realism of the Russian novelists. His milieu was the bohemian life of journalists, of humble trades, and poor neighborhoods. His first play, *My Son the Doctor* (*M'hijo el dotor*, 1903), was an unripened fruit, but it came from a vigorous tree. It dealt with a rural reality like that of so many of the theatrical pieces of the day, except more colorful, fresh and lively, with a living character—the old Creole Don Olegario—and it had a serious purpose: to present to us in intense dialogs a conflict of souls, a set of values, a concept of life, of generations, of city and rural customs, all of which end in a crisis when Julio, the "doctor" son, seduces Jesusa and must answer for his action to Don Olegario. His next rural work, which was more ambitious and more successful, was *The Immigrant's Daughter* (*La Gringa*, 1904). A dialog of great realist strength evokes the Creole ranch, the general store, the immigrant's farm, the customs of the pampa; but this dialog is at the service of an allegory: the Italian immigrants invading the land of the gaucho and the birth of a promising Italo-Creole race. The gaucho Cantalicio and his son Próspero on one side, the Italian Nicola and his daughter Victoria, on the other. But the children, Próspero and Victoria, resolve the conflict with love and with the mingling of bloods in a new racial offspring. In this abstract scheme there are minor symbols, the *ombú* tree, for example, representing the strength of the pure Creole. Situations already dealt with in the theater of the day are repeated: the nationalistic resentment of the Creoles against the *gringos* or European immigrants. But the whole drama is directed toward the exaltation of the new Argentinian race.

Florencio Sánchez has respected the Creole and *gringo* points of view, both are equally legitimate. Cantalicio—gambler, loafer, drunkard, cantankerous, carefree, unreliable—and Nicola—stingy, distrustful—are salvaged through the son that Próspero has with Victoria. Just as Próspero and Victoria unite the Creole and *gringo* worlds through instinct, Horacio unites them intellectually, through his university culture. Horacio is the progressivist, the exemplary man, understanding, good, superior and dramatically empty, as were all "reasoners" of the nineteenth-century drama. Perhaps his mockery of Victoria's romanticism and his view of the Creole as being ugly are the most personal aspects of his character. The construction of *The Immigrant's Daughter* is lax. The drama takes place before our eyes: the spectator sees how Próspero's and Victoria's love begins and how Cantalicio's difficulties develop; but the presentation does not stir the spectator because the scheme is as foreseeable as a geometric theorem.

Florencio Sánchez closed his rural trilogy with *Down Hill* (*Barranca abajo*, 1905), the most somber tragedy of our theater. It does not offer a thesis: at most, it offers a problem, that of the divestiture of the lands of the old Creoles by an oligarchy armed with all the technicalities of the law and police authority. But here, Sánchez has wanted to dramatize not a social theme but the failure of an individual man. The family of Don Zoilo collapses beneath the blows of ill fortune, sickness, sordidness, the deceit of the petty lawyers, and the rot of low passions. It is a masterpiece that gains on stage because it is theater and not literature. Although realist in its dialog, truthful in its rural images and in its details of customs, it is artistically composed, in a crescendo of three acts beginning and ending with deliberate effect. Here, Sánchez dominated, as never before, his scenic art. In the first scene are the four women: the wife, the sister, and Don Zoilo's two daughters. The dialog is interrupted by the apparition of Don Zoilo, who crosses the stage in silence like a phantom, and then, after Robustiana, the good daughter, has left the stage, the three women who will precipitate his downfall speak. Suddenly, Martiniana, a literary descendant of the *Celestina,* another of the Fates, adds her voice to the chorus. Like a tragic chorus, the initial conversation of the women explains the past tragedy (Ibsen's retrospective method) and the crisis which, forebodingly, we are going to witness. The symbols are well chosen: when Zoilo is about to hang himself, the noose becomes entwined in the nest of an *hornero* bird. He struggles in vain to loosen it and exclaims: "God's doings . . . A man's nest is more easily torn apart than a bird's nest!"

The intense pauses in the dialog are more deeply piercing than the words themselves. This dramatist who had heard the speech of the humble people so much and so well knew the value of silence. With an admirable verbal economy he contrasts the animal desire of the landowner Juan Luis for Prudencia ("Come! Woman.") with the charitableness of Aniceto who proposes marriage to the tubercular Robustiana. Occasionally a few simple words loosen emotions, as when Don Zoilo, in scene 5 of Act III, says to Aniceto: "Did the cross stand up all right?"—the only allusion to the death of his daughter who had just been buried. The daughter's death was announced with an equally simple scenic detail: as the curtain rises in the third act, next to the door of the hut, the iron bedstead in which the tubercular had died is seen. They have taken it outdoors so that it might be cleansed by the sun. The prelude to Don Zoilo's suicide is of a sober and certain effectiveness from the moment the curtain is raised on that act. With a backdrop of misery, in front of the dead girl's bed, Don Zoilo is waxing the rope and whistling slowly. This whistling is the melody of death: he will whistle till the final moment. Don Zoilo is all character, with something of an old King Lear about him. A breath of solemn and universal poetry envelops *Down Hill*. The theme of the fall of the house of Zoilo is extended from the country to the city in two of Sánchez' best dramas: *The Family* (*En familia*) and *The Dead* (*Los muertos*), both of 1905. In the score of theatrical pieces he produced there are also farces, plays of suburban environment, and thesis plays *The Rights of the Healthy* (*Los derechos de la salud*, 1907), *Our Children* (*Nuestros hijos*, 1907). Realism triumphed with Sánchez; and he tasted triumph after triumph, which did not save him from the depths of poverty but gave him the intoxication of literary glory.

Other Río de la Plata playwrights and dramatists: PEDRO E. PICO (1882–1945), CÉSAR IGLESIAS PAZ (1881–1922), JOSÉ LEÓN PAGANO (1875), JULIO SÁNCHEZ GARDEL (1879–1937).

Nowhere in Hispanic-America was there another playwright like Florencio Sánchez. Nonetheless, Mexico offers interesting figures. MARCELINO DÁVALOS (1871–1923) is the author of dramas with naturalist themes, such as the hereditary transmission of alcoholism—*Guadalupe*, 1903—or of social matters—*And So They Pass* . . . (*Así pasan* . . . , 1908). And, more cultured and more of a writer, JOSÉ JOAQUÍN GAMBOA (1878–1931) who, after penning several plays, from *Solitude* (*Soledad*, 1899) to *The Day of Judgment* (*El día del juicio*), retired from the theater, only to return to it many years later with even more robust works: a social drama, *The Devil Is Cold* (*El diablo tiene frío*); a high society drama, *The Revillagigedo;* a comedy, *If Youth Knew* (*Si la juventud supiera*); and what appears to be his masterpiece: *The Gentleman, Death and the Devil* (*El caballero, la muerte, y el diablo*, 1931). In *The Same Case.* (*El mismo caso*, 1929) Gamboa tried ingenious novelties. He divided the stage in three parts—"comedy," "drama," "farce"—and in each one he presented the same theme with different denouements.

Other playwrights were EDUARDO CALSAMIGLIA (1880–1918), and JOSÉ FABIO GARNIER (1884), the most productive in Costa Rica. In Chile, VÍCTOR DOMINGO SILVA (1882–1960).

XII. 1910-1925

Authors born between 1885 and 1900

Historical framework: The social Revolution in Mexico opens a new political cycle in our history. In Argentina, new democratic social forces triumph over oligarchy. Effects of the First World War.

Cultural tendencies: The enthusiasm for Modernist artifice having mitigated, writers turn toward a simpler, more human, more American form of expression. There is a group which hurls itself into the adventures of cubism, futurism, creationism, and dadaism. Postwar magazines: "ultraism" and its dissolution.

As we approach our own era, the number of names becomes greater, facts become disputable, and the critical classifications become entangled. It is only natural—we have stopped writing history to write a chronicle. We must now refer to those who have been our own teachers, friends, and even students. These are the embarrassments of every criticism of contemporary—contemporary with the critic—letters. Outrageously, the critic acts in the capacity of both judge and judged. Without sufficient historical perspective it is difficult to place writers in hierarchical orders. Nor is there any room for individual studies. These are the years about which most has been written in our America. At the slightest laxness, the critic falls into mere cataloging.

Since World War I (1914–18) broke out in the middle of these years, some historians speak of prewar and postwar literary groups. But the Great War (in those days these two words did not sound like a hyperbole) was not an occurrence in Hispanic-American letters, but just a pair of field glasses which was used later to look at literature. A drama was being sought, and the effect of the war on literature was exaggerated, dramatically. It will not be denied that the war stirred up writers' minds. But a war is destructive, not constructive. And in the construction of Hispanic-American literature during those years, the forces did not come from the war, but from the spectacle of a culture that was changing rapidly. Nor is it even true that writers clustered together by age; rather, they were drawn together by mutual tastes.

Some writers, the conventional ones, remained loyal to academic letters. If they proposed some intercourse with external things, they would arrive at the last bastions of realism and naturalism and get no farther. If they proposed squeezing the inner pulp of things, all they needed was the wringer of impressionism and symbolism.

Other writers, the adventurous ones, undermined letters through revolutions. They were eccentric, ostentatious, extravagant. They dehumanized (or rehumanized) themselves in unexpected idiomatic and metaphoric pirouettes. They were the "fauvists," the "expressionists," the "cubists," the "futurists." Nonconformists, rebels, these impetuous writers joined those of the third group.

That is to say, they joined the irreverent ones, who inebriated literature and made it dance in the nude or disguised as a rag puppet on the pages of experimental periodicals. "Ultraism" was one of the names of this orgy. It lasted a short time: from 1919 to 1922. Then, the best of them will stop joking, not in their journals, but in books.

This variety of tastes appeared in prose as well as in verse but, naturally, it was more evident in verse than in prose. Why? Because verse is the vehicle of lyricism, and lyricism generally shows up the dominant mood of each poet. For this reason the inner unity of each writer shines through better in verse. Since literature in verse is less objective, less public, less intellectual, less technical than literature in prose, it reveals directly the tastes which gave it life. And, consequently, one can speak of poets of normal tastes, of abnormal tastes, of scandalous tastes.

In prose, on the other hand, these same tastes do not show through so directly. There are also normal, abnormal and scandalous prose writers. The normal prosists expound, realistically, like Rómulo Gallegos. The abnormal prose writers have a penchant for expressionism, like Alfonso Reyes. The scandalous prose writers are the ultraists, like Oliverio Girondo. But a classification of narrative, essay, and theater in these terms would not be very useful. Prose is a form which articulates thought, and thought is generally tied to a world outside the writer. For this reason a more sensible classification of prose would seem to be one based on whether it puts the accent on the subjective, impressionistic, imaginative, free world of the writer, or whether it puts the accent on the objective, real, verifiable world determined by circumstances. But even this classification of idealist or realist novels (or call them what you will) is not sufficiently convincing. One would have to study the principles operating in the construction of the novels: the point of view, the representation of time, the stream of consciousness, the technique, the treatment of themes, the style and the composition. But this cannot be done in groups, but must be done individually, and even novel by novel. A history like the present one cannot be a substitute for individual critical analysis. Since we cannot spin a thread as finely as we would in individual studies, there is no alternative in this history but to wind a thick yarn.

Nevertheless, we would like the reader to keep in mind at every moment the fluid nature of literary phenomena and its unclassifiable character.

How are we to classify, under verse or prose, the man who writes in both genres? So we shall say: "Mainly verse," "Mainly prose," at times placing a writer in one or the other section purely arbitrarily. The same applies to genres: narrative, essay, theater. The same authors may be narrators, essayists, and playwrights.

What shall be done, then, is to divide this chapter into three parts:

    A. The writers who stood out mainly in verse; and

    B. The writers who stood out mainly in prose.

    C. The playwrights.

The first will be grouped, in turn, according to three behaviors, three tastes:

    1. Normality.

    2. Abnormality.

    3. Scandal.

The writers of group B, "mainly prose," will be distributed in two genres:

    1. Novel and short story.

    2. Essay.

And the narrators will be classified into "more subjective than objective" and "more objective than subjective."

A. MAINLY VERSE

1. Normality

In the previous chapter it was seen how the authors who wrote during the height of Modernism (let's say Rubén Darío and his contemporaries) continued to write well into the twentieth century. Death, with its rigorous regularity, was making them relinquish their pens. By

1910 they were all consecrated, and almost all were exhausted. At least one of the poetic wells of the Modernists was drying up: the Parnassian, with its exterior, visual beauties of an artistic museum. Some (Darío, Nervo, González Martínez) were drawing from the symbolist well a deep, fresh, and serene liquid. Others (Leopoldo Lugones and José María Eguren) were explorers of verbal fountains of youth and became rejuvenated when surrounded by the admiration of the young writers. The latter, however, are not satisfied: to them will be reserved the task of making incoherence triumph. Rubén Darío, in spite of his cult to mystery, had been a clear poet. Had not the poetry from 1850 to 1880 been intelligible even in Baudelaire, Verlaine, and Mallarmé? It was true in the most hermetic and the most difficult. After all, when Darío's *Profane Prose* appeared, most of the French symbolists were turning toward a clear, limpid, timid, and even classical expression (Samain, Regnier, Moréas, Jammes). But at the moment when symbolism as an irrational poetry was languishing in France, some of the followers of the old masters, Baudelaire and Mallarmé, reactivated their desire to poetize the obscure: Maeterlinck, Gide, Claudel, Valéry. From this flank will come the expressionists, the cubists, the futurists, the dadaists, the surrealists. In 1910, when Hispanic-American Modernism is subsiding, the scandalous writers of Europe are beginning to rave. Darío met them, mentioned them, but paid no attention. Darío was born when Isidore Ducasse, the Count of Lautréamont, published *Les chants de Maldoror* (1868), but he died without taking note that through this channel would come the inundation of nonsense: Laforgue, Apollinaire, Réverdy, Jacob, and even Supervielle (in passing: Ducasse, Laforgue, and Supervielle were born in Uruguay). Not all the young men who entered literature in 1910 came in the same door. They were born together with the artistic verse and prose of the first Modernist group, that is, between the first Parnassian fruits of 1880 to the ripe *Profane Prose* of Darío in 1896. They grew up with this estheticist literature, in close relation with the books that had become famous, and wished to vie for this fame. The esthetic battle had already been won by their parents: there was no reason for it to be repeated or exceeded. They accepted as ordinary norms that once were extraordinary: the aristocratic function of poetry, knowing how to insinuate with a slight gesture, individualizing oneself with highly finished styles. They succumbed, however, to that "law of imitation" which does so much damage to Hispanic-American letters: imitation of European originals; imitation of Europeanists who managed to express themselves well; even mutual imitation. Due to the discipline of imitation, able poets impressed their contemporaries as being great poets. No one was moved by them, they did not illuminate themselves from within, but they did draw admiration with their cold art of versification and composition. Undistinquished cliques of poets, specializing in fashionable tricks, were convinced they stood at the pinnacle of a Parnassus. More than creative imagination, it was a selection of words, of rhythms, of decors copied in museums and libraries, of experiments the results of which were known beforehand. Many soldiers in dress uniform strolling by on festive days, few captains impassioned by inner combats. Nevertheless, some did exist.

It is impossible to classify the new poetry. Yet, if one hearkens to the best poets of this generation, he will hear distinctive strains.

Some poets turn to a more direct dealing with life and nature. They are simple, human, sober (Fernández Moreno).

Others have an air of wisdom about them, as if they have traveled far and have returned with many classical secrets (Alfonso Reyes).

Others, the most effusive, sincerely confess what is happening to them, their anguishes, their exaltations (Mistral, Sabat Ercasty, Barba Jacob).

There are those who have a sense of humor, as if the children suspected that there had been something ridiculous and sentimental in the family of traditional Modernists (José Z. Tallet).

There are the brainy, severe, circumspect, speculative ones (Martínez Estrada).

Or those devout souls (López Velarde).

And the Creolists, the nativists, those that embrace the land (Silva Valdés, Abraham Valdelomar).

And those having civil and political emotions (J. T. Arreaza Calatrava).

In view of the lack of space we can only pause before a few of these poets. They will be presented with their contemporaries, in national groups, from the Río Grande to Patagonia. This geographic grouping has no critical value; it is just convenient. It gives a rapid account of the minor poets; it places them. The reader will know where to find them. One has no need of guide maps to find the great poets.

(1) *Mexico* / In chapter X it was seen how the language was being rejuvenated with the first Mexican Modernist, Gutiérrez Nájera. It is the epoch of the *Revista Azul*. To the same period belong Salvador Díaz Mirón and Manuel José Othón, solitary travelers. In chapter XI the poets at the pinnacle of Modernism were seen: above all Amado

Nervo and those who were united by his *Revista Moderna*. Urbina, Tablada, Rebolledo, González Martínez, Rafael López, Argüelles Bringas, Manuel de la Parra were crepuscular Modernists. Urbina was a solitary figure. González Martínez was the great poet of the day. The poet who left the Modernist circle in order to seek new ways, and therefore influenced the youth born after 1900, was Tablada. In this chapter González Martínez still dominated the literary groups. But now the generation of the *Ateneo* emerges. In 1909, the *Ateneo de la Juventud* initiated an important renovation in Mexico. The elder poets of the *Ateneo* have been mentioned already: López, De la Parra, Colín, Gómez Robelo, Castillo Ledón, Cravioto. At the beginning of this period, which includes those born after 1885, the finest among the young writers was Alfonso Reyes, who will be studied separately.

A list of all these poets is long and will be of value only to the curious reader: Some went to the bottom during the Modernist shipwreck (JOSÉ DE J. NÚÑEZ Y DOMÍNGUEZ, 1887–1959; RODRIGO TORRES HERNÁNDEZ, 1889–1915; PEDRO REQUENA LEGARRETA, 1893–1918; ALFONSO TEJA ZABRE, 1888–1962) and others changed ship in the hope of reaching a port safely (JORGE ADALBERTO VÁZQUEZ, 1886–1959). Some sang the praises of life in the country (JESÚS ZAVALA, 1892–1957; MANUEL MARTÍNEZ VALADEZ, 1893–1935); LEOPOLDO RAMOS, 1898–1956), of religious sentiments (ALFONSO JUNCO, 1896), of evocations of dreams and memories (GENARO ESTRADA, 1887–1937; RENATO LEDUC, 1898) or of historic and civil themes (MIGUEL D. MARTÍNEZ RENDÓN, 1891); CARLOS GUTIÉRREZ CRUZ, 1897–1930; HONORATO IGNACIO MAGALONI, 1898). Others kept up the music of obscure symbolist melodies (JOSÉ D. FRÍAS, 1891–1936), and others analyzed all the effects of stimulated senses, or wanted poetry to be a feast of beautiful and sonorous words (DANIEL CASTAÑEDA, 1898–1957; VICENTE ECHEVERRÍA DEL PRADO, 1898). But toward 1922, the poet who undoubtedly attracted those who, up to then, had given their attention to González Martínez was López Velarde.

RAMÓN LÓPEZ VELARDE (Mexico, 1888–1921) wrote little: the sentimental verses of *Devout Blood* (*La sangre devota*, 1916), the sensual ones of *Anxiety* (*Zozobra*, 1919) and, posthumously, *The Sound of the Heart* (*El son del corazón*, 1932) which includes his best known poem, "Sweet Fatherland." There are other posthumous tomes: *The Minute Hand* (*El minutero*, 1923), prose of poetic value; *February's Gift* (*El don de febrero*, 1952), essays on diverse subjects; and the miscellaneous book *Poetry, Letters, Documents* (*Poesías, cartas, documentos*, 1952) and *Political Writings* (*Prosa Política*, 1953). We should not reduce López Velarde's stature because his lyrical work was not profuse; and we should not be deceived by the apparently elemental map of his poetic domain: the provinces, Catholicism, his loved one, juvenile anguish. In this domain, which seems so simple on the map, things are occurring that are strange, secretive, complex, and mysterious. For example, López Verlarde's religiosity has an erotic root and his "fearful yearning to intermingle earth and heaven" might scandalize his co-religionists; his love, which he declares to be an only one (love of Fuensanta), is shared by many women; his soft provincial landscapes, painted in a language without softness, in a severe gleaning of extravagant words, unexpected adjectives, and aggressive metaphors; his traditionalism, a screaming war against the commonplace. Yes, López Velarde had more spiritual complexity than his map of poetic themes leads us to believe. He gained in importance with the publication of *Devout Blood,* and even more in 1919 when *Anxiety* appeared. After the liquidation of Modernism, his work, brief and intense, is among the most enduring. He showed a desire for renovation, not a superficial renovation, but one of the inner substance of things—he dug deep into the subjective (his soul) and into the objective (Mexico's inner nature). His amorous inclinations are always present. In *Devout Blood* the two extremes of the love sentiment appear, the pure and ideal, directed toward Fuensanta, and the one of carnal temptation, which is most patent in *Anxiety,* his best book. There are verses here showing the poet submitting himself to love; but the most significant ones are those that reveal his disenchantment and even failure at not being able to satisfy the appetite of his senses or the spiritual communication with his beloved. In *The Sound of the Heart* he is more poised because the poet appears to have struck a balance in his spiritual development, but he is less intense. "Sweet Fatherland" speaks to us of his Mexican province, but the poet does not remain there: without leaving his own garden he visits the literary gardens of other literatures. This is curious "interior exoticism." His veneration for Leopoldo Lugones ("the most sublime, the most profound poet of the Castilian language," he used to say) explains his similarity to other poets of his day, also partisans of Lugones. The Lugones of *Sentimental Lunar Poems* had begun a school for Hispanic-Americans born during the years of the emergence of Modernism. López Velarde, as others, wanted to invent a language that would surprise with unusual images. The danger lay in affectation, in rhetoric, in verbal complexities that lose themselves in obscurity. López Velarde sensed the danger and withdrew in time—although they radiated surprises, his words respected the traditional character of the language and even the shading of the region in which it was born. His humble and even prosaic colloquialisms sallied out to meet the aristocratic verbal inventions, and they embraced happily. In spite of this, López Velarde might have fallen into mannerism, if it had not been for the very personal confessions he had to make. López Velarde conversed with himself, in the voice of the flesh and the voice of the spirit. For him the city was a place of violence and sin; the province, a nostalgic world. And López Velarde writes "Sweet Fatherland," which is not a poem by a country or city dweller, but by a solitary spirit who tenderly and ironically expresses mellow nostalgias and ironic distances. López Velarde, the most Mexican of poets of his generation, takes refuge in "Sweet Fatherland," the best civic poem of Mexico.

(2) *Central America / Guatemala:* Rafael Arévalo Martínez is outstanding, but he will be examined later. Another Guatemalan poet, of Modernist origin, is the battling FÉLIX CALDERÓN ÁVILA. Of later development, but still Modernist, is ALBERTO VELÁZQUEZ (1891).

Honduras: RAMÓN ORTEGA (1885–1932) was a simple poet, a Romantic varnished with Modernism. A writer who stood out in his day was ALFONSO GUILLÉN ZELAYA (1888–1947). He was also one of those who, after his Modernist capers, returned to simplicity: *The Almond Tree in the Patio (El almendro del patio).* He was the first in his country to write social poetry, as in the sonnet "Poet and Beggar." RAFAEL HELIODORO VALLE (1891–1959) published *Thirsting Amphora (Ánfora sedienta)* in 1922, which includes "Niña Lola's School," a delight of agile rhythms, images, and lyrical leaps. His ideal is simplicity, as evidenced by his celebrated composition "Jasmines."

El Salvador: Modernism embraced the poets here so strongly that it left them almost immobilized. First, the initiators CARLOS BUSTAMANTE (1891–1952) and JULIO ENRIQUE ÁVILA (1892). Among those who stand out are JOSÉ VALDÉS (1893–1934), the serene author of *Pure Poetry (Poesía pura,* 1923); RAÚL CONTRERAS (1896), who carried his Modernist devotion to the theater, in *The Princess Is Sad (La princesa está triste,* 1925), a scenic gloss of Darío's *"Sonatina."* The book *Mist (Niebla,* 1956), signed by Lydia Nogales, is Contreras' work. His last title, *Presence of Smoke (Presencia de humo,* 1959). ALBERTO GUERRA TRIGUEROS (1898–1950), a reflexive poet of deep Christian sentiments.

Nicaragua: After having given birth to Rubén Darío, Nicaragua needed a long and merited rest. One can speak, nevertheless, of two movements, both more or less Modernist. In the first we find the landscapist RAMÓN SÁENZ MORALES (1885–1926), the sober and Christian MANUEL TIJERINO (1885–1936), the disconsolate LUIS ÁNGEL VILLA (1886–1907), the solitary LINO ARGÜELLO (1886–1937), the anecdotic ATANASIO GARCÍA ESPINOSA (1886–1938), the gallant GABRY RIVAS (1888), the emotive CORNELIO SOSA (1886), the elegiac ARÍSTIDES MAYORGA (1889), the effusive JERÓNIMO AGUILAR CORTÉS (1889), the impressionist ANTONIO BERMÚDEZ (1889), the sentimental LUIS (1889–1938), and EDUARDO AVILÉS RAMÍREZ (1896) and the poetesses ROSA UMAÑA ESPINOZA (1886–1924), BERTA BUITRAGO (1886) and FANNY GLENTON (1887?). But the major figures were Alfonso Cortés, Azarías H. Pallais, and Salomón de la Selva. ALFONSO CORTÉS (1887) went mad, and his madness gave absurdity to his subtilizations of verses on such metaphysical themes as Time, and to his hallucinatory moods. AZARÍAS H. PALLAIS (Nicaragua, 1886–1954), a priest, sang in the *Witches of Flanders (Brujas de Flandes*) of his medieval, primitive, and ingenuous world. SALOMÓN DE LA SELVA (1893–1959) also lived a long time outside of his country. He wrote some of his poems in English. *The Unknown Soldier* (*El soldado desconocido,* 1922) was written in Spanish, during his Mexican period. If at times he seemed to approach vanguardism, on other occasions he returned to classicism, as in his *Evocation of Horace* (*Evocación de Horacio,* 1948). In the second Modernist movement, more or less from 1914 on, the conquest of flexibility in themes and meters is reinforced. Some of them mockingly resist the first signs of vanguardism. Others prefer, without polemics, a poetic work that is simple and of vernacular inspiration. Oustanding are: NARCISO CALLEJAS (1887?–1917), ROBERTO BARRIOS (1891), ANTENOR SANDINO HERNÁNDEZ (1893), GUILLERMO ROTSCHUH (1894), ADOLFO CALERO OROZCO (1897), JUAN FELIPE TORUÑO (1898).

Costa Rica: Some of the Modernist treasure was inherited by ROBERTO VALLADARES (1891–1920), ROGELIO SOTELA (1894–1943), JOSÉ ALBERTAZZI AVENDAÑO (1892), JOSÉ BASILEO ACUÑA (1897), HERNÁN ZAMORA ELIZONDO (1895). The most brilliant poet was RAFAEL CARDONA (1892). In *Morning Gold* (*Oro de la mañana,* 1916) his preoccupation with the gracefulness of forms was already noticeable. Although he preferred the sonnet, he tried his hand at different meters and strophes, without arriving at free verse. His themes were ambitious—man and his destiny, for example. His impressionism and his initial symbolism yielded later to a more conceptual art. The other Costa Rican poet of significance was JULIÁN MARCHENA (1897), who published his first book in 1941 (*Wings in Flight—Alas en fuga*) but because of his age, his Modernist forms, and the clear logical construction that gives unity to his sentiments, he must be placed here.

Panama: The most noteworthy poet in all its literature is RICARDO MIRÓ (1883–1940). His review *Nuevos ritos* (founded in 1907) was one of the principal organs in the Modernist renovation after the advent of Panama as a republic. He wrought in careful verses—with a preference for hendecasyllables and sonnets—themes of love, of patriotic emotion, and of admiration in the presence of landscapes. He was a poet in minor key, introspective, solitary. His last book of poems was *Silent Paths* (*Caminos silenciosos,* 1929). He also wrote short stories and two attempts at novels. His work has been presented in anthologies: the most recent, *Poetic Anthology* (*Antología poética,* 1951) and *Introduction to the Stories of Ricardo Miró* (*Introducción a los cuentos de Ricardo Miró,* 1957). GASPAR OCTAVIO HERNÁNDEZ (1893–1918) was a Modernist poet who combined the tricks of the trade in almost all his production, but also allowed us to see a personal and popular vein, which expressed in a direct manner his social condition as a patriotic Negro preoccupied with injustice. MARÍA OLIMPIA DE OBALDÍA (1891) intoned, with dignity, her voice of wife, mother, and teacher: *Orchid* (*Orquidea*), *Lyrical Breviary* (*Breviario lírico*), *Children's Parnassus* (*Parnaso infantil*). The emotive JOSÉ MARÍA GUARDIA (1895–1941) completes the family portrait of the Panamanian Modernists of this generation. There were others of lesser Modernist accents such as ANTONIO NOLI B. (1884–1943) and ENRIQUE GEENZIER (1887–1943).

(3) *Antilles* / In Cuba, poetry did not march in the avant-garde either in this period or the following. It may even be said that, after Casal, there was not an energetic Modernism. Rather than great works, the poems of Boti, Poveda, and Acosta—three of the worthiest poets to represent the continuation and renovation of Modernism—are a beautiful awakening. Boti, in spite of his rhythmic audacities,

was placed in the previous chapter because he was born in 1878. In spite of belonging to an older generation, he was the first, after Cuba won its independence from Spain, to shake the dust off Cuban letters and leave the air clean. For his estheticism, directed toward pure poetry, Boti can be coupled with Poveda (although his work endures longer than Poveda's and thus reaches the generation which in 1927 launches the magazine *Revista de Avance*). In JOSÉ MANUEL POVEDA (1888–1926)–*Precursor Verses* (*Versos precursores*, 1917)–there were ostentatious attempts at creating new forms. They are not very new. It was he who was eccentric, not his verses. His eccentricity ("our I above our selves," he used to say) led him to the cultivation of "hysterias," "decadencies," and "satanisms" (these also are his words) and in this way, he restricted himself, together with others, to a cosmopolitan manner. He learned from Europeans (Regnier, Kahn, Stuart Merrill, Laforgue) and from Hispanic-Americans (especially from Darío, Silva, Lugones, López Velarde). The moon to which he sang in a sentimental voice and with ironic little glimpses was the moon that had been seen by Laforgue and Lugones: but the neighborhood from which he saw it, tenderly, was his own. His nervous trembling also made his verses tremble in meters that were freer than those his contemporaries were accustomed to. Like his friend Boti, he too, wanted to renew poetry, but the wise and elegant acoustics of his verses was a thing of sensibility, not just a part of a program of experiments. Nevertheless, he was a technician more than a revolutionary: he employed unusual words, recondite allusions to mythology, difficult notes. Different from Boti and Poveda, for his greater proximity to the things of Cuba, was Acosta. AGUSTÍN ACOSTA (1886) took flight with *Wing* (*Ala,* 1915) and did a few loops in the Modernist sky. He lighted on sentiments of gallant love and on feelings of patriotism (as in his song to Martí) which became even more simple in the mellow and melancholic poems of *Little Sister* (*Hermanita,* 1923). Of more national significance was *Cane Harvest* (*La zafra,* 1926) in which he evokes lyrically, but with social sensitivity, the life of the workers in the sugar industry. It is a poem of a great variety of moods—subjective and realist—with effusions and descriptions that exhibit Acosta's skill as an artisan and—why not say it—his prosaic stumblings. Cuba is converted into one great cane field. "There is a violent smell of sugar in the air," he writes. As the poem proceeds, this smell of sugar cane vaguely suggests warnings, catastrophes, revolutions. Occasionally, a vanguardist image: "on the envelope of night / the moon sets its stamp." But, in general, Acosta's national fervor is frank, realist and even didactic. At the sonorous festivals of rising pyrotechnics that the Modernists used to celebrate, Acosta was a moderate. At each turn he became clearer, simpler: *The Distant Camels* (*Los camellos distantes,* 1936), perhaps his best book, and *The Desolate Isles* (*Las islas desoladas,* 1943). But his orbit was Modernism, and in *The Last Moments* (*Ultimos instantes,* 1941) he invoked, irresistibly, the Darío of "It was a soft air." A Modernism, we repeat, in which there are declamatory, patriotic, religious, sentimental notes, and even touches of a diffused philosophy. After the impetus given by the three leaders, Boti, Poveda and Acosta—their *Mental Arabesques* (*Arabescos mentales*), *Precursor Verses* and *Wing,* respectively, appeared from 1913 to 1917—Cuban poetry was put in motion. Sometimes in reverse, as in GUSTAVO SÁNCHEZ GALARRAGA (1892–1934) and in the brothers FERNANDO (1883–1949) and FRANCISCO LLES (1887–1921), and sometimes circulating around the main avenues of Modernism, as in ARTURO ALFONSO ROSELLÓ (1897), ERNESTO FERNÁNDEZ ARRONDO (1897), RAMÓN RUBIERA (1894).

At times it veered off toward the prose of daily life or, at least, toward ordinary themes. FELIPE PICHARDO MOYA (1892–1957) ran through the geography, the history, and the social activities of the island of Cuba, in "The Poem of the Cane Fields" (*"El poema de los cañaverales"*) or in his compositions on the Negro theme, but he managed to write vanguardist verses in an attempt to place himself within the "new sensibility" of the postwar days. Prosaic, although lively and ironic, was JOSÉ ZACARÍAS TALLET (1893), whose only book, *The Sterile Seed (La semilla estéril*, 1951) appeared hanging from an exclamation by Laforgue: "How humdrum life is!" Tallet used to balance himself on the edge of humble, flavorless, plebeian things and from his balancing board moved either to compassion, or smiled with pessimism and sarcasm. Like Pichardo Moya, Tallet announced the poetry of African themes which will have so much success later. He was a sentimentalist, saddened by the failure of everything, and because of the lucidness with which he faced mediocrity, he arrived at the brilliance of the grotesque. A lyricist? At any rate, a lyricist who now doubts his own individual song: "I am one of the last who says / 'I,' tragically / convinced at once that the password / for tomorrow must be 'we.'" RAFAEL ESTÉNGER (1899) also fits into this deviation of poetry toward a public reality. At times poetry opened into deep crevices of emotion, as in MARÍA LUISA MILANÉS (1893–1919), MARÍA VILLAR BUCETA (1899). At times poetry advanced toward new expressions. The most notable example in this direction of Modernism, of a Modernism that sprang from the Lugones and Herrera y Reissig fountain, was RUBÉN MARTÍNEZ VILLENA (1899–1934). But he was exceptionally gifted, and in *The Sleepless Eye (La pupila insomne)*—his only book, a posthumous one—one admires what he was able to do with the prose of life by dint of sentimental sincerity, bitter humorism, philosophic reflections, and even political irritations, for he was a Communist. Also in REGINO PEDROSO (1896) we find an evolution from early Modernism—*The Route to Bagdad and Other Poems (La ruta de Bagdad y otros poemas,* 1918–23)—to a poetry of social emphasis, "Fraternal Greeting to the Machine Shop," 1927. First, sumptuous images and allegories according to fashion: then, the struggles of the worker, machines, anti-imperialism. A writer of the avant-garde, but more for his themes than for the dislocation of his forms. His humanitarian impulse is despoiled little by little of political propaganda and it leads him to affirm the creative forces of the world. In the end he seems to fall back on the Chinese shadows of his race in *Translations of a Chinese Poet of Today (Traducciones de un poeta chino de hoy).* EMILIA BERNAL (1885), tender, ardent, intuitive, was capable of denying these qualities in herself in order to complicate sounds that brought her close to a poetry which, under the heading "abnormality," will be studied in the second part of this panorama. Those who remain, then, are the Cubans of the "abnormality" —Mariano Brull, Navarro Luna, and others whom we will leave for later.

In the Dominican Republic, the brothers Pedro and Max Henríquez Ureña were the first to openly write, in 1901, Modernist poetry; but both stood out in other genres, so that we will refer to them elsewhere. The truth of the matter is that there was scarcely any Modernism in this country. It arrived late, it was weak and it lasted no time at all. They all turned their eyes toward the "decadents" of France, but some of them were still sighing about their Romantic troubles (as the elegant ALTAGRACIA SAVIÑÓN, 1886–1942). Others, closer to the Rubén Darian sun, shone more brilliantly. VALENTÍN GIRÓ (1883–1949) was the first, with his sonnet *"Virgínea,"* to ignite one of those polemics so necessary to the triumph of new styles. OSVALDO BAZIL (1884–1946) was a Modernist from head to foot, and left at least one sentimental gem: "Little Nocturne." RICARDO PÉREZ ALFONSECA (1892–1950) is remembered above all for his "Ode About an I" ("*Oda de un Yo*"). There were others—such as the tender and simple VIGILIO DÍAZ ORDÓÑEZ, 1895, or FEDERICO BERMÚDEZ, 1884–1921, of social and humanitarian themes—but Modernism in the Dominican Republic was timid. Other names: EMILIO MOREL (1887), BALDEMARO RIJO (1885–1939), RAMÓN EMILIO JIMÉNEZ (1886), ENRIQUE AGUIAR (1890–1947), JOSÉ FURCY PICHARDO (1891), JUAN BAUTISTA LAMARCHE (1894–1956).

Puerto Rico had had its great Modernist poet in Luis Lloréns Torres, whom we have already studied. Modernism was belated and short lived. Those who followed Lloréns were ANTONIO PÉREZ PIERRET (1885–1937), somewhat Parnassian in *Bronzes* (*Bronces*, 1914); ANTONIO NICOLÁS BLANCO (1887–1945), of a minor key; JOSÉ ANTONIO DÁVILA (1898–1941), a good sonneteer; and the best, JOSÉ POLONIO HERNÁNDEZ Y HERNÁNDEZ (1892–1922), who ascended, though always a few rungs lower, the lyrical ladder that Bécquer and Rubén Darío had climbed: melancholic in his sentiments like the former, a verbal craftsman like the latter. His two books, *Couplets of the Bypath* (*Coplas de la vereda*, 1919) and *The Last Combat* (*El último combate*, 1919) speak to us of nature, of death, of love. Love was the inspiration for a madrigal, "To Two Astral Eyes," that made him famous. Evaristo Ribera Chevremont, because of his incursions into the vanguardist poetry of the postwar period, will be shifted to the second half of this chapter.

(4) *Venezuela* / In Venezuela they were wont to speak of the "generation of 1918," which proposed transcending Modernism and raising the cultural level with European norms, but with Venezuelan content. This generation probably was the most resonant, the most effective in the poetic history of the nation. But it was not a generation having a unity of style. One can hear different orchestral ensembles. The Modernist violins are muted, without a clear fortissimo in the postwar saxophones. On the contrary, it is the native flutes that dominate. JOSÉ ANTONIO RAMOS SUCRE (1890–1929) was one of the most outstanding; his books of poems, *The Helmsman's Post* (*La torre del timón*, 1925) and *The Enamel Sky and the Shapes of Fire* (*El cielo de esmalte y las formas del fuego*, 1929), were celebrated as lessons in poetry by the young men of later generations. LUIS BARRIOS CRUZ (1898), with his *Response to Stones* (*Respuesta a las piedras*, 1931), was moving because of the audacious, almost vanguardist way in which he stylized native themes. RODOLFO MOLEIRO (1898), FERNANDO PAZ CASTILLO (1895), LUIS ENRIQUE MÁRMOL (1897–1926) are other members of this generation of 1918 group. (We will see its younger members in the next chapters.)

The most famous of the group was ANDRÉS ELOY BLANCO (1897–1955), rich in timbre, serious and gay, brilliant and diversified, excessive but intimate, capable of classicism but Romantic in his native and folkloric blood. He was popular. His multiple accents sounded in America and resounded in Spain. He was one who crossed geographical frontiers; yet, he himself was a frontier poet. Behind him, Modernism; in front, the desire for change. Since in Venezuela Modernism came late and lasted longer than usual, the vanguardist battle was also going to arrive late.

Other names: ELÍAS SÁNCHEZ RUBIO (1888–1931), PEDRO RIVERO (1893–1958), JULIO MORALES LARA (1894–1952).

(5) *Colombia* / As if it were carrying a glass filled with precious traditions and it were afraid of spilling them at the slightest slip, poetry is seen moving with a very careful step and somewhat to the rear in this country. A poet dressed in the old fashion was AURELIO MARTÍNEZ MUTIS (1887–1954), who always worked with the scruples of a good artisan in the different fields of the narrative, the elegy, and the landscape. He had begun, hardly Modernistically, with the *silvas* of *The Epic of the Condor* (*La epopeya del cóndor*, 1934), but his *Marble* (*Mármol*, 1922) came from the Modernist quarry. Although tied to Modernism by a rubber band, other Colombian poets withdrew a few steps. They are those of the "generation of the Centenary," so called because they began publishing around 1910. They had more of a civic sense than the Rubén Darío esthetes and they were inspired by their national birthright. Nevertheless, the "Centenarian" poets learned their art from Parnassian and symbolist models and, inside Colombia, they continued the work of the Modernists, Valencia, Grillo, and Londoño. The most brilliant were Rivera, Rasch Isla, Castillo, Castañeda Aragón, Gilberto Garrido, Leopoldo de la Rosa, and Seraville.

José Eustasio Rivera was one of the first to lean upon the Colombian landscape from whence his lyricism leaped, but we will deal with him separately below. MIGUEL RASCH ISLA (1889–1951) the confidential poet of *On the Surface of the Soul* (*A flor de alma*), *For Afternoon Reading* (*Para leer en la tarde*), *When the Leaves Fall* (*Cuando las hojas caen*) and *The Apple of Eden* (*La manzana del Edén*). And, the most influential in this constellation, EDUARDO CASTILLO (1889–1939), in an insinuating minor key, a mellow, delicate, sad, resigned poet. His book: *The Singing Tree* (*El árbol que canta*, 1938). Thanks to Guillermo Valencia, whom he humbly admired, Castillo traveled all the routes of Modernism, always correct, on occasion inspired by a personal and powerful lyricism. Rather than a feeling for life, he felt an esthetic theory of life. This theory, of course, came from a European library, rich in French books, poor in Spanish. His readings are more recognizable than his emotions, perhaps because he penetrated his own personality very timidly and, on the other hand, elaborated with great decisiveness a theory of art that became a school in his country.

The Centenarians were about twenty: GREGORIO CASTAÑEDA ARAGÓN (1886) who wrote of the sea and of men of the sea, author of *Corners of the Sea* (*Rincones de mar*); the desolate and recondite ABEL MARTÍN; the soft, musical and enamored ROBERTO LIÉVANO; LEOPOLDO DE LA ROSA (1888); DELIO SERAVILLE [Ricardo Sarmiento] (1885–1936); the melancholy and somber GILBERTO GARRIDO (1887); the brothers BAYONA POSADA (Daniel, 1887–1920; Jorge, 1888; Nicolás, 1902); JUAN BAUTISTA JARAMILLO MEZA (1892), GENARO MUÑOZ OBANDO (1890?); ÁNGEL MARÍA CÉSPEDES (1892), who was acclaimed at the age of sixteen for his poem, "The Blossoming of the Sun," chiseled his poetry in Francophilic fashion; and others. Younger, but still leaning backward, are DANIEL SAMPER ORTEGA (1895–1943), the restrained CARLOS GARCÍA-PRADA (1898), and MARIO CARVAJAL (1896) of classically religious themes, emotions, and vestments.

This listing, which might annoy the reader allergic to the pollen of names, gives an indication, nevertheless, of the great expanse of the Colombian gardens. In the middle of this garden there is a bushy tree, the last in the great Modernist row: PORFIRIO BARBA JACOB (1883–1942). Miguel Angel Osorio, known by his pen names Ricardo Arenales and Barba Jacob, is in fact a notch on the same pole of Colombian poetry on which we had previously notched Silva and Valencia. He was not as delicate and profound as Silva nor as much an artist as Valencia, but his themes were Romantic like the former's and his style was Modernist like the latter's. He is generally considered a bright light in the Colombian firmament. Nevertheless, Barba Jacob, no matter how restless, vehement, or desperate one considers him, did not succeed in poetically airing that inner world that was stifling his heart. In "Light Song" he complained that things were there before his eyes and, yet, he could not give them voice: "and we, wretched poets, / trembling before the vertigoes of the sea, / see the unexpected wonder / and can only yield a sigh." And it was true. Barba Jacob is pained by great interrogations, doubts, discouragements, rebellions, desires, lewdnesses, immoralities; but he stays sick, in the obscurity of his cave, and instead of songs we hear his lamentations. His lyricism is so dense that at times it becomes obscure, as in *"Acuarimántima."* Other times his lyricism clarifies itself in exclamatory poems (the exclamations reveal the poet's emotional charge), in carefully constructed poems (the symmetrical patterns reveal the effect that he wishes to achieve), in narrative poems (the action, in an anecdote or an allegory, reveals the direction of the soul or the idea of the poem). His best songs are those of misconduct, of perdition, of solitude. The legend of his homosexual life does not interest us, although it contributed to his fame, but the legend of his poetry should be revised critically. He exaggerated his wantonness and in his desire for scandal he turned to artistic though not poetic pretenses. Even in his moments of sincerity, he did not always see clearly into his own depths.

Another oddity was JORGE ESCOBAR URIBE (1886–1917), better known as Claudio de Alas (who was so odd, in fact, that before stepping into literary history he stepped into the novel, as the character Braulio Azolas of *A Lost One* [*Un perdido*] by Eduardo Barrios). His ennui for living, after so tempestuous a life, led him to suicide.

(6) *Ecuador* / Modernism struck its spark here in the first decade of the century, though the best of Ecuadorian literature will come later and will appear by preference in prose form. ARTURO BORJA (1892–1912) was one of those who best fanned the new fire. He was sentimental, clear, spontaneous. His influence came

directly from French symbolism: in *The Onyx Flute* (*La flauta de ónix*) one hears echoes of Baudelaire, Verlaine, Rimbaud, Mallarmé, and Samain. Perhaps these readings accentuated his melancholy disposition and made him feel tired of life before living it. He was a solitary, inexplicable sufferer. ERNESTO NOBOA CAAMAÑO (1891–1927) makes us hear Verlaine and Samain in *The Ballad of the Hours* (*La romanza de las horas*) and *The Shadows of the Wings* (*La sombra de las alas*). More harmonious than Borja, though like him, he felt weary of life. He is elegant and moderate despite the intensity of suffering he wished to express. MEDARDO ÁNGEL SILVA (1899–1920), a humble youth who invented his own aristocratic Rubenian atmosphere and who wished to be what he was not, sang his sad melody. Verses by Verlaine, Morèas, and Samain moved in surreptitiously to mix with those that he composed. In *The Tree of Good and Evil* (*El árbol del bien y del mal,* 1918) it is difficult to distinguish his inspiration from that of others. He reflected on the uselessness of existence and then seemed to have found a meaning in his own harmonious song. Borja, Noboa Caamaño, and Silva committed suicide. The one who wanted to live longer, but could not, was the afflicted HUMBERTO FIERRO (1890–1929). He also offered symbolist echoes in *The Lute in the Valley* (*El laúd en el valle,* 1919) and in the posthumous *Night in the Palace* (*Velada palatina*). He was one of the most exquisite poets in his melancholy and in his tedium. He made an effort to leave behind the company of Rubén Darío's followers and to overtake the new writers. These are the four major poets of the best choir that sang in the autumnal parks of Ecuador. They evaded Ecuador, reality, and even life. There were others: JOSÉ MARÍA EGAS (1896), with his amorous and mystical breviary, *Unction* (*Unción,* 1925); REMIGIO ROMERO Y CORDERO (1895), Modernist in *The Pilgrimage of the Caravelles* (*La romería de las carabelas*); MIGUEL ÁNGEL ZAMBRANO (1895), who showed up late, in 1957, with desolate and nihilist poems. And the oldest: AURELIO FALCONÍ (1885) and GONZALO CORDERO DÁVILA (1885–1931).

(7) *Peru* / After Chocano and Eguren, a group of Modernist poets appears which is worthwhile as a group, although no principal figure stood out. JOSÉ GÁLVEZ (1885) began to sing beneath the moon, in a closed garden—*Beneath the Moon* (*Bajo la luna,* 1910); *Closed Garden* (*Jardín cerrado,* 1912)—in the manner of Rubén Darío, although he also followed the example of Chocano's narrative, civil, and American poetry. ENRIQUE BUSTAMANTE Y BALLIVIÁN (1884–1936) visited poetry in the attitude of the intellectual: that is to say, he observed, studied, reflected, experimented. And so it is with his work—without being original, it reflects all the comings and goings of those years: Parnassianism, symbolism, Creolism, indigenism, vanguardism. ALBERTO J. URETA (1885) was the one with most tonal unity: from *Sound of Souls* (*Rumor de almas,* 1911) and *Pensive Torment* (*El dolor pensativo,* 1917) there surges a constant melancholy. ABRAHAM VALDELOMAR (1888–1919), although educated in Modernist estheticism, wrote earnestly of his own land: provincial and family life, landscapes and everyday men. In this way Modernism was shorn of cosmopolitan and fantastic ornaments and, in return, it acquired American objects. In prose he left us short stories of a regional flavor, like the one about *"El caballero Carmelo,"* a gamecock. PERCY GIBSON (1885) composed local poems, with landscapes, anecdotes, and ordinary human types.

Other poets, who had mingled with the preceding ones, separated from Modernism in search of more up-to-date formulas. Within this endeavor at renovation stands ALCIDES SPELUCÍN (1897). In *The Book of the Golden Ship* (*El libro de la nave dorada,* 1926) he gathered his verses written between 1917 to 1921, which spread out like a fan showing the rococo decoration so dear to the Modernists; but there are also sallies toward ordinary, humble, real themes, above all, that of the sea. ALBERTO GUILLÉN (1897–1935) was of a chronic individualism (and an acute egocentrism). He was assertive, optimistic, and even ideological in his barbaric exaltation of force. For the time being, we close this exposition of Peruvian poets—because in the second part of this chapter we will see among others César Vallejo, the best of all—with a few names as suspension points: PABLO ABRIL (1895), ALFREDO GONZÁLEZ PRADA (1891–1943), CÉSAR A. RODRÍGUEZ (1891), FEDERICO MORE (1889), FEDERICO BOLAÑOS (1896), DANIEL RUZO (1900).

(8) *Bolivia* / After the three vertexes of Bolivian Modernism—at the apex Jaimes Freyre and at the base Tamayo and Reynolds—come a few lines of plane geometry. The most enthusiastic propagator of Modernism was CLAUDIO PEÑARANDA (1884–1924), who collected his entire work in *Songbook of Real Experiences* (*Cancionero vivido,* 1919). His "Elegy to Rubén Darío" was, similar to Darío's "Response to Verlaine," a poetic definition. JOSÉ EDUARDO GUERRA (1893–1943) was also one of the "cerebral" poets of Modernism, with philosophic restlessness, and tinges of melancholy and anguish. Others: HUMBERTO VISCARRA MONJE (1898), JUAN CAPRILES (1890–1953), NICOLÁS ORTIZ PACHECO (1893–1953), LOLA TABORGA DE REQUENA (1890).

(9) *Chile* / Chilean Modernism had not given any great poet: only Pezoa Véliz, and also Magallanes Moure. Suddenly, the wind of poetry freshened. Chile will bring the only Nobel Prize for Literature to our America, Gabriela Mistral; it will bring one of the most clamorous innovators of our letters, Vicente Huidobro, and later, Pablo de Rokha and Pablo Neruda, the latter being one of the greatest poets in our language. However, let us not anticipate, but take things in order.

A figure of international stature in this period is Lucila Godoy Alcayaga, or Gabriela Mistral.

GABRIELA MISTRAL (Chile, 1889–1957). Viewing her rugged, disordered poetry, Gabriela Mistral does not appear to derive from the virtuosos of Modernism; nevertheless, her metaphors have the symbolist family habit of leaping into the abyss with torch in hand, illuminating as they fall the recesses of inner life. They are metaphors for readers accustomed to the thrilling spectacle of those mad exercises: anti-intellectual metaphors that do not demonstrate with the slowness of logic but reveal with the rapidity of the immediate gesture and, therefore, require a prepared public. Although different from the Modernists, Gabriela Mistral learned from them—from Magallanes Moure, from Carlos R. Mondaca, from Max Jara. At any rate she wrote for those who had read the Modernists. In "The Sonnets of Death" (*"Los sonetos de la muerte"*), for which she received a prize in the Floral Games of Santiago in 1914, she was already leaving her teachers behind. She introduced provincial ways of speaking (Gabriela was from the Elqui valley), adverbial forms (as in the verse "evil hands entered tragically in him"), and biblical terms. She never stood out as a revolutionary in poetry, in the manner of Huidobro, Rokha and Neruda, but she too, contributed to vanguardist poetry. Her influence was not visible, but like a subterranean river she irrigated contemporary poetry. Her great theme is love; and all her poetry is a variation on this theme. Amorous, amatory poetry, but not erotic. In the first group of these variations, two sad episodes from Gabriela's life are composed in counterpoint. One describes a first love for a man who killed himself for honor and the other, years later, another love that hurt her deeply. These poems were collected under the sections, "Anguish" (*"Dolor"*) and "Nature" (*"Naturaleza"*) of her first book, *Desolation* (*Desolación*) —the first edition, 1922; second, 1923; and the third, 1926, contained additions; the best edition to date is that of Aguilar, 1958. Since neither Gabriela nor anyone else has given the biographical key to these two histories, and the poems are not arranged in two chronological episodes, the reader believes himself to be reading the painful history of a single love: her love for the man who committed suicide. No one has expressed with more lyrical force the awakening of love, the feeling of being enthralled by a man, and the struggle for the right words to recount it; the modesty at being seen by him and the shame of seeing herself in the mirror and finding herself so plain in her nakedness; the sweet warmth of the body; the fear of not deserving her lover, the dread of losing him, jealousies, humiliations, heartbreaks; and afterwards, when he has sent a bullet through his brains, consecrating her life to him, praying to God for the salvation of the soul of the suicide, and the anxiety of wanting to know what lies beyond death and through what shadows does her lover move; the loneliness, the useless waiting in those places that they knew together and, yet, the obsession of feeling him close in supernatural visits; the remorse at still being alive, the wound of remembering; the stamp of virginity and the maternal desire; and time that passes and her own flesh that is slowly drying beneath the dust of the dead bones of her lover, and her reaching thirty years to suddenly realize that she can no longer remember even the dead man's face; and the final poverty following her loss. But we have said that this frustrated love, as moving as it is, is the first suite of the variations on the love theme.

On reaching her thirtieth year—"Already in the middle of my life"— Gabriela Mistral continued with other variations of universal love, love of God, nature, mother, good causes of the world, love of the humble, the persecuted, the sufferers, the forgotten ones; and, above all, of children for whom she wrote rounds, songs, and stories. In *Desolation* she tells how she came to write for the consolation of others: "Your beauty shall be also called grace, and it will console the hearts of men," she says in "Decalogue for the Artist" (*"Decálogo del artista"*); and she formulates the "Vow": "Forgive me, God, for this bitter book, and you men, who feel life as sweetness, you too, forgive me for it. In these hundred poems a tormented past still bleeds, a past in which the song, to alleviate me, was reddened with blood. I leave it behind me in that somber ravine and along these simple slopes I move toward the spiritual plateaus where a wide band of light, finally, will fall upon my days. And from here I shall sing words of hope, without turning to gaze upon my heart . . ." In this way Gabriela, after her purification in suffering, rises toward a candid, pure, and transparent love for her fellow man. She continues in desolation, but now sings of her tenderness. *Tenderness (Ternura,* 1924) is the title of a book of poems, most of which are prunings from *Desolation,* except that these branches have blossomed in a new edition of 1945.

Another of her books—the second original one—*Felling of Trees (Tala,* 1938) is a reprise of the religious theme of *Desolation,* but here Gabriela's vision is more abstract. After her innocence, her passion, and her sad disillusionment in the first contact with poetry, she brings to poetry colorless flowers: symbols, dreams, ideals. Nature is remembered from a distance, or it is the landscape of strange countries where Gabriela moves, caught in the net of constellations that are not her own southern ones. In her exile, in her uprooting, her verses become harder. In the poetry of her third and last book, *Winepress (Lagar,* 1954) her love of land and man is stylized even more. Most of the poems have the rhythms of songs. The fatigue of old age in a strange land makes her remember and yearn for death, and her verses are hard, dry, opaque, even prosaic: "like copious smoke / I am not a flame or burning coal." In reality, *Desolation* is her best work; in it she gave the best of herself, and its themes will always preside in her later works. Her vigor—the vigor of a poet rather than a poetess—is not due to the things she writes about. No. Thousands of weak poets chose strong themes. Her vigor is in raising reality to her lips, spilling it into her inner self, converting it into her blood and then intoning her generous and noble song of love. Her Christian sentiment made her sympathize with the cause of social justice. Posthumous is her *Poem of Chile (Poema de Chile).* She has written poems in prose, essays, letters. Her prose, though very abundant, circumstantial, and unstable in quality, on the day it is completely edited, will not diminish the importance of her verses, which will continue to be fundamental in Gabriela's work; but an anthology of that prose will be surprising for its delightful spontaneity. Some prose titles are: *Messages (Recados); Telling Chile (Contando a Chile,* 1957).

Other Chilean Poets: After Gabriela Mistral, the most important Chilean figures of this period are Vicente Huidobro and Pablo de Rokha. We will find both of them among the poets of "abnormality." But before closing this paragraph on Chile we should mention other significant names. The great Pedro Prado will be studied in another section with the prose writers. Enter MAX JARA (1886), retiring but overbearing, scrimpy but neat, rigorous in a poetry that had few chords: his *Assonants (Asonantes)* of "minor tone" shows his simplicity, result of a profound purification. In a younger group, the first in order of merit is ÁNGEL CRUCHAGA SANTA MARÍA (1893), still illumined by symbolism, personal in his religious sentiment. Each time less effusive, each time more intentional, his most notable collections of poems are *Job* (1922)—expression of the suffering of all things created—and *Night of the Nights (Noche de las noches)* which is interspersed with poetic prose. Then we must remember JUAN GUZMÁN CRUCHAGA (1895), intimate, sad, compassionate; he stands out for his simplicity, for his sobriety: *The Stare (La mirada inmóvil,* 1919), *High Shadow (Altasombra,* 1958). His theater is meant to be read rather than acted. A simple listing of other poets will give an idea of the awakening of Chile in this period: the tender and yet Modernist ROBERTO MEZA FUENTES (1899), the tremendous and multitudinous inquietude of WINETT DE ROHKA (1896–1951), the reflexive and Symbolist JORGE HÜBNER BEZANILLA (1892), the erotic and landscape poet CARLOS PRÉNDEZ SALDÍAS (1892), the priest FRANCISCO DONOSO GONZÁLEZ (1894), and the very human MARÍA MONVEL (1899–1936), whose simplicity in manifesting tenderness love and home life sharply contrasted with the more sophisticated poetry of her contemporaries.

(10) *Paraguay* / Modernism began to manifest itself here when in the rest of Hispanic-America it was already outmoded. The figure of most stature, ELOY FARIÑA NÚÑEZ (1885–1929), approached Modernism and entered; but the distinctively Modernist groups will come later. Fariña Núñez lived abroad, but from a distance sang of themes relating to his country. *Secular Song (Canto secular)* is a long epic poem in blank verse, of a pseudoclassical serenity and coldness. He collected his poetic work in *Poems (Cármenes,* 1922). In reality, he was not a great poet. He cultivated his mind reading and studying European or Europeanized books in the literary circles of Buenos Aires. The idealization of his Guaraní homeland in *Guaraní Myths (Mitos guaraníes)* was the best he produced. He also wrote narrations of Hellenic inspiration in the short stories of *The Vertebrae of Pan (Las vértebras de Pan)* and in the novel *Rodopis,* theater, and several books of essays. Modernism, such as Rubén Darío many years earlier had imposed on the rest of Hispanic-America, took hold in Paraguay in two belated movements. The first was formed around the review *Crónica* (1913–15); the second, around the review *Juventud* (1932–35). Standing out in the first of these movements was GUILLERMO MOLINAS ROLÓN (1889–1945). This Bohemian, talented

but short in poetic production, was a symbolist kindled by the metaphors of Herrera y Reissig. The other two interesting figures of *Crónica* were LEOPOLDO RAMOS GIMÉNEZ (1896), a libertarian poet of violent social mettle in *Sacred Pyres* (*Piras sagradas*), tending more to esthetic forms in *Eros* and *Wings and Shadows* (*Alas y sombras*), and PABLO MAX INSFRÁN (1895), somewhat Parnassian in his desire for formal perfection in exotic and philosophical themes. Later he left poetry for the essay. The most popular poet was MANUEL ORTIZ GUERRERO (1897–1933), popular in part because of the painful legend of his life as a leper, and as a self-sacrificing, idealistic bohemian, without resentment or bitterness. The stamp of Rubén Darío is recognized in his works: *Surging* (*Surgente*), *Eastern Clouds* (*Nubes del este*), *Kernels* (*Pepitas*). He combined exotic and native themes. He also wrote in Guaraní. The rebellious FACUNDO RECALDE (1896), author of *Celestial Kindlings* (*Virutas celestes*) gave himself to social themes. Together with the latter two, we should study Natalicio González, but we prefer to do so when we come to the prosists. A social, militant, and disarranged poet was JULIO CORREA (1890–1955), apparently more meritorious for his Guaraní theater. The second movement around *Juventud,* alluded to above, will be seen in the next chapter.

(11) *Uruguay* / As we have seen in the previous chapter, the miracle of an extraordinary generation emerged in Uruguay: the "generation of 1900," formed by no less than Reyles, Viana, Rodó, Sánchez, Quiroga, Carlos and María Eugenia Vaz Ferreira, Herrera y Reissig. The leading poets of this generation were María Eugenia Vaz Ferreira and Herrera y Reissig. Between them and the poets that belong to this period —those born after 1885—there fell, like a shooting star, DELMIRA AGUSTINI (1886?–1914). The life of a woman of ardent sex, constantly desiring the arms of men, would have no spiritual importance in itself, if it went no further than to tell us, spontaneously, what happens to her organism. Delmira Agustini was like an orchid, humid and warm; one of the themes she repeated was the waiting, in her bed, for the visit of the nocturnal lover. But she transcended her eroticism and the delights of the body were converted to esthetic delights. The beauties of her desires acquired independent value; they became art, with the palpitations of biological life, to be sure, but spiritualized in marvelous images. No woman had dared, up to then, to make confessions of the type found in "Vision," "Another Lineage," "The Brook," in short, in all the poems of her books, from *The White Book* (*El libro blanco,* 1907) until the posthumous *The Stars of the Abyss* (*Los astros del abismo*). But these confessions are of value, not for their anecdotes of life, but for their vision of a transcendental life in which voluptuosity is sublimated in poetry. Her imaginative daring is more amazing than her immodesty. And, well considered, did not her immodesty have a good deal of the fantastic? She had experienced desire, but its carnal satis-

faction, very little: her marriage had scarcely been a month old when she published her work. Her images sprout when least expected, like "gigantic mushrooms."

Of longer life and, consequently, of more completed work are the poets to be presented now. They emerge from the Modernist ebbing and they disbanded at times in opposite directions. In spite of disbanding, those who carried the Modernist emblem over their hearts were PABLO MINELLI GONZÁLEZ (1893) and Juana de Ibarbourou. The most philosophical were the vitalist, Sabat Ercasty, the intellectual, Oribe, and the estheticist, Casaravilla Lemos. With more symbolic intentions, Basso Maglio and Maeso Tognochi either descended dark cellars or climbed clear allegorical towers. Inclined toward national roots are the nativists Silva Valdés and Ipuche and the "Negro-ist" ILDEFONSO PEREDA VALDÉS (1899). And the declamatory ÁNGEL FALCO (1885); the epic writer, EDGARDO UBALDO GENTA (1894); MANUEL DE CASTRO (1896), who, after standing out as an excellent sonneteer, also successfully proved his talent as a novelist; EMILIO CARLOS TACCONI (1895) and many others. But in order not to slip from name to name, let us pause before those poets who will help us to illuminate the atmosphere of those years.

JUANA DE IBARBOUROU (1895) because of the purity of her song was consecrated as "Juana of America." These words come to the mouth of whoever speaks of her: flower, fruit, harvest, gazelle, lark; that is, images of the vegetable and the animal in the joy of living. From these metaphors others emerged; for example, her poetic work passes through the cycles of birth, youth, maturity, and old age. At times the cycles are compared with the four seasons of the year or the four parts of the day. Thus, it has been said that *The Tongues of Diamond* (*Las lenguas de diamante,* 1919) was her introduction to life one spring morning; *Savage Root* (*Raíz salvaje,* 1920) youth, one summer noon; *The Rose of the Winds* (*La rosa de los vientos,* 1930) maturity, one autumn afternoon; and *Lost* (*Perdida,* 1950) old age, one winter night. Metaphors. Because to contemplate oneself is neither vegetable nor animal, but human, and all of Juana de Ibarbourou's poetry is persistent Narcissism. She is a female Narcissus who delights in coquetry but despairs before the mirror of Time where she sees herself older, uglier, and closer to death. Young, spoiled, inviting, she felt in her flesh the power of her beauty. She knew she was admired and desired by men; and for these men she would describe herself, naked, ardent, and pressed on by the certainty that that supreme moment of beauty would never be repeated. "Take me now for it is early still / and I carry new dahlias in my hand," she urges in "The Hour." And what are "Savage," "As Springtime," "The Afternoon" but invitations? In "Fleeting Restlessness" time is not a theme of serious meditation, but a sensual message to the lover, that he not turn his eyes from that "fugitive and restless moment" in which she feels herself as beautiful as a defiant nymph. She fears old age more than death; because after all, death can jell her into that last esthetic gesture. In the sonnet "Rebel" ("Charon, I shall be scandalous in your bark") she sees her naked triumph. She imagines herself as dead in "Life-Hook" but, even dead, she wishes to survive as contemplated beauty: "Make my grave just below the surface," she asks her lover; "I foresee / the struggle of my flesh to return above." The mirthful coquettishness of *The Tongues of Diamond,* her best book, persists in *Savage Root* but it is contained by the preoccupation of encountering something new to do. In *The Rose of the Winds* the verses are no longer easy, simple, clear, pleasant, musical, but they are fanned by the currents of vanguardism, they break in irregular rhythms, they become obscure in mystery, and the images aspire to surrealism. That jubilant Narcissism of before is saddened and bitter. There is less feeling, more thinking. Thinking of time—"the heavy owl of time," "the moss-covered branch of time"—and of the flesh that becomes withered. "What can I give you when my youth is gone?" But she has lost her youth, and is losing her beauty. "I feel the weight of each hour / like a sack of stones upon my back. / Oh! I would free myself of this burden / and return to rosy, agile days" ("Days Without Faith"). In *Lost* Juana continues before her mirror and melancholically thinks matters over.

In 1912 CARLOS SABAT ERCASTY (1887) burned his poems (decadent, crepuscular, Modernist) and from then on sought a healthy, exuberant, and athletic expression. He returned to the primitives, to ancient cultures, and in his first book, *Pantheos* (1917), he sang of the indissoluble unity of God and creation. He was excited at his own prophecies of a powerful Hispanic-America. In *Poems on Man* (*Poemas del hombre,* 1922) man—man as a problematic animal—was its center. He managed to make his poetry a micro-man, in the same way that man is a microcosm. His later books yielded a clamorous, vital, diffuse lyricism that influenced the young Neruda. EMILIO ORIBE (1893) was a poet who discarded the cold Parnassian chisels in order to occupy himself more and more with philosophic problems; in his later years he also discarded his intellectualism to draw out, in *Barbaric Rhapsody* (*Rapsodia bárbara,* 1954), the "essential gaucho who lay dormant in the marrow of his soul." His poetry, as well as his meditations—and in him to poetize and to meditate were simultaneous activities—showed him an interior path, always open, through which he advanced without feeling the necessity of repeating himself as many more sedentary poets do. ENRIQUE CASARAVILLA LEMOS (1889) has a lyrical strength that sometimes goes awry, beats its head against a wall, or strays off through a path of concepts, but when it goes just right it carries him to a high plane of beauty. The rocket of poetry bursts and its trajectory of lights radiates in different directions. FERNÁN SILVA VALDÉS (1887) dazzled young writers—Jorge Luis Borges and others—with *The Water of Time* (*Agua del tiempo*, 1921), an admirable book because of its felicitous picture of the Creole world seen through the eyes of thousands of unexpected metaphors. In this way he launched an ultraist nativism or a nativist ultraism, of great success in the history of our poetry. He won renown also in the short story and in the theater. PEDRO LEANDRO IPUCHE (1889), like Silva Valdés, was an explorer of things Creole in his poems and in his short stories. His roots are in the land, and his poetic flowers, no matter how "metaphysical" they appear, are there too: see his *Dilutions* (*Diluciones*). CARLOS RODRÍGUEZ PINTOS (1895) looks up in search of elevated themes—love, fatherland—and approaches them with changing manners, although always with an aristocratic attitude. VICENTE BASSO MAGLIO (1889) repudiates real things and submits to rigorous and hermetic symbols: through intuitions and reflections he reached a poetry in depth, which influenced the younger groups. Between the essential qualities held dear by the symbolists and the deep images gleaned by the surrealists lies the language of Basso Maglio, one of the most representative poets of these years. His "Song of Small Circles and Great Horizons" (*"Canción de los pequeños círculos y los grandes horizontes"*) is worthy of an anthology. Julio J. Casal will be found farther on.

(12) *Argentina* / In Argentina, earlier than in any other country, writers purged themselves of Modernist artifices. That is, in Argentina, there had been a compact group of Modernists, while elsewhere only isolated voices were being heard; and, conversely, when elsewhere compact Modernist groups appeared, Modernism was dissolving in Argentina, and a group of moderate tone was appearing. Now precious, exotic, morbid, artistic things attract less attention than immediate human themes. They go on being esthetes but their expression is simpler. After Lugones, two great poets showed themselves: the unprolific Banchs and the prolific Fernández Moreno.

ENRIQUE BANCHS (1888) published four books of poems—*The Barks* (*Las barcas*, 1907); *The Book of Eulogies* (*El libro de los elogios*, 1908); *The Falcon's Bell* (*El cascabel del halcón*, 1909); *The Urn* (*La urna*, 1911)—and then was silent, except perhaps for a "few pages not published in book form" that some friends gathered together in 1950. He was not an inventor of images; he did not experiment with forms; he did not affiliate with any group nor look for fame; he did not sing with his full voice nor intervene in the usual literary polemics: and his premature renunciation of letters was his last "no" in this negative series. Yet, positively, he was liked, respected, and admired, even by the youngest poets. Banchs gravitated toward poetry—he says so himself in "The Vow"—"like a pilgrim / full of saintly fears is timid in approaching / the altar, all in linen and light and silver and snow." He wanted perfection, but in a stupefied and trembling attitude would not step past the threshold. His verses, always polished, became thin and transparent until they took on a fragile subtlety. From the Modernists he learned the cult of perfection, but without the ornamental tricks that often were purely substitutions for that perfection. Some of Banchs' sonnets are the best that have been written in Argentina. The one that begins "Hospitable and faithful to his reflection" is of such proficiency that one is impressed that Banchs should renounce this skill in order to write such simple, such elemental, such naked verses as the tender ones in "Stammering" or verses as folkloric as his ballads and songs. He lived in the Castilian, purely Spanish, classical tradition of poetry. He was a pure poet: although occasionally he wrote a verse or two of social cast or realist description. His intimate self was buoyantly revealed when he sang in his first three books of the beauty he saw or imagined. These were the years of wholesome amazement at the harmony of the world, but Banchs still covered himself with symbols, surrounded himself with sumptuous objects, entwined himself in literary language. Then the poet revealed his sadness and his own misfortunes directly. This is when he publishes *The Urn* which contains one hundred sonnets, a book in which we see him uncomplaining, yet meditative and melancholy. The coming of Banchs did not alter the course of poetry, but the coming of Fernández Moreno did.

BALDOMERO FERNÁNDEZ MORENO (1886–1950) wrote steadily from the time he published his first book, *The Initials of the Missal* (*Las iniciales del misal,* 1915) to *Penumbra: The Book of Marcela* (*Penumbra: El libro de Marcela,* 1951). He wrote without moments of decline. His poetry moves always upward, steady, tense, and sustained. We know of very few cases, in his time, of such zealous poetic calling and such successful poetic inventiveness. He went through life in love with humble things and, by simply looking at them, saved them for poetry. He was an impressionist, perhaps the best impressionist in our literature. Those who believed that his poetry was trivial because his themes were trivial—the city of Buenos Aires, the country folk, the fields, the home, his labors and leisure moments, his inner tranquility— did not understand the depth of his imagination. On the surface his verses are elementary, but they are always complex. Simple but not prosaic. Sincere but not ordinary. Fernández Moreno was the type of poet who plants himself somewhere and looks about him, faithful to what he is as a man, and to what things are when seen in their essences. For him there was no one object more poetic than another: all things, the most common, the most insignificant, the smallest and most transitory, could be poetized. Each tiny portion of reality excited his fancy; and with two, three strokes he would give them a surprising meaning.

Like all good impressionists he was fragmentary. But in reading his books one admires the oneness of his ecstatic rapture before the world. There lies the world for him to sing of heartily. The poet may be sad, downcast, and melancholy, but being able to poetize gives joy to life. His sensorial impressions are disrobed by beautiful flashes of light. He had the gift of defining, of drawing in miniature, of synthesizing lyrically. Things take shape in metaphors; the metaphors are softly tinged with the sentimental touch of the poet. There is also ingenuity, which as pure ingenuity can be best seen in his aphoristic prose—*The Butterfly and the Rafter* (*La mariposa y la viga*, 1947). His language—learned because of all he had read and heard—was that of all Hispania. He arrived at simplicity through discipline and his discipline lent a curious air of classicism to his forms and of modernity to his spiritual restlessness. His school has been called "simplism" because, although not noticing it, he had formed a school, not only made up of Bufano, Camino, Mariani, Pedro Herreros, *et al.*, but also of those who admired him, like Alfonsina Storni. The master, of course, surprised everyone because he simplified without impoverishing. In observing what was close at hand, he added to Argentine poetry themes that the Modernists, for having looked in the distance, had not seen. According to his son César, the "simplist epoch" of sentimental spontaneity lasted until 1923 —*Provincial Interlude* (*Intermedio provinciano*), *The City* (*Ciudad*), *Argentine Countryside* (*Campo argentino*); from here to 1937 the "formal epoch," that of greatest preoccupation with artistic canons, opens— *Décimas, Sonnets* (*Sonetos*), *Seguidillas* [or *Dance Tunes*], *Ballads* (*Romances*)—and thence to 1950, the "substantial epoch," in which he deepens his intimate being until he touches the depth of his disillusionment and bitterness—*Penumbra*.

Banchs and Fernández Moreno moved in a traditional, classical, Hispanic current; along this road, another group—Augusto González Castro, 1897; Carlos Obligado, 1890–1949; Arturo Vázquez Cey, 1888–1958; Eugenio Julio Iglesias, 1897; Pedro Herreros, 1890–1937; and Antonio Pérez-Valiente de Moctezuma, 1895—followed, from which we will only tag Cané and Marasso. Luis Cané (1897–1957) gave Creole shading to the old voice of the Spanish people. Gracefully, freshly, and sensually he wrote ballads, couplets, and songs on love and adventure, past and present. Arturo Marasso (1890), a student of the classics, learned from them how to sing about universal themes, especially those of human destiny.

Some poets still clung to Romantic ways, others to Modernist ways. Among those of Romantic tone—because of the intensity of personal confessions—stands Alfonsina Storni (Suiza-Argentina, 1892–1938).

With the embers of her resentment against men, she kindled her poetry, but she also damaged it by leaving too much esthetic ash. She explained it thusly: "I am, in general, superior to the men around me, but physically, as a woman, I am their slave, their mold, their clay. I cannot love them freely: there is too much pride in me to submit to them. I lack the physical means to subdue them. The torment I feel is superior to my desire to write poetry . . ." She saw herself a humiliated, conquered, tortured woman, but, nonetheless, with a pagan need for love. She searched for it desperately. She had no illusions: she knew what a man was. "Your catacombs inundated by dead / obscure, muddy waters were / by these hands felt." Love of men but at the same time disillusionment and even disgust. An original note, therefore, in erotic feminine poetry. The theme: a disdainful, ironic, and always frustrated love of the male, "master of the world," for whom a woman is nothing but a "feast." The books of this first manner ran from *Sweet Mischief* (*El dulce daño*, 1918) to *Ochre* (*Ocre*, 1925), perhaps her best. In the end, Storni triumphs in her struggle against the male, but at the cost of her sensitivity. It is the triumph that the plant wins over its sap by drying up. (Can this be called a triumph?) The most tale-telling symbol had been, up to *Ochre* (*Ocre*), that of a violent and almost paradisiacal spring, as if Alfonsina always felt her flesh flowering. She abandoned her eroticism in *The World of Seven Wells* (*El mundo de siete pozos*, 1934) and also the Modernist make-up of her verses—looking for images hidden in things, she disarranged all the drawers of her verse and became a belated companion of the vanguardists. Life is not worth living, she seems to want to tell us. She had had easy literary success, because there were people who sympathized with her human struggles. But she, who had valiantly proclaimed her liberty as a woman, was also valiant in literature: she renounced her successes, she renounced her admirers and began a new type of poetry—tortured, intellectual, of different rhythms—that brought her away from her old public but brought her no new public. Now she stylized her non-passionate, serenely deceptive experiences in symbols of obscure keys: *Mask and Trefoil* (*Mascarilla y trébol*, 1938). She knew she was through. She wrote a sonnet—"I go to my sleep"—and went to the sea, to drown herself.

Also of Romantic tone is ARTURO CAPDEVILA (1889), although more eloquent than lyrical. First a tone of anguish (from *Melpomene*, 1912, to *Book of Night—El libro de la noche*, 1917). Then, beginning in *World Holiday* (*La fiesta del mundo*, 1922) his tone was resigned and even happy, and he spoke of his adolescence, of his voyages, of his civic emotions, and his language—rich in nuances—often flows spontaneously as does sincerity itself: then, we are moved. In his best instances—e.g., *Melpomene*—his verses quiver with the mystery of human depth.

This group closes with ENRIQUE MÉNDEZ CALZADA (1898–1940), HÉCTOR PEDRO BLOMBERG (1890–1955), and PEDRO MIGUEL OBLIGADO (1888).

In the second group, the poets of Modernist ways, the best are Ezequiel Martínez Estrada and Arrieta. The first will be studied later with the essayists of this generation. RAFAEL ALBERTO ARRIETA (1889) is a lyricist without excesses, limited, but within whose limits one sees, hears and feels things. He is elegant, demure, cold, and brief. *Soul and Moment* (*Alma y momento*, 1910), *The Mirror of the Fountain* (*El espejo de la fuente*, 1912), *Golden Nights* (*Las noches de oro*, 1917), *Fugacity* (*Fugacidad*, 1921), *Highland Summer* (*Estío serrano*, 1926) and *Captive Time* (*Tiempo cautivo*, 1947) are the subtle and veiled confidences of a distinctive spirit, more Nordic than Latin, who polished symbolist crystal so much that he tends to give it the transparencies of pure poetry. His is a poetry in a minor key, sweet and elegiac. This group closes with FERNÁN FÉLIX DE AMADOR (1889–1954) and ÁLVARO MELIÁN LAFINUR (1893–1958). And still another group could be opened here, those poets immersed in their American regions, such as JUAN CARLOS DÁVALOS (1887–1959), ALFREDO R. BUFANO (1895–1950) and ATALIVA HERRERA (1888–1953).

2. Abnormality

Let us now pass on to a group which, on leaving Modernism, slammed the door thunderously. It cannot be said that they were the best writers of their generation, but they were indeed the most audacious, the ones who best responded to the esthetic changes in all the arts of Europe. On opening this chapter we tried to put into proper perspective the relations between this literature and the effect of the war. The gestation of vanguard literature took longer than has been assumed. And conversely the effect of the war on it was far less decisive that has been supposed. The war was a concomitant event and not a cause. Long before the war, literature—and all of the arts—was becoming more and more insolent. Symbolism had taught a kind of revolutionary magic and, when it disappeared, the sorcerer's apprentices were not able to dominate their own revolutions. Not because painting can explain literature, but because it is easier and quicker to see changes in style on the walls of a museum than to disembowel them from the library stacks, the reader is invited to remember what happened in the plastic arts beginning about 1900: "fauvism," "expressionism," "cubism," Italian "futurism," French "orphism," Russian "irradiantism," "dadaism," "surrealism," etc. Think of the prodigious restlessness of Picasso which fills an entire history of picturesque "isms," and one has an idea of what was happening in European consciences long before the first World War. An analysis of the arts—or of the philosophic theories of the vitalists, irrationalists, neo-idealists, mystics, existentialists—would carry us to the same place: the spiritual energy with which the logical scaffolding raised by the common sense of the nineteenth century is demolished, in order that the plural dimensions of life should triumph. Ever since the days of symbolism, writers were convinced that literature was a permanent revolution. We have said already that in Hispanic-America Modernism is just that: a feeling that all fashions, all new manners, were worthy. In French literature Apollinaire, Salmon, Réverdy were demanding new revolutionary processes. First of all, the liquidation of symbolism. They took from the symbolists precious necklaces of metaphors in order to break the thread of meaning: let each metaphor roll where it will, like a loose pearl. Not only had the new writers completed the liberation of the so-called free verse of the symbolists, but they also carried symbolist irrationalism to its ultimate consequence: they denied the logical principle of identity, they denied causality, they denied the a priori concepts of time and space. Prior to 1914 then, there existed a disintegrating literature —in Spain the "greguerías" of Ramón Gómez de la Serna. But the first World War, from 1914 to 1918, exacerbated everyone. The instability of civilization, the power of political violence, the deprecation of man, the feeling of the absurdity of existence and of the world, the disillusionments with the pretensions of the seriousness of past art, produced an eruption of incoherent expression. The "isms" in painting had their equivalents in literature: expressionism, cubism, futurism and, during the war years, Dadá, the onomatopoeia of incoherence. Tristan Tzara, Paul Eluard, André Breton, Louis Aragon, Paul Morand, Blaise Cendrars, Drieu La Rochelle, Valery Larbaud, Max Jacob were the best known writers in Hispanic-America. The dadaists discovered that the subconscience was a source of esthetic pleasure: if verbal incoherence illuminates abysses of the soul, they used to say, why look for beauty? Far better to free the obscure and spontaneous forces. They wanted to touch the very sources of artistic creation, hence their attraction by the art of primitive peoples. Once this problem was posited, the dadaists prepared "surrealist" poetry, poetry dictated by the subconscious— André Breton, Philippe Soupault, Aragon. Artistic will diminishes and the esthetic pleasure of dreams and psychic automatisms increases. Many dadaists were swallowed up by this non-art. Those who survived profited by the obscure discoveries, for the purpose of constructing works sufficiently clear to mean something—Cocteau, Morand, Salmon.

The surrealist movement was more orderly and productive than the dadaist, but both concurred in their anti-materialism, in their aspiring for a more absolute reality than the one perceived normally, in the rejection of logical intelligence, in their yearning for escape, travel, adventure, dreams. In Hispanic-America this literature influenced some of the writers we studied in the first group. But now we shall separate the most exasperated. In almost all of the poets to be studied in this chapter we will notice strange things. The truth of the matter is that strange men moved in Modernism or, at least, men who had a strange manner of moving. But the strange ones who will occupy our attention now—Vallejo, Huidobro, Greiff, Girondo—move in the same direction; they meet, conspire, proselytize, and reach out to take hold of the banner that is to wave in the avant-garde. In what order shall we have them file by? In the order of poetic merit? Then César Vallejo would move to the head. In the order of greatest repercussion of their novelties? In that case, Vicente Huidobro. In the order in which they, slowly, slackened off from Modernism? Well then, Mariano Brull, Casal. In the order in which they gave their first fruits? Then, Huidobro again. This would be fine if one had only to consider a few individual poets, but we must give data on a multitude. Let them file by following the same order as in the previous chapters.

(1) *Mexico* / There were not in Mexico any César Vallejos or Vicente Huidobros. In any event, there was the aging José Juan Tablada, who was still experimenting in the war years with new forms of metaphors—synthetic poems, Japanese *haikais* —and he therefore influenced the abnormal cult of the free metaphor that now concerns us in this chapter. The stridentists (Maples Arce and List Arzubide) and the group from the review *Contemporáneos* (Pellicer, Gorostiza, Villaurrutia, Torres Bodet, Novo) do not fit here. We shall glance at them in the third part— "scandal"—and, more dilatorily, in the next chapter in the 1925 to 1940 literature.

(2) *Central America* / The few poets who were aware of an "avant-garde," of a "new sensibility," realized their vocation better in prose: Max Jiménez and Rogelio Sinán. In addition, they belong to the next period, from 1925 to 1940, where we will see them. The names to be dropped here are: VICENTE ROSALES Y ROSALES (El Salvador, 1894), who published his anthology in 1959, left Modernism, went on in search of new forms, and ended by speaking the language of the vanguardists. ANDRÉS RIVAS DÁVILA (Nicaragua, 1889–1930) was one of those who prepared the outburst of the avant-garde, with something of stridentism: *The Kiss of Eratus* (*El beso de Erato*).

(3) *Antilles* / In Cuba it was MARIANO BRULL (1891–1956) whose sails were swollen with the first winds of the new poetry. He began with a serene lyricism: *The House of Silence* (*La casa del silencio*, 1916). Attracted by the ideals of pure poetry—to liberate verse from

anything that could be said in prose, according to Valéry's definition—
Brull got into the vanguard with *Waning Poems* (*Poemas en menguante*,
1928). These were the years in which the new poets, gathered to celebrate the third centennial of Góngora, discovered that Gongorism was
present, and not past, and that at the light of this high moon they could
write better than ever a poetry of pure images and beautiful themes.
Afterwards Brull published *Rotund Song* (*Canto redondo*, 1934), *Rose
Solo* (*Solo en rosa*, 1941), *Time in Torment* (*Tiempo en pena*, 1950).
There is no evolution in his work, nevertheless—it is monotonic (and
even monotonous). Brull helps each thing—the rose, the sea, the stone,
the eyes of children—bring to light a metaphor. Beautiful metaphors,
but they leave the bowels of the world, from where they came, in ruins.
Brull permitted himself one game: the free invention of sounds as the
dadaists had done. He believed, as the dadaists did, that everything
could be said in poetry, provided it sounded different from what older
poets had written. His punishment was that the readers paid more
attention to the mere sound effects of some of his word plays—e.g.,
"Green Cajolery" (*"Verdehalago"*)—than to the imagination, beauty,
serenity, and tenderness of his poems. From one of his games—*"Fili-
flama alabe cundre / ala olalúnea alífera / alveolea jitanjáfora / liris
salumba salífera"*—Alfonso Reyes took the word *"jitanjáfora"* and made
it famous as a reference to those stupid and sonorous sisters of metaphors that erupted in this deliberately infantile poetry.

Other Cubans accompanied the youths in their vanguardist subversion: Regino
Pedroso, Juan Marinello and, above all, MANUEL NAVARRO LUNA (1894) who,
beginning with *Furrow* (*Surco*, 1928) basted metaphors onto diminutive allegories
and drew calligrams.

The Dominican Republic, late with its Modernism, received early the tendencies
of postwar vanguardism, due to the advent of "posthumism." The word "posthumism," like "futurism" and "ultraism," manifested the impossible desire to write
the literature of the-day-after-tomorrow. But the posthumists diluted Dadá's wine.
In their tiny country they seemed quite daring to themselves, but in comparison
to what was being done elsewhere, they were scarcely extravagant. They thought
they were iconoclasts because they neglected the language; they were enthralled
with free verse and did not study the great poets of the past. But they lacked the
mischievous, playful, and irreverent spirit of the vanguardists. *From the Posthumous Movement* (*Del movimiento postumista*, 1922) was the first anthological
pamphlet. The posthumists were legion, and in their stampedes they wanted any
ridiculousness to pass as poetry. One of them, nevertheless, the Supreme Pontiff
of Posthumism, was the best poet that had been produced up to then on the island
of Santo Domingo: DOMINGO MORENO JIMENES (1894). His first booklet of new
poetry was *Psalms* (*Psalmos*, 1921). He ignored the traditional forms of the verse,
and with his melancholic humor he would soften and work up ideas. Anarchic
and uneven, he looked about him, and the landscape of his country entered his

poetry, detail after detail. His nativist, landscapist, and folklorist realism is his greatest merit. After all, it was something his predecessors had not done. And as for his elegiac sentiments and ideas, they miscarried because his language was plain, opaque, lax, and poor in imagination. When he does synthesize his ideas in an image, he manages a very personal poem, and at these moments one phrase has the power of an entire poem. Later they bestowed the title of Supreme Pontiff of Posthumism on RAFAEL AUGUSTO ZORRILLA (1892–1937), author of micro-poems of keen sensibility, but it is only Moreno Jimenes who is saved. Despite all, posthumism has been one of the most consequential, combative, and durable movements on the island. Related to it were: JULIO ALBERTO CUELLO (1898), ANDRÉS AVELINO GARCÍA SOLANO (1899), MANUEL LLANES (1899), RAFAEL AMÉRICO HENRÍQUEZ (1899) whom we shall see later.

In Puerto Rico the promoter of new tendencies was EVARISTO RIBERA CHEVRE-MONT (1896). When he returned from Spain in 1924, where he had been for five years, he diffused the poetry that he had become acquainted with in ultraist circles. His "vanguardist page," which appeared for ten years in *La Democracia*, was an organ of esthetic propaganda and also a laboratory for poetry. His program was to break with the excessively eloquent, solemn, and heavy forms that pre-dominated. But he did not affiliate with the Puerto Rican "isms" nor with Vicente Palés Matos' "euphorism" and "no-ism" nor with Graciany Miranda Archilla's "watchtowerism" ("*atalayismo*"). Ribera Chevremont liked to experiment with new techniques—*Hebe's Glass* (*La copa de Hebe*, 1922) was his free verse experiment—but in reality he felt more attracted to tradition, as is obvious in his *Poetic Anthology* (*Antología poética*, 1924–1950). He was a universalist; he respected what the Parnassians and symbolists had done. Traditionally Hispanic forms per-sisted in him; and although he did not allow himself to be suffocated by native subjects, neither did he yield to the revolutions that followed dadaism.

(4) *Venezuela* / Except for timid vanguardist prancings by Andrés Eloy Blanco or Fernando Paz Castillo, writers jumped from the "normality" we studied in the first section to the "scandal" we will study in the third.

(5) *Colombia* / Between the poets of the Centennial that we have seen already and the "new ones," whom we shall see, can be placed, all alone, LEÓN DE GREIFF (1895). Complex, introverted, Narcissistic, sarcastic, discontented, imaginative, with explosions of rhythms, words, and madness, always lyrical, León de Greiff was, among the best Co-lombian poets, the one who cut the tape at the vanguardist bridge. From *Tergiversations* (*Tergiversaciones*, 1925) to *Farrago* (1955) he never stopped his contortions. Actually from 1915, in the review *Panida* of Medellín, he had already begun to amaze with a poetry that resem-bled nothing known in Colombia. Later, both in Spain and in Hispanic-America, poets appeared that left León de Greiff in the shade—but he came first and what he did came from his own head. Youthful in his lyrical rapture, the years pass, but he continues to enjoy the respect of the youths, generation after generation. He is not easy to read, how-ever. He handles words like musical instruments and distributes them

as to an orchestra. His free verse is contained by the musical structures of the rondel, counterpoint, and others which make it sound forth with repetitions that, although inevitable, are at the same time surprising. The words—archaisms, onomatopoeias, neologisms, cultisms— the capricious repertory of themes—legends, reminiscences of strange authors, Scandinavian landscapes—the sudden changes in mood, and the constant excitement also contribute to the difficulty, not of understanding, but of enjoying his work.

(6) *Ecuador* / HUGO MAYO (1898) imitated the dadaists and the creationists somewhat. Although reluctant to publish in books, he is still respected for his original personality.

(7) *Peru* / It has been shown already how some Peruvian poets broke lances with Modernism. Added must be RICARDO PEÑA BARRENECHEA (1893–1949). In *Flowering* (*Floración,* 1924) he was still a sentimentalist of the old school, but later he disciplined his poetry and made it move along recently opened trails. Like Góngora, whom he admired and emulated, he cultivated cultist and popular lyrics. At times he was seen in the poetic vanguard with those younger than he. His lyricism flitted about graciously telling us about his loves, without convincing us when he became serious. He was proud of his poetic licenses and images, inspired by Góngora, "supreme acrobat of Spanish syntax, juggler of hyperbaton, unicyclist of color." Also to be added is JUAN PARRA DEL RIEGO (1894–1925), who during the years of World War I, took possession of the images of the new language of speed, machinery, sports, jazz, and violent action. His "Ode to the Motorcycle" was epoch-making. His "polyrhythms" as well. Nevertheless, all this was still not vanguardism. José Carlos Mariátegui, an essayist who focused on serious social problems with Marxist lenses, had said in 1924 that futurism, cubism, dadaism, and pirouettes of the decadent bourgeoisie would not emerge in Peru. It is curious that of all the vanguardist reviews—the vanguardism of the first of these, *Flechas,* 1924, could hardly be said to have been impetuous—*Amauta* (1926–30), directed precisely by Mariátegui, would be the one that lent itself most to these pirouettes. However, in addition, other enthusiasms were aired. Mariátegui was in sympathy with the idea of revolution and it did not matter whether the revolution be in politics or in letters. *Amauta,* in consequence, being leftist, published everything. For many years the books of a Peruvian, ALBERTO HIDALGO (1897), were arriving from Buenos Aires. A "futurist," like Marinetti, he sang to war, energy, violence, anti-democracy, the machine, and speed, extravagant in his manipulations of all the "isms." He believed himself to be an ingenious poet. He had less stature than his megalomania led him to believe. After his *Chemistry of the Spirit* (*Química del espíritu,* 1923) he collected through distillation, *Simplism* (*Simplismo,* 1925): here he proposed his own "ism," which consisted of reducing poetic substance to pure metaphors. "In the air our glances graze / many flocks of metaphors," he used to say. "Let the world stand on its head; let evil people govern it; let the strong crush the weak: it matters not to me. I am but a poet and only build metaphors! Poetry is necessary, but it is useless, u-s-e-l-e-s-s!" But, in the vanguardism of those years, no one was able to rise as high nor go as far as Vallejo had in *Trilce.*

CÉSAR VALLEJO (Peru, 1892–1938) left on his first poetic voyage—
The Black Heralds (*Los heraldos negros,* 1918)—away from the esthetics
of his forefathers, Rubén Darío, Herrera y Reissig, and the Lugones
of *Sentimental Lunar Poems,* carrying in his pockets, like gifts of candy,
many verses from the Modernist cupboard. But the lad, though he
keeps eating the candy on the way, withdraws from cosmopolitanism
to head toward national, regional, popular, and indigenist areas. Mestizo the author, mestizo the poetry. His Parnassian and symbolist blood
circulates through his verses mixed with that of Peruvian realism. His
themes are erotic or family love; the daily life in his land of *cholos* or
mestizo laborers; and his mood is one of sadness, disillusion, bitterness,
and suffering. Man suffers fatal, undeserved blows: "There are blows
in the world, so hard . . . I don't know! / Blows like the hatred of
God." He was born without wanting to be; and until death may come,
he cries, and sympathizes with his fellow man who also suffers, and
when a blow does not strike him he feels guilty knowing that that blow
has fallen on another unfortunate. This impulse for human solidarity
will take him later to political rebellion. Meanwhile, his next book is
of pure poetic rebellion: *Trilce* (1922). It was an explosion. Literary
traditions burst into pieces, and the poet advanced in search of liberty.
Free verses, to begin with, but not only free in meters and rhythms,
but also freed of syntax and logic, with images fleeing freely in all
directions without looking at each other, and with such speed that at
times they are lost in the darkness without the reader being able to
recognize them. Cubism? Creationism? Ultraism? Surrealism? Vallejo
had read the French symbolists in translations; and in a translation by
Cansinos-Assens, published in 1919, he must have read Mallarmé's *"Un
coup de dés,"* a poem which animated all the avant-garde of Europe
and which seems to have left its mark on the hermetic construction
of *Trilce.* This book, his most important, has many unsuccessful poems.
In the worst instances we come across merely external caprices: grammatical and typographical irregularities; meaningless sounds; unnecessary verbal mechanisms; ugly mixtures of technical and popular terms,
hackneyed expressions and obscure neologisms (the title *Trilce* was,
for example, a whimsical neologism invented from an insignificant circumstance). But these same caprices become ennobled—that is, they
stop being caprices—when they contribute to the expression of a deep
intuition of life. In these cases the poems reveal the serious, tormented,
desolate soul with which Vallejo, convinced of the absurdity of existence,
recalls his lost home, his dead mother, and his early sufferings. The

poems in *Trilce* are irrational and unintelligible; only those in which Vallejo has elaborated sentiments common to all men move us. The value of this book is primarily historical. In 1922 Vallejo was thirty years old, but he exhibited some of the traits of adolescent vanguardism that appeared after World War I. Later on we will refer to this vanguardism. However, Vallejo's poetry is not dehumanized. His feeling, his subconscious shadows, his experiences of poverty, orphanhood, and suffering in prison, his protest against injustice, his feeling of pious brotherhood toward all the oppressed, rise through the crevices of his versification.

After *Trilce* Vallejo left his country (he was not to return to Peru, ever) and withdrew from poetry: he wrote short stories, novels, dramas, and many newspaper articles. He lived in France, Spain, Russia, and other countries. He was now a Communist and wrote literature of Marxist, revolutionary propaganda. The Spanish civil war forced out the *Human Poems* (*Poemas humanos*) which were published posthumously in 1939. The old pity he felt for the underprivileged now turns to action; the old desolation, to hopeful combat. And the poet, as he sings of his own belligerency and that of the masses, arrives, naked and free, at the deepest part of his being—his incoherent emotions. Of his prose works the stories were the most significant part. *Savage Speech* (*Fabla salvaje*) is the history of a neurasthenic, the peasant Balta, who feels himself followed, pursued by the shadow of a human form which he occasionally surprises in the mirror or in the reflections of a stream, watching him from behind. Hallucinations, forebodings, and doubt grow in his mind while in his wife's womb a child is growing: just when the child is born, he, Balta, harassed by the shadow, falls over a cliff and dies. The unfortunate atmosphere depicted with magical realism tends to shine with poetic images. With the title of *Musical Scenes* (*Escenas melografiadas*) he collected some loose pages: prison memories, poems in prose, fantastic stories ("*Los Caynas*"), all in a prose verdant with verbal buds, with dadaist and surrealist phrases, with expressionist fantasies. After his first trip to Russia (1928) he abandoned this artistic attitude and served the Communist Party with a propaganda novel: *Tungsten* (*Tungsteno*, 1931). The hero is the blacksmith Huanca, whom we see in the last pages preparing the social revolution with Marxist catchwords. The action takes place a little before 1917. A United States company has bought the tungsten mines in the province of Cuzco. We are presented with the exploitation of the Indians, the political corruption, the brutality of the police, the debauchery of priests and bourgeoisie, the servility of the intellectuals, in truculent scenes of sex, misery, drunkenness, and death. The prose is journalistic, discursive, plain; also conventional is the lineal composition of the story. All leads to one end: to exalt the example of Lenin, to promote world revolution, and, in Peru, to dignify the Indians and to give political power to the workers and peasants. The intellectuals are assigned a role: "to place themselves at our orders and at the service of our interests," says the worker Huanca.

(8) *Bolivia* / RAFAEL BALLIVIÁN (1898) falls here in view of his cosmopolitanism that looks for novelty—*The Illumined Path* (*La senda iluminada,* 1924).

(9) *Chile* / The most notable Chileans in this panorama of "abnormality" that we are offering are Huidobro and Rokha. When the anthology *Lyrical Forest* (*Selva lírica*) is published in 1917, Rokha seems to be closer than Huidobro to Marinetti's futurism and other vanguard tendencies. Rokha is better represented in this anthology than Huidobro. Alongside him Huidobro seems insipid. But with time, Huidobro keeps growing until he becomes the Chilean poet of most significance.

PABLO DE ROKHA (1894) is a poetic personage more than a poet. An abnegator who is contusive, emphatic, affirmative, he drowns in his own words. He had an influence on other Chilean writers: one of those influenced was no less than Pablo Neruda (the older Pablo however is a desperate poet whom we shall not take seriously; and Pablo the younger, on the other hand, is a serious poet who will never convince us that he is really desperate). The demoniacal and disoriented Rokha has the voice of a Romantic. Like the Romantics he confronts what he calls the "infinite," the "eternal." And while he moans and roars he feels like a titan. He howls a foreboding of death. His emphasis determines the quality of everything gigantic, tremendous, colossal. A volcanic eruption that releases its pressure in a long enumeration of images broken in pieces, or molten in formless lava. Poetic gems in prosaic slag. The disorder of his poems does not always render, legitimately, the vision of a disordered world—at times it is just a failure in the composition. The undulation of his verses does not always release what is shaking him from within: at times it is just free-versism. For this reason his gigantism tends to resemble the characteristic diffusion of gas. His best poems ("Circle," etc.) combine lenses that make objects appear farther away as well as closer; and as the images are mixed, they superimpose in enlargements and miniatures (century and scarf; world and skirt; God and bottle, and so on). He is very Chilean and understands the obscure meanderings of the Creole soul and the meaning of popular language. Because he loved the people, he wrote civic, political poetry (which he believed to be Marxist). He stopped feeling like the "illumined one," "the terrible megalomaniac of metaphors" in order to dedicate his soul to the "social service, which is its truth"—"Allegory of Torment" (*"Alegoría del tormento"*). In spite of his love of the populace—manifested in folkloric subjects and communist catchwords—his excessive invectiveness and megalomania have prevented him from being truly popular: *Ode to the USSR* (*Oda a la USSR*), *Morphology of Fright* (*Morfología del espanto*).

VICENTE HUIDOBRO (Chile, 1893–1948) has claimed for himself the honor of being the father of Creationism. Not everyone concedes it to him. Be that as it may, he was one of the first poets in our language who was in the vanguard of European literature and, among other happy innovations, he proffered this one: a poetry that magically obliterates the real world and, in the emptiness that remains, raises, almost magically, a new ideal world. This is poetry, then, as absolute creation—"creationist" poetry. This pride in creation—"The Poet is a little God," says Huidobro—is as old as poetry itself, but it was contained or dissimulated in those styles which for centuries imitated nature or imitated imitations of nature. With symbolism, from Mallarmé to Apollinaire, the poet denies the purely adjectival function of qualifying a reality outside himself and, on the other hand, he affirms energetically his substantive function of inventing objects inside his own conscience. Huidobro incorporates himself into the host of poets having this divine vocation; and he was so precocious that in a few years he skipped several stages of a long historical process. On arriving at this point, the historian must be very cautious, since the documents relative to the theoretical formation of Creationism are those that Huidobro himself administered later, and it is possible that he forged lectures and non-existing editions. It is known that the vanity of writers who wish to act as masters of ceremonies of literary schools tends to antedate their opinions and their poems. In all events, it seems that at the outbreak of World War I, in the manifesto *Non serviam* (1914) read in Chile, he begins to undertake the road that Apollinaire had opened in 1912 in *Esthetic Meditations*. Apollinaire had spoken of the "servitude" to nature, and that "it is time we were our own masters." Huidobro says: "*Non serviam*. I shall not be your slave, Mother Nature; I shall be your master ... I shall have my trees, and they will not be like yours; I shall have my mountains, I shall have my rivers and my oceans, I shall have my sky and my stars. And no longer will you tell me: that tree is bad; I don't like that sky ... , mine are better;" "Until now we have done nothing better than imitate different aspects of the world, we have created nothing. What has come from us that was not first standing in front of us, all around us ... ? We have raised our hymns to Nature (something that matters very little to her). We have never created our own realities ... We have accepted, without further reflection, the fact that no other reality exists other than the one around us, and have not thought that we too can create realities in a world of our own, in a world that awaits its own fauna and its own flora."

In short, instead of imitating Nature, the poet must proceed as she does, and create. During the war, in a lecture given in the city of Buenos Aires in 1916, it seems he said, "all history of art is no more than the history of the evolution of mirror-man to god-man;" a work of art "is a new cosmic reality that the artist adds to Nature." And less than ten years later Huidobro remembers: "That is where they baptized me with the name *creationist* for having said in my lecture that the first condition of being a poet is to create, the second to create and the third to create." A month later he published the booklet, *The Water Mirror* (*El espejo de agua,* this edition of 1916 can not be found), where his famous "Poetic Art" appears: "Why sing to the rose, oh Poets! / Let it bloom in your poem." The composition that gives the title to the booklet beautifully illustrates his esthetic manner. Toward the end of 1916 Huidobro arrived in Paris and joined the group led by Apollinaire and the review *Nord Sud,* which also counted among its contributors Pierre Réverdy, Tristan Tzara, Paul Dermée, and Max Jacob. Huidobro is not just a simple follower because he collaborated on an equal level. Huidobro published poems in French, which escape the confines of this history, though in many of them there are definite outlines of his Creationism: *Horizon carré* (1917), *Tour Eiffel* (1917), *Hallalli* (1918), *Saisons Choisies* (1921), *Automne régulier* (1924), *Tout à coup* (1925). Huidobro is the one who brings us new French axioms, the one who speaks the new French poetic language. That is, due to Huidobro the new French style becomes Hispanic-American. In 1918 he arrived in Madrid, and immediately his Creationism marked another direction in the desire to travel new esthetic roads that he urged upon the youth. He perturbed some, enthused others; he was envied and feted. And the poetry of the generation of '98, even Juan Ramón Jiménez', suddenly appeared pallid (although no less beautiful) alongside the daubed face of Huidobro. His presence (after a trip to Chile, he was in Madrid again in 1921) assisted at the birth of what was to be known as Ultraism. When one reads the poems of Spanish and Hispanic-American ultraists, he imagines that they all, at one time, passed over the Huidobro bridge. The bulk of the Huidobro rockets began to burst in Castilian literature with *Arctic Poems* (*Poemas árticos*) and *Ecuatorial,* both of 1918. The musical poets were those who became annoyed at all the ruckus. The visual poets, accustomed to silent movies, noticed on the other hand that those rockets were signal flares or fireworks which, with their firecrackers, girandoles, sparklers, Bengal lights and pyrotechnic castles, gave the night its festive air. They looked upon the rain of images with an admiring, ah! Thundering rockets, but also sparkling rockets: "A nightingale in his down pillow / beat his wings so much / that he loosed a downpour of snow;" "I made rivers run / that never existed. / With a cry I raised a mountain / and around it we danced a new dance."; "I am the old mariner / who sews the severed horizons" (*Arctic Poems*). "The wind rocks the horizons / that hang from the rigging and the sails"; "Slowly the captive cities pass by / sewn together one by one with telephone lines"; "The black slave / opens his mouth quickly / for his pianist master / who makes his teeth play" (*Ecuatorial*). Huidobro had rejected Marinetti's Futurism—for being too muscular and extroverted—and André Breton's Surrealism—because its source was mental debility and its medium a feigned automatism—in order to promote his esthetics of Creationism that went deep into the inner self to produce autonomous poetic objects that could not be compared to the objects of nature.

Only the Poet, he says, "possesses the vertiginous mirrors that surprise the metamorphoses as they pass by." His formula: "To make a poem like nature makes a tree." What does this mean? It means that the poet must create, invent new things like the forces of nature but without imitating nature. How? With the metaphor. Things are despoiled of their real being and imaginatively fused with another being. Creationism, then, was a way of metaphorizing. He supressed comparisons and the logical connection of fantasy to reality and he established as truth the fact that "slowly the captive cities pass by / sewn together one by one with telephone lines." What seems to be a simile, becomes real, the image becomes object. The world that our intelligence accepts and arranges Huidobro counters, in good humor, with an invented world. This is what poets have always done, but Huidobro surprised all with his chaotic enumerations, his neologisms, his manifold deluding images, his free verses capriciously spelled, his cult of meaningless words and unconnected letters of the alphabet, his capers mocking literature. The humor of the dadaists had freed poetry from an excessive weight of melancholy. Huidobro, too, gives freedom to poetry through his humor. His humor is neither comical nor somber: it is poetic. Huidobro continues to grow, and with him grows his ambition. He strives for longer and more confidential poems. The more he confesses, the more surrealist become his creationist images. He tells us of his life, his yearnings, his disillusions. This is the best Huidobro, the anguished Huidobro who, in denying God in order to take his place as a divine poet, finds himself in a void. He can, of course, create his own world of images, but it is a fallacious creation. With his mind full of inventions, in his imagination he feels he is falling toward death. This is the Huidobro of *Altazor* (1931), *See and Feel* (*Ver y palpar*, 1941) and *The Citizen of Oblivion* (*El ciudadano del olvido*, 1941). The *Last Poems* (*Ultimos poemas*, 1948) are posthumous. According to Huidobro he composed those books between 1919 and 1934. Here, through the openings of his Harlequin's mask, Huidobro's eyes are looking at death. Once the things we call real are abolished, Huidobro casts his metaphor-glances to fill the great void; and he casts them —here lies his seriousness—with the deliberate and conscious intent of being "an absolute creator, a god-artist." His metaphor-glances fly, because this flight figures in his theoretical program—poetry as flight— and because flight was the rising impulse of Huidobro's aerial nature. "Flight" and "Travel" are the two beautiful constellations in his metaphoric zodiac: sky, wings, light, angels, airplanes, birds, meteors, wind, arrows, indicate that Huidobro, on nullifying reality, flies through the air to the center of his subjectivity. What has wings is positive: adventure, play, life. What does not have wings is negative: sadness, sickness, downfall, death. *Altazor or Voyage in Parachute* (*Altazor o El viaje en paracaídas*) tells us of this fall down to the depths of oneself, this tumbling toward death. It is one of the worthiest poems of this period; and in his verses, as in the prose of *Satyr* (*Sátiro*), Huidobro proves that Creationism was not a game, but the anatomy and physiology of his theory of poetry, a theory lived and not thought up. Altazor is Huidobro himself, *alto azor* or hawk on high, "hawk fulminated by the heights," "Vicente anti-poet and magician."

He wanted to live with things, but how was he to sustain himself in a world of imaginary creation, of pure vision without meaning, a world dreamed by a small god who does not believe in the great God, a nothing-world, in a word? One afternoon he took up his parachute, he explains in the preface, and leaped into the hollow spaces of the void. "My parachute began to fall giddily. Such is the force of the attraction of death and the open grave." And as he falls he recited his poems, "aerial feats." Throughout seven cantos Altazor-Huidobro renounces the world, falls in "an eternal traveling into the interior of himself," falls to the depths where death awaits him. "Justice," he exclaims, "what have you done with me, Vicente Huidobro?" And the fallen angel, in its "fall without end, of death in death," tragically "challenges the void" and transforms the universe in an incessant metaphoric re-creation. The poet gives us his biography as a magician of words with his anxieties and insurrections. And in the fall his words, little by little, become mad—"a beautiful madness in the zone of language"

—lose their grammar, change into pure sound, break up into loose letters and in the final canto they fuse in the chaos: "*Lalalí* / Io ia i i i o / Ai a i ai i i i i o ia." In *See and Feel,* the same tone. In "Song of Livingdead" ("*Canción de la muervida*") he speaks of the dead who "are exiled from earth and enheavened in the skies." "Let us fly to nothingness / . . . / Fly like a sensitive bird when death comes nigh." "I fall from my soul / and I break into pieces of soul upon the winter." In the first poem in *The Citizen of Oblivion,* when he takes an account of his thirty years, he asks "what madness has made us be born, / from whence this substance of bitterness comes"; and when he remembers his life as the poet who sang within his enigmas, he adds that then "I did not know the weight of my death." In another poem, "In Time's ear," he says "I contemplate from such heights that all becomes air"; and then the world crumbles into nothingness, a nothingness that only those who agonize can feel. In "Transfiguration": "the universe only discovers its alliances / moving through the insides of yourself. / In this amalgam of echoes / I am living and I will be dead." He also wrote theatrical pieces and novels. Of the former, *In the Moon (En la luna,* 1934), "a little guignol," is a political farce which ends with the collectivist revolution in which the intellectual of the 1930's believed. His novels were more interesting. *Cagliostro* was published in fragments between 1921 and 1922; the first edition is of 1934; we have seen the second edition of 1942. A "film-novel" Huidobro calls it. If this is so, it looks more like a joke played on the movies, since the plot is absurd, truculent, mysterious in the bad sense. Huidobro's ironic posters have not been sufficient to convert Cagliostro's adventures into literature (if one follows this Cagliostro to the end it is because interest in him existed before, when we first met him in Alexander Dumas). Then came *Mio Cid Campeador* (1929). But the novel that interests us most for its professional revelations is *Satyr or The Power of Words (Sátiro o El poder de las palabras,* 1939). The novel intertwines two themes: the double development in the neurotic Bernardo Saguen of a literary vocation and an unbridled sexual desire for ten-year-old girls. Since in poetry a word creates a reality—this is Huidobro's creationist credo—the word "satyr," hurled unjustly in the face of Bernardo (chapter II), results in creating in him a real satyr. His efforts to be a writer and not a satyr, and the failure of both efforts, are the sum total of the novel. An interior novel, then, in which there are lightning strokes of "creationist poetry." In general, a novel more reflexive than introspective. For a few fleeting moments, nevertheless, Huidobro tries the direct interior monolog that reveals the stream of Bernardo's consciousness.

(*10*) *Paraguay* / We will gather the poets later, when we study Campos Cervera.

(*11*) *Uruguay* / Julio J. Casal (1889–1954) broke the soft Modernist line of his first books, and from 1921 he became attached to ultraism, more in sympathy than in verses. From *Tree* (*Árbol*, 1923) to *Musical Hillock* (*Colina de la música*, 1933) Casal went about looking for poetry, finding it, losing it, and then once again looking, finding, and losing. Three poets already mentioned could be brought into the picture here: Carlos Rodríguez Pintos, who looked into the metaphoric shops of the postwar period; Silva Valdés, nativist, but with images of a new quality; Parra del Riego, Peruvian, but who showed up at the salons of Uruguayan poetry.

(*12*) *Argentina* / A partial Lugones—the one of the *Sentimental Lunar Poems*— and a complete Macedonio Fernández was the farthest reach of the Modernist generation: and this is recognized by the young postwar ultraists. Between these two Modernists and the young ultraists, there were poets who were coming and going, and the abnormality consisted of this coming and going. Of those born during the last fifteen years of the nineteenth century, some approach ultraism. Ricardo Güiraldes, in *The Crystal Cowbell* (*El cencerro de cristal*, 1915), had poems which anticipated the watchwords of ultraism—"to drink what comes / to have the soul of a prow," can be read in "Travel"—and, in fact, he joined in the revision of *Proa* and *Martín Fierro;* however Güiraldes will be studied as a writer of prose. It has been stated already that Alfonsina Storni, in *World of Seven Wells* (1934) became a vanguardist. The anomaly of Évar Méndez (1888–1955) is not in his own work—four books of poems that would not have alarmed Rubén Darío—but in his enthusiasm for the work of the younger group. He directed *Martín Fierro*, introduced some ultraist poems, and paraded the banner of an esthetic movement not his own. For his playful wit and his acrobatics, mention can be made of Emilio Lascano Tegui (1887). He made himself a "viscount" for the same caprice that Ducasse had made himself "count of Lautréamont." His verses *The Shadow of la Empusa* (*La sombra de la Empusa*, 1910); *The Singing Tree* (*El árbol que canta*, 1911); *Boy from San Telmo* (*Muchacho de San Telmo*, 1954) and his prose works *On Elegance While One Sleeps* (*De la elegancia mientras se duerme*, 1925) are fanciful, humorous, dextrous. An *enfant terrible* was Oliverio Girondo (1891). He was not a child when he committed his first mischief: *Twenty Poems to Be Read in the Trolley* (*Veinte poemas para ser leídos en el tranvía*, 1922). But he did approach the postwar boys, formed an ultraist gang; and when the boys grew up and became serious, Girondo stayed a child. He grew old without growing in ultraist stature. He is the Peter Pan of Argentine ultraism. He edited the manifesto of the review *Martín Fierro* (1924): a nationalist program by a reader of Apollinaire, Morand, and Max Jacob. Girondo is aphoristic, explosive, disoriented, metaphoric, dadaist, and surrealist in verse *Decalcomanías* (*Calcomanías*, 1925) as well as in prose *Scarecrows* (*Espantapájaros*, 1932). In *Persuading Days* (*Persuasión de los días*, 1942) and above all in *Our Fields* (*Campo nuestro*, 1946) it looked as if he might change; but in *The Moremarrow* (*La masmédula*, 1954) he returns to his own, which is a bell-ringing lyricism.

3. Scandal

It has just been seen how some of the inheritors of Modernism, having used up their inheritances, began to build up new fortunes.

There were poets younger than these, born without this inheritance, who dedicated themselves to the new industry: that of the metaphor to the ultimate, that of the ultraistic metaphor, that of ultraism. It was a scandal. But even scandals, no matter how sudden and unexpected they may seem, in literature, above all in Hispanic-American literature which is so timid in its experiments, come after practices, tests, imitations. In 1918 after the end of the war, some poets who were over forty caught glimpses of the flames from the conflagration in which the expressionists, the cubists, the futurists, and the dadaists had burned the libraries and museums. And, in order to take part in the madness in some way, they leaped in the air, clicked their heels, and cut capers. We have spoken of Lugones and his *Sentimental Lunar Poems,* of Herrera y Reissig and his "Moonlight Gathering," of Eguren and his *Symbolics,* of Tablada and his *Ideographic Verses.* Following the obscure vein of symbolism, they at least came close to the "creationism" that Huidobro was to impose later. There were among the poets who were less than forty years old at the end of the war some who occasionally or belatedly felt the desire of doing what the Europeans had done, from expressionism to dadaism: Alfonso Reyes, López Velarde, Peña Barrenechea, Ibarbourou, Storni. Others, who were around thirty years old when the war ended, were more violent, decisive, and conscious of their desire to scandalize: Vallejo, Huidobro, Girondo, Greiff.

But the first poets to emerge completely from the negation of Modernism and its styles were those who were less than twenty years old when the war ended: Borges and Co. This movement was concomitant with the one in Spain; and the Spaniards and Hispanic-Americans put their heads together to formulate a new esthetic program, like the brothers-in-law Borges and Guillermo de Torre. GUILLERMO DE TORRE (Spain–Argentina, 1900) imposed the happy word "ultraism" to illustrate the literature of the avant-garde: his 1925 book *European Literatures of the Avant-Garde* (*Literaturas europeas de vanguardia*) was the first panorama offering a synthesis of the new tendencies, leveling off, and integrating European, Hispanic, and Hispanic-American elements. By 1919 the whole group, Spaniards and Hispanic-Americans, is called "ultraist." "Ultraism" alludes to a youthful and liberating point beyond, a desire to go beyond goals. "Here is our motto: Ultra, in which all advanced tendencies will fit." This word remained as the landmark which indicated, not the birth of a current, nor that the current passed by the mark, but that that current existed. The official ultraist group—with the exception of the Spaniard Garfias and the Hispanic-American Borges—did not have any great poet in the few years it lasted, from 1919 to 1922. And these two were great not just during these years but afterwards. One could say: ultraism does not exist. But no doubt loose vanguard currents existed in poets who were foreign to ultraism. In any case, ultraism existed in reviews, not in books. From 1919 on, the reviews already in existence become ultraist (*Grecia* and *Cervantes*, from 1919 to 1920) and those that come to light are born ultraist (the Spanish *Ultra*, 1921–22; the Argentine *Proa*, 1922–23, *Prisma*, 1921–22, *Martín Fierro*, first period 1919, second 1924–27; the Mexican *Horizonte*, 1926–27, and *Contemporáneos*, 1928–31; the Cuban *Revista de Avance*, 1927–30; and the Uruguayan *Los Nuevos*, 1920, and *Alfar*, which lasted until 1954). Ultraism was a most happy word. There were many other labels: simplism, creationism, vanguardism, cubism, dadaism, posthumism, surrealism, stridentism, advanceism, and so forth. When new explosive esthetics were lacking, they made simplicity itself explode in "simplism" (Évar Méndez). It was said that ultraism lay "beyond all other 'isms'"—that is, it was an "ism" to get away from all other "isms." The "isms" that appeared were branches of the great industrial plant situated in Europe. But this time, the Spanish-American writers who had been born around 1900 wrote simultaneously with the Europeans. Never before had we been so close to synchronizing our clocks with those of Europe. But they were clocks bought at local bazaars. Those who were adolescents when the World War ended wound up the clocks, set the alarms, and let them go off noisily so that everyone might believe that a new literary hour had begun.

It is difficult to study these "isms" because, at first, they did not intend to exist as literature. They must be studied in two steps: the first in "little magazines," the second in books. This chapter is concerned with the first, which was the really scandalous one. These magazines are interesting not so much for a history of literature as for a history of literary life. In them are found all the excesses, madnesses, nonsense, badinage, nihilisms, and scandals. Poetry could not move like this. It had to accept coherence. After all, no matter how irrational a poem may be, it must offer a minimum of sense in order to be generic and understandable. Some poets, obstinate in their folly, disappeared or became shadows or stayed to beat in the drum sections of jazz bands. Others saved themselves in books, seeking an honorable conciliation between fantasy and logic. Those poets who were able to save themselves will be looked at in the next chapter. But it would be unjust to scorn the negation of the literary past by the first vanguardists, no matter how senseless it might be. In looking for the naked metaphor and eliminating well-known verse forms, they were fulfilling a necessary function. The bad part of these inflamed metaphors was that, without being aware of it, they gave in to a superstition: that of believing that metaphors, through some magic virtue, had value in and of themselves. They searched for them rather than found them. And if they found them, they tended to forego direct mention of what they wanted to say, which would have been more poetic. The metaphors did not express the intimate being of the poet. This was true because the vanguardists started from a disrespect for literature. They had no faith in poetry. They did not believe it was serious. They were ashamed of it. They preferred badinage. The metaphoric creation, in spite of being essential, occupied a subordinate position. There was a certain insincerity in this because, on mocking serious poetry, they earned a notoriety in reverse: the easy notoriety of those who deny something worthwhile. They wrote against. Against pleasant perspectives, against the dreams of Modernism. And in writing against, they surrendered to the loose verse, to the idolatry of images, and to the mania of collecting these metaphoric idols, to changes in the grammatical functions of words, to deliberate barbarisms, to the over-production of neologisms. And this excessive preoccupation with forms—negative preoccupation, but preoccupation after all—changed to rhetoric, and the rhetoric corrupted what good they brought to literature, which was the feeling that beauty need not be dreamed of in other lands, but can be seen in the simple, ordinary life of the cities and countryside of Hispanic America. We know that every style is penetrated by a particular outlook of the world; or, if we please, that every outlook of the world prefers to mold its own style. In those periods when man sees an integral cosmos, he tends to compose with closed forms, with clearcut limits, with well-defined words, with independent and proportioned details, with clarity and repose. But now there were writers who felt themselves to be in sharp conflict with the world in which they lived.

The result was that forms shook loose from each other, they became disorganized and broken, and sentences began to sound as though they were coming from the mouth of a schizoid. Eyes saw chaos. That is, it was a kind of blindness, and in this way a literature, less visual than that of the Modernists, emerged; on the other hand, more visceral, more tactile sensations were projected. Feeling that the universe was hostile or, at least, that it turned its back on human understanding, these writers were anti-realists who preferred to project abstract schemes in which they could distort things with violent emotions and with freedom of fantasy. In Europe, during the first World War and the years immediately following, philosophic anthropology advanced in great strides. Thus, at the same time that philosophers, sociologists, psychologists, and biologists were looking for answers to the question "what is man?" the vanguard writers, independent of anthropology, contributed to it with their own explorations, one of which was surrealism. The problem was not posited in anthropological terms, but their purpose was to illumine the obscure zones that literature had never illumined before. The style of these writers was as chaotic as the object they were describing: human chaos.

In Mexico the scandal, at least the noise, broke out in 1922 with the "stridentism" of Manuel Maples Arce, Germán List Arzubide, Salvador Gallardo, Luis Quintanilla, and Arqueles Vela. They launched manifestoes and reviews and even left the chronicle of their disdain for the bourgeoisie and for literature in List Arzubide's *The Stridentist Movement* (*El movimiento estridentista,* 1926) and in Vela's *Nobody's Coffee* (*El café de nadie,* 1926). They had heard the stuttering of Tristan Tzara's dadaism and they were enchanted by its irrational aspects. They were defiant, mischievous youths for whom poetry was a rack on which to hang their hats: hats that buzzed with a mental beehive of metaphors. Good literature did not emanate from the stridentists, but from the group of the *Contemporáneos* review (1928–31), where three excellent poets stood out, Villaurrutia, Gorostiza, and Pellicer, and also Torres Bodet and Salvador Novo. They wrote with classical desires for perfection, but when final accounts are taken, it is the voice and not the outcry that makes poetry move. The stridentists, for trusting too much in the notion that street speech is easy, in the end communicated nothing; on the other hand, the solitary writers of *Contemporáneos,* in interiorizing themselves, converted their ivory towers into lighthouses that irradiated messages. They will be received in the next chapter.

In all Hispanic-America, Argentina (or better, Buenos Aires) was in truth the circus of vanguardism. The world was breaking into smithereens, but the Argentinians felt quite confident of the future in those years of prosperity. That is why the literary vanguard was not a political vanguard and they wrote to enjoy themselves and to tease the sacred Lugoneses and Capdevilas. In a letter to Juan Pinto (published in 1958) the refined Carlos Mastronardi said: "In spite of the world war the generation to which I belong knew a stable world. Only later did the pillars of that moral and spiritual world, which went into bankruptcy during the last World War [1939–45], falter. Even up to

1920 the principles that made up a sort of organic system of life were still in force; we inserted ourselves in this system, without violence and without bitterness. The innovating spirit was fulfilled precisely because it leaned on a firm and delimited reality. The aggressive nihilism of the vanguardist schools that emerged in that period was identified with a certain volition for unscrupulous play. The sense of humor, of an epoch that insisted on Progress, subsisted." Order and tradition permitted them to play with adventures and the future. Oral, mural, and printed magazines were happy activities. Borges used to go to printing shops and stick in grotesque errata in the poems of his friends. González Lanuza used to write epitaphs to Lugones, and Alfredo Brandán Caraffa to González Lanuza. They would lasso the most brutish and pesky animals—an English soap, a patio faucet, the grinding sound of a trolley—and bring them, tamed, into the corral of the printed page. They twisted the language to poke fun in the faces of the grammarians. They would invent authors in order to jibe at the pedants. They would invade cafés with masks on. They would stick out their tongues. They were promiscuous in love. Taunts and gags for the professors and for the serious audiences. Jeering. Carnivalades. Jesting. Facing these good-humored youths (Girondo, Borges, González Lanuza, Marechal, Norah Lange) were those worried over the moral decadence of the world and over the suffering of the proletariat (Yunque, Barletta, César Tiempo), but even from here, furious clowns such as Raúl González Tuñón and Nicolás Olivari broke out.

So, the postwar "isms" planted their fabricated canes in the soil of Hispanic-America; and on occasion the cane sprouted like the branch of a tree. The stick was becoming a plant. It was almost a mistake; but mistake or no, those "isms" transplanted to Hispanic-America were productive. For example, educating an artistic eye for primitive, subconscious, elementally creative and mythical forms made possible the respect for Afro-Antillian folklore and for indigenous arts, although the meaning of the Maya paintings and the Mexican bas-reliefs was ill-interpreted.

A table of scandals in the postwar literature would include these peculiarities:

1. *Cosmopolitanism.* The language meridian passes through all cities, not only Madrid. Writers continue to look toward Europe, but it is no longer the idealizing Europeanism of the Modernists, but an irreverent Europeanism which made it possible to sing, in any corner of Hispanic-America, of humble local things. The streets of every city form an international network more true to life than the network of

the Academies—the Academies now serve to provoke anti-academism.

2. *Attitude toward literature.* Although they were more productive in theory than in practice, the young writers were in agreement in their desire for insurgence, nihilism, and iconoclasm. Literature was a purposeless game. Refusal to give explanations. Talk for its own sake, without meaning. The abolition of ornamentation. Carefully sought obscurity. Schematic forms.

3. *Wit.* Reality becomes an arena where one tests his ingenuity and imagination. Aphorisms. Cult of novelty and surprise. They did not clearly define the logical categories they used, but they had recourse to a gradation of analogies that became on each occasion more vast until they lost themselves in empty symbols.

4. *Sentiment.* Dehumanization of art, thus obliterating the sources of all sentimentalism. They destroyed the "I" by substituting the psychology of man for what they imagined to be the lyricism of matter. They heeded their instincts and, when they gave vent to their feelings, there were feelings of scorn, sarcasm, confusion, and humorism.

5. *The cult of the ugly.* In their desire to achieve the maximum of disorder, they cultivated the grotesque, the extravagant, the revolting, the deformed, or things traditionally ugly. Poetry intended to be a new mode of understanding, uninterested in the manipulation of a beauty already known.

6. *Morphology.* It did not matter to them if language lost its communicative practicality, so they managed to empty it of its meaning. Being in disagreement with the language, they would rupture it or substitute for it mathematical and musical signs. They reduced it to pure matter (the "letterism" in which each letter of the alphabet was no more than a scrawl); they made it sound like a jester's jinglebells (*jitanjáforas*). In poems, white space was worth as much as words. They abandoned capital letters and punctuation. Typography was set in several planes simultaneously. Words were printed on the page to form the shape of the things they were describing, in calligrams.

7. *Syntax.* They destroyed syntax by setting down the nouns according to the happenstance of their birth. Words set free. Verbs in the infinitive. Intransitive verbs became active. The adjective enlisted as a noun. Abolition of adjective and adverb. The redoubling of the noun analogically: Man-torpedo, Woman-gulf, Multitude-undertow. Connective words and interlocking phrases were eliminated. A return to medieval script, without capitals or punctuation.

8. *Metrics.* Abandonment of strophic molds, of rhyme, of measure, of rhythm. The loose verse, the loose word, for the purpose of giving

maximum liberty to the poet. In this way what poetry had inherited from music was renounced.

9. *Themes.* Exclusion of the narrative and the anecdote. The description of the landscape as an artificial backdrop. Inanimate things become protagonists. Introduction into literature of elements, until then neglected: noise, weight, smell. Presence of the machine and of social movements.

10. *Imaginism.* Instead of the musicality of external things—the rhyme and rhythm of the Modernists—the ultraists violently searched for another kind of poetry, one reduced to metaphor. The image for the image's sake, at all costs. They shipped in carloads of metaphors without constructing the house: the poem's unity—if it existed at all—remained in the mind of the poet, and what was visible were metaphoric fragments. Bombardment of metaphors. The algebra of metaphors. Metaphors in long unconnected series or mixed metaphors.

We have tried to give the theory, the history, and the stylistic traits of the literary scandal that took place during the years of the first World War. The writers born between 1885 and 1900 who took part in it were confused with those who were adolescents or almost adolescents when the next period begins: 1925. After all, there was not much difference in age between Girondo (1891) and Borges (1899), between Huidobro (1893) and Neruda (1904). The writers who remained amidst the pure scandal belong—we repeat—to the history of literary customs, not to achievements. The others, born from 1900 on, will be passed to the next chapter. A good deal of what we have said in this paragraph is valid also for the next chapter. At times it is proper for historians to mix the chapters: in this way the reader, who was beginning to accustom himself to a conventional scheme, will be obliged to take notice of the fluidity of the historical process.

B. MAINLY PROSE

The reader should not be surprised to find the name of a poet here in a list of prose writers or vice versa. Let us then pass on to the prose writers where we will continue to find poets. Because in this generation, daughter of Modernist esthetics, there were brilliant prosists (Alfonso Reyes). They continued writing novels and short stories with the ideals of lyrical prose dating from the time of Rubén Darío (Pedro Prado). And even in the realist narratives, there is still the memory of the great parade of artistic prose which had filed by with its torches, its brass bands and colorful streamers, through the streets of 1900, showing everyone how to write with esthetic decorum and impressionistic techniques (Gallegos, Rivera, Güiraldes, Guzmán, Barrios). But realism and naturalism, of course, continued in their own direction, ever more certain, more masters of themselves, more decided to narrate actions that interest everyone (Gálvez, Lynch, Azuela). Also in the theater, the realism of Florencio Sánchez was enriched by new contributions (Ernesto Herrera). The essayist prose of thinkers and humanists was important (Pedro Henríquez Ureña, Martínez Estrada, Vasconcelos, Reyes).

1. Novel and Short Story

In accordance with the explanation at the beginning of this chapter, narrative production will be divided into two families of writers: one, the more subjective, the other, the more objective. The two families tend to intermingle. Moreover, a narrator might shift his focus and write different narratives, some being oriented toward the subjective world and others toward the objective. Even more, in the very same novel they frequently alternate pages of introversion and pages of extroversion. One can see then the difficulty of marking the thousands of narrations with only two labels. And if we were to add other labels— Europeanism and nationalism; cosmopolitanism and regionalism; urbanism and ruralism; idealism and realism, and so on—we would not gain a great deal. If we were to be hypercritical, we would end up by classifying nothing, since all classification is false. On the other hand, if we do not classify, we will lose ourselves in the chaos. The only solution is to try some divisions and to beg the reader not to follow them to the letter of the law.

In the history of prose narrative two undulating lines seem to cross each other. In one line are the narrators who sing lyrically of their intuition of the world. They interiorize, and their words restrict themselves to the very act of seeing. They reveal the singularity of their vision, and in general they cultivate art for art's sake. In the other line are those narrators who reflect upon their intuition of the world. They exteriorize, and their words restrict themselves to the things seen. They describe the nature of the objects, and in general their art is converted into a social function.

(*a*) *Narrators More Subjective than Objective* / We repeat: here will be recorded the efforts that, more or less, approach artistic, expressive, poetic, imaginative, personal, intimate fiction. Instead of a contemplation of the world, these narrators confide in us an auto-contemplation; instead of a reality unfolded on large surfaces, a reality folded back onto the depths of the imagination. That is to say, a de-realized reality. Although these narrators cannot help but relate what happens to certain men who dream or struggle in the midst of problematic social situations or in the midst of nature, they do not lean on the reality they are describing, but dive into themselves.

(1) *Mexico* / The most brilliant: Alfonso Reyes. Like quicksilver, he escapes through our fingers. He escaped from verse to prose; and, within prose, he escapes from the narrative. We will corner him among the essayists, although he deserves a prominent place as a poet and a narrator. Another very refined Mexican: JULIO TORRI (1889). He has published very little: *Essays and Poems* (*Ensayos y poemas,* 1917); *On Executions* (*De fusilamientos,* 1940). His prose is sharp, intentional, malicious. It restrains smiles. But he who does not divine the smile is deceived. Intelligence shows up with such grace that one greets it as if it were the poetry itself. His poetic prose is really made with intelligence: fantasy allows itself to be shaped by it. *The Flight of Illusion* (*La fuga de la Quimera,* 1915) by CARLOS GONZÁLEZ PEÑA (1885–1955), was one of the first novels which denounced, directly or via the characters, the unnecessary violence of the Mexican Revolution. But the Revolution is not its theme, but only one of the circumstances. The theme is—as the title indicates—the evasiveness of the illusions of love. The novel is not realistic. It retells the events in a logical order and with clear architectonic lines. Only the attention rendered to the psychological life of the characters—at times using indirect interior monologs—the esthetic quality of the descriptions—countryside scenes and human figures—and the care of the sentence—Latinizing syntax, rich vocabulary, and abundant images—situate the novel among the modernist.

(2) *Central America* / *Guatemala:* RAFAEL ARÉVALO MARTÍNEZ (1884), poet and novelist. Let not the simplicity of some of his poems ("Clean Clothes") or the invoking of simple good fortune ("Dream of Good Fortune") or simple traditional themes (religion in "Prayer to the Lord") distract us—Arévalo Martínez is not a poet of simple soul, but he is twisted in nervous and sickly convolutions. More than in his verses—from *Juggleries* (*Juglerías,* 1911) to *Along This Little Path* (*Por un caminito así,* 1947) passing through his celebrated *The Roses of Engaddi* (*Las rosas de Engaddi,* 1927)—he revealed himself in his stories and novels. Above all in *The Man Who Looked Like a Horse* (*El hombre que parecía un caballo,* 1914), which was the most original story of his generation. It is said that that selfish, strong, arrogant, blasphemous, and amoral man-horse was the caricature of the poet Barba Jacob. But a caricature is judged worthy in relation to its model; whereas the story we are commenting is valuable in itself, as a delirious vision. It has a nightmarish and poetic atmosphere which we knew in Jean Lorrain and today we recognize in Franz Kafka. He wrote other psycho-zoological stories, namely, *The Colombian Troubadour* (*El tro-*

vador, 1914), whose main character is a tame, humble, loyal man-dog. We also have "the man who looked like an elephant," and "the man who looked like a tiger." Many years later Arévalo Martínez tells us that a spiritualist friend gathered, in one of her trips to the world beyond, two stories written by a witness to the events that "date back to olden times, millennia ago, when the earth had but one continent, Atlán, which preceded Lemuria and Atlantis": both these Utopias, *The World of the Maharachías* (*El mundo de los maharachías*, 1938) and *Voyage to Ipanda* (*Viaje a Ipanda*, 1939), are interweaved. The first is the more poetic: in the same way that the shipwrecked Gulliver found among the Houyhnhnms a civilization of creatures that looked like horses, the shipwrecked Manuol finds a civilization of creatures that looked like monkeys that were also superior to men. They are the *"maharachís,"* whose tails are almost spiritual organs. Contrary to Swift, Arévalo Martínez' tone is not satiric. One can picture the good-humored smile, and no more, with which the author lyrically described the love of Manuol for Aixa and Isabel, the warm land of philosophic monkeys and the beauty of their sensitive tails. The novel is not successful, however. The thought does not keep in line with the fantasy. When in *Voyage to Ipanda*—which is an outgrowth of *The World of the Maharachías*—this thought attempts to construct a Utopia with intellectual and political pretensions, the result is worse. Even less interesting, as a novel, is the political outline of *The Torlanian Ambassador* (*El embajador de Torlania*, 1960).

FLAVIO HERRERA (1892). "I'm of Romantic origin," says one of the characters in *Ashes* (*Cenizas*), stories written in 1923. "I have read Bourget," says another. In this sentimental zone, and, with a touch of the psychological narrator, Flavio Herrera tells his stories, all about love, with a varied gallery of women as a background. The unraveling of each story throws light on the psychology of the characters. The prose runs rapidly and nervously, but along an old artistic river bed: a Frenchified, Modernist river bed, with measured turns. As a poet, his lyrical temperament was put into practice in Japanese *haikais*. In a poetic prose he also described peasant surroundings. His works: *The Tiger* (*El tigre*), *The Storm* (*La tempestad*), *The Seven Birds of the Rainbow* (*Los siete pájaros del iris*), *Seven Petty Lawyers in Flux* (*Siete rábulas en flux*), *Chaos* (*Caos*). CARLOS WYLD OSPINA (1891–1958) forms, with Arévalo Martínez and Flavio Herrera, a trio of the best Guatemalan narrators of the artistic style. Like his colleagues, he was a poet: *The Simple Gifts* (*Las dádivas simples*, 1921) is a serene and elegant song to sowing time and to tillers of the soil. Then he wrote short stories: *The Land of the Nahuyacas* (*La tierra de las nahuyacas*, 1933) and novels: *The Gonzagas' Manor House* (*El solar de los Gonzagas*, 1924) and *The Immigrant's Daughter* (*La Gringa*, 1935). In a precise, disciplined prose, proud of itself, he depicts scenes of the tropics and tells of Creole life. Even the pages that appear naturalistic are measured with an artistic yardstick. Although not a novelist, but deserving of a place of honor among poetic prose writers, is another Guatemalan, JOSÉ RODRÍGUEZ CERNA (1889–1952), author of the. beautiful landscapes in *Lands of Sun and Mountain* (*Tierras de sol y de montaña*).

Costa Rica: FRANCISCO SOLER (1888–1920) was a Modernist in his themes of the Italian Renaissance. MANUEL SEGURA MÉNDEZ (1895) was a poet and novelist. MOISÉS VINCENZI (1895), an essayist of philosophic themes, published several novels intellectually conceived, with thematic and technical novelties: they go from *Atlante* (1924) to *Elvira* (1940).

Panama: JOAQUÍN DARÍO JAÉN (1893–1932) published stories and novels with morbidities that remind one of Vargas Vila.

(*3*) *Antilles / Cuba:* No one will deny, merely because part of his career was spent in Spain, a place in our history to ALFONSO HERNÁNDEZ CATÁ (1885–1940). He is a short story writer conscious of the formal dignity of his genre, with a richness of observation for external detail and for psychological meanings, with a sense of "pathos" which takes him toward melodrama but which is sufficiently sober to stop in time and remain on this side of the line, the tragic side. His favorite theme is abnormal psychology, sometimes treated with irony, sometimes with compassion. When least expected Cuba appears in the stories. In his first book, *Passionate Stories* (*Cuentos pasionales,* 1907) he brings to mind Maupassant. His mature works were *The Seven Sins* (*Los siete pecados,* 1918), *Acid Fruits* (*Los frutos ácidos,* 1919), *Precious Stones* (*Piedras preciosas,* 1927), *Insane Asylum* (*Manicomio,* 1931). One of his best books was *Zoo* (*La casa de fieras,* 1919). A lively, sensual, juicy, warm, opulent, noble prose dominates throughout. He writes well; that is, he knows how to embroider and emboss a sentence so as not to confuse it with another. He knows the secrets of the trade of the short story writer, as attested to by these anthological stories: "The Witness," "The Guilty Woman," "The Pearl," "The Chinese," "The Little Galician Girl." As a novelist he did not stand out: *Pelayo González* (1909), *The New Death* (*La muerte nueva,* 1922), *The Drinker of Tears* (*El bebedor de lágrimas,* 1926), *The Angel of Sodoma* (*El ángel de Sodoma,* 1927). And he achieved even less as a poet and playwright.

ARMANDO LEYVA (1885–1940) was a short story writer affiliated with Modernism, with ironic fondness for mysteries *à la* Poe.

Dominican Republic: ABIGAÍL MEJÍA DE FERNÁNDEZ (1895–1941), author of works of imagination, such as *Dream, Pilarín* (*Sueña, Pilarín,* 1925) of psychological analysis.

(*4*) *Venezuela /* The education of RÓMULO GALLEGOS (Venezuela, 1884) in Modernist literature and his perception of crude Venezuelan reality appear contrasted in the themes of his novels—the fight between civilization and barbarism in hamlets, plains, forest, coffee plantations, rivers and lakes—as well as in the double onslaught of his style: artistic impressionism and descriptive realism. He had already published his short stories *The Adventurers* (*Los aventureros,* 1913) and his novels *The Last of the Solars* (*El último Solar,* 1920) and *The Creeper* (*La trepadora,* 1925) when Gallegos established himself with *Doña Bárbara* (1929) as one of our few novelists who satisfy the expectations of an international public. *Doña Bárbara* receives its movement from the traditional springs of the nineteenth-century novel. Against a background of implacable nature the action brings out, Romantically, almost melodramatically, the heroic endeavor. The symbols—exaggerated even in the names of the characters: the barbarism of Doña Bárbara; the saintly light and ardor (*"santa luz y ardor"*) of the civilizing Santos Luzardo—are too obvious. The composition with symmetries and antitheses—which at times lean to allegory—tend to go from the artistic to the intellectual: the mare and Marisela are tamed in parallel and simultaneous processes; the civilized man has all the dexterity of the barbaric one; the "sleeping beauty" is savage and lovely at the same time; the idyl in a counterpoint of voices; Doña Bárbara agonizes between good and evil; the burden of witchcraft, black auguries and curses end by yielding to a happy outcome. The scenes are violent and deliberately sensational: the deflowering of Bárbara; the father who runs a lance through his son and then dies with his eyes open; the burial in the room, with an abominable bat; the drunkenness of Lorenzo and Mr. Danger; mother and daughter fighting; the cadaver hanging from the horse. Yet, *Doña Bárbara* is a great novel. The prose runs like the grazing lands of Venezuela. The author's lyrical, folkloric, psychological, sociological attitudes change in the course of the story, and in each perspective he achieves admirable pages. Who has described better than Gallegos the landscape of the plains, the horse-taming, the round-up time?

The subject matter of *Cantaclaro* (1934) is the couplets, stories, superstitions, and legends that are heard on the Venezuelan plains. All of these are incarnated in the wandering musician, Florentino, nicknamed Cantaclaro. He is a friendly, loyal, haughty young fellow, infallible in his feminine conquests. At the heart of the action is the conflict of conscience in Doctor Payara, a man of rigid moral precepts, who feels he should remove Rosángel from his life, so that the relationship between them, apparently that of father and daughter, will not end in something that he deems to be incestuous. Actually, Rosángel is not his daughter, but the daughter of his dead wife. Cantaclaro carries the girl off with him, but not for himself: he will give her refuge in his home, and will then continue his life as a solitary, nomadic adventurer. But the novel does not coagulate around a plot; rather, it is a succession of sketches of customs, of descriptions, of psychological portraits, of ethnographic and sociological lessons, of poetic moments. The attitude of Gallegos is that of the intellectual—he even gives an aphoristic quality to the dialog of the plainsmen—but the folkloric quality of this novel does not permit him to offer ethnic or political messages as manifest as those in the earlier *Doña Bárbara* or in *Canaima,* which followed it. *Canaima* (1935) is another of Gallegos' good novels. The scene: the cities which lie near the jungle, and the jungle itself, in the great valley of the Orinoco River. The time: the present. The subject: the struggle of life. The theme: "the Male, semigod of the barbarous lands," against Canaima, the malignant god "of the anti-human, satanic jungle." The protagonist: Marcos Vargas. The novel is constructed in the form of a vast and complex sketch of customs. The first and last chapters (I and XIX) serve as the frame. The first chapter contains an exposition of preceding events: we see the landscape around the mouth of the Orinoco and, emerging from Ciudad Bolívar, the childhood and adolescence of Marcos Varga, a boy fascinated by the legends and adventures of the jungle. In the middle of the picture (chapters II–XVIII), the action begins when Marcos, at twenty-one years of age, sets out "for the open road, to confront life." He is all male, violent, generous, with a sense of justice that leads him to identify himself with the workers, and later, with the Indians, but he is basically more vital than rational, confused, unadaptable, and without heroic stature. Avenging the death of his brother by killing Cholo Parima is all he accomplishes. He looks for adventure simply for the sake of adventure. We lose sight of him when he is twenty-seven years old. The last chapter, which repeats some landscapist notes from the first chapter, completes the framework with an epilog: twelve or fourteen years have gone by, and we see another Marcos Varga, a child, on the road to Caracas, where he will be educated. The thesis of the novel, more insinuated than formulated, seems to be in the inverse trajectories of these two children, the child of the first chapter, torn from civilization by the witchcraft of the jungle, and the child of the last chapter, who comes out of the jungle to be saved by civilization. Can the thesis of *Canaima* be that only a Europeanizing civilization can save Venezuela?

In his last novels—*Poor Negro* (*Pobre negro,* 1937) and *Upon the Same Earth* (*Sobre la misma tierra*)—Gallegos enriches the gallery of his regional paintings: in the first, with the unsolved social problems of

the Barlovento region; the second, with some unhappy Indians searching for pasture lands on the boundaries of Coquivacoa. In *The Stranger*
(*El forastero*)—whose rough draft was anterior to *Doña Bárbara*, but
was published much later—the political theme dominates. Different
from other Gallegos novels, in this one nature's action on the characters is diminished. There are fewer descriptions, more characters
and dialog, since the author is preoccupied with the problem of despotism. *The Wisp of Straw in the Wind* (*La brizna de paja en el
viento*) takes place, not in Venezuela, but in Cuba.

Delightful Teresa de la Parra (1891–1936) makes us feel time as
if it were a substance. And, in fact, time is the substance of her literature. She describes the backward life of the old society. She tells us
how it is falling apart. The aristocratic class to which she belongs is
a moment of history already spent. She says good-by to things so cor-
dially that we can see them moving off into the past, wrapped in their
hours. Or in contrast, she evokes her childhood; and landscapes, events,
and people come from afar, wrapped in their years. Time, always
time. But, above all, it is the subjectivism of her prose, quivering with
impressions and metaphors, that makes the passing of time so striking.
It is known that inner life is a temporal flux, a process of lived time;
so, whatever Teresa de la Parra speaks of, the subject is always herself.
Proust was one of her masters in the art of shading the undulating
succession of memories. Her first novel was *Iphigenia: Diary of a Young
Girl Who Wrote Because She Was Annoyed* (*Ifigenia: Diario de una
señorita, que escribió porque se fastidiaba*, 1924). In whispers—because she is confessing and gossiping about others—but with the fluidity
of an elegant conversation, Teresa de la Parra comments on the unjust
social position of Creole women. Better yet was her second, and best,
novel, *The Memoirs of Mamá Blanca* (*Las memorias de Mamá Blanca*,
1929). It is a novel, because the episodes, as scattered as they may
appear, cannot be pruned away from the central trunk of the narrative.
The branches and twigs would dry up. The characters develop maturity chapter after chapter, like a novel. The artifice of presenting
the *Memoirs* as a manuscript left in legacy to the author by the old
woman, Mamá Blanca, is also novelistic. These are the memories of a
happy childhood on a sugar cane plantation near Caracas. The tenderness, the melancholy, the vivid imagination, the human sympathy, the
sensitivity for registering the gentleness of the world, the charm of
writing and narrating have no equal in our literature. Childhood remembrances, but not naive ones. Her intelligence, smiling and ironic,
watches over all. The emphatic and the commonplace would not be

permitted to enter these pages. The style seems spontaneous because Teresa de la Parra, wisely, ingeniously, laboriously, has dug deep into the hardness of the language in order to strike an original well of metaphors.

Although JESÚS ENRIQUE LOSSADA (Venezuela, 1895–1948) wrote stories on rural surroundings or of satiric intent, more personal were his stories of intellectual problems, with incredible themes or characters that move from lyricism to delirium. He is the author of *The Happiness Machine* (*La máquina de la felicidad*, 1938).

(5) *Colombia* / The excessive respect for European forms had an ill effect even on the best Colombian novels, the Romantic ones as well as the realist and Modernist ones. Suddenly there sprouted the pages of a novel having the strength of native trees: those of Rivera's *The Vortex* (*La vorágine*). The seeds blew about, and little by little other novels emerged with Colombian themes and individual styles.

JOSÉ EUSTASIO RIVERA (1888–1928) wrote admirable sonnets: *The Promised Land* (*Tierra de promisión*, 1921). The fixed structure of the sonnet lends itself to a tension wherein verse after verse the action is developing in a rigorous centralized movement which keeps the reader alert to what is coming. The action that Rivera depicts in his sonnets is that of the Colombian nature: animals, plants, rivers, mountains, the colors of the sky. The last verse closes the action and leaves it perfect, like a painting full of color. What one sees in this painting is a virgin territory for poetry—no one, prior to Rivera, had laid it open with such intensity, from such a beautifying angle. But the literary technique of painting the things of nature with such cleanness of profile, of shading, of gesture, and of framing them in an aristocratic form, is Parnassian. The words selected by the poet ennoble the brute substance of nature and transform it into precious material. Rivera was one of the forces of nature. His humanistic culture was poor in comparison to his extremely fruitful temperament. But at least he had a cultured way of contemplating himself: his passions, his peculiarities, his need to live in the country among trees, animals, and rivers were all dressed with the raiment of the sonnet. When Rivera wrote *The Vortex* (1924) he maintained his high poetic tension but changed his perspective. Instead of contemplating pictures, he placed himself within nature itself and startled the beauty of fear. Framed, in order to make us believe in its objectivity, between a prolog by Rivera and an epilog by the Consul, *The Vortex* pretends to be an autobiographical book. With the old procedure of feigning to edit the memoirs of another—"I respected his style and even his errors"—he lets Arturo Cova narrate in the first person, except when the narrative shifts to other characters. (The novel, therefore, is one-voiced, although the "I" is displaced rhetorically on occasion: the "I" becomes "you" when Cova speaks to himself; the "I" becomes "he" when Cova speaks as if he were Lesmes; the "I" opens on a gallery of mirrors that reflect other "I"s, as when Clemente Silva speaks.) The plains of the Orinoco River and the lowlands of the Amazon form the setting. The action takes place in little more than seven months—it begins with the impregnation of Alicia and ends with the abortion of the seven-month fetus. The action is rapid and continuous, but the story, divided into three parts, advances in intermittent lines.

First part: the exposition. Arturo Cova, a young Colombian poet, already celebrated for his intelligence and for his "sculptured" poems (even in the wilds, the sordid Barrera, the drunkard Gámez, and the prostitute Clarita will admire his fame) has an easy love affair with Alicia. He seduces her, without loving her, and flees Bogotá with her. He flees from the threat of marriage made by her parents, the judge, and the priest. Then a series of adventures, with touches of the crime novel, follows. Alicia and Cova live in La Maporita with Franco and his wife, "Griselda" (these two also have a police record). Arturo, because of his loyalty to Franco, resists Griselda's sensual overtures and, out of spite, begins to become impassioned for Alicia. Enters Barrera, a scoundrel who robs, lies, kills, betrays, and wants to seduce the women. A furious Arturo leaves in search of Barrera. Arturo is stabbed in a squabble over a game of dice. A prostitute nurses him to health. On his return to La Maporita with Franco, he finds out that Barrera has gone off taking Griselda and Alicia with him. They set La Maporita on fire.

Second part: the action is knotted with social condemnations. Arturo, accompanied by Franco and others, goes into the jungle after Barrera and the two women to avenge himself. He lives among Indians —which occasions ethnographical scenes and a contemporary "Indian chronicle." He listens to the grievances of some of those with him— which constitute a hair-raising documentary on the sufferings of rubber plantation workers. The painful history of the Colombian Clemente Silva takes up more than half this part. Third part: denouement. The rubber worker, Silva, ends his story and goes off in search of his son's bones; now Cova is on the move again, not only for personal vengeance, but also to fight against the injustices of the big bosses and to redeem the rubber workers. His infirmities begin to depress, madden, and paralyze him. He falls into the sensual arms of the Turkish Zoraida.

New characters open new circles in the green hell: el Váquiro, Cayeno, Ramiro, the swindler Lesmes. Cova starts to write a sheaf of accusations to send to the Consul of Colombia. It will be a panorama of miseries, an "imposing register of ills in a style, seething and precipitous like the waters of a torrent." The threads of the story intertwine and are pulled firmly together. Cova comes across Griselda, who tells of her misfortunes with Barrera and how Alicia had slashed his face. The violent scenes mount until they take away the reader's breath: horrendous tortures, mutilations, pools of blood, Cayeno's cadaver floating in the river while a dog is disemboweling it, Barrera bitten to death by fish, Alicia's abortion, the final march where "the jungle devoured them" without leaving a trace.

The Vortex (the novel of the vortex, that is, the jungle) is built on two levels, one of social protest and the other of psychological characterization. Rivera seems to have written it with a double purpose and even with two distinguishable themes. On the first level he defends the Colombians, prisoners of the jungle, and the sovereignty of Colombia, menaced by invasions and depredations. For this he used historical data, word of mouth experiences, anecdotes that he had read, and others that he had lived, and his own travels to the Orinoco and the Amazon. These pages of obvious social and political intentions are not his best—scenes of local customs, moral reflections, satiric phrases, and deviations from the story damage the unity of composition and style. His best literary achievement on this level is the interesting case of the interior duplication of the novel: that is, that while we read the memoirs, not only do we hear the intimate revelations of how Cova is inspired by nature and the difference between the traditional conventions of literature and the sincere artistic expression, but also we see him in the very act of writing them, looking after them, and sending them to the Consul. The second level is superior. Rivera has created a character of marked mental complications, obsessed by his failure: "I am not what I could have been." Since Rivera made Cova a poet, not only his reactions, exaltations, and torments are convincing, but also the lyrical tone of his memoirs is authentic. Cova is passionate, irascible, theatrical, imaginative, bold, hysterical, crotchety, with adolescent and neurotic tendencies. The violence of his actions harmonizes with the violence of his metaphors, and the bloodiest and most macabre things are illuminated with esthetic lights: "the frenetic sight of the shipwreck shook me like a wind of beauty," he says. And he composes the most truculent scenes of torture, infamy, death, and human bestiality and filthiness with the eyes of an artist. From Casanare, until he loses himself in the Brazilian jungles, Cova traverses inhospitable regions: from plain to plain, from river to river, from village to village, from tribe to tribe and from rubber plantation to rubber plantation, he learns of the horrors of a most devastating environment and of a most degrading humanity. Serpents, ants, infra-men, all appear in one repulsive mass. Occasionally, there is a prose poem on the beauty of the landscape; but generally, he gives us a lyricism of nightmare, fever, and grotesqueness. He is a refined poet, but of barbaric drive. He gives nerves to the Colombian landscape and, when it becomes convulsive and tragic, we are seeing Cova's soul as well. At any rate, we see the jungle about to swallow Cova, but we see it through the eyes of Cova himself. Cova's complex personality is expressed in the first person. Rivera, however, does not attempt interior monolog. It is, rather, a long soliloquy in which Cova analyzes himself psychologically. His dreams, feverish deliriums, unbridled fantasies, and abnormal sensations do not appear in the dim stream of consciousness and of subconsciousness, but are thoroughly explained, arranged, and illumined in a prose whose most daring sorties are metaphors, impressionistic descriptions, synesthesias, and expressionistic personifications, as in the vengeance of the rubber trees against the workers.

Notwithstanding the intense artistic stimulus of *The Vortex,* Colombian novelists moved along the branches of realism, naturalism, and the depiction of social customs. These writers will be seen later. Here we must deal with psychological, fantastic, intellectualist novels and those of lyrical intonation, which also existed, although in small numbers. The three most subjective novelists are López de Mesa, Alvarez Lleras, and Restrepo Jaramillo. The first two were not really novelists—the first an essayist, the second a dramatist. Regardless, they must be mentioned here. Luis López de Mesa (1884) wrote his *Book of Apologs* (*Libro de apólogos,* 1918), related to the parables of Rodó, with esthetic pomp. He also attempted the idealist novel with *The Tragedy of Nilse* (*La tragedia de Nilse,* 1928) and *The Biography of Gloria Etzel* (*La biografía de Gloria Etzel,* 1929), in which there are psychological analyses, a diffused spiritualism, and more or less philosophical chats on individual perfectibility. Antonio Alvárez Lleras (1892–1956) left one of the best novels of this period: *Only Yesterday . . .* (*Ayer, nada más . . . ,* 1930), on the milieu of the Colombian capital, with studies of decadent characters and strolls through mental labyrinths. More important is José Restrepo Jaramillo (1896–1945), daring in his experiments with the art of narrating and in the esthetic focus of complex psychologies. He delights in the spectacle of his own creative imagination, novelizes the very act of novelizing. He looks at his characters from multiple perspectives. He takes the obscure, irrational depths of life by surprise and describes them lyrically. Titles: *The Novel of Three* (*Novela de los tres,* 1924), *David, Son of Palestine* (*David, hijo de Palestina,* 1931). We close this list with Félix Henao Toro (1900), author of "the first psycho-analytical novel in Spanish": *Eugeni the Handball Player* (*Eugeni la pelotari,* 1935); M. F.

SLIGER, who dealt in the genre of science fiction: *Interplanetary Voyages That Will Take Place in the Year 2009* (*Viajes interplanetarios que tendrán lugar en el año 2009*, 1936); GREGORIO SÁNCHEZ GÓMEZ (1895–1943) with his phantasmagoric *Life of a Dead Man* (*Vida de un muerto*, 1926); and RAFAEL JARAMILLO ARANGO (1896) with his stories of escape into the unreal worlds of animals and of children.

(6) *Ecuador* / One of the respected prose writers of this generation was GONZALO ZALDUMBIDE (1885). For many years he was esteemed for his critical works on Rodó, Montalvo, D'Annunzio. He is also the author of an extraordinarily chiseled novel on youth, *Tragic Eclogue* (*Égloga trágica*). He wrote it in 1910–11, published some of its segments in different newspapers from 1912 to 1916, and it was not until 1956 that he edited it, completely, and published it in the form of a book, without retouching the style. The youth Segismundo, after traveling for several years through the capitals of Europe, where he lived all the refinements of the life of an artist without ever having experienced a real love, returns to his native corner of the earth, Ibarra, and its surroundings. He becomes enthused over the beauties of the landscape, he helps the peasants at work, he observes the customs of the Indians, he reflects on the problems of Hispanic-America, he comes to know the disasters of a political revolution, he ardently enjoys a churlish little Indian girl. His uncle Juan José, a forty-year-old giant, lord of the land, takes him to visit Marta, a pretty young girl, sweet, anemic. Marta lives with her insane mother, Dolores. (Dolores had had a clandestine love affair with a German; one night, on finding them embraced, Dolores' father fired a shot at the German; Dolores, now insane, gave birth to Marta; Juan José, Dolores' cousin, became the protector of the two women.) In view of a raging civil war, Juan José lodges Dolores and Marta in his house. Dolores dies. Segismundo and Marta fall in love. Juan José feels an incipient, desperate passion for Marta and in the throes of jealousy threatens Segismundo with death. The latter, because of his love for his uncle, decides to return to Europe. On the point of leaving, he receives a letter in Quito from Marta who has guessed what happened between the two men and who is saying good-by before taking her own life. Segismundo returns to his uncle's house to remain. Juan José dies; Segismundo lives on with the memory of Marta, "symbol of the happiness that no one achieves." The story is melodramatic: that is, an action that seeks effects, but softened by a musical background. The structure of the novel is traditional: the protagonist Segismundo narrates; the descriptive first part and the second part which sets the conflict are slow; the last two parts rush forward tragically. But the exceptional part of *Tragic Eclogue* is the quality of its prose—a Modernist prose, with cadenced steps and rare good choice of the right word and of the lyrical image. The description of nature and of intimate sentiments is brilliant, impressionistic, imaginative. Zaldumbide does not propose to reproduce real things nor to analyze psychological states, but to stylize his poetic vision in admirable prose poems. Due to this artistic view, *Tragic Eclogue* can give delight even today to the pursuers of images; his literary language, nevertheless, produces a strange effect of mixed epochs, with old Romantic structures and the modern ones of the beginning of the century. CÉSAR ARROYO (1890–1937) directed the review *Cervantes* in Madrid, which at one time was the organ of the creationists; but in spite of his admiration for anything new, the chronicles and narrations he left us are still Modernist.

(7) *Peru* / VENTURA GARCÍA CALDERÓN (1886–1959) is a prose artist who rendered a good diplomatic service by showing Europeans, who believe Hispanic-Americans to be a picturesque people from whom they expect only regionalism—no matter how unpolished and mediocre it might be—an excellently written regional literature. *The Vengeance of the Condor* (*La venganza del Cóndor,* 1924) contains stories of violence, death, horror, superstitions, and unrestrained passions. His good prose combines all this reality (raw in other narrators) as on a stained glass, brilliant and cold. This man of Parisian culture relating barbaric episodes, or describing hair-raising regions, is smiling with a refined and almost imperceptible irony. Those rather dull souls who need explanations, theses, declamations, believed that García Calderón had not seen his Peruvian land: indeed he had, and he understood its problems, but with artistic moderation. After him (better said against him) came the pro-Indian narrators. If García Calderón had exaggerated the defects of the Indians, they exaggerated the virtues. However, García Calderón wrote better.

(8) *Bolivia* / ARMANDO CHIRVECHES (1883–1926) began as a Modernist (from *Lilí,* 1901, to *Nostalgias* (*Añoranzas,* 1912) but we are grateful to him for having decided to write novels: *Sky Blue* (*Celeste,* 1905), *Manor House* (*Casa solariega,* 1906) and *Tropical Flower* (*Flor del trópico,* 1926). Because of its exceptional merit, we shall consider *The Candidacy of Rojas* (*La candidatura de Rojas,* 1909) separately. In this novel can be discerned one of the Modernist phenomena already noted: once the dazzlement of European artificial lights had passed, there were writers who, without rejecting cosmopolitan refinements, wrote Hispanic-American literature. The protagonist, Enrique Rojas, says that his favorite authors are the Spaniards, Pereda and Palacio Valdés. That may be so. But it is evident that Chirveches formed his style on French artistic prose, from Flaubert on. The novel is about the abortive political adventure of Rojas, who leaves La Paz with the ambition of being elected representative, and ends up by marrying his cousin Inés in a provincial corner of the country. The Bolivian reality of city, country, intellectual groups, and uncivilized masses, of Spaniards, Creoles, mestizos, and Indians, is masterfully described. Chirveches, as only a few have done, symphonically orchestrates all of the instruments and tonalities of the literature of his time: lyrical and humoristic pages, idealization of things and brutal and malodorous naturalism, mischievous wit, and severe critical thought, satiric and idyllic themes,

Spanish-American Literature: A History

the will to create literature and at the same time mockery of literature, exquisiteness of landscape, and yet rapidity of action. Chirveches knows how to tell a story. He has psychological keenness. The most significant details of each scene do not escape him. He has created, objectively, a character with such life that the reader, deceived by the fact that the narrative is in the first person, might believe that Rojas is Chirveches himself. He is not: Rojas is a novelistic creation.

(9) *Chile* / Eduardo Barrios (1884). In his juvenile dramas (from 1910 to 1916) there were thoughts of social reforms or, at least, preoccupations with social problems: religious hypocrisy, bureaucracy, politics, and woman's disadvantageous position in family life. Later he abandoned the theater, and in his novels he became more interested in people than in things, and more interested in their souls than in their adventures. In *The Boy Who Went Crazy With Love* (*El niño que enloqueció del amor,* 1915) he was already showing his capacity for psychological analysis: it is the diary of a hypersensitive boy of ten who falls in love with a woman, suffers, becomes ill and then demented. A more penetrating novel, was *A Lost One* (*Un perdido,* 1917), in which he analyzes the history of the unfortunate Lucho who, from failure after failure, sinks into misery and vice. At the same time that he delves into the psychology of Lucho and many other characters, Barrios constructs his work with the ability of an architect; it is a psychological novel, but so crammed with observations on the social life of Chile that it is also a novel of customs. In *Brother Ass* (*El hermano asno,* 1922) once again the tense narrator of rare psychological cases is seen. These loose, impressionistic pages, written in the present tense and in the first person, take the form of an intimate diary. It is written by Friar Lázaro. When he begins his diary, he has already spent seven years in a Franciscan monastery, but he has not been able to forget the world. In this outer world he was called Mario and had loved a woman, Gracia. When Gracia married a pianist, Mario became Friar Lázaro. One day Friar Lázaro thinks he sees Gracia in church. No, it isn't Gracia: it is her sister María Mercedes. She was eleven, twelve years old when Gracia abandoned Mario, and she was then romantically in love with him. Now she is twenty; between María Mercedes and Friar Lázaro is born a sentiment of friendship, even of love, which he tries to control. Gracia and her mother become alarmed. The pages in which Friar Lázaro records his days are interlaced with others in which he describes Friar Rufino. The latter has shown such proof of abnegation and love that people begin to revere him like a saint. This attribution of saintliness disturbs Friar Rufino. He feels he does not

deserve it. He wonders whether there is not deep within him a feeling of vanity. Furthermore, he feels he is carrying "a brother ass," that is, a body capable of baseness and temptation. Finally he assaults María Mercedes in the darkness of the chapel, and before he dies he confesses that he wanted to rape her. Was this the lustfulness of "brother ass"? Could it have been the desire to humiliate himself, to have himself hated so as to destroy the notion of saintliness? Or perhaps a way of saving his friend Friar Lázaro by separating him from María Mercedes? Or perhaps a moral mistake in following the advice of the devil, disguised as a Capuchin monk? Or plain madness? The two tresses of the story—and even a third, the description of monastery life and the different types of monks—form a well-wrought braid which ends in a firm knot: Lázaro takes Friar Rufino's guilt upon himself and, ironically, the monastery for its own convenience decides that Friar Rufino is to be venerated in spite of his desires and sacrifices.

Since Friar Lázaro, before becoming a monk, was a man of letters— one of his favorite books was *The Boy Who Went Crazy With Love*, by Barrios himself, and its manuscript begins with some verses of Amado Nervo—it is plausible that his diary would contain beautiful pages of fine impressionism, rich in metaphors of interior and exterior vistas. In two decades, Barrios produced nothing of great value until *Tamarugal* (1944), in which he continued his description of Chilean life in the desolate fields of the north. In *Gran señor y rajadiablos* (1948), Barrios constructed a pentagonal pantheon to the memory of José Pedro Valverde, whom he imagined as having died close to his eightieth year of life. The novel has five parts: evocations of childhood, adolescence, youth, maturity, and old age. With an artistic prose—rich in perceptions and in brilliant descriptions—he painted on each tympanum of the vaulted arch scenes from the long life of this rich landowner (*"gran señor,"* in the feudal sense), virile, powerful, violent, cock-brained, Catholic, haughty, donjuanesque, enterprising, fearsome, likeable, intelligent although anti-rational. The character of the protagonist, nevertheless, is seen less clearly than the social and historic panorama of the Chilean landscape from the middle of the nineteenth century until the advent of the "democratic and leftist rabble of the twentieth century." Not that Barrios is more of a sociologist than a psychologist, it was merely that he conceived of his hero as a representative figure of Chilean progressive oligarchy. Unfortunately, those actions which best lent themselves to the novelistic treatment—bandit fights, the raping of women, the wars with Bolivia and Peru, political changes, adventures—were not actually presented, but merely alluded to. We learn of what has taken place, without having seen it happen. We have used the "psychological" concept in connection with Barrios so much that it would be well to warn that his novels, more than psychological, are subjective. The fact is that Barrios uses narrative conventions that are not always plausible, and at times they are incredible from a rigorously psychological point of view. Barrios' subjectivism in the creation of characters takes place along with his impressionism in the creation of expressions. His last novel—*Man's Men* (*Los hombres del hombre,* 1950)—re-creates the inner torture of a husband who doubts he is the father. "You suddenly get the notion," says another character in the novel, "that Charlie is not your son. Why? Because an English friend, his godfather, dies without heirs and leaves him a million."

PEDRO PRADO (Chile, 1886–1952) first was a verse poet, but prose poetry was his widest and longest avenue. Verses: *Thistle Flowers* (*Flores de cardo,* 1908). In 1949 an *Anthology* (*Antología*) and *Old Unedited Poems* (*Viejos poemas inéditos*) were published. Prado's poetry does not exhibit efforts at a formal renovation. Although he was one of those who introduced free verse in Chile, he prefers traditional ways, the sonnet. In a language faithful to normal grammar, he puts the reader in tension but does not take him into unexplored worlds. In "Love's Abodes" the dominating motif is the amorous one. During his last years, he gathered poems from different books and with them he initiated a new phase: *The March of Time* (*Camino de las horas,* 1934), *Autumn in the Dunes* (*Otoño en las dunas,* 1940), *This Beautiful Poisoned City* (*Esta bella ciudad envenenada,* 1945), *Just One Rose* (*No más que una rosa,* 1946). Prado is a reflexive spirit, given to meditation with philosophic preoccupations. He poetized a philosophy of life in parables—*The Abandaned House* (*La casa abandonada,* 1912) —and even in prose poems—*The Birds Errant* (*Los pájaros errantes*). His purest lyrical pages are imbued with a thought process refined into tenuous symbols. In applying his philosophic ideas to social life he arrived at a combination of anarchism and Tolstoyism: through the path of simplicity in conduct, confidence in intelligence and the cult of beauty and goodness, mankind would be liberated. His first novel— *The Queen of Rapa Nui* (*La reina de Rapa Nui,* 1914)—is a beautiful fantasy set on a lost island of the South Pacific. He followed with *Alsino* (1920), one of the best poetic novels in our literature, in which some critics see a libertarian or anarchical allegory. Alsino is a little Chilean boy who wants to fly. He falls from a tree and becomes hunchbacked from the fall. His hunch sprouts wings. And Alsino flies, inebriated with air, trees, birds, liberty, happiness, and song. It is a story of magical adventure, which takes place among the things and men of this world. Fantasy and reality beat like Alsino's two wings: "One of my wings," says Alsino, "takes me to the right; the other to the left; my weight to the earth; and my eyes to every point of the compass." The novel traces the trajectory of Prado's lyrical flight; the author gives himself joyfully to nature but goes beyond it in a desire to be everywhere, to observe from extra-human perspectives and to fuse with the universal air. The imagination that warped the thick threads of the marvelous history of the little hunchback worked each mesh of the cloth exquisitely: it is a precious, compact style of original poetic visions. *A Rural Judge* (*Un juez rural,* 1924) relates from street level the daily life of a slum, but the scenes are not realistic: the author has come down to the street surface but his eyes bring an idealism from above. After *Karez-I-Roshan*—a literary hoax that attempted to pass off some of Prado's prose poems as those of a Persian poet—he published *Androvar* (1925), a "tragedy in prose" with a metaphysics on personality: Androvar, his wife, Elienai, and his disciple, Godel, fuse in a single conscience; when Godel dies the two others can see beyond death.

Also in Chile, also in the narrative literature that does not surrender to realism, must be recorded JENARO PRIETO (1889–1946). In his novel, *The Bad Judgment of a Dead Man* (*Un muerto de mal criterio,* 1926) a judge dies and continues to pass sentence on "cases" in a court in the world beyond: the cases are absurd, grotesque, phantasmagorical. The rapid parade of farcical scenes at times sparkles with good imaginative art. The nightmare ends when the judge is resuscitated (or, if one prefers a realist explanation, when by a series of injections he recovers his consciousness) and begins to write the novel of the world beyond the grave which is, precisely, the one we have just read. Very superior was his novel *The Partner* (*El socio,* 1928), related by an omniscient author capable of showing us simultaneous actions and of depicting different characters. Nevertheless, Jenaro Prieto is intentionally close to his protagonist, Julián Pardo (notice that the names of author and character have the same initials), and by means of indirect interior monologs, he follows him even in his most intimate thoughts. Julián Pardo, at one time a poet, now a real estate agent, invents a partner, Mr. Davis, in order to lighten his responsibilities. All Chilean society accepts the hoax, and the ideal Mr. Davis begins to take on life, body, independence, and effectiveness. He humiliates Pardo, threatens him, destroys him. In the end a beaten Pardo becomes demented, believes in his own creation, and commits suicide— Mr. Davis appears to be the murderer. The police, naturally, then look for Mr. Davis. It is possible that the novel's situation may have been suggested by Oscar Wilde, whom he cites (remember how Algernon invents Bunbury in *The Importance of Being Earnest*). The scholar might propose a long list of possible sources, because the variants on the interior duplication in fiction are innumerable: the novel within a novel, the character who invents another character, the fictitious situation that becomes real, the imaginary hero who rebels against the author and proclaims his autonomy. When one speaks of this theme people always remember Pirandello (*Il fu Mattia Pascal, Sei personaggi in cerca d'autore*). But the fact is that Spanish literature was one of the first to deal with it (splendidly in *Don Quijote de la Mancha*) and there is no reason to go far from home: remember in Galdós *Misericordia* how Benina invents "Don Romualdo," who suddenly appears and intervenes in the action, or in *El amigo Manso*, also by Galdós, or in Augusto Pérez from Unamuno's *Niebla*. The hypostatization of the fictitious Davis is part of a more complicated game: Anita and Julián invent a novel of adultery which they eventually incarnate; Anita invents a Madame Duprés just as Julián Pardo had invented a Mr. Davis, and Madame and Mister will have loves from which will be born a child; a fortuneteller predicts that Anita will marry a nonexistent man, and so Anita has to fall in love with Mr. Davis. Therefore, it is not a psychological novel, with Julián as the "case," but rather a humoristic, and occasionally satiric, novel on the symbolic medium in which all men live, on our myth-making capacity, on imagination as the fabric of an ideal world. Everyone believes in the fictitious Mr. Davis, and they even see him. And the reader himself, in certain pages when he has doubts as to whether Davis exists or not, is also converted into a character of the novel. It is an expressionist novel, then, which in the form of a farce shows how the most absurd ideas are objectified. The prose is rapid, alive, natural, of rare imaginative quality. The metaphors—mainly Modernist, at times ultraist—are constantly and forcefully catching fire. The book is disrespectful, original, with humoristic winks, but with a serious purpose: to bring to light man's deceitful nature. His book of memories was posthumous—*The Old House* (*La casa vieja*).

(10) *Paraguay* / LEOPOLDO CENTURIÓN (1893–1922) and ROQUE CAPECE FARAONE (1894–1922), both initiated into the Modernist group of the review *Crónica* (1913), wrote short stories in a Modernist, colorful prose with precious French brush strokes.

(11) *Uruguay* / ADOLFO AGORIO (1888) colored with fantasy and exoticism the prose narrative of *Rishi-Abura* (1920), a "voyage to the land of shadows." This swamp witch emanates from the superstitions of India.

(12) *Argentina* / RICARDO GÜIRALDES (Argentina, 1886–1927) presented, with the verses of *The Crystal Bell* (*El cencerro de cristal*) in 1915, his credentials as a reader of French poetry and daring poet: as a reader, he preferred the symbolists and, above all, Jules Laforgue; as a poet he tried a good deal, succeeded at times, and managed some advances which later were to be called "creationism" and "ultraism." *Stories of Death and Blood* (*Cuentos de muerte y de sangre*), also of 1915, were in reality "anecdotes heard and written because of affection toward the things of our land." These *Stories* were not well constructed nor well written. But the "affection for things of our land," for the Argentinian countryside and its folk, was to inspire better works. Two interesting novelettes were *Raucho* (1917), in whose protagonist we see the same educational upbringing as in the author who, wearied of Buenos Aires, wearied of Paris, was attracted to the country, and *Rosaura* (1922), a simple, sentimental, and melancholy story of small-town loves. The second is of especial interest because the constructive and emotional unity are much more obvious than in all his other works. Quite apparent, also, is the influence of Laforgue on his poetic, metaphoric, impressionistic language, ironic in its expression of tenderness. Güiraldes appreciated the prose poem—in Baudelaire, Flaubert, Villiers de l'Isle-Adam, Aloysius Bertrand—and in poetic prose he published in 1923 his most characteristic book: *Xaimaca,* which is typical of his double and harmonic aptitude as a lyricist and narrator. The novel *Xaimaca* —a voyage from Buenos Aires to Jamaica, with a love adventure—was forgotten because of the success of *Don Segundo Sombra* (1926). There were factors foreign to purely literary merits that entered into this success, such as the nationalist feelings of the reader, the surprise of finding, in gaucho clothes, a metaphoric language fashionable in postwar literature, and a conception of the novel, also fashionable in those years, according to which the poetic tone was more important than the action and the characterization. The reality is contemplated through a curious esthetic lens that retires objects to a distance, yet enlarges them. The cattleman Don Segundo, for example, is a "phantom, a shadow, an idea" that appears to be emerging from tradition. He is not the gaucho of the *Facundo* nor of the Martín Fierro epoch, but he does come from those backgrounds and the narrator admires, with historical emotion, his legendary aura: "What a leader of the bushwhackers (*montonera*) he would have been." Although we see him as a laboring and civilized cattleman, he is not a contemporary man, but "something that is passing." The novel, in this regard, is in the form of a farewell. It is an Argentina that is passing and the narrator takes leave of it with the tenderness of a poet. One by one the scenes

of country life make up an album of poetic customs: the small town, the general store, the saddle-breaking, natural love, the slaughtering of cattle, the square dance, folkloric tales, cockfights, scenes of Creole politicking, fairs, encounters of old friends in the nomadic life of the Argentine plains, horse harnessing, the round-up, knife duels, horse racing for money, stampedes. Within this body of evocations—of customs, but lyrical ones—there is a novelistic skeleton and musculature. That is, these lyrical evocations of customs move at a novel's pace, but with a simple, minimal action. In the form of memoirs Fabio Cáceres relates details of his life.

There are twenty-seven chapters that might be divided into three parts, though not all the readers will agree in the location of the joints of this tripartition. Those who like symmetry might propose three parts of nine chapters each. First: an orphan boy of fourteen, who does not know who his father was and who, up to now, has roamed the streets of a country town like a rogue, is suddenly fascinated by the appearance of the gaucho, Don Segundo Sombra, and decides to hang on to him like a burr. He runs away from home and is initiated into "the most manly of occupations": steer-herding on the pampas. This exposition, into which a family secret is inserted, comes to a close with an interruption in the narrative sequence. Second part: five years have passed, and our protagonist-narrator tells us that Don Segundo Sombra has made a gaucho out of him. From this point, the following nine chapters are nine sketches of rural customs. This part, descriptive not only of customs but also of landscapes, culminates in chapter XVIII, when the protagonist-narrator, on coming to from a fainting spell, has the rare experience of seeing into the future: he hears, or believes he hears, what he will indeed hear in chapter XXVI, that from a cowhand he has become a rich cattleman. Third part: his labors as a cowboy continue, with a few adventurous sketches included. The protagonist returns to his home town and there finds out who his father had been. He inherits his name and property, becomes a cultured man, and has the urge to become a writer. The book ends with Don Segundo Sombra's farewell. This symmetrical division, although defensible, suggests a rigorous structure that the novel is far from having. An asymmetrical division is one composed of three retrospective moments that the protagonist-narrator himself proposes: first chapter, in which, at the edge of a brook, the fourteen-year-old youth evokes his childhood; tenth chapter, in which, at the shores of a river, he evokes his five years of living with Don Segundo Sombra; chapter XXVII, in which, on the banks of a lagoon, he evokes his three years as the owner of a ranch.

There are other structural elements in the novel: the appearance and disappearance of Don Segundo Sombra (chapters II and XXVII), both actions occurring at dusk and described almost with the same words ("I thought I had seen a phantom, a shadow, something that is passing and is more an idea than a person"; "What went off into the distance was more an idea than a man"); the narrator's premonition of the future —encased in another supernatural episode, that of Don Sixto, the invisible devil, and the death of his son—and the repetition of the scene, nine chapters later; the narrator's family mystery that opens the novel, and its final clarification. But let us not exaggerate: *Don Segundo Sombra* is not a novel of a complex and harmonic architectural structure. The order is rather that of a collector of scenes and landscapes who wants to complete an album of pages linearly juxtaposed. The action changes pace, it moves slowly, it hurries along, and it even leaps over time, only to return later to complete itself in a flashback (the separation of the two lovers in chapter VI, which closes the love scene begun in chapter V); but it never reaches the fluidity of the psychic life of the narrator. "Gradually my recollections had brought me up to the present," Fabio says in his first retrospection (chapter I). How coincidental that recollections should be organized in such a logical sequence! These are memories written like a clear and coherent soliloquy that arranges the episodes with the object of moving the urban reader with a stylization of country life. There are no interior monologs to directly reveal the profound life of the narrator. "Brief words fell like ashes of inner thoughts," Fabio tells us; but either we do not hear them or, if we do, they have already lost their fleeting intimacy. Nevertheless, the greatest achievement of the novel rests in the oneness of its point of view. "Enclosed within a character that did not allow me to pour myself in him except with great prudence," Güiraldes explained to Valery Larbaud, "I have been obliged to restrain my desires to perfect my expression." And, in fact, what elegant temperance this, of holding back from yielding to the temptation of displaying his powers as a cultured writer. "I don't wish to speak about that," says the narrator referring to his education and travels to the world's capitals, "in these simple, straightforward lines." He avoided dissonances between the style and the theme, and his efforts were dissimulated and always subtle. And so, as he wrought the usual gaucho similes transforming them into new metaphors, he also thinned down the sulky, malicious speech until it took on literary subtlety, as in "I have lost a ring in the cornfield," spoken by the girl, chapter IV, in which "ring"—as in Chaucer —means virginity.

But the protagonist's change in social position, with his subsequent literary education, capably solves the problem that intrigues the reader from the very first pages: May not the reader ask?—What will happen farther on to make the little gaucho who is telling us his memoirs acquire a perspective on his own life that is so literary, so wise in metaphoric procedures? Because the perspective with which the protagonist is contemplating the countryside, its men, and his own adventures is always idealizingly poetic. At times he looks down upon himself from the sun: "the first look from the sun found me sweeping"; more normally he looks at himself from a moon, high and distant, illumined by cosmopolitan literature. It has already been noted that among the many refinements that Güiraldes puts in the soul of his protagonist—metaphors, rare sensations, synesthesia—there is evidence of that literature that offers cases of parapsychological states, telepathy, and paramnesias. It is true that the little gaucho Fabián always had a delicate nervous constitution (with esthetic delights, superstitious shudderings, propensity to tears, and the imagination of one who enjoys hearing the stories that Don Segundo elaborated in his campfire chats), but without that jump from cowhand to ranch owner—and, consequently, without the time distance between the adventures he experienced and the memories he evoked—the book would not be convincing. In his evocative flights the protagonist considers as feats what to Don Segundo were everyday events: to lasso, to break horses, to wrangle steers were feats for one who, through later education, learns that the cultured public of the city, having read about them in many books, would also consider them as such. A stylistic analysis would show the complicated inventive operations with which *Don Segundo Sombra* was created. Operations that were very subtle, very lyrical, very cultured; but one of these intended to objectify the collective soul of the traditional Creole Argentina, and this achievement in descriptive transparency is what gained international recognition for the novel. It was thought to be a realist novel, almost a telluric novel. Not at all. Güiraldes, a rich ranch owner, educated in the latest currents of French literature, did not express the real viewpoint of the cattlemen: as he let Fabio Cáceres speak, he put symbols of distance in his mouth ("for those old timers"), extemporaneous judgments, philosophical reflections foreign to the world of the gaucho and, especially in chapter XXVII, scorn for the wealth and comfort that falsified the social reality of the Argentine countryside. But, in spite of this social falsification, the novel has an admirable stylistic truthfulness. Fabio Cáceres, now a mature man and writer, relives his cowboy years and describes them with a language of refined expressive dignity and, yet, true to the actual vision of country life. The vision is that of a lyrical poet, but the things he sees are only those that are there before him. No matter how original his metaphors may be, they never escape the horizons of the pampa: they fuse and transmute things familiar to cowboys and cattlemen. Even the most realistic details are doubly artistic: because they are beautiful and revealing. Güiraldes combined the language spoken from birth by the Creoles with the language of the Creolist educated in European impressionism, expressionism, and ultraism. In spite of his realist dialogs, his folklore, his rural comparisons, his pampa dialect of cowhands and cattlemen, *Don Segundo Sombra* is an artistic novel. Cáceres, without leaving his pampa, strives for a style rich in rare and brilliant images.

Before going off into realism we should record the fantastic narrations of SANTIAGO DABOVE (1889–1951). A friend of Macedonio Fernández and of Borges, a reader of Horacio Quiroga and of Leopoldo Lugones, he wrote a few stories of horror, neurasthenia, madness, alcohol, and metamorphosis, with themes from science fiction and characters obsessed with death.

(*b*) *Narrators More Objective than Subjective* / Whether they reacted against Modernism, or ignored it, or in respecting it did not feel it viable for what they wished to say, the fact is there was a family of narrators of unimpeachable realist souls. Some studied life in the cities, but in their majority they worked with folkloric and regional material. Most of them profited by the interest that readers had in these matters: the reader tended to have illusions. Literary disorderliness led him to believe that the author was sincere; the morose description of customs led him to believe that what the author was saying had the value of reality; indigenous words used profusely led him to believe that the author was giving a correct vision of the Indian. Many novelists, instead of creating persons, used to propose names and then tell us that those who carried these names were living and moving on some part of this earth. They would add a "problem" from outside and when they had reached a certain number of pages the novel was done. The reader was deceived into believing that these men existed as persons, that those "problems" converted the novels into vigorous allegations. As he studies the novels and short stories the critic, assailed by a sudden dizziness—the authors are in the hundreds, the titles in the thousands— looks for some support to lean on in order to keep from falling. One of these supports might be a thematic arrangement: stories of the city, the country, the jungle, the mountain, the coasts; or of work in the mines, in workshops, in fruit mills; or of the Indian, the mestizo, the Negro, the Creole, the *gringo;* or of history, ethnography, sociology, politics, anti-imperialism, psychology. We must remember that what is valuable in literature is not the themes, but what the novelists do with these themes. For this reason we have separated the authors who apparently built their novels on the same reality; namely, the Argentinians Güiraldes and Héctor Eandi or the Colombians Rivera and Uribe Piedrahita or the Mexicans González Peña and José Rubén Romero. But even those narrators who used the same realist techniques cannot be grouped by themes. If such were done the same authors would appear several times with different labels, since they often changed themes.

(1) *Mexico* / The Revolution of 1910 in Mexico, one of the few Hispanic-American revolutions to really change the economic and social structure of a country, stirred up a whole novelistic cycle. It falls within the jurisdiction of the novel to describe real anecdotes and not to judge ideal intentions. The intentions of the Revolution were noble, its anecdotes, dreadful. And so the novelistic cycle of the Revolution, because of its valiant realism, seemed to be anti-revolutionary. A simple paradox to solve: the desire for justice is also the desire for truth and, because they were revolutionaries, these writers denounced without hypocrisy the brutalities of a people in arms.

The cycle was opened by Mariano Azuela, whom we have studied already. Some narrated the fighting itself; others, its consequences. Novelists of both these phases in this period were Guzmán, López y Fuentes, Romero, Muñoz, Mancisidor, Urquizo (in the following period these will be added: Icaza, Campobello, Iduarte, Rojas González, Magdaleno, Ferretis). After Azuela came JOSÉ RUBÉN ROMERO (1890–1952) with *A Villager's Notes* (*Apuntes de un lugareño,* 1932) and *Disbandment* (*Desbandada,* 1934), both pictures with autobiographical strokes. Beneath the comicality of his types, the situations in which he puts them, and the language he makes them speak, there is, in Rubén Romero, a bitter undercurrent. In *Anticipation of Death* (*Anticipación a la muerte,* 1939) that underground river of bitterness comes closer to the surface than in his earlier novels; e.g., *The Useless Life of Pito Pérez* (*La vida inútil de Pito Pérez,* 1938) presents, during the years of social dissolution which followed the Revolution, a rogue from the lower class who convinces through his typical Mexican traits. The malicious novel *My Horse, My Dog and My Rifle* (*Mi caballo, mi perro y mi rifle,* 1926) is perhaps the best. Only because of the common theme of the Mexican Revolution shall we invite here MARTÍN LUIS

GUZMÁN (1887) who, for his more artistic style, should be treated apart. He published the biography of *The Youthful Mina, Hero of Navarre* (*Mina el mozo, héroe de Navarra,* 1932), *Memoirs of Pancho Villa* (*Memorias de Pancho Villa,* 1940) and *Historical Deaths* (*Muertes históricas,* 1959). (The *Memoirs* are not autobiographical: Guzmán: who never concealed his sympathy for Villa—whom he knew personally —makes him speak as he must have spoken, imagining here and there where documents are missing, but imagining with so much knowledge of the fountainhead that these *Memoirs,* apocryphal and all, are more authentic than those set down by politicians and militarists.) By then he was famous for *The Eagle and the Serpent* (*El águila y la serpiente,* 1928) and *The Shadow of the Caudillo* (*La sombra del caudillo,* 1930). *The Eagle and the Serpent* is not a novel but a bouquet of stories, all of them having blossomed from the revolutionary experiences of the author. The prose is vigorous and vigorously resists the very dangerous temptations of this type of literature, that of falling into political chronicle. Stylistic vigor, then, which is the only kind that counts in a history of literature. His impressionism, especially outstanding in its pictorial technique, does not disturb the rapidity of the action. Guzmán lifts his theme with the muscles of a well-trained style. *The Shadow of the Caudillo* surpasses this one because it is literarily more ambitious, better organized as a work of art. But, since it is a novel and not an ensemble of chronicles, like *The Eagle and the Serpent,* one is more demanding. And because of this artistic demand—a demand which tends to remain unsatisfied—the taste of the reader vacillates for a moment and he does not know which of the two books best measures the real talent of the author. *The Shadow of the Caudillo* begins with artistic phrases that are rich in impressionistic word pictures. But the whirlpool of action snatches the prose and drowns it in a chronicle of infamy, treachery, ignominy, crimes, abuses, vices that take place during the political intrigues of the Obregón and Calles era, toward the end of 1927 in the city of Mexico and its environs. The Mexican Revolution appears here in its farcical electoral process. There is not a single noble figure: not even Axkaná is convincing, since he is also involved in the shady intrigues of others, though he has more scruples. And one is horrified at the cold precision with which Guzmán describes gun-rule in Mexican politics. He has not created any memorable characters because his interest was more sociological. The novel has no unity. The early chapters suggest a situation (Rosario-Aguirre) that later has no development nor importance. Nor does it have stylistic unity: impressionistic preciosity in the early chapters, objective prose later. The most important part, in keeping with the tone of a novel, is in the intrigue, the conspiracy, the violence at the end. A good novel, all in all.

Little by little, the novel of the Revolution lost part of its violence and attended more to social problems. At times the living conditions of the Indians were brought to light, or the ups and downs of political life, or the revolutionary repercussions in the provinces. And even the uprising of the Catholics against the Revolution, as in *The Virgin of the Cristeros* (*La Virgen de los Cristeros*, 1934) by FERNANDO ROBLES (1897). FRANCISCO L. URQUIZO (1891) was a chronicler of an elaborate style. One of the best novels in this period is *They Took the Cannon to Bachimba* (*Se llevaron el cañón para Bachimba*) by RAFAEL F. MUÑOZ (1899), who relates in loose episodes, but in sequence, the revolutionary apprenticeship of a boy of thirteen in the ranks of the "*colorados*" who fought against the government of Madero in 1912. It recalls something of *Don Segundo Sombra*, not only because of the boy's devotion to Marcos Ruiz (the general fighting for Orozco), but also because of the idealization of the landscape and of the military feats, and for the richness of its images. But of course, Muñoz' novel has a violence foreign to Güiraldes'. Here, the civil war is related in the midst of revolution. The character Marcos Ruiz would have been more authentic if Muñoz had not put, especially toward the end, moral, political, and revolutionary discourses in his mouth. The novel's action is rapid, like the war, although the author never surrenders his slow-paced description of things, scenes, fields, and villages. And to be certain, the best of the prose, notable for its precision and for the energy of its images, lies in the description. His imagery is not just adornment but impressions of all his senses, experienced by the author and efficaciously used throughout the story. So that together with the military action, we are given always the imaginative visions of the protagonist-narrator. The equilibrium between the novel's action and the poetic contemplation is well achieved. JOSÉ MANCISIDOR (1895–1956) sacrificed the art of his best works to Marxist politics. *The Riot* (*La asonada*, 1931) interprets the Revolution from the Communist point of view: his denunciations of imperialism, militarism, and religious fanaticism respond to the aims of political propaganda. His novel *Frontier by the Sea* (*Frontera junto al mar*, 1953) opens with the struggle of the people of Vera Cruz against the United States' invasion. The characters are intentionally scarcely individualized. Then he published *Dawn in the Chasms* (*El alba en las simas*) and *María Kainlová Told Me* (*Me lo dijo María Kainlová*, 1956). GREGORIO LÓPEZ Y FUENTES (1897) has written a number of novels of the Mexican scene; the scene—political, anthropological, folkloric, social—tends to be more interesting than the novels themselves. At times the novels study the characters psychologically: *My General!* (*¡Mi general!*), *Huasteca*, *The Compliant One* (*Acomodaticio*), *Mezzanine* (*Entresuelo*). But his preference for social study is more obvious: *Encampment* (*Campamento*), *Land* (*Tierra*), *The Indian* (*El indio*), *Muleteers* (*Arrieros*) and recently, *Cornfield, Cattle-Ranch and Mountain* (*Milpa, potrero y monte*, 1951) where he denounces the sufferings of the field worker, the cowhand, and the deer hunter personified in three brothers. *The Indian* (1935) is made up of loose scenes—basted together with a tenuous thread of a plot, which is the history of the Lame One—on the life of an indigenous Indian tribe during the years of the Revolution. It deals with ethnography (superstitions, customs), sociology (social intercourse, work and property matters, class struggles) and above all politics (the exploitation of the Indians, their claims and the inter-play of vested interests). It presents such an abstract attitude that it blurs the individuality of the characters: they don't even have proper names (the hunter, the old man, the teacher, the girl). But this is not an abstraction that a man of science would deal with, because everything is constructed in the form of a political allegation where one protests—with bitter reflections, or simply in the manner of setting up the episodes—against injustice. The revolutionary and social substance that nurtured these novels also sustained the theater and the short story. In its place we shall refer to the theater of Magdaleno and Bustillo Oro.

The Revolution shook intellectual life to such a degree that many of those who would have preferred to stay on their sun roofs looking over European fashions from a distance had to come down quickly, plant their feet firmly on the ground, travel about the territories, find out what was going on, and understand the peo-ple, their customs, their folklore. Among these intellectuals that rediscovered Mexico there were those with the souls of historians. Alongside pro-Indian and revolutionary literature, then, there were those who, about 1917, looked back to the Colonial period. They are called the "colonialists": Genaro Estrada, Francisco Monterde, Artemio de Valle-Arizpe, Julio Jiménez Rueda, Ermilo Abreu Gómez. The satirist of the group was GENARO ESTRADA (1887–1937), author of four books of verse, very Mexican in their polished transparency—though the crystal may have tinges of Góngora and García Lorca—published from 1928 to 1934, and of a comely novel, *Pero Galín*, 1926, intelligent in bringing the old and new face to face. Estrada, an antique collector, a bibliographer, a colonialist, seems to have carica-turized himself in his character, a man with a mania for the archaic, oblivious of the present, who suddenly marries an ultramodern young girl, breaks into the movie world, and is cured of his anachronism. The novelistic elements are min-imal; the essayistic prose, sharp and good-humored, is what entertains the most. ARTEMIO DE VALLE-ARIZPE (1884–1961) never strayed from his path: painting beautiful pictures with the dust of archives, museums, and libraries of the Colonial period. Of his many books perhaps the most vital one is *The Newsboy* (*El Canillitas*, 1942). FRANCISCO MONTERDE (1894) is a poet, dramatist, and novelist. The scholar within him pulls him toward criticism, and his personal literature veers toward the historical. His theater is important and has represented the political, social, and psychological themes of the rural environment with fine lyrical intui-tions. As a novelist, he began with revolutionary themes; then he wrote novels of the viceregal period—*The Madrigal of Cetina* (*El madrigal de Cetina*) and *The Secret of the "Escala"* (*El secreto de la "Escala"*). He is one of the best culti-vators of the historical novel in this generation—*Montezuma, the One of the Golden Chair* (*Moctezuma el de la silla de oro*), *Montezuma II, Lord of the Anáhuac* (*Moctezuma II, señor del Anáhuac*); the narrative of *The Fear of Hernán Cortés* (*El temor de Hernán Cortés*) reveals serious study, a desire for a critical revi-sion of the past, and a fresh imagination. ERMILO ABREU GÓMEZ (1894) began in the theater with themes of colonial Mexico: *Long Live the King* (*Viva el rey*, 1921), *Humanities* (*Humanidades*, 1924), *Ballads of Kings* (*Romances de reyes*, 1926). Later without abandoning the theater—*A Play of Scorn* (*Un juego de escarnio*, 1943); *A Parrot and Three Swallows* (*Un loro y tres golondrinas*, 1945) —he extended his alert and novel prose to other themes and genres: poetic stories on the lives of Mayan heroes—*Canek* (1940); stories for children—*Juan Pirulero* (1939) and *Three New Stories About Juan Pirulero* (*Tres nuevos cuentos de Juan*

Pirulero, 1944). Of greater scope are *Quetzalcóatl, Dream and Vigil* (*Quetzalcóatl, sueño y vigilia,* 1947), stories on the life of the indigenous god. One of his best works is *Shipwrecked Indians* (*Naufragio de indios,* 1951), a novel about a little Mexican village that protests the invasion of the French. Maximilian's emissaries arrive in town to recruit troops—the rich cede, the poor resist, youths conspire, women pray. The story advances by means of a savory language. The episodes are like watercolors with incisive lines and variegated quantities of color. The title of the first page alludes to the tragedy of the last page: a French ship sinks with its cargo of Indian prisoners. In *Tata Lobo* (1952) he has created, in a gracious style of archaic and popular flavor, if not one of those anti-heroes of picaresque literature, in any case a rogue-hero lost in the chaos of Mexican life; he sloughs along from adventure to adventure, but at times he leaps as though he were flying. In the form of a letter-novel he began his memoirs in *Day Was Dawning . . .* (*La del alba sería . . . ,* 1954). In *The Conspiracy of Xinum* (*La conjura de Xinum,* 1958) he novelizes the violence of the indigenous uprisings in the Yucatán peninsula.

(2) *Central America / Guatemala:* CARLOS SAMAYOA CHINCHILLA (1898) is the author of *Mother Cornfield* (*Madre Milpa*) and *Four Chances* (*Cuatro suertes*). His *Stories and Legends* (*Cuentos y leyendas,* 1936) penetrates the Guatemalan reality by several paths: the Mayan legend, the still-active folklore, the country's history, the direct observation of customs, his own experiences. Samayoa Chinchilla moves along any of these paths with a dignified and cultured bearing, making no concessions to plebeian notions. Yet, he is not original: his literature is the same as that cultivated in many other countries, not the material elaborated, but the style.

Honduras: CARLOS IZAGUIRRE (1894–1956) took advantage of his novel, *Beneath the Cloudburst* (*Bajo el chubasco*), to pass on his political ideas.

El Salvador: ALBERTO RIVAS BONILLA (1891) writes narratives on local customs in rural environments: *Doings and Ill-Doings* (*Andanzas y malandanzas*), *I Mount My Colt* (*Me monto en un potro*).

Nicaragua: HERNÁN ROBLETO (1895) in *Blood in the Tropics: The Novel of Yankee Intervention in Nicaragua* (*Sangre en el trópico. La novela de la intervención yanqui en Nicaragua,* 1930) gave us the chronicle of the civil war between liberals and conservatives in 1926. Sandino is absent from these pages. The United States appears as the invading force, on the side of the conservatives. Robleto, who took part in this war on the liberal side, does not dissimulate his partiality. He makes propaganda, not against the people of the United States, but against the influence of Wall Street on the foreign policy of the State Department. The United States is represented as a giant intervening between two quarreling dwarfs (liberals and conservatives) in order to protect one of them. Robleto seems to admire the Americans and even wishes to win their good will. The novel ends with a sentimental episode: Sergeant Clifford Williams, who had raped a little Creole, searches her out at the war's end and marries her. In a political framework, this chronicle—for it is a novelistic chronicle, more than a novel—records the sufferings of men, the violence of the struggle, and, the most impressionable part, the devastating action of nature on its social ills. A prose without imagination: communicative, objective, descriptive. In *The Stranglers: Yankee Imperialism in Nicaragua* (*Los estranguladores. El imperialismo yanqui en Nicaragua,* 1933) he re-accentuated his position.

Costa Rica: The person who distinguished herself most for her direct observation of local reality and for profiting from folklore was María Isabel Carvajal, who signed her books CARMEN LYRA (1888–1951). She was a school teacher and militant in political movements favoring the working class. Her love for children and for people shows through her books: *The Fantasies of Juan Silvestre (Las fantasías de Juan Silvestre)* and *In a Wheelchair (En una silla de ruedas),* both of 1918, and *The Stories of My Aunt Panchita (Los cuentos de mi Tía Panchita,* 1920). This last book has given her the most fame. It is a collection of traditional stories, from written and oral sources, refurbished in popular Costa Rican language. Worthy of note are GONZALO SÁNCHEZ BONILLA (1884), ANIBAL RENI (1897), GONZALO CHACÓN TREJOS (1896). And separately, for his artistic stylization of the Costa Rican reality, LUIS DOBLES SEGREDA (1891–1956), author of *For the Love of God (Por el amor de Dios), Mystic Rose (Rosa mística),* and *Wild Cane (Caña brava).*

Panama: The short story was cultivated first, and not until the year 1930 did a group of novelists emerge. On the realist side loom JOSÉ MARÍA NÚÑEZ (1894) with his *Creole Stories (Cuentos criollos)* and JOSÉ E. HUERTA (1899) with his stories of local customs in *Peasant Soul (Alma campesina).* Less significant is MANUEL DE JESÚS QUIJANO (1884–1950).

(3) Antilles / Cuba: Political preoccupations, the spirit of social documentation, the will to protest and reform inspired a series of novels. LUIS FELIPE RODRÍGUEZ (1888–1947) planted in his stories and novels the roots of peasant life with its enchantments, but above all, with its miseries and injustices; more than in his novels—*What Damián Paredes Thought (Cómo opinaba Damián Paredes,* 1916), *Swamp (Ciénaga,* 1937)—he was successful in the short stories in *Home Town Easter (La pascua de la terra natal,* 1923) and *Marcos Antilla,* 1932, his best book. Nor is he a creator of characters, but rather he is an outliner of sections of collective life. His defense of the peasants, his attacks against the latifundium system or imperialist plundering, his bloody endings, his liking for documentation, and his theses give his pages a movement more appropriate to the essayist than to the artist. He influenced the young writers. FEDERICO DE IBARZÁBAL (1894–1953), a poet of dockside themes, also preferred themes of the sea in his narrations. A literary sea, but evoked with sober effectiveness and with a sense of adventure and exoticism. Others: JOSÉ ANTONIO RAMOS (1885–1946), taken up with Cuban reality: *Coaybay, Caniquí:* CARLOS FERNÁNDEZ CABRERA (1889), and MIGUEL DE MARCOS (1894–1954).

Dominican Republic: Noteworthy for his historical evocations is MAX HENRÍQUEZ UREÑA (1885), author of a sober series of *Dominican Episodes (Episodios dominicanos,* 1951). He is also an essayist and poet: he collected his verses in *Claw of Light (Garra de luz,* 1958). MIGUEL ÁNGEL JIMÉNEZ (1885) is a novelist for his *The Daughter of a Nobody (La hija de una cualquiera,* 1927). SÓCRATES NOLASCO (1884) cultivated the Creole story, of folkloric roots, of rural customs: *Stories of the South (Cuentos del sur,* 1939) and his edition of *Wild Stories (Cuentos cimarrones,* 1958) collected directly from oral tradition. FRANCISCO MOSCOSO PUELLO (1885) documented in *Sugar Canes and Oxen (Cañas y bueyes,* 1936) the hard work of the sugar plantations. More than a novel, it is a succession of objective frames that follow the manufacturing process step by step, from cutting the trees to clearing the ground, up to the most unjust phases of exploitation.

RAMÓN EMILIO JIMÉNEZ (1886), a poet and narrator of jovial mood. JOSÉ MARÍA PICHARDO, "Nino" (1888) cultivated the national short story, *Flower Bread* (*Pan de flor*), and the novel, *Inland* (*Tierra adentro*, 1917). ENRIQUE AGUIAR (1890) cultivated the Indianist historical novel, *Don Cristóbal*, 1939, and also that of national landscapes, *Eusebio Sapote*, 1938. MIGUEL ÁNGEL MONCLÚS (1893), narrator of *Things Creole* (*Cosas criollas*, 1929), *Creole Scenes* (*Escenas criollas*, 1941) and a novelist with *Cachón*, 1958.

(4) *Venezuela* / The novels of JOSÉ RAFAEL POCATERRA (1889–1955) were declarations of war against Modernism. He was aware of his power: to novelize—he used to say—"people on the street, on corners, in church, in intimate life, from the sidewalk across the street." He was also aware of his weaknesses: he admitted his "defects in form and composition." Was he aware that his novels failed because he insisted on not "drawing persons, but in fixing types?" *Doctor Bebé* (*El doctor Bebé*, 1917) for example, presents a bourgeois family elevated by the political boss or *caudillo*, Bebé, and subsequently dragged down by him to dishonor and misery. But what is presented are types: Bebé, the political boss, sensual, unscrupulous, abusing; the cowardly, intriguing and servile Pepito; the poor women, ambitious but fearful of scandal, in love, but browbeaten: Josefina, with her illegitimate daughter, is the one who is most moving. This corrupt society is heard in typical speech, and not in individual voices. The prose is hard and opaque: only in moments of cruel irony does it acquire expressive vigor, and that is when it strikes one most. Being a naturalist, Pocaterra shows the animalistic, the instinctive, the sordid aspects of life. In their irate and aggressive Creolism, his novels—*Obscure Lives* (*Vidas oscuras*), *Beloved Land of the Sun* (*Tierra del sol amada*)—are not as easily read as his *Grotesque Stories* (*Cuentos grotescos*, 1922). Others: JOSÉ ANTONIO RAMOS SUCRE (1890–1930), ENRIQUE BERNARDO NUÑEZ (1895), JULIO GARMENDIA (1898), JULIO ROSALES (1885) and LEONCIO MARTÍNEZ (1888–1941).

(5) *Colombia* / In returning to the land—in part because of the example of Rivera's *The Vortex*—many narrators became mirrors in which local settings and customs were reflected. When they did intervene in reality, it was to denounce social ills and to take up the claims of the humble masses. Their optimism in wishing to improve things was clothed in apparently pessimistic preferences for misery, suffering, and pestilence. The sociological view of this type of novel focused on sordid human groups and on trivial types. The desire to propagandize led them to seek out the mass public, and the exaltation of the mediocre led to an unimaginative language. Only the most outstanding of these works of fiction need be cited here. EDUARDO ARIAS SUÁREZ (1897–1958) divided *Growing Old and Selected Short Stories* (*Envejecer y cuentos de selección*) into two portions: "sentiment" and "humorism." His humorism recalls that of the sketches of customs, somewhat sarcastic and even critical in intent. Among the stories grouped in the category of "sentiment" he placed his novelette *Growing Old*. There is also humorism here in the reflection of every detail of life. Arias Suárez observes and then comments on his observations with intelligence, imagination, and wit. CÉSAR URIBE PIEDRAHITA (1897–1951) gave us with *Toá* (1933), rather than a novel, a chronicle on the life of the rubber workers in the Amazon basin of Colombia. No character takes on sufficient relief, not even the protagonist Antonio. And the double action—the fights between the Colombian rubber workers and the intruders from Peru plus

the love between Antonio and Toá—is also insufficient. The jungle—which should be in the background with its diseases, its beasts, and its Indians—is moved to the foreground. The book has value as a document for the natural sciences, ethnography, and a little, very little, for sociology; but its value as a novel is minimal. The intention seems to be not to novelize the cruelties of nature, but the cruelties of man that vex nature itself: "the white man, lascivious and covetous, bestially violated Nature and in this way tried to dominate it." But only the intention remains. The interest in *Toá* is derived from the natural, social, ethnographical reality it describes, not from the art of novelizing. The prose is simple, communicative, realist, on occasion like a chronicle or scientific report. His other novel, *Oil Stain* (*Mancha de aceite*, 1935), comes face to face with the imperialistic interest of the petroleum industry.

(6) *Ecuador* / BENJAMÍN CARRIÓN (1898) in 1926 published a novel about the failure of an intellectual, *The Disenchantment of Miguel García* (*El desencanto de Miguel García*), but later he definitively turned to the essay and criticism. FERNANDO CHAVES (1898?) in his novel *Silver and Bronze* (*Plata y bronce*, 1927) showed the suffering of the highland Indians under the injustices of the parish priests and the feudal lords. Thus, with Chaves, the indigenist novel, which will acquire more importance under the pen of Jorge Icaza, arises in Ecuador.

(7) *Peru* / We have already referred to Abraham Valdelomar. AUGUSTO AGUIRRE MORALES (1890) reconstructed, with the experienced hand of an archeologist, the life of the Incas—*The Sun People* (*El pueblo del sol*). CÉSAR FALCÓN (1892), who in *The City without God* (*El pueblo sin Dios*, 1928) displayed national woes in a style that strove to simulate current literary styles, gives in *The Good Neighbor Sanabria U* (*El buen vecino Sanabria U*, 1947) in an ordinary and traditional style a picaresque history with a political theme: imperialism and the "good neighbor policy" of the United States as it functions in Hispanic-America.

(8) *Bolivia* / ANTONIO DÍAZ VILLAMIL (1897–1948) worked the popular clay of folk legends, stories, theater, and novels. In *The Apple of His Eye* (*La niña de sus ojos*, 1948) he novelized a social situation, in La Paz: the young lady, of Indian origin, provokes race prejudice and class resentments as she prospers in her social status. ALFREDO GUILLÉN PINTO (1895–1950) wrote naturalist novels in defense of the Indian and the proletariat of fields and mines: *Indian Tears* (*Lágrimas indias*, 1920); *Utama* (1945); *Mina* (1953). Also indigenist, but more conventional, are the narrations of SATURNINO RODRIGO (1894). Of a pedagogical purpose is the novel, *The Sense of Life or The Life of Jorge Esteban* (*El sentido vital o La vida de Jorge Esteban*, 1931) by RIGOBERTO VILLARROEL CLAURE (1890). GUSTAVO A. NAVARRO (1898), who penned his name "Tristán Marof," enjoyed a fleeting success—partly because of his personality as a political fighter—with *Suetonio Pimienta: Memoirs of a Diplomat of the Carrot Republic* (*Suetonio Pimienta. Memorias de un diplomático de la República de Zanahoria*, 1924). Irony, sarcasm, and cynicism run like an open faucet, too easily and too superficially. Since the jokes touch on current matters—the theme: five years in the lives of Hispanic-Americans living in Paris—the novel is boring. Marof has humor, but no wit. There are intentions toward social criticism and political reform, but without originality or keenness. The sentences are short, quick, but unfortunately, for one who wished

to be the chronicler of what he had seen or lived, Marof did not display any inventive faculties. The indications of a will to renovate remain in the realm of political thought, not in literary know-how: denunciation of vanity, prostitution, falsehood, holidays, diplomatic hypocrisy, playboyism, etc.

(9) *Chile* / The "more subjective than objective" narrators, as we have called them, at times were fairly realistic, as Barrios was in *A Lost One*. And those whom we now qualify as "more objective" at times show a good deal of interest in psychology, as did Edwards Bello and Maluenda. Nor do the geographical categories of "country" and "city" or the economic-political categories of "lower classes" and "upper classes" solve the difficulty of classification, for there are narrators who belong to all these categories. One might be tempted to group them according to whether they specialized in the description of the landscape (Creolists like Latorre), in psychological peculiarities (Manuel Rojas) or in social circumstances, with all their economic and political implications. The worst of it is that these rings, since they are too abstract, fit no one's finger. The only defensible critical arrangement is that of pointing out the artistic merit of each one, and this we will attempt in the individual commentaries. Let us see what can be done.

The regionalists used to go out into the open air, and there they noticed that men were less free than elsewhere: man seemed to appear to them determined, molded, or overcome by nature. This is not exactly applicable to RAFAEL MALUENDA (1885), who has eyes for seeing through to souls, and even magnifying lenses for psychological breakdowns. He comes and goes between the short story and the novel—he succeeds when, halfway between, he writes long stories or short novels—and he always probes deep within his characters. He has created a rich gallery of characters. In it, rare, eccentric, and complicated personalities abound. He is especially excellent in the drawing of feminine figures—*Miss Ana, Confessions of a Schoolmistress* (*La señorita Ana, Confesiones de una profesora*). He began with *Scenes of Country Life* (*Escenas de la vida campesina*, 1909), but also novelized scenes of urban life—*Urban Beehive* (*Colmena urbana*, 1937?). The social scale on which he places his narratives is also varied—from the humble classes to the powerful. A good specimen of his irony, of his wit, of his art, is the story "The Pachacha," whose characters are chickens. His theatrical works are not unworthy of his narrative talent. Another great narrator is FERNANDO SANTIVÁN (1886). Santibáñez is his real name. He joined D'Halmar, Prado, and Magallanes Moure in the foundation of a Tolstoy colony (see his *Memoirs of a Tolystoyan* [*Memorias de un tolstoyano*, 1955] and also the *Confessions of Enrique Samaniego* [*Confesiones de Enrique Samaniego*, 1933] which, in approaching something between a novel and an autobiography, in passing, light up literary history). Santiván does not invent extraordinary things nor select extraordinary cases from country life; he takes a "piece of life" and his literary effort consists in preserving its palpitations. *Palpitations of Life* (*Palpitaciones de vida*, 1909) is precisely the name of one of his first collections of stories—one of the last: *The Forest Starts Its March*

(*El bosque emprende su marcha,* 1946). In his novels he made incursions into the city, into the middle class, into artist and writer circles; but he distinguished himself most in the interpretation of rural life with *The Bewitched* (*La hechizada,* 1916). It is a novel of country environment. A city youth visits the country, falls in love with a girl, fights his rival, and wins her—not in a duel, but in a farm feat. But in the end he discovers that she is "bewitched"; in spite of all, she loves the bad man. The conception of the hero Baltasar and his contrast with the villain Saúl is Romantic; and so is the "case" of the girl Humilde. And even the descriptions of the landscape would be Romantic if it were not that certain decorative metaphors remind us that Santiván, on writing *The Bewitched,* left behind not Romanticism but Modernism. Nevertheless, despite this Romanticism and Modernism, *The Bewitched* can be considered as toned down realism. The Chilean novels and short stories that described life in the country in realist modes were the most abundant. They were realist yet preserved something of the descriptive ways of Modernism. Because they admired the landscape, the fauna, and the flora of each region excessively, these narrators tended to forget their characters and their conflicts. They formed a regionalist, Creolist school. The leader of this school was MARIANO LATORRE (1886–1955). He observes, he lists, he documents; seldom does his literature give birth to characters that have the vitality of real men. Although he has written good novels, such as *Zurzulita* (1920), a somber, tragic love story that depicts the cowboy of the coastal ranges, his collections of stories are the more worthy: *Ully* (1923), *On Panta* (1936), *Men and Foxes* (*Hombres y zorros,* 1937), *Mapu* (1942), *Viento de mallines* (1944) and many others. It is as if his long series of volumes wanted, tirelessly, to exhaust the description of the soil of Chile, span by span: the landscape of Chile appears in his last book, *Bird Island* (*La isla de los pájaros*).

In the Creolist school headed by Latorre we find LUIS DURAND (1895–1954). His characters are peasants. He surrounds them with landscape. When he hears them speak he reproduces their rustic voices unadornedly. He was a short-story writer, somewhat careless in the art of composition, but prolific (see his anthological *Seven Tales* [*Siete cuentos,* 1955]). He was also successful as a novelist: *Frontier* (*Frontera,* 1949). ERNESTO MONTENEGRO (1885) is not easy to place. He elaborated the folklore of his land without literarily retouching what was handed to him by tradition: *My Uncle Ventura: Popular Tales of Chile* (*Mi tío Ventura. Cuentos populares de Chile,* second edition, augmented, 1938). Different from the Creolists, sketchers of customs, and regionalists, there were those who, without renouncing realism, brought a greater complexity to the novel—the complexity of large cities, of political agitation, of spiritual life, of uncommon themes, of new techniques in the art of storytelling, of irony and imagination. The two outstanding figures were Edwards Bello, at the beginning of the period, and Manuel Rojas, at the end. JOAQUÍN EDWARDS BELLO, (1886) is a psychological novelist, though not as artistic as Barrios. He is always on the lookout for abnormal human types, unbalanced because of their impulsiveness or their lethargy, excited by action or by delirium. The social conduct of his characters is observed, nevertheless, through the combined perspective of psychology and sociology. After several attempts he succeeded with *The Down-and-Outer* (*El roto,* 1920), an "experimental novel" on the bawdy houses and the underworld of Santiago de Chile. Later Edwards Bello turned his travel experiences into novels: *The Chilean in Madrid* (*El chileno en Madrid,* 1928) and *Creoles in Paris* (*Criollos en París,* 1933). In the novels set in

Chile, the attack on national vices is merciless. There is, down deep, a love for the country and its people, but on the surface one only sees a discontented and reforming soul. Whether he is evoking memories of his own life—*In Old Almendral: Valparaiso, Windy City* (*En el viejo Almendral: Valparaíso, ciudad del viento,* 1931)—or showing a life of false luxury through a woman—*The Girl from Crillón* (*La chica del Crillón,* 1935)—Edwards Bello is amazing for the ease of his narrative movement. Yet, he was not a great novelist. The carelessness of his hurried writing left his characters obscure and pieces of his story unhinged, not counting what fell beyond the artistic heart of the novel itself, such as social theses, sketches of customs, journalistic material.

We have left for the end, because he is singular in every respect, MANUEL ROJAS (1896). He was born in Argentina but as an adolescent went to Chile. In this epoch, the sketches of customs of Santibáñez and his generation dominated the scene. Though his parents were Chilean, Rojas was not looked upon as a Chilean, nor were his experiences totally Chilean. He therefore remained outside the circle of writers of social customs. He told stories, mixing the Argentinian with the Chilean. Rojas was not worried about being atypical. He was not interested in becoming a painter of customs. On the contrary. For him, the mission of the short story or of the novel was not to overwhelm insignificant men with landscapes. What he wanted was to show what man feels, thinks, and is. And to describe this man he did not turn to linguistic naturalism. Of course, his characters spoke naturally, but he did not insist on putting words taken from the outlying corners of society into their mouths. He aspired to be read by a public beyond the region that he was describing. His narrative material consisted of men as they are, and of the situations they are in. Nature enters only in relation with the characters. The description of nature must be essential to the narrative, not a mere decoration, luxury, or virtuosity. But he looks at men as a group on the march. He does not seek to create a great character. There was almost no influence of Hispanic-American writers on him (he admired Horacio Quiroga most). On the other hand, some Americans did influence Rojas: Hemingway, and above all, Faulkner. From Faulkner he learned to avoid the heavy novelistic techniques of the nineteenth century, where all the action is explicitly described; Rojas preferred to reveal the action with interior monologs and time shifts without having to explain it to the reader. An able narrator in every setting—sea, country, city—he created in his innumerable short stories a whole population of characters. They are collected in various books that go from *Men of the South* (*Hombres del sur,* 1927) to *The Biretta from Maule* (*El bonete maulino,* 1943), and in various novels, from *Launches in the Bay* (*Lanchas en la bahía,* 1932) to *Son of a Thief* (*Hijo de ladrón*, 1951). This last one, in the tone of memoirs, is considered one of the best in all Hispanic-America. *Son of a Thief* is the first of a trilogy. The third, *Better Than Wine* (*Mejor que el vino*, 1958), relates in the third person (because of modesty?) the love experiences of the protagonist; the second is on his intellectual and political formation (Rojas became an anarchist together with González Vera). *Son of a Thief* relates, in the first person, the life of a boy from his first recollections until his seventeenth year: his poverty, his orphanhood, his sufferings, his trip to Chile, his hunger, his participation in a popular uprising, his unjust imprisonment, his hard labors, his friendships. All the material related is real—even the filthiest scenes—but the narrative manner is not typical of realism. His sympathy for strange lives leads him to paint, with very imaginative tints, a whole gallery of eccentricities. His taste for strange people in strange situations makes the narrator veer from his line of memoirs. But, moreover, the whole novel is unhinged from the inside. There is no narrative sequence. The narrator follows the flow of his evocations. Capriciously, the action is sent forward or held back. This rupture in the order of events increases the reader's interest, especially if the procedure is a novelty to him. If, on the other hand, the reader already was acquainted with the use of dislocations of planes in the masters, James Joyce, Aldous Huxley, William Faulkner, and others, he may notice the huge difference: in Rojas the technique of looking at one life from different levels of time does not form part of an original and poetic vision of the world, but it is, rather, an easy way of composing a novel in a restful position. The interior monologs, the indirect free style, the stream of consciousness do not succeed, in Rojas, in penetrating profoundly the intimate being of each character.

Among those writers who were more complex than the Creolists—we have just named Edwards Bello and Rojas—one notices a tendency toward sociological realism. It had come down from Baldomero Lillo; now we see it headed by Edwards Bello. We will see its immediate continuation in González Vera; and, in the following chapters, Godoy, Guzmán, and others will carry on. José Santos González Vera (1897) wrote scanty, sober, delicate works that had the virtue of being directed to minorities, even though his themes go deep into the humble and dispossessed masses. *Minimal Lives* (*Vidas mínimas*, 1923) carries the story of a tenement house; *Alhue* (1928) are simple stories of a country village; *When I Was a Boy* (*Cuando era muchacho*, 1951) is the autobiography of his poverty. Alberto Romero (1896), with naturalist tenacity, depicted in *The Tenement House Widow* (*La viuda del conventillo*, 1930) a reality similar to that of *The Down-and-Outer* of Edwards Bello, that is, the slums of Santiago. In other novels his preferred theme was the life of the middle class. Other writers, excited by social and political commotions, were: Juan Modesto Castro (1896–1943), author of *Stagnant Waters* (*Aguas estancadas*), and WALDO URZÚA ÁLVAREZ (1891–1944), author of *A Man and a River* (*Un hombre y un río*). Of those Chilean narrators who fit here because of their age, it suffices to mention EDGARDO GARRIDO MERINO (1888), whose novel *The Man of the Mountain* (*El hombre de la montaña*) places him in Spanish literature; VICTORIANO LILLO (1889) who leans toward psychological and even fantastic themes.

(10) *Paraguay* / NATALICIO GONZÁLEZ (1897) stands out here. In his country he initiated a poetry directed at vindicating the Indian. His attitude was more nationalistic than esthetic. His poetry, beginning with *Guaraní Ballads* (*Baladas guaraníes*) up to *Elegies of Tenochtitlán* (*Elegías de Tenochtitlán*, 1953) passing through *Motifs of the Red Land* (*Motivos de la tierra escarlata*, 1952) in which he included his Guaraní ballads together with other personal and political compositions, remained hidden, however, under the weight of a large prose production. As a prose writer—essay, narration—he was quite vigorous. He is the author of *Stories and Parables* (*Cuentos y parabolas*, 1922) inspired by indigenous legends, and *The Errant Root* (*La raíz errante*, 1953), a novel that takes place in the jungle about the sociological theme of the divestiture of lands from the original owners. A prose larded with Guaraní language. JUAN STEFANICH (1889) in *Aurora* (1920) novelized the fight of university students against a petty tyrant, with the bourgeois life of Asunción as a background. Other narrators: LUCIO MENDONÇA (1896) and JUSTO PASTOR BENÍTEZ (1895).

(11) *Uruguay* / ADOLFO MONTIEL BALLESTEROS (1888) is one of the more complex—in genres, themes, intentions, and moods. He was outstanding in his pictures of the life of the soil, which were true in narrative but rich in imagination and lyricism. ALBERTO LASPLACES (1887) a good teller of popular stories.

(12) *Argentina* / There are novels from every region, with European urbanity and Creole rusticity, evocative of the past or belligerent in the present, sweet and bitter, written with careful art or with peevishness. Here are some of the authors. First, those who narrate the life of the city. VÍCTOR JUAN GUILLOT (1886–1940), in *Stories Without Importance* (*Historias sin importancia*), *Terror*, and *The Soul in a Pit* (*El alma en el pozo*). GUILLERMO ESTRELLA (1891–1943), in *The Egoists and Other Stories* (*Los egoístas y otros cuentos*, 1923) and *The Owner of the Fire* (*El dueño del incendio*, 1929), ironically captured happenings of life in Buenos Aires. Other narrators of this type: SAMUEL GLUSBERG (1898), JOSÉ GABRIEL (1898), HECTOR OLIVERA LAVIÉ (1893), ERNESTO MARIO BARREDA (1889). In his *Three Stories About Buenos Aires* (*Tres relatos porteños*, 1922) ARTURO CANCELA (1892) feigns a subtle and cold humorism. Cancela is not laughing as he writes: all the effectiveness of his pages is due to his impassivity. The style seems simple, and no doubt it is; at moments it seems to flow from his pen, in a conversational tone, but suddenly one is aware that an effort has been made—the effort to become serious without reproof, bitterness, or mockery. The first of his stories, "Herrlin's Coccusbacilus" (*"El cocobacilo de Herrlin"*), is a caricature of Argentine bureaucracy. The second, "A Week on a Spree" (*"Una semana de holgorio"*), is better because the satire is less obvious, and the story, in the first person and in the present time, creates an atmosphere of fantasy and even poetry. Nevertheless, the satire is there: it alludes to the events of the "tragic week in January" (1919), when young patriots, taking advantage of workers' agitation following

the Russian Revolution, murdered Jews and identified the ideals of Argentina with those of the Jockey Club. But the satirical observations appear as the little bones of an airy literary body that moves with the grace and vivacity of stories similar to those of Chesterton, whom, let it be said in passing, Cancela read in English and whom it is not unlikely he imitated. The third story, "The Cult of Heroes" (*"El culto de los héroes"*), is on its way to being a novel, and perhaps because it promises to be a novel, it satisfies less as a short story. Some of the narrators of the city, because of their preference for humble lives and cases of poverty, form the "Boedo group," after Boedo Street which was then a so-called proletarian street. Their organ was *Los Pensadores* (later *Claridad*), and their function, to dignify the working class literarily.

To this group (there were other younger ones who are waiting for us in the next chapter) belong Yunque, Mariani, and Castelnuovo, three readers of Russian literature; the first, of Tolstoy, the second, of Chekhov, and third, of Dostoevski. Álvaro Yunque (1893) believes that the suffering of one man makes society unjust. His literature is a long lament. During those years, these laments were called "social ferment." Of an anarchic mind and apostolic sentiments, he spoke to men with very simple words. His tenderness toward the sad lives of poor children was the most moving: *Bichofeo.* Other titles: *Scarecrows* (*Espanta-pájaros*), *Zancadilla.* Roberto Mariani (1893–1946) also wrote to serve man and yearned for goodness and justice, but he was more complex. In *Office Stories* (*Cuentos de oficina*) he observed the lowest and grayest layers of the bourgeoisie, but his preoccupation with death gave his pages a deeper dimension: in *Aggressive Love* (*El amor agresivo*), *Death's Visitations* (*La frecuentación de la muerte*), *In the Penumbra* (*En la penumbra*), *Return to God* (*Regreso a Dios*) he penetrated his characters, even those most entrapped by circumstances. He also wrote for the theater: *A Child Plays With Death* (*Un niño juega con la muerte*) and *Twenty Years Later* (*Veinte años después*). Elías Castelnuovo (1893) was the most naturalistic of the group. Not only did he denounce social inequality but also the curse that falls on the insane, the lepers, and other shattered humans: *Darkness* (*Tinieblas*, 1923), *The Cursed Ones* (*Malditos*, 1924), *Among the Dead* (*Entre los muertos*, 1925), *Cannon Fodder* (*Carne de cañón*, 1926), *Calvary* (*Calvario*, 1929), *Grubs* (*Larvas*, 1931) are his happy titles. Let us now pass on to those narrators who describe life in the country, provincial towns, and villages. Some move on from place to place. Alberto Gerchunoff (1884–1950) who in *The Jewish Gauchos* (*Los gauchos judíos*) described rural life in an Argentine province, with poetic grace; in the novel, *The Important Man* (*El hombre importante*), he described the life of a contemporary political boss, Hipólito Irogoyen, with satiric grace. The quick and pleasant pen of Bernardo González Arrili (1892) has evoked, in novels and collections of stories, an Argentina of wide breadth, of long history, and of a rich variety of themes: the customs of the northern provinces —*The Calchaquí Venus* (*La Venus calchaquí*), politicking—*Protasio Lucero,* the conflicts between labor and capital in the refrigerator store-houses of Barracas— *The Red Pools* (*Los charcos rojos*), historical episodes—*The Invasion of the Heretics* (*La invasión de los herejes*), Creole devotion—*The Virgin of Luján* (*La Virgen de Luján*), memories of childhood in Buenos Aires—*Corrientes Street Between Esmeraldas and Suipacha* (*Calle Corrientes entre Esmeraldas y Suipacha*). Julio Vignola Mansilla (1891) re-elaborated the folklore material of several provinces in a series of short stories. A rare gift of phrase is evident in the *History of* an *Absurd Passion* (*Historia de una pasión absurda*) by CARMELO M. BONET (1886). From the mountainous region of northern Argentina came some good narrative books. *The White Wind* (*El viento blanco*) by JUAN CARLOS DÁVALOS (1887–1959); *The Regionalists* (*Los regionales*) by FAUSTO BURGOS (1888–1952); *The Long-Suffering Race* (*La raza sufrida*) by CARLOS B. QUIROGA (1887); *The Gold Prospector and Other Stories* (*El buscador de oro y otros cuentos*) by JULIO ARAMBURU (1898); *Wild Horses* (*Baguales*) by JUSTO P. SÁENZ (1892); *The Night Patio* (*El patio de la noche*) by PABLO ROJAS PAZ (1896–1956); *The Water Well* (*El pozo de balde*) by ROSA BAZÁN DE CÁMARA (1892). From the coast area and the pampa: *Wanderers and Capable Men* (*Errantes y hombres capaces*) by HÉCTOR I. EANDI (1895); *Gringo Pampa* (*Pampa gringa*) by ALCIDES GRECA (1896).

2. Essay

Throughout this chapter we have been occupied with writers who, in passing, gave the essay literary category. Those whom we are about to see are predominantly essayists. We noticed that verse and prose are like two stories of the same building: the writers who live in it go from one floor to another and write a poem as easily as a novel. And there are houses not of two but of ten stories, where the polygraphers, like Alfonso Reyes, live.

ALFONSO REYES (Mexico, 1889–1959)—as did Prado, Güiraldes, Rivera, Arévalo Martínez—overflowed from verse to prose. No one better than he can link the poetry pages of this chapter to the pages on prose; since he is as illustrious in one as in the other, he could be placed in either section. But it would not be proper to sever his work and study it separately because, as in no other writer, his verse and his prose form a crystalline unity. His poetic books appeared so widely interspersed in almost unavailable editions, so overwhelmed by his greater prose production, with such versatility of style, themes, and tonality, that very few readers have a clear image of the poet Reyes. When he finally published his poetic works *Poetic Constancy* (*Constancia poética*) in which he collected earlier books and added unedited poems, it was patent to all, not just to a minority, that Reyes was excellent. He groups his poetry under three headings. The first is a "Poetic review," then the topical verses, and finally, those books of poetry which have a certain unity: "Cruel Iphigenia" (*"Ifigenia cruel"*), "Three Poems" (*"Tres poemas"*), "Day's Sonnets" (*"Jornada en sonetos"*), and "Deaf Ballads" (*"Romances sordos"*). His first poems, from around 1906, were Parnassian. Having learned respect for verse forms in this school, Reyes struck out for himself. Like other Modernists, he penetrated the obscurities of his own being, sometimes to bring color to it, sometimes to question, and even in order to touch its dark and silent depths. Serious symbolism alongside of which, after the first World War, rhythms and images of juvenile vanguardism begin to play. There were even poems describing sensual African dances. Actually, nothing was outside the pale of his poetry which was "fickle in theme and style." His themes were as varied as the turns of his own life: autobiographical evocations, the homeland, friends and loves, works, and death. His styles come and go between the laboratory in which the hermetic poets distill their verse and the clear, open road where the people walk. Reyes was not afraid to prospect along dangerous trails: for example, along the prosaic trail (in case they "jumped him" he was well armed— see his "Prosaic Theory," where he declares "I prefer to be promiscuous / in literature," "the popular ballad / of the neighbor / with the rare quintessence / of Góngora and Mallarmé"). Difficult or simple he always demands the attention of the reader, because earlier, he was demanding of himself and gives only essences.

His poetry is concise, sober, insinuating. His prose is beaten gold. The virtues of intelligence and esteem that tend to come separately in people in Alfonso Reyes are integrated in gracious and subtle light. He is erudite in the field of philology and sparkling in witty sallies; he writes stories, chronicles, sketches, and penetrating critical glosses. His prose is impish and prying. The multiplicity of Reyes' vocations (a man of the Renaissance) is not only measured by the vast repertory of motifs, but also by the stylistic richness of each turn. Reyes' restlessness transmits to his style a zigzagging, jumpy, prankish, and sensual movement. Before leaving Mexico in 1913, his writer's hand was already educated: from this period, with a single exception, are the stories and dialogs of *The Oblique Plane* (*El plano oblicuo*, 1920), a most original book in the Spanish language because of its rapid shifts from the real to the fantastic ("The Supper"—"*La cena*") and because of its expressionist procedures. From 1914, except for a brief stay in France, he was to live in Spain until 1924, probably the most productive period of his career: *Vision of Anáhuac* (*Visión de Anáhuac*, 1917), *The Eves of Spain* (*Las vísperas de España*, 1937), *The Suicide* (*El suicida*, 1917), *The Hunter* (*El cazador*, 1921), *Real and Imaginary Portraits* (*Retratos reales e imaginarios*, 1920), and the five series of *Sympathies and Differences* (*Simpatías y diferencias*, 1921–1926). This is a consummate work that links on different pages, and at times on the same page, impressionist sentences, fantasies, elegances, narrative flights of fancy, biographical sketches, notes, and reflections. His norms appear to be these: to express himself in miniatures; to not lean too much on actual things; to subjectivize everything, whether it be through his sensibilities or through his imagination; to intermingle life and culture; to address himself to a sympathetic reader who possesses the same qualities that the writer possesses, and to converse with him; to watch each word. Later still in the diplomatic service, Reyes continued his travels: France, Hispanic-America (1925–1938), and his final return to Mexico in 1939. From among his personal, imaginative, and expressive prose works, let us mention here, *The Testimony of Juan Peña* (*El testimonio de Juan Peña,* 1930), *A Train of Waves* (*Tren de ondas,* 1932), *The Seven Above Deva* (*Los siete sobre Deva,* 1942), *Works and Days* (*Los trabajos y los días,* 1945), *In Pencil* (*A lápiz,* 1947), *The Literary Experience* (*La experiencia literaria,* 1952), *Fireworks* (*Árbol de pólvora,* 1953), and *Fifteen Presences* (*Quince presencias,* 1955). Characteristic of his fictional work is its preference for exciting the imagination of the reader with suggestive details rather than satisfying his curiosity with a plot or a denouement. It is fantasy for sharp readers, already accustomed to and perhaps tired of reading so many novels. His essays are always lyrical, even those of didactic or logical themes, because the manner in which he treats his object is personal, not public. In *Sundial* (*Reloj de sol,* 1926) Reyes confessed: "The historian I carry in my pocket will not allow me to waste a single datum, a single document." But it is not so much a desire to recoup a past public as it is to reconstruct an intimate diary whose leaves had fallen out along the road of life. Like Echo, the quartered nymph, the diary that was buried here and there by Reyes throughout his work lives on in a constant murmur. No matter how impersonal a Reyes theme may appear, one can always perceive the vibration of a confidence about to be revealed. Even though he was one of our most exquisite, most original, most surprising writers, Reyes founded his work on healthy experiences. Others would like to look at the world upside down, to see if a world askew will tell them something new: they mutilate themselves or give value to their mutilations; they give themselves over to sophistic frenzy or to lethargy; they corrupt honor, deny light, betray the heart. Not Reyes. Alfonso Reyes is a classical writer because of the human integrity of his vocation, because of his serene faith in intelligence, in charity, in the eternal values of the soul. The uniqueness of Reyes' poetic universe is not extravagance, but the refinement of the normal directions in man. Each one of his volumes is a collection of unsurpassed pages. To date, the Fondo de Cultura Económica of Mexico City has published thirteen thick volumes of *Complete Works.* On contemplating this grandiose monument to his effort, a literary critic states a bundle of problems that should be studied carefully: the problem of a writer who fails in spite of being extraordinarily equipped for success; that of a secret sterility that is disguised by incessant labor; that of an intelligence which, because of its propensity for dialog, remained with its face toward the best spirits of its time, but with its back to its own works; that of a classic of our literary history who, nevertheless, left no great books. Is there in the air of Hispanic-America something lethal to literary creation? Why did not the author of *The Testimony of Juan Peña* give us the novel he promised? Why did not the author of "The Supper" give us the collection of stories he promised? Why did not the author of *Cruel Iphigenia*, of *Footprints*, give us the drama, the book of poems he promised? Indeed, the fruits yielded are sufficient. But for those of us who had the privilege of being his friends, it is clear that Alfonso Reyes could have given more, much more than that, to the great genres of literature. Where he did succeed was in the essay. Alfonso Reyes is without any doubt the keenest, most brilliant, versatile, cultured, and profound essayist in our language today.

Other Essayists / PEDRO HENRÍQUEZ UREÑA (Dominican Republic, 1884–1946) began as a critic—*Critical Essays* (*Ensayos críticos*, 1905), *Hours of Study* (*Horas de estudio*, 1910)—and this is the most visible stamp on his work, which is so pithy in philological research, in literary history, in the disquisition and synthesis of general questions, in the preparation of anthologies and bibliographies. But he was also an imaginative and sensitive writer: verses of Modernist flavor, poetic prose, travel descriptions, the *Birth of Dionysus* (*El nacimiento de Dionisus*, 1916), "an essay of tragedy in the ancient manner," beautiful stories. He did not write enough in this vein to be incorporated into a purely literary history. Nevertheless, the artistic sense puts its seal on everything he wrote including his rigorously technical works. His prose was masterful in precision, economy, and architecture. He was a humanist formed from all literatures, from all philosophies; and in his curiosity for things human, he did not neglect even the sciences. His written work, though important, scarcely reflects the value of his talent. He gave his best to his friends, in conversations, in teachings. Wherever he lived, there grew atmosphere, intellectual groups, disciples. He had classical, rationalist preferences: and even in his socialist ideas, in favor of a new social order based on economic equality, and on personal and national liberty, these preferences for clear and constructive thinking appeared. See *Critical Works* (*Obra crítica*, 1960).

Let us pay a call on another essayist of this period, VICTORIA OCAMPO

(Argentina, 1893). She delights in confessing her limitations; but there is in the confession a quick smile of pride: "Had I had less memory, perhaps I would have been less indolent, and today I could have spoken to you of things learned during my studies, and not all the details that I discover when I pull to the surface of my consciousness—as the fisherman who hauls in his net full of fish—what still lives on, in the depths of my unexplored memories." But the reader knows this is not indolence. To convey personal memories at times requires more effort than to transmit learned ideas. And what is most admired in her series, *Testimonials* (*Testimonios*), are the personal memories of Victoria Ocampo. Her whole intellectual world, wide and bright as a summer hat, is pinned to her head with anecdotes. Would it be just to separate EZEQUIEL MARTÍNEZ ESTRADA (Argentina, 1895) from the poets and place him among the essayists? His books of poetry, from *Gold and Stone* (*Oro y piedra*, 1918) to *Humoresque* (*Humoresca*) and *Light-Footed Puppets* (*Títeres de pies ligeras*, both 1929), are among the best that Hispanic-America produced in this generation. Moreover, after Lugones, he is probably the most complex Argentinian poet. His is a poetry of somber humor, but capable of humorism, very imaginative, but wrought with philosophic rigor, born of an original hypersensitivity, but in reference to the world of culture. Martínez Estrada's intellectual tone is not pedantic: he dialogs with simplicity. What happens is that he converses with a reader who is also very intellectual. Humor, imagination, sensibility, intelligence, all strike hard blows, and the reader who can return blow for blow will enjoy a manly sport invented by Martínez Estrada. Public recognition of his talent came late, when he had already abandoned poetry and was writing only essays. His reputation, then, is that of an essayist, although his talent is that of a poet. In 1933 he published *X-Ray of the Pampa* (*Radiografía de la Pampa*), an interpretation of Argentine reality as profound as that of *Facundo*, but without Sarmiento's optimism. No doubt there is a good deal of his own temperamental nature—and also of contact with the pessimistic currents of literature—in Martínez Estrada's hopeless vision. But what is proper in his book is due to the moral crisis into which Argentina fell in 1930. Neither the masses nor the oligarchy were helping the country. Up came the *X-Ray of the Pampa*, which is the bitterest book ever written in Argentina. In a magnificently baroque prose, full of metaphor and witticisms that keep the reader in constant tension, Martínez Estrada drew the picture of Argentine miseries. There is nothing in Argentina that is spared. The detail and the rapid philosophic reflections that follow it about like a shadow give the book an extraordinary poetic quality. Its aphoristic force heaves the reader and, if the reader happens to be Argentinian, throws him in the air, in a grotesque whirl, and then lets him fall in the mire where he can do nothing more than cry in humiliation. A sad book which saddens. A book of tragic humor, taciturn, severe, unpardoning. Unconnected essays, held together by the common theme, the "microscopy of Buenos Aires," are those in *Goliath's Head* (*La cabeza de Goliath*, 1940). When he attempted theater, he failed. *What We Don't See Die* (1941), *Shadows* (1941) and *Hunters*—published in the volume, *Three Dramas* (*Tres dramas*, 1957)—are verbose, confused, sickly. Although enveloped in a Scandinavian mist, very nineteenth centuryish, they lack Ibsen's or Strindberg's tragic sense of life. As in Ibsen, when the curtain rises, the drama has already taken place, and all we witness is its revelation through the dialog and the final crisis. But this retrospective method (and an occasional situation dear to the heart of Ibsen, like the man who vacillates between two sisters of very different character and fails in marriage for having made the wrong choice) is the only Ibsen noticeable. His dialogs do not have dramatic force. The words bubble forth from the author's neurasthenia, not from the tormented conscience of the characters. In *What We Don't See Die* we are aware of Pablo's failure (failure in art, in business, in matrimony), and we are present at the catastrophe: Marta, Pablo's wife, commits suicide; and Pablo, humiliated, runs away from the broken home. But the tortured, mournful confessions of these consciences do not obey a profound analysis of life, but respond to pure morbidity. In *Shadows* and in *Hunters* the same theme of matrimonial failure is also unsuccessful. During these last years he published a series of stories: *Three Stories Without Love* (*Tres historias sin amor*), *Holy Saturday* (*Sábado de gloria*), *Marta Riquelme*. In the tone of a biblical prophet, he thrusts himself into the discussion of the heated political problems of his time. His contributions to literary criticism are important: *Sarmiento, Death and Transfiguration of Martín Fierro* (*Muerte y transfiguración de Martín Fierro*), *The Marvelous World of William Henry Hudson* (*El mundo maravilloso de William Henry Hudson*), *Brother Quiroga* (*El hermano Quiroga*), and others.

Critics, with assets in literary creation, in poetry, in fiction, or in theater are MANUEL ANDINO (*El Salvador*, 1892–1938); the Cubans JOSÉ MARÍA CHACÓN Y CALVO (1892) and FÉLIX LIZASO (1891); the Venezuelans MARIO BRICEÑO IRAGORRY (1897–1958) and LUIS CORREA (1889–1940); JOSÉ DE LA RIVA AGÜERO (Peru, 1885–1944); the Chileans HERNAN DÍAZ ARRIETA, "Alone" (1891), ARTURO TORRES RIOSECO (1897), ARMANDO DONOSO (1887), and DOMINGO MELFI (1892–

1946); ALBERTO ZUM FELDE (Uruguay, 1888) and the Argentinians ROBERTO F. GIUSTI (1887), JOSÉ MARÍA MONNER SANS (1896), and BERNARDO CANAL FEIJÓO (1897).

Less attentive to pure literature are the essayists SAMUEL RAMOS (Mexico, 1897–1959); the Salvadorians JUAN RAMÓN URIARTE (1884–1934) and NAPOLEÓN VIERA ALTAMIRANO (1894); OCTAVIO MÉNDEZ PEREIRA (Panamá, 1887–1954); MEDARDO VITIER (Cuba, 1886–1959); ANTONIO S. PEDREIRA (Puerto Rico, 1898–1939); JOSÉ CARLOS MARIÁTEGUI (Peru, 1895–1930); GUSTAVO ADOLFO OTERO (Bolivia, 1896); MANUEL DOMÍNGUEZ (Paraguay, 1896–1935), and FRANCISCO ROMERO (Argentina, 1891–1962), an elegant prose writer, a philosopher of German formation, preoccupied with the problem of spiritual life as the supreme level of transcendency toward truth and value—*Theory of Man* (*Teoría del hombre,* 1952).

C. THE THEATER

Of the hundreds of authors well known in the history of the stage, a few also enter into the history of literature. We shall see them from north to south. Naturally, some of them will not appear here for having been mentioned in the other genres.

After a long decline, the theater had a resurgence in Mexico with the works of JULIO JIMÉNEZ RUEDA (1896–1960) and FRANCISCO MONTERDE (1894), who were placed earlier among the "colonialists." These names should be added: CARLOS NORIEGA HOPE (1896–1934), CATALINA D'ERZELL (1897–1950), and VÍCTOR MANUEL DÍEZ BARROSO (1890–1930), the latter, in *Conquer Yourself* (*Véncete a ti mismo*), played with the real and the imagined in an ingenious and effective manner.

In Central America, J. EMILIO ARAGÓN (El Salvador, 1887–1938) and H. ALFREDO CASTRO (Costa Rica, 1889).

In the Antilles the most eminent names are Cuban. Above the heads of Sánchez Galárraga, Sánchez Varona, Louis A. Baralt, Marcelo Salinas, and Montes López, stands the robust JOSÉ ANTONIO RAMOS (1885–1946) with his theater of ideas. The ideological preoccupation of the polemicist and the reformer stifled the dramatist; in play after play he fought the prejudices against the rights of women, the superstitions of mealy-mouthed people, political corruption, cowardice, hypocrisy, foolishness. His is a theater of careless forms until he gave his masterpiece, *Tembladera* (1917), in which he put forth a serious Cuban problem—the sale of sugar mills and plantations to foreigners and the squandering of the money obtained therefrom. The economic suicide, the loss of sovereignty, indolence, irresponsibility, and parasitism of the families that live in mansions in the city, with no love for the land. The thesis rises from the dialogs and the plot situations, and also the hope for a solution symbolized in Joaquín and Isolina. His predilection for symbols was revealed more in the daring drama, *In the Hands of God* (*En las manos de Dios,* 1932). Of greater psychological refinement was his theatrical sketch *The Legend of the Stars* (*La leyenda de las estrellas,* 1935), somewhat Pirandellian in its epistemological relativism.

In Venezuela, LEOPOLDO AYALA MICHELENA (1894).

In Colombia the most important figure was ANTONIO ÁLVAREZ LLERAS (1892), author of *Social Vipers* (*Víboras sociales,* 1911). For him the theater is spectacle and also literature, a school that must fulfill the social mission of analyzing conflicts and proposing theses.

In Peru, FELIPE SASSONE (1884).

In Bolivia, ANTONIO DÍAZ VILLAMIL (1897–1948) and ADOLFO COSTA DU RELS (1891). The latter, a narrator and theatrical author, has written in Spanish, and for this reason he appears here, but he obtained his greatest successes with plays in French.

From Chile ARMANDO L. MOOCK (1894–1943). Several plays had already been presented in Chile when he decided to move to Argentina. Of his two hundred plays, some had an international success, like *The Serpent* (*La serpiente,* 1920)— the serpent is a woman, Luciana, who squeezes her prey to death and then looks for another victim—which was made into a movie in the United States. DANIEL DE LA VEGA (1892), fertile poet, good essayist, occasional short-story writer and author of one successful novel—*Cain, Abel and a Woman* (*Caín, Abel y una mujer,* 1933)—produced various plays with ironic overtones.

In Uruguay, after Florencio Sánchez, the spotlight falls on JOSÉ PEDRO BELLÁN (1889–1930), and especially on ERNESTO HERRERA (1886–1917). Herrera is in the naturalist vein of rural drama. *The Blind Lion* (*El león ciego,* 1911) presents in three acts the unsuccessful life of a political boss who led a faction in the Uruguayan civil wars: he is old, blind, and ridiculed by his own coreligionists. Herrera, with his anarchist ideas, could not sympathize with the brutal customs and passions he was describing; on the contrary, he communicates his repugnance. But unfortunately, he did not sympathize artistically with his sanguinary lion, and therefore, Gumersindo comes out psychologically dwarfed. The realist and lively dialog is of more interest to the philologist than the drama to the critic. *The Morals of Misia Paca* (*La moral de Misia Paca*) was first shown in its definitive version of three acts in 1912: before this, only the embryo in one act and its re-elaboration in two acts were known. It is a drama of ideas, but without revolutionary spirit, dealing with ill-mated women among the Creole bourgeoisie. The plot is not original—a young girl married to a sick old man—but Herrera operates in the "case" with the instruments of a surgeon. It has been said that his best play was *Our Bread* (*El pan nuestro,* 1913?) about a broken-up Madrid family of the middle class.

In Argentina the list of significant authors is long. Also, in these years the world of theatrical troupes settles itself in Buenos Aires, noisily, actively, brilliantly, and abundantly: VICENTE MARTÍNEZ CUITIÑO (1887), ROBERTO GACHE (1892), FRANCISCO DEFILIPPIS NOVOA (1891–1930), JOSÉ GONZÁLEZ CASTILLO (1885–1937), FEDERICO MERTENS (1886), CLAUDIO MARTÍNEZ PAIVA (1887), IVO PELAY (1893), RODOLFO GONZÁLEZ PACHECO (1886–1949).

The most important dramatist of the professional theater was SAMUEL EICHELBAUM (1894). His family, his literary family, came from Russia and northern Europe: Dostoevski, Chekhov, Ibsen, Strindberg. His theatrical style is realist. Eichelbaum's realism, however, does not consist in reproducing on the boards of the theater a piece of real life, but rather in showing how the characters suddenly become aware of the dramatic situation they are in without having been aware of it until then. The perspectives in which the characters see each other in the dramas of Eichelbaum are converted into the spectacle itself. The best scenes are invariably those with dialogs containing dense pauses between two characters. Family life is his preferred raw material. He has created, then, a theater of conflicting consciences, with soundings in the subconscious. Eichelbaum is serious, analytical, concentrated, cerebral, inquisitive, somber. He is not a pessimist because his plays have an ethic nerve that reacts actively in defense of spiritual liberty. Profound? More than profound, he is subtle. He selects a few behavioral motivations, the stranger the better, and then promotes a discussion on them. At times he seeks out exceptional situations in order to sound out sentiments that are also exceptional, as in *Clay Pigeon* (*Pájaro de barro*, 1940): Felipa, a poor peon's daughter, gives herself to the sculptor Juan Antonio: a child is born; when Doña Pilar wants to force her son Juan Antonio to marry Felipa, the latter, out of pride, denies his paternity; since the father engendered the child without love, he was born as if he were "a' orphan." Felipa is worthy, but Eichelbaum, determined to present her as misunderstood, paints her with shadings difficult to understand. In *A Turn-of-the-Century Tough* (*Un guapo del 900*, 1940), the moral springs are also surprising: Ecuménico, a professional killer, has placed his knife in the service of a political boss; the latter's wife makes him a cuckold with no one less than his political rival; Ecuménico kills this rival because he cannot serve a man who has been dishonored by his wife. All this, as well as having made a mythical hero of the assassin. In *Two Burning Coals* (*Dos brasas*) the artifice is even greater. Two coals from hell, two misers, husband and wife, sacrifice their lives to the cult of Mammon. The dramatic structure is weak; the United States atmosphere is false; the plot situation, absurd; the psychology of the characters, abstract; the dialogs, wordy; the denouement—the husband strangles the wife—futilely sensational.

XIII. 1925-1940

Authors born between 1900 and 1915

Historical framework: Political and economic consequences of the first World War: on one hand, greater participation in government leadership on the part of the masses, with Communist propaganda and Fascist conspiracies; on the other hand, "strong governments" which defend oligarchy, especially during the depression which begins in 1929. Also affecting Hispanic-American life are the fall of the Republic in Spain, the triumph of international Fascism, and the outbreak of World War II.

Cultural tendencies: After the first World War "vanguardist literatures" with a "new sensitivity" appear. Modernism being exhausted, styles are now violent and hermetic. The will to break with all the literary norms of the past predominates. Ultraism and its dissolution. The lost generation of those born around 1910. Pure poetry and surrealism.

Literary Groups / One of the themes considered here is the disintegration of so-called postwar literature, the literature which after 1918 called itself vanguardist. In the previous chapter we have already outlined the theory, history, and intent of this literature. But, as we said, the most scandalous writers calmed down after their first few books and, little by little, became more serious in their desire to express their true originality. The mere chronicling of this literary effort is difficult enough, not to mention trying to form a critique on it, not only because of its lack of seriousness, its crazy disorder, and the brevity of its duration, but also because there were other tendencies, and they all ran together. Ultraists unto death, renegades from ultraism, enemies of ultriasm. But do not believe that ultraism was the key signature for these years. There were excellent poets who grew up as though ultraism had never existed. The prose writers complicate the panorama even more, because in stories and novels it is possible to have styles with their faces prettily painted, homely styles and—as a most extravagant novelty—"ugliest" styles. That is, a deliberate poetization of everything ugly, frightful coagulations of "esperpentic" metaphors, the passage from calology to cacology. Writers lived between 1925 and 1940 as though they formed part of two opposing groups. No one today would insist on the *raison d'être* of these groups. As an example of how these groups broke up, of how these writers changed the sign under which they wrote, it suffices to recall the street of the "stridentists" and that of the "contemporaries," in Mexico; and in Argentina, the two streets, Florida (with its magazine *Martín Fierro*) and Boedo (with its review *Los Pensadores,* afterward called *Claridad*). What we have said of Argentina and Mexico could be extended to take in the intermediary countries; everywhere the pot of literature boiled over. It would be useless to try to trace the outline, the duration of each bubbling up. Interesting as they may be to the history of each country, these activities are insignificant from the point of view of a history of this type which looks at all of Spanish America and can only pause for the major figures.

We have already characterized the postwar vanguard in the previous chapter by referring to the "scandal." To put things in balance we will now characterize the writers whose works began to appear after 1930. Those authors immediately preceding had gloried in a "new sensitivity"; these were to brag about being "newists." What was this sensitivity? No one was able to distinguish it, much less define it. But by this time Ortega y Gasset had imposed his idea of "the vital sensitivity of each generation," and those born around 1910 were determined to belong to a generation. The Generation of the Centennial of the Independence? The Generation of the Sighting of Halley's Comet? The event, whether historical or astral, was the least important. What was important was to be a generation, a brand new generation. And the desire was so great that, since then, there has been no cessation in the invention of generations: that of "40," of "45," of "50," and of "55." Many more generations than can humanly fit into such a short passage of time. The youths who appeared during the decade of 1930 did not bear the aforementioned "anti's" into the lists as all generations customarily do when they present themselves. They were no anti-Modernists because Rubén Darío was already a bibliographical item, dead and buried in the literary curricula of the secondary schools. Modernism was an exercise, a remnant of the classical past, for today's classrooms. Neither were they anti-vanguardists because they did not take the orgy of postwar "isms" seriously. This literature had denied itself; it was not possible for them to deny it further. The more serious ultraists were showing promise of making amends for their first practical jokes, with solidly constructed works. The youths who were beginning to publish after 1930 could not be in opposition to this promise. Be it, then, that the past had become impregnably classical, or that it had disintegrated of itself until it no longer offered resistance, or that it had requested a moratorium, the fact is that in 1930 it was necessary to leap into literature without springing from the "anti" trampolin. At most, it could be said that they were against the post-Modernist generation, partly because they saw them full-face, seated in the chairs of literature of the high schools and universities. Perhaps because those born around 1910 appear around 1930 without the slightest uproar, without declaring war on anybody, they arrive unnoticed. Nevertheless, their silent, slow, sure, serious work, without the lavishness of Modernism, and without the childish pranks of the ultraists, might be visible if we look at it. They had the feeling that the others, "the previous ones," had swept and cleaned their house. Excellent servants. They were grateful to them. But they were not going to wield the same brooms. What for! The house having been cleaned, it was now necessary to get down to studying and producing.

Unfortunately, they studied more than they produced. There was much to study. The feigned disdain for culture on the part of the *enfants terribles* of the pre- and postwar periods no longer convinced anyone. New philological disciplines, new literary theories, new philosophies, new literatures. Everything interested them. There had never been in our America a group so well informed on such a vast field of cultural activities as that which appeared after 1930. And the more they studied, the less they wrote. It was not unjust, therefore, that they should not be considered a productive literary group. On the other hand, the 1930 authors, upon maturing, preferred drawing nearer to the younger writers; while the younger writers, in turn, drew together into their own generation, ignoring the near past, attentive to the distant past, that of the ultraists. A bridge was stretched between the irrationalism of the 1914 postwar period and the irrationalism of the 1939 postwar period; and the men of the 1930's remained beneath it. They were not irrationalists. But when they were, they took no joy in the disarticulated cry. Rather they sought the underlying reasons for life. They were closer to Ortega y Gasset than to Unamuno, nearer to the builders of literature than to its destroyers, closer to originality than to novelty. Let it not be forgotten, if we wish to explain why this group was not clearly distinguishable, that from 1930 onward the times were not propitious for literature. The writers that had burst forth after the first World War imitated the wry face of disillusionment of the Europeans without actually feeling disillusioned. They pretended to be a sacrificed generation, but they lacked a menacing catastrophe. After 1930, on the other hand, storm clouds were gathering in the sky. The first sign was the great depression that convulsed the entire world, and with it, the crisis of liberalism. Let us take the case of Argentina where the military revolution of that year gave strength to anti-democratic nationalism. The Catholic Action, stimulated by the Eucharistic Congress of 1933, adopted Italian fascist professions of faith. The growing successes of Hitler after 1934 were enough to make one's hair stand on end. The Civil War in Spain and the downfall of the Republic proved that the cause of liberty in the world was lost and that a new era of violence, tyranny, and stupidity had begun. Then in 1939, the war. There was no literary life. People read no books but searched in the newspapers for the grim notices of war. In 1943 another military revolution put the rightists in power; first, theocratic attempts, then demagogic, but in the end, fascism triumphed and intellectual liberty was at an end.

This series of blows, in all of Hispanic-America, not just in Argentina, made the creation of literature difficult, and once created, it found no public. Such was the uproar of the world. Let us have all those born around 1910 take hands and form a line. Does it not seem to be a dividing line? And though it may not indicate the division between esthetic stages, it does, at least, indicate this division: from here on what we have to say is no longer history. Actually, we should at this point consider that our historical framework for Hispanic-American literature is done. With this reservation, that our literary history is finished and that what follows is a gathering of friends—with exclusions and inclusions that do not always have critical worth—we continue with our chronicle of the latest years. We are not going to describe any "ism" as an abstraction, rather, as it appears as a concrete force in each individual poet. Let the reader of this history make his own synthesis. However, it would not be honest to simplify the literary whirlwind of this decade merely for comfort's sake. We will, rather, follow a very tenuous line—so tenuous that at times we may lose sight of it—of writers who wrote mainly in verse, those who wrote mainly in prose, and those who wrote for the theater, descending the geographical stairway from Mexico to Argentina. We will divide the prosists into the usual two categories: narrative and essay. Within the narrative genre we will follow the line from anti-realism to realism. It will be seen that we cannot follow even this simple outline faithfully.

A. MAINLY VERSE

The historian who would give form to the poetry of these years finds before him the ungrateful task of fitting together a jigsaw puzzle from the pieces of many puzzles. Some of the Modernist and post-Modernist poets are still active. Some follow their unvarying path; others attempt to cross over to the vanguardist ranks. They are not always old men; there are also young ones. The same thing happens with the vanguardists. There are those who are consistent to their dying day, and those who abandon ultraism, now to return to traditional and classical ways, now to advance toward new neo-Romantic and existentialist movements. And, at the end of this period, around 1930, when only a few fading echoes of ultraism remain in the air, there are youths, born about 1910, who set out to speak of themselves and of their own patriotic circumstances in a grave, sentimental voice, but in a language of pure poetry or of surrealism. That the pieces of this jigsaw puzzle come from various puzzles can be proved by observing the use of the metaphor. In the Modernist poets the metaphors are like doves caged in allegories, in apologs, in clear, beautiful images. The ultraist poets loose their metaphoric doves in order to shoot them down with rifle blasts, and we are left without knowing the final course of their flight. The neo-Romantic and existentialist poets began to see that all of the charm was in breeding carrier pigeons which were capable of returning alive to the intimate dove cote from which they had flown. We have already mentioned the heading "neo-Romanticism." Because of its vagueness, this heading may not remain. But we can understand why some poets called themselves "neo-Romantics." Romanticism never died; it was transformed into symbolism, into surrealism, into existentialism. The intent to transform a state of being into poetry (evident since 1930) was common to Spain and to the Hispanic-American countries. The advent of the Spanish Republic and the interest in Hispanic literature of a popular and effusive tone were not a casual coincidence.

The Spaniard García Lorca and the Chilean Pablo Neruda will be the two poets who most strongly influence the poets who appear in the 1930's. It is interesting to find, on all sides, the effort to restore the classical forms of Spanish literature (ballads, *décimas*, and sonnets) while using spontaneous surrealist images. What those born in 1910 are doing, those born in 1900 were also doing. As we have said, many of the 1900 group had deserted the ranks of ultraism and had accepted the rigors of rhyme and meter. Before reviewing the lyric contributions of each country, we shall say a few words about the pure poetry and the surrealist poetry of these years, as they stand most in need of clarification since the other types, the circumstantial, the descriptive, the civil, the folkloric, and the epic, which were also being written at this time, are already well known. The Parnassians and the symbolists had already spoken of pure poetry, and Valéry, in 1920, had discoursed upon it with the most talent of all. But Henri Bremond chose the term *"poésie pure"* in order to expound upon his personal theory, and thus, between 1925 and 1930, a debate was loosed in France that had repercussions even in Hispanic-America. The premise was this: that reason cannot explain poetry. We can enjoy a poem without understanding it logically. Poetic experience is analogous to mysticism in religion. In this sense, poetry is the fountain of consciousness. What remains of a poem after we strip it of all that is not poetry is a mysterious, supernatural reality: let us call it "pure poetry." Yet, it is easier to define the impure than to speak of the pure. The impure is the superficial, the human content of a poem: to think, to feel, to desire, to imagine, to teach, to move, that is, the ideas, the themes, the elocutions, the forms, the moral intents, the description of real things. Words are not poetic, but they can transmit a mysterious power of pure poetry. A poem energizes our deepest self and numbs our superficial self: it is the shock of the current that passes through the poem and electrifies us before the impure elements of our ordinary human activities can reach us. The poem which happens to be a good conductor of poetry delivers its essence even before the reader has understood it, and even before he has finished reading it. That which poetry delivers to us is not mere pleasure in the presence of beauty, but a knowledge of the supernatural. The mystic state, the ecstatic union with God, is first in the hierarchy of knowledge. Next comes the poetic state which communicates to us, through a poem, an original experience. Farther down are the lesser poetic states, lesser because they are abortive or superficial. And even farther down the scale is the knowledge of physical things which is better gained through contemplating a landscape than by reading about the same scene in a descriptive poem. Thus, pure poetry aspires to silence.

Other anti-rational theoreticians were speaking at the same time about a poetry not directed toward the supernatural, but toward the super real. Surrealism saw the universe as being in disorder, and to communicate this vision, it forged a language which itself was as disordered as the universe. André Breton and his companions proposed, through psychic automatism, to plumb the deepest abysses of man and of the cosmos. They gathered awesome sentences, totally destitute of meaning, but poetic because of the subconscious mystery from which they sprang. They did not deny reality: they deepened it in their attempt to seize the spontaneous workings of the life of the mind. From 1919 to 1925 surrealism was a scandalous, nihilist, polemic movement. From 1925 on, surrealism, with a certain gravity, oriented itself toward philosophy and politics. There were convergences with Marxism which attracted through its promises of violence and subversion. The two Utopias: that of economic communism and that of psychic communism. Communism, however, was much more interested in the social condition of man (hunger) than in his human condition (the subconscious). Some surrealists continued to interest themselves in communism's politics of the masses; others, more faithful to their individual esthetics, broke with the party. After 1930 surrealism flourished, submitting itself to the dominion of literary forms. Its technique is that of a composition which allows for the free association of words. There is no need to trouble oneself over language for its own sake. After descending to the subterranean depths of consciousness, language will emerge after all, and in the proper manner. Grammatical syntax is a stumbling block to the free affirmation of things marvelously apprehended in their disconnection. Thus, the language of surrealism corrects the false, logical structure of reality. With the disjointing of the grammar, the musicality and, in fact, all traditional forms become disjointed too. On the other hand, images grow and multiply which can only be assimilated through emotion. Metaphors free themselves from the things that are recognizable to us through a process of rational thought; they exile themselves from the world and reveal an interior reality created entirely by the poet. These two ideals of poetry—pure poetry and surrealist poetry—combined with other less irrational, but equally difficult types, in helping to create in Hispanic-Amerca an art so hermetic that even the critics could not understand it. Many poets, through their excessive admiration for certain surrealist automatisms—the doing away with punctuation marks, the denial of the semantic value of words, the breaking up of syntax, the segregation of stray images—dozed in an expressive irresponsibility: each reader could see what he wanted to in a poem since the poet had not filled his verses with his own precise images, but with a diffuse, vague vapor. That is, each reader was to react in the face of the invisible. It is natural that he should be mistrusting. We all remember the story of the two thieves who said they were weaving a cloth that could only be seen by the well-born. We do not dare say "we do not see anything" for fear of being taken for fools. But neither are we sure that there are others capable of seeing this invisible beauty. There was a certain amount of fraud during the ultraist generation. They poked fun at the reader. Today the reader is wary. In spite of this, some readers sincerely and trustingly like the invisible. What do they see? The definers of "pure poetry" have always given us tautological answers: poetry is what remains after we purify it of its impurities. Well: in the hermetic poetry of these years, at times in the best of instances, we do not find impurities: and this not seeing what is not poetry overtakes us as if it were poetry itself. The reader feels an emotion similar to that of faith. Faith in an absolutely poetic, though invisible, reality. It must be divined, apprehended through the purgative, illuminative, unitive discipline of the ascetic and of the mystic. Thus the reader admires a cryptic poetry. Some beautiful images, a few sagely surprising adjectives, various allusions, which, because we are drawn to them we hunt down on the wing, prove to us that behind the poem there is a poet deserving of our respect. And that is enough for us although we are only intermittently able to profit from what he tells us. Furthermore, we admire the courage of this poet who plays his game of poetry with a single card. After all, this poet, by being so hermetic is risking the sense of that about which he writes. Without timidity, without thinking of the consequences, with no quarter given to reason, blind and delirious, he proceeds toward suicide. Thus many of the poets that we will mention (as was the case with many that we have already mentioned) may leave no other testimonial in history than the admiration felt for them by their contemporaries. The most ungrateful task for any literary critic is to have to face the poetry of these recent years. There are too many poets and all too few of them have realized a finished form. We lack the perspective for distinguishing those values which may become permanent. At times the critic becomes impatient and tends to diminish the significance of this poetry, seemingly less vital than the other literary genres.

(*1*) *Mexico* / In Mexico the "isms" of the postwar period caught on as they did in the rest of the world. Only, the Mexicans—unlike the writers from the Río de la Plata area—did not deny the past. Each poet respects his elders, and the esteem they feel for the Othón-Díaz Mirón-Gutiérrez Nájera-Tablada-González Martínez-López Velarde-Villaurrutia-Paz string of writers threads the generations together in a rare continuity.

It has already been seen in the previous chapter, when we spoke of the "scandal," how little the stridentism of ARQUELAS VELA (1899), GERMÁN LIST ARZUBIDE

(1898) and LUIS QUINTANILLA (1900) left. Its major figure was MANUEL MAPLES ARCE (1900). Ever since *Interior Scaffoldings* (*Andamios interiores*, 1922), he proposed rhyming, not the present, but the future action, and believed that this was to be done by presenting a landscape of machines, industrial products, and technical nomenclatures: motors, propellers, airplanes, movies, automobiles, cables, voltaic batteries, triangles, vertices. And this with calls to labor and political action. Maple Arce gradually lost his mechanical toys, and in *Memorial to Blood* (*Memorial de la sangre*, 1947) he attempts a more human poetry. Stridentism was a fleeting adventure.

Of greater vitality, both in intent and result, were the friends who ended by grouping around the magazine *Contemporáneos* (1928–31): Villaurrutia, Gorostiza, Torres Bodet, Ortiz de Montellano, Jorge Cuesta, Owen, Novo, González Rojo, Barreda . . . and although they did not form part of this group, we must add the names of Pellicer and Nandino. In comparison with the stridentists, the *Contempóraneos* group had a greater artistic decorum, a surer instinct for appreciating the values of European literature and for selecting its models. They were cultured, moderate, well disciplined. They did not permit social unrest to adulterate their art. For them poetry was a play of images and abstractions motivated by intuition, intelligence, and irony. The first few years of youthful grace gone by, they retired into themselves, and in the depths of their solitude they drank in bitter dregs. The more important poets were Pellicer, Gorostiza and Villaurrutia. With the exception of Pellicer, the dominant theme of the group was death—the *Nostalgia of Death* (*Nostalgia de la muerte*) of Villaurrutia, the *Death Without End* (*Muerte sin fin*) of Gorostiza, the *Death of Blue Sky* (*Muerte de cielo azul*) of Ortiz de Montellano, *Mirror of My Death* (*Espejo de mi muerte*) of Nandino. More interesting than studying the movement as a whole is following a few individual trajectories, among the most brilliant of all the continental literature of this time.

The poet who in worth came after López Velarde was CARLOS PELLICER (1899). In spite of the fact that they belonged to two different groups because of their age, they both brought loose poems to light in the same years. Those books which Pellicer held in the greatest esteem, however, are his last: *The Hour of June* (*Hora de junio*, 1937), *Antechamber* (*Recinto*, 1941), *Subordinations* (*Subordinaciones*, 1948), *Practice for Flight* (*Práctica de vuelo*, 1956). The collected works of Pellicer, from 1918 to 1961, have just been published: *Poetic Papers* (*Material poético*, 1962). On reading Pellicer, one has the impression that Pellicer is making an effort to limit himself; his good health, his resonant voice, his sensitivity, his sumptuous tropicalism, his interest in the world and in men are all submitted to a forced fining down. The poet puts his lyricism on a diet because he admires the dehumanized silhouette—impossible to him—of others of his generation: in "Desires" he beseeches the tropics to "allow me for one moment only / not to be cry and color." He describes his perceptions of the landscape with such objectivity that at times they seem to be faithful descriptions, not of his own impressions, but of something exterior to him. He rejoices good humoredly in nature like a grateful drunkard. The joy of being alive, the joy of living; and beyond this love for the light and air that envelop him with the natural world, the love of the supernatural heavens. Religious faith is another of his fountains of happiness. He is witty, agile. A musician of the word, and his words are always music from his senses. But not music alone: he brings the brilliant color of painting, the grandiose volume of sculpture, and even the eloquent gesture of him who makes a tribunal in his own small corner and speaks to all the men of his time. A solid builder who, with his lyrical materials, has erected a beautiful city of great monuments and delicate miniatures. His scruples as an artisan of verse never robbed him of spontaneity. His metaphors lend brilliance, velocity, magic, gaiety, surprise, like birds who, flying over the ocean, suddenly hurl themselves at the sun. A lyric flight in which all of life is praised, and in life, God. In the religious sonnets of *Practice for Flight* religion is no mere theme, but a beating of wings and a celestial journey. Perhaps not quite, because Pellicer is a man, not an angel; he is not even an ascetic man. His religious sentiment is that of a man who can only open his arms in the form of the cross without being able to fly on the spread wings of mysticism: "May the wind at my back give flight! / I live completely on earth. You are sky. / You blue, and I in the emptiness of myself." Very rarely do the eyes of the poet seem to go blind with ecstasy. More than being a mystic union with God, this poetry gives us images of the love of God. His eyes, not bewildered by rapture but open and perceptive, see in life the azures and rose hues of a Fra Angelico, or the shadows of the baroque tenebrists. Thus the intensity of faith does not lead to silence as with the mystics, but to eloquences: a lyrical eloquence without concepts, without Scholasticism, but active in its desire for grace. Each image is concrete and surprising, like details from a geographical chart of the soul.

XAVIER VILLAURRUTIA (1903–1950) appeared in his first poems as though he were going to follow the path of López Velarde. *In Reflections* (*Reflejos*, 1926), however, he revealed a more graceful and witty spirit. There were sudden religious invocations or melancholy reflections, but on the whole his images are flamboyant and gay. There were also unusual metaphors without the hurly-burly of the ultraists. Later he drew closer to intelligent, imaginative masters: Proust, Gide, Cocteau, Giraudoux. From his varied spectrum of themes—landscape, love, mystery, goodness, art, travel—he chose, for his lucid analysis, the saddest band of color. His intelligence observes, selects, and orders the emotions that are to go into his poetry, emotions which come to him on contemplating and understanding the secret expressions of things. His best work: *Nostalgia for Death* (*Nostalgia de la muerte,* 1939–46). It was a splendid work. Villaurrutia foresaw that life is a dream and that death will be an awakening: "I doubt! And I dare not ask / if it is the awakening from a dream, or is my life a dream." Not at all, Death tells him, life is "the dream in which you would like to believe you live without me, when it is I who draws it and who erases it." And the poet in yet another poem: "The night pours down its mystery upon us, / and something tells us that to die is to awaken." Instead of being paralyzed by fear like a man who suddenly discovers that he is only a phantom in the night, Villaurrutia departs from this basic intuition, and with intelligence and with fantasy creates metaphysical hypotheses. There are innumerable plays of words and sounds. But these plays are converted into plays of concepts. They are the themes of fantastic literature which in another less anguished tone other writers are trying out during these same years (Borges, for example). Themes of the double man and of the unfolding of consciousness, of mirrors facing one another repeating infinitely the same image, of empty bodies which receive mysterious visitors, of autonomous human shadows, of gods who dream into existence men who are dreaming others into existence, of the absurd fear of nonexistence, of solipsist universes, of corrupt angels, of death that surreptitiously haunts us, that all men are one man and that we simultaneously are and are not, of metamorphosis and labyrinths. Villaurrutia disintegrates the real world and falls into the lonely emptiness, where he begins to invent another world, and anguishes because not only does he know it not to be real, but also he doubts even his own personal existence. His hypotheses are floating upon the humor with which he thinks about Death. The ten *décimas* of "The Tenth Death" (*"Décima muerte"*) are classical in construction, Baroque in their sharpness of conceit, and existentialist in the idea that death is a proof of existence, and that in the final analysis we live nourishing a personal death. Villaurrutia, calculating and cold when it came to composing his ideas and his verses, was upset by the presence of death. In his last years—*Song to Spring and Other Poems* (*Canto a la primavera y otros poemas,* 1948)—his emotions no longer obeyed the reins and simply bolted. In his theater there is no passion, only sentiment—sentiment limited by intelligence. Ironic flashes indicate the design of the plot. We are presented with a world of artifice rather than reality. His *Profane Mystery Plays* (*Autos profanos*, 1943) are five dramatic sketches, so finely drawn that it can easily be seen that they are directed toward an elite and not the public in general. In his three-act pieces—*Ivy* (*La hiedra*), *The Legitimate Woman* (*La mujer legítima*), *Invitation to Death* (*Invitación a la muerte*), *The Incandescent Error* (*El yerro candente*), *Poor Bluebeard* (*El pobre Barba Azul*), *Dangerous Game* (*Juego peligroso*)—the dialogs are richer, and in the mouth of each character, intelligence shows the same smile.

José Gorostiza (1901) is one of the best crystallizers of poetry of this generation: *Songs to Be Sung in Barks* (*Canciones para cantar en las barcas*, 1925), *Death Without End* (*Muerte sin fin*, 1939). In his clear verses of popular rhythmic sketches there is such depth and lyrical complexity that the reader, upon coming across the obscure half of his poetry later, goes on, confident that he is not being deceived with false complications—as it was the custom of the prestidigitators of this generation—and that he will arrive finally at a subtle and authentic zone of the spirit. Thus it is. With his wings Gorostiza touches folklore, the cultured poetry of the period from Garcilaso to Góngora, and the pure poetry of Juan Ramón Jiménez, but these wings interest us for their flight, not for the objects they brush against. Gorostiza mounts to a height where what was invisible on the ground because of its excessive subtlety is seen clearly illuminated. *Death Without End* was the most important Mexican poem which, until that time, had appeared in his generation. It is only one moment from an enduring agony. The poet suffers his solitude, lost in a world whose meaning escapes him. He does not know whether he is surrounded by God or by nothing. Upon contemplating himself—"my slow, searching steps through the mire"—the poet recognizes himself in the image of the water; although this water might acquire form in the rigors of the glass, this form gives it neither knowledge nor consolation. On the contrary, life, thus contained by the consciousness, is an unending death. All of the universe disintegrates in this poem which runs like a river, in waves of solitude and time, liberty and death, life and intelligence, impulse and form, God and chaos. The glass (intelligence and the word) molds and throttles the water of life. Disillusioned, the poet ends—prosaically, which corresponds with his disillusionment—with a challenge to death who is lying in wait for him behind sleepless eyes: "Come on, little slut with the frozen blush, / let's go to the devil."

JAIME TORRES BODET (1902) came on the literary scene with a book of verses: *Fervor*, 1918, containing a prolog by González Martínez. His tastes were still conventional, respectful of French symbolism and of Hispanic Modernism. Little by little, in dialogs with his "contemporaries," and leafing through the *Revista de Occidente* and the *Nouvelle Revue Française*, he began to understand the jargon of his time: Gide, Proust, Joyce, Antonio Machado, Dostoevski, Cocteau, Juan Ramón Jiménez, Giraudoux, Ortega y Gasset, Morand, Soupault, Girard, Lacretelle, Jouhandeau, Jarnés . . . From 1922 to 1925 he had published seven volumes of verse: from these he selected the best for *Poetry* (*Poesías*, 1926). Suddenly, without abandoning verse, he became enthusiastic about prose. He wrote essays—*Contemporáneos*, 1928—but his most promising passages we find in narrative form—*Margaret of the Mist* (*Margarita de Niebla*, 1927)—in which a minimum of plot sustains interplays of sensitivity and fantasy between two girls and a young professor, who is the one telling the story; *Proserpine Rescued* (*Proserpina rescatada*, 1931), also "dehumanized art," in which the characters walk like Bengal lights and burn in spark-spluttering sentences; and *The Birth of Venus and Other Tales* (*Nacimiento de Venus y otros cuentos*), written between 1928 and 1931, but published in 1941, whose first pages—about the shipwrecked Lidia—have the cold, lovely light of the window of an elegant shop, on the most luxurious street in the city. Afterwards, Torres Bodet traveled all over the world with important, official duties. He continued to write books of verse: *Without Respite* (*Sin tregua*, 1957), *The Four Leaf Clover* (*Trébol de cuatro hojas*, 1958), essays: *Three Inventors of Reality* (*Tres inventores de realidad*, 1955), memoirs: *Sand Time* (*Tiempo de arena*, 1955). Each one was more opaque than the other. His best moments were those in which his imagination let its hair down, but with an elegance that equaled any coiffeur's. Disheveled images streaming in the wind of madness. Madness? Let us look at them, one by one. They make sense. They startle, because we had never heard before that "ladies / take from their encyclopedic cases / with the missing fingers of Venus de Milo— / an articulated smile / for the head of what Victory of Samothrace?" They are images that go against the grain of intelligence, with allusions to an artistic culture of good repute, humorously frivolous, ironically lyrical, related to very acute states of the spirit. This poetry, of minor tone, anti-climactic, more European than Mexican, without moral or political contaminations, passes triumphantly from verse to prose.

BERNARDO ORTIZ DE MONTELLANO (1899–1949) has written poems in prose— *Net* (*R. d*), stories—*Five Hours Without a Heart* (*Cinco horas sin corazón*), dialogs

—The Big Hat (*El sombrerón*) and, naturally verses. The edition *Dream and Poetry* (*Sueño y poesía,* 1952) gathers his books together and adds new verses. He began with a muffled voice, but little by little he dared to speak more firmly on the impure, on solitude, on shadows, dreams, and death. He embarked for the murky country of his *Dreams* (*Sueños,* 1933): he never arrived, at least he never reached the last islands of surrealism. But he was able to communicate the sensation of seasickness which is common to those who travel on this ocean. His best compositions are of a grave and hopeless intonation like the sonnets of *Death of Blue Sky* (*Muerte de cielo azul,* 1937). He explored, not so much his dreams, but his amazement before these dreams when he was awake: "Hymn to Hipnos." SALVADOR NOVO (1904) is the circumstantial and humorous poet of the group. Like his companions, he was born into letters to fly metaphors. He went, nevertheless, to the very edge of the prosaic and leaned over so far that some of his verses crumbled beneath his feet. His accomplishment was in not falling into the abyss himself. In *Poetry* (*Poesía,* 1955) gusts of irony can be seen, lyricism, impassioned impetus, and bitter desolation. He also wrote stories and theatrical pieces. ELÍAS NANDINO (1903) gathered his verses into *Poetry* (*Poesía,* two volumes: 1947–48) and without pause continued to publish those which occurred to him after that. He excels in his sonnets; their tone—monotonous—is breathless. His themes: love, solitude, death. The tormented JORGE CUESTA (1903–1942) and the skeptic GILBERTO OWEN (1905–1952) bring this group to a close. CONCHA URQUIZA (1910–1945), whose voice humbly seeks dialog with Fray Luis de León and San Juan de la Cruz, came later.

(2) *Central America / Guatemala:* LUIS CARDOZA Y ARAGÓN (1904) occupies with Asturias the seat of highest honor in letters in his country. While he lived in France, he became familiar with surrealism, an experience which left traces in such works as *Luna Park* (1943), *The Tower of Babel* (*La torre de Babel,* 1930), *Maelstrom* (1926), *The Sleepwalker* (*El sonámbulo,* 1937) and *The Little Symphony of the New World* (*Pequeña sinfonía del Nuevo Mundo,* 1949). He is a difficult poet because of his vertiginous images and his explorations through fugitive worlds, but his awareness of living in one of the critical periods of history and his preoccupation with the destiny of mankind illuminate his work. He is also a brilliant essayist, as can be seen in *Guatemala: The Lines in Her Palm* (*Guatemala. Las líneas de su mano,* 1955). Another poet: CÉSAR BRAÑAS (1900), author of one of the most beautiful elegies of the generation: *Black Wind* (*Viento negro*).

Honduras: The three best poets of this generation are Barrera, Cárcamo, and Laínez. CLAUDIO BARRERA (1912), through the path opened up by Vallejo and Neruda, threw himself into a poetry of political tone, of American themes, as for example, in his poem "The Double Song" (*"La doble canción"*). JACOBO CÁRCAMO (1914–1959), also with metrical liberty, sang to the "Pines of Honduras" and to the "Ahuehuete" of Mexico. DANIEL LAÍNEZ (1914–1959) was the most spontaneous, the most popular. Other poets were MARCO ANTONIO PONCE (1908–1932), RAMÓN PADILLA COELLO (1904–1931), JOSÉ R. CASTRO (1909), and ALEJANDRO VALLADARES (1910).

El Salvador: One of the most lyrical presences is that of Claudia Lars (1899), who wrote under the pseudonym of Carmen Brannon. She began with the poems of *Stars in the Well* (*Estrellas en el pozo,* 1934), which were followed by other books. For a while, the influence of García Lorca could be noted in her work, for example, *Ballads of North and South* (*Romances de Norte y Sur,* 1946), but from the sonnets *Where Footsteps Carry* (*Donde llegan los pasos,* 1953) her originality sings with its own voice: intelligence, with insinuations, sharpen her aim and her metaphors hit the lyrical mark. Other outstanding poets: ALFREDO ESPINO (1900–1928), a landscapist in *Sad Ballads* (*Jícaras tristes*); SERAFÍN QUITEÑO (1906), the vehement poet of *Corasón With an S* (*Corasón con S*); and LUIS MEJÍA VIDES (1909). Compromised by political struggles were CARLOS LOVATO (1911) and PEDRO GEOFFROY RIVAS. The latter was the author of an "impure poetry" deliberately impure, because the poet gave himself over to the popular leftist tide.

Nicaragua: There were poets who, although they belong to this chapter because of the dates of their birth, maintain a tone of the Modernist past (like AGENOR ARGÜELLO, 1902, who was incorporated into Salvadorian literature, or LÉON AGUILERA, 1901), or who cautiously approach vanguardism (HORACIO ESPINOSA ALTAMIRANO, 1903–1945; ABSALÓN BALDOVINOS, 1903–1938; SANTOS CERMEÑO, 1903; ISRAEL PANIAGUA PRADO, 1905–1950; ALÍ VANEGAS, 1905; JOSÉ FRANCISCO BORGEN, 1908). Nicaragua is the home of Rubén Darío. The group of youths that we are about to discuss no longer has any reverence for Rubén Darío. "Our beloved enemy" they called him. José Coronel Urtecho presided over the group and was accompanied in his vanguardist campaigns by LUIS ALBERTO CABRALES (1902), MANOLO CUADRA, Pablo Antonio Cuadra, and Joaquín Pasos. Before stopping to study them we will try to assemble the frame. Literarily, they poured the usual sentiments—the feeling for the soil, native experience, personal arrogance—into ametric verses, rich and verbose. Politically, they were Catholic, anti-liberal, and anti-democratic. The literary sheet, *Vanguardia,* dated from 1928. As well as those already mentioned, JOSE ROMÁN and ALBERTO ORDÓÑEZ ARGÜELLO (1914) made up the vanguardist group. This group had an immediate influence on the national literary movement. In search of a national expression, they cultivated folklore, gathering the Hispanic tradition and elaborating it with their own creations. Some of them disseminated their poetic works in magazines and appear in anthologies without ever having published a book. Other poets of these years: EDGARDO PRADO (1912), NAPOLEÓN ROMÁN (1906), AURA ROSTAND (1908), CARMEN SOBALBARRO (1908). Now let us bring to the fore those who demonstrated the most value. First of all, JOSÉ CORONEL URTECHO (1906). He was one of the most versatile poetic temperaments of all Hispanic-America: an iconoclast, but hard working in the creation of new icons. Well informed on the latest tendencies of all literatures and determined to scandalize all of the consecrated tastes, he began by sarcastically greeting Rubén Darío: "And so, Rubén / my inevitable countryman, I greet you / with a flip of my derby / that the rats ate in nineteen hundred and 20 / five, Amen." The poetry of Coronel Urtecho is disconcerting because of its ceaseless innovations and changes of direction. The only permanent feature is his Catholic faith: in all else he is a experimenter with forms and modalities. He is simple or hermetic, clear or surrealistic, severe or humorous. In search of a popular expression he cultivated folklore and took rhythms and themes from traditional songs and stories. The "Little Ode to Uncle Coyote," for example, is based on a "wayside tale" (that is, a children's story): Uncle Coyote is an animal who robs fruit from orchards. When he is told that the moon, reflected in the water, is a cheese, he tries to eat it and is drowned. Upon this folkloric canvas, Coronel Urtecho embroiders a comic-lyric figure: Uncle Coyote is to be a deluded figure like Don Quijote or the Chinese poet, Li-Tai-Po. PABLO ANTONIO

435

CUADRA (1912) is the most active and productive regional poet: *Nicaraguan Poems* (*Poemas nicaragüenses*, 1933), *Temporal Song* (*Canto temporal*, 1934), *A Crown of Goldfinches* (*Corona de Jilgueros*, 1949), this, not counting his plays, most of which were produced; one successful piece was *Along the Roads Go the Peasants* (*Por los caminos van los campesinos*), a work with political intent. He sings to men, landscapes, and Nicaraguan customs. An evocation of mysterious indigenous population inspired his recent *The Jaguar and the Moon* (*El jaguar y la luna*). JOAQUÍN PASOS (1915–1947), a writer of harsh sentences, schematic in form, experimented with new poetic ways: "Choral Poems," was written to be recited by several voices, with such effects as simultaneous and contrapuntal words.

Costa Rica: The dense ALFONSO ULLOA ZAMORA (1914); the simple FRANCISCO AMIGHETTO (1907); the cordial FERNANDO LUJÁN (1912); the landscapist GONZALO DOBLES (1904); ARTURO AGÜERO CHAVES, the most notable regionalist; FERNANDO CENTENO GÜELL (1908), removed from national themes; RAFAEL ESTRADA (1901–1934), a beautiful promise that died; ARTURO ECHEVERRÍA LORIA (1909), and MANUEL PICADO CHACÓN (1910).

Panama: DEMETRIO KORSI (1899–1957), who waylaid postwar literary restlessness, took his themes from city life and treated them with irony and a carefree cheerfulness. His poetic production—begun in 1920 with *Strange Poems* (*Los poemas extraños*)—earns for him one of the highest positions in his country. Nevertheless, much of what he wrote at the beginning and at the end of his career had something of the air of imitative exercises. His intervening work—let us say, that done between the ages of thirty and fifty—is more spontaneous in its song to the neighborhood, to everyday human types, to the aspects of life as daily lived in the city. Country poets were MOISÉS CASTILLO (1899), SANTIAGO ANGUIZOLA D. (1899?), and in a lesser measure LUCAS BÁRCENA (1906). After 1929 there is evidence that the current of vanguardism has settled in Panama: Rogelio Sinán— whom the reader should look for among the prosists—was the one who produced the first wave in this current. *Wave* (*Onda,* 1929) was his book of poems. Panamanian vanguardist poetry, purer, more universal than that which up to this time had been cultivated, flowed from the pens of ROQUE JAVIER LAURENZA (1910), the most learned in the postwar schools; DEMETRIO HERRERA SEVILLANO (1902–1950), who, with the liberty of the ultraists, gave popular rhythms to his ill-bred muse; and RICARDO J. BERMÚDEZ (1914), more ambitious in his themes, with lyric and declamatory images, was, at the same time conscious of the dignity of his song.

(3) *Antilles* / In Cuba, vanguardist literature was called "de avance," because one of its speakers in 1927 was the *Revista de Avance*. The young men felt weighed down beneath a mental inertia and the moral baseness of their country and they reacted vehemently. Even the apparently playful forms carried a feeling of social rebellion. In the words of Jorge Mañach, one of the founders of *Avance:* "The lower case letters, the outrageous images, the meaningless plays of sound, the typographic cabriolets, the plastic deformations, were merely the concrete expression of that mood"; "vanguardism, as a polemic movement, succumbed among us as soon as our consciences felt that they had found the real opportunity for expression in the field of politics." Beneath

the ensign of vanguardism—rebellious but futile—two groups of poets form: the pure poets (Eugenio Florit) and the poets of social protest (Nicolás Guillén). There are comings and goings from one group to the other (Ballagas). Even Negroid poetry fluctuates between lyricism and documentation. At the end of this period another group appears: the transcendentalists (Lezama Lima).

We shall pause, upon retracing the road that we have just drawn, on a few representative poets from each group.

From the group of pure poets—SILVERIO DÍAZ DE LA RIONDA (1902); RAFAEL GARCÍA BÁRCENA (1907–1961); DULCE MARÍA LOYNAZ (1903) —we are going to choose one of the finest lyricists of his time: EUGENIO FLORIT (1903). In the *décimas* of *The Tropics* (*Trópico*, 1930), the syntactic thought, vagabond but quick, spins images of the Cuban countryside and sea, images which fuse, also with quick strokes, concrete perception and abstract concept. Traces of Gongoristic poetry, traces of popular poetry. *Double Accent* (*Doble acento*, 1937)—the cold accent, measured and classical; the burning accent, overflowing and romantic—is a complex book. At times, as in "The Martyrdom of Saint Sebastian" (*"Martirio de San Sebastián"*), the descriptive, the narrative, the lyrical, and the mystical are joined: the saint is described at the moment when he is about to suffer his torture, and his lyric monolog is narrated from his invitation to the arrows: "Yes, come to my arms, little doves of iron," "Come, yes, hard angels of flame, / small cherubim with tenséd wings"—until the final arrow, the death arrow, that which will unite him mystically with God—"I know that my last dove is coming . . . / Ah! Now all is well, Lord, I shall bring it to you / buried in a corner of my bosom!" In *Kingdom* (*Reino*, 1938) the poet wishes to render his impression of the landscape—be it a subjective insight or an objective view—exact, in its purest essence, and to do this, he outlines it in brief, clean, tense brush strokes. In the new poems of his anthology *My Poem* (*Poema mío*, 1947) his verse becomes simpler, more sentimental: childhood memories, religious unction, solitude, meditations by the sea. *Final Assonance and Other Poems* (*Asonante final y otros poemas*, 1956) is a conversation, also about memories and meditations. But now Florit, since he is conversing—"Conversation with my father"—broadens out his verse and, no longer having to follow a strict course, his thought wanders along with simplicity and even humor. But this verse, although colloquial, is not prosaic. In "Final Assonance"—where the poet allows the occasional images of his consciousness to flow freely, and, as in a mirror, he sees himself in the act of writing—poetry is a close-knit part of the most ordinary phrases. Poetry of tenderness, goodness, of the sad smile, of resignation, and of confidence in God. Poetry which touches little things with a dart of light; the commonplace, the everyday things, thus touched, light up, marveling. His *Poetic Anthology* (*Antología poética,* 1930–1955, published in 1956) traces the most outstanding features of his art.

Negroid poetry—to which we later make special reference—had at times purely esthetic norms, but at other times, on denouncing the conditions in which the Cubans of African heritage lived, it became social and even political. The best representative of this combative poetry is NICOLÁS GUILLÉN (1902). He began, in *Motives of the Sound* (*Motivos de son,* 1930) with the rhythms of the Negro dance, drawn in the manner of the sketchers of customs and with an ironic stylization of popular speech. A circumstance, a deed, a sentiment are commented upon in few words while the musical outline of the *son* keeps time with the laughter and gaiety. In *Sóngoro Cosongo* (1931) Negro folklore is integrated with the Hispanic tradition, but, better than this, we find verbal creation, lyrical metaphors, serious moods, that is, true poetry. *West Indies, Ltd.* (1934) intensified the civil, polemic, anti-imperialist tone which was before only occasional: here are some of his good poems, lived from the depths of his mulatto sensitivity, of a solidarity with the oppressed Negro. His *Songs for Soldiers and Dances for Tourists* (*Cantos para soldados y sones para turistas,* 1937), with the simple speech of the humble people and with the rhythm of the *son,* give vent to the aspirations of the dispossessed class. Like Neruda, like Vallejo, Guillén also took the side of the Republic during the Spanish Civil War, and from this fighting position—which will carry him over to Communism—came the poems on *Spain* (*España,* 1937). His mastery affirms itself in 1947–48 in two *Elegies* (*Elegías*)—to Jacques Roumain, and Jesús Menéndez. The book which best rounds out Guillén is *The Complete Sound* (*El son entero,* 1947), of a popular tone, rarely political, more national than racial, having a rhythmic fruition without the comicality of his first *sons.* Here we have a mature synthesis of the personality of Guillén, with all of his traits as an observer and as a sensitive man, as a singer of tradition and of the lyric cult, as a sculptor and musician, attentive to primitive magic, and at the same time to social reclamation. After years of silence, Guillén reappeared, without any surprises, in *The Dove of Popular Flight* (*La paloma de vuelo popular,* 1958): again, the double face of the political agitator and of the traditional lyricist. We prefer the lyrical Guillén, of course. In spite of his interest in the poor and humble folk, in spite of his enthusiasm for folklore, in spite of his themes of everyday, elemental life, of the false rhythm of popular song, and his political messages, Guillén is an aristocratic poet because of the delicate profile with which his lyricism cuts the air. We have said that some poets would swing between pure poetry and social poetry. The Afro-Cuban poets also swung between estheticism and protest.

EMILIO BALLAGAS (1908–1954) is extremely notable among those who can be studied in one group as well as in the other. *Jubilation and Flight (Júbilo y fuga, 1931)* is pure poetry, angelic in its disengagement and capacity for flight, playful in its sounds without meaning, sensual, but with the sensuality of pastoral poetry. Afterwards, in *Eternal Taste (Sabor eterno, 1939)*, his emotion is amatory and elegiac, as in the Romantics. Classically structured in sonnets, *liras*, and *décimas, Our Lady of the Sea (Nuestra señora del mar, 1943)* is religious poetry. Along with this theme, and without being a Negro, Ballagas cultivated verses on the life of the Negro perceived from outside: *Notebook of Negro Poetry (Cuaderno de poesía negra, 1934)*. In Ballagas, then, we find a poetry of verbal sensuality, a pure poetry, a poetry of Negro theme. Like other poets of his country, with the same leanings, the same themes, of the same generation, Ballagas, on writing Negro poetry shakes the seeds of his maraca-words or invents jingling words, and in the end, more than poetry, we hear babblings, interjections, drum rolls, rhythms, onomatopoeias, melodic stimuli to the conditioned reflexes of a popular choreography. Ballagas leans toward the picturesque, the exterior, the playful; his sympathy for the Negro is a projection, through social means, of his old desire to arrive, by way of poetry, at a candid, pure, and primitive reality.

RAMÓN GUIRAO (1908–1949) also wrote pure and somewhat surrealist poetry —*Poems (Poemas, 1947)*—but his place in literary history is that of the initiator of Afro-Cuban poetry—"The Rumba Dancer" (*"La bailadora de rumba"*) is from 1928. Nevertheless, he had neither the vital interior force of Guillén nor the exterior descriptive force of Ballagas: his book of Negro poems, *Bongó* (1934). Other poets of Afro-Cuban poetry during these years should be mentioned: lyricism upturned into social themes in MIRTA AGUIRRE (1912), the somewhat Nerudian eroticism of JOSÉ ÁNGEL BUESA (1910), FÉLIX PITA RODRÍGUEZ (1909), who went through the initiation rites of French, Spanish, and Hispanic-American surrealism; and, above all, Feijóo who, because he is a solitary figure, can just as well be put in with the group of this chapter as with that in the next, since no particular group attracted him, and Lezama Lima, who, because of his age comes here, but should be put with those born after 1915 because of his affinities. SAMUEL FEIJÓO (1914) is a neo-Romantic who treats intimate sentiments and Cuban landscapes. Inward and outward poetry, but with gardens on both sides, and at times we do not know whether these flowers are spiritual or vegetable. Narcissism which contemplates itself in the mirror of nature, of pampered trees, hills, ocean, sky, all asking to be caressed by the poet. The island of Feijoo is neatly ornamented with a veil drawn over it to soften and render it even more enchanting: glance at his books, from *Celestial Comrade* (*Camarada celeste,* 1944) to *Face* and *The Poet's Leaf* (*Faz, La hoja del poeta,* 1956). The poet isolates himself within the landscape and notes down his impressions in an intimate diary of poems and poetic prose; effectively, he published *Travel Diaries* (*Diarios de viajes,* 1958). José LEZAMA LIMA (1912) was a promoter of magazines—namely, *Orígines*—of literary circles, and of a new poetic manner. He withdrew from everything that had been done and was being done by the Cuban generation that we have just finished describing, but his solitude was of short duration: his first books of poems—*The Death of Narcissus* (*Muerte de Narciso,* 1937) and especially *Inimical Murmuring* (*Enemigo rumor,* 1941)—had scarcely appeared when they seduced the younger poets, making him, from that moment, the master. The ascendency which he exercises over other writers seems to be due to the example of a life monstrously consecrated to literature. Moreover: a life made of books, bibliophilistic and bookish. His vast library is cataloged in his essays: *Analect of the Watch* (*Analecta del reloj,* 1953), *The American Expression* (*La expresión americana,* 1957), *Treatises in Havana* (*Tratados en la Habana,* 1958). But even between the lines of his poetry the shelves of books were to be seen, with some volumes more dog-eared than others: baroque Spaniards (especially Góngora and Quevedo), symbolists (Valéry, Rilke), Catholics (Chesterton, T. S. Eliot, Claudel), surrealists (Neruda). His poetry—hermetic—is vital in its impulse, but because this vitality, as we have said, is completely identified with literature, the verses which result are more literary than poetic. He knocks things over in order to discover what is hiding behind them, but he refuses to let us know what he sees. His sight is metaphysical, even theological. Man, through Original Sin, is exiled from absolute reality: he longs to return, but sees that poetry is inaccessible, an "inimical murmuring." There is therefore something sacred in taking up one's pen. The true poet—Lezama believes—is not the one who contents himself with the appearances of things, nor with a sentimental effusion, but the one who, in spite of a certain resistance, advances toward Poetry which in turn gazes at us from a distance, always from a distance, like the absolute and pitiless creature that it is. *Steadfastness* (*La fijeza,* 1949)—his most complex and difficult book—alludes to this fixed, transcendental character of poetry. We question poetry: the answer it gives is lost even as the poet tries to note it down. His language is hard in its rhythm, its syntax cracked, abrupt in metaphor, leaving a frozen wake. His poems try to be organs of metaphysical perception, but they do not allow themselves to be perceived; they want to be objective, but are so liquefied in subjectivity that we can no longer make out their profile. Lezama whets himself down to such a point that he weakens, loses authority, and his words give themselves up to a captious madness. His last book of poems: *Giver* (*Dador,* 1960). Other poets: MERCEDES GARCÍA TUDURÍ (1904); GUILLERMO VILLARRONDA (1912), ÁNGEL I. AUGIER (1910).

Dominican Republic: Between the posthumism of Moreno Jimenes (which we saw in the preceding chapter) and the magazine *La Poesía Sorprendida,* 1943 (which we will see in the next chapter), arise the first imaginative, novel, complex, generally anti-realist poets, educated, if not in Góngora, at least in the Gongorism of García Lorca. The one to receive and join, in a cordial reunion, the poets of the generation of Moreno Jimenes with those of the generation of Fernández Spencer is the lyricist, FRANKLIN MIESES BURGOS (1907). Whether it be with free verse or with the rigorous form of the sonnet, he seduces us with an insinuating melody which uncoils into metaphors. His poetic world is as limpid as a happy dream, with lasses, roses, beams of moonlight, crystals, angels, and mystery. Sometimes, however, his voice swells with emotion and he declaims. It is an elegiac emotion, like that of *Without a World Now and Wounded by Heaven* (*Sin mundo ya y herido por el cielo*, 1944), which seeks the beloved shadow through death. Other titles: *Climate of Eternity* (*Clima de eternidad*, 1947), *The Presence of the Days* (*Presencia de los días*, 1949), *The Hero* (*El héroe*, 1954). RAFAEL AMÉRICO HENRÍQUEZ (1899)—author of "Earth Rose" (*"Rosa de tierra"*) —gathers together materials from the landscape, carries them to his ceramic workshop and tries to give them shape, to color and polish them. His Baroque grammar sometimes makes his images ugly. In spite of all this, his abundant metaphors are the index of his originality. TOMÁS HERNÁNDEZ FRANCO (1904–1952), who captured life by the sea in *Songs of the Happy Coast* (*Canciones del litoral alegre*, 1936), stands out for his "Yelidá" (1942), an expressionist poem, half narrative and half allegorical. It is the history of a mulatto girl, the daughter of a Norwegian father and an Antillian mother. His poetic imagination coins itself into sentences, strangely brilliant. His dynamism carried him to the story—*Cibao*, 1951—in which he continued being an impressionist poet.

MANUEL DEL CABRAL (1907) sings with an unmistakable Antillian voice: *Tropic of the Negro* (*Trópico negro*, 1942), *Older Blood* (*Sangre mayor*, 1945), *On This Side of the Sea* (*De este lado del mar*, 1948), *The Secret Guests* (*Los huéspedes secretos*, 1951), *Planetary Lapidation* (*Pedrada planetaria*, 1958). One of his most famous books is *Pal Mon* (*Compadre Mon*, 1943), an epic-lyric poem in which he creates the myth of a popular hero. This book, nevertheless, represents a stage already passed: later, Cabral combined human and metaphysical touches in his poetry. His two anthologies—*Anthology of the Land* (*Antología tierra*, 1959) and *Key Anthology* (*Antología clave*, 1957)— reveal a vast gamut of themes and tones. Manuel del Cabral has also created a poetic prose: *Chinchina Searches for Time* (*Chinchina busca el tiempo*, 1945) and *30 parábolas* (1956). He is out of orbit. He gets lost and finds his way again only to get lost and find himself once more. The creative force of his popular lyric vein always pulls him up after one of his falls. His Negroid poetry is important also, but he sings ambitiously too, to the men of other races and, in *Planetary Lapidation*, his Hispanic-American voice shouts into space (*"Monolog of Sputnik I"*).

Another poet of these years was the exalted HÉCTOR INCHÁUSTEGUI CABRAL (1912). He comes forth into the world and greets the native landscape and, above all, his fellow man, with a potent voice. He laments human misery and calls for a more just social order. He has a philosophy of life with an active moral spur, and in his will to communicate it, he often obliges his verse to assume the functions of prose. Eloquent verses, more sonorous than musical. His expressive impetus, nevertheless, saves him. Detail arrives in time to variegate that which was becoming discolored into an abstract idea. Like other vanguardist poets he disdained the traditional forms: ten books of poems, from *Poems From a Single Anguish* (*Poemas de una sola angustia*, 1940), to *Vegetable Rebellion and Other Less Bitter Poems* (*Rebelión vegetal y otros poemas menos amargos*, 1956). Also associated with this movement, to which we will refer with more detail in the next chapter, were the vanguardists of social accent PEDRO RENÉ CONTÍN AYBAR (1910) and PEDRO MIR (1913).

Puerto Rico: There is something in the atmosphere of this country that reins in, moderates, and rounds out the advances that arrive from the literary world. An example of this is JOSÉ AGUSTÍN BALSEIRO (1900): in *Captive Purity* (*La pureza cautiva*), *Homesickness for Puerto Rico* (*Saudades de Puerto Rico*) and *Eves of Shadow* (*Vísperas de sombra*) unity is gained through love of the native island, through clear song, and from sentiments contemplated in the light of a conscience, serene in spite of its preoccupations. In general, the poetic spirit did wave in the breeze of popular fashion. Nevertheless, the "isms" of vanguardism proliferated. First, in 1921, the *diepalism* of JOSÉ I. DE DIEGO PADRÓ (1899) and Luis Palés Matos, a movement which proposed an onomatopoeic poetic language. Afterwards, in 1923, the *euphorism* of VICENTE PALÉS MATOS (1903). In 1925, *noism* (from "no"), also initiated by Vicente Palés Matos. In 1928, the *atalayism* of GRACIANY MIRANDA ARCHILLA (1910), FERNANDO GONZÁLEZ ALBERTY (1908) and iconoclasts and individualists who made up a literary circle with something of the bohemian hermeticism of dadaism and something of pure poetry. Later, LUIS HERNÁNDEZ AQUINO (1907) founded *integralism,* a leaning toward the vernacular, the autochthonous. His poetry is simple, deep, with Hispanic roots: he begins with *Lyric Mist* (*Niebla lírica*, 1931) and ends with *Island For Anguish* (*Isla para la angustia*, 1943). Of a Creolist persuasion are SAMUEL LUGO (1905), FRANCISCO HERNÁNDEZ VARGAS (1914), anecdotic in *The Trail* (*La vereda*, 1937); FRANCISCO MANRIQUE CABRERA (1908), more original, more agile, more profound in his free way of capturing the Puerto Rican essence: look at his *Poems of My Land, Land* (*Poemas de mi tierra, tierra*, 1936) and *Shadow-Footprint and Song* (*Huella-sombra y cantar*, 1943). One of the major poets is JUAN ANTONIO CORRETJER (1908). He also followed the *integralism* line in *Love of Puerto Rico* (*Amor de Puerto Rico,* 1937). His nationalist ideals are expressed with simple, human, everyday effects. The homeland is for him a beloved woman, and in his lyricism, the dreams, the exhalation of the land, and the vital impulse are all given in an admirable unity, from *Agüeybana* (1932) to *Affectionate Don Diego* (*Don Diego en el cariño*, 1956). Feminine poetry was conspicuous. Above all, JULIA DE BURGOS (1914–1953) moved in her unsatisfied passion for life, so deep that at times she touches on metaphysical themes with a sharp sense for the nature and beauty of love, from *Poem in Twenty Furrows* (*Poema en veinte surcos*, 1938) to the posthumous *The Sea and You* (*El mar y tú*). CLARA LAIR was the most erotic, the most passionate, the most daring in her confidences about surrendering to a man and about the solitude in the midst of these fires: *Bitter Tropics* (*Trópico amargo*). On the other hand, CARMEN ALICIA CADILLA (1908) was circumspect in her intimate revelations—*Songs on a White Flute* (*Canciones en flauta blanca*, 1934)— and in CARMELINA VIZCARRONDO (1906) love of country is at least as great as the other kind of love. The last "ism" of these years was *transcendentalism,* piloted after 1948 by FÉLIX FRANCO OPPENHEIMER (1912), author of *Man and His Anguish* (*El hombre y su angustia,* 1950). The aim was "to elevate man to a plane of high spirituality, without letting him forget his human reality." We will see the younger companions of this movement in the next chapter. Among all these movements go FRANCISCO RENTAS LUCAS (1910), OBDULIO BAUZÁ Y GONZÁLEZ (1907), DIONISIO TRUJILLO (1912), PEDRO JUAN LABARTHE (1906), MANUEL JOGLAR CACHO 1898), and various others. But the one who, together with Lloréns Torres, Dávila, and Ribera Chevremont, is a principal pillar in Puerto Rican poetry is Palés Matos.

LUIS PALÉS MATOS (Puerto Rico, 1898–1959) is one of the most original poets of this era. He began by writing Modernist poetry— *Azaleas,* 1915—but sought his own path and, after 1926, he published poems of Negroid themes which immediately placed him in the vanguard of Hispanic-American literature. Those Negroid poems were previous to, or in any event independent of, those which were flourishing in Cuba. But Palés Matos gathered his into a book much later, after having displayed them in periodicals. His first book of Negroid poetry was *Shoe-blacking of Kinky Hair and Negro Themes* (*Tuntún de pasa y grifería,* 1937), and it was enough to consecrate him definitely. Whether or not the Negroid content of this literature was authentic or of national significance is an ethnographic and sociological problem outside the pale of literary criticism. The important thing is to indicate its extreme poetic merit. With eminent rhythmic skill Palés Matos makes us hear an entire people, real or not. It is like the verbal imitation of the movements of the Negro dances: rhythms, syncopations, repetitions, onomatopoeias, alliterations, and rhymes accented on the last syllables. The vocabulary gathers together expressions either heard, read, or invented; and the proper names, the geographic terms, the mythological references, the descriptions of beliefs, customs, and Afro-Antillian rites end up by creating the illusion of a magic world. All kinds of sensorial perceptions are blended into metaphors that are not simply tinsel ornaments, but deep, lyrical intuitions. In his huge orchestra an ironic contrapuntal melody can be heard; because Palés Matos is not a Negro, but a white man, and he smiles wistfully at the contrasts in both cultures, in neither of which does he really believe. Precisely in this refined note of irony, skepticism, and melancholy does he differ from the other poets who write of Negro themes. He does not copy a popular reality exactly as it exists in a particular country, rather he interprets the Negro motifs from his position as an imaginative poet with all the artistry of a distant disciple of the Spanish Baroque. Although his Negroid poems brought him fame, they are only one facet of his personality. The reading of his book *Poetry* (*Poesía,* 1915–1956, published in 1957) revealed a complete Palés Matos to the reader. It became evident that many of his verses are not merely superficial elaborations on the Negro theme; they go deeper, revealing intimate, personal moods. Thus one understands that those Negro poems —"Negro Dance" (*"Danza negra"*)—are episodes in a single protracted expression of a sad insight into primitive life and of human dissolution into nothingness—"The One Called" (*"El llamado"*).

Before leaving the Antilles, we will pause on that which was most different in Negro and mulatto poetry. Folklore is extremely rich in old rhythms and Afro-Antillian themes, but only after 1925 did all this acquire a worthwhile esthetic value. The stimulus came from Europe. The Afrological investigations of Leo Frobenius; the Afrophilism of Paris in the "fauves," expressionist and dadaist paintings, literature and ballet; examples of Negro art in the United States; the use of the gypsy, the African, the folkloric by García Lorca and others in Spain, indicate that the Negro theme was in style during the years of ultraism. The actuality of Negro race and culture in the Antilles favored the fad. Furthermore, in the Antilles, it was less a fad than a self-discovery. But that the stimulus should have come from European literature explains the surprising poetic quality of Nicolás Guillén, Palés Matos, Ramón Guirao, and Emilio Ballagas.

(4) *Venezuela* / First of all, among the youngest members of the "generation of 1918" whom we discussed in the previous chapter, JACINTO FOMBONA PACHANO (1901–1951) was the first to stand out. *Shiftings* (*Virajes,* 1932) was a book of genuine Creolist poems, notable for its freshness and lyricism. Years later he composed his most vigorous book, *The Unguarded Towers* (*Las torres desprevenidas,* 1940), in which are reflected the preoccupations and problems of a humanity tormented by a war which was not experienced at first hand, but was felt on all sides. MANUEL FELIPE RUGELES (1904–1959) in all of his books, from *Pitcher* (*Cántaro*) to *Golden Season* (*Dorada estación*), sings of the neighborhood in which he was born, trying to grasp its spirit in clear images. Other poets of this generation: ENRIQUE PLANCHART (1901–1953), PEDRO SOTILLO (1902), ENRIQUETA ARVELO LARRIVA. Until 1930 the voices of the vanguardists are heard (Arraiz, Otero Silva), and toward 1936 those of the group of the magazine *Viernes,* headed by ÁNGEL MIGUEL QUEREMEL (1900–1939) who returned from Spain with the ultraist incentives which Gerardo Diego, Alberti, and García Lorca left him with. (Earlier, the influential Spaniards had been Antonio Machado and Juan Ramón Jiménez.) The magazine *Friday* (*Viernes*) was a laboratory for contradictory esthetics, all experimental. VICENTE GERBASI (1913), OTTO D'SOLA (1912), PASCUAL VENEGAS FILARDO (1911), JOSÉ RAMÓN HEREDIA (1900), PABLO ROJAS GUARDIA (1909): hermetic lyricism, somewhat surrealist, metaphysical fever, renovation. There were others who opposed this poetry, completely encased in obscure symbols. This opposition came from various sides. One, from the partisans of regular and even

classical forms: Luis Beltrán Guerrero, 1914 and Juan Beroes, 1914, who was among the first to give classical structure to his poems, with an ear trained to the measures and rhythms of the Golden Age. Another side, from the partisans of an objective poetry of normal themes: Alberto Arvelo Torrealba, 1904. Another, the partisans of the native soil, folklore and regional themes (Juan Liscano, 1915). Also, isolated voices, some of them from the provinces: Héctor Guillermo Villalobos (1911), J. A. de Armas Chitty (1908), Luisa del Valle Silva (1902), Manuel Rodríguez Cárdenas (1912), Miguel Ramón Utrera (1910), José Miguel Ferrer (1904) and Luis Fernando Álvarez (1902–1952).

(5) *Colombia* / The "New Ones"—that is, the poets who grouped around the magazine, *Los Nuevos,* published by Jorge Zalamea and Alberto Lleras Camargo—drew away from the Modernists, but not very far. At any rate, they did not break with them as the youths of other countries had. Colombians have always been very circumspect in the use of language. Modernism, in its respect for good form, had reinforced this traditional sentiment for grammar. Thus Modernism went on to form a part of this tradition, and the desire for linguistic perfection of the Parnassians continued to dominate until after the first World War. The vanguardist movements scarcely altered the Modernist, Parnassian course of the "New Ones." One of the essayists of this generation, Jorge Zalamea, said: "To suppress the books of Valencia and Silva would be to suppress the current moment of Colombian literature." Thus the "new poets" leaped over the immediately preceding generation of "Centenarists" without recognizing their mastery. For example, they felt that José Eustasio Rivera had put political propositions, nationalistic sentiments, and a vague humanitarianism, wrapped up in a conservative philosophy, in his book *The Vortex.* As for his sonnets of *The Promised Land,* the "new poets" found them to be too labored. The "Centenarists" had not familiarized themselves with the literary course from Proust to Breton. The "New Ones," on the other hand, although they also prolonged Parnassianism, at least cast a glance at distant vanguardists, from Europe and from some South American cities. In general, they did not disencumber themselves of the past, but it is enough that there should have been among them a few exceptions in order for us to be able to distinguish them from the "Centenarists." These few exceptional poets leaped into the future with arrogances, obscurities, music, and challenging ideas. Some were pure esthetes who with childish sprightliness played with literature, dehumanizing it. Others, won over by socialist ideas, proclaimed bellicose programs of political revindication (Luis Vidales). There was one group of skeptics who remained on the sidelines of ideology and another group that supported order and authority (Silvio Villegas, Eliseo Arango,

José Camacho Carreño, Augusto Ramírez Moreno). León de Greiff, upon establishing himself in Bogotá, lent force to the "New Ones." He was a unique personality, inimitable in his perpetual youth. He attracted followers to himself.

For example, Luis Vidales (1904), who in 1926 disturbed the atmosphere with *Bells Are Ringing (Suenan timbres)*, a book of poetry connected with the power house of electrical and unexpected images that functioned throughout the Western world after the first great war. Vidales was the one who profited most from the mischievous, *gregueristic* genius which was cultivated in Spanish letters after Gómez de la Serna. But Colombian literature did not allow itself to be seduced by the postwar "isms." Certainly not the two major poets of these years: Maya and Pardo García. Rafael Maya (1898), moderate, intelligent, extended the mastery of his poetry, but without changing its character. His sensations and images became more vertiginous; his rhythms disbanded and there was more liberty and more space in his verses. But all this without exhibitionisms. The same contemplation of nature, harmonious, tender, simple, grew deeper with the years without there being the necessity for breaking noisily with the manners of the prewar literature. He is of that classical temperament which reflects upon its emotions and obliges them to assume an equilibrium between the new and the traditional. Without ignoring the French, Maya reads the Spanish classicists with pleasure. His last book, *Nocturnal Navigation (Navegación nocturna,* 1959), is an examination of conscience. Maya smashes his soul to pieces, as though it were a time glass, and in each splinter the light of a memory is reflected; afterwards, he tries to reconstruct himself from these fragments, and the image that he recovers is that of desolation. But in this solitude the poet feels himself beneath the shelter of God and in the face of a vocation for creating his own world, with words. The presence of God gives order, unity, and harmony to what he has created, and the poet admires the beauty of this creation in the landscape. Pain from the thorn that he carries in his heart, agony in his expression, happiness in his contemplation of the world: behold his sentimental frames of mind. The soul of the poet flows in time, undivided, and changing, and his voice joins with that of all other poets in singing the multiple histories of mankind. He longs for ancient clarity, not modern confusion. A confidential and simple voice which, by dint of reflection, clarifies even the darknesses of its own being. More than living, to feel alive. Poetry is for him not impressionism, but knowledge of essences, gathered together in time, ready for death. His images, propelled by intelligence, order themselves into beautiful expressionist allegories, stories, literary glosses and fables—always in a lyric tone. Germán Pardo García (1902) sees three steps in the fourteen volumes that go from *Will (Voluntad,* 1930) to *Star Without a Shore (Lucero sin orillas,* 1952). Afterwards, he published five more. It went from the approved forms of the past to verbal audacities. In their depths can be heard the same desolate song. When he is not clear it is because he has opened his eyes in a zone of shadows, but he wants to see clearly, and even his sorrow comes out in regulated verses. There is something Romantic in his tone: his exaltation of mysteries and anguish is that of a Narcissus who feels himself to be a titan, and he shouts his protest against injustice and war. One of his last books: *There Are Stones Like Tears (Hay piedras como lágrimas,* 1957). In the group of the "New Ones" these also stood out: José Umana Bernal (1899), Juan Lozano y Lozano (1902),

CIRO MENDÍA (1902), OCTAVIO AMÓRTEGUI (1901), RAFAEL VÁZQUEZ (1899), CARLOS LÓPEZ NARVÁEZ (1897), ALBERTO ÁNGEL-MONTOYA (1903), VÍCTOR AMAYA GONZÁLEZ (1898).

The group of the "New Ones" was succeeded, toward 1935, by the "stoneandskyists" (*"piedracelistas"*), so-called because of their note-books of poetry named "Stone and Sky." That they should have taken as a name the title of that book of Juan Ramón Jiménez was already a definition. Nevertheless, there is not only the influence of Juan Ramón Jiménez there. It was a generation that had had its origin in the Spanish poets of '25 (Alberti, Diego, Salinas, García Lorca) and also in the Hispanic-Americans (Huidobro, Neruda). The "stoneandskyists" (*piedracelistas*) formed a group with unity of style: the vocabulary and the syntax, the meters and the strophes, the metaphors and even the themes indicate that, although each one had his own personal accent, they all departed from the same poetic position. The block influence of the "stoneandskyists" over Colombian literary history stems from this fact. Their verses were svelte and moved through the air with light and flexible grace. On fleeing from pomp and eloquence, they did not turn to a magic, dreamy, or intellectual language, rather they cultivated a poetry of dignity and circumspection, more artistic than vital.

The promoter of the "stoneandsky" group was EDUARDO CARRANZA (1913). In *Songs for Beginning a Fiesta* (*Canciones para iniciar una fiesta,* the Madrid edition is of 1953) he gave a selection from his poetic work which he had begun in 1936 with a book of poems of the same title. Carranza is one of the best poets of these years. He jubilantly affirms all things and even exalts them beyond their own intimacy: "All is well . . . / All of creation, except my heart, all is well." It seems that, mistrusting his own voice, he would like to move things, align them, use them, so that they, thus placed, might speak for him. He sings to the reality that envelops him (the native landscape, the history of the fatherland), he sings of his own reality (memories, loves), he sings to Christ. He has an air of awe before the essence of man and of the world; but his expression is not metaphysics (fortunately), but poetry. JORGE ROJAS (1911) is among the excellent ones. His sonnets, of classical rigor and mysterious meaning, are among the most impeccable of his generation. He documented his admiration for Juan Ramón Jiménez with the title of his first book of poems: *The Form of His Flight* (*La forma de su huida,* 1939). At the entreaty of his verse the great themes of metaphysics stand up. Pure poetry, of solitude and dreams: *Water Rose* (*Rosa de agua,* 1941–48), *The Water Maiden* (*La doncella de agua,* 1948), *Solitudes* (*Soledades,* 1948). The work of ARTURO CAMACHO RAMÍREZ (1910), is also enduring. The list of names of the "stoneandsky" group is completed with DARÍO SAMPER (1909), TOMÁS VARGAS OSORIO (1908–1941), GERARDO VALENCIA (1911), and CARLOS MARTÍN (1914). All of these "stoneandskyists" imposed an art of verbal subtleties and esthetic experiences that until then had been resisted by the public. Its renovating function was, then, important. During these years there were other Colombian poets who did not belong to the "stoneandsky" group, nor were they typical of it: JORGE ARTEL (1905), in Negro poetry; ANTONIO LLANOS (1905), of religious unction, who exercised influence because of his delicacy and poetic purity; and, above all, AURELIO ARTURO (1909), who sings of the landscape of his country and of the events of his days and nights with such simplicity and sincerity that his voice is, during these years, the one most frequently heard by the youth of his country.

(6) *Ecuador* / Two clear voices: Carrera Andrade and Escudero. Born far from the main highways of the world, JORGE CARRERA ANDRADE (1902) left his corner of the earth and wandered all over the world: he wrote poetry about his travels and, of course, about his return to the homeland. Educated in a primitive country town, he sought out difficult books and disciplined himself in French literature: Hugo, Baudelaire, Francis Jammes, Jules Renard. Romantics, symbolists were his teachers. He did not give in to the surrealism of Breton or Eluard. He was interested in immediate reality, that of the consciousness and of all things. And, in effect, his poetry is clear. He experiments, changes, grows young again, but remains clearly sentimental. He can be seen in all these various phases, gathered together in *Registry of the World* (*Registro del mundo,* 1940), an anthology from 1922 to 1939, and in *Place of Origin* (*Lugar de origen*). His poetic impressionism has given us his vision of the landscape in surprising vignettes. GONZALO ESCUDERO (1903) is a poet of great vigor: from *Helices of Hurricane and Sun* (*Hélices de huracán y de sol,* 1934) to *Statue of Air* (*Estatua de aire,* 1953) tonal changes can be noted. That grandiloquence of images and abstractions (at times fused into hyperboles) has become more lyrical and moderate.

ALFREDO GANGOTENA (1904–1945), associated with vanguardist tendencies, wrote in French (from *Orogénie,* 1928, to *Nuit,* 1938) but he also showed us, in Spanish, his *Secret Storm* (*Tempestad secreta,* 1940); JORGE REYES (1905), a carefree and playful spirit, wrote his *Quito, City in the Sky* (*Quito, arrabal del cielo,* 1930) in a climate of vanguardism; the tranquil and sad AUGUSTO ARIAS (1903); the abortive MIGUEL ANGEL LEÓN (1900–1942) and IGNACIO LASSO (1912–1943); the Indianist G. HUMBERTO MATA (1904); the tragic AUGUSTO SACOTO (1910); the abundant but refined CÉSAR ANDRADE Y CORDERO (1902); and JOSÉ ALFREDO LLERENA (1912), also a good prosist.

(7) *Peru* / When vanguardist tendencies imposed themselves on Peru, no one was capable of surpassing Vallejo. A large part of the production of the youths who imitated the dadaists, creationists, and surrealists was more ingenious than poetic. It simulated a new sensibility. Its stridence, of which they were so proud, sounded like that of a large

armaments factory. And it was: a factory of metaphors. The molds of literary expression were shattered with nonsense. Such excess had to be moderated. Something of this habit of excess always remained. Some poetic lines were traced with a heavier hand than others. They, as a result, can be seen more clearly: (a) a line of pure poets; (b) another of Peruvianist poets; (c) another of political poets. Even these lines cross, run parallel, and become one. Do not blame the critic for this confusion.

In the line of pure poetry the program is personal, intimate, disinterested, gratuitous, inactive. Eguren had set the example. CARLOS OQUENDO DE AMAT (1909–1936) followed him with his *5 Meters of Poems* (*5 metros de poemas*, 1927), notable for the sincerity of its vanguardist esthetics. His words came loose from real objects and fluttered through the air of fantasy: "In your dreams, elephants graze with their flower eyes / and an angel rolls rivers of hoops." MARTÍ ADÁN (1908) was careful with verbal extravagances from the beginning and ended by regulating them: for example, *Crossing of Seas Beyond Seas* (*Travesías de extramares*, 1950). Old forms of Spanish verse—sonnets, *décimas*, ballads—were redressed in vertiginous metaphors, in simultaneous impressions, in uneven enumerations, in a new, magic lyricism, content with its creative powers. Even in those moments in which he is most free and seems to be writing against form—his "anti-sonnets," for example—it can be seen that his verbal torments also have a grammar, a code of laws. One of his most important books, *The Cardboard House* (*La casa de cartón*, 1928), was not poetry, but narrative prose. The one most conscious of European techniques was XAVIER ABRIL (1905), who not only practiced them, but also formulated them. He was a strange one. Through the quality of his imagination, through his audacities, through his vitality, he would have been an effective poet if it had not been for the fact that at times he slackens his effort and falls into vanguardist rhetoric. His hermetic poetry opens an occasional pore and allows the oxygen of social feeling to enter. As he is an intellectual, he is also capable of prying into the great past of Spanish literature, as in his "Vague Elegy in the Ancient Tone of Jorge Manrique" (*"Elegía oscura en el viejo tono de Jorge Manrique"*). Works: *Difficult Labor* (*Difícil trabajo*, 1935), *Discoveries of Dawn* (*Descubrimientos del alba*, 1937). ENRIQUE PEÑA BARRENECHEA (1905), brother of the already mentioned Ricardo, took advantage of the calls to liberty of the new tendencies in order to bury himself in his dreamy, neo-Romantic forms of expression. This "wounded intellect," that of *The Aroma of Shadow* (*El aroma de la sombra*, 1926), *Cinema of Pure Sense* (*Cinema de los sentidos puros*, 1931), and *Elegy to Bécquer* (*Elegía a Bécquer*, 1936), was a poet of dreams but not a surrealist poet; and we find him comfortably established in forms that come from the Golden Spanish century. Of purist tendencies were JOSÉ ALFREDO HERNÁNDEZ (1910) and VICENTE AZAR (1913), the latter, a pseudonym for José Alvarado Sánchez, author of *The Art of Forgetting* (*Arte de olvidar*, 1942). Extremely important to Peruvian surrealism is CÉSAR MORO (1904–1956). His real name was Alfredo Quíspez Asín. That part of his poetry which is written in French is outside of this history. Moro lived in that international hotel of poetry which was surrealism. In another room was EMILIO ADOLFO WESTPHALEN (1911). It seems that he gives us only those splinters that were broken off his poems in the process of writing them. And as we look at each splinter, we can still hear the noise with which his poems had burst. In *Strange Islands* (*Insulas extrañas*, 1933), less than splinters: dust, only dust. Not even the structure of a simple sentence, much less the structure of a verse has remained. Without punctuation, without syntax, without images. A dust of words blown about by a dark wind of emotion. In *Abolition of Death* (*Abolición de la muerte*, 1935) his poetry has more than one corpuscle to lean upon: the imagery offers a wider surface, and at times the face of the poet is reflected in it, serious, contracted, preoccupied with the time, the existence, and the Beyond. There were poets who took rooms in other houses. We have already said that there was an avenue of Peruvianist poetry. Along this avenue, the first predominating theme, after 1926, was the revindication of the Indian, which had been commenced by González Prada, but which was now formulated through a collective style. In general, this style was that of postwar European vanguardism. There is no need to mention the fact that the Indians were left out of this hermetic Indianist literature. The best representative here was ALEJANDRO PERALTA (1899), author of *Ande* (1926) and *El Kollao* (1934). The Indians appeared as though sculpted from visual metaphors; but the poet also sees the social injustice. Others: EMILIO VÁZQUEZ (1903), GUILLERMO MERCADO (1904), NICANOR DE LA FUENTE (1904), and LUIS DE RODRIGO (1904). This exaltation of the Indian was a false, limited, empty reality. The mestizo or the civilized Indian had greater possibilities. LUIS FABIO XAMMAR (1911–1947) was the most representative of this type of literature dealing with the civilized Indian. He told us, simply, and in a flavorful and popular language, his love of the fields and their men, from *Thoughtfully* (*Pensativamente*, 1930) to *The High Mist* (*La alta niebla*, 1947). The literature of the *cholo* (civilized Indian) continued after the exhaustion, around 1930, of the Indian theme, and its label was no longer the incoherent one of European vanguardism, but that of traditional Spanish forms touched by the vanguardist spirit, as in the ballads of García Lorca in Spain. Along the lines of political poetry, they took the part of the oppressed classes; or, at least, they expressed the emotions they felt on witnessing the social struggles. MAGDA PORTAL (1901) and SERAFÍN DELMAR [Reynaldo Bolaños] used poetry as an instrument. Others were LUIS NIETO (1910), JULIÁN PETROVICK (1901), and RAFAEL MÉNDEZ DORICH. Social messages, although not political, were written by LUIS VALLE GOICOCHEA (1908–1954), who revived poetically all of the emotions of his childhood and adolescence, of provincial conditions and landscapes, of traditional songs, all in a clear language; MANUEL MORENO JIMENO (1913), whose poetry is made dramatic by his compassion for mankind upon seeing it before the difficult crossroads of our time; and AGUSTÍN TAMAYO VARGAS (1914), who in "Lyric Entry to Geography" (*"Ingreso lírico a la geografía"*) announced a "poetry, not of I, but of We." To sum up, the poetry of Peru centered on the mestizo, on the *cholo*, on their national originality, and it preferred the traditional manner, at times brilliant with imagination, at times in deliberately muted tonalities. To the list of local themes, political poetry added the Civil War in Spain and the Fascist and Nazi aggression which unleashed the second World War. Other poets: JULIO GARRIDO MALAVER (1909), JOSÉ VARALLANOS (1908), FELIPE ARIAS LARRETA (1910–1955), FRANCISCO XANDOVAL (1902).

(8) *Bolivia* / After the three most outstanding Bolivian poets—Jaimes Freyre, Tamayo and Reynolds—came a generation of greater number. OCTAVIO CAMPERO ECHAZÚ (1900), in the popular and traditional forms of Spain and America, cap-

tured the landscapes and loves of his region: *Amancayas* (1942), *Voices* (*Voces,* 1950). GUILLERMO VISCARRA FABRE (1901), who in *Climate* (*Clima,* 1918) preferred to suggest vaguely, and in *Creature of the Dawn* (*Criatura del alba,* 1949) presented clear images of what he saw in the landscape and in the depths of his own sadness. Given over to Indianism, the good poet ANTONIO ÁVILA JIMÉNEZ (1900). Others: JAVIER DEL GRANADO (1913), LUIS MENDIZÁBAL SANTA CRUZ (1907–1946), RAÚL OTERO REICHE (1905), LUCIO DÍEZ DE MEDINA, AMELLER RAMALLO, the VILLA GOMEZ brothers, and JESÚS LARA.

(9) *Chile* / Poetry had touched Chile, and after Gabriela Mistral, there was never a time when there were no poets. We have seen Huidobro and Rokha. And in this chapter we will see the greatest lyricist of them all, the vibrant, famous, and influential Pablo Neruda. After the four names cited above—the most resonant—Rosamel del Valle, Humberto Díaz Casanueva, and others follow at a respectful distance.

PABLO NERUDA (Chile, 1904) has marked off the steps of his poetry. The first is that of the *Song of the Festival* (*La canción de la fiesta,* 1921) and *Crepusculary* (*Crepusculario,* 1923). The second is that of *Twenty Poems of Love and One Desperate Song* (*Viente poemas de amor y una canción desesperada,* 1924) and *The Attempt of Infinite Man* (*Tentativa del hombre infinito,* 1925). The third is of *The Enthusiastic Slinger* (*El hondero entusiasta,* 1933), of his *Residence on Earth* (*Residencia en la tierra,* Vol. I, poetry from 1925 to 1931; Vol. II, poetry from 1931 to 1935), and *The Furies and the Pains* (*Las furias y las penas,* written in 1934 but published in 1939). The fourth is that of *Third Residence* (*Tercera residencia,* 1947), *General Song* (*Canto general,* 1950). The fifth is that of *Elemental Odes* (*Odas elementales,* 1954) and the extravagant book *Far Wanderings* (*Estravagario,* 1958); the fourth volume of odes, *Embarkings and Returnings* (*Navegaciones y regresos*), is of 1959.

Let us attempt a characterization.

(1) The tone is still Modernist. Conventional language, traditional forms. In *Crepusculary* the original Neruda appears, but he still sings in tune with other voices in the literary chorus which he prefers; moreover, at times he is still, and other voices—that of his admired Sabat Ercasty above all—are heard singing in his verses. In "Final" he confesses that "other voices than mine are mixed in."

(2) The *Twenty Poems,* in many ways, are a continuation of *Crepusculary;* they seem to come before *The Slinger.* More regulated verses, simple, contemplative; images, not in eruption, but laced together in structures of logical patterns; their impetus suppressed through respect for traditional literary tastes. It is Neruda's first personal book: less literature, more sincere in his intimate revelations as a lover. *The*

Attempt of Infinite Man acknowledges the will to break with the past. Free verse, syntax, and spelling; verbal chaos begins.

(3) We are now confronted with the complete Neruda. He hurls us into his imaginative volcano. Obscure poetry, because the poet has not given his intuitions complete configuration. Embryos, larvae, sparks, germs of ideas, attempts, promises of poetic expression. It is useless for the critic to try to understand how and from where they come. Neruda dives deep into his sea of sentiment: each time he comes to the surface for air and joins those of us who are watching him from the shore, he brings a fish-image. These images become more and more monstrous as he dives deeper and deeper into his own depths: first, images which we recognize for their literary value (stars, moon, etc.); next, "ugly" or non-literary images (brooms, rags, spittle, underpants). In *Residence* he confronts his existence and allows his emotion to remain hermetic. He does not objectify, does not externalize his sentiments into a structure which is comprehensible to all. His tone runs from sadness to anguish; and his anguish is torn from a desolate vision of the world and of life: death, decay, failure, chaos, senselessness, ash, dust, endless ruin, infinite disintegration. He does not disintegrate reality into literary *greguerías,* rather he sees a reality already disintegrated. And he sees it without literature. At least, without much literature. For this reason there are so many failures of expressiveness, so many howls, so much dissatisfaction, so much emotional material not esthetically developed. As a surrealist, Neruda wanted to ensnare profound life, show its spontaneous fluidity, bring to light the irrepressible movements of the subconscious. The act of making a poem gave him more pleasure than beholding the finished poem. The circumjacent world is in such a ruined and murky condition that the poet has to look away. Then he sees himself: he sees himself as a pile of broken and dirty mirrors where his violent feelings are reflected in fragments. That is, the poet neither goes out into the world nor enters into his passion. Stripped and shattered, he bends in sadness over the most subterranean courses of his subconscious. There, he allows his poems to be carried by the current, bearing their desires and memories with them. Words do not aim at extrinsic objects: there are no fixed points of reference. Neither do his metaphors have the clear fullness of a vision: they are ugly phantoms wandering through a disordered night. And all of this poetry horrifies the reader just as the dismantled world must have horrified the poet; and as we read Neruda, we find pieces of wreckage from which we reconstruct, with our imagination, the beauty of the cataclysm. The novelty of Neruda is in his allowing

himself to fall inward, to drown himself, to deform himself. Poets and intellectuals were enthusiastic about his *Residence* precisely because they saw Neruda's soul as a busy workshop, in that moment when sentiment, and the poetic intuition of that sentiment, had not yet reached a state of equilibrium. To read Neruda is to penetrate within the creative process of a poet.

(4) The spectacle of death and injustice in the crushing of the Spanish Republic by the military awakened the political conscience of Neruda: with *Spain in the Heart* (*España en el corazón*, 1937) his voice began to be heard, less and less hermetic, more and more didactic. From his *Third Residence* to *General Song*, the oratorical breadth in the poetry of Neruda grows wider, while the weight of lyric images diminishes. Because the poet becomes politically excited, he becomes metaphorically tranquil. There are fewer surprises because now his metaphors are threaded together by universal concepts and sentiments. Neruda becomes a militant communist. One must proselytize, one must defend the Party, one must denounce the enemy. Before, the poet, very romantically forlorn, viewed chaos from within: Nature was monstrous or, when humanized, it acquired the form of an anguished soul, and culture was a cancer which rapidly multiplied its diseased cells, driving man either to utter madness or to total annihilation. Now, the poet, politically organized, leaps away from the chaos. He leaves his enemies to lose themselves in the debris, while he seeks salvation in the order of the Communist Party, which remakes and implants values in a society. Society, no longer chaotic, becomes a springboard from which he hurls himself toward the future. Lyricism was Neruda's forte, not the epic. For this reason he slips into creating heavy chunks of prose in verse, utilitarian broths which have nothing to do with literature, in an anti-historic detonation of Russian names which he includes in his songs to indigenous Hispanic-American themes. His *General Song* (*Canto General*) is a portrayal of America: botany, zoology, archeology, conquerors and liberators, the ups and the downs of politics, the history of the past and the chronicles of the present. In some passages—"The Heights of Macchu Picchu" and "General Song of Chile" —it can be seen how Neruda, a powerful poet even though he is sacrificing his lyricism to politics, is capable of intense poetry.

(5) In *Elemental Odes* and *New Elemental Odes* Neruda's rejection of his own past is definitive. His anguished vision of a world buried in quicksand, his tragic solitude, his proud surrealism are left behind: now the poet wants simply to reach the simple man. Thus, he gives the order to his poetry to march toward the masses. Between the thighs

of this marching poetry—that of the passion for the Communist International, that of the passion for the American Indian—are seen the themes of ardent sex. The poems he is at present producing are like fragments of an intimate yet public diary which contains impressions and events that sometimes border upon trivia. Has Neruda ceased to be the great poet he was? His conversion to communist realism in his later years causes him to be given to the exaltation of three uglinesses: arrogance, demagoguery, and insincerity. In *Far Wanderings* and in *Embarkings and Returnings,* there is a gross and noisy superficiality: nevertheless, his creative force is always impressive. What endures in Neruda is his romantic vein; it follows along all his themes whether they be of passionate love, melancholic hopelessness, delirious nightmares, or political utopia. His narrative prose *The Inhabitant and His Hope* (*El habitante y su esperanza,* 1926) adds nothing to his work.

Other Chilean Poets / Rosamel del Valle and Humberto Díaz Casanueva should be studied together, in spite of their differences. They are at least joined by friendship, by the vanguardist magazines they founded, by a certain common poetic air, and by their common devotion to poetry. ROSAMEL DEL VALLE (1901) is the more spontaneous of the two. His free-versifying demolishes the structure of poetry until the poet is left standing amid the nocturnal ruins, singing the hallucinations and mysteries of his solitude. And one of the poems from his book, *The Communicable Vision* (*La visión comunicable,* 1956) is named, precisely, "The Lonely Head." With meters that fluctuate between seventeen and twenty-one syllables, the poet converses with a tired, digressive, and occasionally prosaic air on the affinity between persons and phantoms, and upon the solitude to which the real and concrete existence of those who surround us condemns us. When he wishes to communicate, he does so by prophesying thoughts or myths—like that of *Orpheus* (*Orfeo,* 1944). HUMBERTO DÍAZ CASANUEVA (1906) converts the dark mass of his profound life into ideas and song. He is an inquisitive poet: Who am I, what is this Being that surrounds me? He is open to his subconscious, to his dreams, to the nocturnal side of his being: "I must always write when the stars come out, to write my / marks which, like birds, chirp on the side of death"—*Sleeping Beauty* (*La bella durmiente*). In "The Vision" he tells us how "he lay, in the shadow, with his eyelids closed toward the terrible," and suddenly he understood that his "forehead was formed over a vast dream / like a slow scab over a wound that oozes unceasingly." Unlike the surrealists, who show the current of shadows in all of their spontaneity, Díaz Casanueva leaves his subconscious in order to contemplate what he has seen there, and after thinking about it, guards his images in a sealed coffer of symbols. Public recognition has distinguished other poets. We will mention a few. JUVENCIO VALLE (1905) is the pure lyricist, of noble vocabulary, with musical, insinuating, and subtle charms. Plants, sap, flowers, and fruits, all lend their forms to a dynamic necessity of growing toward the sky. Vegetable freshness and flights of birds, water and land elevated with grace, liberty and beauty. The aerial, ascendant impulse of Juvencio Valle, shepherd of clouds, tight-rope walker without a tightrope, is one of the happiest of his generation. OMAR

CÁCERES (1906–1943) was one who influenced the younger writers. JULIO BARRE-NECHEA (1910), GUSTAVO OSSORIO (1911–1949), ANTONIO UNDURRAGA (1911), GLADYS THEIN (1911), and ALDO TORRES PÚA (1910–1960) merit more attention than we can give them here.

(10) *Paraguay* / An extemporaneous movement of still Rubén Darian Modernist poets gathered, in these years, around the magazine *Juventud* (1923). To it belonged HERIBERTO FERNÁNDEZ (1903–1927) who died just when he was beginning to renew himself in *Sonnets to My Sister* (*Los sonetos a la hermana*) and JOSÉ CONCEPCIÓN ORTIZ (1900), of a bright intimacy. There was a nativist poetry—like that of VICENTE LAMAS (1909) with a certain descriptive, if occasionally superficial, grace, but always of correct form—and a social poetry—like that of MANUEL VERÓN DE ASTRADA (1903), the author of *Banners in the Dawn* (*Banderas en el alba*). A poetess born in the Canary Islands, but definitely associated with Paraguayan literature, took off in new directions: JOSEFINA PLA (1909). Her first book of poems was in 1934: *The Price of Dreams* (*El precio de los sueños*). She enriched herself with new experiences in poems of which only a few were collected in *The Root and the Dawn* (*La raíz y la aurora*, 1960). Later, she stood out in the theater. For Pla, poetry is always free and disencumbered, going before social events, not pushed by them. But the greatest Paraguayan figure of these years was HERIB CAMPOS CERVERA (1908–1953). He left only one book: *Ashes Redeemed* (*Ceniza redimida*, 1950). He arrived late, and for this reason some of his surrealist images failed to surprise anyone but Paraguayan readers; but inside Paraguay, Campos Cervera initiates a movement which will be carried on by Roa Bastos, Elvio Romero, and others. He is a poet without gaiety. Shaken by presentiments of death and wounded by the pains of the world, Campos Cervera vacillated between a poetry of intimate, confessional value and one of social service. He wrote exiled from his native land, torn away from his friends; and his best compositions were not those inspired by episodes of war, politics, labor, collective life, or erotic themes, but those in which he lyrically expressed his nostalgia—"A Handful of Earth" (*"Un puño de tierra"*)—and his memory of a lost friend—"Small Litany in a Low Voice" (*"Pequeña letanía en voz baja"*).

(11) *Uruguay* / There were—it was inevitable—ultraist buzzers, bells, and wooden rattles. Nevertheless, the most common trait of the Uruguayan poets of these years was the desire for a rigorous esthetic form. At times, those values seen in the best light were religious; at times, they were social ones. A wide register runs from the estheticizing sensitivity of some, to the deliberate prosaicness of others. The minstrels were Fusco Sansone and Ferreiro. NICOLÁS FUSCO SANSONE (1904) announced with *The Trumpet of Happy Voices* (*La trompeta de las voces alegres*, 1925) that he had come simply to celebrate the joy of living. His lustrous lyricism illuminated book after book, although life put a shade over him from time to time, and a few shadows blurred his work. ALFREDO MARIO FERREIRO (1899) was a clown—*The Man Who Ate a Bus* (*El hombre que se comió un autobus*, 1927)—with something of the ultraist in his selection of images, and now and then a sad face in the midst of the machines of the modern city. Those who moderate the voice of these times are Pereda, Esther de Cáceres, and Roberto Ibáñez. FERNANDO PEREDA (1900), without having published a single book, was admired for the exactitude of his poems, above all, his sonnets. Never satisfied with the words

which offered themselves spontaneously, he drove away the more servile ones, and kept the egotistical ones. Furthermore, Pereda tied them together according to a secret code that he kept hidden in the coldest corner of his heart. Neither pure poetry nor surrealist poetry, but certainly a poetry enclosed in itself, like a geometric volume. In ESTHER DE CÁCERES (1903) religious faith became song. Her simple, sincere sentences, interrupted by fervor or ecstasy, are directed at God. Thus her books—from *Strange Islands* (*Las ínsulas extrañas*, 1929) to *Footstep in the Night* (*Paso de la noche*, 1957)—are like a musical murmur. ROBERTO IBÁÑEZ (1907), already personal in *The Dance of the Horizons* (*La danza de los horizontes*, 1927), continued reducing his expression, not in order to dehumanize it, but to purify it. His *Mythology of the Blood* (*Mitología de la sangre*, 1939) transfigures his vital experiences—anxieties for permanence, the snares of fate, the certainty of death—into symbols in which sense and sound harmonize delicately. JUVENAL ORTIZ SARALEGUI (1907) gives us a lyricism without surprises, but with lovely figures: all is visible and recognizable, even the manner of setting up the poem. SARA DE IBÁÑEZ (1910?) was already famous for her first *Canto* (1940). The prolog was by Neruda. Therefore, some noted a Nerudianism in *Canto* and in *Blind Hour* (*Hora ciega*, 1943): rapidity and dispersion in the firing of metaphoric fusillade, words in conflict that assailed one another with the energy of voltaic batteries. Only Sara de Ibáñez has the mastery of meter, of accent, of rhyme, of strophe. She submits the madness of her lyricism to the rigor of perfectly formed verses. It is as if life had suddenly become a cold decoration. The obscurity of her images is not due to the fact that they remain in disorder in the depths of her subconscious, just as they appear, but to a process of distillation from which a labored mental process leaves a quintessence that remains in hermetic symbols. Sara de Ibáñez penetrates into things and allows them to penetrate her; her verses are hermetic because she refers to this violent interpenetration and allows herself to be caught at a frontier where words change their value. *Pastoral* (1948), in three "tempos," each one with its own tone and strophic form, causes a river of lights, flowers, fish, wheat, and dogs to flow musically to this frontier and to pass over it. The poem *Artigas* (1951) comes more out into the open and leans on a more public subject matter; but it does not draw too far away, and lyricism is, after all, more powerful than the epic. CLARA SILVA (1910?), a poetess bearing a neo-Romantic stamp in her intermittent surrender to emotion, lately has produced religious poetry—religious but not mystical, because her soul strives to reach an ever-elusive God. The poetess remained unanswered, but at least she succeeds in facing God. Attentive to the social theme is ILDEFONSO PEREDA VALDÉS (1899). His first book of poems: *The Lighted House* (*La casa iluminada*). He was still a sentimentalist. Enthusiastic over ultraism, he collaborated in its magazines. In 1929 the sufferings of others became a preoccupation with him. It was then that he decided to sing of the Negro, not as an historical figure, but as a living element of the fields and of the cities. From this sentiment of sympathy for the Negro arose the most characteristic trait of his poetry.

It has been said that the continuity of the Uruguayan poetry of these years was interrupted by Falco and Cunha, who were held in more esteem by the youths who came after them than by their contemporaries. LÍBER FALCO (1906-1955) left us a posthumous book: *Time and Time* (*Tiempo y tiempo*): poor poetry, gray, clumsy, with themes of friendship, solitude, poverty, death. He confesses his emotions in a loud voice or stammers about them prosaically. JUAN CUNHA (1910) is in the first line of Uruguayan poetry. His variety seems to be due at times to the observation and study of the manner of other contemporary poets (Spaniards like García Lorca, Hispanic-Americans like Vallejo). His forms either change in continuous experiments or lean toward folkloric rhythms and stanzas. Words, verse measures, tone of images are renewed, while the poet, beneath this apparent variety, always pursues the same intuition: that of the fluctuation between the exterior and the intimate, between the communion with man and solitude. And it is this unity in his vision of life that is most worthwhile in him. Cunha appeared with *The Bird Who Came From the Night* (*El pájaro que vino de la noche*, 1929), but his continued production is rather more recent; after his anthology *At the Foot of the Harp* (*En pie de arpa*, 1950) he published several volumes. We will finish this picture with ÁLVARO FIGUEREDO (1908). *At about Dusk* (*A eso de la tarde*, 1961) the poet, now mature, reminisces on his past life.

(*12*) *Argentina* / In 1925—which is the date upon which the doors of this chapter open—the poets who enter these doors come from different neighborhoods. Two neighborhoods, above all, were being mentioned a great deal then: that of Florida Street and that of Boedo Street. Florida, the stylish street, centrally located, elegant, cosmopolitan, was frequented by the "vanguardists" who wanted to reform literature and who created a literature (art for art's sake) that had learned many things from Europe: Borges, González Lanuza, Marechal, Molinari, Norah Lange, Bernárdez, Mastronardi. Boedo, the street of the gray suburb, run-down, of the Creole-immigrant, was frequented by revolutionaries who wanted to reform the world, and who created, with a formula of sociological art, a literature that had learned many things from Russia: Barletta, César Tiempo, Nicolás Olivari, Raúl González Tuñón, Gustavo Riccio, Enrique Amorim, Santiago Ganduglia, Roberto Mariani. The Florida clique made fun of the bad artistic taste of the Boedo clique; the Boedo clique, more resentful, condemned the lack of socialist ideals in the Florida clique. The first group wrote in *Inicial, Prisma, Proa,* and *Martín Fierro;* the second group, in *Los Pensadores* (which later was called *Claridad*). The first group stood out for its verse; the second group produced more in the novel and short story. For a characterization of the vanguardism of the first group, see the section on "the scandal" in the preceding chapter. The sects which we have indicated were not homogeneous and ended by intermingling. Ultraists who took classicists and Romantics as their models. Pure poets who turned into poets of the sacristy. Poets of political theme who went over into art for art's sake. Revolutionaries of the Boedo group who became Fascists; aristocrats from Florida who joined up with Communism. Needless to say, each band, in its turn, subdivided into factions, magazines, anthologies and quarreling manifestoes. The dissolution of ultraism began in 1922 when the writers turned from magazines to books: of 1923 is *Fervor of Buenos Aires* (*Fervor de Buenos*

Aires) of Borges; of 1924, *Prisms* (*Prismas*) of González Lanuza; of 1925, *The Street of Afternoon* (*La calle de la tarde*) by Norah Lange and the *Falcon's Perch* (*Alcándara*) by Bernárdez; of 1926, *Days Like Arrows* (*Días como flechas*) by Marechal; *Red Mill* (*Molino rojo*), by Jacobo Fijman; *The Violin of the Devil* (*El violín del diablo*) by Raúl González Tuñón; and of 1927, *The Religious Painter* (*El imaginero*) by Ricardo Molinari. Moreover, the military revolution of 1930—which made it necessary to take sides, not only in the Argentinian struggle between oligarchy and the people, but in the ideologies of the world, liberal, socialist, and fascist—ended by undoing the literary ranks and from that time the Florida and Boedo groups lost their meaning. (It should not be forgotten that in the provinces distant from Buenos Aires, although there were also committed and uncommitted literatures, the polemic was not as intense and some poets were not even aware of it.) As they developed along their individual trajectories, the poets grew away from ultraism. Ultraism fell behind: it was regarded as a collective style of the past, a school of metaphors where one could obtain diplomas to hang on one's wall, an institution to be rejected just like any other academy. And, in fact, ultraism was rejected. There were some poets who drowned in the ultraist shipwreck; others swam to safety and appeared on the shore, cured of ultraism.

There were also those who did not run aground. They preferred to follow the solid path of poetry. They were content that Lugones should have followed the same path. (Lugones, in his polemic against the partisans of verse without rhyme, of a poetry reduced to strings of metaphors hung up like a braid of onions or garlic, wrote sympathetically about Horacio Rego Molina, Conrado Nalé Roxlo, Luis L. Franco, José Pedroni. On the other hand, the ultraists—Marechal, Borges, González Lanuza—attacked Lugones.) The independent poets—that is, the ones who did not follow on the watchwords of art for art's sake nor of art as a social function—without realizing it and without meaning to, formed the following literary families. The family of those who pursued their own cordial impulses: Abella Caprile, María Alicia Domínguez, María de Villarino, Juan L. Ortiz, Silvina Ocampo, José Sebastián Tallón, González Carbalho, Pedro Juan Vignale, Horacio Esteban Ratti, Ulyses Petit de Murat. The family of those who did not celebrate their own lives, but who concerned themselves with social problems: Aristóbulo Echegaray, José Portogalo, Córdoba Iturburu, Nydia Lamarque, César Tiempo, Carlos M. Grünberg, Raúl González Tuñón. The family of the heirs of Modernism: López Merino, Rega Molina. The family of those knowledgeable in the popular or classical tradition: Estrella

Gutiérrez, Amado Villar, Alberto Franco, Salvador Merlino, Ignacio B. Anzoátegui, Elías Carpena. The family of the regionalists: Jijena Sánchez, Pedroni, Carlino, Antonio de la Torre.

Let us pass in review those poets who left a considerable work. We propose that the major lyricists are Borges, Molinari, Nalé Roxlo, González Lanuza, Ledesma, and Bernárdez. In the Argentinian literature of these years, the first name, because of his quality, because of his influence, should be that of Jorge Luis Borges. First in poetry, first in the short story, first in the essay. Because his stories profit equally from his ability as a poet and as an essayist and stand, therefore, at the center of his literary work, we will study Borges in the section dedicated to narrative prose. Let it be known, however, that he would merit the place of honor even in this section.

RICARDO E. MOLINARI (1898) appeared with the ultraist group, close to Borges, but his roots more eagerly penetrated the earth. He avoided easy regionalisms austerely. His language always showed a sound education in the Spanish classicists and in the European symbolists. Nationalism heightens his poetry, and in order to catch its essences, his language becomes so refined that it is hermetic. He elaborates his expression with extreme care. At times he flows over in odes of free verse, at times he builds his structures in the sonnet form, at times he cultivates the popular verse form. His verbal economy tends to make him monotonous. His insistence on certain images tends to give them a hardness of symbol. His ear sometimes fails him in the measure of his verses. But the series of books which he began with *The Religious Painter* (1927) and those which he collected in *Early Morning Worlds* (*Mundos de la madrugada*, 1943) and that later reached a high point with those that go from *The Guest and Melancholy* (*El huésped y la melancolía*, 1949) to *Night United* (*Unida noche*, 1957) is poetry of admirable intensity. Intensity of his odes on themes of love and death, the intensity of his windings along the shores of metaphysics. Of the group of vanguardists, Molinari is the one most respected by the youths of today: he has taught them to discipline themselves by pursuing rigorous forms and by attending not only to the geography, but to the history of Argentina.

EDUARDO GONZÁLEZ LANUZA (1900) appeared under the big top of the ultraist circus, but, like the others, he left it in time and straightened out his life. "My poems are worked over," he had written in his ironic manifesto in *Prisma* (1924), and since then it has, in fact, been seen that Lanuza is a hard-working poet who has analyzed himself and ordered the abundance of his imagination. González Lanuza has proven to be one of our good poets, passionate, free, unimpeachable, moody, so individualistic that he has remained alone. His continued meditation on what is the world, what is life, and what is poetry has given González Lanuza such profundity that in order to astonish he had no need of the acrobatics to which the ultraists resorted, in order to gain attention. A sense of the ephemeral quality of all terrestrial things, of the imminence of nothingness, of the insecurity of our lives and of our consciousness, but also the feeling that men are capable of powerful song when they grasp the time that flows within them, these feelings have found no more powerful expression in Argentina than they have in González Lanuza. The will to be obscure is not in him; in spite of the fact that he has taken the enigma of existence as his theme, González Lanuza is clear. Neither does he have the will to play with his verses, which are of classical form or free verse, according to the melody of each intuition, and always with infallible rhythmic mastery. He did not care to restore that which the ultraists had condemned: rhyme, meter, strophe. His purpose, from which he never swerved, was to reveal himself sincerely.

Roberto Ledesma (1901), natural, identified with the elemental forms of reality, conversant with the telluric, intense in his elegies and romantic expressions, sings, not of unfixed essences, but of the things from which these essences have become detached. *The Flame* (*La llama,* 1955), a selection of poetic works, is shown as a thing (an admirable thing) which is added to an admired reality. The poet baptizes the world each time he looks around him. In *The Bird in the Tempest* (*El pájaro en la tormenta,* 1957) he has continued to go deeper and deeper and to take more and more consciousness of his originality, as in "On the Sand." Some of Ledesma's sonnets are the most beautiful in our literature.

Francisco Luis Bernárdez (1900) came into the new poetry with *Sunrise* (*Orto,* 1922), *Bazaar* (*Bazar,* 1922), *Kindergarten* (1924), and *The Falcon's Perch* (*Alcándara,* 1925). Later he left this cryptic poetry of assorted images and sounds—with something of the silent movie and of a broken victrola playing jazz—and cultivated what ultraism had forgotten: the extensive poem, clear syntax, classical strophes, the balanced Thomist idea of the world. *The Boat* (*El buque,* 1935) was a theological poem: it is the theme of grace, which like a boat, visits the spirit. These ascetic stanzas skipping over *Land Sky* (*Cielo de tierra,* 1937) were followed by the amorous lyrics—serene, limpid—of *City Without Laura* (*La ciudad sin Laura,* 1938) in sonnets and other regular forms. In *Elemental Poems* (*Poemas elementales,* 1942)—perhaps his best book—Bernárdez raised his voice even louder, doubtless to reach the heights of his Catholic themes. Elemental poems, because they sing to the elements: "earth," "evil,"، "wind," "fire." When Bernárdez gives in to Scholasticism, his verses become syllogistic, hard, insipid, poor; but when he gives in to the impulse of his love (not that of St. Thomas, but that of St. Francis) his religiosity deepens and reveals to us the faith, the grace, the tenderness of his contemplation of the world. His poems elongate with the undulation of a prayer of supplication, at times in meters of twenty-two syllables with fixed accents. In his best poems, religious feeling runs like a subterranean river: its freshness is felt without seeing its form. In *Flesh and Blood Poems* (*Poemas de carne y hueso*, 1943) Christian humility turns into an asceticism of poetic expression. His repertory of motifs is ennobled (the cardinal loves of man: his sons, his faith, his flag, the tomb of General San Martín, etc.), but he slides into logical, non-poetic mechanisms. His last titles go from *The Nightingale* (*El ruiseñor*, 1945) to *The Flower* (*La flor*, 1951). Bernárdez chose the poetic family to which he wanted to belong: San Juan de la Cruz, the two Luises, Lope, and even the more remote Galician-Portuguese troubadours. Nalé Roxlo, whom we will study farther on, also traveled with these major lyricists. Others to be mentioned: Mastronardi, Marechal, Villar, and Luis L. Franco.

CARLOS MASTRONARDI (1901) was a cautious ultraist. He drew away from those who, with a deaf ear for music, thought it was enough to look through all kinds of metaphors. Neither was he seduced by styles that reduced poetry to states of being. For him, to intuit was to attune spiritual and linguistic forms with the material of his recollections. The language of his first books, *Awakened Land* (*Tierra amanecida*, 1926) and *Treatise on Anguish* (*Tratado de la pena*, 1930), was more temperate than that of his companions of *Martín Fierro* and *Proa*, and he displayed a clean pleasure in all the things of his province. In *Knowledge of Night* (*Conocimiento de la noche*, 1937) his beloved province of Entre Ríos is the subject of his poems: with a circumspect lyric tone, with ordered poetic forms, he sang of fields, villages, men, beasts, days, labor, seasons of the year, pains, joys. His poem "Light of the Province" is dedicated to anthologies.

LEOPOLDO MARECHAL (1898) also belonged to the ultraistic group during the days of *Days Like Arrows* (*Días como flechas*, 1926), but he later turned to the themes of human love and divine knowledge and wandered over the same paths that had been traversed by Spanish Christian poetry of the Golden Age. Even the forms of these paths were copied in his verses. After *Labyrinth of Love* (*Laberinto de amor,* 1936) and *Sonnets to Sophia* (*Sonetos a Sophia,* 1940) the poet became a militant Catholic. Even in *Five Southern Poems* (*Cinco poemas australes,* 1937), dedicated to his memories and to his country, religious anxiety prevails. He also published a novel: *Good-by Buenos Aires* (*Adíos Buenosayres,* 1948), with symbolic intentions: in spite of its uglinesses, it is important because he makes a mythology of his "Martín Fierro" generation.

AMADO VILLAR (1899–1954), a colorist and an engraver in *Verses with Sun and Birds* (*Versos con sol y pájaros,* 1927), in *Marimorena* (1934) he preferred to capture transparent, almost invisible realities: air, water, crystal. LUIS L. FRANCO (1898) began as a lyric poet who took his vital and happy inspiration from his peasant life: its landscape, its loves, its bodily health, its people. In *Addition* (*Suma,* 1938) and in *Bread* (*Pan,* 1948) he shows himself to be more committed to social philosophies, but his impulses toward liberty and justice, his rebellion, his solidarity with those who suffer, in spite of a few lapses in rhetoric, usually have that fresh lyricism that always vibrates in sincere temperaments. His images are as vigorous as his concepts and also shake his prose: *Small Dictionary of Disobedience* (*Pequeño diccionario de la desobediencia,* 1959). Other poets claim individual commentary. Unfortunately we have no space for any more.

We have said that after 1930—the date of the military coup that caused Argentina to stumble in her march toward liberalism—the literary groups broke up. During this time, political factions were more prevalent than poetic ones. All of the poets whom we reviewed at the beginning of this chapter had produced significant works before 1930. New writers appear after 1930. They are the ones born around 1910. Before characterizing them we should put here, parenthetically as it were, between Borges and his contemporaries, whom we have discussed, and the contemporaries of Enrique Molina and Ferreyra Basso, whom we are about to discuss, an excellent poet who demands a special place: VICENTE BARBIERI (1903–1956). He entered letters late in life: his first book of poems is *Fable of the Heart* (*Fábula del corazón*) of 1939. Barbieri had—as did Neruda, from whom he took a few of his forms—the gift of firing his metaphors with such energy, and from such profound areas of his being, that they awaken in the reader emotional resonances which are difficult to analyze. Many of these metaphors, by dint of repetition, are converted into symbols. At times we do not know whether they are symbols or decorative, scenographic, heraldic, aquatic toys. Reading his books— for example, *The Column and the Wind* (*La columna y el viento*)—one gets the impression that Barbieri is not a surrealist, but that he uses the literary conventions of surrealism. That is, his words do not flow directly and spontaneously from the dark springs of his being, rather, they have an order; however, this order is not clear and intelligible, but of a rhetoric deliberately disordered. Barbieri appears to write his poems with ideas, with messages; and if we were to compile a "dictionary of symbols," we would be able to decipher them. They are ambiguous. He points at one thing and calls it another. His code is secret. Not for this reason is his poetic world any less well constructed. He does not free the obscurity of existence but gives us charades instead. Those writers born around 1910, and who appear in the literary field around 1930, were much more moderate than the vanguardists. Cured of fright, they searched for equilibrium. They were familiar with extremes. They proposed being more serious. A philosophy whose preoccupation was the understanding of man led them to the old theme: sentimental life. This neo-Romanticism will end by speaking in a loud voice in the following generation, that of 1940. ENRIQUE MOLINA (1910) grew with his books—from *Things and Delirium* (*Las cosas y el delirio*, 1941) to *Wandering Habits or The Roundness of the Earth* (*Costumbres errantes o La redondez de la tierra*, 1951)—until he achieved the greatest height of any of his group. His vision is desolate. He presses his wounds. He seeks the confirmation of his suspicion that all is mire and pain. And, naturally, he is surprised to find that from the depths of the ruins, his own life being so sad, he can still admire the beauty of the world. His demoniacal, destructive strength breaks up into disordered images. He became more and more surrealist and spontaneous in the way he accentuated his impassioned nostalgia and denuded his dreams and imperious longings. JORGE ENRIQUE RAMPONI (1907), one of the notable lyricists—above all in *Infinite Stone* (*Piedra infinita*, 1948)—braided his harsh concepts and images with surrealist vapor. ERNESTO B. RODRÍGUEZ (1914), was also a surrealist. JUAN G. FERREYRA BASSO (1910) gathered landscapes, especially those of the countryside, into the mirror of his soul. The landscape is real; his love of the land is real; nevertheless, everything remains drawn as on a fantastic dream. Works: from *Clay Rose* (*Rosa de arcilla*) to *The Countryman Who Died in a River* (*Paisano muerto en un río*). CÉSAR ROSALES (1910), a lyricist who through his cantos gave shape to the love of country. RAUL GALÁN (1913), telluric, elegiac, traditionalist; the regionalist, CARLOS CARLINO (1910); FERNANDO GUIBERT (1912), ambitious enumerator of the turbulent life of a big city —*Poet at the Foot of Buenos Aires* (*Poeta al pie de Buenos Aires*, 1953). OSVALDO HORACIO DONDO (1910), who curbs his sentiments (his words) with a determination for exactitude. FRYDA SHULTZ DE MANTOVANI (1912), who contains herself and veils her sentiments with an attitude which is more intellectual than lyrical; an attitude which is to carry her to other genres. MIGUEL ÁNGEL GÓMEZ (1911). ARTURO CAMBOURS OCAMPO (1907).

B. MAINLY PROSE

Our aim in the early pages of this book was to make a compendium of all works done in verse. Naturally, we have had to mention the prose works written by the poets whom we have mentioned. From this point on, we propose to make a compendium of the production in prose, and naturally, we will have to give an account of the verses written by story writers, novelists, and playwrights. We are not writing a history of literary genres, but of the most interesting literary figures. Genres can be divided and subdivided, because they are abstract; not so with personalities, because they are concrete, complete, and alive. Many writers slip over from poetry to prose: we have already seen this in the preceding pages. But let us not become paralyzed by our own scruples. We now must study the prose written by those born between 1900 and 1915, and we will necessarily have to mention names that might well have figured among the poets of the early pages.

1. Novel and Short Story

Many novels appeared tranquilly, with a nineteenth-century bill of lading; and if they were modified at all, it was with such gentility that the modification passed unnoticed. French and Russian realism still retained their clientele. But more or less, around 1930, European novelistic changes began to have their effects on Hispanic-America. Because, it must be said, it is an Hispanic-American trait that our writers do not experiment with new forms, but apply, late and diffusely, European innovations. France continued to be the exporting center for the new art of novelizing. From Russia the writer who continued to take on most importance was Dostoevski, but now Germany and England enter the picture; the United States—Faulkner and Hemingway—will have its influence a little later on; Italy, after the second World War; Spain—Benjamín Jarnés and his contemporaries—did not produce anything of any influence. The French novel seemed to be a drunken compass, Proust, Gide, Mauriac, Duhamel, Romains, Thérive, Giraudoux, Cocteau, Green, Jaloux, Fournier, Martin du Gard, Montherlant offered an invitation to adventure, simultaneously indicating all points on a circular horizon: the evocation of a personal psychological time and the leaps of a tourist-cricket around the planet, the dreamy lyricism of solitary adolescents in their provincial towns, and the tumult of the masses in the large cities, the impetus of imagination and of politics, rightists and leftists, the Original Sin of the Catholics, the denunciation of evil by the socialists, preciosities, uglinesses, fragmentary novels, cyclic novels . . . Germany had been, from 1910 to 1920, the laboratory of the expressionist novel. Instead of impressionism, which had attempted to note down the blows of exterior reality upon the senses of the writer, now the creative energy of the writer was developed in such a way that nature was fought back under the blows of imagination, intelligence, will, emotions, and instincts. And the writer rebelled against the society of his time, he judged and condemned it and threw its traditions into crisis; not only the old ones, the religious traditions, but also the more recent ones such as nineteenth-century liberalism. Radicalism was not just political, nor did it dwell only on social disintegration; but besides it took root in speculations on the destiny of man, his guilt and his redemption, his tragic condition, his failures and his renewed charges on life. It was not a matter of describing outward appearances, but of causing what the writer "experienced" in the face of these appearances to explode into violent language. It was similar to naturalism in the brutal and fearless way with which it came into contact with the most foreboding things, but what stood out was the symbolization of nature, not its photograph.

In the thirties, Hispanic-America was reading the narratives of Franz Werfel, Arnold Zweig, Leonard Frank, Franz Kafka, and in the theater they were seeing the works of Franz Wedekind, Ernest Toller, Georg Kaiser. We have mentioned authors of the German language because it was from Germany that expressionism had departed; but we have already mentioned that this artistic upheaval was universal, and that it arrived in Hispanic-America from everywhere. In some circles, the English novel was replacing the French: D. H. Lawrence, with his instinctive challenge to civilization; Aldous Huxley, the superintellectual; the evanescent and monologous Virginia Woolf with her slow shifts in time; and above all, James Joyce, the most revolutionary in the technique of the novel, with his Dublin internalized into a stream of consciousness. Thus, the Hispanic-Americans of these years wrote novels at a time when the general consensus was that the novel had gone to pieces. Its architecture had broken down. Its planes collapsed. There was no order in its episodes. Its characters had no identity. At times there was nothing to tell. The preoccupation with time converted the space where the novel took place into pure metaphor; or it caused the chronology of events to be sacrificed so that different lives or different moments of the same life could be presented simultaneously. The point of view was mobile, unforeseeable, microscopic and telescopic, localized and ubiquitous. A linguistic empire was established, and not a single word, neither the basest nor the most cultured, nor the most neologistic, was foreign to it. In Hispanic-America no single author presented a complete picture of these technical experiments, but in many of them, various of these experiments are to be recognized: Yáñez, Labrador Ruiz, Marechal, Mallea, Uslar Pietri . . . But let us not anticipate. It is necessary to put the work of our narrators in order. How? We shall begin with those works which most disfigure exterior reality and pass to those which are a more faithful reflection of it.

Is it necessary to dwell on the fact that literary "idealism" and "realism" are no more than logical categories designed to give order to a disordered mass of books? Not only can a single author produce both verse and prose narrative, but the narrative itself can then be pigeonholed under various headings. Moreover, a single novel might be filed in different drawers. It does not make any difference. Therefore, do not expect a scientific classification. First we will tie together those authors who are most disdainful of ordinary reality. They cannot do without it since they are writing about the lives of men, but their

Spanish-American Literature: A History

dependence on reality will be minimal and reluctant. What they seek is
to retire to the farthest depth of their souls, shake loose from the net
of natural determinations, free themselves from the things that surround them. Thus, they make unreal the human, physical, social reality
upon which the novel is constructed and, on the other hand, objectify
pure thoughts. Later, we will put into one group those writers who
apply their vision of the world and life to a reality which, as imaginative as it might be, we will recognize as being exterior, public, common.
Prose becomes transparent for them in order that the reader might see
the articulations of an objective reality: characters, mental conflicts,
social problems, dialogs, descriptions of nature or of society, historical
processes, real or fictitious situations.

(a) *Narrators More Subjective than Objective* / We have already
characterized their style in the previous chapter and in the preceding
pages. These are the ones who give greater emphasis to their personal
vision than to the things seen. When it is not pure fantasy, it is an
intellectual game or an expressionist allegory. Realism is either magic
or is so stylized that things take on a lyric quality. The sense of time—
especially in evocations of childhood or adolescence—the characterization of complex psychologies, the description of strange impressions,
the anguishing analysis of existentialist experiences, the unquenchable
flow of bleeding images, and the mobility of the narrative point of view
impose a poetic rhythm on this literature. And, in fact, many of the
writers who make up this group are poets, and we might well have
studied them in the section in which we studied verse. Some of them,
although they are not presenting fantastic characters or situations, en-
fold reality in an atmosphere so dense with imagination that one sees
it from afar, as in a dream. In others, superstitions, myths, and folkloric legends are colored with strange, fictitious flowers. Another non-
realist expression, one that disfigures reality into fantastic symbols, was
that of the bestiaries. Science fiction stories and novels and battles of
wits between murderers and detectives balance on the trampolin of
reality ready to leap into the air and cut curlicues. There were narratives in which the imagination journeyed to other times, to other places,
and to other animal species. All of reality, finally, evaporates into poetic
metaphors.

(1) *Mexico* / We have already referred to Torres Bodet and other poets of the
Contemporáneos group who wrote poetic narratives. We add here *A Novel Like
a Cloud* (*Novela como nube*, 1928) of GILBERTO OWEN (1905–1952) and the
dreamy *Storm Over Nicomaco* (*Cerrazón sobre Nicomaco*, 1946) by EFRÉN HER-

NÁNDEZ (1903–1958). FRANCISCO TARIO (1911) is a story teller of the grotesque, of madness, of painful obsessions, novelist of a rich and terrible imagination, huntsman of aphorisms: from *Down Here* (*Aquí abajo,* 1943) to *The Door in the Wall* (*La puerta en el muro,* 1946).

We would like to pause on AGUSTÍN YÁÑEZ (1904), who has maintained a high level as a narrator. His lyric, poetic tendency is comfortable with autobiographic evocations, and even in his most objective works one is conscious of the intervention of the author in the lives that he is creating. In *Passion and Convalescence* (*Pasión y convalecencia,* the text is dated 1938) nothing moves, unless it be the amplifications—sometimes rhetorical—that the author gives to each of his lyric fragments: a feverish invalid; his convalescence; his visit to the family dwelling; vacillation between the country and the city and the final decision to return to the city. Delirious images, evocations of childhood. A poematic novel in which subjective reactions rather than objective actions are recounted. Unfortunately, Yáñez has so many "pretentious phrases" that he cannot make them all happy. His most ambitious novel is *At the Water's Edge* (*Al filo del agua,* 1947). The title is a popular expression which, in its figurative sense, alludes to an impending event: in this novel, it is the Mexican Revolution of 1910 which is the impending event. Yáñez is describing the collective lethargy of a little southern town whose every crevice is filled with religiosity. It is a negative religiosity, dark, morbid, resentful, ascetic, which undermines life, until life can hold out no longer and topples, crushing all, even Father Dionisio. It is he who ends the novel sadly, as he celebrates his final mass with a heart broken by the awareness of his failure and of the failure of all he represents. The plot—if one can speak of it as such—is unknit. Thousands of loose ends. Each character is a loose end dancing grotesquely in the burning wind of superstition. None of them attains the fullness of a vital creation, but occasionally their destinies join—always in order to suffer—and thus they seem to be virtualities of possible novels, whose most oft-repeated themes would be those of eroticism, neurosis, and violence. Yáñez does not propose a thesis. He limits himself to depicting an atmosphere. At most, in this huge impressionist canvas, an occasional brush stroke seems to smile ironically. The structure of *At the Water's Edge,* deliberately broken into parallel planes, intersecting planes, juxtaposed planes, or dispersed entirely, gives a notable fluidity to the action. At bottom, it is not the stream of reality, but the stream of consciousness that Yáñez seeks to depict. To this end he uses, and well, the techniques of the interior dialog, direct and indirect, of the soliloquy, of the dialog within a tormented mind, of symbols, allegories, and even suggestive typographical changes. The weightiness of the novel is due to its excessive verbosity; because Yáñez, instead of impersonalizing himself in order to leave bare the multiple perspectives of the flock of the Mexican archbishopric and—inviting the reader to put himself into the plot and imagine for himself—he mixes himself into the batter of the rich, slow prose, and tries to say everything. From *At the Water's Edge* Yáñez chose a situation—Gabriel vacillating between two women, Victoria and María—and he prolongs it into *The Creation* (*La Creación,* 1959). Twenty years have gone by: Gabriel, who under the protection of these two women has studied music in Europe, now returns home with the sole purpose of rooting himself in Mexican reality and expressing himself artistically. The novel proceeds to follow his steps from 1920 to 1935. Gabriel's fountain of inspiration seems to be the "feminine essence." After succeeding with his "erotic symphony" (inspired by Diotima of Plato's *Symposium*) Gabriel commences to work on a symphonic poem in which his numerous experiences with all types of women will be molded into the image of Helen of Troy. In the course of the novel we have a parade of well-known politicians, intellectuals, artists, and writers; and we also have portraits of Mexican cultural life, from Vasconcelos onward, with the ideals of each group. The novel is left flooded and devastated by the incessant downpour of names which are dropped from a too-easy history of culture. In spite of the fact that the theme is the creative force of art, Yáñez here fails as a creator. Gabriel's character is not convincing and the story-line is frequently ruptured by flashbacks and interior monologs. Consequently, the novel is more artificial than artistic. In the same cycle is *Prodigal Earth* (*Tierra Pródiga,* 1960).

(2) *Central America / Guatemala:* Poet and novelist is MIGUEL ÁNGEL ASTURIAS (1899). He published his own anthology, *Poetry: Pulse of the Skylark* (*Poesía. Sien de alondra,* 1949). In it can be seen his esthetic changes: bucolic poetry of village life, fleeting emotion, and the return to the vernacular. Other books of poems followed, such as *Poetic Exercises in the Sonnet Form on Themes from Horace* (*Ejercicios poéticos en forma de soneto sobre temas de Horacio,* 1951). He was a poet of minor tone, visual, attentive to the relationships between things, to the essence of the mineral and the vegetable, with a gift for shadings. In *Legends of Guatemala* (*Leyendas de Guatemala,* 1930) he elaborated the magic vision of the Mayas with his own images. They belong to the first stage of his career, when, in Paris, under the direction of Georges Raynaud—translator of *Popol-Vuh*—he specialized in

anthropological studies of the Mayan civilization. He also has written theater: *Soluna* (1957). But his novels have brought him more fame. *Mr. President* (*El señor presidente*, 1947) describes the diseased—morally diseased—life of an Hispanic-Américan country. He does not mention it, and the reader has no right to assume that it is a Guatemalan document, because all of our America suffers from the same symptoms. What is certain is that Asturias, on writing it, recalled his fears as a child, living under the dictatorship of Estrada Cabrera (from 1898–1920). Nevertheless, it is not the biography of a dictator, but the caricature of all dictators. The sad thing is that the novel is dirtied by the purulences which he describes. This reality of homosexuals, beggars, the venereal- and malaria-ridden, idiots, drunkards, misers, the louse-ridden, the degenerate mulattoes and other human vermin who cling to the tatters of a society undone by hate, intrigue, despotism, prostitution, and servility, overflows the artistic borders of the novel: it moves us in a practical sense without moving us with the same artistic force. It is an extremely bitter novel, not only because the author has written it in bitterness, but also because the reader reads it embittered by the frightful picture of misery which it paints. It is, nevertheless, not a realist novel, but "esperpentic," to use a term which would apply also to *Tirano Banderas* of Valle Inclán. Asturias, although he contorts things in the same warped mirrors that Valle Inclán used, lacks the latter's underlying humor. The novel is completely tense, with the political philosophy of the author cocked, aimed, and ready to fire. Expressionist exacerbation is noted more than the scientific impassiveness of the naturalists. At times, there are deliberately ugly recourses. At other times, the poet Asturias bejewels his sordid material with verbal and fantastic luxuries. And thus, thanks to the creative power of his tremendous imagination—because here, imagination is more tremendous than life—*Mr. President* becomes an artistic novel. Asturias, like Quevedo, does not disdain to use any facet of language. In his descriptions he assaults with words, accumulating them, molding them, playing with them in *jitanjáforas*, neologisms, alliterations, refrains. He exploits metaphors, rich in impressions and ideas. Although the omniscient author intervenes in the development of the plot, he frequently installs himself inside his personages and reveals to us the stream of consciousness through interior dialogs. *Men of Corn* (*Hombres de maíz*, 1949) are stories in which legendary and real elements are given structure, their counterpoint at times being a bit out of tune, because the author did not clarify his artistic intent in his own mind: one of his aims seems to be to show the conflict between the Indians who planted corn only as a food, and the Creoles who plant it commercially, impoverishing the soil through their greed. In the trilogy of his last novels there is a predominance of the sociological over the purely novelistic: *Strong Wind* (*Viento fuerte,* 1950), *Green Pope* (*Papa verde,* 1954), and *The Eyes of the Interred* (*Los ojos de los enterrados,* 1960). He denounces United States imperialism, inspires protests, and puts a partisan stamp on his political thought. He frees himself from the traditional novelistic technique, but the weight of a regional material, not very well worked out, ends by weakening his underpinnings. And so, his novels are wrapped in a soft air of poetry, shot through with expressionism and surrealism. *Week-end in Guatemala* (*Week-end en Guatemala,* 1956) are stories of a frankly political intent. *The Little Jeweled Boy* (*El Alhajadito,* 1961), a prose work more poetic than narrative, reconstructs the memories of a childhood paradise. Asturias is doubtless one of our major novelists, for the vigor of his imagination, the audacity with which he complicates the interior structure of his tale, and the violent or tender lyricism with which he evokes the lands of America.

El Salvador: In the *Stories of Mud* (*Cuentos de barro*) by SALARRUÉ (1899)—his real name is Salvador Salazar Arrué—there are suffering, sad superstitious Indians and exploited workers, but the unities of action are so well etched that they leave sociology and politics aside. Salarrué looks at reality without being a realist; he has something of the somnambulist who walks with his eyes open. His style is impressionistic, imaginative. Each "tiny tale"—as the author calls them—groups the Indians around a propitious situation, so that, on speaking, their sparse, dialectical words insinuate all that is going on inside.

Costa Rica: The major novelist of this generation here was JOSÉ MARÍN CAÑAS (1904). He wrote four novels. The first, *Steel Tears* (*Lágrimas de acero,* 1929), has a Spanish background. The second was *You, the Impossible: Memoirs of a Sad Man* (*Tú, la imposible: Memorias de un hombre triste,* 1931), written during those years when novels against novels were being written. The novelist proved to his colleagues that he knew how to write, that he had imagination and sensitivity. He wrote novels without saying anything; or if they said anything, they said it in such an intricate, jerky manner that the ordinary reader became disoriented. The novelist of these years, moreover, wanted to prove that he was superior even to literature itself: from this stems the humoristic tone, the habit of taking everything lightly in metaphors that blow up in the middle of the story. The author-protagonist, Juan Arocena, gives the esthetic key of this literature when he speaks of himself as a "mannered writer, seeker of striking big words"; "I narrate with a furious emotion, in which images seem to be like shots." The syntax of this prose is normal, but the style is very metaphoric, and the composition being on various levels gave the novel of those years a new look. There are several points of view: that of Marín Cañas, of Juan Arocena, and of the heroine, Chidy. These *Memoirs,* then, are disarticulated. Putting them back together, a romantic story of love appears, an impossible love between a poor, married writer and a girl of eighteen years, rich and innocent. The action takes place in Spain, even though the protagonists are Hispanic-Americans. The lyricism at times crystallizes into poems in prose; more frequently, it laughs at itself with those images that had pleased the ultraists. The gift for words is greater than the novelistic gift. More serious was his novel, or rather chronicle, *Green Hell* (*Infierno verde*, 1935). It pretends to have been written by a Paraguayan soldier in the Chaco War. A war that was completely South American, but Marín Cañas, on describing it, joins the cycle of anti-war literature that arose after the war from 1914 to 1918. That is, Marín Cañas applied the technique and spirit of European literature to a South American war. Also its style. Some of these novels were written with an expressionist style. On the side of ultraism in poetry and expressionism in prose, this metaphoric restlessness came in Marín Cañas. There are, in Marín Cañas, clichés and a certain stylistic monotony, but withal, it is evident that he sallies forth to the encounter of reality as it impresses him, and he fells it beneath the weight of his enterprising personality. One of his enterprises is politics: he does not take sides in favor of either Paraguay or Bolivia, but he shows both nations as victims of international capitalism, of patriotic myths, and of an irresponsible citizenry. Esthetics and politics do not contradict one another in a style that might be called expressionist, because both depart, without contradicting each other, from the creative energy of the author. His last novel was *Pedro Arnáez* (1942), with Central American landscapes, through which the hopeless and complex Pedro wanders and suffers. His life is seen—on the three occasions on which Death stalks him—through the doctor-narrator. He also wrote stories and various theatrical pieces. MAX JIMÉNEZ (1900–1947) has given us a curious Utopia: *The Flea Trainer* (*El domador de pulgas*, 1936). He has concocted a society of fleas redeemed by the blood of the trainer, the Christ of fleas. Poor trainer! He dies bloodless and repentant. He has sacrificed himself uselessly: the freed fleas copy the bad passions of human beings. Unfortunately, these acrobatics built on nonsense failed, because the author based his stunt on a hamstrung prose. Max Jiménez lived in Paris and traveled all over the world. He was one of the postwar subversives in the plastic arts and in fiction. His poems were less revolutionary. His last book, *El jaul* (1937), is a novelistic series of peasant tales, somewhat naturalist in its barbarous personages, in the crudity of their voices, and in the exaggeration of its terrible landscapes. Not realists, or at least of a mild realism, were ARTURO CASTRO ESQUIVEL (1904) and EMMANUEL THOMPSON (1908).

Panama: It was the globe-trotting ROGELIO SINÁN (1904) who headed vanguardism. He began his campaign in favor of the new poetry with *Wave* (*Onda*, 1929) which was followed by *Fire* (*Incendio*, 1944) and *Holy Week in the Fog* (*Semana santa en la niebla*, 1949). Nevertheless, he stood out more for his narratives: *Full Moon* (*Plenilunio*, 1947), *The Red Beret and Five Stories* (*La boina roja y cinco cuentos*, 1954), and *The Birds of Sleep* (*Los pájaros del sueño*, 1958). Introspective, preoccupied with the problem of personality, a delver into the subconscious, ironic in his treatment of sexual themes (read, for example, his story "All a Conflict of Blood"), Sinán was an experimenter. Another Panamanian of the estheticist group was MANUEL FERRER VALDÉS (1914).

(3) *Antilles / Cuba:* There was a group of narrators who took their themes from the lives of the Negroes and the mulattoes. Those who faced these themes as a part of the complex of social problems we will see later, among the realists. We

are only concerned here with the more imaginative writers, those who interested themselves in Afro-Cuban legends and superstitions, or, at least, those who wrote with a non-realist attitude. Among them are RÓMULO LACHATAÑERÉ (1910–1952), RAMÓN GUIRAO (1908–1949), whom we saw among the poets, and LYDIA CABRERA (1900), who collected in *Negro Stories of Cuba* (*Cuentos negros de Cuba,* 1940), and *Why* (*Por qué,* 1948) a rich store of ethnographic material, revealing the magic conception of the world which the African slaves brought to the lands of America.

Another narrator who touched on the Negro theme in his early works but who, when on opening out onto a more ample reality, became the major novelist of his generation was ALEJO CARPENTIER (1904). He traveled a great deal, not only geographically (Europe, above all), but through culture (music, folklore, literature) and, within letters, through verse and prose. He narrates, generally, the things of his country—as in *Ecué-Yamba-O* (1931), "an Afro-Cuban history"—but he does so experimenting with the style and structure of the novel. *The Kingdom of This World* (*El reino de este mundo,* 1949) presents the Antillian landscape with "esperpentic" and surrealist techniques. In the novel *The Lost Steps* (*Los pasos perdidos,* 1953), there are adventures—a journey from civilization to a primitive corner of the equatorial jungle which turns out to be more of a trip into the depths of prehistoric American time—adventures that just as soon leave us in the dark as illuminate with lightning flashes of intelligence. *The War of Time* (*Guerra del tiempo,* 1958)—the title alludes to the words of Lope de Vega, that man "is a soldier in the war of time"—collects three stories and a novel, all, in fact, penetrated by the obsession of time, be it historical or personal, put there as the theme itself or as a narrative form. The three stories—"The Road to Santiago," "Journey to the Seed" and "Similar to Night"—have an air of being a magic game: the most far-fetched one is the second, in which is described how a life travels back over the course of time in "a journey to the seed" (an old man becomes a child, re-enters the womb, and with a world on his shoulders disappears into the world beyond). The novel is *The Pursuit* (*El acoso*). If we were to remake it into a continuous story-line we would have a novel of violence, betrayal, and vengeance: in the years of the downfall of the dictatorship of Machado and of the political chaos that followed it, a young boy from the provinces goes to study at the University of Havana, he joins a subversive, terrorist organization, informs on his companions, flees, and is hunted down and killed in a concert hall where he has been listening to the Eroica Symphony of Beethoven. But his material is divided into three parts. The first and the third take place within one hour: the action begins slightly before and ends slightly after the performance of the Eroica Symphony. There are two points of view which shape the narrative material: that of the ticket seller and that of the hunted man. They are two parallel lives, and certain common experiences draw them together. The second part takes place within a period of two weeks, but, thanks to the interior monologs of the hunted man, we are made aware of the preceding events and of the present situation of the novel. *The Pursuit* is a puzzle with its pieces carefully mixed: the reader apprehends, little by little, in each fragment, the total design. The concordance between the interior monologs, direct and indirect, and the objects, characters, and episodes of the central action is admirably thought out. Carpentier does not explain, but he leaves all the clues so that the reader can identify the characters, recompose the chronology, reorder the logical sequences, and find the exit from the labyrinth. In spite of the fact that the material, because it is made up of mental processes, appears to pulverize or evaporate, Carpentier, subtly, organizes it into an ironic spectacle, to which the Catholic religion, the music of Beethoven, and the Electra of Sophocles all lend symbols and allegories. The novel is not subjective. Rather than analyzing the psychology of his characters, the author limits himself to describing deeds just as they occur, random, partial, harsh: let the reader find their meaning. In this, Carpentier is doing in our literature something resembling that which was being done in Europe, after 1950, with the so-called objectivist novel.

ENRIQUE LABRADOR RUIZ (1902) has published "gasiform" novels—*Labyrinth* (*Laberinto*, 1933), *Cresival* (1936), *Anteo* (1940); little, misty novels—*Chimeric Flesh* (*Carne de quimera*, 1947); and a "fabulation"—*Trailer of Dreams* (*Trailer de sueños*, 1949); later, he changed his theme and his manner and wrote *Hungry Blood* (*La sangre hambrienta*, 1950) and *The Rooster in the Mirror* (*El gallo en el espejo*, 1953), narrations in which he no longer evades reality, nor does he allow himself to be dragged along by it. LINO NOVÁS CALVO (1905) does not seem to add imaginative festoons to reality; on the contrary, it could be said that he reduces it to elementary outlines. But he could not be called a realist because the slow displacement of his figures, the suggestive power of gestures, words, and even silences, the decomposition of the plot into planes, startles the reader and obliges him to intervene imaginatively in what he is reading. He has also written *The Ninth Moon and Other Stories* (*La luna nona y otros cuentos*, 1942), *I Do Not Know Who I Am* (*No sé quien soy*, 1945), *Cape Canas* (*Cayo Canas*, 1946), *In the Backyard* (*En los traspatios*, 1946). "I have Faulkner in my blood," he has said. He is a witness buried in the inconsistencies of life and society.

The short story enjoyed a period of exceptional popularity during these years, and one of the directions it took was the fantastic, whether free or lyrical or even of the existentialist type. We will have to repeat here names that we saw in the paragraph on poetry. FÉLIX PITA RODRÍGUEZ (1909), "esperpentic," magic, poematic, but strong in his blows at the drama of man in our time. José LEZAMA LIMA (1912), hermetic, geometric—that is, a darkness with interior guide lines— that makes the power of his poetry play in the story. DULCE MARÍA LOYNAZ (1903) went from verse to the novel without diminishing her poetic spirit. After *Verses* (*Versos*, 1938) and *Water Games* (*Juegos de agua*, 1947)—poetry in which an insinuating interior music wrapped the words and impressions received from reality in mystery—she wrote a "lyric novel," *Garden* (*Jardín*, 1951). It is the history of Bárbara, a hypersensitive, overimaginative woman, obsessed by the garden which has her imprisoned. We see her first, shortly after her twentieth birthday, looking over some old photographs. Later we see her reading some old love letters of an adolescent boy written to her great-great aunt, whose name was also Bárbara. Identifying herself in this way, with a romantic past, she awakens to love. Finally, we see her in love with a playboy yachtsman. She runs away with him, sees the world, has children; and years later, on returning to the house where she was born, alone, the vengeful garden destroys her during a phantasmagoric dawn. The structure of the novel is defective, but the style is startling because of its intimate and delicate images.

Of the novels of CARLOS ENRÍQUEZ (1907–1957), we shall concern ourselves only with *The Fair of Guaicanama* (*La Feria de Guaicanama*). Throughout it is a tale of passion: the impulsive Juan Lope swoops away Palmenia and, with her submissive in his arms, he violently challenges social conventions. Enríquez slowly discloses an obscure message: anarchism, vitalism, and irrationalism. This inter- vention of the author damages the novelesque plot. The exhaltation of sexual impulses—in which we discern the influence of D. H. Lawrence—the belief in super- natural forces and extrasensory perceptions, the extremely romantic manner in which he presents his hero—hero of the barbaric against the civilized—the lack of intel- lectual discipline revealed in the characters' discussions, a style overloaded with images and hyperboles, and a careless composition are all the more lamentable when we know the author to have more personality and expect from him a better expression of his fantasy.

Dominican Republic: The best storyteller in the artistic direction was TOMÁS HERNÁNDEZ FRANCO (1904), whom we have already seen among the poets.

(4) *Venezuela* / The first information on cubism, ultraism, and sur- realism arrived in Venezuela very late, compared to the other countries. When it arrived, a group of story writers and novelists, headed by Uslar Pietri, not being able to deny reality nor wishing to copy it, hit upon the art of noting down the poetic quality which is enmeshed in all things. ARTURO USLAR PIETRI (1905) set the example with a prose rich in sensual impressions, in lyric metaphors, in symbols which suggest a new interpretation of Hispanic-American reality. His first narratives were in 1928: *Barrabás and Other Tales* (*Barrabás y otros relatos*). In the two books that followed, an evolution from the cult of the very imaginative phrase toward an art more attentive to description and vernacular things can be noted: *Net* (*Red*, 1936), *Thirty Men and Their Shadows* (*Treinta hombres y sus sombras*, 1949). He has written, in

addition, an excellent historical novel on the war of independence in Venezuela: *The Red Lances* (*Las lanzas coloradas*, 1931). Historical novel? Bolívar does not appear. Nevertheless, the figure of Bolívar frames the novel. In the first pages, Presentación Campos, the major-domo of El Altar, gets up, bothered by the voice of a slave who is telling an adventure of Bolívar; in the last pages, Presentación Campos falls dead without having been able to appear at the window in order to see the triumphal entry of Bolívar. But within this elemental frame-work the novel unfolds in barbarity and chaos. The characters live in psychological plenitude: the belligerent, animal, proud will of Presentación Campos; the sweet and dreamy Inés; the lethargic Fernando; the curiosity for life and the desire to live it completely of the English-man, David . . . In addition, there are magnificent figures, like that of Boves, fighters and women. But this humanity, so well outlined in his personal bas-reliefs, is not forged in the manner of the traditional novel. Pietri passes by the precipices opened by Romantic literature; but he never falls over the edge. On the contrary. His creatures are lost amidst the furious masses of the war. Destinies do not cross, but separate. Inés wanders over the plains, gone mad, disfigured by the fire, search-ing for Campos in order to avenge herself: but she will not find him. Fernando will not see his sister, will not fight for the Republic in which he believes; he will not fall with his friends, neither will he avenge himself on Campos. Pietri gives us the movements of crowds, not of heroes. The heroism of Boves, of Díaz, of Campos is—as in the epics —a reddish light scarcely visible in the gleam of the lances, stained crimson with blood that covers the plains like an outrageous death. Incarnations of devastation. This perspective which deliberately con-fuses everything into disorderly and unattached blotches is that of impressionism. Pietri has put the delicacies of impressionist art at the service of a barbarous theme. The metaphors—audacious, pictorial, fresh—save the reality which is evoked from the logical interventions of the novelist. Pietri does not construct a novel along political or moral principles. He is not with Boves nor with Bolívar. The novel thus gains in esthetic virtues. *The Road to El Dorado* (*El camino de El Dorado*, 1948), more than an historical novel, is the novelized biography of the diabolic conquistador, Lope de Aguirre; and it is even poetized geography.

Uslar Pietri was followed by José Salazar Domínguez (1902), Nelson Himiob (1908), Arturo Briceño (1908), and Carlos Eduardo Frías (1906). These narrators accept the reality in which they live, but upon this foundation they raise a high and well-constructed literature, full of life and with windows ventilated by a breeze of poetry. The same can be said of those who come later. JULIÁN PADRÓN (1910–1954) wrote some stories that slid off toward realism: *Summer Fires* (*Candelas de verano*), *Peasant Clamor* (*Clamor campesino*), *This Desolate World* (*Este mundo desolado*). But his best works were those in which he gave a poetic tone to his memories of childhood and adolescence: *La Guaricha* (1934), *Dawn* (*Madrugada*, 1939), *Nocturnal Spring* (*Primavera nocturna*, 1950). His perception of the landscape—a little town, a river, a road, a cornfield, the mountains, trees and clouds—is so acute that, at times, responding to it, Padrón forgets the action of the novel and the plot suffers. But his suggestive power, the minuteness of detail, and his introspection save the novel even in those moments when its unity breaks down. There is an autobiographic background to his narrations, especially in *Nocturnal Spring*, a novel of the city which, because of its poetic tension and its wealth of symbols, opened new paths in the field of the novel in his country. GUILLERMO MENESES (1911) captured sympathetically the lives of the Negroes, mulattoes, and zambos in his three novels, *The Sloop Isabel Arrived This Afternoon* (*La balandra Isabel llegó esta tarde*, 1934), *Song of the Negroes* (*Canción de negros*, 1934) and *Champions* (*Campeones*, 1939). His portraits of humble men, the way he pictures Venezuelan scenes—popular scenes with natural backgrounds—indicate a firm sense of reality, but we place him among our artists because of the singular vivacity with which he showed the inner, psychological side of his characters. The first-mentioned work, *The Sloop Isabel Arrived This Afternoon*, was a small masterpiece. *Three Venezuelan Stories* (*Tres cuentos venezolanos*) are close to being psychological studies: through a youth of fifteen years ("Adolescence"), a Negro ("Drunkenness"), and an Indian ("Moon") Meneses presents the problem of the need for women and its final satisfaction. Other works: *The Mestizo José Vargas* (*El mestizo José Vargas*), *The False Notebook of Narciso Espejo* (*El falso cuaderno de Narciso Espejo*). JOSÉ FABBIANI RUIZ (1911) is something of a potter in the way he creates his stories in *Salt Water* (*Agua salada*, 1939) and his novels *Deep Valley* (*Valle hondo*, 1934) and *The Swell of the Sea* (*Mar de leva*, 1941). He forms his figures as from clay, squeezing, economizing, smoothing here and there, bringing out the necessary relief. *The Painful Childhood of Perucho González* (*La dolida infancia de Perucho González*, 1946)—told by himself—is a clouded novel. Wisps of novel, like scattered clouds. At times clouds that more or less envelop lyrically scenes from the life of a poor, unfortunate, adventurous, and imaginative child. At times, the clouds are gray and form when the style evaporates, impeding our view of the story. *On the Shores of Sleep* (*A orillas del sueño*)—a novel which won the National Prize for Literature in the biennium 1958–59—presents the lives of adults, children, and adolescents; the latter being the protagonists, whom we see in all their solitude, misunderstood and unprotected. ANTONIO PALACIOS (1908) with her book *Ana Isabel, a Decent Girl* (*Ana Isabel, una niña decente*, 1949) puts herself in line with *Iphigenia*, by Teresa de la Parra.

(5) *Colombia* / EDUARDO ZALAMEA BORDA (1907), in his powerful and original novel *Four Years On Board Myself* (*Cuatro años a bordo de mí mismo*, 1934), tells in the form of a diary of his crossing over and stay at the semiabandoned salt mines of La Guajira. The narrator is a vital and jubilant spectator of himself and of the world, an analyst of sensations: "I like to look slowly at things, little by

little, as though I were savoring noises, colors and perfumes, with all the intensity of my senses." Life is lived intensely—one's sexual life is part of this intensity—but a free and blithe imagination converts these vital experiences into a lyric expression. Zalamea Borda does in prose what the "stoneandskyists" were doing in verse: a new poetry of impressions, symbols, and fabulous figures. ANTONIO CARDONA JARAMILLO (1914) is a story writer saturated with the landscape of his district in Caldas: *Mountain Range (Cordillera*, 1945). He penetrates into the spirit of the people and makes them speak in a natural dialog. His descriptive prose is agile, complex, artistic, and imaginative. He puts a poetic language at the service of rude themes, and he is at times violent in his vanguardist imagery.

(6) *Ecuador* / PABLO PALACIO (1906–1946), in the stories of *A Man Kicked to Death (Un hombre muerto a puntapiés*, 1927), penetrated into human life with irony and a biting humor. He was a strange person, and his literature, strangely artistic. He created a dehumanized, anti-sentimental humor, which accepted without question the "abnormalities" of his characters: "This business of being a cannibal is just the same as smoking, or being a pederast, or an erudite"; ". . . being crazy, just like being a political office-holder, a schoolteacher, or a parish priest." He was a spontaneous monologist. Palacio was losing his mind, but before he went completely insane, he was able to publish the novels, *Débora* (1929), of a sentimental tone, and *The Life of the Hanged Man (Vida del ahorcado*, 1932), exacerbated, anguished. Also a narrator of artistic prose was ALFONSO CUESTA Y CUESTA (1912), notable for his creation of juvenile characters. Stories: *The Arrival of All the Trains in the World (Llegada de todos los trenes del mundo).*

(7) *Peru* / Although in narrative prose there were poetic whitecaps, in general, the most important writers will be seen when we study realism. Perhaps we should mention MARÍA ROSA MACEDO (1912) here because of the expressionism of a few of the pages in *Cane Huts (Ranchos de caña)* and *Cane Stubble (Rastrojo).*

(8) *Bolivia* / FERNANDO DÍEZ DE MEDINA (1908) published *The Masked One and Other Inventions (La enmascarada y otras invenciones*, 1955), fantastic stories without much originality, with a prose more inflated than poetic; but in his best moments, the author frees himself from reality, either in the form of Aimará Indian traditions or by leaping off into absurd spheres using procedures from poetry and the movies.

(9) *Chile* / In this country, where the story and the novel have been generally in the realist vein and descriptive of the surroundings, one can note during these years a deflection toward obscure, irrational, and subconscious themes. The highest—which is the same as saying the most poetic—expression of this literary mode is MARÍA LUISA BOMBAL (1910), author of *The Last Fog (La última niebla*, 1934) and *The Shrouded Woman (La amortajada*, 1941), where the human and the superhuman appear in a magic, poetic zone, by dint of vision rather than through a tricky style. The reader sees just what the characters of the novel see. Subjectivity. Things appear in a cloud of impressions. In the first of the mentioned novels, a woman loves in a zone between reality and dream. In the second, a dead woman sees, feels, and evokes the memories of her loves and her family life with a definitive certainty and total understanding which is now useless. Other women,

although with not so much intensity, rejected the themes of Creolism and the mechanical reproduction of things. MATILDE PUIG, given to psychopathological revelations, aberrations, surrealism, and Kafkaisms. CHELA REYES (1904), also a poetess: MARCELA PAZ (1904), who in *Papelucho* probed child psychology with delicacy; MAGDALENA PETIT (1900), imaginative in her manner of handling biography and history (cf. *The Pincheiras Family—Los Pincheiras*, 1939) and in her invention of purely novelistic situations (*Caleucha*, 1946; *A Man in the Universe—Un hombre en el universo*, 1951). MARÍA FLORA YÁÑEZ (1898)—who signed her first novels with the pseudonym "Mari Yan"—tended to spiritualize and even to make myths of certain aspects of reality. MARÍA CAROLINA GEEL (1913) was daring in her psychological penetrations, as in *The Sleeping World of Yenia* (*El mundo dormido de Yenia*, 1946) and *The Adolescent Perces Was Dreaming and Loving* (*Soñaba y amaba el adolescente Perces*, 1949). Some writers escaped from reality on the side of the sea, adventure, dreams, science fiction, historical evocations, and stories for children. SALVADOR REYES (1899), for example, in *The Night Crews* (*Los tripulantes de la noche*), tells an adventure of love and contraband in a lyric tone; the poetic images are not very disturbing to the plot because the action is also poetically conceived. Although JUAN MARÍN (1900) is the author, among many other books, of a description of the painful existence on the *53rd Parallel, South* (*Paralelo 53° Sur*), he also has a fantastic dimension, as can be seen in his *Stories of Wind and Water* (*Cuentos de viento y agua*). HERNÁN DEL SOLAR (1901) with his stories for children; BENJAMÍN SUBERCASEAUX (1902), the one who wrote the slightly historical, slightly philosophical novel *Jemmy Button;* and LUIS ENRIQUE DÉLANO (1907), with *Port of Fire* (*Puerto de fuego*), complete this group of imaginative writers.

(10) *Paraguay* / We prefer to put José S. Villarejo with the realist group.

(11) *Uruguay* / FELISBERTO HERNÁNDEZ (1902) was, in *No One Was Lighting the Lamps* (*Nadie encendía las lámparas*), an excellent storyteller. He presents an unhinged reality, with areas of mystery ("The Balcony," "The Usher"), or he reduces it to the absurd ("Except Julia," "Hydrangeas"). On occasion, surrealist images are freed through the analysis of sensation. GISELDA ZANI (1909), in her short stories *Through Subtle Bonds* (*Por vínculos sutiles*, 1958), criticizes high-class society by giving a free hand to her fancy.

One of the most vigorous writers of later years figures just as strongly in Uruguayan literature as in Argentinian literature: JUAN CARLOS ONETTI (1909). He novelized enclosed lives: the confinement of the city (Montevideo, Buenos Aires), of enclosed spaces (rooms, cabarets, offices); if life comes out into the open air, the action remains enclosed by the night; circumstances enclose the characters with their stains of filth . . . These characters are solitary failures. They have been thrown out upon a hostile world, which from waste to waste precipitates itself toward death. There is nothing remaining for them but to encounter reality, torture themselves, or try to escape inwardly. The more they escape into the memories of a lost childhood, in their dreams, the deeper they are thrust into solitude. There is an air of pessimism, fatalism, demoralization. Ideals are moth-eaten; friendship is a misunderstanding; love is converted into sex. The similarity between some of Onetti's novels with others of Sartre has been noted. But he set out on the road to existentialism through his reading of Celine and the North American novelists, Dos Passos and, above all, Faulkner. The raw materials of his first novels open out into introspective meanderings in his later ones. In *Short Life* (*La vida breve*) even fantastic meanderings are opened. They are novels made up of fragments: each fragment, with an interior eye. Thus, the novelistic vision is multiple, simultaneous, or contradictory in various narrative stages and in various temporal stages. *The Well* (*El pozo*), *No Man's Land* (*Tierra de nadie*), *For Tonight* (*Para esta noche*), *Short Life*, *A Dream Realized and Other Stories* (*Un sueño realizado y otros cuentos*), *Good-byes* (*Los adioses*) all show Onetti as being a novelist of the senselessness of city life. *Short Life* (1950) seems to be written in a turbid, pasty prose: a paste of language with globs, mentally translated from foreign languages. This unctuousness and heaviness of its sentences contribute to the reader's sensation of being inside a nightmare. The novel *Short Life* is that nightmare, and the reader, lost among the crevices and rubbish, suddenly feels it incumbent upon himself to write the novel which Onetti did not want to write. As in all nightmares, this effort to give order to the disordered fails time and time again. The narrator—Brausen—lives several lives, and the story weaves them together. Brausen becomes Arce in order to possess another woman. Brausen fabricates a character Díaz Grey. A heavy atmosphere of sexuality, sadism, prostitution, perversion, crime, cancer, morphine addiction, madness, and ugliness sordidly disfigures things and men. These men, always seeking to put themselves into a horizontal position, in bed, seem to be reptiles. Nevertheless, there are lyric moments, in part because Onetti—using the literary procedures of the interior dialog and showing reality from different perspectives and spatial and temporal planes—is able to lay surprising intimacies bare. Peevishly written in a very Río de la Plata vernacular (as though he were saying to the reader: "If you understand me, fine; if not, tough: I'm not going to knock myself out for you.") his *Short Life* is a curious case of ill-used talent and theme. His creative imagination—capable of originality—is weakened through neglect and through the lack of discipline. Now it appears that his best novel is *The Shipyard* (*El astillero*, 1961). Another important novelist: ALFREDO DANTE GRAVINA (1913).

(*12*) *Argentina* / It has already been seen in the preceding chapters (and it will continue to be seen in the chapters to come) that non-realist prose was cultivated in this country with more vigor than in any other Hispanic-American country.

JORGE LUIS BORGES (Argentina, 1899). As we explained before, Borges is one of the major writers of our time and, if we place him here and not among the poets or essayists, it is precisely because his stories, for the manner in which they combine the essences of his lyricism and his intelligence, give us the key to his entire work. Borges had lived in Switzerland (also in Spain) during the war years: he returned to Buenos Aires in 1921. He contributed to the mischief of *Prisma, Proa,* and *Martín Fierro.* But during his stay in Geneva, he had become acquainted with German Expressionism, which struck him as being much more serious and renovating than the frivolous esthetics of the avant-garde which were being voiced and practiced in the Hispanic world. His literary knowledge was amazing, his lucidity, even more so. Over the years this knowledge and this lucidity have become so enriched that, more than being amazed, we are troubled at the spectacle of a new kind of madness. He began with two rites: the funeral of "Ruben Darianism" and the baptism of "ultraism." Childish things. When he became more mature and decided even to bury ultraism, he did not wish to have recourse to any other rite: he simply let it fall into the hole, covered it with the best literature he was capable of—he was the most capable of his entire generation—and cultivated an orchard of strange fruit on the site. When he spoke, in 1932, of the "dead ultraist whose ghost continues to haunt me," we were not sure exactly when it had died. We do know that he repented for having written "arid poems of the sect, of the ultraist mistake." His first formula had been this: "the reduction of lyricism to its primordial element: the metaphor." Fortunately he did not follow it in his books of poems *Fervor of Buenos Aires* (*Fervor de Buenos Aires,* 1923), *The Moon Across the Street* (*Luna de enfrente,* 1925), *San Martín Notebook* (*Cuaderno San Martín,* 1929): books of poems which were selected, retouched, and gathered together with "other compositions" in his volume *Poems* (*Poemas:* see the second edition enlarged—1923-1958—in *Complete Works,* 1958). Metaphors, yes, stacks of them; and each one with "its unedited vision of some fragment of life," to put it in the words of the ultraist Borges. But these metaphors were neither primordial nor reductive of the lyricism of Borges. There was something else. Like all lyricists, Borges sang to and of himself. And he chose the traditional genre for lyricism, which is verse. But it was soon seen that, although he sang to himself,

Borges did not stay with the old themes: love, death, pain, solitude, nature, happiness, the past of his own country, the reality of his own city, rather, he included in his range of themes preoccupations more appropriate to metaphysics: time, the meaning of the universe, the personality of man. One could see that Borges was singing to himself and thinking at the same time. An intellectual lyricism, then. Even those poems which were humbly Creole in theme were reinforced with an inner framework of universal philosophy. He said it in *Fervor of Buenos Aires:* his lyric was "made of spiritual adventures." From this book of poems comes *"El truco"* [a card game] that contains the idea—a favorite one with Borges—that all men are but a single man. In Borges, metaphysics and lyricism are one and the same thing. Dissatisfied with the limits which tradition imposed on verse, Borges sought himself in the essay and later in the short story. The same breath of lyricism blew across all these genres. His richly inquisitive essays and, above all, his stories assure him of the highest of places in contemporary literature. Essays he had written from the time he was very young: *Inquiries (Inquisiciones,* 1925), *The Size of My Hope (El tamaño de mi esperanza,* 1926), *The Language of the Argentinians (El idioma de los argentinos,* 1928), *Evaristo Carriego* (1930), *Discussion (Discusión,* 1932), *History of Eternity (Historia de la eternidad,* 1926), *Other Inquiries (Otras inquisiciones,* 1952), and so on. But his work as a short story writer—to which he owes his definitive glory—was late, timid and experimental. They were at first merely narrative sketches, almost essays. In *Universal History of Infamy (Historia universal de la infamia,* 1935) he borrowed and even translated the stories of others, although there was at least one original story, the admirable "Man on the Pink Corner." Little by little he affirmed himself in the mastery of the new genre, and soon he amazed everyone with the stupendous stories in *The Garden of Bifurcated Paths (El jardín de senderos que se bifurcan,* 1941), *Fictions (Ficciones,* 1944) and *Aleph* (1949). The edition of his "complete works" adds some new stories. Others are found in *The Maker (El Hacedor,* 1960) and in *Personal Anthology (Antología Personal,* 1961). Reading the works of Borges in order, one can see how his style is decanted: from a Baroque aggressiveness, sarcastic and disorderly, to a terse simplicity in which intelligence and admiration are as direct as light. In his later years, losing his sight, he had to dictate, and his stories are penetrated more and more by the framework of oral language. Borges' theory of literature has progressed through various stages. First, an ostentatious period: the cult of the metaphor for the metaphor's sake. Later, a playful period: expression by transforming concept into image or image into concept. And, lastly, a reflexive period: limiting oneself to allusion or mere mention, as if the writer were trying to say something but not saying it ("this imminence of a revelation which does not appear"—states Borges now—"is perhaps the essence of Esthetics"). If esthetic value were like economic value, which grows with scarcity and diminishes with abundance, it would be a simple thing to explain the exceedingly high artistic merit of Borges. What he gives us is rare. In fact, if we glance at narrative all over the world from 1918 to 1949—the date *El Aleph* was published—we can verify the rarity of Borges' work. His originality could be studied in his moody metaphysical cavils, in his poetic intuitions, and in his logical rigor.

Borges, at heart, is a skeptic, but the keen critic should be wary of placing him in all the forms of skepticism which are recorded in the history of culture. There are skeptical positions which are definitely alien to Borges. Not being a scholar of philosophy, but rather a hedonistic reader, Borges sometimes uses terms that do not correspond to his essential skepticism. He does not contradict himself, but the reader is often left confused by Borges' verbal complications. For Borges, the essence of truth does not lie in the relation between thought and the object, but rather something in agreement with thought and itself. Sometimes he adopts epistemological idealism and, even its most extreme form, solipsism. Berkeley, Hume, Kant, Schopenhauer, Croce, and all the idealists in general are his favorite philosophers—which is not to say, however, that he identifies himself with any of them. What interests Borges is the beauty of theories and myths, beliefs that he really disbelieves. It is "an Esthetics of the Intellect," to say it in his own terms. The critic should fully understand the difference between Borges' "essential skepticism" and Borges' "esthetic delight in dealing with myths," as Borges himself has stated again and again. If the critic is not aware of Borges' playfulness and sophistry, he might confuse the artistic structure of the short stories with the author's actual conception of life. The fact that a chess player is defending the king on the chessboard does not mean necessarily that, once the game is over, he is a royalist. Borges belongs to that lodge of writers which, in all times, disbelieved the established, universal order, and remained out in the open air. The world is for him an absurd chaos. But his vision of that chaos is diaphanously communicated. He is not a surrealist trafficking in the bird-droppings of the subconscious, but an expressionist who re-creates reality with the energy of a consciouness illuminated by all the lights of reason. Neither is he an existentialist: he does not feel himself hurled into life once and for all, committed to realize one sole project from a given circumstance, but rather he is free to choose—within his mind, which for him is the absolute—a multiplicity of simultaneous paths. Instead of crying out his anguish, like the existentialists, Borges prefers to reason out his suspicions. His greatest suspicion is that the world is a chaos: and that within this chaos man is lost as though in a labyrinth. Except that man, in his turn, is capable of constructing his own labyrinths. Mental labyrinths made of hypotheses that seek to explain the mystery of that other labyrinth, the one in which we are wandering, lost. Each mind fabricates its own reality and tries to give it meaning. There are thinkers who propose simple hypotheses: God, Matter, and so forth. Borges prefers to complicate his. He is a radical skeptic but he believes in the beauty of all theories; he collects them, and on stretching them to their farthest inferences, he reduces them to the absurd. The dogmatists, who believe that their personal metaphysical ideas, or their myths, are universally true, tend to be annoyed at the agility with which Borges leaps from one hypothesis to another. The agnostic outlook of Borges is expressed in a good-humored dialectics. He encloses the reader in a linguistic labyrinth and plays with him until he defeats him. In his esthetic fruition, nevertheless, overtones of anguish can be distinguished, an anguish which springs from his knowledge that he is unique, solitary, raving, lost, and perplexed inside of a blind Being. Aware of his originality, Borges renounced popularity. He created a literature that ignores the common reader. Not through vanity, but through rigor. Rigor in the selection of the theme and even in the choice of words; rigor in the structure of the story; rigor in his dialog with the reader. If he writes something on so popular a theme as the detective story, he takes it to such a high plane that it reaches a rarefied atmosphere where the reader cannot breathe. A game which delights the intellectual but which humiliates the ingenuous realist. The stories of Borges demand a great deal of knowledge: a knowledge of culture (because of their allusions to the history of literature), a knowledge of philosophy (because of their allusions to ultimate problems), and a knowledge of the work of Borges himself (because of their allusions to this or that page of his works). Let us pause a moment on this requirement: that of having to have a knowledge of the complete work of Borges in order to understand one of his stories. In his stories the same themes constantly reappear: the universe as a chaotic labyrinth, the infinite, the eternal return, the transmigration of souls, the obliteration of the I, the biography of one man coinciding with the history of all men, the changes which unreal ideas impose on real things, pantheism, solipsism, liberty, and destiny.

His stories are all connected to each other, and all, in turn, to his essays. For example, the essay, "The Total Library" (*"La biblioteca total"*) becomes the story "The Library of Babel" (*"La biblioteca de Babel"*). From his essays we could extract explanations to put as foot-notes in his stories, and from his stories, illustrations to clarify his essays. One story is placed within another. The same outline is re-peated or inverted. Here, he merely sketches what there he completes. He attacks a theme from two different perspectives; thus the stories are complementary. The precision of Borges manifests itself in the struc-ture of each narrative, in which each piece is knowledgeably accom-modated to the others. He challenges the reader to an intellectual com-petition, and if it is he who always wins, it is because he does not allow himself to be distracted even for a moment. Part of the perfection of the framework of a short story is the stylistic perfection of each sen-tence. He startles us by using just the right word. Whoever proposed to do so could point out the constellation of writers to which Borges belongs. Ideas, situations, denouements, the art of deceiving the reader, yes, all these have the same family traits: Chesterton, Kafka, and ten more. But Borges, in this constellation, is a star of first magnitude. He has written stories that do not have a match in our literature: "Tlön, Uqbar, Orbis Tertius," "Funes, the Man with the Prodigious Memory," "Death and the Compass," "The Secret Miracle," "The Dead Man," "The Aleph," "The Circular Ruins," "The Library of Babel." No one would take the sophisms of Borges seriously; but his malicious dia-lectics fertilize his stories, which no one could help but take seriously. A powerful mind, Borges. A powerful lyricism of the intimate beauty which he discovers in Argentine life, in the houses, patios, and streets of Buenos Aires, in historical incidents, in wanderings through the suburb, in the pampa that is still present in the city, in the rose-colored general store, or in a vestibule. A powerful imagination which lives each impression of its senses until it is prolonged into a fabulous and allegorical plot. A powerful intelligence which comes and goes with-out getting lost, through the maze of sophistry. A powerful metaphysics which triumphs over the problems of Chaos, Mind, and Time. A pow-erful gift for words which our language had not seen since the Baroque writers of the seventeenth century. A powerful moral sense, capricious when viewed from a distance, but always sincere, daring, and con-sistent if we watch Borges' behavior as a writer. A powerful intellectual knowledge, which is hedonist, because Borges reads only what gives him pleasure and enriches him, without yielding to the reputations established by the handbooks of literary history, yet as strict and serious as that of any scholar.

Other Argentine Narrators / We will occupy ourselves first with writers of inner lives and moods. A five-pointed star: Villarino, Lange, Sofovich, Gándara, and Levinson. MARÍA DE VILLARINO (1905) wandered up an *Out of the Way Street* (*Calle apartada*), verses written in 1930, and came out in a *Town in the Mist* (*Pueblo en la niebla*), stories written in 1943 which were followed by those in *A Rose Should Never Die* (*La rosa no debe morir*, 1950). NORAH LANGE (1906) turned up another street: *The Street of Afternoon* (*La calle de la tarde*), her first book published in 1924. She was one of the ultraist poets of the *Martín Fierro* group. Modes of expression from her poetry reappeared years later in her prose—evocations of childhood, literary memories—even in novels and quasinovels, such as *People in the Living Room* (*Personas en la sala*, 1950), in which an adolescent author-protagonist magically projects her own phantom and feminine personages; in *Two Portraits* (*Los dos retratos*) the atmosphere is dusty with poetry, as though Lange were declaring her love for ordinary things at the instant in which they fall into dust. LUISA SOFOVICH (1912), in the novel *The Bouquet* (*El ramo*, 1943) and in her *Deer Stories* (*Historias de ciervos*, 1945) is one of those who renovated from within (from the retina, from the skeleton of the sentence) the forms of the story. In CARMEN GÁNDARA (1905?) her psychological explorations go beyond the natural and touch an almost metaphysical depth, from which a vapor of mystery rises and envelops and obscures the narrative action: *The Place of the Devil* (*El lugar del diablo*, 1948); a novel—*The Mirrors* (*Los espejos*, 1951). LUISA MERCEDES LEVINSON (1912?) has recently published a novel, *In Me—A Concert in E Flat* (*Concierto en mí*, 1956), which is an intense soliloquy, and short stories, *Pale Rose in Soho* (*La Pálida Rosa de Soho*, 1959). One of these stories, "The Haven," is a jewel in which the light is violently polarized. Three narrators turned inwardly: Bianco, Sábato, and Mujica Láinez. JOSÉ BIANCO (1911), already esteemed for his stories *The Small Gyaros* (*La pequeña Gyaros*), gained even more esteem with *The Rats* (*Las ratas*, 1943). In this psychological novel (in the sense in which the novels of Henry James can be called "psychological") a soul advances by degrees toward the poisoning of Julio Heredia. What is worthwhile is the complex personality of the protagonist-narrator: no less worthwhile, nevertheless, is the complex action and the premeditation of each step, up to the final surprise. ERNESTO SÁBATO (1911) went from science to literature, and within literature, from the essay to the novel, but he always remained more of an intellectual than an artist. In *The Tunnel* (*El túnel*, 1948) the protagonist, Castel, announces that he has committed a crime of passion and proceeds to tell about it. His confession is interesting, not because of the crime, but because each word is a symbol of the progress of his madness, and his madness is the symbol of a desperate metaphysics. The madness of Castel is rational, at times, intellectual: at bottom it is that he can no longer communicate with the world, not even with his lover, María (who is, incidentally, the first heroine of an Hispanic-American novel to read Sartre). He is like a man lost in a tunnel: at times the walls of the tunnel become transparent and he can see the movement of other lives, but it is his solitude, his inability to communicate, which is the anguish of the confession of the painter, Castel. The world is seen through the eyes of an unattached "I," almost pure subjectivity, incapable of communicating with its surroundings. The style also moves swiftly—displeasing, temperamental, and unbalanced. His second novel is *On Heroes and Tombs* (*Sobre héroes y tumbas*, 1961). MANUEL MUJICA LÁINEZ (1910)—in *The Idols* (*Los ídolos*), *The House* (*La casa*), *The Travelers* (*Los viajeros*, 1955)—has novelized with nostalgia, in the ironic and elegant manner of Marcel Proust, the search for a lost golden age, that age of wealthy people, in an oligarchic Argentina. Not only does he imagine an impressionist and metaphoric style, but in the second of the mentioned novels, he arrives at the point of imagining that it is the house itself, speaking in the first person, that narrates its history.

Unfortunately, we must now draw back from the window—although a parade of the following narrators is coming down the street: MANUEL KIRSCHBAUM (1905), author of *The Exasperated Diversions* (*Las diversiones exasperadas*), ALEJANDRO DENIS-KRAUSE (1912), MARIO A. LANCELOTTI (1909)—in order to converse with one of the most important novelists of these years: Mallea.

Existentialism, or at least that anguished meditation which we associate with the existentialism of Kierkegaard—the meditation on the human creature, concrete, singular, tormented by the sense of his responsibility—inspired stories and novels. It was neither idealist nor realist literature; its originality lay precisely in the fact that it refused to separate consciousness to one side and the exterior world to another. It wanted to understand human existence as a vital situation in the world, not as an essence. Oriented in this direction, our America contributed a great novelist: EDUARDO MALLEA (Argentina, 1903). He began playfully with *Stories for a Desperate Englishwoman* (*Cuentos para una inglesa desesperada*, 1926), but after ten years of silence, he reappeared with a tremendous seriousness. *European Nocturne* (*Nocturno europeo*, 1934) was a confession in the third person; in this person—Adrián—Mallea commenced to go deep into his anguished conception of life. In *The History of an Argentine Passion* (*Historia de una pasión argentina*, 1935) he showed his anguish in its Argentine setting. An autobiographic book, vibrant, heated. Imprecation against the fattened oligarch, against the powerful classes that control Argentina through fraud and asphyxiate the authentic life of the people. Tenderness for the profound voices of the laboring, loyal nation. Hope in Argentine generosity and austerity, capable of shaping a new world. In his stories of *The City Beside the Immobile River* (*La ciudad junto al río inmóvil*, 1936) Mallea attempted to describe the secret of Buenos Aires: characters conscious of their solitude and desperation, with their moral roots in the air. After *Fiesta in November* (*Fiesta en noviembre*, 1938) Mallea, who until that time had expressed himself in monologs, began to construct his novels with dialogs in counterpoint, with multiple personages, each with his own perspective. But in all of the novels that followed, beginning with *The Bay of Silence* (*La bahía de silencio*, 1940), the characters and their attitudes toward life, as varied as they may be, are always inhabited by Mallea who, from each created soul, continues to probe into what it means to be a man, to be a woman, in a living Argentinian situation. Ágata Cruz, the protagonist of *All Greenery Will Perish* (*Todo verdor perecerá*, 1941), is a good example of how Mallea creates his characters. What is happening in the novel is less interesting than what is happening inside of Ágata. Ágata, motherless, in a little town in the south of the province of Buenos, grows up at the side of an odd person—a Swiss doctor, insatiable reader of the Bible—marries a man she does not love: the taciturn Nicanor Cruz, who is beaten year after year in his agricultural battle against nature. Each failure separates them more. In the distance, hate begins to grow. When he is ill with pneumonia, she, in order to end everything, opens the doors and windows of the house to the cold wind. But only he dies. Ágata survives. She goes to Bahía Blanca; she feels the necessity of leaving her doldrums, of knowing a man, of loving. In an atmosphere of frivolity and luxury—in Bahía Blanca—she falls in love with a lawyer, Sotero. They become lovers for several weeks. Then Sotero goes to Buenos Aires. She falls once more into solitude. She returns to her home town, growing more insane day by day. She ends by going completely mad and perhaps committing suicide. But, contrary to what this clumsy resumé leads one to believe, Ágata's solitude, which is described in the novel, is not a solitude determined by circumstances; rather, it is the solitude of human existence or, if you wish, that of the personal, unique existence of Ágata. Mallea will describe the flow of that existence; and even more, he will describe its stream of consciousness. In order to do so, he disconnects the novel into two temporal planes: the present action, which takes place within the space of little more than a year, and the evoked action, thanks to which we are familiar with the life of Ágata from the time of her earliest memories. The action, the present as well as the evoked action, follows a successive line in the order of the calendar and of the clock. Mallea, the omniscient author, intervenes between the character and the reader. Not only does he gather together the interior monologs of Ágata, but he also explains and even judges them.

In *The Enemies of the Soul* (*Los enemigos del alma*, 1950) there are various souls in agony. The theological title—the world, the flesh, and the devil as the enemies of the soul—might lead the reader astray in his interpretation of the novel. Because the "M" of Mario could be the "M" of *Mundo* 'world,' and the "C" of Cora the "C" of *Carne* 'flesh,' and the "D" of Débora the "D' of *Demonio* 'Devil.' Nevertheless, a theological interpretation of the novel would reduce to dry symbols what, in reality, is the tragic sense of several concrete, very Argentinian lives. Mallea, without abandoning his purpose in besieging the Argentine essence, participates completely in the assault on the human essence. It is one of his most intense novels. In *The Eagles* (*Las águilas*, 1943) Román Ricarte returns, a failure, to what remains of his ranch, and with his memories—plus flashbacks that Mallea adds—the novel of three generations of rich Argentinians (from 1853 until the present) takes shape. The protagonist is Román, an indecisive, weak person with a noble but unhinged soul. The entire novel appears to be made up of the weaknesses of Román, victim of the social ambitions of his wife and children. Mallea is a shy narrator. Each time he comes to a point in the narrative where it would be propitious to accelerate the action, he veers off into long psychological disquisitions, or more or less philosophical reflections. His style is also evasive, indirect; and although in these digressions he succeeds in creating a few good passages, in general his sentences are clouded. His tone of preoccupation, of sadness, and, at times, of grief over the conditions in which the Argentinians live, is the same which dominates his other novels. *Chaves* (1953) is more a short story than a novel because of the unique situation it offers us: Chaves, whom suffering—failures, the deaths of his wife and children —has refined spiritually, giving him a distinguished superiority, works as a laborer in a sawmill where he is surrounded by the hostility and hate of his fellow workers who mistake his silence for proud disdain. Only at the end of the story, in the last line, do we hear a single word from Chaves: when he is asked "Aren't you ever going to say anything?" He answers, "No." Pain has eaten up all his words. The narrative, in which Mallea has installed himself inside of Chaves—indirect discourse—is a braid of two threads of action: the present action from the time Chaves arrives and asks for a job, and the underlying, evoked action from his adolescence to the death of his wife.

Simbad (1957) is a novel about Fernando Fe, a playwright. It is also the drama that Fernando is writing—identification of the playwright's life with that of his hero: "it was as if life, having impeded that work, had condemned him to live it." There are two temporal planes. The first relates the days of Fernando's solitude after his separation from Magda; this portion, from the twenty-eighth to the thirty-first of December, 1952, is composed in italics and is divided into fragments, each one of which will head one of the five parts of the novel. The second temporal plane is the actual body of the novel—composed of flashbacks with which Fernando, during these secluded days, reconstructs his past—from the time he is twelve way back in 1914 to the moment that Magda returns and the confidence of being able to finish his "Simbad" is reborn. In the last pages, both temporal planes are mingled. The three main themes—the promiscuous amorous life with both Magda, who needs protection, and Lea, who inspires him; the endeavor to dignify with a classical repertoire the Argentine theater; and a description of the process of dramatic creation—are braided chronologically. Mallea places himself within the novel in the figure of Gustavo Villa, character and witness. In *Simbad,* we find some of Mallea's most beautiful pages. Yet, judging it as a novel, it is not nearly as convincing as *Todo Verdor Perecerá,* probably because the dissonance between Fernando's moral tone and his double adultery is not compensated for by a concrete analysis of the artist's psychology. The narrative, much too vague and abstract, robs Fernando Fe of his authenticity.

Those subversive to the real order of things we have left for last. We have already mentioned the poets who, on abandoning verse for prose, continued to disfigure reality so that the figures of their free imaginations could be better seen. From among those not mentioned, let us bring forth SILVINA OCAMPO (1905?). She has alternated books of verse with books of short stories. Her verses—collected in *Small Anthology* (*Pequeña antología,* 1954)—are desolate, but without the rhetoric of desolation, made up of bright memories, but without our being able to tell whether they have been lived in a dream or while awake. She was more of an innovator in her fantastic stories, *Forgotten Voyage* (*Viaje olvidado,* 1937), in which the lyricism of metaphysical origin is moving because of its nakedness, although the author tends to be a little careless in her narrative composition. In *The Fury and Other Stories* (*La furia y otros cuentos,* 1959) Silvina Ocampo has chosen to tell about cruel situations. She seems to have taken them from reality which she has either lived through or observed. However, we see them as though distorted by thick lenses. MANUEL PEYROU (Argentina, 1902) cultivated the short story in the manner of Borges, although he did not need Borges in order to read Chesterton. His stories from *The Sleeping Sword* (*La espada dormida,* 1944) charm the reader, opening caves in reality, full of ingenious characters, enfolding these characters in situations whose secret the author retains until the end. *The Thunder of Roses* (*El estruendo de las rosas,* 1948) is a detective story (in which the order of discovery is given) although it begins as a police story (in which the order of criminal events is given). In fact, we see a man assassinated; only it turns out that this man is the double of another, who was already assassinated the day before. The uninterrupted and exciting accumulation of events demonstrates very quickly that Peyrou, unlike Chesterton, is not interested in the philosophy nor in the psychological motives of his characters, but in the game. A chess game in which each move on one side of the board is counterarrested by one from the other side. His stories from *The Repeated Night* (*La noche repetida,* 1953) also play at being literature, although they are more successful at being a game than at being literature. In *The Rules of the Game* (*Las leyes del juego,* 1959) a man

489

kills another in self-defense. Afterwards, he learns that the woman who caused this misfortune is unworthy of him. Prompted by a feeling of remorse on one hand and a bit of vengeance on the other, he decides to confess the crime to the police. The accent of the novel, thus, is placed on the criminal's psychology and Peyrou analyzes it with sympathy, but without idealization. The major artistic merit, however, is in the composition. Just as the rules of the vital game plot the destiny of the characters, so the rules of the narrative game plot the novel. Two rules, two games, two plots: on the one hand, circumstances which become disordered and complicated by the irrational impulses of the protagonist; on the other hand, episodes which are ordered and simplified by the logical plan of the author. In this logical plan upon which the novel's plot is constructed, we can see a reflection of Peyrou's interest in detective stories. The action is linear and is recounted in realistic prose, rapid in its characterizations and in its dialogs. Buenos Aires is seen as a diorama with its streets, restaurants, cafés, movie houses, etc.; and above all we are given a documentation of the moral prostration of Perón's Buenos Aires. The bitter and indignant tone, the irony and sarcasm with which Peyrou criticizes the immorality during the Peronist regime is tempered by his love of Buenos Aires and by his recognition of at least one Argentine virtue: the cult of friendship.

It was in Argentina that fantastic literature arose more conspicuously than anywhere else, with its preference for lyric and sophistic play of imagination. The fantasies of Borges and Silvina Ocampo responded to a new enthusiasm. An enthusiasm for a difficult, anti-realist, analytic literary art, which proposed problems in order to then solve them according to set laws. The great reputation of Borges has led to the belief that he had a direct influence on this group; nevertheless, the influences which Borges himself received from French, English, and German literature are the same which acted directly upon the others. By the side of Jorge Luis Borges, it is necessary to put his friend and collaborator, Adolfo Bioy Casares (1914). He was an admirable inventor of fabulous worlds constructed in accordance with strict laws. In his novel *Morel's Invention* (*La invención de Morel*, 1940), he tells us of an apparatus which captures the appearances of reality and then, with a projector, reproduces that reality in space and time. But in narrative literature, absolute originality is impossible: Horacio Quiroga in "The Vampire" and Clemente Palms in *XYZ* had already spoken of similar apparatuses. *Plan of Evasion* (*Plan de evasión*, 1945) was the twin of his previous novel: the same implicit philosophy—absolute idealism—the same setting—an island—the same conception and the same art of giving verisimilitude to the absurd. The stories in *The Celestial Plot* (*La trama celeste*, 1948) are so intellectual that the ideas in it do not even take the precaution of disguising themselves. The same thing could be said of the stories gathered together in *Prodigious History* (*Historia prodigiosa*, 1956). In *The Dream of Heroes* (*El sueño de los héroes*, 1954) a magic adventure is embroidered on a realist framework. Gauna, a worker in a mechanic shop, and some undesirable friends celebrate the festivities of the 1927 Carnival over a period of three days and three nights. Gauna, drunk, will scarcely remember a few disconnected scenes of that dark adventure. He seems to remember, for example, fighting, knife in hand, with a tough of the old school. Three years later, when Carnival time comes, Gauna decides to go over the same route with the same companions to see if he can capture the meaning of the adventure. Suddenly, as though a miracle had occurred, the years 1927 and 1930 converge, and what in

1927 had been a mirage in Time—the fight with a knife—now comes to pass: Gauna dies in a knife fight. The force of destiny? Bioy insinuates that it is rather the evil spell of a demiurge or blind god that the wizard Taboada—a friend of Gauna— was able to break the spell in 1927, but which in 1930, when the wizard has already died, must be fulfilled. In a sordid atmosphere, the voyage of Gauna through the districts of Buenos Aires flashes fantastically like that of Jason and the Argonauts: these are the heroes that Gauna has dreamed of. The novel proceeds on two levels, like a mischievous child who walks with one foot on the curbstone and the other in the street. The style is as careless as that of a friendly chat, but with smiles and ironic winks. He wrote, together with Borges, *Six Problems for Don Isidro Parodi* (*Seis problemas para Don Isidro Parodi*, 1941), under the pseudonym of Bustos Domecq. Parodi is a prisoner who, from his cell, solves the crimes that are brought before him with the deductive procedures of the classical criminal detective. They are ingenious stories, notable for their parody of detective-type stories and above all for their satire of Argentine types and situations, told in a language that imitates the commonplaces and affectations of the intellectuals and pseudo-intellectuals. In collaboration with his wife, Silvina Ocampo, he wrote a "whodunit," *Those Who Love, Hate* (*Los que aman, odian,* 1946), without distinction within the genre, other than a biting humor: all of the investigators fail, only the narrator's hypothesis is correct and is confirmed by the written confession of the criminal, a neurotic child. It can be seen that this type of analytic, chess-game literature has nothing to do with the science fiction, the mysteries, or the detective stories which, in the United States, are directed to the mass public. Borges, Peyrou, Bioy Casares, and others write for readers with alert minds, informed on metaphysics, with an enthusiasm for analysis, disciplined in the rules of a refined game. These writers are familiar with all literature, especially the Anglo-Saxon literatures; but if they were to be translated into English, they would not be popular among the masses. We have almost forgotten about another Argentinian writer of this group. In *Vigil* (*Vigilia,* 1934), a poetic novel about an adolescent; *The Proofs of Chaos* (*Las pruebas del caos,* 1946), lyric short stories; *Fugue* (*Fuga,* 1953), a novel on the feeling of "false recognition" and the idea of the "eternal return"; and *The Magic Book* (*El grimorio,* 1961), fantastic and playful stories, he has compressed himself into a thin line of purely imaginative expression. His narratives are like those Chinese feet, tortured into tiny shoes, which take their art from their very torture. But even though they always cause the author much pain, they do not always appear beautiful to the reader. This author, like Velázquez in *Las Meninas,* upon painting the historic portrait of his generation, has left a blank corner on the canvas in order to paint himself with his brushes in hand. It is as the signature on the picture: ENRIQUE ANDERSON IMBERT (1910).

(*b*) *Narrators More Objective than Subjective* / We saw among the previous writers authors who were either able to free themselves from their circumstances or were flayed by them. On the other hand, the majority of the Hispanic-American novelists accentuated their circumstances, and there were even stories and novels in which everything was circumstance. They did not contain men, or, at least, men were unimportant. A great part of this literature implied a materialistic philosophy. At times that philosophy was dogmatic: Marxism, for example. The Communist Party directed the pens of many of these writers and then organized the propaganda in their behalf in order to put them before the public eye. Remember that in the decade of the 1930's the world seemed headed toward Communism. Then reactionary groups arose and the world turned around toward fascism. The Creole fascists also had their literature, but it was less effective: as fascists, they had nothing to say in a literary style. In general, the "committed" but more independent novelists—the liberals, the socialists—were the better writers, although not always the most successful. All, some more, others less, presented a situation barren of men, or, if you wish, full of masses of men rather than individuals. Their descriptive techniques were those of naturalism and realism, although there were those who combined them with a detonator of ultraist metaphors, a taste for allegory, and the "messages" of German expressionism. These novels of protest have been classified by critics according to their central themes. Novels concerned about the position of the Indian in our society. Regionalist and rural novels with their conflicts between the landowner and the laborer, between the laborer and a hostile nature. Novels about the rapid changes in our economic life. Novels about our political disasters: wars, revolutions, dictatorships. Novels about the invasion of foreign capitalists, the exploitation of markets and men, and the evils of imperialism. Novels on the tormented life of the great cities, and the agitations of the bourgeoisie and the proletariat. To impose a certain order on the novelistic mass of this generation, we will show a couple of national groups, from Mexico to Argentina.

(1) *Mexico* / The literature surging from the Mexican Revolution was not, in general, revolutionary either in its technical procedures or in its style. And at times it was not revolutionary even in its spirit. We viewed before the emergence of this thematic narrative. Let us now continue with other figures.

JORGE FERRETIS (1902–1962), from *Calid Land* (*Tierra caliente*, 1935) to *The Colonel who Killed a Cock-Pigeon and Other Stories* (*El coronel que asesinó un palomo y otros cuentos*, 1952), was a keen observer of the conflict between civilizing ideals and civic degradation in our Hispanic-American countries; he is not satisfied with a mere description of rural life but posits social problems, with intentions aimed at reform. Among the writers of social themes, the most outstanding was FRANCISCO ROJAS GONZÁLEZ (1905–1951). He also wrote novels: *The Negress Angustias (La negra Angustias), Lola Casanova.* But his col-

lections of short stories—the last one, posthumous, was *The Beggar*
(*El diosero,* 1952)—lent themselves to his talent which was more apt
in observing than in constructing. Although he started writing these
short stories about a big-city milieu, his best deal with country life.
There are, however, weighed down by a good deal of artistically unas-
similated ethnographic material.

The realist current ran along the ditch of the revolutionary theme,
but it also ran over into the surrounding terrains. The least superficial,
the most ambitious among them is JOSÉ REVUELTAS (1914). *Human
Mourning* (*El luto humano,* 1943) contained promises and youthful
awkwardness. What he had learned from Faulkner he was not able
to apply properly, and the result is that, because of his experiments
with shifts in time and perspective, the structure of the novel is frac-
tured. The action is simple: some country people, men and women,
with a dead baby in their arms, try to save themselves from a flood;
some die, drowned; and vultures hurl themselves at the anguished survivors who are on the roof-terrace. The complexity is not in the action,
but in the intertwining of memories. The same author has also written *Days of the Soil* (*Los días terrenales,* 1949) and *In Some Valley
of Tears* (*En algún valle de lágrimas,* 1956). In this last novel, he
tells of a few hours in the contemptible life of a man in his fifties, but
since the author follows him step by step, and thought by thought, the
novel becomes one long interior monolog of the protagonist.

ANDRÉS IDUARTE (1907), in the terse and moving pages of *A Child of the Revolution* (*Un niño de la revolución,* 1951), and NELLIE CAMPOBELLO (1912), in
Cartridge Belt (*Cartucho,* 1931) and *Mother's Hands* (*Las manos de mamá,* 1937),
gave us the juvenile view of the revolutionary movement. XAVIER ICAZA (1902)
novelized the themes of the Revolution and, in *Panchito Chapopote* (1928), satirized
"Yankee imperialism." Other names: ANTONIO ACEVEDO ESCOBEDO (1909), CIPRI-
ANO CAMPOS ALATORRE (1906–1934), RODOLFO BENAVIDES (1907). More removed from the revolutionary theme were JUAN DE LA CABADA (1903), author of
short stories—*Street of Lies* (*Paseo de mentiras,* 1940)—and RUBÉN SALAZAR
MALLÉN (1905), who, in his novels *Waste Land* (*Páramo,* 1944) and *Eye of Water*
(*Ojo de agua,* 1949), reflects, respectively, on the life of the lowest levels of the
city and of the country. ANDRÉS HENESTROSA (1906)—author of a delicate "Portrait of My Mother" (*"Retrato de mi madre,"* 1940)—collected, re-created, and
invented in *The Men That the Dance Dispersed* (*Los hombres que dispersó la
danza,* 1929) graceful, theogonic legends of his Zapotecan land. This literature,
about Indians or pro-Indian in tone, is a kind of service which was paid to the
Indian in order that he might express his vision of things. It is significant that one
of the best attempts at this type of literature was not that of a novelist or a poet,
but of an anthropologist: RICARDO POZAS (1910), with his *Juan Pérez Jolote* (1952),
creates an anthropological study which is similar to literature, and along the way,
comes across literature which is similar to anthropology.

(2) *Central America / Guatemala:* MARIO MONTEFORTE TOLEDO (1911) gives local variations on the theme of the battle between man and nature, with protests over social evils and the exploitation of the peasant class: after *Anaité* (1940), the vigorous novels *Between Stone and the Cross* (*Entre la piedra y la cruz,* 1948) —perhaps the best, about an educated Indian in the conflict between two worlds, the primitive and the civilized—*Where the Paths End* (*Donde acaban los caminos,* 1953), and *Invisible Walls* (*Los muros invisibles,* 1957). He has also written stories: *The Cave Without Peace* (*La cueva sin quietud,* 1949).

Honduras: The most outstanding of the regionalists was MARCOS CARÍAS REYES (1905–1949). He wrote thesis novels, such as *Tropic* (*Trópico*), in which he denounces the political mistreatment of the rural peoples. Others: JORGE FIDEL DURÓN (1902), author of *American Stories* (*Cuentos americanos*) and ARTURO MEJÍA NIETO (1900), an expatriate who barely touched on national themes. ARGENTINA DÍAZ LOZANO (1909) wrote, in a simple prose, stories and novels on national themes, *Mayapán,* and a novelized autobiography, *Pilgrimage* (*Peregrinaje*).

El Salvador: Within realism, the following stood out for their descriptions of regional surroundings and for their sharp consciousness of social ills: RAMÓN GONZÁLEZ MONTALVO (1908), for his stories in *Pacunes* and his novels *The Jars* (*Las tinajas*) and *Verbascum* (*Barbasco*); NAPOLEÓN RODRÍGUEZ RUIZ (1910), whose novel, *Jaraguá,* with its lively, popular dialog and its clear landscapes, calls attention to the problems of the field; MANUEL AGUILAR CHÁVEZ (1913–1957) and ROLANDO VELÁZQUEZ (1913).

Nicaragua: The writing of novels was part of a literary exercise undertaken in various genres. There were not, therefore, any pure novelists; neither were there pure novels, because social and political life intervened in them. We could give as an example of this tendency ADOLFO CALERO OROZCO (1899), in the novel *Sacred Blood* (*Sangre santa*) and in the *Aromatic Stories* (*Cuentos pinoleros*); EMILIO QUINTANA (1908) in the stories of *Banana Trees* (*Bananos*); MANOLO CUADRA (1907) in his tales *Against Sandino in the Mountain* (*Contra Sandino en la montaña*) and *Starch* (*Almidón*). More attentive to the inner workings of their characters were JACOBO ORTEGARAY (1900) and MARIANO FIALLOS GIL (1907).

Costa Rica: The major novelist, in the direction of proletariat literature, was CARLOS LUIS FALLAS (1911). His political position is to the far left. His novels denounce the working conditions on the banana plantations, in the jungles, and on the farms. *Mamita Yunai* (1941), which organizes chronicles that appeared originally in communist periodicals, is a protest against imperialist action and the exploitation of the rural masses. *People and Little People* (*Gentes y gentecillos*), *Marcos Ramírez,* and *My Godmother* (*Mi madrina*) followed. His style is ironic, sincere, direct, elemental. More stylized is the realism of CARLOS SALAZAR HERRERA (1906), in his *Stories of Anguish and Landscapes* (*Cuentos de angustias y paisajes*), and of ABELARDO BONILLA in *Clouded Valley* (*Valle nublado*).

Panama: The realist narrators were IGNACIO DE J. VALDEZ (1902), whose *Panamanian Stories of Field and City* (*Cuentos panameños de la ciudad y del campo*) attempted a faithful portrait of the people, using antiquated procedures: GRACIELA ROJAS SUCRE (1904) and GIL BLAS TEJEIRA (1901) of greater literary quality; JOSÉ ISAAC FÁBREGA (1900), who states, although schematically and ingenuously, the national problems; historical novelists like JULIO B. SOSA (1910-1946) and LUISITA AGUILERA PATIÑO (191?); regionalists like CÉSAR A. CANDANEDO (1906), or those who wrote descriptions of city life, like RODOLFO AGUILERA (1909). It is after 1930 that the writers of more substance break in. There is less sentimentalism and more social sense; vernacular themes, yes, but with reformist points of view that coincide with movements all over the continent. One of the novelists who has understood Panamanian life in broader vistas is RENATO OZORES (1910): in *Deep Beach* (*Playa honda*, 1950), the idleness of the rich, with frivolous women and love intrigues; in *Bridge of the World* (*Puente del mundo*, 1951), the formation of the country, with the contribution of foreigners; in *The Dark Street* (*La calle oscura*), the humble life in the lower-class districts; this does not include his shorter narratives, written with good humor.

(3) *Antilles* / As everywhere, the Antilles yielded a narrative literature, rooted in the land and in the social problems of the worker, of race, and of sex.

Cuba: The social current is represented by CARLOS MONTENEGRO (1900). He gathered his stories into *The Offshoot* (*El renuevo*), *Two Boats* (*Dos barcos*), and *The Heroes* (*Los héroes*). He also has a novel: *Men Without Women* (*Hombres sin mujer*). With strong agility, he leaps from the prison to themes of the sea, from the anti-imperialist war, to psychological probings: in these leaps he assumes intense realistic postures. ENRIQUE SERPA (1899), who began as a poet of Modernist taste, put his strength into realist narratives. Realist in their subject matter, but the attention that he gives to the psychological, his preference for interior monologs, and his careful phrasing, polish and attenuate reality. The novel *Contraband* (*Contrabando*, 1938) is a good example of this. In the novel *The Trap* (*La trampa*, 1956), he falls, nonetheless, into the writing of political customs. His stories— from *Felisa and I* (*Felisa y yo*, 1937) to *Night of Fiesta* (*Noche de fiesta*, 1951)— acknowledge a progression toward expressive simplicity. GERARDO DEL VALLE (1898), the author of stories—*Fragments* (*Retazos*)—about Negro and mestizo superstitions and beliefs, about the lower depths of city life, on ancient legends and myths, on spiritualist themes. Other realist narrators: ONELIO JORGE CARDOSO (1914), OFELIA RODRÍGUEZ ACOSTA (1906), DORA ALONSO (1910), MARCELO POGOLOTTI (1902), ALBERTO LAMAR SCHWAYER (1902–1942), JOSÉ M. CARBALLIDO REY (1913), AURORA VILLAR BUCETA (1907), ROSA HILDA ZELL (1910).

Dominican Republic: JUAN BOSCH (1909) has published the major part of his work outside of the country. He has written a novel *The Cunning One* (*La mañosa*, 1936), but his greatest merits are those of the story writer: *The Royal Road* (*Camino Real*, 1933), *Indians* (*Indios*, 1935), *Two Dollars' Worth of Water* (*Dos pesos de agua*, 1941), *Eight Stories* (*Ocho cuentos*, 1947) and *The Girl from El Guaira* (*La muchacha del Guaira*, 1955). He prefers to narrate the simple life of the Antillian peasant. He uses the language of these people with veracity, but he interprets his themes with the tenderness and ironic humor of an observer who has withdrawn to a distance from reality, in order to interpret it with the eyes of the artist. MANUEL A. AMIAMA (1899) evoked the customs of the capital city in his novel *The Trip* (*El viaje*, 1940). HORACIO READ (1899) novelized with vigor the period of United States intervention, in the *Civilizers* (*Los civilizadores*, 1924). Afterwards, he wrote other narratives in a different style: *From the Shadow* (*De la sombra*, 1959). ÁNGEL RAFAEL LAMARCHE (1900), of impressionist, sentimental prose: *The Stories That New York Doesn't Know* (*Los cuentos que Nueva York no sabe*). VIRGINIA DE PEÑA DE BORDAS (1904–1948), author of *Toeya*, a novel of Indianist theme, and of *Stories for Children* (*Cuentos para niños*). ANDRÉS FRANCISCO REQUENA (1908–1952), wrote, in *The Enemies of the Land* (*Los enemigos de la tierra,* 1936), of the moral suffering of the peasants who want to leave their land to go to the city. In *Path of Fire* (*El camino de fuego,* 1941) and *Cemetery Without Crosses* (*Cementerio sin cruces,* 1949), he denounced political bossism. RAMÓN MARRERO ARISTY (1913) is a story writer of strong realism in *Balsié* (1938) and also a novelist in *Over* (1939). The latter is a notable novel in which social problems are stated with reference to the exploitation of sugar cane. The title, taken from the jargon of the sugar refinery, alludes to the extortion which the stores employ to abuse the worker. The author himself is a peasant, unskilled in literature, but has lived through these same experiences with a combative spirit. FREDDY PRESTOL CASTILLO (1913), a Creole story writer of social theme, creates in his novel *Pablo Mamá* a good character, untamed and solitary on the frontier. HILMA CONTRERAS (1913), more of an artist, more surprising in her *Four Stories* (*Cuatro cuentos,* 1953).

Puerto Rico: ENRIQUE A. LAGUERRE (1906) wrote novels about the soil. When *Sudden Flame* (*La llamarada,* 1935) appeared, some believed that in it were revealed the sugar cane area of Puerto Rico, the sufferings of the worker, the force of nature, collective problems, human insular types . . . What was revealed was a good novelist. He does not give unity to his book, but with unconnected episodes and scattered characters, he has created an artistic illusion of real life. In *Montoya Farm* (*Solar Montoya,* 1947) he completed the vision of the Puerto Rican field and proposed a program of agricultural rehabilitation. In *Undertow* (*La resaca,* 1949) he writes about the conspirators who wanted to free Puerto Rico from the Spaniards during the last years of the Colony and who are overthrown by the apathy of the people. Laguerre sees his theme panoramically; and, in fact, the land is what dominates his novels. The souls of his characters remain floating like telluric emanations. *The Five Fingers of the Hand* (*Los cinco dedos de la mano,* 1951) and *The God-Tree in the Pot* (*La ceiba en el tiesto,* 1956) are his last titles. His novels, one after the other, describe all of the landscape of the island, all of its activities, all of its social classes, and always, at the heart of his work, his preoccupation is for the fortunes of his country. In *The Labyrinth* (*El laberinto*), a quite recent work, the action takes place in New York and in a foreign country.

Other narrators worthy of note are: TOMÁS BLANCO (1900), *The Bards* (*Los vates,* 1930); JOSÉ A. BALSEIRO (1900), *Vigil While the World Sleeps* (*En velo mientras el mundo duerme,* 1953), EMILIO S. BELAVAL (1903), *Stories to Encourage Tourism* (*Cuentos para fomentar el turismo,* 1936), ERNESTO JUAN FONFRÍAS (1909), *By the Heat of the Fire* (*Al calor de la lumbre,* 1936), VICENTE PALÉS MATOS (1903), *Wind and Foam* (*Viento y espuma,* 1946).

(4) *Venezuela* / MIGUEL OTERO SILVA (1908) novelized in *Fever* (*Fiebre,* 1939) the student fight against the dictatorship of Gómez. It

was a document, political and literary, on the generation of '28. The first pages were written in an exalted style, when he was twenty years old, living in the midst of the same events that he was describing: the last pages—which are better—were written in his maturity. The structural crack between the two styles is obvious, and even the thematic development is lacking in unity. But the breath of poetry that blows across his landscapes, the vigor with which he describes the agony of his protagonist, the fevered atmosphere of the ending incorporate him with all honors into the body of the Venezuelan novel. *Dead Houses* (*Casas muertas,* 1955) is an album of sad prints on the city: the city of Ortiz, previously a prosperous capital, has become a dilapidated and desolate cemetery for dead houses. Pestilence—yellow fever, malaria, hematuria—have destroyed the city. But, as the teacher Berenice says, if pestilence were able to destroy it, it was because political decay had already weakened its resistance. These were the years of Gómez' tyranny and in this album, together with the sketches of illness, are those on the abuses and violence of the dictatorship. ANTONIO ARRAIZ (1903) is a poet and a capable novelist of naturalist bent, esteemed for his animal stories which, in a magic world, reveal the plebeian Venezuelan soul with more efficacy than do many pages of direct description: *Uncle Tiger and Uncle Rabbit* (*Tío Tigre y Tío Conejo*). Even in his last novels we can recognize the poet's fingers under the claws of the narrator: *Real Men* (*Puros hombres*), where he documents the experiences of the political prisoners during the dictatorship; *The Sea Is Like a Colt* (*El mar es como un potro*)—whose former title was *Dámaso Velázquez*—describes the life of the fishermen; *They All Were Disoriented* (*Todos iban desorientados*) follows the decadence of several families. LUCILA PALACIOS (1902) novelized the marine ambient in *The Sea Divers* (*Los buzos*) and *The Courser With the White Mane* (*El corcel de las crines albas*); her last novel is *The Day of Cain* (*El día de Caín*). RAMÓN DÍAZ SÁNCHEZ (1903), in his novel *Mene* (1936), composed with the technique of the reporter—the theme is the rapid transformation of a rural village into an oil well camp—had demonstrated a restlessness that finally led him toward the psychological theme. He is now more interested in man than in the landscape, and he reacts against Creole primitivism. In his novel *Cumboto*, of a Negroid setting, Díaz Sánchez delves into the crudest of Venezuelan realities, but with a fine brush paints an atmosphere of poetry, terror, and magic symbols. His description of the customs and geography of Venezuela does not continue the line of Romero García or Picón-Febres, nor that of Gallegos. It is enough to compare the manner of conceiving

497

the landscape in *Doña Bárbara* and in *Cumboto* to see the great difference between styles in the treatment of the regionalist theme. Others: ARTURO CROCE (1907), MANUEL GUILLERMO DÍAZ (1900–1959), better known by his pseudonym Blas Millán, and PABLO DOMÍNGUEZ (1901).

(5) *Colombia* / The naturalism of JOSÉ A. OSORIO LIZARAZO (1900) has specialized in the sordidness of tenement houses, crime, alcoholism and in degenerative diseases, in the superstitions and ignorance of the peasants, in the vices and evils of the bourgeoisie. His purpose was sociological, didactic, and also one of protest. But this novelist of human failure has failed himself, in the creation of his characters. Perhaps his best work was *Man Beneath the Earth* (*El hombre bajo la tierra*, 1944). It is the life, realistically told, of the miners who dig gold from a Colombian valley. Some details are naturalist—the bestiality of man, his physiological needs, his submission to his surroundings—but there is no thesis of social reform or protest. The most violent scenes—knife duels, sex, gambling, drunken sprees, death, and madness—all appear as part of the cult of "he-manism." This *"machismo"* is the dominant theme: an adolescent, Ambrosio Munero, having run away from his bourgeois life in Bogotá, hides in the mine and there learns to be a "he-man." ADEL LÓPEZ GÓMEZ (1901) published some six collections of stories: those of 1956 are his *Selected Stories* (*Cuentos selectos*). He is a realist, not a naturalist (that is, the real, not the repulsive side of the real). He offers an ample gallery of characters: cowardly and courageous, stupid and intelligent. And they are not characters all of one piece, but persons with interior shadings. The plot is not important. At times it is nonexistent. Spiritual states more than action. The art of storytelling adjusts to psychological veracity. He is a balanced author. He does not illustrate any extreme esthetic position, even though all of them are represented. His center appears to be in the sentimental.

One of the good novels of this period, *Risaralda* (1935), was written by BERNARDO ARIAS TRUJILLO (1905–39). It is like a film—filmed in reels—on the life of "Negroidism and cowboyism." In the middle of the jungle, mulattoes, Negroes, and zambos work, dream, kill, grow violently impassioned, and smile gently. The ethnography is idealized. The prose is swollen with poetry and also with eloquence. EDUARDO CABALLERO CALDERÓN (1910) has published various novels—*Tipacoque*, *The Penultimate Hour* (*La penúltima hora*)—with an occasional experimental technique. There is nothing experimental in the best of them: *Christ With His Back to Us* (*El Cristo de espaldas*, 1952). A young priest, recently ordained, sets out for the first time from the seminary to serve as parish priest to a little town lost in the Andes. It is as though he were visiting hell or dreaming a nightmare. In less than five days he comes to know all the horrors of infamy, of ugliness, injustice, stolidity, violence, and misery. They are years of civil war between the conservatives and the liberals. Caught in the middle of that fight, a boy is condemned for a crime which he did not commit: he is accused of having assassinated his father, the conservative chieftain. The priest hears—without being able to reveal it—the confession of the true assassin, the sexton. Everyone is against this devoutly dedicated priest, the only honorable person in the whole novel. Even the bishop judges him wrongly. Since the priest has failed, he is punished by being sent back to the seminary. The bishop believes that "Christ has turned His back" on the priest; the priest knows that it is man who has turned his back on Christ. The prose is plain, realist, documental, composed with the old technique of the author who narrates in the third person, following the order of events (except for a few pages of exposition and retrospection to knot the line of the narrative). The first five chapters are vigorous: the last three lose their narrative force because they become too discursive and moralizing. The essayist HERNANDO TÉLLEZ (1908) figures also among the better story writers: *Ashes For the Wind and Other Tales (Cenizas para el viento y otras historias,* 1950). In this collection there is "Foam and Nothing More," which is surprising for the artistic sobriety with which it narrates a violent situation. Others: ANTONIO GARCÍA (1912), of political intent, and ALFONSO LÓPEZ MICHELSEN (1913), the author of *The Elect (Los elegidos,* 1953); AUGUSTO MORALES PINO (1912) and HUMBERTO JARAMILLO ÁNGEL (1908).

(6) Ecuador / This country produced a body of novels compactly realist. Except for Mera and Montalvo—isolated cases—the only notable novelist of Ecuador had been Luis A. Martínez, with the powerful naturalism of *Toward the Coast (A la costa).* But only twenty years later, a whole family was to rise from naturalism. In only a few years a group of writers, for the most part militant communists and socialists, imposed itself, writing to denounce the living conditions of the people and to protest against the injustices of the social system. Crude language, exaggeration of the dark and the sordid, bravery in the exposé of shameful national conditions, sincerity of combative purpose give this literature more moral than literary value. From the Ecuadorian reality they set aside certain themes that they considered bourgeois and chose others that they considered vigorous and wrote novels filled with suffering Indians, with abominable latifundia, with the miserable peons of the coast and of the mountain, with filthy cities, malignant beasts, local epidemics and disasters.

JOSÉ DE LA CUADRA (1904–1941) was the most able storyteller: *The Love That Slept (El amor que dormía,* 1930), *Consoles (Repisas,* 1931), *Oven (Horno,* 1932), *The Sangurimas (Los Sangurimas,* 1934), *Guasinton* (1938). He was a moderate socialist, comprehensive, flexible, and at times ironic. His themes were taken from poverty, injustice, suffering, human bestiality, and hostile nature, but they were not monotonous. The stories of *Guasinton* are very diverse, in theme, humor, and perspective (there are even poetic ones like "A Girl Is Lost"), and even in his most unified collections (such as *The San-gurimas,* whose tales end with incest, rape, madness, and death), the author does not allow himself to be dragged down by an easy trucu- lence. His prose, sharp, rapid, and precise gives a frigidity to the observed reality. A novelist of international fame is JORGE ICAZA (1906). He published, between *Clay of the Sierra* (*Barro de la sierra,* 1933) and *Six Tales* (*Seis relatos,* 1952), a series of novels, dramas, and tales that tried to transfer pieces of coarse matter into literature. The read- ing of *Huasipungo* (1934), his most famous novel, which is badly con- structed, can only satisfy those who seek sociological documentation or political feelings rather than literary virtues. In it Icaza novelizes the exploitation of the Indian by his masters; the Indian is not a con- crete person, but an abstract mass-man. The title refers, in Quechua, to the parcel of land that the landowners ceded to the Indian in return for tilling the rest of the farm. They strip the Indian of his "huasipungo" when they sell the land to a foreign enterprise. The novel uncovers the avarice and despotism of the landowners, the corruption of the parish priest, the brutality in the use of weapons to put down the in- digenous uprising, bestiality of customs, sex, misery, crude language, and, nevertheless, a certain haughty coldness, that of the critical intel- ligence of the author. Another of his Indianist novels, of a political theme, was *Hairapamushcas.* ALFREDO PAREJA DÍEZ-CANSECO (1908), on the other hand, has novelized the city: *The Wharf* (*El muelle*), *Baldomera, Three Rats* (*Las tres ratas*). At times, however, he came out of his urban enclosure: *La Baldaca.* He does not write propaganda, although he is interested in the evils of his country and describes them. He is more conscious of his technique as a novelist. He draws his fig- ures with agility and makes them speak in lively dialogs. If his femi- nine characters are most convincing, it is because one of his novelistic themes is the impact of social injustice on sexual relations. Among his best novels: *The Wharf* and *Three Rats.* He has recently begun an all-inclusive novel, *The Nine Years* (*Los nueve años*), of which the volumes "The Warning" ("*La advertencia*") and "The Air and Mem- ories" ("*El aire y los recuerdos,*" 1958) are already known. That long novel reflects the shiftings of Ecuadorian society after 1925. *The Wharf* is a naturalist novel, of improvised style and weak composition, facile, sober, and even agile in its descriptions and dialog. It deals with the misery of Juan and María, two mestizos from Guayaquil, with scenes of prostitution, theft, sickness, administrative corruption, lack of work or work that is hard and ill-paid, abuses, and violence. The first few chapters take place in New York: the depression, workers' protests disbanded beneath the blows of the police, contraband. Conclusion: society is badly constructed, as much in Guayaquil as in New York, and the poor worker has no avenue of escape.

DEMETRIO AGUILERA MALTA (1905) prefers to relate the sufferings of the Indians, mestizos, and zambos of the Ecuadorian fields. In general, he chooses moving situations in which the social problem dominates over the psychological: *Don Goyo, Canal Zone, The Virgin Island* (*La isla virgen*). He seems to have abandoned the novel for the theater. HUMBERTO SALVADOR (1907) seemed, at the beginning of his career, to be going to dedicate himself to the theater, but what appeared were stories—*Chess* (*Ajedrez*) and *A Cup of Tea* (*Taza de té*)— and novels—*In the City I Have Lost a Novel* (*En la ciudad he perdido una novela*), *Comrade* (*Camarada*), *Workers* (*Trabajadores*), *November* (*Noviembre*), *The Interrupted Novel* (*La novela interrumpida*), *Clear Fountain* (*Fuente clara*). He is a sober, humorless chronicler of the city life of his time. He studies circumstances and psychology. At times this fundamentally urban novelist does both things at the same time and psychoanalyzes the city of Quito. If in his first novels the dialog could be heard, in his later ones, we are listening to the interior monologs of his characters. ENRIQUE GIL GILBERT (1912) conceived of the novel as a political pamphlet at the service of the revindication of the workers. *Our Daily Bread* (*Nuestro pan*, 1941), is a novel about the exploitation of the rice laborers. He later abandoned literature to dedicate himself entirely to politics. JORGE FERNÁNDEZ (1912), a novelist of the peasant theme in *Water* (*Agua*, 1937) and of the urban theme in *Those Who Live By Their Hands* (*Los que viven por sus manos*, 1951), in which he describes the vicissitudes of bureaucracy and unemployment, mediocrity, vice, and humiliation. JOAQUÍN GALLEGOS LARA (1911– 195?) gave us the painful history of Guayaquil in *The Crosses Upon the Water* (*Las cruces sobre el agua*). GERARDO GALLEGOS used the Antilles—where he lives —as the setting for some of his novels and Ecuador for others. He is a two-fisted novelist, with some good descriptions of landscapes. ANGEL F. ROJAS (1910) brought new techniques to the novel: in *Exodus from Yangana* (*Éxodo de Yangana*) he describes how an entire town disbands and buries itself in the jungle in search of justice. There is nothing stranger than to find humor in the lugubrious climate of the Ecuadorian novel. ALFONSO GARCÍA MUÑOZ (1910) was a humorist in his series of *Sketches of My City* (*Estampas de mi ciudad*). Others: LUIS MOSCOSO VEGA, MANUEL MUÑOZ CUEVA, GONZALO RAMÓN (1912?), and ARTURO MONTESINOS MALO (1913?).

(7) *Peru* / The novelist with the greatest reputation among the realists is CIRO ALEGRÍA (1909). His sympathy for the outcast, the humble, the Indian, for the worker flows generously. His prose is simple, powerful in the impetus it gives to the mass of the novel. In *The Golden Serpent* (*La serpiente de oro*, 1935), *The Hungry Dogs* (*Los perros hambrientos*, 1939), *Broad and Alien Is the World* (*El mundo es ancho y ajeno*, 1941), although nature and the masses are visible, artistically created characters also move through the novel. The title of the novel

is explained at the end of the book in a kind of Marxist discourse. It means that, for the poor, the world is wide, and that is why the privileged class pushes them from side to side, but the world is also alien because the poor never even receive a salary sufficient to live on. It deals with the sufferings of a community of Indians in the hills of Peru, more or less from 1910 to 1928. The landowner, Alvaro Amenábar strips the Indians of their land, persecutes and destroys them. Mayor Rosendo dies in jail, beaten to death. The rebel bandit, Fiero Vázquez, is beheaded. The social insurrection of Benito Castro is smothered in blood beneath the government guns. In order that there should remain no doubt as to the inhuman conditions to which the Indian is subjected, the novel takes us for a look at Peruvian geography: valley, mountain, jungle, coast, even to the city of Lima, and shows us the labor in the fields, in the mines, and on the rubber plantations. The main line of action of the novel is simple but irregular: there are disconnected scenes, biographies of Indians, historical episodes, stories, legends, songs. There is also a chapter (the twentieth) in which are aired ideas on what social functions art, folklore, and literature should serve in Peru: the Americans, Dreiser, Sinclair Lewis, John Dos Passos, and Upton Sinclair appear as models in the field of literature. And, naturally, the "dialectical materialism" of Marx is included, taught to Benito Castro by a director of the workers' syndicate. The population of an entire town moves through the novel; yet no one character succeeds in coming alive with all the force of art, although it can be seen that Alegría made the attempt with the ancient Indian mayor, Rosendo Maqui. He failed because of his excessive idealization. Interior monologs, soliloquies, flashbacks, and impressionist techniques put the action within the souls of the Indians, but in spite of everything, it is always the mass that is seen. The novel uses clap-trap from the nineteenth century, although there are also spatial-temporal cuttings characteristic of the twentieth. The structural innovations are timid: what dominates is the realist, explicative prose, which in moments of enthusiasm for the beauty of the landscape, or some of indigenous scene, succeeds in being more sentimental than lyrical. A novel of protest, without unity of tone, but readable and efficacious.

FRANCISCO VEGAS SEMINARIO (1903) is a novelist in the old style. He narrates without formal discipline, without desiring to experiment; he reads as easily as a nineteenth-century novel. Whether he is narrating episodes about the country or about the city, his realist program is obvious: he wants to illustrate social problems, and to do so he takes average people and stereotypes them. ROSA ARCINIEGA (1909) wrote, among other novels of exasperated political feeling, *Gears* (*Engra-*

najes, 1931). The title indicates that human lives are so many gears in the great wheel of Labor. First, in the smelting ovens, then in the mines, warehouses, and factories, Arciniega shows the horrors of social injustice: hunger, sickness, prostitution. Arciniega believed that one of the new roads for the novel was "to allow oneself to be taken up by the great, collective conflicts," to present the masses, "the man—millions of men," "the case—millions of cases." But it is not a novel of political propaganda. Manuel, the protagonist-narrator, is a proletariatized bourgeois; and at the end, he wants to destroy the existing order with bombs, not in order to redeem the people, but in order to install nothingness. The novel takes place in Spain. The prose is simple, rapid, elliptic; but since she does not create individual characters nor singular situations, the novel is monotonous. FERNANDO ROMERO (1905)—*Twelve Jungle Novels* (*Doce novelas de la selva*), *Sea and Beach* (*Mar y playa*)—is a regional storyteller of a tragic vein. His last collection— *Rosarito Says Good-bye and Other Stories* (*Rosarito se despide y otros cuentos*, 1955)—contains a rare and hidden lode of relative good humor. JOSÉ DIEZ CANSECO (1904–1949), a novelist of the lower levels of life in the city and in its port, in *Duke* (*Duque*) whiplashes the decadence of Lima society.

A novelist of good reputation is JOSÉ MARÍA ARGUEDAS (1913), author of stories and novels that deal with the Indian theme in a sober but intense lyricism. He spent his first years in an Indian community and only later did he learn Spanish. Both languages are useful to him in his literary creation. He began with a collection of short stories: *Water* (*Agua*, 1935). In *Yawar Fiesta* he narrated the strength with which certain cruel rites have impregnated the customs. *The Deep Rivers* (*Los ríos profundos*, 1959) is a novel about a mestizo boy raised by the Indians and later educated in the dull and sad atmosphere of a provincial small-town high school: from the depths of poverty, injustice, and suffering there emerges an optimistic lyricism. In *The Sixth* (*El Sexto*), he describes the degradation of jail; but even there, Arguedas knows how to find moral values. Although he can and does describe vigorously violent climates, Arguedas becomes tender with his native landscape or with his brother Indians. There is definitely something positive in his vision of man, no matter at what depth of the social squalor he views him.

(8) *Bolivia* / The war between Bolivia and Paraguay (1932–35) opened a novelistic cycle. OSCAR CERRUTO (1907), in *Rain of Fire* (*Aluvión de fuego*, 1935), mixed the reality of the war with revolutionary political ideals and also with the ideals of a literary expression. AUGUSTO CÉSPEDES (1904) collected disconnected tales on episodes from the war in *Mestizo Blood* (*Sangre de mestizos*, 1936); ten years later he wrote *Metal of the Devil* (*Metal del diablo*), a novel against the tin magnates. AUGUSTO GUZMÁN (1903) in *Prisoner of War* (*Prisionero de guerra*) gives us the history, in two parts, of a soldier, the campaign and his capture. LUIS TORO RAMALLO (1898–1946), in *Cutimuncu* and *Inca Gold* (*Oro del Inca*), has novelized the Bolivian Indian in his landscape of plateaus. CARLOS MEDINACELI

(1899–1949), relates in his novel, *The Chaskañawi*, the love of a student for an Indian girl; in passing, he also describes provincial customs.

(9) *Chile* / Creolism, such as we saw it in Latorre, degenerates a bit during these years, at least as a school. This Creolism, in filling the narrative with landscapes and documents, deprived the characters of freedom of movement; or, when it presented social problems, it simplified them with facile political formulas. Now it will be seen that the realist writers insist on representing a turbulent epoch in all of its shades. Man, struggling between nature and society, seems integrated into a total reality; and this totality is changing, menacing, confused. Of course, as understanding as these realists might be, for them, the connection between man and his environment is always more important than man himself.

In the Creolist direction, MARTA BRUNET (1901) stands out. She has a powerful dramatic, and even tragic, vision; she is valiant and one of her valiant acts was to create good literature with shocking material; she stylizes—as artists do—the material that in the hands of the naturalists remained unhewn. Her *Toward the Mountain* (*Montaña adentro*, 1923) was the masterful beginning of extensive narrative works on peasant themes. Her last novel is *María Nadie* (1957). DANIEL BELMAR (1906), in his best novel, *Coirón*, harmonizes an artistic evocation of the landscape, man, and his customs, with a just feeling for social problems. There are countless writers who originate from the people, observe social evils, and write to denounce these evils. They are so conscious of the collective social process, and so attentive to the consequences of industrial changes, that they generally propose political catchwords. In the preceding chapter, we saw that sociological realism, which recognizes the elder Lillo as its master, continued with Edwards Bello, González Vera, and Alberto Romero. In the period that we are now reviewing, this direction is affirmed in those whom we mention here. Among the most talented, FRANCISCO COLOANE (1910) stands out. He wrote about what he had observed and lived through in the southern regions of South America, on land and at sea. Although disorderly, his literature is truly estimable: stories, *Cape Horn* (*Cabo de Hornos*, .1941), *Tierra de Fuego* (1956); a novel, *The Last Cabin Boy of the "Baquedano"* (*El último grumete de "La Baquedano,"* 1941). NICOMEDES GUZMÁN (1914) made a novelistic study of a poor district in *Dark Men* (*Los hombres oscuros*, 1939) and of a family of laborers in *Blood and Hope* (*La sangre y la esperanza*, 1943). Pestilence, rape, death, human filth do not disgust him. He approaches ugliness burning with faith in the proletariat, with hope for the regeneration of the people; in his prose, naturalism is mixed with lyric metaphors, as in *Light Comes From the Sea* (*La luz viene del mar*). JUAN GODOY (1911) also occupies himself with the lower classes in *Gluttons* (*Angurrientos*, 1940). In his work, more than in the work of Guzmán, can be noted the stamp of a style common to many Hispanic-American novelists of these later years: naturalist and socialist material written with a poetic rhythm, seen with the eyes of many metaphors, glimpsed in visions pleasing to surrealism, moved by hidden resources which, at least in the time of Joyce and Aldous Huxley, were anti-conventional. ANDRÉS SABELLA (1912)

—author of *The Great North* (*Norte Grande*)—was able to braid together success-fully a literature of protest against social injustice with a literature of lyric imagina-tion: naturally, he tied allegorical tufts to that braid. Let us put a foundation of names and titles under the structure of this paragraph: CARLOS SEPÚLVEDA LEYTON (1894–1944), *Ahijuna;* LAUTARO YANKAS (1902), *The Flame* (*La llama*); RUBÉN AZÓCAR (1901), *People on the Island* (*Gente en la isla*); EUGENIO GONZÁLEZ (1902), *Farther Out* (*Más afuera*); DIEGO MUÑOZ (1904), *Coal* (*Carbón*); JACOBO DANKE (1905), *The Red Star* (*La estrella roja*); GONZALO DRAGO (1907), *Purgatory* (*Purgatorio*); NICASIO TANGOL (1906), *Huipampa;* OSCAR CASTRO (1910–47), *Mine-Dust of Blood* (*Llampo de sangre*); LEONCIO GUERRERO (1910), *Feluccas* (*Faluchos*); REINALDO LOMBAY (1910), *Ranquil;* LUIS MERINO REYES (1912), *Bitter Bosom* (*Regazo amargo*).

(10) *Paraguay* / We have already said that the Chaco War (1932–35) provoked, in Bolivia, a narrative cycle. Paraguay did not produce novels and stories of high esthetic quality on this theme. ARNALDO VALDOVINOS (1908), with more passion than art, wrote tales on the war with Bolivia in *Crosses of Quebracho Wood* (*Cruces de quebracho,* 1934); even more militant was his narrative *Beneath the Boots of a Blond Beast* (*Bajo las botas de una bestia rubia,* 1932). In this genre, JOSÉ S. VILLAREJO (1907) produced the best work: *Eight Men* (*Ocho hombres*), a novel of personal experiences, with good descriptions. He is a correct prosist and also writes in the short story: *Ojhóo the Sayoiby* (1935). Among the depicters of cus-toms, the nativists, we could also mention EUDORO ACOSTA FLORES (1904), CARLOS ZUBIZARRETA (1903), JUAN F. BAZÁN (1900), RAUL MENDONÇA (1901), PASTOR URBIETA ROJAS (1905).

We close this paragraph with the best Paraguayan novelist of this period: GABRIEL CASACCIA (1907). He published stories—*The Well* (*El pozo,* 1947); *The Guahú,* 1938, and novels—*Mario Pereda,* 1939; *Men, Women and Marionettes* (*Hombres mujeres y fantoches,* 1930). In *The Driveler* (*La babosa*) he has made an inventory—since nat-uralism does not allow him to invent—of the drivel of gossip, moral corruption, physical misery, and the degradations of a little town near Asunción. The characters, who speak in Spanish and in Guaraní (with translations at the foot of the page), form part of a large, collective body.

(11) *Uruguay* / JUSTINO ZAVALA MUNIZ (1898), bombastic in his theatrical plays —*The Cross on the Highways* (*La cruz de los caminos*)—showed more vigor in the novelized chronicle: *Chronicle of Muniz* (*Crónica de Muniz*), *Chronicle of a Crime* (*Crónica de un crimen*), *Chronicle of the Window Grille* (*Crónica de la reja*). FRANCISCO ESPÍNOLA (1901), with gaucho motifs—*Blind Race* (*Raza ciega,* 1927)—and from the lower classes of society—*Shadows Over the Land* (*Sombras sobre la tierra,* 1933)—created exceptional characters, or rather, characters excep-tionally well-conceived: characters shaken by violent discharges of passion and de-scribed with a dramatic vision. The dramatism of Espínola led him to experiment with the theater, in the *Flight in the Mirror* (*La fuga en el espejo,* 1937), a sur-realist mystery play. In 1961 he collected his *Short Stories* (*Cuentos*). JUAN JOSÉ

Morosoli (1899–1957), who began with two books of verse—evocative poetry on his childhood and adolescence—found his true talent in a series of narratives: *Men* (*Hombres,* 1932); *The Bricklayers* (*Los albañiles de los tapes,* 1936); *Men and Women* (*Hombres y mujeres,* 1944); *Perico,* 1947; *Lads* (*Muchachos,* 1950); *The Living* (*Vivientes*). He captured the life, inside and out, of the humble folk of the field. Other realiest narrators: Santiago Dosetti, Eliseo Salvador Porta (1912), and Víctor Dotti.

Enrique Amorim (1900–1960), a Uruguayan, also belongs to Argentine literature. He was a novelist of fields and cities, although he gained his greatest success with a series of rural novels. After *Tangarupá* and *The Cart* (*La carreta*), he attained a good reputation with *Countryman Aguilar* (*Paisano Aguilar,* 1934). The theme of this novel is simple: Aguilar, brought up in the country and educated in the city, returns to the country, as the owner of a small ranch. He feels insecure, a failure in the face of the enticements of the two different kinds of life that he knows so well, until little by little he gives in to the inertia of the surroundings, vegetating in the end, like a gaucho. This simple theme, however, unravels into disconnected episodes. A novel, then, without a solid structure; neither are the inner workings of Aguilar clearly illuminated. The best part of the novel is the sharp observations scattered through it. Many of these observations are formulated in metaphors that belong to the literary family of "vanguardism." However, in Amorim these new metaphors, even the most audaciously expressionist, enter into the narrative naturally, without changing their tone of voice, without bumping into the story-line. Amorim is an intelligent observer, moderate but worried because of the lack of spiritual orientation of his time: this is the theme of *The Uneven Age* (*La edad despareja,* 1939). In *The Horse and Its Shadow* (*El caballo y su sombra,* 1941) the action goes at a gallop, as though it were following the "splendid golden sorrel" who comes, with his biological potency, to enrich Azara's ranch. Azara is a landholder of the old style, a cattleman, not a farmer, who tries to impede the path of agriculture. By prohibiting the people to cross his fields, he causes the death of a child. The father of the child, an Italian, fights with Azara and stabs him to death. The Italian, who in *Martín Fierro* never fought, here, stands face to face with the Creole and defends himself. In *The Moon Was Made From Water* (*La luna se hizo con agua,* 1944), the author looks at the rural area from the perspective of today's city. In *Victory Does Not Come By Itself* (*La victoria no viene sola,* 1952)—notice that the title is taken from a statement by Stalin—Amorim attempts to write a political novel. Social injustice suggests an abstract problem to Amorim;

and from it, his characters arise, also excessively abstract. His crude novel, *Open Corral* (*Corral abierto*, 1956) has value as a document: juvenile delinquency in the filthy, corruptive districts. Indefatigably, Amorim constructs his tower of novels, from which he observes the social structure of South America: his last novels are *Anything Can Happen* (*Todo puede suceder*, 1956), *The Mountaineers* (*Los montaraces*, 1957), and *Outlet* (*La desembocadura*, 1958).

(12) *Argentina* / The realist novels helped to point out the social peculiarities of a prosperous and democratic country, without Indians or Negroes, populated by European nationalities, of a fundamentally agricultural and cattle-growing economy, but with powerful industrial centers. But although its reality was of a cleaner and more pleasing cut than that of other countries, many of its novelists sought its more harrowed aspects. The novels, as much the type that proposed a documentation of nature or society as the type that went deep into the motivations of its characters and into their moral and political reactions, prided themselves on their veracity more than on their art. And if these novels did not comprehend the whole truth, there is no doubt that in their observations they were sufficiently direct to be of service to scholars. They are useful to geography and ethnography, since they describe the life of all the regions of the country.

Buenos Aires had always been the center of literary activity, and from its streets the following gathered their novelistic materials: JULIO FINGERIT (1901), ARTURO CERRETANI (1907), ISIDORO SAGÚES, JOAQUÍN GÓMEZ BAS, ENRIQUE GONZÁLEZ TUÑÓN (1901–1943), and ROGER PLA (1912). Writers emerged from the inner corners of the country: from the islands of the Delta (ERNESTO L. CASTRO), from Patagonia (LOBODÓN GARRA, 1902; ENRIQUE CAMPOS MENÉNDEZ, 1914); from the pampas (ARISTÓBULO ECHEGARAY, 1904); from the provincial towns and cities (ANTONIO STOLL, 1902; JUAN MANUEL VILLARREAL, 1905; and SILVERIO BOJ, 1914?). At times it was a case of the same author changing his locale. These novels were useful as history and sociology also, because they describe the successive moral breakdowns that were weakening the national fiber. And finally, they were useful to political science because they put into action traditionalist, liberal, fascist, anarchist, and communist ideologies and platforms. We can scarcely mention a few who stood out.

Above all, ROBERTO ARLT (1900–1942). He was the one who, with most originality, continued the work begun by the "Boedo Group": Alvaro Yunque, Roberto Mariani, Elías Castelnuovo, Lorenzo Stanchina. Like the others, he had read the Russians and certainly he was the little Dostoevski of the family. Neurotic, preoccupied, irritable, imaginative, impassioned, he appeared with *The Furious Plaything* (*El juguete rabioso,* 1927) in the years when the masses were beginning to take over the country. From this tumultuous life in which he was spectator and actor he took his novels. He attracted attention with *The Seven Madmen* (*Los siete locos,* 1929), wherein he created the personality of Erdosain, and its continuation, *The Flamethrowers* (*Los lanzallamas,* 1931). They were followed by *Love, the Sorcerer* (*El amor brujo,* 1932), the chronicles and stories of *Etchings of Buenos Aires* (*Aguafuertes porteñas,* 1933) and *The Little Hunchback* (*El jorobadito,* 1933). His theater is also interesting: *Africa, 300 Million* (*300 milliones*), *The Desert Island* (*La isla desierta*). For Arlt "human beings are monsters waddling in the shadows," overwhelmed, lost, failures in the murkiest spots of a vulgar city. He created exasperated characters as a pretext for airing his own hate and protests in the face of a Buenos Aires which he regarded as one huge brothel. He was the novelist of the frustrated hopes of the Argentinian middle class during the historic pathfinding days of 1930. But he was no mere chronicler of social events. He was a tortured person, and he tortured the reality of his novels. He believed in evil, and his imagination elevated a world of panderers, perverts, and prostitutes to art. They seem to have been dreamed rather than seen. Dreamed with resentment, with bad words, in a nightmare from which Arlt suffers. These human shadows are too dirty for their rebellions to be heroic. They eat themselves up and at the same time, they are the termites of the world in which they live. Arlt's sincere impulse, unfortunately, had failings in the art of composing a narrative. Arlt was popular; and far from being forgotten, he is constantly gaining new readers.

LEONIDAS BARLETTA (1902) is another of those who form the "Boedo Group." His debut as a writer with *Royal Circus* (*Royal Circo*) was as mediocre as the things which he was describing, but in *The City of a Man* (*La ciudad de un hombre*) he successfully created a good realist novel. He wrote his stories and novels with a slow, popular, simple, unpretentious prose, which was nevertheless powerful because it was the vehicle of his love for the most humble of lives. More humanity than literature, more nobility of spirit than esthetics, but in spite of his ungrateful theme—people of the poor districts, without refinement, huddled in depressing little houses—Barletta is capable of converting poverty into poetry. Although he is afflicted by the grief of his characters (the consequences of social injustice) and by their loneliness (the consequence of a lack of solidarity between men) his mood is not pessimistic. He believes that man is fundamentally good, and he assumes that a proletariat revolution (Russia, which gave him his literary models, also provides his political direction) would assure complete human dignity. Meanwhile, he describes in a gray tone the contrasts of black and white that he sees in his photographic negatives. Others among the biographers of human misery: Lo-RENZO STANCHINA (1900), author of *The Bedeviled* (*Endemoniados*) and *The*

Eccentric (Excéntricos), in the caves of the city. Of a more imaginative realist technique is MAX DICKMANN (1902). His selection of detail joins in the interpretation of social life and in the understanding of his characters. The novels— *Mother America (Madre América)*, *People (Gente)*, *Bitter Fruit (Frutos amargos)*, *This Lost Generation (Esta generación perdida)*, *The Mutiny of the Deluded (El motín de los delusos)*, *The Inhabitants of Night (Los habitantes de la noche)*— have a complex and dynamic structure. JUAN GOYANARTE (1900), the vigorous novelist of the fight of man against nature in *Argentine Lake (Lago argentino)*, is also a novelist of the moral horrors of the city of Buenos Aires in *Carnival Monday (Lunes de carnaval)* and *Three Women (Tres mujeres)*. An agile, sparkling narrator with a deep sense of humanity: LUIS GUDIÑO KRAMER (1898), *Fond Solitude (Aquerenciada soledad)*, *Foreign Land (Tierra ajena)*, *Horses (Caballos)*. FERNANDO GILARDI (1902) is a careful prosist who in *Silvano Corujo* captured the spirit of the old suburb. AUGUSTO MARIO DELFINO (1906–1960) internalizes his tales: situations, things come from the city, but he absorbs them into psychological material. *Márgara Who Came from the Rain (Márgara que venía de la lluvia)*, *End of the Century (Fin de siglo)*, *Stories of Christmas Eve (Cuentos de Noche Buena)* and *In Order to Forget the War (Para olvidarse de la guerra)* have a rhythm of interior time. The realist writers who lived between the two revolutions, the oligarchic fascist revolution of 1930 and the popular fascist revolution of 1945, with the spectacle of the second World War before them, were completing, with broad brush strokes, the mural of Argentina. BERNARDO VERBITSKY (1907) describes the customs of the city, with a preference for adolescent characters and always attentive to the social fact: from *It Is Difficult to Begin to Live (Es difícil empezar a vivir, 1941)* to *Misery Village Is Also America (Villa Miseria también es América, 1957)* he has written seven novels. One humorist, at least, in all this group: FLORENCIO ESCARDÓ (1908), of an elaborated, intellectualized humor, very personal in its content and form: *Oh, New Ohs (Nuevos Oh)*, *Things of Argentina (Cosas de argentinos)*.

2. Essay

Thanks to the successes of André Maurois, Stefan Zweig, Emil Ludwig, and others, the novelized biography came into vogue in Hispanic-America, as did essays of the historical or sociological type. Along these lines LUIS ALBERTO SÁNCHEZ (Peru, 1900) stood out, the author of *Don Manuel* (1930) and *La Perricholi* (1936). MARIANO PICÓN-SALAS (Venezuela, 1901) appeared with Uslar Pietri in the vanguardist group shortly after the first World War. Like Uslar Pietri, he was a narrator: *Night Dealings (Los tratos de la noche)*, his novel, was written in 1955. But his narratives, which are very intellectual, occupy a minor spot within his vast labor as an historian, critic, and essayist. His cultural histories are excellent, for instance, *From the Conquest to the Independence (De la conquista a la independencia, 1944)*. He has also cultivated the novelized biography: *Pedro Claver, the Saint of the Slaves (Pedro Claver, el santo de los esclavos, 1950)*. His collections of essays reveal one of the most alert intelligences of the continent.

GERMÁN ARCINIEGAS (Colombia, 1900) is an agile and brilliant essayist, with points of view which are always unforeseen. He tried to write a novel, *Halfway Along the Road of Life* (*En medio del camino de la vida*, 1949), but it is obvious that he only feels comfortable when he takes the floor and gives opinions A journalist with a tremendous grasp of things, his opinions usually appear in the form of short articles. Later, he gathers them together, and in this manner he puts out collections of disconnected essays, such as the admirable *The Student of the Round Table* (*El estudiante de la mesa redonda*, 1932), *America, Terra Firma* (*América, tierra firme*, 1937), and *In the Land of Skyscrapers and Carrots* (*En el país de rascacielos y las zanahorias*, 1945). At other times, his pages follow a central theme and are organized into unified books, such as *The Commoners* (*Los comuneros*, 1938), *The Germans in the Conquest of America* (*Los alemanes en la conquista de América*, 1941), *This American People* (*Este pueblo de América*, 1945), *Biography of the Caribbean* (*Biografía del Caribe*, 1945). Whatever the exterior form of his writings, Arciniegas' work reveals a profound unity: that of a lucid, original mind, preoccupied with the problem of our America. With a sympathy for the Indian and for the lower classes, with a lively sensitivity for the historic past and for its heroic figures, with a militant faith in the good purposes of democracy, culture, and progress, he has been progressively writing a versatile encyclopedia of America. In Arciniegas, knowledge is not mere erudition: it is combined with a vision, rich in good humor, in lyricism, and in meaningful anecdotes.

One of the favorite essay topics is the clarification of the essences of each national reality: within this class, the following stand out: the Mexicans DANIEL COSÍO VILLEGAS (1900), FERNANDO BENÍTEZ (1910), and LEOPOLDO ZEA (1912); the Cubans JORGE MAÑACH (1898–1961), JUAN MARINELLO (1898), FRANCISCO ICHASO (1900), RAÚL ROA (1909), and JOSÉ ANTONIO PORTUONDO (1911); the Puerto Ricans ANTONIO S. PEDREIRA (1899–1939) and TOMÁS BLANCO (1900); the Venezuelans HUMBERTO TEJERA (1901?) and EDUARDO ARROYO LAMEDA (1902); the Colombian JORGE ZALAMEA (1905); the Ecuadorians BENJAMÍN CARRION (1898) and LEOPOLDO BENITES (1909); the Peruvian HÉCTOR VELARDE (1898); the Argentinians CARLOS ALBERTO ERRO (1903), DARDO CÚNEO (1914), ROMUALDO BRUGHETTI (1913)—who, in *Prometheus* (*Prometeo*, 1956) has made this mythical person speak in such a manner that his autobiography is converted into the history of liberty.

There are notable essayists, critics, and students of literature. Mexico: ARTURO RIVAS SÁINZ (1905), JOSÉ LUIS MARTÍNEZ (1918). Puerto Rico: CONCHA MELÉNDEZ (1904), NILITA VIENTÓS GASTÓN (1908), MARGOT ARCE DE VÁZQUEZ (1904). Venezuela: JOAQUÍN GABALDÓN MÁRQUEZ (1906), PEDRO PABLO BARNOLA (1908). Chile: RICARDO LATCHAM (1902?). Bolivia: GUILLERMO FRANCOVICH (1901). Argentina: LUIS EMILIO SOTO (1902), RAIMUNDO LIDA (1908), MARÍA ROSA LIDA

DE MALKIEL (1910), ANÍBAL SANCHEZ REULET (1910), ANA MARÍA BARRENECHEA, and MARÍA HORTENSIA LACAU.

C. THE THEATER

The theater of these later years lives from the professionals who seek economic success, from the authors who, with nobility and dedication, give themselves entirely to experimenting with new forms in small halls before reduced audiences, and from the outstanding novelists or poets who, on writing comedies and melodramas, are apt to occasionally lend dignity to the field of dramatic literature. There were autonomous theatrical movements, particularly in Argentina and Mexico.

Mexico: These were years of maturation for the existing realism and for experimentation with European and United States techniques. History and the Mexican political revolution fed the theatrical renovation which JUAN BUSTILLO ORO (1904) and MAURICIO MAGDALENO (1906) undertook together in the Teatro de Ahora [Present-Day Theater] group. Being anti-individualistic, one might expect this problematic type of theater to be of scant psychological value. This is not so, however. Magdaleno, who in his novels of social protest showed himself to be a good observer of human conflict and very capable of creating his characters from it, brought psychological keenness to his *Mexican Revolutionary Theater* (*Teatro Revolucionario Mexicano*): *Pánuco 137, Emiliano Zapata, Tropic* (*Trópico*). But it is undeniable that his purpose is socio-political, and not that of delving into the soul or creating theatrical contrivances. The same could be said of *Shark* (*Tiburón*), *Those Who Return* (*Los que vuelven*) and *A Lesson For Husbands* (*Una lección para maridos*) of Bustillo Oro.

Of all of the Mexican authors, the most professional, the most often translated, is RODOLFO USIGLI (1905). Plays about customs, social and political satires, psychological and historical dramas reveal Usigli's scenic mastery and also his intellectual restlessness. The action of *The Child and the Mist* (*El niño y la niebla*, 1936) is weakly interlaced with certain episodes of Mexican political life: the assassination of Venustiano Carranza and the designation of De la Huerta as president in 1920. Unfortunately, the technique of the drama itself antedates its historical reality: Usigli has recourse to the spent procedures and themes of the nineteenth century (hereditary madness, the armed sleepwalker . . .). In *The Impersonator* (*El gesticulador*, 1937), "a piece for demagogues," using a situation that Pirandello would have treated as a farce (he dealt with a similar one in *Enrico IV*), Usigli made a melodrama. César Rubio, a professor of history, passes for César Rubio, a general of the Mexican Revolution who had been assassinated many years before. At first, it is merely an impersonation done to get money and to avoid poverty; but later, it becomes a patriotic identification with revolutionary ideals. Ironically, Professor César Rubio dies at the hands of the same person who had assassinated General César Rubio. When Usigli criticizes the violence and sordidness of Mexican politics, he does so with solemnity. Usigli did himself harm when he publicly acknowledged his admiration for Bernard Shaw. One can see this admiration in *The Family Dines at Home* (*La familia cena en casa*, 1942), but the comparison of Usigli with Shaw is cruel. Usigli begins his career at the point where Shaw ended his: pure dialog, without construction. Furthermore, Usigli lacks a philosophy—at least, an original philosophy—a dialectic capacity, and even a sense of humor. On the other hand, he has too much of what Shaw had no appreciation for: sentimentalism. *The Family Dines at Home*, although it takes place in Mexico, contains little that is Mexican. If he presents a problem, it is that of mixing different social classes at cocktail parties: an aristocracy of the rich, the diplomats, and the old families; the *nouveau riche*, and the lower social level of prizefighters, bullfighters, and cabaret dancers. The problem, in Mexico, presents itself in a different manner. Neither is the central plot convincing, because Usigli is careless with detail and fails to make it believable. *Crown of Shadow* (*Corona de sombra*, 1943) is one of his most ambitious works. It is an anti-historical work, he says, with an historical theme: the tragic trajectory of the lives of Maximilian and Carlota. It is not, in truth, anti-historical. In any case, we could call it defectively historical. Usigli at times uses known events as a point of departure or interprets them in a manner which would be of little satisfaction to an historian. His work would indeed be anti-historical if he had shown irreverence for historical truth, or if he had used anachronisms in order to illuminate his theme with the light of a personal philosophy. But Usigli has written scenes using effects from historical melodrama and dialogs in which the sentences follow the conventional lines of an historical melodrama. The most anti-historical feature of his work lies in the fact that his characters speak in an altogether too solemn manner, as though they had read a treatise on the Empire of Maximilian written by Rodolfo Usigli. It is a shame, because the scenic conception of *Crown of Shadow*—the title alludes to the madness that sat upon the brow of Carlota for sixty years —calls for a more novel, original, and brilliant treatment. The action is well multiplied into planes of times: it occurs in 1927, the date of the death of Carlota, and agile flashbacks evoke scenes from the Empire of Maximilian. The thought, however, was not as felicitously complicated into dialectic planes.

CELESTINO GOROSTIZA (1904) began by writing about subtle psychological and intellectual conflicts, but later turned to dramatizing Mexican social life. One of his more celebrated works is *The Color of Our Skin* (*El color de nuestra piel*, 1952). His technique is that of the old realism: a mimetic scenography, shriveled and dry dialogs, exaggerated sensationalism, character-rationalizations, with their store of reflections and theses. The theme also appears to be a realist theme: the color of the skin of the mestizo seen as a social problem. It is a problem—rather, a pseudo-problem—because it produces an inferiority complex in those whose skin is dark, and a sense of pride in those who are fair-skinned; it is a problem because, according to Manuel, who is the rationalizer of the work, Mexico feels insecure, and by disdaining the Indian, it falls into a stupid admiration of the foreigner, who does not interest himself in the slightest in the growth of the nation. A simple thesis, an affirmation of the mestizo base of Mexican nationality. It is likewise defended in a simple manner. There is nothing ingenious, brilliant, paradoxical, or surprising in the point of view. It is the type of thought expected from any well-meaning person. Moreover, what is surprising is that Gorostiza, who shows evidence of such good sense, should not have realized that his theme, although a true one, is altogether obvious. It is especially obvious in Mexico. EDMUNDO BÁEZ (1914), in his play *A Pin in the Eyes* (*Un alfiler en los ojos*, 1950), dramatized with only a few symbols—one of them is the bird whose eyes were pierced with pins so that it would sing better—the forbidden passions of love and hate: the love for one's brother-in-law and hatred for one's mother, passions which lead Quintila to suicide. Neither the plot, nor the characters, nor the dialog is sufficiently convincing. Other playwrights: FEDERICO S. INCLÁN (1910), MARÍA LUISA OCAMPO (1907), MIGUEL N. LIRA (1905), MAGDALENA MONDRAGÓN (1913), and RICARDO PARADA LEÓN (1902).

Central America: The Guatemalan MANUEL GALICH (1912) and the Costa Rican MANUEL G. ESCALANTE DURÁN (1905) stand out.

Antilles: In Puerto Rico, EMILIO S. BELAVAL (1903) and MANUEL MÉNDEZ BALLESTER (1909).

Venezuela: CÉSAR RENGIFO (1905) and LUIS COLMENAREZ DÍAZ (1902).

Colombia: RAFAEL GUIZADO (1913).

Peru: JUAN RÍOS (1914).

Bolivia: JOAQUÍN GANTIER (1900).

Uruguay: JUAN CARLOS PATRÓN.

Argentina: Among the better professional writers in the theater are ENRIQUE GUASTAVINO (1898), ARMANDO DISCÉPOLO (1887) and ROBERTO A. TÁLICE (1902). Others who contributed valuable works to the theater were not professionals, but came from the fields of poetry, the novel, or other literary activities.

Let us set one apart from the others: CONRADO NALÉ ROXLO (1898). We will study him here as a playwright, but he is above all a poet, and before referring to his theater we should make mention of his poetry. *The Cricket* (*El grillo*, 1923) has youthful grace, lyric mischief, freshness, innocent gamboling: "My eclogic and simple heart / awakened as a cricket this morning." This Nalé Roxlo is still charmed by Lugones, his literary father, and Darío, his literary uncle. As he grew, he lost his resemblance to his father and uncle. On the other hand, he preserved his similarity to his literary grandfather, Heine: lyric tenderness and pungent humor. In *Clear Vigil* (*Claro desvelo*, 1937) the mood is more grave, reflexive, melancholy, and even bitter. Surrealism lends him something from its dark cupboard. This man, who just yesterday had told us that his heart "awakened as a cricket," now tells us: "I do not know who I am, nor do I know why I exist." He tells us that he is "pointlessly writing vain words." In *From Another Sky* (*De otro cielo*) the poet, already mature, continues to grow, producing ever sadder fruit. The three books that we have already mentioned seem to be a single book; and, in fact, the first of them was perfect, and the other two only added to that perfection. Nalé, so serious in his poetry, has left us a series of humorous books: he signs them "Chamico." What interests us here is his theater. In *The Mermaid Tail* (*La cola de la sirena*, 1941), Nalé plays up and down his entire keyboard: the lyric and the humorous. As a lyricist, from the joy of living to bitter disillusionment: as a humorist, from the joke to subtlety. A siren, in love with Patricio (the theme of a story from Andersen), throws herself into the fishermen's nets and allows herself to be caught after Patricio comes to believe in her. She is so in love that she wants to be a woman and allows herself to be operated upon in order to be a woman. But Patricio loves what was wondrous in her, not what was human. Now Alga—so the siren is named—can no longer sing nor swim. Patricio falls in love with another woman—an aviatrix—because she seems to him to be a marvelous bird. Alga, understanding that she has lost the battle, throws herself into the sea, where she will be punished. At depth, the theme is the impossibility of love, or, at least, the impossibility of man's loving. Men fall in love with their dreams; when these dreams, on becoming real, become mutilated, they are pushed aside with displeasure. *A Difficult Widow* (*Una viuda difícil*, 1944) is a "farce" because the accumulation of so many abnormal situations is improbable, but upon this base, Nalé has constructed a fine comedy about colonial Buenos Aires shortly before the Revolution of 1810. In the drama *Cristina's Pact* (*El pacto de Cristina*, 1945) the theme appears elemental: Cristina, in love with a crusader who is leaving on a mission to reconquer the Holy Sepulcher, makes a pact with the Devil in order to gain the crusader's love; Cristina and Gerardo marry, but when she realizes that the price she must pay to the Devil is the son who will be conceived on her very wedding night, she commits suicide, a virgin still. Nalé Roxlo wanders among themes, situations, and traditional characters; but, nevertheless, he does not allow himself to fall into common pitfalls. His paradoxical wit surprises us just at the moment in which we were beginning to recognize an old medieval scene. That the love of Cristina, human rather than divine, should be so pure that the Devil should not want to buy her soul is a new touch; that the miracle of the fallen beech tree should appear to Gerardo to have come from God, and to Cristina, from the Devil, is another; that the pact should have been useless, since Gerardo loved Cristina anyway and the intervention of the Devil was superfluous, is an able variation on folklore; that the Devil hoped Cristina would give birth to the Antichrist is an unusual theological conundrum. Thus could we continue to enumerate the lively intelligence, the lyrical innovation, with which Nalé Roxlo composed the details of his drama. A beautifully worked jewel. The last plays of Nalé are *Judith* (1956), *El neblí* (1957) and *Reencounter* (*El reencuentro*).

XIV. 1940-1955

Authors born between 1915 and 1930

Historical framework: The second World War ends with the victory of the liberal nations, but in Hispanic-America some totalitarian dictatorships continue. They do not fall until the end of this period. The "cold war" between the United States and Russia forces new political alignments. In general, under the dictatorships as well as under the democratic regimes—which alternate in successive revolutions—the new phenomenon seems to be an evolution toward planned economies.

Cultural tendencies: Surrealism. Existentialism. Neo-naturalism. Committed literatures and gratuitous literatures, with neo-naturalist and existentialist styles predominating on one hand and classically inspired styles on the other.

Those who were born after 1915 had to become writers in the midst of horrors. The second World War had a different effect on them than the first World War had had on the ultraists. Those of the 1914 postwar period showed up as acrobats and clowns. They made fun of literature. They wanted to dehumanize it. They cultivated the absurd. They despoiled the verse of any regularity. Later they repented and tried to justify their nihilism. They discovered that at the bottom of their defiance of all literary conventions there was a pathetic sentiment: nothing less than the discontentment of the world. The youths born after 1915 did not experience this early stage of frivolity; they appeared on the scene pathetically. They even made a great fuss about the acrobatic contortions of their elder brothers. Poetry, no matter how obscure it may be, now aspires to delivering a message. Earlier poetry had been absurd; now, without ceasing to be absurd, it proposes to demonstrate that existence itself is absurd. An almost tragic accent is heard in the new literature: youth lives with a preoccupation with moral problems, because when it opened its eyes, it saw that human values had crumbled to the ground.

Surrealism, which the ultraists had reached only after becoming serious, was the point of departure for these young writers. The fact is that the embers of surrealism had just burst into flame again in France and everywhere. But this surrealism now was combined with existentialist philosophies. In the Spanish language we had our own existentialism, Unamuno's, Antonio Machado's, and Ortega y Gasset's. But it was Heidegger, Sartre, *et al.* who imbued youth. Style strove to be "essentially lyric," it strove to express "the truth of being." In addition, there were stylizations of popular elements (like those of García Lorca in the preceding generation). Between personalism and popularism surged neo-Romantic and neo-naturalist tendencies. They wrote "gratuitous literature" and "committed literature," with spiritualisms and materialisms, with the beautiful and the ugly, with hopeless anguish and revolutionary ire. Babel years. Has not literary life always been this way? Indeed it has. The historian knows very well that on putting his ear to each epoch, he will hear the confused Babel of literary languages. Nevertheless, the years to be reviewed here have been more Babelian than ever. Literature was now becoming complicated by new phenomena. The greatest demographic density in the republic of letters—never have so many persons written so much in our America as now—provided an example for every taste. It was as though an earthquake had unearthed all the geological strata and had juxtaposed them. Without perspective, we do not know which is the topmost. Furthermore, the culture of the world has been restructured with violent changes in national prestige, with a multiplicity of creative centers having conflicting values among themselves. The techniques of communication each day offer a complete universal panorama. Literature no longer depends on Paris, not even on London, New York, Madrid, Moscow, or Rome: it is planetary. The result is that in every minor literary circle there is a microcosm where everything is found. Nor is it even possible to exclude "badly written" literature, because to write badly— uglyism, the "what-do-I-care," the open faucet from whence filthy water is still issuing—does give expression to the desperate spirit of our times. In the three directions of contemporary literature—a literature committed to non-literary realities, a literature directed from outside of literature, and a literature regulated by purely literary laws—all stylistic attitudes are struck.

A. MAINLY VERSE

The poets who make their appearance during these years, in general, have a melancholy, elegiac, serious, pessimistic, introspective tone. These could be called neo-Romantics, provided we quickly add that their favorite poets were not Romantics, but surrealists like Neruda, symbolists like Rilke, concentrated poets like T. S. Eliot, fabulists like Saint-John Perse and, if they looked to the past, it was to admire the Spanish poets of the Renaissance. These influences, in themselves contradictory, are even more complex if we observe them closer. Surrealism for example is transformed into a kind of existentialism; in others, because of the social and political way of Neruda and Vallejo, it is transformed into a more or less lyrical communism; in still others, in a Catholicism which, because of its cult of tradition, leads to a cult of one's country.

Respectful of the innovations of vanguardism, they preferred to continue them in earnest. Hence, they admired Neruda, who did not play with literature—the Neruda of the last period, from *Third Residence* on, the Neruda who affirmed the existence of real things, who did not propose or intend to create them. It is a return to reality, but not directly, rather through the suburbs of metaphysics. The result was that many of those who claimed they were affirming human, national, and vital elements became lost on the road and never reached reality. Instead of creationist metaphors, they stated the things themselves: they believed that this was "founding poetry ontologically," although it was evident that these statements were also metaphors, basically. For example, it is a metaphor to affirm that "poetry does not create," but that "it discovers and recoups what is being shipwrecked in the obscurity of our being." The Catholic poets, for their part, affirmed life in an attitude of care and even love for man and all his assets. Real things offered themselves to the Catholic poets in order to enter their songs, and in this way to be honored. Only that, in thusly founding reality, they recognized the supernatural, the link with mystery.

To judge this poetry is impossible in a brief history. It is easier to point out mutual praise, collective evaluations, the energy with which some poets radiated on their contemporaries with radiations which, like uranium, perhaps before long will lose their radioactivity and return to lead. The sensation of the critic on reading these poets, is similar to the sensation of *"déjà vu, déjà lu";* it is quite natural, for we are looking at an abundant material not yet sorted, from which the dregs have not been sifted.

(1) *Mexico* / In this country of uninterrupted and diverse poetic production, none of the roads of pure poetry remained deserted: pure esthetes, contemplators of the world, worriers about social problems, explorers of the subconscious, those proud of their hermeticism and those of a transparent air and classical tastes, the religious ones, the new Romantics. The poets of the generation of *Contemporáneos* are followed by the generation of *Taller* (1938–41); Paz, Huerta, Quintero Álvarez, Beltrán. They move through the same paths: European culture, artistic conscience, technical rigor. Their experiences nevertheless are different. Marxism, surrealism, the desire to revolutionize man and society by means of love and poetry.

One of the leading poets of this generation is OCTAVIO PAZ (1914), a profound poet determined to interiorize himself. He began as an adolescent with *Savage Moon* (*Luna silvestre*, 1933) and matured quickly during the civil war in Spain with *They Shall Not Pass!* (*¡No pasarán!*, 1936). The books that followed were definitive: they have been collected in one volume, *Parole: Poetic Works* (*Libertad bajo palabra. Obra poética*, 1960). The title of one of his books ("at the world's shore") and the keynotes of his poems ("shore," "limit," "frontier," "mirror," "river," "instantaneous") show, not that the world has turned indifferently away, but the tragic and painful sentiment of wishing to identify with it. The pathetic poems of an exile who, by dint of feeling the world beyond himself, re-creates it with the ardor of an anguished flame. Paz gives body to the languid mists from which other poets of similar language never emerge. His imagination—and not all is imagination, there is an intelligence disciplined in devising metaphysical themes—is profoundly serious. He feels that his existence emerges from the Being, but he cannot know anything about the Being. It is the obverse, the zero. His existence is the only illuminated part of the Being. Between Being and Existence there is an immense mirror, the last wall of the consciousness, against which we stumble and despair. But this desperate solitude of our existence is pure Time; and we can objectify and eternalize each instant of our existence in Poetry. In Poetry, as in a mirror, we find ourselves and lose ourselves. In his most ambitious poem, *Sun Stone,* Paz gives us a synthesis of his lyricism. With a continuous river of images that twists along a cyclical bed, as fully shaped as a human personality, intuitions flow that only seem contradictory if we think them out logically: deep-rooted solitude and the transcendence that seeks companionship, the world of subject and the world of object, rebellion in one's intimate galleries and rebellion in the ruins of society, the minute and the millenium, the oneness and the wholeness, and love, in which a woman and a land proffer their forms and go off, as a single wave, along the undulating river of Paz's lyricism. A lyricism whose secret lies in a desire to resolve thesis and antithesis in a synthesis that might re-establish the lost unity of man. Between solitude and communion, Paz sings lyrically to each instant of his experience, but he is concerned with society, he is introverted and extraverted, hopeless and hopeful, given to blasphemous impulses toward destruction, but having faith in salvation. His will to transcend to other lives tends to assume erotic intensities. He has passed through the intellectual experiences of our time: Marxism, surrealism, the discovery of the Orient. But his thought seeks new paths. This thought is displayed in penetrating essays: *The Labyrinth of Solitude* (*El laberinto de la soledad*), *The Bow and the Lyre* (*El arco y la lira*), *The Pears of the Elm* (*Las peras del olmo*).

EFRAÍN HUERTA (1914), who had first written poems of love, went down to the street, mixed with the masses, spoke to them in verse, and incited them to proletarian revolution. His political purpose at times runs into unsuccessful messages. Mere external circumstances swallow them without a leftover. In *Star on High* (*Estrella en alto*, 1956) his two notes are heard, love and hatred. NEFTALÍ BELTRÁN (1916) poured out in his well-turned sonnets many lyrical wines: love, death, forlornness. His book: *Inimical Solitude* (*Soledad enemiga*, 1949).

A new group, the one of the review *Tierra Nueva* (1940–42), took up the lessons of pure art that had been given by Villaurrutia and his colleagues. They bolted the door against the din of social struggles and toasted to the pleasure of the naked poetic word. The most important is ALÍ CHUMACERO (1918). He offers an intelligently constructed poetry; he is a lyricist attentive to his sentiment but one who knows that a poem must appear with an austere structure. The cultured themes he mentions are not disguises, but classical moments in which the substance of his poetry will crystallize. The spontaneity of *Waste Land* (*Páramo de sueños*, 1944) is guarded in *Exiled Images* (*Imágenes desterradas*, 1948) and, now totally disciplined, it was concentrated in *Words at Rest* (*Palabras en reposo*, 1956). As a poet he is more essential than sensual, more confidential than imaginative, more pensive than raving. His desire to enclose his meditations within strict measures is the cult of a solitary poet. The loving impulse, the dense perception of time, the scorn for vulgarity, the knowledge that death is with us, the laceration of the soul are reflected in the intelligent mirror of his consciousness and from there classically organized images emerge. Chumacero takes possession of himself in the poetic form and is calm.

Central America

JAIME SABINÉS (1926) is also among the personal ones, that is, among those not easily grouped. Bitter, skeptical, derisive, suffering, unadaptable, pessimistic, he speaks to us of himself, especially of his enamored flesh. His eyes, more than seeing, seem to touch things: *Horal, The Sign (La señal), Confusion (Tarumba)*. MARGARITA PAZ PAREDES (1922), a poetess of intimate shades, of love, of maternity, of human solidarity, and social betterment: eight volumes of poetry among which are: *Shadow Scaffolds (Andamios de sombra)* and *Dimension of Silence (Dimensión del silencio)*. RUBÉN BONIFAZ NUÑO (1923) began with a poetry of impeccable classical cut—*Images (Imágenes,* 1951). Then, in *The Devils and the Days (Loe demonios y los días)* he went down to the people, with verses of social content and occasional prose forms. His book of love poems *The Mantle and the Crown (El manto y la corona,* 1958) balances these two movements of his lyricism. Bonifaz Nuño does not overflow like a river, but orderly he flows along a bed of well-constructed verses. As he constructs his poetry in careful forms, he also constructs his image of life. He feels that man, in his solitude and in the midst of the evils of contemporary civilization, becomes deformed or loses his plenitude. Down deep, his bitterness is optimistic, since he affirms a future in which man will stand consummate and high-minded in a society rebuilt on a new base. ROSARIO CASTELLANOS (1925) goes to her poetic confessional with one of the most sincere, serious, and interesting voices of this generation. Her confession speaks of herself—amours, lamentations, heartaches—and also of her origins, of the whole land and race of Mexico. In addition to her poems—*Of the Sterile Vigil (De la vigilia estéril), The World's Ransom (El rescate del mundo), To the Letter of the Law (Al pie de la letra)*—she published an excellent novel: *Balún Canán*. TOMÁS SEGOVIA (1927), if he is not a pure poet, is at least a poet of great purity, having achieved this purity by dint of contemplating his soul until he calmed it: *Provisional Light (La luz provisional), Seven Poems (Siete poemas), Light From Here (Luz de aquí)*. Other poets of these years: JAIME GARCÍA TERRÉS (1924), sober, measured, deep but circumspect, constructs his verses with clear understanding, in contrast to poets of fluid obscurity; JESÚS ARELLANO (1923) began with poems of distress, but later others flourished that were more optimistic and combative; JORGE GONZÁLEZ DURÁN (1918), who with daggers of ice dissects his soul, scorched with disenchantment; the nostalgic and elegiac JOSÉ CÁRDENAS PEÑA (1918); MANUEL CALVILLO (1918), one of the most delicate in the nuances of tenderness and memory; MIGUEL GUARDIA (1924) who descends to everyday prose—as he descends his verses become accordingly prosaic—complains of social oppression and, in sympathy for his fellow man, seeks to dialog with possible comrades; MARGARITA MICHELENA (1917), EMMA GODOY (1920), JORGE HERNÁNDEZ CAMPOS (1921), GUADALUPE AMOR (1920).

(2) *Central America / Guatemala:* During these years the review *Acento*, organ of the "generation of '40," broke out fighting. Its contributors had formed their tastes reading Rilke, Joyce, Valéry, Kafka and in Spanish, Neruda, Alberti, García Lorca; but their tone was one of open democratic affirmation, of clear human optimism. Prime movers: RAÚL LEIVA (1916), the most productive, came out of desolate and obscure poetry into the streets of a more popular poetry—*Anguish (Angustia,* 1942), *Ode to Guatemala (Oda a Guatemala,* 1953) and *Never Oblivion (Nunca el olvido,* 1957); CARLOS ILLESCAS (1919), author of *Autumn Frieze (Friso de otoño,* 1959); ENRIQUE JUÁREZ TOLEDO (1919), author of *Dianas for Life (Dianas para la vida,* 1956); OTTO RAÚL GONZÁLEZ (1921), inspired by noble

521

human causes: *Clear Wind* (*Viento claro*, 1953), *The Forest* (*El bosque*, 1955), and various books of poems of like distinction. Then came another wave: the Saker-Ti group, more militant in its leftist movement, more oriented toward the people. HUBERTO ALVARADO (1925) was the standard .bearer and he was accompanied by RAFAEL SOSA, MIGUEL ÁNGEL VÁZQUEZ, WERNER OVALLE LÓPEZ, MELVIN RENÉ BARAHONA, OSCAR ARTURO PALENCIA, ABELARDO RODAS.

Honduras: One can distinguish the voices of CARLOS MANUEL ARITA and DAVID MOYA POSAS.

El Salvador: CLARIBEL ALEGRÍA (1924), of a sincere and simple lyricism— *Vigils* (*Vigilias*, 1953); *Aquarium* (*Acuario*, 1955)—was also a prose writer with *Three Stories* (*Tres cuentos*, 1958). DORA GUERRA (1925), who has become silent lately. ALFONSO MORALES (1919). OSWALDO ESCOBAR VELADO (1919–1961), first an amatory poet, then turned to social poetry. In social poetry, committed to leftist political parties, are such figures as JORGE A. CORNEJO (1923), EDUARDO MENJÍVAR (1920?), MATILDE ELENA LÓPEZ (1923), and various others.

Nicaragua: Continuing enthusiastically the vanguard tendencies unleashed by Coronel Urtecho and others studied in the preceding chapter, a new generation appeared concurrently: the one made up of Ernesto Cardenal, Ernesto Mejía Sánchez, Carlos Martínez Rivas, and María Teresa Sánchez. ERNESTO CARDENAL (1925) is a spontaneous poet with the clarity of a prose writer. He has determined to form his sentiments so as to be understood, rather than to win admiration with his pure form: *Zero Hour* (*Hora o*), *Gethsemane Ky.* (1960). He lives in a monastery. ERNESTO MEJÍA SÁNCHEZ (1923), one of the most penetrating and rigorous poets, is author of *Spells and Exorcisms* (*Ensalmos y conjuros*, 1947) and *Contiguous Flesh* (*La carne contigua*, 1948). In his acuteness and rigor there is also a game of complex meanings and surprises that oblige the reader to respond with his intelligence, not just with emotion. CARLOS MARTÍNEZ RIVAS (1924) with deep, inner well-springs. MARÍA TERESA SÁNCHEZ (1918), of a delicate quality. Others: ERNESTO GUTIÉRREZ (1929), FERNANDO SILVA, and RODOLFO SANDINO (1928).

Costa Rica: A splendid poet of this period is ALFREDO CARDONA PEÑA (1917). His production, in verse and prose, is copious: his most important books were published in Mexico, where he lives, although the memory of his childhood, of his native land, continues to inspire him: *First Paradise* (*Primer paraíso*, 1955). He is a cultured, emphatic, eloquent poet, versatile in traditional and free rhythms. Other names: EDUARDO JENKINS DOBLES (1926); ARTURO MONTERO VEGA (1915) of social cares; MARIO PICALO UMAÑA (1928), original and disconcerting seeker of new ways; SALVADOR JIMÉNEZ CANOSSA (1922).

Panama: The new poetry offers these names: the monotonous EDUARDO RITTER AISLÁN (1916) and the polytonal ESTHER MARÍA OSSES (1916); the precise TOBÍAS DÍAZ BLAITRY (1919); the vital STELLA SIERRA (1919); and the withdrawn TRISTÁN SOLARTE [Guillermo Sánchez] (1924), author of a good novel, *The Drowned One* (*El ahogado*). Also there are HOMERO ICAZA SÁNCHEZ (1925), JOSÉ DE JESÚS MARTÍNEZ (1928), JOSÉ ANTONIO MONCADA LUNA (1926).

(3) *Antilles / Cuba:* Amazed by the quantity that he had read, Cuban youths selected Lezama Lima as a guide for their reading, and with their mouths open they almost lost their tongues. When they pulled

themselves together and were able to speak, they did so with obscure and arduous subtleties. They were anti-realists; or, if one pleases, they desired to pass beyond what we call reality and approach the absolute. As one of them, Cintio Vitier, had said, they were not determined to advance, like those of the *Revista de Avance* of 1927, but to submerge in search of origins—and *Orígenes* (1944–56), in fact, is the name of the review around which they gathered. They gave their esthetic credo the name of "transcendentalism" because they did not enjoy those immediate experiences easily expressed in words, but they departed into the unknown in search of absolute entities. The first to stand out were Gaztelu, Piñera, Baquero, and, to one side, Rodríguez Santos. They entered literature in two platoons.

The first was led by GASTÓN BAQUERO (1916). He reluctantly writes to tell us that he and we, and all of us, are constantly transforming. As in dreams, we are present at the metamorphosis of the world, but the final form will be that of death. Not even the forms of art will save us. After *Poems* (*Poemas*) and *Saul on His Sword* (*Saúl sobre su espada*, both of 1942) the poet abandoned his vocation prematurely. He had already told us about his disillusionment with poetry in the "Sonnet For Not to Die." Learned in Latin and Spanish classics, Father ÁNGEL GAZTELU (1914) gave us in his *Lauds Gradual* (*Gradual de laudes*, 1955) poetic exercises on Catholic themes, Cuban landscapes, and on his readings. VIRGILIO PIÑERA (1914), hard and angry in his verses, preferred prose, and as a narrator we shall see him in his place. JUSTO RODRÍGUEZ SANTOS (1915) is more of an esthete than any of those mentioned, veering less from the lyrical road and telling beautifully of the visits we receive from the world through our senses and also in what mood we receive them. Rodríguez Santos has an elegiac spirit. And others: ALCIDES IZNAGA (1914), ALDO MENÉNDEZ (1918):

The second platoon was led by CINTIO VITIER (1921). All of his work from 1938, published and unedited, was gathered in *Vespers* (*Vísperas*, 1953). His work is unhewn, scraggy, irregular, with shaded precipices (in whose depths Cintio Vitier broods) and sharp pinnacles that raise things (places, nostalgia) until they are carried to a sky of beauty. The theme of his poetry is that of feeling out of sorts with the world, the futile desire to capture it, and, within this desire, a resorting to his most obscure experiences. *Plain Song* (*Canto llano*, 1956) is reflective poetry—that is, a poetry made on reflections of what the poet is seeing inside himself. It is like a playing with mirrors to multiply the objects: the Cintio Vitier who is writing the poetry reflects on the Cintio Vitier who is living. The images, as they bounce from mirror to mirror, tire and weaken. Because of its reflective attitude *Plain Song* is rich in definitions, esthetic programs, theories on literary creation, confessions, and professional secrets. We could use this "plain song" as a key to his earlier books. The key, in itself, is not hermetic— it serves to open up his hermeticism.

Certain of her own poetic visions, FINA GARCÍA MARRUZ (1923) in *Lost Glances* (*Miradas perdidas,* 1951) allows herself the luxury of a plain though not simple expression, natural though artistic, human though not common, always sincere in her religious beliefs, in her memories, and in her impressions of the landscape: "Who shall gather thee, fleeting dust, lost afternoon / that leaves in my soul the sensation of the lily." OCTAVIO SMITH (1921) feels the presence of God in the quiver of all things. Each thing is an adjective made of the substance of God. Touched by this universal radiation, the poet's verses also ascend to vibrant adjectives: *Of the Furtive Exile (Del furtivo destierro,* 1946). Others: RAFAELA CHACÓN NARDI (1926), ELISEO DIEGO (1920), LORENZO GARCÍA VEGA (1926). The last two will also be found among the narrators.

Dominican Republic: The most important event in this period was the founding of the review *La Poesía Sorprendida* (1943–47). Its originators, directors, and collaborators belong to three generations. The Chilean poet Alberto Baeza Flores, together with Rafael Américo Henríquez and Franklin Mieses Burgos, already mentioned, and Freddy Gatón Arce, who will be mentioned, founded it. It was also edited by Lebrón Saviñón and Fernández Spencer. Among others, the editorial board was formed by Manual Llanes (1899), AÍDA CARTAGENA PORTALATÍN (1918), MANUEL VALERIO (1918), MANUEL RUEDA (1921), and JOSÉ MANUEL GLAS MEJÍA (1923). The tone of *La Poesía Sorprendida* was esthetically demanding— it got rid of the weight of local themes and the coercion of traditional forms, not to yield to easy ways but to impose upon itself a new rigor. It remained attentive to novelties in the literary world and in this way it refined its imaginative modes. Surrealism passed through its pages, but there was no one single esthetic that prevailed. On the contrary, it sought the integration of ancients and moderns, of Europeans and Hispanic-Americans, of symbolists and existentialists. It respected anything that incited effort and coordinated Dominican culture with that of the world.

One of the more famous poets in these years is ANTONIO FERNÁNDEZ SPENCER (1923). He opens his mouth with a naive gesture and sings of his amazement at life, nature, love, and death. He is plain, frequently prosaic, always spontaneous and affectionate. "To relate what happens in life" was his definition of poetry. Fortunately, he recited more than he related in *Interior Winds (Vendaval interior,* 1942) and *Beneath the Light of Day (Bajo la luz del día,* 1952). FREDDY GATÓN ARCE (1920) began in *Vlía* (1942) with obscure, bubbling, demoniacal prose poems. But on passing on to verse, without calming down, he stepped up to an illuminated podium and there recited his lyrical meditations. MARIANO LEBRÓN SAVIÑÓN (1922), an inspired musical poet, also tried a drama. The desolate MANUEL RUEDA (1921), masterful sonneteer and theatrical author, is one of the most interesting personalities. In other poetic groups we find poets as dissimilar as SÓCRATES BARINAS COISCOU (1916), RUBÉN SURO GARCÍA GODOY (1916), MANUEL DE JESÚS GOICO CASTRO (1916), HÉCTOR PÉREZ REYES (1927), CARMEN NATALIA MARTÍNEZ BONILLA (1917).

Puerto Rico: One of the most enraptured voices, not only for his lyricism, but also for his patriotic ideals, is that of FRANCISCO MATOS PAOLI (1915). His is a poetry that at times surprises us for its purity and hermeticism—*Inhabitant of the Echo* (*Habitante del eco*), *Theory of Forgetfulness* (*Teoría del olvido*)—and at times, for its profound grasp of things Creole—*Peasant's Thistle* (*Cardo labriego*). No sooner do we see him sensually yielding to the solicitations of his flesh and of the tropical landscape than he is singing to his solitude, his chaste spiritualism, his deep preoccupations. A great poet in all his moments.

Other poets worthy of consideration: Francisco Lluch Mora (1925), author of *Of Siege and Closure* (*Del asedio y la clausura*, 1950) and *Desperate Song to Ashes* (*Canto desesperado a la ceniza*, 1955) and Juan Martínez Capó (1923).

(4) *Venezuela* / Those who appeared in 1940, though they may not have formed a single group with a single program, had in common at least the will to withdraw from nativist, vernacular poetry as well as from the surrealism and free versism of the generation of the review *Viernes*. They aspired, on the other hand, to the expression of universal human values with formal rigor. They cultivated the sonnet, the *lira*, and other forms that they admired in the Castilian classics. They were cultured youths, most having a university education, who prepared themselves intellectually for the creation of their poems.

Aquiles Nazoa (1920) is a popular poet. He comes from the people and it is to the people that he sings with lively good humor, and with a serious voice too: *The Flute-Playing Burro* (*El burro flautista*), *Poems for Coloring* (*Poesía para colorear*). Morita Carrillo (1921), the highest expression of poetry written on children's themes. And also Luis Pastori (1915), Pedro Francisco Lizardo (1920), Tomás Alfaro Calatrava (1922–1953), Alarico Gómez (1922–1958), Ana Enriqueta Terán (1920). A few years later, around 1945, another group of poets came to reinforce the work of those we have just characterized. More lyrical than formalist, more vital, more free, at times more mischievous, were Benito Raúl Lossada (1923), Jean Aristeguieta (1925), Luz Machado de Arnao (1916), J. A. de Armas Chity, Ernesto Luis Rodríguez, Arístides Parra, Rafael Ángel Insausti (1916), José Ramón Medina (1921), Pedro Pablo Paredes (1917), J. A. Escalona-Escalona (1917), Eliseo Jiménez Sierra (1919). Later come Pedro Lhaya (1921), Rafael Pineda (1926), Francisco Salazar Martínez (1925), Rubenángel Hurtado (1922), Ali Lameda (1920), Dimas Kiew (1926), Palmenes Yarza (1916), Juan Manuel González (1924), Manuel Vicente Magallanes (1922). One of the most original poetesses, because of the expansive power of the lyricism which radiates in her verse—*Poems* (*Poemas*), *The Magic Wand* (*La vara mágica*), her theater, *Juan Palomo's Daughter* (*La hija de Juan Palomo*), *Belén Silvera*, and her narrative, *Fearless Juan* (*Juan sin miedo*), is Ida Gramcko (1925). Even her most intense sentiments, the amorous ones, are delicately sublimated into metaphysical material. Her imagination elaborates myths, dreams, and vital experiences, but it is respectful of forms. Her creative power is extraordinary for the abundance and facility with which she converts the slightest incitation—a remembrance, an overheard word, a stone, or a bird—into a motif of lofty poetry. Toward 1950 a group of poets appears which is difficult to separate into two chapters because of the few years that separate its members. Those who fit into this chapter are: simple and nativist, Lucila Velazquez, 1929, and Rafael José Muñoz, 1928; intellectual or hermetic, Francisco Pérez Perdomo, 1929, and Juan Salazar Meneses, 1929; sentimental and affirmative, Carlos Gottberg, 1929, and Miguel García Mackle, 1927.

(5) *Colombia* / After the "stoneandsky" group, but without the same cohesion of style, a new generation appeared, less brilliant but more preoccupied with the position of man in the world. More than Juan Ramón Jiménez they read Antonio Machado. They also read the surrealists. And the English poets. And the theoreticians of poetry. They reproached the "stoneandsky" group for having confided too much in the virtue of an oft-repeated poetic preciosity; in their more critical probing of the problems of existence, they used colloquial, everyday language. Because they wished to communicate with the public, they did not assume the arrogance of the hermetic poets.

The most listened to of these Colombian poets are (without counting those who will be mentioned in other sections) FERNANDO CHARRY LARA (1920), of the yearning but serene *Nocturnes and Other Dreams* (*Nocturnos y otros sueños*); MEIRA DELMAR (1922), MARUJA VIEIRA (1922), HELCÍAS MARTÁN GÓNGORA (1920), CARLOS CASTRO SAAVEDRA (1924), and OSCAR ECHEVERRI MEJÍA (1918). *If Tomorrow I Awake* (*Si manaña despierto*) by JORGE GAITÁN DURÁN (1925–62) contains both verse and prose penetrated by an intelligence poetic in nature, by intellectual emotions artistically elaborated: the most recurrent themes are those of eroticism and death.

(6) *Ecuador* / On the first level: CÉSAR DÁVILA ANDRADE (1917), a lyricist of great imaginative intensity, even with something of the magician, has also written some good short stories; FRANCISCO TOBAR GARCÍA (1920), Catholic, original in his human impetus, is also a dramatist; JORGE ENRIQUE ADOUM (1923), a leftist, Nerudian, vital, and overflowing; and ALEJANDRO CARRIÓN (1915). The latter is a disillusioned soul who gives us the chronicle of his disillusionments. But he reasons, enumerates, and repeats; and under these weights his lyricism becomes slow-paced. There is a noble lyricism, nevertheless, in *Poetry of Solitude and Desire* (*Poesía de la soledad y el deseo*, 1946)—defining title—and in *Agony of Tree and Blood* (*Agonía del arbol y la sangre*, 1948). As a prose writer he gathered in *The Damaged Apple* (*La manzana dañada*) stories of childhood evocation. He is ironic, of facile phraseology, though in his novel *The Thorn* (*La espina*, 1959) the theme of solitude is treated with black disorder. Other poets: ALFONSO BARRERA VALVERDE (1925?) and EDUARDO VILLACÍS MEYTHALER (1925).

(7) *Peru* / The pure poets now write with seriousness, with gravity, with responsibility. They write of all the emotions they feel worthwhile, without limiting themselves to fashionable themes, without mutilating the totality of man. They write in all modes, be they traditional or very new. At times, very free verses; at times, verses measured in every aspect. Further, one notices in them a respect for well-structured poetic forms. They are: JORGE E. EIELSON (1922), author of *Realms* (*Reinos*) and JAVIER SOLOGUREN (1922), author of *Circumspections* (*Detenimientos*) and *Sleeping Daedalus* (*Dédalo dormido*). In the nativist vein one of the most distinguished is MARIO FLORIÁN (1917). Both pure and nativist tendencies occur in the work of some poets, like WASHINGTON DELGADO (1926), of proven quality, and ALBERTO ESCOBAR (1929). Poets no longer think of Indians

and mestizos as racial groups, but as a "new Hispanic-American man," crucible of all ethnic metals. They also acknowledge the desire to use classical meters and strophes. Among the more recommendable social poets are: ALEJANDRO ROMUALDO (1926) and GUSTAVO VALCÁRCEL (1921), who is also a novelist: *The Prison* (*La prisión,* 1951) is a document on the sufferings of youths persecuted by reactionary forces. Within a tenuous and melancholy surrealism lies BLANCA VARELA (1926).

(8) *Bolivia* / First to be called on is YOLANDA BEDREGAL (1916), a lyricist of religious tone who writes about children and laments human suffering: *Nadir,* 1950, *Of the Sea and Ash* (*Del mar y la ceniza,* 1957). The novelty of these years is the springing up of a generation which is the most numerous in the history of Bolivian poetry: it is called "*Gesta Bárbara.*" Let us pull aside at least three significant poets. JULIO DE LA VEGA, making a way for himself between classical forms and the form of surrealism, entertained the noble causes of the world with a sense of Hispanic-Americanism. No sooner does OSCAR ALFARO appear with his tenderly lyrical poems of childhood recollections than he disappears in poems of political passions: *Alphabet of Stars* (*Alfabeto de estrellas*). ALCIRA CARDONA TORRICO is a deep, sincere voice, preoccupied with human destiny. One might add the names of ENRIQUE KEMPFF MERCADO (1920); GONZALO SILVA SANGINÉS, of tormented tonality; CARLOS MONTAÑO DAZA, who cultivated children's poetry; JORGE ALVÉSTIGUE, soft, delicate; CARLOS MENDIZÁBAL CAMACHO and JACOBO LIBERMAN, poet of social theme.

(9) *Chile* / After 1938 (Neruda and Rokha were already fixed in the firmament, the Alpha and Beta of Gemini) two new constellations appeared. One we will identify with the surrealist, Braulio Arenas, and the other with the popularist, Nicanor Parra. Braulio Arenas was the leader of the group gathered around the hallucinatory magazine, *Mandrágora* (six issues from 1938 to 1941), which sought a weird marriage between an unreal world and an irrational poetry. In its labyrinth, geography lost its frontiers, history only evoked deeds of invented creatures, literature proclaimed that the melting of forms was necessary for human liberty. At times their tricks turned out to be magic, at others, failure. The Mandragorists elbowed their way through, savagely breaking everything: screams, taunts, insults with no preoccupation over good forms. The other principal figures who accompanied Arenas were ENRIQUE GÓMEZ CORREA (1915) and JORGE CÁCERES (1923–1949). Gonzalo Rojas joined the group. Without becoming part of it, Gustavo Ossorio collaborated with *Mandrágora.* Among the Mandragorists one could name TEOFILO CID (1914) and FERNANDO ONFRAY (1922).

The leader, BRAULIO ARENAS (1913), does not construct objective images, like the Creationist Huidobro, nor does he envelop his spontaneous images in a full-blown emotion, like Neruda; but he inebriates his speech and lets it ramble, fagged and stammering, incapable of communicating anything to anyone. His initial forms were violent, but other poets accepted them with such tranquil souls, that in 1941 Arenas, unhappy over the peace that had settled, broke with *Mandrá-gora* and founded *Leitmotiv* (three issues from 1942 to 1943). These were wrenching years for Europe. Hitler had invaded France; France became mute; the surrealists took refuge in the United States and, guided by Duchamp, Breton, Char, and others, they invented a new letter of the alphabet, the triple V, not the simple V for Victory, and founded the review *VVV*. Braulio Arenas, fighting against the provincial spirit, becomes one with international surrealism. In order to prevent the death of the Spanish language, he converts it into the true agent of poetry, daringly and with greater liberty. See *Poems* (1960).

In his nocturnal strolls between Huidobro and Neruda, GONZALO ROJAS (1917) occasionally joined the somnambulists in the *Mandrágora* group. Then without leaving his element, the darkness, he began to speak more about his emotions than about his nightmares. A matter of accent, because everything was present in his introspective poetry: Romanticism, Creationism, Surrealism, Existentialism. His moods are dejected, with the exception of some beautiful, erotic moments: he feels lost in a stupid and cruel reality that does not reveal to man his destiny or who lent him his body. It is not the certainty of death that torments him, but the uncertainty of living in an indissoluble solitude. Thrust into the void, he feels ephemeral and poetizes while he, "a worm," is undone in the "beautiful darkness," "daughter of the chasms." The title *The Wretchedness of Man* (*La miseria del hombre*) is the key to his book dated 1948.

While in the *Mandrágora* movement, freed images beat their wings and gave poetic intensity to the darkness, poets of the other movement gave us a clear poetry, clear, not because it was configured by reason, but because it was aware of the continuous sentiment that inspired it. In general, the clear, natural, and popular poets turned to the native landscape and, as with the Romantics, they converted it into their sweet confidante. They were Nicanor Parra, Luis Oyarzún, Oscar Castro, Jorge Millas, ALBERTO BAEZA FLORES (1914), Venancio Lisboa, Vicario. They did not move along the trail of artistic renovation: but rather they backtracked so as to be better understood by the mass public. Nevertheless, they were different.

OSCAR CASTRO (1910–1947), connoisseur of the Spanish ballad, produced a provincial, nativist poetry. JORGE MILLAS (1917) and LUIS OYARZÚN (1920) attempted a philosophic poetry; Oyarzún is, in addition, a notable essayist of philosophic and esthetic themes. Parra was the one who felt the attraction for folklore most. NICANOR PARRA (1914) is the most complex. He began with popular and picturesque ballads—*Song Book Without Name* (*Cancionero sin nombre,* 1937) —and at each new turn he accented his lament and sarcasm before the absurdities of daily life—*The Long Dance* (*La cueca larga,* 1958). His most famous experiment was that of the antipoems. They consist of traditional poems composed with narrative material which, after drinking several glasses of surrealism, are stood on their heads. The everyday world, seen from feet up, appears grotesque. "Life has no meaning," he concludes prosaically in "Soliloquy of the Individual." Colloquial phrases deliberately ordinary, and an imagination that prefers to be ingenious rather than lyrical, communicate the pessimism and the irony of the antipoet (Huidobro had called himself "antipoet and magician"). The first edition of *Poems and Antipoems* (*Poemas y antipoemas*) dates from 1954. We have seen Gonzalo Rojas emerge from nocturnal poetry with alabaster words and Nicanor Parra from diurnal poetry with ebony words. The fact is that there are not poetic groups: there are poetic destinies, and their individual trajectories, no matter how much they ignore each other, end by crisscrossing. On the margin of these groups, then, we should study the Catholics EDUARDO ANGUITA (1914), the more important, and VENANCIO LISBOA (1917). We should also mention the egotist MAHFUD MASSIS (1917). While the generation of 1938, which we have just characterized, matured in poets like Braulio Arenas, Nicanor Parra, and Gonzalo Rojas, another youthful generation was growing up. Some of the young poets are still close to the older ones. They are JOSÉ MIGUEL VICUÑA (1920), ANTONIO CAMPAÑA (1922), RAQUEL SEÑORET (1923), ELIANA NAVARRO (1923), and JUAN LANEA (1925).

Then came poets who firmly manifested their disagreement with what had been done by the immediately preceding generation. For these young writers the free versism of Huidobro, Rokha, Neruda, Díaz Casanueva, and Rosamel del Valle, the nightmarish babblings of Braulio Arenas, and the guitar-twanging of Nicanor Parra were subterfuges to escape from the only responsibility of the poet: to compose poems with maximum formal rigor. What these youths wish is to continue the great tradition of Hispanic poetry, to respect rhythm, rhyme, and strophe and to renounce the non-esthetic activities of the spirit, to withdraw from themes appropriate to prose and to preserve the lyrical grace that wells up from one's intimate self. Poetic pressure must be disciplined until it acquires a clearcut visual and linguistic structure. Even free verse must have an interior architecture. The sense of composition can be exercised in regular as well as irregular verses: the important thing is the unifying projection of a worthwhile vision, that the images remain secured to a central nucleus.

One of the most decisive—and lucid—in the theory and practice of this program was MIGUEL ARTECHE (1926), a formalist poet of great purity and intensity in the expression of religious sentiment: his last books of poems are *Solitary One, Look Toward Absence* (*Solitario, mira hacia la ausencia*, 1953) and *Other Continent* (*Otro continente*, 1957). Arteche represents the cult of form that is reminiscent of the Golden Age of Spanish literature, even to his religious themes. Alongside Arteche are ROSA CRUCHAGA DE WALKER and DAVID ROSENMANN TAUB (1926): the latter does not disguise his artful artisan's trade. Other poets, such as ENRIQUE LIHN (1929), applied themselves more to expressions of passion, solitude, anguish, and affliction with free verse and simple words. Others, more direct, sang as all poets have sung who feel themselves close to the land, to the people, and to common speech: ALBERTO RUBIO (1928) and PABLO GUÍÑEZ (1929).

(*10*) *Paraguay* / Various poets appeared after Campos Cervera. They are Augusto Roa Bastos, who is to be found also among the prose writers; Hugo Rodríguez Alcalá (1919) who in *War Prints* (*Estampas de la guerra*) gave us a type of chronicle in verse on the Chaco War. Other poets of this same persuasion: Jesús Amado Recalde (1921), taken up with social problems; José Antonio Bilbao (1919), given to eclogues; Ezequiel González Alsina (1922), culturally oriented toward France; Rodrigo Díaz Pérez (1924), with his love for all things human. Another group followed immediately with Elvio Romero (1927) in the forefront. He is a social poet of exceptional expressive strength. He has published: *Broken-up Days* (*Días roturados*), with themes from the civil war of 1947; *Arid Sun Glares* (*Resoles áridos*), *The Bonfires Awaken* (*Despiertan las fogatas*), and *The Sun Beneath the Roots* (*El sol bajo las raíces*). His view of life is dramatic: this means he animates the conflicts between nature and man, and within man, between the forces of good and evil. Metaphysical rather than social is the poetry of Elza Wiezell de Espínola (1927). Others: Julio César Troche (1928), José Luis Appleyard (1927), Ricardo Mazo (1927), Ramiro Domínguez (1929).

(*11*) *Uruguay* / As in other parts of Hispanic-America the poets of these years visit the tourist nerve centers of poetry: Spanish poetry (Antonio Machado, García Lorca, and, of course, Juan Ramón Jiménez, Salinas, Guillén, Aleixandre), French poetry (from Valéry to Supervielle), our poetry (Neruda, Vallejo). But the poets of value are those who return from their tours and begin to live their lives.

First, these: Pedro Picatto (1914–1950) continues in a poetic language of images which have always been celebrated for their beauty and for their compassionate, soft, and occasionally doleful language. Carlos Denis Molina (1917) began as a poet surrounded with surrealist decors, similar, in his self-demanding attitude, to his countryman Fernando Pareda, and then he veered off to the theater —*If the Murderer Were Innocent* (*Si el asesino fuera inocente*) and the poetic novel—*It Will Always Rain* (*Lloverá siempre*). Luis Alberto Varela (1914) diagnosed his heart in the book entitled *The Saddened Side* (*Costado triste*, 1958). In his readings of the surrealist poets he discovered the possibilities of the symbol and the metaphor, but he knew how to reject verbal facility and withdrew into his sadness in order to arrange it ever more poetically. Others: Alejandro Peñasco (1914), Walter González Penelas (1915), González Poggi (1915), Beltrán Martínez.

The poets who make themselves known when the World War ends are neither optimists nor pacifists. On the contrary, with impassioned souls they decide to carry on their own war against reputations and styles that up to then had been respectable. This common negative attitude united them. Their mood was elegiac and hopeless. For this reason they were displeased with the overflowing vitality of Sabat Ercasty, Ibarbourou, Silva Valdés and, of the poets of the past, they only tolerated the taciturn ones, like Basso Maglio. The Uruguayan roots of this new poetic blooming are to be found rather in Cunha and in Liber Falco. In general, the postwar poets withdrew from society and, immersed in their inner selves, disdained or ignored the Church, the political Party, and the State. The style is human, direct, rugged, unarranged; it seems they feel that to insist on the perfection of esthetic forms is an insincerity. They absorb all the humors, even the prosaic ones, of everyday life and avoid rhythms, rhymes, strophes, and sumptuous metaphors. Time ticks tragically in them; as they ramble through ruins and rubbish they stop occasionally to write of a happy moment, but suddenly they stumble and think of death (Vilariño, Vitale, Brandy, Paseyro). Even the least afflicted are far from the optimism of the preceding generation (Sarandy Cabrera, Ariel Badano, Hugo Emilio Pedemonte, Silvia Herrera, Dora Isella Russell, Orfila Bardesio).

Perhaps the one who best illustrates the poetic mood of this generation is IDEA VILARIÑO (1928). She appeared in 1945 with *The Suppliant* (*La suplicante*) and since then, in poetic booklets, she has given us the poetry which leaves us with a bad taste, the taste of death. Yet the voice intones its breathlessness with broken and moving rhythms. It is hard, intense, obsessed with the impassioned hold that death has on us, tortured by sickness, suffering and desolation. IDA VITALE (1925), since she wrote *Light of This Remembrance* (*La luz de esta memoria*, 1949), has been registering the strong tones of her sensitivity. CARLOS BRANDY (1923), when he disposes of affected surrealist manners and when he is able to discard certain stylish formulas, denudes his body of its original feeling of existence and goes ever deeper, ever melancholically, into its experience. He also poured poetry into social themes. RICARDO PASEYRO (1927), melancholy, tortured, caretaker of his flame and his form. SARANDY CABRERA (1922), though he wrote in the manner of Neruda and Vallejo in his first book (*Onfalo*, 1947), he fixed his eyes on things with such a will to recognize them, one by one, as familiar objects of a universal disorder that he ended up by creating a convincing lyrical world. When later he delved into social themes, he did not break the unity of that world. SILVIA HERRERA (1927) is quick and precipitate in her confidential verses of sadness and tenderness. AMANDA BERENGUER (1924) who in *The River* (*El río*, 1952) had achieved an unimitative poetry of living experience (memories, travels, loves) is manifestly concentrated, intractable, wearisome in the eight poems of *The Invitation* (*La invitación*, 1957). She is a despondent woman conscious of her despondency in the midst of a life that invites her to be festive. Opaque images, deafening sounds. Because she knows her own sincerity and her own unmistakable tedium, she is not afraid of prose and allows it to be expressed by turns of ordinary language: *Contracanto*, 1961. DORA ISELLA RUSSELL (1925) is copious and adheres to traditional forms. The classical architecture of her poems is aired by a breeze from her inmost being. Her subjectivity—desires, presentiments of love, heartbreaks—at times touches a metaphysical depth. A careful technique holds her sentiments in check, and rather than describe them she suggests them to us. ORFILA BARDESIO keeps watch over her love poetry by fleeing from the episodic. And in conclusion there is CECILIO PEÑA (1925).

(*12*) *Argentina* / In 1940 a group appears—the "generation of '40"—which finds the immediately preceding poets too formal and too balanced, and from the past, it esteems only Borges, Molinari, and Mastronardi. They are grave, melancholy, elegiac, prudent. They have seen the world in shambles, and have no desire to play at literature. They did not cultivate wit for wit's sake nor the metaphor for metaphor's sake. They prefer traditional forms (like the sonnet) and at times popular inspiration. They know existentialism and when they are not writing about the visions of their immediate locale they write of the universal themes of existence.

Among the first to step to the front and center were JORGE CALVETTI (1916) and LEÓN BENARÓS (1915) who represent narrative poetry; OLGA OROZCO (1920); ROBERTO PAINE (1916); DAMIÁN CARLOS BAYÓN (1915); MARÍA GRANATA (1923). MIGUEL D. ETCHEBARNE (1915) wrote *John Nobody: The Life and Death of a Tough* (*Juan Nadie: vida y muerte de un compadre*, 1954) with an abstract, universal, and even allegorical intention. Although the subject matter does not have greatness, many of the stanzas are most expressive: images which colorfully describe, ingeniously define, and lyrically sing. Borges' enthusiasm for this poem—"it is the book that I should have liked to write, but couldn't" he told me in 1959—proves not so much the value of the book itself, but the effort to make of the *compadre* (bully, tough guy, ruffian, hoodlum) what Hernández had made of the gaucho. Juan Nadie is to the city what Martín Fierro had been to the country. JUAN RODOLFO WILCOCK (1919) begins, with a Romantic onrush, to speak of his own sentiments but he arranges them through respect for classical norms—a rare equilibrium by one who is not ashamed of the intensity of his nostalgia nor of the strength with which ancient meters and rhymes shape his expression. One of the poets of this group whom we have read most is DANIEL DEVOTO (1916). He is graceful, imaginative, cultured, technically masterful, and deeply lyrical from the dark roots deep in his solitude to the bright flower at the height of his song. *The Archer and the Towers* (*El arquero y las torres*, 1940) was his most metaphoric moment. In it the intermittent, hard, obscure, provocative images require that the imagination and sensibility of a sympathetic reader penetrate them like an electric current, but suddenly the light of the voltaic battery leaps from image to image; thus the solitude and melancholy of the poet are illumined. One notes that in *The Book of Fables* (*El libro de las fábulas*, 1943) Devoto has learned, while meditating on his own sadness, that down low we touch on fear, and lower still, the void. Shadows crawl on his recollections. Rather, shudders of shadows. But as his lyricism rises, it washes the wounds and cures them. Devoto, piously, kindly, optimistically, seeks the partial beauty of things and wants to save them. In his "David's Canticle" he is grateful for what in others is a source of anguish. Later Devoto applied himself to formal problems. In *Song Against Change* (*Canciones contra mudanza*, 1945), *Disheveled Songs* (*Canciones despeinadas*, 1947), *Two Rondels for Xylophone* (*Dos rondeles con maderas del país*, 1948), *Summer Songs* (*Canciones de verano*, 1950), *Hexasyllables from the Three Realms* (*Hexasílabos de los tres reinos*, 1959) he reconciled extreme complication of forms with maximum expressive facility. It is a program of technical rigor, with acrostics ciphered in accordance with a code of difficult keys, surprising crisscrosses, counterpoints of short and long, regular and free verses, interweaving of rhymes, playful experiments, and manipulations of perspectives. But at the bottom of this creation and re-creation of metrical movements, one hears a doleful voice that has become poetry. On one hand, love awakens torment in him, and on the other, poetry. *In Songs for No One (Canciones para nadie)* the verse clings closer to pure intuition. MARIO BINETTI (1916), discontented with his own epoch, travels through the ages: Greco-Latin classics, Dante and Petrarch, Garcilaso and Fray Luis, the great European Romantics, the symbolists; and while he travels, he writes of his solitude in ten books of intimate material that go from *The Good Shadow (La sombra buena,* 1941) to *The Book of Returning (El libro de los regresos,* 1959). The work of this initial group is prolonged by poets who line up in two tendencies: the one, more conservative and national; the other, more experimental and European.

In the first—well served by hinterland poets—we select among the most important, EMILIO SOSA LÓPEZ (1920), RAUL ARÁOZ ANZOÁTEGUI (1923), MANUEL J. CASTILLA (1918), NICOLÁS CÓCARO (1926), ALFREDO A. ROGGIANO (1919), HORACIO ARMANI (1925), AMÉRICO CALI (1915) LEDA VALLADARES (1920?), MARIO BUSIGNANI (1915), NICANDRO PEREYRA (1917), ANTONIO ESTEBAN AGÜERO (1918), FRANCISCO TOMAT GUIDO (1922). JORGE VOCOS LESCANO (1924), with architectonic forms, has celebrated sentiments of human and divine love, conscious of belonging to an illustrious family of Spaniards (from Garcilaso and San Juan de la Cruz to Góngora, Bécquer, and Juan Ramón Jiménez) and of Argentinians (from Banchs to Bernárdez and Molinari). GUILLERMO ORCE REMIS (1917) had a double theme: man, tormented and unprotected; and God, awaiting us.

In the other tendency, of lesser national tradition, the nonconforming, anti-conventional poets look to see what is being done elsewhere: Eliot, Pound, Luc Deaunes, St.-John Perse, René Char, Vallejo, Ungaretti, Aleixandre. Earlier they used to speak of Creationism, now they speak of inventionism—JUAN JACOBO BAJARLÍA, EDGAR BAYLEY (1919), RAÚL GUSTAVO AGUIRRE (1927), MARIO TREJO (1926), and JORGE ENRIQUE MÓBILI (1927). Also on this side, though not necessarily along the same route, move OSVALDO SVANASCINI (1920), MIGUEL A. BRASCÓ, and HORACIO JORGE BECCO (1924). The latter, in *Countryside Poems (Campoemas,* 1952) without juvenile ostentations of vanguardism (although with the liberty that this movement had won) tranquilly, with a sincere tone that had no pretensions even of being musical, poetized his observations and emotions of rural Argentina. He evokes figures from the past as easily as he stretches out toward things, in an attitude of waiting. He receives rural material in his hands and with it forms surprising miniatures, metaphors independent from one another, all of them rich in inventiveness and visuality. During the last years two poets approached surrealism. CÉSAR FERNÁNDEZ MORENO (1919), who in *Blind Rooster (Gallo ciego,* 1940) evoked his nostalgias with unadorned voice, in *Twenty Years Later (Veinte años después,* 1953) he intoned the broken murmur of that unarticulated voice that the surrealists preferred. EDUARDO A. JONQUIERES (1918) began with serene, simple, sincere poetry: *Permanence of Being (Permanencia del ser,* 1945), *Growth of the Day (Crecimiento del día,* 1949), *The Monsters (Los vestiglos,* 1952). In *Song Trials (Pruebas al canto,* 1955) his expression is aggravated with grimaces of inner torment. Others: ALDO PELLEGRINI, CARLOS LATORRE. And now, one of the better poets of this generation: ALBERTO GIRRI (1918). Without the expressive automatisms of surrealism, but urged on in his irrational depths, Girri wants to reveal himself in images that capture essences. His images tend to be hermetic; they tend to become cold; they tend to become hard. But one can glimpse that behind them the poet is apprehending the temporal sense of existence. From *Deserted Beach* (*Playa sola,* 1946) up to *Scandal and Solitude* (*Escándalo y soledades,* 1952), *Magic Attributes* (*Propiedades de la magia,* 1960), Girri sought the exact, hard, cold word in which his vision as a passionate, sensual, tragic, solitary soul would remain implacably carved. Murena—also a poet—will be seen among the prose writers. We close our panorama with the names of CARLOS F. GRIEBEN, CARLOS VIOLA SOTO, EDUARDO CIOCCHINI (1922), GREGORIO SANTOS HERNANDO (1921), DAVID MARTÍNEZ (1921), GUILLERMO ETCHEBERE (1917).

B. MAINLY PROSE

1. Novel and Short Story

A new realism, a new naturalism appears. It will be remembered that in the previous chapter the dissolution of the novel was discussed —the novel such as it had been practiced up to 1910. Proust, Joyce, Mann, Faulkner, Kafka, Woolf, Huxley, and others broke its framework. And in Hispanic America novels appeared that seemed only to intend to go counter to reality. But now, after those experiments, there was the will, once again, to grasp reality. Except that one could no longer return to the naturalism of the nineteenth century. Zola and his followers had written with the desire to prove a more or less scientific doctrine. But the young novelists of 1940 to 1955 no longer read Zola. Nor the Russians. In any case, they did read the Italian, French, and American neo-naturalists. Especially the Americans. Instead of describing, they wanted to convey reality: to produce reality as something alive, disordered, in bulk, something that is going on between the novelist and the reader. That is, the novelist no longer aspires to control the reader. The narrator as the omniscient witness, as the operator who arranged things from the inside in order that we may understand them better, as producer and impresario of a spectacle to which we are invited for our entertainment, disappears. The novel seethes, as life itself. The characters are scarcely glimpsed because there is no one who sees them totally. And since the characters only glimpse each other and do not clarify for us (how could they, if the characters do not know they are characters of a novel, if they don't know that we, the readers, are reading them!) the mobile situations from which they espy each other, the chronological and spatial orders become confused. Thus is reality: absurd.

Although this realism does not look like that of the nineteenth century, it is realism. Further: it is a daring, raw, aggressive, shocking naturalism. Things are not narrated or described by an author who feels the esthetic form of the novel, but presented by an author who feels the formless anti-novelistic ugliness of everyday life. Something is put forth and something is hidden at the same time: a reality is put forth but the artistic connections are hidden. The experiments that a few had undertaken earlier now are repeated as if they were not experiments but established modes of novelizing: representation of time, alteration of the narrative sequence, multiple perspective, the technique of the stream of consciousness, and simultaneous, retrospective, crisscrossed actions on various planes. Novels, then, with a minimum of plot, characterization, and description. It is as if the novelistic structure had disintegrated. Either the stuff of the narrative remains dumped in the mind of the author or of the characters—as was done in James Joyce's generation—or the psychology is eliminated and autonomy is taken on by the objects themselves—as is done in Alain Robbe-Grillet's generation. It goes without saying that in the novels, or anti-novels, that resembled pieces of chaos Creolism was abandoned. Creolism seemed to identify Hispanic-America with an agrarian reality. This could have been convincing up to the second World War; but then literature had to become aware that the cities had grown at the expense of the countryside, that the tone of life was that of the industrial society, that realism had to reflect class struggles with more urbane styles.

Another interesting phenomenon is the emergence, at the end of the fifties, of a Catholic group of narrators who, without detouring from the traditional beliefs, illuminate with a crude light and experimental techniques the sinful state of man (in Argentina, for example, Dalmiro Sáenz, Helen Ferro, Federico Peltzer, Bonifacio Lastra, and others). There is no bigotry in them. On the contrary, they often dare to treat themes of sex, crime, violence, and infamy, and they accomplish this with free ingenuity and good humor. Rooted in an ancient Catholicism, but displaying avant-garde techniques, these narrators resemble an opposing group, the Marxists, who also explain reality dogmatically, but who now practice ways of writing they had considered "bourgeois" and "decadent" in the thirties and forties.

(1) *Mexico* / Two principal figures: Arreola and Rulfo. JUAN JOSÉ ARREOLA (1918) has a preference for fantastic short stories and for intellectual games rich in humor, problems, and paradoxes: *The Whole Fabulous Book* (*Confabulario total,* 1962). He also published a theatrical farce, *Everyone's Day* (*La hora de todos,* 1954), in which he satirized the life of a potentate, with mobile and innovating scenes.

JUAN RULFO (1918) molded regional life—its landscapes, its names, its words and its situations of innocence, crime, adultery, and death— in his short stories *The Plain in Flames* (*El llano en llamas,* 1953). Later, in *Pedro Páramo* (1955), he worked on his rural themes with a complicated novelistic technique which owes something to William Faulkner. The complication is due to the fact that the story is told in leaps, forward, backward, to the sides, and from several points of view. The eye that knows all and sees all belongs, naturally, to the author; but that eye enters the novel following Juan Preciados who narrates, in the first person, how he went on behalf of his dying mother to a place called Comala to straighten accounts with his father, Pedro Páramo. However, Juan Preciados finds that Comala is a ghost town: in the rarefied air only voices, echoes, and murmurings of phantoms are heard. Juan Preciados dies and his shade continues to dialog with other souls in purgatory. The author, who has come down to Comala like one who goes down to Hades, completes the story of Juan Preciados in the third person. The voices, echoes, and murmurings that Juan Preciados had heard are explained by means of the scenes conjured up by the author. The atmosphere is supernatural, but not subjective. Time does not flow: it is eternalized. Because of the apertures cut into this eternity we can see and hear the dead, caught in instants that do not succeed each other in a straight line but are dispersed in disorder: only the author gives them meaning. The narrative nucleus is the life of Pedro Páramo, from his infancy to his death, in his old age, in the years that run from Porfirio Díaz to Obregón. His life is violent, despotic, brutal, covetous, vengeful, treacherous, sensual, but dignified by his great love for Susana, his childhood companion, who is half-crazed when he takes her with him. The reader is chilled in horror, as if he were dreaming an absurd nightmare; the images, which occasionally are of great poetic force, tragically evoke the annihilation of a whole Mexican town.

Other narrators: ALBERTO BONIFAZ NUÑO (1915), SERGIO FERNÁNDEZ (1926), LUIS SPOTA (1925), RAFAEL SOLANA (1915) and CARLOS VALDÉS (1928).

(2) *Central America / Guatemala:* The most outstanding short-story writers of the group around the review *Acento* is AUGUSTO MONTERROSO (1921), who has published *Complete Works and Other Stories* (*Obras completas y otros cuentos*) of manifest irony. Also a short story writer, ironic in his observations on social inequities, is GUILLERMO NORIEGA MORALES (1918). JOSÉ MARÍA LÓPEZ VALDIZÓN, author of *The Letter* (*La carta,* 1958), cultivated the realist short story on social themes.

Honduras: The best short story writer of these years is VÍCTOR CÁCERES LARA (1915): his *Humus* is sad but moistened by a certain soft humorism. With short and agile brush strokes he tells us about farm laborers and city workers. The novel of the social problems involving the abuses of the great fruit companies began with *Green Prison* (*Prisión verde*) by RAMÓN AMAYA AMADOR. Another of his novels, *Builders* (*Contructores*), raises its scaffolding in the city.

El Salvador: HUGO LINDO (1917) is one of the most outstanding figures. He is a poet—*Book of Hours* (*Libro de horas*), *Symphony of the Limit* (*Sinfonía del límite*)—but is situated here because the depiction of customs that dominated literature almost everywhere in Hispanic-America was enriched with psychological depth by his narrative work: *Sugar Brandy and Champagne* (*Guaro y champaña*, 1955), short stories, and *God's Fishhook* (*El anzuelo de Dios*, 1956), a novel. RICARDO TRIGUEROS DE LEÓN (1917), a fine sonneteer in *Presence of the Rose* (*Presencia de la rosa*), distinguished himself for his impressionistic prose, artistically shaded.

Nicaragua: FERNANDO SILVA ESPINOZA (1927).

Costa Rica: After the already-discussed Marín Cañas and Fallas, another pair of novelists of note appeared. FABIÁN DOBLES (1918), with his Marxist forceps, delivered several novels from the painful reality of injustices, privileges, and social miseries. *This Thing Called People* (*Ese que llaman pueblo*, 1942) is the story of the hardships of a young peasant. In *In the Valley* (*El sitio de las abras*) one of his favorite themes appears: the unjust sequestration of the peasants' lands. A *Bubble in Limbus* (*Una burbuja en el limbo*), even more than previous novels, shows the personal and literary side of Dobles. He has cultivated, likewise, the short story and poetry. Also in a frank political attitude, JOAQUÍN GUTIÉRREZ (1918) has novelized themes of imperialism and of banana plantations, but he does it at times with the techniques of the interior monolog. *Grove of Mangroves* (*Manglar*, 1946) follows the steps—and the thoughts—of Cecilia in her daily incidents as a teacher and woman, in the city and in the highlands. *Puerto Limón* (1950), less poetic, is rich in observations, though what is observed more is the mass and not the individual. He has published *Poetry* (*Poesía*, 1937) and children's stories (*Cocorí*, 1954). On the more subjective side, and with a more complex style, YOLANDA OREAMUNDO (1916–1956) distinguished herself with the representation of her experiences of time with techniques of psychic flux in *Terra Firma* (*Tierra Firme*) and in *The Route of Its Evasion* (*La ruta de su evasión*).

Panama: In their majority, the narrators of this generation concentrated on the national reality, urban or rural, and with faith in the people; but with their eyes opened to the evils of society, they converted literature into a means of protest. What they lacked in esthetic concentration, they made up in practical militancy. Overestimation of the popular element at the cost of artistic merit. JOSÉ MARÍA SÁNCHEZ B. (1918)—author of *Three Stories* (*Tres cuentos*, 1946) and *Shumio-Ara*, 1948—has described, in the violent landscape of a certain Panamanian region, the life of laborers and the social injustices they experience. MARIO AUGUSTO RODRÍGUEZ (1919) has selected as his setting that band of land where the city and the country defend a mutual frontier from each other. MARIO RIERA (1920) and CARLOS FRANCISCO CHANGMARÍN (1922) are also rural narrators, nonconforming and sentimental. JOSÉ A. CAJAR ESCALA (1915) in *The Head-Man* (*El cabecilla*, 1944) writes a novel about an abortive uprising of peasants. Different from those mentioned previously are writers of urban themes: JUAN O. DÍAZ LEWIS (1916), FERMÍN AZCÁRATE (1922). But Panamanian writers generally felt that the cities denied nationalism or that, in any case, the only thing that could justify a novel about the city would be its descriptions of the masses. We have purposely left to the end two of the best novelists of this realist group: Beleño and Jurado. JOAQUÍN BELEÑO (1921) in *Green Moon* (*Luna verde*, 1951) records his own experiences as an aggrieved worker in the American Zone of the Panama Canal. It is a picture of misery and dereliction, in contrast with the falsely prosperous city of Panama—a picture drawn with undisguised resentment. RAMÓN H. JURADO (1922) works with sundry themes. *San Cristóbal* (1947) is the slow and occasionally poignant novel of the exploitation of sugar. *Deserters!* (*¡Desertores!*, 1952) reconstructs the "thousand day war" (between 1899 and 1902) with the legendary indigenous leader Victoriano Lorenzo. In *The Attic* (*El desván*, 1954)—basing himself on the strange book by Francisco Clark, *By Way of Torment* (*A través del tormento*, 1931)—Jurado analyzes the psychology of a person who is a witness to his own horrendous and macabre ankylosis.

(3) *Antilles / Cuba:* VIRGILIO PIÑERA (1914) has an ironic, hopeless, anguished, and philosophizing attitude. In his *Cold Stories* (*Cuentos fríos*)—a hellish cold—his imagination carries him to torment. Although hermetic, he polishes his images with such care that through them we see, magnified, the meaninglessness of the world and the absurd movements of our existence. The stories of HUMBERTO RODRÍGUEZ TOMEU (1919) move in an irrational current, floating on the absurdity and grotesqueness of life. GUILLERMO CABRERA INFANTE (1929) is a narrator of inner life (at least those aspects illumined by his favorite American authors: Faulkner, for example). LORENZO GARCÍA VEGA (1926) evokes personal recollections in his *Spirals of the Cuje Poles* (*Espirales del cuje*, 1951). SURAMA FERRER (1923) is a novelist in *Romelia Vargas* (1950) and a short story writer in *The Sick Sunflower* (*El girasol enfermo*, 1953). RAMÓN FERREIRA (1921) delves into Cuban life, but seeks psychological apertures and chiaroscuro atmospheres: *Shark and Other Stories* (*Tiburón y otros cuentos*, 1952). RAÚL GONZÁLEZ DE CASCORRO (1922), after his rural and endearing narrations, has dedicated himself to the theater *Trees Are Roots* (*Arboles son raíces*, 1960).

Dominican Republic: The tendency to reflect national life with its social problems predominated. JOSÉ RIJO (1915), whose short stories are neat and circumspect; NÉSTOR CARO (1917), in his stories *Black Sky* (*Cielo negro*, 1949) sketches lives of humble people; RAMÓN LACAY POLANCO (1925), a poet, short story writer, and novelist: *The Woman of Water* (*La mujer de agua*, 1949), *In the Mist* (*En su niebla*) and *Southern Point* (*Punto sur*, 1958); and ALREDO FERNÁNDEZ SIMÓ (1915), author of the novel *Guazábara* (1958). J. M. SANZ LAJARA (1917) has traveled throughout Hispanic-America and from his observations have come several collections of realist stories: *Cotopaxi* (1949), *Aconcagua* (1950), and *The Padlock* (*El candado*, 1959).

Puerto Rico: A half century of United States domination could not remove Puerto Rico from its Hispanic base. Even more: if not the will for political independence, at least the will to preserve Puerto Rican essences was growing. Literature reflected a divided opinion: supporters of United States annexation, supporters of total autonomy. In 1952 a juridical formula of conciliation is reached: the majority of the people voted in favor of an Associated Free State. There were dramatic national gestures, bloody incidents, polemics. The affirmation of the historical personality of the island and the defense of its values will be one of the themes of Puerto Rican narrative.

One of the best story writers is RENE MARQUÉS (1919). In *Another of Our Days* (*Otro día nuestro*, 1955) death, time, anguish, disgust, fear, consciousness of being, the absurdity of life, liberty—topics much viewed and reviewed by the existentialists—insert themselves like a corkscrew into Puerto Rican political reality in Quixotic or heroic episodes of nationalism. Marqués is a man of political concerns, worried over national sovereignty, but subtle, complex, and capable of stylistic surprises. His novel *The Eve of Man* (*La víspera del hombre*, 1959) is a tormented history of love, the love of Pirulo not only for a woman, but also for the land and his humble village. The action takes place in 1928, and one of the threads of the plot is tinged with the red of political passion. One of its highlights is the dialog between Pirulo, who prefers the republic, and Raúl, agreeable to North American domination. In addition to excelling in narrative literature, Marqués is important in theatrical production. *The Little Cart* (*La carreta*, 1952), in three acts, presents the story of a family which is uprooted from the land, moves to a city slum in San Juan and then to New York. He has collected in one volume, *Theater* (*Teatro*, 1959), *Maimed Suns, A Blue Boy for That Shadow* and *Death Does Not Enter the Palace*. He also published the drama *The Sun and the MacDonald's*, a "pantomime" *Johnny Simpleton and the Lady From the West* (*Juan Bobo y la dama de occidente*, 1956), and the play *House Without Clock* (*La casa sin reloj*, 1962). Another of the good narrators is ABELARDO DÍAZ ALFARO (1920), author of the stories in *Terrazo* (1948), rural in atmosphere. Within a realist style his phrases are pleasant and at times contain overtones of protest over social hardships; in some pages he symbolizes human conflicts by using animals. A biographer of city life was JOSÉ LUIS GONZÁLEZ (1926). He has several collections of stories: *In the Shadow* (*En la sombra*, 1943), *Five Stories of Blood* (*Cinco cuentos de sangre*, 1945), *The Man in the Street* (*El hombre en la calle*, 1948), *On This Side* (*En este lado*, 1954). His novelette *Paisa* was written in 1950, but he re-edited it and modified it a good deal in 1955. Here he capably interweaves a story and an evocation. The story: two Puerto Ricans hold up a store in New York. The flashback: the one made by Andrés, the *paisano* or *paisa* [countryman] of his own life, from his hungry childhood in Puerto Rico to his hungry adolescence in New York. The technique of interweaving and certain expressions of vivid imagination and even poetry require that we respect José Luis González, the writer. Nevertheless, the novelette suffers for the impatience with which the author gives vent to his political zeal without first having stylized it artistically. The political outlines—of Marxist type—are obvious: the suffering of the working class, social injustices, Yankee imperialism, racial discrimination, banditry as an immediate defense, and revolutionary struggle as an ultimate solution. Perucho, the other bandit, is the "reasoner," the one who raises an optimistic slogan from the depth of the tragedy in *Paisa*. PEDRO JUAN SOTO (1928), in *Spicks* (1956), also tells us stories of Puerto Ricans in New York, written in a nude prose, somewhat in the manner of Hemingway. He has written novels—*Anonymous Dogs* (*Los perros anónimos*), *Usmaíl*—and theatrical pieces. GUILLERMO COTTO-THORNER (1916) is another of those inspired by the Puerto Rican colony in New York: *Tropics in Manhattan* (*Trópico de Manhattan*, 1951). CÉSAR ANDREU IGLESIAS (1918?) is one of the novelists of strong personality; he related in *The Defeated* (*Los derrotados*, 1956) the terrorist actions of the nationalists when they attacked government representatives in Washington. Later he published another novel: *A Drop of Time* (*Una gota de tiempo*, 1958). EMILIO DÍAZ VALCÁRCEL (1929) delves into depressing, morbid, and disgusting realities and comes up with stories of great narrative strength. *The Siege and Other Stories* (*El asedio y otros cuentos,* 1958) is a black anthology of horrors: lesbianism, suicide, macabre scenes, prostitution, morphinomania, homicide, misery, injustice, thievery, sickness, sexual impotence. Only in one story—"The Toad in the Mirror"—the repugnant situation enters with a light of fantasy: the soldier without legs who turns into a toad and croaking, advances in little leaps headed for his wife's sex. But even in the other stories, molded from real mire, Díaz Valcárcel knows how to impose upon them a violently artistic form; he only fails in two discursive and moralizing monologs. The interior monologs, intercalated in the course of the action, are more effective. The most powerful aspect of the book is its keen comprehension of solitude. José Luis Vivas stands somewhat apart from the previous group for his more sentimental, more combative stories: *Lights in Shadows* (*Luces en sombra,* 1955). Other names: Edwin Figueroa (1925), Salvador de Jesús (1927), Violeta López Suria, Manuel Toro (1925), Jorge Felices (1917).

(4) *Venezuela* / In the year 1940 a generation of short story writers breaks out. They differ among themselves; some soak in national life, in the country and the city, others turn to self-contemplation or follow foreign literary examples. Gustavo Díaz Solís (1920) is a good landscapist, but his stories turn to shambles when they come to the city: *Sea Swell* (*Marejada,* 1941), *It Rains On the Sea* (*Llueve sobre el mar,* 1942), *Stories of Two Times* (*Cuentos de dos Tiempos,* 1950). His stories, however, although composed straightforwardly, have strength and lyrical suggestion. Oscar Guaramato (1918) paints well the basics of nature—landscapes, animals—and tenderly presents in the foreground his human characters: *Biography of a Beetle* (*Biografía de un escarabajo,* 1949). His social themes are usually the same ones preferred by the realists, but he treats of them with more artistic care. Humberto Rivas Mijares (1919) is an artist of well-disciplined style, precise and concise in his description of things: *Eight Stories* (*Ocho relatos,* 1944), *The Blind Man Who Clings to the Wall* (*El murado,* 1949). Antonio Márquez Salas (1919) takes nature by surprise in its most dramatic moments and a lyrical aura envelops his characters: *The Man and His Green Horse* (*El hombre y su verde caballo,* 1947), *Ants Travel at Night* (*Las hormigas viajan de noche,* 1956). He was one of the most influential figures of his generation, in part because of the innovations he used in composing his narratives. Appearing later were Héctor Mujica (1927), Roger Hernández (1921), Alfredo Armas Alfonso (1921), Andrés Marino Palacio (1928), Oswaldo Trejo (1928), a story writer of strange and original vision and techniques, Francisco Andrade Álvarez (1920), Eduardo Arcila Farías (1918), Horacio Cárdenas (1924), Mireya Guevara (1923). Ramón González Paredes (1925) has distinguished himself in various genres: poetry, theater, essay, and, in the narrative, for his short stories *Extraordinary Crime* (*Crimen extraordinario,* 1945), and the novels *The Imaginary Suicide* (*El suicida imaginario*) and *Genesis*. Carlos Dorantes (1929) is a short story writer.

(5) *Colombia* / As everywhere else, there were narrators who tightened the natural bonds of life with reality, and narrators who loosened these bonds in order to see inside man, and there were even those who cut them so that men would come free from their circumstances, thus becoming free as fantasy. Another way

of classifying writers would be by their narrative technique: those who are safely relying on the effectiveness of a clear, continuous, logical traditional art; others risking calculated disorder. JESÚS BOTERO RESTREPO (1921) was the novelist of the jungle in *Andágueda* (1947). NÉSTOR MADRIDMALO (1918) in *Luck at Seven O'Clock and Other Stories* (*Suerte a las 7 y otros relatos*, 1955), is one of those who broke loose from the formulas of the depicters of social customs and, in a simple prose, approached men to study their psychologies. EDUARDO SANTA (1928) made himself known with *The Lost Province* (*La provincia perdida*, 1951). Is it a novel? Only in the sense that one can say that Juan Ramón Jiménez' *Platero y yo* is a novel. Poems in prose? Only in the sense that one can say that the "confessions of a little philosopher," in "the towns" of Azorín are so. Rather, it is an album of vignettes of life in Aldeópolis as they are evoked by a well-educated adolescent. Or, better yet, an intimate diary. Scenes, types, customs, landscapes, real things, but the reality that always imposes itself is the sensibility of a wandering and artistic author. In his novel *The Sunflower* (*El girasol*), Santa later analyzes the obscure movements of an abnormal psychology. JAIME IBÁÑEZ (1919) has narrated episodes of civil wars: *Where Dreams Dwell* (*Donde moran los sueños*) and, in a more poetic style of human suffering at the hands of a nature that destroys itself, *Each Voice Carries Its Anguish* (*Cada voz lleva su angustia*). MANUEL MEJÍA VALLEJO (1923), impersonal, exact in his version of the things that he sees in American lands, has a novel *We Were the Land* (*La tierra éramos nosotros*, 1945) and stories, *Time of Drought* (*Tiempo de sequía*, 1957). Other realists: CLEMENTE AIRÓ (1918); CARLOS ARTURO TRUQUE (1927); JESÚS ZÁRATE MORENO (1915), a short story writer about peasant life; ELISA MUJICA (1918); and PRÓSPERO MORALES PRADILLA (1920). Less dependent on reality are the following: JAIME ARDILA CASAMITJANA (1919) poured the material of his novel *Babel* (1943) into the head of an intellectual protagonist and made a keen analysis of the perception of time and of the confused states of personality. Worthy of note is *Withered Leaves* (*La hojarasca*, 1955) by GABRIEL GARCÍA MÁRQUEZ (1928). The novelist cedes the storytelling to three witnesses of the corpse of a suicide: the boy, the mother, and the grandfather. Through their interior monologs—simultaneous and twined together in less than an hour, in 1928—the reader ties the loose ends and is apprised of what has happened in more than a century. The action advances, retreats, zigzags. It is the story of a strange French doctor, of a family, of a whole town ruined. RAMIRO CÁRDENAS (1925), author of *Twice Dead and Other Stories* (*Dos veces la muerte y otros cuentos*, 1951), handles the techniques of the stream of consciousness, the sudden shift in point of view, the latticing of event and evocation in such a way that reality dissolves into a strange atmosphere. ÁLVARO CEPEDA SAMUDIO (1926), who is well aware of the path that contemporary fiction took after the experiments with time, interior dialogs, narrative focal points, and the crumbling away of plot, renovated, albeit moderately, the traditional form of the short story: *We Were All Waiting* (*Todos estábamos a·la espera*, 1954). ARTURO LAGUADO (1919) is one of the few Colombian writers with a rarefied and fanciful atmosphere: *The Morris Rhapsody* (*La rapsodia de Morris*, 1948), *Dance for Rats* (*Danza para ratas*, 1954). Another: ALBERTO DOW (1923).

(6) *Ecuador* / ADALBERTO ORTIZ (1914) made his appearance in 1942 with *Juyungo,* one of the best Hispanic-American novels. The

dominant theme is the Negro race and its mixing with Indians and whites: prejudices, resentments, hatreds. But the purpose of the author is to superimpose upon the concern for the sufferings of his race the more universal sufferings caused by social injustice and war. The current of action effaces the characters, as if they were drawn on water. One character remains, Ascensión, the *"Juyungo"* Negro, whom we see from infancy to death, during the Peruvian invasion of Ecuador in 1941. Light falls upon the terrible nature and the primitive customs of Negroes, Indians, mulattoes, and zambos. Everything else, by contrast, seems dark. The exploitation of the poor, political baseness, sickness, superstition, violence, death, and the arduous work in the jungles and rivers of Esmeraldas occupy the greater portion of *Juyungo*. But there are also noble political ideals, idyls, patriotic reflections, hopes for betterment. The novel does not have stylistic unity; imaginative expressions go hand in hand with worn-out clichés. A disarranged novel and not always because the author wishes it so. The episodes succeed each other needlessly, in a line of continuous points. Each chapter is preceded by a fragment of what the "eye and ear of the jungle" see and hear. There is, then, an attempt at artistic composition. And in fact, the lack of plot and the accumulation of so many dialectal words, of so many strange scenes, of so many unknown things, terminate by creating a poetic atmosphere. Later Ortiz collected eleven stories in *The Bad Shoulder* (*La mala espalda*, 1952). They have a lyrical realism, especially in the description of the landscape, but nature does not drown out the voice of men. In a climate of violence, the weak perish; the strong survive. The motivations are fear, avarice, elemental passions, jealousy. Even here, the preoccupation with racial tensions appears and the procedure that represents the stream of consciousness. Recently he published his poetic anthology: *The Wounded Animal* (*El animal herido*, 1959).

PEDRO JORGE VERA (1915) appeared as a poet: *New Itinerary* (*Nuevo itinerario*), *Early Morning Ballads* (*Romances madrugadores*), and *Illuminated Tunnel* (*Túnel iluminado*). Then he gave his novel *Pure Animals* (*Los animales puros*, 1946), which instead of gliding along the surface of Ecuadorian reality—as other novelists did—went into the depths of its characters. He followed with a book of short stories: *Eternal Mourning and Other Stories* (*Luto eterno y otros cuentos*, 1950), simpler but also dense in introspective glances. We take leave of Ecuador with NELSON ESTUPIÑÁN BASS (1915), a cultured novelist, and RAFAEL DÍAZ ICAZA (1921?), a poet who was later outstanding for his short stories.

(7) *Peru* / Here, as in almost all the other Hispanic-American countries, the novel as a document of a badly organized society—generally

a rural one—fell into decline, and the characterization of people was sacrificed to the necessity of proving a thesis. Now social themes make up the narrative, but at least there was more artistic consciousness, more of a will to be current with the renovation of novelistic techniques. Some writers went along the road of indigenous themes, treating them with lyrical force. They were urged on by the example of José María Arguedas.

ELEODORO VARGAS VICUÑA (1924) stands out among this group. He has culti-vated the rural story, but does it in the form of poetic vignettes: *Nahuín*. Putting himself within the sensitivity, the beliefs, the points of view of his mountain char-acters, he makes them speak in a convincing local language. Also writing in this same vein is CARLOS E. ZAVALETA (1928), one of the most notable writers of his generation. His stories, from *The Cynic* (*El cínico*, 1948) to *The Ingars* (*Los Ingar*, 1955), deal with the problem of the Indian, not from a sociological point of view, but rather with an emphasis on psychological nuances. His knowledge of Amer-ican literature, especially Faulkner, has enriched his technique. The characters, each one from various perspectives, talk or break the narrative continuity with their testimonials. The reader often is lost in the disorder, or becomes discouraged by the difficulties of reading the book. In *The Villenas Christ* (*El Cristo Villenas*) the plurality of different reports on the same violent reality is resolved more suc-cessfully. There is another group that lards its narrations with experiences about the city. They are realists who criticize social iniquity, but are attentive to the different planes of human personality and to the necessities of renovating the art of composition. We mention, above all, JULIO RAMÓN RIBEYRO (1929). He was successful with his novel *Chicken-Hearted* (*Los gallinazos sin plumas*, 1955), a novel about two boys who live in a miserable section of Lima, gathering filth to feed their grandfather's pig. The note of violence, sordidness, and cruelty tends to crop up in his *Topical Stories* (*Cuentos de circunstancias*, 1958). He is fol-lowed by CARLOS THORNE (1924) and ALFONSO LA TORRE. A third group of nar-rators cultivated humor and fantasy, like JOSÉ DURAND (1925), an irrepressible caricaturist in his stories, *Cats Among Us* (*Gatos entre nosotros*). Also LUIS FELIPE ANGELL, LUIS LEÓN, FELIPE BUENDÍA, and CARLOS MINO. MANUEL MEJÍA VALERA (1925) published *The Evasion* (*La evasión*, 1954) and some of his pages were collected in *Canvases of Dreams* (*Lienzos de sueños*, 1959), which are nar-rative sketches: one of them, the one that gives its title to the volume, is imitative of Borges in the play of forms within forms.

(8) *Bolivia* / From the predominantly social novel RAÚL BOTELHO GOSÁLVEZ (1917) stands forth: *Green Drunkenness* (*Borrachera verde*, 1938), *Cocaine* (*Coca*, 1941), *Plateau* (*Altiplano*, 1945), *It Is Worth a Fortune, Interlude* (*Vale un Potosí*, *entremés*, 1949), *Untamed Land* (*Tierra chúcara*, 1957). His novel *Cocaine* is the history of the failure of Álvaro, a young aristocrat who returns to La Paz from the Chaco War morally destroyed. He goes to the jungle in search of gold, has love affairs with two equally passionate women, although of opposite social classes; he is debased by the cocaine habit and ends by committing suicide. Botelho Gosálvez unites, without amalgamating, socialist realism with an estheticism that is still Modernist, even in the Valle Inclán's brand of it. The most frequent theme is the erotic.

(9) *Chile* / In general, one can say that the narrators of this period wanted nothing to do with the Creolists, at least with the Creolists who limited themselves to making an inventory of external events. What interested them more from the Chilean past was the psychological, urbane direction of D'Halmar-Barrios-Prado-Maluenda-Edwards Bello-Manuel Rojas. But if in the beginning this rejection of a literature that was excessively vernacular, excessively loaded with geography, botany, zoology, and ethnography unites them, they again part company because of the way they accentuate their narrations—accents that are social and political, imaginative and formalist. The changes brought by industrialization, planned economies, the violent aspiration of the masses to govern, and the second World War, plus the changes of literary technique resulting from the experiments undertaken ever since the generation of James Joyce and company, modified the form and content of the novel and the short story.

The principal writers in this new narrative mode were CARLOS DROGUETT (1915) with *100 Drops of Blood and 200 of Sweat* (*100 gotas de sangre y 200 de sudor*, 1961); and GUILLERMO ATÍAS (1917), who novelized in *Banal Time* (*El tiempo banal*, 1955) lives from the various social echelons, paying special attention to the psychological aspects. FERNANDO ALEGRÍA (1918), distinguished by his novelesque biographies, turned to the novel itself in *Chameleon* (*Camaleón*, 1950) which, if not a political novel, is at least politically loaded. After his stories, *The Poet Who Turned into a Worm* (*El poeta que se volvió gusano*, 1956)—also in a political vein—he wrote a picaresque-type novel on the life of an Hispanic-American in San Francisco: *Jack of Hearts* (*Caballo de copas*, 1957). The plot interweaves three threads: the history of a horse, the love of Mercedes and the narrator, and the strike of the stevedores led by Marcel, Mercedes' father. Afterwards came: *Hunter's Nights* (*Las noches del cazador*, 1961). VOLODIA TEITELBOIM (1913), a militant Communist, denounces the exploitation of the working class and the struggle against foreign companies. ROBERTO SARAH (1918), pseudonym of Andrés Terbay; EDMUNDO CONCHA CONTRERAS (1918); CARLOS LEÓN (1916); PABLO GARCÍA (1919); is a short story writer of a lyrical impact, a penetrating psychological insight, and a violent style: *The Boys and the Pompeya Bar* (*Los muchachos y el bar Pompeya*, 1958). These, and others, are approaching what has been called the "generation of 1950." One of the traits that characterize them is their resistance to the claims of nationalistic or social realism. In order that their narratives be more personal, they give them a conscience and a point of view: from this process stems their autobiographical quality and their air of interior monologs. At times, the meaning of the novel is illuminated by symbols, allegories, and myths. The one who defined this generation is ENRIQUE LAFOURCADE (1927). His literature—poetic prose, short stories, novels—refuses to let itself be corraled in any rural theme; he also refuses to propose for the problems of literature solutions that are not, above all, literary ones. His last book is *The Prince and the Sheep* (*El príncipe y las ovejas*, 1961). JOSÉ DONOSO (1925) after the stories in *Summer Vacation* (*Veraneo*)—distantly related to Henry James, Faulkner, Truman

Capote—wrote one of the best novels in recent years: *Coronation (Coronación,* 1957). He depicts a traditional home of Santiago's upper class and shows its decomposition and ruin in contrast with the strength of the masses. The prose and his constructive processes are personal. José Manuel Vergara (1928) gained notoriety with his novel *Daniel and the Golden Lions (Daniel y los leones dorados,* 1956), an immersion in contemporary life in England and Spain from the Catholic point of view, akin to that of Graham Greene in the analysis of religious psychology. His last book: *The Four Seasons (Las cuatro estaciones,* 1958). Claudio Giaconi (1927), encouraged by the reading of international literature (especially in the English language, such as Faulkner, Wolfe, and others), rejected the regionalist costume of Chilean narrative and appeared in letters with the impetus of a rebel, revisionist, and indicter; he created lively characters in his stories: *Difficult Youth (La difícil juventud,* 1954) and *Amadeo's Dream (El sueño de Amadeo,* 1959). Herbert Muller (1923) leans in *Perceval and Other Stories (Perceval y otros cuentos,* 1954) to the schematic, subtle stories, bound to his characters without external descriptions. Later he published a novelette: *Without Gestures Without Words Without Tears (Sin gestos sin palabras sin llanto,* 1955). Armando Cassigoli (1928) looks at life with a festive eye, taking pleasure in the absurd and in the social criticism: *Confidences and Other Stories (Confidencias y otros cuentos,* 1955), *Angels under the Rain (Ángeles bajo la lluvia,* 1960). Jaime Laso (1927?) in his novel *The Stocks (El cepo,* 1958) as well as in his short stories composing *The Disappearance of John Di Cassi (La desaparición de John Di Cassi,* 1961) narrates the cases of a senseless life. María Elena Gertner (1927), Catholic, has successfully turned from poetry and drama to the novel: *Islands in the City (Islas en la ciudad,* 1958). Others: Margarita Aguirre (1925?), Guillermo Blanco (1926), Mario Espinosa (1924), Alfonso Echeverría (1922), Luis Sánchez Latorre (1925), Jorge Guzmán (1929), Jaime Valdivieso (1929), Miguel Serrano (1917), and Jorge Ibáñez (1926).

(*10*) *Paraguay* / Augusto Roa Bastos (1918), a poet in *The Ardent Orange Grove (El naranjal ardiente),* is the most representative of the Paraguayan narrators of this generation. *Thunder in the Leaves (El trueno entre las hojas,* 1953) consists of seventeen stories that describe the violence and misery of national life. The prose adheres to regional speech (a mixture of Spanish and Guaraní) as easily as it twists with literary artifices. He protests against the social and political situation in his country, and his tone is one of hope for the revindication of the oppressed classes. In *Son of Man (Hijo de hombre,* 1959) he relates, animates, and explains the life of the Paraguayan people.

José María Rivarola Matto (1917), in *Foliage in the Eyes (Follaje en los ojos,* 1952), novelized the exploitation of the *"yerba"* plantations. Another narrator: Néstor Romero Valdovinos (1916).

(*11*) *Uruguay* / The narrators might be divided into two families: one with roots in the native soil, with simpler emotions, realist, of careless style; the other of more rigorous and intelligent techniques, polished in the minor forms of expression and in the construction of the overall architecture.

In the first Luis Castelli (1918) and Julio C. da Rosa (1920) are distinguished for their nativist stories. The latter has matured since the stories in *Uphill* (*Cuesta arriba,* 1952) to those in *From Sun to Sun* (*De sol a sol,* 1955), though within the limits he imposed on himself: the country, the village, humble creatures tied to humble tasks, sad anecdotes, conversational rather than literary words. In the second family, that of more esthetic ambitions, belong Carlos Martínez Moreno (1917), intelligent and complex: after his short stories *The Days Left to Live* (*Los días por vivir,* 1960), he wrote a novel, *The Wall* (*El paredón*) where Uruguayan scenes are interlocked with those of the revolutionary Cuba of 1959; Ángel Rama (1926), the author of *Oh Puritan Shadow* (*Oh sombra puritana,* 1951); José Pedro Díaz (1921), who phantomizes reality in his story *The Inhabitant* (*El habitante,* 1949); María Inés Silva Vila, with her stories of fantastic themes and artistic style: *The Snow-White Hand* (*La mano de nieve,* 1951); Clotilde Luisi in *The Return and Other Stories* (*El regreso y otros cuentos,* 1953) is a story writer of fantastic vein; Mario Arregui (1917) maintains his constructive tension and his intelligent selection of words even in the moments when he describes plebeian customs: *Night of St. John and Other Stories* (*Noche de San Juan y otros cuentos,* 1956); Mario Benedetti (1920) is a good observer of the souls of his characters, generally seen in their city surroundings. He is also a poet and essayist, but his narrative production is considerable: *This Morning* (*Esta Mañana,* 1949), *The Last Trip and Other Stories* (*El último viaje y otros cuentos,* 1951), *Which of Us* (*Quién de nosotros,* 1953), *Montevideans* (*Montevideanos,* 1959), and *The Truce* (*La tregua,* 1960).

(12) *Argentina* / One of the most outstanding figures of this generation—in poetry, essay, and novel—is that of Héctor A. Murena (1923). Even more, he has been one of the thinking leaders, one of the definers of his generation. His trilogy *History of a Day* (*Historia de un día*)— "The Fatality of Bodies," "The Laws of Night," and "The Inheritors of the Promise"—and his short stories—*The Center of Hell* (*El centro del infierno,* 1956) give us a desperate and despairing vision. He engages reality and describes it with rawness; but in the stories mentioned, in order to better communicate his feeling that the world is hostile to us, he has preferred to give it a fantastic dimension. Horror and the unknown are not for Murena pleasures of the imagination, but torments. It is as if he were narrating consumptions of the body, exhaustions of the soul; and he does it with unsavory and vinegary gestures. He is displeased with life, tired of the senselessness that surrounds him, and he lets himself go and sinks into the obscure, into tedium, into solitude. Atmospheres of failure and degradation. Another of the more excellent writers is Julio Cortázar (1916). He attracted attention with *The Kings* (*Los reyes,* 1949), a dramatic prose poem. It is a prose of marked strength in the definition of images and ideas. In it he proposed a curious variant of the myth of the Minotaur. Arianna, in love with her monstrous brother the Minotaur, gives the thread to Theseus,

not so he may leave the labyrinth safely, but so that the Minotaur might destroy it and thus escape. But the Minotaur prefers to die. He lets himself be killed so as to survive vaguely in the dreams and instincts of Arianna, and further, in the dreams and instincts of all men. From that moment on, the Minotaur will live in our blood and hold sway over us like a genie. Already in *The Kings* we recognize Cortázar's favorite theme: the monstrous, the bestial, mysteriously clenched to human destiny. Notice the very significant title of the book that followed: *Bestiary* (*Bestiario*, 1951), fantastic stories. And in *End of the Game* (*Final del juego*, 1956), also a collection of stories, the theme reappears in "Axolotl," wherein the narrator has the feeling that he is one of the monsters that he is looking at in the aquarium. Although the theme of his stories is not animal life, Cortázar will animalize man in cruel descriptions, as in the nightmarish story "The Maenads." It is possible that an unattentive reader, in allowing himself to be impressed by the sharp perception of details with which Cortázar begins his stories, may believe that he will be dealing with everyday men and things. He will soon notice, however, that an air of hallucination and poetry seeps into the apertures of reality, envelops the episode, and makes it end in phantasmagoria. In "The Band" there is satiric intention: that ugly, sordid, absurd, grotesque "reality" is that of Peronism. The protagonist, Lucio, "understood that that view of life could extend itself to the street, to the coffee shop, to his blue suit, to his evening date, to his office work tomorrow, to his savings plan, to his summer vacation, to his girl friend, to his old age, to the day of his death." And, disgusted, he exiled himself from Argentina. One suspects that this inundation of vulgarity leaves its mark also on the language of writers educated in refined literatures and politically against the Peronist movement, but who feel, all of a sudden, that to speak like the masses is "cute" (Bioy Casares and Borges, in *Isidro Parodi*) or vigorously real (Cortázar). Cortázar does not construct in his stories. He writes with a certain displeasure and is careless with his composition. The same can be said of his collection of stories: *Secret Weapons* (*Las armas secretas*, 1959). Perhaps the best of them is "The Persecutor." The atmosphere—jazz, vice, delirium, sordidness, etc.—is well done: it is the beat generation, the lost and disoriented youths of recent years. But the moral slackness of customs also slackens the style of the storyteller. Bruno, a jazz critic, has written a book about the music of his friend Johnny, an erotic saxophonist, drunkard, and marihuana smoker. He is preparing a second edition: he listens carefully to what Johnny has to say about his own music and on the book that he, Bruno, has written. But Johnny is so incoherent that he says nothing in reality: he barely alludes to certain themes (time, God) and there is no evidence that behind his mumblings there is really any deep meaning (nor is there any evidence that Cortázar feels these themes deeply). Johnny finally dies; and so, with a chronological note to that effect in the second edition, the novel closes; and that is it. In spite of what has been said, Cortázar is one of the good short story writers of Hispanic-America, and critics will have to keep an eye on his future work. See his novel *The Prizes* (*Los premios*, 1961).

A great many of the story writers and novelists of these years insist on presenting human life niched into a world seen in its totality. The human constants that they prefer to describe are sex, violence, and death. Figuring in this group are FRANCISCO JOSÉ SOLERO—*Guilt* (*La culpa*); JUAN C. MANAUTA (1919)—*White Lands* (*Tierras blancas*); ALBERTO RODRÍGUEZ (1925)—*Where God May Be* (*Donde haya Dios*); NÉSTOR BONDONI—*The Mouth on Earth* (*La boca sobre la tierra*), and a few others. In reading them it would seem that violence is necessary in a condemned, hellish America. One of the most "committed"—that is, one who not only describes what he sees but also participates in what he tells, is DAVID VIÑAS (1929), who just lately declared himself a Marxist: *He Fell on His Face* (*Cayó sobre su Rostro*, 1955); *The Cruel Years* (*Los años despiadados*, 1956); *A Daily God*, 1957); and *The Landlords* (*Los dueños de la Tierra*, 1958). Some narrators evoked the years of adolescence, poetically, like JULIO ARDILES GRAY (1922) in *Elegy* (*Elegía*, 1952) and in his novelistic cycle *Faraway Friends* (*Los amigos lejanos*), *The Crevice* (*La grieta*), *The Blind Dunes* (*Los médanos ciegos*). BEATRIZ GUIDO (1924) is another of the novelists of adolescence: *The House of the Angel* (*La casa del ángel*, 1954), *The Fall* (*La caída*, 1956), *The Wind-up* (*Fin de Fiesta*, 1958). She also has some short stories: *Hand in the Trap* (*La mano en la trampa*, 1961). Except for a weak attempt at complicating the perspective (Adolfo is alternately the narrator-protagonist and a character seen by another narrator who speaks in the third person) *The Wind-up* brings no technical novelties. The old naturalism (at least new in a woman) uncovers the rubbish-can of a powerful family in the political oligarchy of 1930–45. The "fiesta" that the military revolution of 1943 brings to a wind-up is not really a fiesta: it is sex, crime, moral decadence, ugliness, bad customs of society, government, and church. The axis of the action is the city of Avellaneda. Everything turns rapidly, but only the surface is seen. Although the prose does not have descriptive vigor, it is believable in the dialogs. There is no creation of characters, only situations in which the characters have fun or suffer. SILVINA BULLRICH (1915) began with poetry—*Vibrations* (*Vibraciones*, 1935)—but her road is the novel: *The First Angel's Flask* (*La redoma del primer ángel*, 1943), *The Third Version* (*La tercera versión*, 1944), *Crystal Wedding* (*Bodas de cristal*, 1952), *The Line Is Busy* (*Teléfono ocupado*). In *The Third Version* we have the autobiography that Paul, a writer with no calling nor talent and somewhat upset by skeletons in the family closet, addresses to his girl friend Claudia. He gives us the two versions of the failure of his father, a Spanish violinist (also called Pablo); the version of the mother (also called Claudia) according to which she deliberately ruined his father's genius through her jealousy, and the prosaic version of the doctor friend, according to which he was a mediocre musician who died accidentally. When the doctor, on his deathbed, offers the third version, the real one, Paul refuses to hear it. The novel falls apart in the unraveling, although it is at that moment that the poetic tone—maintained through the novel—comes to the fore. Excellent in the presentation of a soft atmosphere of mystery, it fails in the construction of its towers: "the symmetry of destinies" (the two Pauls, the two Claudias) is not novelistically resolved. ESTELA CANTO (1920), in *The Marble Wall* (*El muro de mármol*, 1945) as well as in *The Man at Dusk* (*El hombre del crepúsculo*, 1953), has distinguished herself for the psychological understanding of her characters. (In *Night and the Mud* [*La noche y el barro*] she is also attentive to mass psychology.) In this psychological direction lies the curious novel of CARLOS MAZZANTI (1926), *The Substitute* (*El sustituto*), a completely interiorized monolog. JUAN CARLOS GHIANO (1920) with his *Strange Guests* (*Extraños huéspedes*), *Histories of the Deceased and the Traitors* (*Historias de finados y traidores*), and *Memories of the Scarlet Land* (*Memorias de la tierra escarlata*) seemed to have decided in favor of narrative, but later he achieved greater success in the theater. In the police genre—which had given its best moments with Borges, Bioy Casares, Silvina Ocampo, Leonardo Castellani, Manuel Peyrou, and Abel Mateo—the standouts in this generation were ADOLFO PÉREZ ZELASCHI (1920), RODOLFO J. WALSH (1927), and MARÍA ANGÉLICA BOSCO. MARCO DENEVI (1922) had an instantaneous success with his novel *Rosaura at Ten O'Clock* (*Rosaura a las diez*, 1955). A murder has been committed in a cheap hotel in Buenos Aires—the victim, a young girl. The police question several witnesses. The successive testimonies of four of these witnesses constitute the novel. In the fifth part, the puzzle is completed when a document is introduced that not only absolves the accused but also uncovers the real murderers. This clarifying letter is one that the murdered girl had left half written. The procedure of showing the same reality from four different perspectives permits Denevi to exercise his psychological penetration, his humorism, and, above all, his ability in making an ever-anxious reader clutch the book and not let go till the very end. The hazy and complicated past reveals itself little by little. At ten in the evening (hence the title) Rosaura enters, in flesh and blood, into the world of the boarding hotel where the important characters live. Her mysterious personality—fictitious and real, innocent and vile, veiled and revealed—lights a light in the midst of the ugliness of the incidents. The theme of an invented character who suddenly appears before his very creator (this was pointed out in reference to Jenaro Prieto's *The Partner*) is here developed in a realist fashion. DALMIRO SAÉNZ (1926?) sees life through Catholic eyes and describes it with realist force. His short stories *Seventy Times Seven* (*Setenta veces siete*) and *No* had immediate popular success. Other narrators: LUIS MARIO LOZZIA (1922), *Sunday Without Football* (*Domingo sin fútbol*); VALENTÍN FERNANDO (1921), *From This Flesh* (*Desde esta carne*); ABELARDO ARIAS (1908), *The Great Coward* (*El gran cobarde*) and *Felled Poplars* (*Álamos talados*); JACOBO FELDMAN (1917), *Story of a Flight* (*Relato de una fuga*); ADOLFO JASCA, *The Bitter Sprouts* (*Los tallos amargos*); DAVID JOSÉ KOHON, *The Black Circle of the Street* (*El negro círculo de la calle*); GLORIA ALCORTA (1916), *The Hotel of the Moon and Other Fabrications* (*El hotel de la luna y otras imposturas*); GREGORIO SCHEINES, *The Lost Visage* (*El rostro perdido*); EMMA DE CARTOSIO, *Stories of the Angel That Guards Well* (*Cuentos del ángel que bien guarda*); FEDERICO PELTZER (1924), *Shared* (*Compartida*); and JORGE MASCIANGIOLI (1929).

2. Essay

This is the most abundant genre in Hispanic-America. We set down just a few of the names closest to literature, leaving aside those who specialize rather in other disciplines—historical, philosophical, or sociological.

In Mexico, RAMÓN XIRAU (1924), ANTONIO ALATORRE (1918). In Central America, LUIS GALLEGOS VALDÉS (El Salvador, 1917). In Venezuela, OSCAR SAMBRANO URDANETA (1929), GUILLERMO MORÓN (1929), JOSÉ LUIS SALCEDO BASTARDO (1924), and ORLANDO ARAUJO (1928). In Colombia, ANDRÉS HOLGUÍN (1919), DANIEL ARANGO (1920), JAIME TELLO (1918), who are also poets; and OTTO MORALES BENÍTEZ (1920). In Peru, ANTONIO PINILLA (1924), FRANCISCO MIRÓ QUESADA (1918), and ALBERTO WAGNER DE REYNA (1915). In Chile, in literary criticism one of those who work with analytic rigor is ALFREDO LEFEBVRE (1917); in the philosophic essay, FÉLIX MARTÍNEZ BONATTI (1928). In Uruguay, EMIR RODRÍGUEZ MONEGAL (1921), CARLOS REAL DE AZÚA (1916). In Argentina, ALBERTO M. SALAS (1915), EMMA SUSANA SPERATTI PIÑERO (1919).

C. THEATER

The efforts of writers to convert themselves into professionals of the theater are obvious. On leaving the experimental theaters—which treated a minority public to stage pieces of literary quality—to embrace professionalism, some playwrights and dramatists began to serve up typical dishes for the national palates. This, of course, is generally speaking; for there also was theater of great artistic integrity. University groups or groups connected with intellectual circles tried to renovate the gimmicks of spectacle. With the growth of cities, stage activity also grew. Some authors have already been mentioned for their contributions in other genres and, therefore, will not appear here.

In Mexico one of the most original authors is ELENA GARRO (1917); her plays —several were collected in a volume *A Solid Home* (*Un hogar sólido*, 1958)— drew out of traditional material a magical, poetic, evocative, ironic, and somewhat surrealistic conception. LUISA JOSEFINA HERNÁNDEZ (1928) is important for the sustained quality of her continual production. We have seen *The Deaf and Dumb* (*Los sordomudos*, 1953). There is only one deaf-mute—the servant girl. But the title refers to the moral deaf-and-dumbness of a middle-class family in a Mexican province. The home is broken by hatred, resentment, incompatibility. They are like deaf-mutes. They barely communicate with one another. In the end the children disperse and the cynical father remains alone with the servant. Later Hernández gave better plays: *The Fallen Fruits* (*Los frutos caídos*) and, especially, *The Real Guests* (*Los huéspedes reales*), one of the few good tragedies of this entire generation. We have also seen *Ash Wednesday* (*Miércoles de ceniza*) by LUIS G. BASURTO (1920): the dialog languishes on discussions about religious sentiment. EMILIO CARBALLIDO (1925) knows his trade down to the fingertips.

He likes to fathom the provincial souls of the middle class. Among his better works are *Rosalba and the Turnkeys* (*Rosalba y los llaveros*) and *The Dance the Tortoise Dreams* (*La danza que sueña la tortuga*). SERGIO MAGAÑA (1924) is one of the more problematic. In *The Signs of the Zodiac* (*Los signos del Zodiaco*) he presents the moral disorientation of youths in a Mexico City slum. A solid promise is that of JORGE IBARGÜENGOITIA (1928), with his play about customs, *Clotilde at Home* (*Clotilde en su casa*). WILBERTO CANTÓN (1923) and IGNACIO RETES (1918) also stand out.

In Central America, ALFREDO L. SANCHO (1922). In the Antilles the Puerto Rican FRANCISCO ARRIVÍ (1915) who, with new techniques, brought themes of national life to the stage; he has several plays, from *The Devil Becomes Human* (*El diablo se humaniza*, 1941) to *Club for Bachelors* (*Club de solteros*, 1953). In Venezuela, leaving aside the extraordinary Ida Gramcko, whom we have seen among the poets, stands RAFAEL PINEDA (1926), pseudonym of Rafael Ángel Díaz Sosa. In Colombia, ENRIQUE BUENAVENTURA (1925). From Peru there is SEBASTIÁN SALAZAR BONDY (1924). Intelligent, cultured, deeply emotional, preoccupied with the problems of man and the social conditions of Hispanic-American life, he has excelled in several genres: the essay, poetry, the narrative—*The Shipwrecked and the Survivors* (*Náufragos y sobrevivientes*, 1954); *Poor People of Paris* (*Pobre gente de París*, 1958). But his theatrical talent demands that he be placed in this section of our history: *Meadow* (*Rodil*, 1952), *There Is No Happy Island* (*No hay isla feliz*, 1954), and others. Another of Peru's theatrical values is ENRIQUE SOLARI SWAYNE (1918), author of the realist drama *Collacocha*. In Chile one of the most distinguished is LUIS ALBERTO HEIREMANS (1928). In addition to his collections of short stories, with "strange children" and characters held incommunicado from "each other," he has produced plays with which he has been more successful. The best dramatist: EGON WOLF (1926). Other Chileans: SERGIO VODANOVIC (1928), ENRIQUE MOLLETO (1922), ISIDORA AGUIRRE (1919), FERNANDO DEBESA (1921) and FERNAND JOSSEAU (1924). In Uruguay the three most important are ANTONIO LARRETA (1922), author of *The Smile* (*La sonrisa*); CARLOS DENIS MOLINA, of whom we spoke in the poetry section; and JACOBO LANGSNER (1924), an experimenter of forms. Langsner is the author of *The Incomplete Man* (*El hombre incompleto*), *The Ridiculous Ones* (*Los ridículos*), *The Rebellion of Galatea* (*La rebelión de Galatea*), *Iphigenia's Game* (*El juego de Ifigenia*). Also worthy of mention are HÉCTOR PLAZA NOBLÍA, ALEJANDRO PEÑASCO, ANGÉLICA PLAZA. In Argentina the group of theatrical authors is numerous. OMAR DEL CARLO (1918) is the author of *Electra at Daybreak* (*Electra al amanecer*), *Proserpine and the Stranger* (*Proserpina y el extranjero*), *Where Death Plants Its Banners* (*Donde la muerte clava sus banderas*), *Ash Garden* (*El jardín de ceniza*). In *Proserpine and the Stranger* the myth of the rape of Proserpina penetrates like a ray of light into the sordid reality of a Buenos Aires slum and it refracts in strange poetic reflections. The sun on a muddy pool that shows emeralds in the putrid water. The personified Myth moves on the stage and speaks to us: his words conjure rapid transmutations. Hell changes to Buenos Aires; the Acheron is the immobile, dirty Río de la Plata; Hades, king of the subterranean world becomes Porfirio, the gangster, king of the underworld; the deity Proserpina, daughter of Demeter, is now Proserpina, a girl from the country who falls into surroundings of baseness and prostitution. Del Carlo capably fuses myth and reality, and together they create dramatic art. The characters are creatures of the Argentina of today;

and yet, their gestures and their words have a strength that comes from the depth of time. And the landscape of wheat fields where Demetria and her daughter Proserpina lived, strikes an Argentinian chord even though we know that those are the wheat fields of the deity Demeter. The linking of the myth of Proserpina raped in Hell, with the figures of Claudius and Flavia, representing respectively the lowest moral point of pagan power and the driving impetus of the expansion of Christianity, adds the attempt at religious allegory to the drama. The salvation of Proserpina in the end thus acquires the value of moral symbol. Omar del Carlo breaks out of the framework of modern theatrical composition and sets the action at liberty: rapid movements of vivid, loose, naked, changing scenes. The fluidity of the Greek theater or of the theater of Lope de Vega and Shakespeare (after the freezing of realist décors) now returns to flow down the river bed of the new forms of the contemporary theater: forms learned from the movies, but without imitating them. *Where Death Plants Its Banners* (1959) seems to be inferior. The theme, as old as the biblical Amnon and Tamar, of the incestuous love between brother and sister, reappears in the Argentina of Mitre and Urquiza, on the eve of the battle of Pavón. The father of the incestuous pair, who must pay for his own violent past out of the vengeance of a woman, rebels against God and dies. The idea is Catholic, and the conception of the drama has a rapid scenic movement, with choruses. But the spectacular qualities go beyond the content of the drama. CARLOS GOROSTIZA (1920) is human, preoccupied with social ills; he was successful in *The Bridge* (*El puente*) and then continued in an uneven career, until *The Last Dog* (*El último perro*). JULIO IMBERT (1918) acquired with *The Earthworm* (*La lombriz*), *The Hand* (*La mano*), *This Place Has a Hundred Fires* (*Este lugar tiene cien fuegos*), *The Tooth* (*El diente*), *Ursula Sleeps* (*Ursula duerme*), *The Longest Night of the Year* (*La noche más larga del año*) a deserved reputation. Running through the plays are characters in vivid dialogs, well-linked scenes, fateful atmospheres, psychological delvings, use of symbols, themes of horror and repugnance. Other important figures: AGUSTÍN CUZZANI, TULIO CARELLA, OSVALDO DRAGÚN, PABLO PALANT, JUAN CARLOS GENÉ, VITO DE MARTINI.

XV. 1955-1963

Authors born since 1930

Historical framework: The popular masses strive to attain political power—masses more interested in an immediate distribution of wealth than in revolutionary ideologies. The governing classes (even those traditionally conservative, as are the Military and the Clergy) attempt to adjust to this new climate.

Cultural tendencies: A keener awareness of the literary craft leads the writers to experiment with new techniques or to exhume classical forms. Be they violent or serene, nihilistic or affirmative, cynical or candid, all seem to sense the imminence of a great change in values.

It is evident that these writers are directing their steps somewhere. But where? This is not so evident. The group is too young: neither its direction, nor its quality, nor even its significant names can be known yet. In general they impress one for their serious, discontented, and resentful looks. They came out of their shells when the second World War had already ended, and what did they see? They saw a new political order jelling, divided into two colossuses—the United States and Russia—armed with atomic bombs, rockets, and gases capable of exterminating the human race. They saw that the hatred of nations against nations was being fomented and that the "cold war" was being brought to the very brink of universal suicide. They witnessed a new spectacle: astronauts orbiting our planet and preparing themselves for trips to the moon. They saw how the European or Europeanized powers, which earlier had justified their actions in the name of the expansion of civilization, now were doing so in the name of the necessity to survive in the midst of disintegrating old empires, and how Africa, China, India, and the rest of Asia were bringing the cycle of colonialism to an end and were changing the balance of power. They saw the United Nations where, around the same table, were seated countries that were accelerating to an extraordinary degree the Technological Revolution (in the last fifteen years), countries that were just entering into the Industrial Revolution (which was already 150 years old), and countries still living in the period of the agrarian revolution (some 10,000 years). They saw that the rebellion of the masses—with nationalist and communist labels—convulsed every corner of the globe. They saw the population explosion (in Hispanic-America, with a population of 185 million, the growth index is an annual 2.5 per cent, while that of the world as a whole is 1.6 per cent) and the inevitability of a radical change in the economic, social, and political structure. In Hispanic-America they saw totalitarian regimes succeed one another, with different concepts of what the State should be, from the fall of the Perón regime in Argentina to the installation of the Fidel Castro regime in Cuba. They saw all of this with pessimistic and agonizing eyes, without understanding at times that the birth of a new moral order, in spite of its chaotic appearance, is a blessing in comparison with the immoral order promised by the Fascist program of 1936 to 1945. They were too young to understand that. And so, while technology was decreasing the size of the world, in their minds, the idea of *world* increased, and within such a mental framework they suffer in their very flesh the crisis of individualism.

In the panorama of letters they saw impotence, desperation, and bitterness everywhere. They emitted Romantic laments, but they were no longer the laments of titans: rather pygmies nostalgic for a great past. They felt not more alone—because writers have always felt alone—but less in communication than ever. It was a new type of aloneness, helpless but desirous of communion, even if it takes orgies. A grumbling solitude. As when a boy tells a girl: I give myself to you, you give yourself to me (sex as culmination), and the two of us will send the world to the devil. It is an effort at communication—no longer as a safety valve for subjectivity, but as a reaction against the objective world—oriented toward contacts with the remote recesses of life, heretofore disdained by the elite, or in forms of political militancy, either in favor of order or of disorder. The answer to an absurd world is arbitrariness; there are no golden dreams of the future, and one is writing, not for posterity, but for the present. Thus these angry young writers tend to behave scandalously, as though they were trying to be characters in a novel thought up by the public. There is nothing new in this: what is new, however, is that it should have acquired importance as an index of a social state, of a direction in the historical process, of a taste shared by the majority. Neo-naturalism, existentialism, Communist and Catholic propaganda, the expression of the telluric in nationalist movements, the cult of brutality and even of ugliness on the part of groups that denounce the liberalism of the bourgeoisie convince them of the necessity of a "committed literature": an active literature by means of which a stand can be taken in the face of our own times, thus freely affirming the program of our personal lives. One of the means of committing oneself is by submitting the past to an inexorable critical revision. They deny a great deal of excellent but, according to them, devitalized poetry, elegiac or having an excessive virtuosity in its verbal display. Verse loses its old power. At any rate, poetry is cultivated without building any hopes on it, as one did in the days of its primacy in the field of letters. On writing poetry, they cannot help but repeat some of the researches of previous writers. For example: the "inventionism" of today—to invent worlds verbally—is similar to the "creationism" of yesterday. At bottom lies the same impulse to produce surprising things through the use of images. Others wrap themselves in anguish, and from there, try to give their surrealist spirals of smoke the configuration of art. Revisionism also alters the hierarchies of prose: in the judgment of many youths, the stylists dissolve the art of storytelling into a mere unfurling of clouds. On the other hand, these youths propose violence without style, violence for the sheer joy of being violent. There is a preference for the novel (which field the Americans dominate, especially Faulkner), conceived of now as being a cesspool in which all of reality is made up of putrefactive material. Along with the "patricides," the denouncists, the prosecutors, the rebels, other more serene artists are writing: those who escape reality by becoming wrapped up in themselves, or in the cult of the past. In this manner, forms and formulas of the Renaissance are reborn. There is a professional air about learning the disciplines so as to write better; there is more awareness of the craft. To sum up: some disbelieve in individual heroism and give themselves up to the masses; others resuscitate a heroic sense in the cult of the classics. Authoritarian personalities in the name of prevailing majorities, and free personalities in the name of the great geniuses of history. Our respect goes to the individualists who do not equivocate with "isms" nor seek customers in easy political gatherings. Our respects to those who by expressing new visions renew art. What else can one do in the space of this appendix than to list names.

A. MAINLY VERSE

(1) *Mexico* / The most numerous group is that of the politically-oriented poets. Lyricism seeps through the apertures of those windows that face the problems of peace, class struggles, the Indian, solidarity, justice. The purpose, however, is to communicate with the people in simple words that refer to an immediate reality. There are other directions, nevertheless. Rubén Bonifaz Nuño and Rosario Castellanos were seen in the last chapter, and also Tomás Segovia.

During these recent years the poet is MARCO ANTONIO MONTES DE OCA (1931). He allows his mind to run freely through his words; and this stream of consciousness is rich in the sensation of time. In *Testimonial Document,* metaphoric constellations shift as in a dream. *The Birds Sing Before the Light* (*Delante de la luz cantan los pájaros,* 1959)—a book where earlier books are gathered—he shows his imaginative skill and preoccupation with man. Montes de Oca's creative imagination deluges the world with myriads of marvelous dewdrops. The entire world becomes iridescent with so many metaphors of sharp poetic light. Dewdrops, that is, full, minimal, rapid, fluid intuitions that surprise one for their originality. Liberty, but not that of the spontaneous surrealist, who mixes gem and mud, but that of the lucid forger of miniature myths, a proud gold-beater of limpid forms. If one had to record the shop of his apprenticeship, it would be that of Huidobro rather than that of Neruda.

(2) *Central America* / In Guatemala these men were joined together in *Poemario* (1957): JULIO FAUSTO AGUILERA, IVÁN BARRERA, MARIO EFRAÍN HERNÁNDEZ, DONALDO ESTRADA CASTILLO, MARTÍN GOMAR, JUAN FRANCISCO MANRIQUE, HÉCTOR GUILLERMO PINEDA, and CARLOS SIPPEL Y GARCÍA. In Honduras, OSCAR ACOSTA (1933), with his *Minor Poetry* (*Poesía menor*) is clear, communicative, even conceptual, and POMPEYO DEL VALLE (1930). In El Salvador, a combative generation arises from leftist quarters. One of the most capable among these militant poets was WALDO CHÁVEZ VELASCO (1933), author of "Biography of Bread" (*"Biografía del pan"*), "Four Songs of Love for Future Peace" (*"Cuatro cantos de amor para la paz futura"*) and other poems committed to the themes of the sufferings of the people, human solidarity, and social justice. Also important in this group is ÍTALO LÓPEZ VALLECILLOS (1932). Others: ORLANDO FRESEDO

(1932?), Eugenio Martínez Orantes (1932), Álvaro Menéndez Leal (1931), Mercedes Durand (1933), Irma Lanzas. In Costa Rica, Virginia Grütter (1929) and Enrique Mora Salas (1930), known for his "three sonnets to the Rose." In Panama those standing above the crowd are Guillermo Ross Zanet (1930), Demetrio J. Fábrega (1932), Edison Simons Quirós (1933), José Franco (1931), and Álvaro Menéndez Franco (1933).

(3) *Antilles* / In Cuba, there are Fayad Jamis (1930), Rosario Antuña (1935), and Roberto Fernández Retamar (1930), who celebrated the struggles for Cuban liberation in *Return of Old Hopes* (*Vuelta de la antigua esperanza,* 1959): one of the most moving poems, "The Other." In the Dominican Republic the most promising voices are those of Abelardo Vicioso (1930), Juan Sánchez Lamouth (1929), Rafael Lara Cintrón (1931), Abel Fernández Mejía (1931), Juan Alberto Peña Lebrón (1930). In 1957 Máximo Avilés Blonda (1931), Lupo Hernández Rueda (1931), and Rafael Valera Benítez (1938) became known in *Trio.* In Puerto Rico, Jorge Luis Morales (1930).

(4) *Venezuela* / The young writers begin to produce around 1950, with the feeling that they were leaving behind easy themes of folklore, nationalist conventions, cultural demagogy and, on the other hand, that they were approaching universal currents. They proposed—sometimes violently—revising the past and defending the right to a purely artistic vocation. But actually they were not of equal talent, nor did they travel down the same roads. Some are explicit, nativist (Jesús Rosas Marcano, 1932); others are more hermetic, intellectual, or universal (Ramón Palomares, 1935; Alfredo Silva Estrada, 1934; Edmundo J. Aray, 1936; Alfredo Chacón, 1937; Guillermo Sucre Figarella, 1933; Régulo Villegas, 1930); others are sentimental, affirmative (Juan Ángel Mogollón, 1932; José Joaquín Burgos, 1933; Hely Colombani, 1932; Victor Salazar, 1940; and Enrique Guedez). Let us turn to two examples of this poetry. Juan Calzadilla (1931) whetted his mastery of classical forms into a present-day sensitivity, leaning hard on the land, attentive to the claims of life—*The Tower of the Birds* (*La torre de los pájaros*); he also cultivated prose in *The Red Herbarium* (*Los herbarios rojos*). Pedro Duno (1933), in *I Shall Not Silence Thy Voice* (*No callaré tu voz,* 1955), spoke to us of his dissatisfactions in phrases expressed intermittently because of his dispiritedness: the limitations of man, the impossible aspects of a monotonous life, failure, sadness. The strength of his sincerity lifts the simple almost conversational language to a tower of images that are rich for their inventiveness. This sincerity is that of a solitary man who, as revealed in the poem that gives its title to the volume, wants to communicate with ordinary life.

(5) *Colombia* / In recent years two new voices are heard: Héctor Rojas Herazo (in the "Psalm to Defeat" we have read this hoarse lament: "We fall, yes, we fall, / inwards we fall. / With no charity towards ourselves we contribute to our destruction. / Happily we destroy ourselves"), and Eduardo Cote Lamus (1930), who meditates with simplicity and unwilling sadness; his are meditations so attached to personal experiences and to the things he describes that, fortunately, they do not desert poetry to go over to philosophy, but do, nevertheless, tend to become prosaic: *Everyday Life* (*La vida cotidiana,* 1959).

(6) *Ecuador* / New writers appear who continue families of poets that either open their eyes to reality, or explore inner life: JACINTO CORDERO ESPINOSA, DAVID LEDESMA VÁZQUEZ (1934), HUGO SALAZAR TAMARIZ, CARLOS EDUARDO JARAMILLO, RUBÉN ASTUDILLO (1939?).

(7) *Peru* / In the social vein influenced by César Vallejo are GONZALO ROSE (1928) and MANUEL SCORZA (1929). In the vein of introverted lyricism, PABLO GUEVARA (1930) who, in *Return to the Creature* (*Retorno a la creatura*, 1957), strikes a very personal tone. AUGUSTO LUNEL (1930?) and C. GERMÁN BELLI (1930?) tread close to surrealism.

(8) *Bolivia* / JORGE SUÁREZ (1932), FÉLIX ROSPIGLIOSI NIETO (1930).

(9) *Chile* / Let us separate from the busy mass of youths a few figures who show a real vocation as poets. The one who affirms life with most transparency, in direct words, is EFRAÍN BARQUERO (1931). In *The Companion* (*La compañera*, 1956) and *The Swarm* (*El enjambre*, 1959), through natural situations, he has gone deeply into his vision of man: conjugal love, offspring, contact with things. JORGE TEILLIER (1935) is such an imaginative lyricist that, while he sings to himself, he transforms things, animating them, personifying them, imbuing them with his own nostalgic and melancholy spirit. It is appropriate to mention here also PEDRO LASTRA (1932), ARMANDO URIBE ARCE (1933), and XIMENA SEPÚLVEDA (1932).

(10) *Paraguay* / CARLOS VILLAGRA MARSAL (1932), capable of epic themes and tones, as in his "Letter to Simón Bolívar" ("*Carta a Simón Bolívar*"). Others: RUBÉN BAREIRO SAGUIER (1930), JOSÉ MARÍA GÓMEZ SANJURJO (1930), LUIS MARÍA MARTÍNEZ (1934), FRANCISCO PÉREZ MARICEVICH (1937), MIGUEL ÁNGEL FERNANDEZ (1938), and CARMEN SOLER, the first of the militant social poets of her country.

(11) *Uruguay* / MAIA CIRCE, NANCY BACELO and SAÚL IBARGOYEN ISLAS.

(12) *Argentina* / Independent of the surrealist group (obscure spontaneity of dreams) and the "inventionist" group (intelligent vigilance of dreams) are those who seek a personal expression, namely, JUAN JOSÉ HERNÁNDEZ (1930), in whom landscape and soul are wedded—*Clarity Overcome* (*Claridad vencida*, 1957), and MARÍA ELENA WALSH (1930), who, in *Almost Miracle* (*Casi milagro*, 1958), confirmed what she had augured in a book written in her adolescence: a dazzling poetic capacity, full and happy in the expression of pure instantaneousness ("I am what it occurs to me to be when I sing"). The youngest, and one of the most promising: RODOLFO ALONSO (1934).

B. MAINLY PROSE

1. Novel and Short Story

(1) *Mexico* / After Arreola and Rulfo and emerging from the last group of narrators (Rosario Castellanos, Josefina Vicens, Luis Spota, Sergio Galindo, Jorge López Páez), the most notable is CARLOS FUENTES (1929). His book of short stories, *The Masked Days* (*Los días enmascarados*, 1958), was followed by the

novel *The Most Transparent Region* (*La región más transparente,* 1958). Having plunged into the currents of the experimental novel, from Joyce and Faulkner on, Fuentes presents the mental processes of his multiple characters and interweaves a series of events. The protagonist is the city of Mexico, seen in various social classes, human types, activities, and forms of sensitivity. The technique with which he handles the constructive elements of the novel—and even the mechanical resources of typography—is complicated, ambitious, and exhibitionist. Later, in *The Good Consciences* (*Las buenas conciencias,* 1959)—which initiates a quartet of novels: "The New Ones"—Fuentes puts his shop in order, sets aside the unnecessary tools, and with the frugality of a nineteenth-century novelist tells the story of a bourgeois, conservative, Catholic family in Guanajuato, from the epoch of Porfirio Díaz, and the biography of the adolescent Jaime Ceballos, his intellectual friendship with the Indian Juan Manuel, his religious scruples, and his rebellion against Pharisaic hypocrisy. Others: TOMÁS MOJARRO (1932), *The Cannon of Juchipila* (*Cañón de Juchipila,* 1960), stories written in regional Mexican language; ERACLIO ZEPEDA, *Benzuzul* (1959), stories of Indian themes; and VICENTE LEÑERO.

(2) *Central America* / FERNANDO CENTENO ZAPATA (Nicaragua, 1935?), ÁLVARO MENÉNDEZ LEAL (El Salvador, 1931).

(3) *Antilles* / NIVARIA TEJERA (Cuba, 1930). MARCIO VELOZ MAGGIOLO (Dominican Republic, 1936).

(4) *Venezuela* / First of all is SALVADOR GARMIENDIA (1931), the most serious novelist of his time up to now. He drew attention with his novel *The Little Beings* (*Los pequeños seres,* 1959); later, he wrote *The Inhabitants* (*Los habitantes*) in which he novelized the inability of the members of a family to communicate with one another, as seen through a single day of their existence. The others are mainly short story writers: ADRIANO GONZÁLEZ LEÓN (1931), restless, with touches of magical realism in *The Highest Bonfires* (*Los hogueras más altas,* 1957), and HÉCTOR MALAVÉ MATA (1930).

(5) *Colombia* / The nihilist GONZALO ARANGO (1930), FANNY BUITRAGO (1939), and EDUARDO ARANGO PIÑERES (1931), who cultivates the fantastic short story.

(6) *Ecuador* / Of the narrators closest to today's youth we have mentioned Pedro Jorge Vera, Adalberto Ortiz, and Jorge Fernández. Now to name the most recent: EUGENIA VITERI (1935?), authoress of *The Ring* (*El anillo*); JORGE RIVADENEIRA (1930?), with more political than literary intent; and WALTER BELLOLIO (1933?).

(7) *Peru* / Youth cultivates the short story more than the novel. It is no longer the regionalist, folklore story of years back, but of a realism very conscious of techniques in style and composition. Along this realist line, one of the most proficient is MARIO VARGAS LLOSA (1936), short story writer—*The Bosses* (*Los jefes*). ENRIQUE CONGRAINS MARTÍN (1932) did not distinguish himself with his stories *Kikuyo* (1937) or *Lima, Zero Hour* (*Lima, hora cero,* 1958), but did with his novel *Not One But Many Deaths* (*No una sino muchas muertes*). His realism is down-to-the-bone, a little in the manner of Moravia, applied to suburban life.

Mario Castro Arenas (1932) in *The Leader* (*El líder,* 1960) novelizes a problem of the city: that of the housing situation. Others are proficient along the expressionist, fantastic, or paradoxical line: José Miguel Oviedo (1934), who stylizes reality with artistic purpose; and Luis Loayza (1931?), intelligent and cultured short story writer. Oswaldo Reinoso (1933?), in his short stories *The Innocents* (*Los inocentes*), describes the world of the rock-and-roll teenagers—violent, aggressive, and without direction.

(8) *Bolivia* / The narrative production of these years has remained in magazines without yet being collected in book form.

(9) *Chile* / The young narrators seemed to be more preoccupied with form. Two tendencies are drawn, both rejecting coarse regionalism: one, with urban themes and a more subtle and more designing language; the other, with a deformation of reality through abnormal and occasional pathological perspectives. A good step forward has been taken by the short story writer Jorge Edwards (1931), author of *The Patio* (*El patio,* 1952) and *City People* (*Gente de la ciudad,* 1961); Cristián Huneeus (1937), *Chamber Stories* (*Cuentos de cámara,* 1961); Poli Délano (1936), *Lonely People* (*Gente solitaria,* 1960); and Carlos Morand (1936), *A Long Wait* (*Una larga espera,* 1961).

(10) *Paraguay* / José María Gómez Sanjurjo (1930), a delicate and intimate poet, has also brought attention to himself with the novel *The Department Store Spaniard* (*El español del almacén*).

(11) *Uruguay* / Juan Carlos Soma (1930).

(12) *Argentina* / In the realist tendency of urban themes, more attentive to the psychological than to the social, Jorge Onetti (1931) and Roberto Hosne (1931) excel. One of the better recent novels is *January* (*Enero*) by Sara Gallardo (1934?): a moving youthful love, in the Argentine country, told with deep comprehension and sincere prose.

2. Essay

In Mexico, José Emilio Pacheco (1939), Carlos Monsivais (1936). In Colombia, Alberto Parra (1937). In Chile, Juan Loveluck (1929) and Cedomil Goic (1928). In Venezuela, Gustavo Luis Carrera (1933).

C. THE THEATER

In Mexico Héctor Mendoza (1932), who has staged the problems of adolescence in *The Simple Things* (*Las cosas simples*); Juan García Ponce, with *The Song of the Crickets* (*El canto de los grillos,* 1957); Héctor Azar, somewhat in the manner of Eugene Ionesco, with *Apassionata;* and Eduardo García Máynez (1938).

In the Antilles, the Dominican Franklin Domínguez (1931) is the most productive: he has written a score of plays of which he has already staged five.

In Venezuela the theater is probably the most limited of all activities. Of the young men, he who has stomped on the boards of the theater most firmly is ROMÁN CHALBAUD (1933), author of *Adolescent Cain (Caín adolescente)* and *Requiem for an Eclipse (Requiem para un eclipse)*.

In Chile, ALEJANDRO SIEVEKING (1936).

In Uruguay, MAURICIO ROSENCOF (1933).

Names, names, names . . . They do not belong to history yet, but some of them will make history.

BIBLIOGRAPHY

We offer to those who commence their study of Spanish-American Literature this elementary bibliography.

I. General Histories

General histories are so numerous that there are even bibliographies made of them. See for example ROBERTO P. PAYRÓ, *Historias de la literatura americana,* Washington, D.C., Pan American Union, 1950.

We recommend, first of all, PEDRO HENRÍQUEZ UREÑA, *Literary Currents in Hispanic America,* Harvard University Press, 1945. Very useful are the histories by LUIS ALBERTO SÁNCHEZ, *Nueva historia de la literatura americana,* Buenos Aires, Editorial Guarania, 1950, fifth edition; and by ARTURO TORRES-RIOSECO, *The Epic of Latin-American Literature,* University of California Press, 1959. J. A. LEGUIZAMÓN has now published separately the *Bibliografía general de la literatura hispanoamericana,* Buenos Aires, 1954, which was what made his two-volume *Historia de la literatura hispanoamericana,* Buenos Aires, 1945, useful before. ALBERTO ZUM FELDE has divided his history according to genre. Until now: *Índice crítico de la literatura hispanoamericana,* Volume I: *Los ensayistas,* Mexico, Editorial Guarania, 1954; Volume II, *La narrativa, ibidem,* 1959. Two recent additions: CARLOS HAMILTON, *Historia de la literatura hispanoamericana,* 2 vols., New York, 1961; ANGEL VALBUENA BRIONES, *Literatura hispanoamericana,* Madrid, 1962.

There have recently appeared histories written in other languages: ROBERT BAZIN, *Histoire de la littérature américaine de langue espagnole,* Paris, 1953; CHARLES V. AUBRUN, *Histoire des lettres hispanoaméricaines,* Paris, 1954; JOÃO-FRANCISCO FERREIRA, *Capítulos de literatura Hispano-Americana,* Porto-Alegre, Brazil, 1959; UGO GALLO-GIUSEPPE BELLINI, *Storia della letteratura ispanoamericana,* Milano, 1958; MATEO PASTOR-LÓPEZ, *Modern Spansk Litteratur. Spanien och Latinoamerika,* Stockholm, 1960.

In the Spanish translation of GIACOMO PRAMPOLINI's *Historia universal de la literatura,* Buenos Aires, Uteha Argentina, 1941–42, in Volumes XI and XII, there are a few "amplifications" of the national panoramas of our literature made by critics like Roberto F. Giusti, José María Chacón y Calvo, Alfonso Reyes, Pedro Henríquez Ureña, Isaac Barrera, and others. A similar project is the *Panorama das literaturas das Americas* edited by JOAQUIM DE MONTEZUMA DE CARVALHO. Until now three volumes have been published (Edição do Município de Nova Lisboa, Angola, 1958–59). It is a collection of monographs contributed by different historians on national literatures. The Pan American Union has initiated a

Diccionario de la literatura latinoamericana: already the volumes corresponding to *Chile, Bolivia, Colombia,* and *Argentina* have been printed (Washington, D.C., 1958–61).

General histories that are limited to certain periods, tendencies, genres, or themes are numerous. We need name only a few.

Periods and tendencies: MARIANO PICÓN-SALAS, *De la Conquista a la Independencia: tres siglos de historia cultural,* México, Fondo de Cultura Económica, 1944; IRVING A. LEONARD, *Books of the Brave,* Cambridge, Harvard University Press, 1949, and *Baroque Times in Old Mexico,* Ann Arbor, The University of Michigan Press, 1959; EMILIO CARILLA, *El Romanticismo en la América Hispánica,* Madrid, Gredos, 1958; MAX HENRÍQUEZ UREÑA, *Breve historia del Modernismo,* México, Fondo de Cultura Económica, 1954; A. BERENGUER CARISOMO and JORGE BOGLIANO, *Medio siglo de literatura americana,* Madrid, 1952.

Genres: FEDERICO DE ONÍS, "La poesía iberoamericana" (in *España en América,* Universidad de Puerto Rico, 1955). ARTURO TORRES-RIOSECO, *La novela en la América hispana,* Berkeley, 1939, and *Grandes novelistas de la América hispana,* Berkeley, 1949, 2nd ed.; FERNANDO ALEGRÍA, *Breve historia de la novela hispano-americana,* México, Ediciones De Andrea, 1959; LUIS ALBERTO SÁNCHEZ, *Proceso y contenido de la novela hispano-americana,* Madrid, Gredos, 1953; H. D. BARBAGELATA, *La novela y el cuento en Hispanoamérica,* Montevideo, 1947; ARTURO USLAR PIETRI, *Breve historia de la novela hispanoamericana,* Caracas, 1957. JOSÉ JUAN ARROM, *El teatro de Hispanoamérica en la época colonial,* La Habana, 1956; WILLIS KNAPP JONES, *Breve historia del teatro latinoamericano,* México, Ediciones De Andrea, 1956. ROBERT G. MEAD JR., *Breve historia del ensayo hispanoamericano,* México, Ediciones De Andrea, 1956; FRANCISCO ROMERO, *Sobre la filosofía en América,* Buenos Aires, Editorial Raigal, 1952; MEDARDO VITIER, *Del ensayo americano,* México, Fondo de Cultura Económica, 1945.

II. National Histories

(1) *Argentina:* ARTURO GIMÉNEZ PASTOR, *Historia de la literatura argentina* (2 vols.), Buenos Aires, Editorial Labor, 1948. RICARDO ROJAS, *La literatura argentina* (la edición de Buenos Aires, 1948, trae índices). *Historia de la literatura argentina,* directed by Rafael Alberto Arrieta. Monographs by JULIO CAILLET-BOIS, ROBERTO F. GIUSTI, RAFAEL ALBERTO ARRIETA, RICARDO SÁENZ-HAYES, EZEQUIEL MARTÍNEZ ESTRADA, ÁNGEL J. BATTISTESSA, JUAN P. RAMOS, JULIO NOÉ, LUIS EMILIO SOTO, CARMELO BONET, CÉSAR FERNÁNDEZ MORENO, AUGUSTO RAÚL CORTÁZAR, LUIS FRANCO, RICARDO CAILLET-BOIS, DOMINGO BUONOCORE, Buenos Aires, Ediciones Peuser, 1958–1959, 6 vols.

(2) *Bolivia:* FERNANDO DÍEZ DE MEDINA, *Literatura boliviana,* La Paz, 1953; ENRIQUE FINOT, *Historia de la literatura boliviana,* México, 1943.

(3) *Colombia:* ANTONIO GÓMEZ RESTREPO, *Historia de la literatura colombiana* (4 vols.), 2nd ed., Bogotá, 1945. BALDOMERO SANÍN CANO, *Letras colombianas,* México, Fondo de Cultura Económica, 1944.

(4) *Costa Rica:* ABELARDO BONILLA, *Historia y antología de la literatura costarricense,* San José, 1957. Vol. I, *Historia.*

(5) *Cuba:* JUAN N. JOSÉ REMOS Y RUBIO, *Historia de la literatura cubana* (3 vols.), La Habana, 1945; O. OLIVERA, *Breve historia de la literatura antillana,* México, Ediciones De Andrea, 1957.

(6) *Chile:* Arturo Torres-Rioseco, *Breve historia de la literatura chilena,* México, Ediciones De Andrea, 1956; Hugo Montes-Julio Orlandi, *Historia de la literatura chilena,* Santiago, 1955; Alone, *Historia personal de la literatura chilena,* second edition, Santiago de Chile, 1962; Raúl Silva Castro, *Panorama literario de Chile,* Santiago de Chile, 1961.

(7) *Ecuador:* Augusto Arias, *Panorama de la literatura ecuatoriana,* 2nd ed., Quito, 1948. Isaac J. Barrera, *Historia de la literatura ecuatoriana,* 4 vols., Quito, Casa de la Cultura Ecuatoriana, 1955.

(8) *El Salvador:* Luis Gallegos Valdés, *Panorama de la literatura salvadoreña,* San Salvador, 1962.

(9) *Guatemala:* David Vela, *La literatura guatemalteca* (2 vols.), Guatemala 1944–1945. Otto-Raúl González, "Panorama de la literatura guatemalteca" (in *Panorama das literaturas das Américas,* vol. III, 1959).

(10) *Honduras:* Humberto Rivera Morillo, "La literatura hondureña en el siglo xx" and Jorge Fidel Durón, "La prosa en Honduras" (in *Panorama das literaturas das Américas,* vol. II, 1958); Luis Mariñas Otero, "Formación de la literatura hondureña" (in *Universidad de Honduras, Tegucigalpa,* septiembre de 1959, número 14).

(11) *México:* Carlos González Peña, *Historia de la literatura mexicana,* 7th ed., México, 1960. Alfonso Reyes, *Letras de la Nueva España,* México, Fondo de Cultura Económica, 1948, and *Resumen de la literatura mexicana* (*siglos xvi–xix*), México, 1957; Julio Jiménez Rueda, *Letras mexicanas en el siglo xix,* México, Fondo de Cultura Económica, 1944. José Luis Martínez, *Literatura mexicana. Siglo xx* (2 vols.) México, 1949.

(12) *Nicaragua:* Juan Felipe Toruño, "Sucinta reseña de las letras nicaragüenses en 50 años: 1900–1959" (en *Panorama das literaturas das Américas,* vol. III, 1959).

(13) *Panamá:* Leonardo Montalbán, *Historia de la literatura de la América Central* (2 vols.), San Salvador, 1929–1931. Rodrigo Miró, "La literatura panameña de la República" (en *Panorama das literaturas das Américas,* vol. III, 1959).

(14) *Paraguay:* Carlos R. Centurión, *Historia de las letras paraguayas* (3 vols.), Buenos Aires, 1947–1951. Rubén Bareiro Saguier, "Panorama de la literatura paraguaya: 1900–1959" (en *Panorama das literaturas das Américas,* vol. III, 1959).

(15) *Perú:* Luis Alberto Sánchez, *La literatura peruana* (6 vol.), Buenos Aires, 1951. Alberto Tauro, *Elementos de literatura peruana,* Lima, 1946.

(16) *Puerto Rico:* Josefina Rivera de Álvarez. *Diccionario de literatura puertorriqueña,* Universidad de Puerto Rico, 1955. ("Panorama histórico de la literatura puertorriqueña," pp. 3–153.) María Teresa Babin, *Panorama de la cultura puertorriqueña,* San Juan de Puerto Rico, 1958; Francisco Cabrera Manrique, *Historia de la literatura puertorriqueña,* San Juan, 1956.

(17) *República Dominicana:* Max Henríquez Ureña, *Panorama histórico de la literatura dominicana,* Río de Janeiro, 1945. Joaquín Balaguer, *Historia de la literatura dominicana,* 2nd ed., Ciudad Trujillo, 1958.

(18) *Uruguay:* Alberto Zum Felde, *Proceso intelectual del Uruguay y crítica de su literatura,* Buenos Aires, 1941.

(19) *Venezuela:* Mariano Picón-Salas, *Formación y proceso de la literatura venezolana,* Caracas, 1940.

III. Genres and Periods

Besides the bibliographical sources already mentioned, the following national histories of genres and particular periods have been most useful:

Poetry: JUAN CARLOS GHIANO, *Poesía Argentina del siglo xx*, México, Fondo de Cultura Económica, 1957. ROBERTO FERNÁNDEZ RETAMAR, *La poesía contemporánea en Cuba*, La Habana, 1954. CINTIO VITIER, *Lo cubano en la poesía*, La Habana, 1958. FERNANDO ALEGRÍA, *La poesía chilena*, México, F.C.E., 1954. RAÚL LEIVA, *Imagen de la poesía mexicana contemporánea*, México, 1959. LUIS MONGUÍO, *La poesía postmodernista peruana*, México, F.C.E., 1954. CESÁREO ROSA-NIEVES, *La poesía en Puerto Rico*, 2nd ed., San Juan, 1958. JOSÉ RAMÓN MEDINA, *Examen de la poesía venezolana contemporánea*, Caracas, 1956. JUAN PINTO, *Breviario de literatura argentina contemporánea*, Buenos Aires, 1958.

Narrative: ANTONIO CURCIO ALTAMAR, *Evolución de la novela en Colombia*, Bogotá, 1957. RAÚL SILVA CASTRO, *Panorama de la novela chilena*, México, Fondo de Cultura Económica, 1955. ÁNGEL F. ROJAS, *La novela ecuatoriana*, México, Fondo de Cultura Económica, 1948. JOAQUINA NAVARRO, *La novela realista mexicana*, México, 1955. JOSÉ FABBIANI RUIZ, *Cuentos y cuentistas*, Caracas, 1951. PASCUAL VENEGAS FILARDO, *Novelas y novelistas de Venezuela*, Caracas, 1955.

Theater: ERNESTO MORALES, *Historia del teatro argentino*, Buenos Aires, 1941. JOSÉ JUAN ARROM, *Historia de la literatura dramática cubana*, New Haven, 1944. ANTONIO MAGAÑA ESQUIVEL and RUTH S. LAMB, *Breve historia del teatro mexicano*, México, 1958.

IV. Anthologies

Due to lack of space, we shall only indicate general anthologies that comprehend all the Spanish-American countries. The best and most useful are, however, those which are limited to one country, or to one period in that country.

Literatura hispanoamericana. Antología e introducción histórica by ENRIQUE ANDERSON IMBERT and EUGENIO FLORIT (New York, Holt, Rinehart and Winston, 1960) comprehends various genres (excepting the novel and theater).

(a) *Verse:* MARCELINO MENÉNDEZ Y PELAYO, *Antología de poetas Hispanoamericanos*, Madrid, 1893–95. FEDERICO DE ONÍS, *Antología de la poesía española e hispanoamericana* (1882–1932), Madrid, 1934. CARLOS GARCÍA PRADA, *Poetas modernistas hispanoamericanos*, Madrid, 1956. JULIO CAILLET-BOIS, *Antología de la poesía hispanoamericana*, Madrid, 1958.

(b) *Short Story:* See BERNICE D. MATLOWSKY, *Antología del cuento americano. Guía bibliográfica*, Washington, D.C., Unión Panamericana, 1950. Some examples: VENTURA GARCÍA CALDERÓN, *Los mejores cuentos americanos*, Barcelona, s. f. ANTONIO R. MANZOR, *Antología del cuento hispanoamericano*, Santiago de Chile, 1939. ENRIQUE ANDERSON IMBERT and LAWRENCE B. KIDDLE, *Veinte cuentos hispanoamericanos del siglo xx*, New York, 1956. RICARDO LATCHAM, *Antología del cuento hispanoamericano*, Santiago, 1958.

(c) *Novel:* Francisco Monterde, *Novelistas hispanoamericanos* (*del pre-rromanticismo a la iniciación del realismo*), México, 1943. Angel Flores, *Historia y antología del cuento y la novela en Hispanoamérica,* New York, 1959.

(d) *Essays:* Aníbal Sánchez Reulet, *La filosofía latinoamericana contemporánea,* Washington, D.C., Unión Panamericana,. 1949. José Gaos, *Antología del pensamiento hispanoamericano,* México, 1935.

V. Bibliographic Indexes

Those who wish further information may turn to: Cecil K. Jones, *A Bibliography of Latin American Bibliographies,* second edition, Washington, 1942; *Bibliographies of the Belles-Lettres of Hispanic America prepared by the Harvard Council of Hispano-American Studies* (several volumes), Cambridge, from 1931 to 1937; *Handbook of Latin American Studies* prepared annually since 1936 in The Hispanic Foundation in the Library of Congress, Washington, D.C. The last volume, 1962, is edited by the University of Florida Press. For the period before 1935, which is when the works of the *Handbook of Latin-American Studies* begin, Sturgis E. Leavitt has compiled a bibliography: *Index to the Literary, Linguistic and Folklore Materials in Fifty Spanish-American Magazines.* José Manuel Topete's *Spanish-American Bibliography* has been just revised. There are bibliographies of the content of various magazines (*Nosotros, Sur,* etc.). See also the systematic bibliographies published by the *Revista Hispánica Moderna,* New York, Columbia University, and other specialized publications.

INDEX OF AUTHORS

Alarcón, Abel (Bolivia, 1881), 311
Alarcón, Félix de (Peru; 18th cent.), 104
Alarcón, Pedro Antonio de, 250
Alas, Claudio de. See Escobar Uribe, Jorge
Alatorre, Antonio (Mexico; 1923), 550
Alberdi, Juan Bautista (Argentina; 1810–1884), 141, 163, 166–167, 175
Albertazzi Avedaño, José (Costa Rica; 1892), 335
Alberti, Rafael, 444, 447, 521
Alcedo y Bexarano, Antonio de (Ecuador; 1735–1812), 113
Alcorta, Gloria (Argentina; 1916), 549
Alegre, Francisco Javier (Mexico; 1729–1788), 100, 108, 113
Alegría, Ciro (Peru; 1909), 501–502
Alegría, Claribel (El Salvador; 1924), 522
Alegría, Fernando (Chile; 1918), 544, 562, 564
Aleixandre, Vicente, 530, 533
Alemán, Mateo, 54, 55, 67
Alfaro, Oscar (Bolivia; 20th cent.), 527
Alfaro Calatrava, Tomás (Venezuela; 1922–1953), 525
Alfaro Cooper, José María (Costa Rica; 1861–1939), 230
Alfieri, Victor, 143, 178
Almafuerte. See Palacios, Pedro B.
Alone. See Díaz Arrieta, Hernán
Alonso, Dora (Cuba; 1910), 495
Alonso, Manuel A. (Puerto Rico; 1823–1889), 184, 290
Alonso, Rodolfo (Argentina; 1934), 557
Alonso y Trelles, José (Spain–Uruguay; 1857–1924), 231
Altamirano, Ignacio Manuel (Mexico; 1834–1893), 215–217, 223
Althaus, Clemente (Peru; 1835–1881), 184
Alva Ixtlilxóchitl, Fernando de (Mexico; 1578–1648), 58, 59
Alva y Monteagudo, Mariano José de (Cuba; 1761–1800), 130
Alvarado, Huberto (Guatemala; 1925), 522
Alvarado Quirós, Alejandro (Costa Rica; 1876–1945), 293, 305
Alvarado Sánchez, José (Peru; 1913), 449
Alvarado Tezozómoc, Hernando (Mexico; ca. 1520–ca. 1600), 24

Álvarez, José Seferino (Argentina; 1858–1903), 259
Álvarez, Luis Fernando (Venezuela; 1902–1952), 445
Álvarez Chanca, Diego (Spain; 15th–16th cent.), 13
Álvarez de Toledo, Hernando (Spain; born 1550), 48
Álvarez de Velasco y Zorrilla, Francisco (Colombia; 1647–died after 1703), 79
Álvarez Lleras, Antonio (Colombia; 1892–1956), 385, 419
Alvéstigue, Jorge (Bolivia; 20th cent.), 527
Alzate, José Antonio (Mexico; 1729–1799), 100, 119, 120
Amador, Fernán Félix de. See Fernández Beschted, Domingo
Amarilis (Peru; 17th cent.), 92
Amaya Amador, Ramón (Honduras; 20th cent.), 537
Amaya González, Victor (Colombia; 1898), 447
Ambrogi, Arturo (El Salvador; 1875–1936), 291, 293
Ameller Ramallo (Bolivia; 20th cent.), 451
Amiana, Manuel A. (Dominican Republic; 1899), 495
Amighetti, Francisco (Costa Rica; 1907), 436
Amor, Guadalupe (Mexico; 1920), 521
Amorim, Enrique (Uruguay; 1900–1960), 457, 506–507
Amortegui, Octavio (Colombia; 1901), 447
Anabalón Sanderson, Luisa (Chile; 1896–1951), 345
Anacaona (Santo Domingo; 16th cent.), 19
Anacreon, 129
Ancona, Eligio (Mexico; 1836–1893), 173, 190, 226
Anderson Imbert, Enrique (Argentina; 1910), 491, 564
Andino, Manuel (El Salvador; 1892–1958), 417
Andrade, Mariano (Ecuador; 1734), 109
Andrade, Olegario (Argentina; 1839–1882), 201
Andrade Álvarez, Francisco (Venezuela; 1920), 540

The manuscript was edited by Patricia Davis. The book was designed by Richard Kinney. The text typeface is Linotype Caledonia, designed by W. A. Dwiggins in 1940. The display faces are Latin Wide cut by Stephenson Blake & Company, Limited, and Mistral designed by Roger Excoffon for Fonderie Olive in 1953.

The book is printed on Glatfelter's R R Antique paper and bound in Bancroft's Linen cloth. Manufactured in the United States of America.

The manuscript was edited by Judith Davis. The book was designed by Richard Kegan. The text window is a bookmaker designed by W. A. Dwiggins in 1938. The display type used is Stephenson Blake & Company. Printed and bound and dressed by R. Donnelley. Printed in Ohio, to wit.

The work is printed on Gladfelter's R Antique paper and bound in Roxite Linen cloth, both manufactured in the United States of America.